FOUNDATIONS OF PUBLIC INTERNATIONAL LAW

General editors: Malcolm Evans and
Phoebe Okowa

INTERNATIONAL LAW AND THE USE OF FORCE

Third Edition

International Law and the Use of Force

Third Edition

CHRISTINE GRAY

OXFORD

UNIVERSITY PRESS

OXFORD

UNIVERSITY PRESS

Great Clarendon Street, Oxford OX2 6DP
United Kingdom

Oxford University Press is a department of the University of Oxford.
It furthers the University's objective of excellence in research, scholarship,
and education by publishing worldwide. Oxford is a registered trade mark of
Oxford University Press in the UK and in certain other countries

First published 2008
Reprinted 2013

British Library Cataloguing in Publication Data
Data available

Library of Congress Cataloging in Publication Data
Data available

ISBN 978-0-19-923915-3

General Editors' Preface (3rd Edition)

There is no difficulty in making the case for the appearance of a new edition of Professor Gray's seminal study on the use of force in international law: the importance of the subject and the standing of this work, the first edition of which was published in 2000, combine to make that case compelling. This third edition is thoroughly updated and fully revised to take account of the numerous significant developments both in state practice and in the jurisprudence that have taken place since the 2nd edition was published in 2004. These developments include the Israeli invasion of Lebanon in 2006, attacks by Turkey on the Kurdish separatist forces (PKK) in northern Iraq, Ethiopia's use of force against Somalia and, of course, the on-going ramifications of the US-led invasions in Iraq and Afghanistan. Particular attention is also paid to the conflict in Darfur.

Most importantly, this new edition offers a critical account of the jurisprudence of international tribunals on the use of force. In addition to the decisions of the International Court of Justice, there is also extensive coverage of the decisions of the Eritrea-Ethiopian Claims Commission. Throughout this new edition there are a number of new sections that offer helpful insights into this most important area of Public International Law. In each case Professor Gray has supported her analysis by extensive reference to state practice, including detailed consideration of what states claim for themselves or object to in the context of international litigation. There can be no doubt that this new edition will be greeted with the enthusiasm that it richly deserves and that it will continue to provide a guide to the law which is clear, challenging, and authoritative.

Malcolm D Evans
Phoebe N Okowa

General Editors' Preface (1st Edition)

Few topics in international law arouse as much interest as the use of force. Indeed, the very origins of the discipline lie in attempts to wrestle with the question of when force might legitimately be used within the international arena. It shapes and defines the subject. It is, then, most fitting that the first volume to appear in the Foundations of Public International Law Series should address international law and the use of force.

Since 1945 there has been a sustained attempt to place limitations upon unilateral use of force by states and it was envisaged that this would be balanced by the capacity of the UN Security Council to exercise a monopoly over the use of force for the common good of the international community. This, of course, proved to be unattainable for most practical purposes during the Cold War years. The Cold War is over, but other problems have emerged which ensure that the perennial problems surrounding the legality of the use of force will remain the subject of fierce debate and fundamental doctrinal difference.

In keeping with the aims of the series, Christine Gray surveys and explores the current pattern of legal regulation in a manner which combines clarity in presentation with rigour in academic scrutiny. If the issues raised are themselves timeless, the point of departure is clearly contemporary and firmly grounded in recent state practice as well as the pronouncements of the International Court of Justice. Indeed, one of the hallmarks of this work is the way in which state practice is drawn into the jurisprudential debate, producing a synthesis which is both stimulating and satisfying. Difficult questions are posed and challenging conclusions are drawn and this is as it should be. Even if the law in this area were easy to state—and it is not—it would still be difficult to apply. It is a sign of the increasing maturity of international law that it is able to face up to this truth whilst continuing to search for a way forward that preserves and enhances the rule of law within the international community. If that means replacing the platitudinous orthodoxies of a previous era with the ever-more complex and perplexing outcomes of evolution and innovation in law and practice, then this a price well worth paying. One does, however, need a reliable guide through the resulting thickets and this volume is offered in the expectation that it will not only fulfil that function with distinction, but will itself mould the manner in which the legal regulation of the use of force is perceived and examined for years to come.

Malcolm D. Evans
Phoebe N. Okowa

Contents

Abbreviations   xv

1. Law and force   1
Identification of the law   6
Effectiveness of the prohibition of the use of force   25

2. The prohibition of the use of force   30
Humanitarian intervention   33
Kosovo: a new role for NATO   39
    Legality of Use of Force: the case before the International
        Court of Justice   44
    The subsequent debate   47
A responsibility to protect?   51
Darfur   53
A right of pro-democratic intervention   55
Force and self-determination   59
Other claims under Article 2(4)   65

3. Invitation and intervention: civil wars and the use of force   67
Recent application of the law on intervention in
   civil wars: Africa after the Cold War   68
The *Nicaragua* case   75
Armed activities on the territory of the Congo (*DRC v Uganda*)   78
The right of a government to invite outside intervention   80
    Classification of conflicts   82
    Invitation by governments in practice   84
Intervention and protection of nationals   88
Intervention in response to prior foreign intervention   92
    Chad 1975–1993   96
    The identification of the government entitled
      to invite intervention   98
Forcible intervention to assist the opposition   105
Intervention and counter-intervention in Angola
   and Mozambique   107
The end of the Cold War and the start of the 'War on Terror'   110

4. Self-defence   114
Introduction   114
The academic debate   117
The role of the Security Council   119

The duty to report to the Security Council   121
Self-defence as a temporary right   124
Security Council measures and self-defence   126
The scope of self-defence   128
    Armed attack   128
        Cross-border action by irregular forces   132
            Turkey, Iraq and the Kurds   140
            Iranian Oil Platforms case   143
            Gravity of attack   147
        Necessity and proportionality   148
            Accumulation of events   155
        Protection of nationals   156
        Anticipatory self-defence before the 'Bush doctrine'   160
Conclusion   165

5. **Collective self-defence**   167
    The *Nicaragua* case   171
    The meaning of armed attack   173
        The actions of armed bands and irregular forces   173
        The supply of arms   175
    Frontier incidents   177
        The distinction between armed attack and frontier
            incident in the *Nicaragua* case   178
        Criticism of the distinction between armed attack
            and frontier incident   179
        Arguments for the distinction between armed attack
            and frontier incident   180
        The distinction and the *Definition of Aggression*   182
    Other limits on the right of collective self-defence   184
        Third state interest?   187
        The duty to report to the Security Council under Article 51   188
    Conclusion   189

6. **The use of force against terrorism: a new war
    for a new century?**   193
    Previous practice   195
    The impact of 9/11   198
        The concept of armed attack after 9/11   199
        Necessity and proportionality   203
            Operation Enduring Freedom   203
        Pre-emptive self-defence   208
        How far has *Operation Enduring Freedom* been a turning
            point in the law on the use of force?   208

The Bush doctrine of pre-emptive self-defence 209
Iraq and pre-emptive self-defence 216
    Allegations of links between Al Qaida and Saddam Hussein 217
    Pre-emptive self-defence against the threat of Iraq's
        weapons of mass destruction 218
The next steps: North Korea and Iran 222
    North Korea 222
    Iran 224
Terrorist attacks after 9/11 and the international response 227
Intervention after *Operation Enduring Freedom* 228
Regime change 231
The 'War on Terror' extends 234
    Israel, Syria and Lebanon 2001–2006 234
    Israel/Lebanon 2006 237
        Non-state actors 239
        The role of the UN 240
        Proportionality 241
    Ethiopa/Somalia 2006 244
Conclusion 252

7. The UN and the use of force 254
The UN in the Cold War 255
    Chapter VII action 255
    The division of powers between the Security Council
        and the General Assembly 259
    Peacekeeping during the Cold War 261
A New Legal Order? Chapter VII after the Cold War 264
Article 41: transformation 266
Peacekeeping after the Cold War 272
    The end of Cold War conflicts 274
    The start of new conflicts 278
Peacekeeping and enforcement action in Yugoslavia
    and Somalia: the blurring of traditional distinctions 281
    The extension of peacekeeping 281
        Yugoslavia 282
        Somalia 286
    Contemporaneous peacekeeping and
        enforcement operations 289
Rwanda 292
The relation of UN peacekeeping and Chapter VII 294
    Consent to peacekeeping 298
    The use of force by peacekeeping operations 302
Reform of UN peacekeeping 306

The *Brahimi Report* and its implementation   307
Sierra Leone and the DRC   312
Recent peacekeeping operations   319
Peace Operations 2010   323
Conclusion   326

8. **Security Council authorization for member
   states to use force**   327
   Express authorization   327
      Member state operations in Africa (2003–2007)   334
      Europe in Africa   340
         Chad and the Central African Republic (CAR)   340
      Kosovo   341
      Afghanistan   343
         The multinational force in Iraq (2003)   345
   Implied (or revived) authorization to use force   348
      Iraq 1991–2002   348
      The 1999 Kosovo operation   351
   Operation Iraqi Freedom (2003)   354
      Security Council Resolution 1441 (2002)   356
      The 'coalition' case for action   358
   Conclusion   366

9. **Regional peacekeeping and enforcement action**   370
   Introduction   370
   Cooperation between the UN and regional organizations   372
      The UN and the AU   376
      The AU in Somalia: AMISOM   378
      The AU in Darfur: AMIS   380
      Joint operations   382
   'Regional arrangements and agencies'   383
   The constitutional bases for regional peacekeeping   387
      ECOWAS action in Liberia   392
      ECOWAS action in Sierra Leone   395
   The legality of regional action in terms of the UN
      Charter and general international law   396
      ECOWAS action in Liberia (1990–97)   400
         The legality of the operation under the UN Charter   400
         Consent of the host state   401
         The impartiality of ECOMOG   402
         Enforcement action   403
         ECOWAS cooperation with a UN force   405
         Conclusion   406

The former USSR 407
   Tajikistan 407
   Abkhazia, Georgia 409
ECOWAS action in Sierra Leone 411
A reinterpretation of Article 53 of the UN Charter? 417
   A regional right to use force to restore democratic
      government? 418
      Côte d'Ivoire 419
      Liberia (2003) and the Central African Republic 421
Security Council authorization of use of force by regional
   organizations 423
Conclusion 426

Index 429

Abbreviations

ADF	Arab Defence Force
AMIB	AU Mission in Burundi
AMIS	AU Mission in Sudan
AMISOM	AU Mission in Somalia
ANC	African National Council
ASEAN	Association of South-East Asian States
AU	African Union
AUPSC	AU Peace and Security Council
BONUCA	UN peace-building office in the Central African Republic
BYIL	*British Year Book of International Law*
CAR	Central African Republic
CARICOM	Caribbean Community
CEMAC	Communauté Économique et Monétaire de l'Afrique
CEN-SAD	Community of Sahel-Saharan States
CIA	Central Intelligence Agency
CIS	Commonwealth of Independent States
CSCE	Conference on Security and Cooperation in Europe
CSTO	Collective Security Treaty Organization
DPKO	Department of Peacekeeping Operations
DPRK	Democratic People's Republic of Korea
DRC	Democratic Republic of Congo
ECCAS	Economic Community of Central African States
ECOMIL	ECOWAS Mission in Liberia
ECOMOG	Economic Community of West African States Monitoring Group
ECOWAS	Economic Commnity of West African States
FMLN	Frente Farabundo Marti para la Liberación Nacional
FNLA	Frente Nacional de Libertaçã de Angola
FOMUC	Force multinationale en Centrafrique
FRY	Federal Republic of Yugoslavia
IAEA	International Atomic Energy Agency
ICJ	International Court of Justice
ICTY	International Criminal Tribunal for the Former Yugoslavia
IEMF	Interim Emergency Multinational Force
IGAD	Intergovernmental Authority on Drought and Development
ILC	International Law Commission
ILM	International Legal Materials
IPTF	United National International Police Task Force
ISAF	International Security Assistance Force
MIF	Multinational Interim Force

MINUCI	United National Mission in Côte d'Ivoire
MINURCAT	United Nations Mission in the Central African Republic
MINUSTAH	UN Stabilization Mission in Haiti
MISAB	Inter-African Force in the Central African Republic
MLC	Movement for the Liberation of Congo
MNF	Multinational Force
MONUA	United Nations Observer Mission in Angola
MONUC	United Nations Observer Mission in the Democratic Republic of Congo
MPLA	Movimento Popular de Libertação de Angola
NAM	Non-Aligned Movement
NATO	North Atlantic Treaty Organization
NPFL	National Patriotic Front of Liberia
NPT	Treaty on the Non-Proliferation of Nuclear Weapons
OAS	Organization of American States
OAU	Organization of African Unity
OECS	Organization of East Caribbean States
ONUB	UN Operation in Burundi
ONUC	United Nations Operation in the Congo
ONUCA	United Nations Operation Observer Group in Central America
ONUSAL	United Nations Observer Mission in El Salvador
OSCE	Organization for Security and Cooperation in Europe
PKK	Kurdish Workers Party
PLO	Palestine Liberation Organization
RENAMO	Resistencia Nacional Moçambicana
RPF	Rwanda Patriotic Front
RUF	Revolutionary United Front
SADC	Southern African Development Community (formerly SADDC)
SOFAs	Status of Forces Agreements
SWAPO	South West Africa People's Organization
TCCs	Troop Contributing Countries
TFG	Transitional Federal Government
TSZ	Temporary Security Zone
UAR	United Arab Republic
UIC	Union of Islamic Courts
UN	United Nations
UNAMET	United Nations Mission in East Timor
UNAMI	United National Assistance Mission
UNAMIC	United Nations Advance Mission in Cambodia
UNAMID	AU/UN Hybrid Operation in Darfur
UNAMIR	United Nations Assistance Mission for Rwanda

UNAMSIL	United Nations Mission in Sierra Leone
UNAVEM	United Nations Angola Verification Mission
UNCRO	United Nations Confidence Restoration Operation in Croatia
UNEF	United Nations Emergency Force
UNFICYP	United Nations Peace-keeping Force in Cyprus
UNGOMAP	United Nations Good Offices Mission in Afghanistan and Pakistan
UNIFIL	United Nations Interim Force in Lebanon
UNITA	União Nacional para a Independência Total de Angola
UNITAF	Unified Task Force
UNMEE	United Nations Mission in Ethiopia and Eritrea
UNMIBH	United Nations Mission in Bosnia and Herzegovina
UNMIH	United Nations Mission in Haiti
UNMIK	United Nations Missioin in Kosovo
UNMIL	United Nations Mission in Liberia
UNMISET	United Nations Mission of Support in East Timor
UNMOGIP	United Nations Military Observer Group in India and Pakistan
UNMOP	United Nations Mission of Observers in Prevlaka
UNMOT	United Nations Mission of Observers in Tajikstan
UNMOVIC	United Nations Monitoring, Verification and Inspection Commission
UNOCI	UN Operation in Côte d'Ivoire
UNOMIG	United Nations Observer Mission in Georgia
UNOMIL	United Nations Observer Mission in Liberia
UNOMOZ	United Nations Operation in Mozambique
UNOMSIL	United Nations Observer Mission in Sierra Leone
UNOMUR	United Nations Observer Mission Uganda/Rwanda
UNOSOM I & II	United Nations Operation in Somalia
UNPREDEP	United Nations Preventive Deployment Force
UNPROFOR	United Nations Protection Force
UNSCOM	United Nations Special Commission
UNTAC	United Nations Transitional Authority in Cambodia
UNTAES	United Nations Transitional Administration for Eastern Slovenia
UNTAET	United Nations Transitional Administration in East Timor
UNTAG	United Nations Transition Assistance Group
UNTS	UN Treaty Series
UNYB	UN Year Book
WEU	Western European Union
WMD	Weapons of mass destruction

1
Law and force

Conflict continues in Iraq and Afghanistan at the start of 2008, on what US President George W Bush describes as 'the frontlines in the war on terror'—a war he proclaimed after the September 11, 2001 terrorist attacks on the World Trade Center and the Pentagon.[1] This 'war on terror' was to be 'a new war for a new century'—a rather less inviting prospect than the New World Order proclaimed by his father at the end of the Cold War. The language of the 'war on terror' has also been used with regard to the recent use of force by Israel against Lebanon, by Ethiopia against Somalia and by Turkey against the PKK in Iraq. The question arises how far this language is simply a rhetorical device, designed by the USA to legitimate domestic repression, the increase in military spending, the expansion of bases round the world, the imposition of pressure on certain states, and the pursuit of US foreign policy actually driven by other considerations.[2] President Bush has said that 'The war against terrorists is a global enterprise of uncertain duration'.[3] What precisely does this involve?[4]

It is clear that the 'war on terror' is not a technical legal term,[5] and it is argued by many officials to be a misleading and unhelpful term.[6] There is a danger that the language of the 'war on terror' will not only glorify those more properly regarded as criminals, and exaggerate the threat that they pose, but that it will also distort our understanding of particular conflicts, just as during the Cold War the perception of many conflicts in ideological terms distorted their true nature and obstructed their effective solution.

---

[1] Hereafter 9/11. See Chapter 6 below.

[2] For criticism of the use of the language of 'war', see Megret, 'War? Legal Semantics and the Move to Violence', 13 EJIL (2002) 361. For an opposing view, see Dinstein, *War, Aggression and Self-Defence* (4th edn, 2005); Dinstein argues throughout his book for a wide and very controversial concept of the state of war.

[3] Covering letter to *US National Security Strategy*, September 2002, 41 (2002) ILM 1478. He referred to the 'war on terror' as 'the defining ideological struggle of the twenty-first century' in his 2008 State of the Union address, available on <www.whitehouse.gov>.

[4] For a detailed critique of the strategy of the 'global war on terrorism', see Record, *Bounding the Global War on Terrorism* (2003); Record argues that 'The Global War on Terrorism as it has so far been defined and conducted is strategically unfocused, promises much more than it can deliver, and threatens to dissipate scarce US military and other means over too many ends. It violates the fundamental strategic principles of discrimination and concentration.'

[5] UK Materials on International Law, 72 BYIL (2001) 690, 697; Bellinger, US State Department Legal Adviser; <www.opiniojuris.org/posts/1168811565.shtml>. See also, Greenwood, 'War, Terrorism and International Law', 56 Current Legal Problems (2003) 505.

[6] Keesings (2005) 46729, *The Guardian*, 10 December 2006, 24 January, 17 April 2007; *The International Herald Tribune*, 22 July 2007.

This danger is intensified when leaders speak of the 'war on terror' as one against a single enemy.[7] Moreover, it is open to doubt whether the use of force is an appropriate and effective response to terrorism. The experience of Afghanistan and Iraq, Lebanon and Somalia does not suggest that the use of force has proved effective in securing stability. And the UN Secretary-General has expressed concern that the war against terrorism will detract from other equally, if not more, pressing dangers—sometimes categorized as 'soft threats'—such as threats of extreme poverty, unsafe drinking water, the disparity of income between and within society, the spread of infectious diseases or climate change and environmental degradation.[8]

Nevertheless, the rhetoric of the 'war on terror' has some significance for the law on the use of force in that it has been used to justify a wide right of self-defence against non-state actors, and to threaten pre-emptive action to prevent certain states, accused of state sponsorship of terrorism, from developing nuclear weapons. There are significant differences between states, and between commentators, on these issues. In pursuit of those responsible for the terrorist attacks of 9/11, and on the basis of a right of self-defence against terrorist attacks, the USA initiated *Operation Enduring Freedom* in Afghanistan, an operation which continues today. But President Bush then widened the focus of the war against terrorism beyond Afghanistan. In his famous *State of the Union* Address of January 2002 he singled out the states of the 'Axis of Evil'—Iran, Iraq and North Korea—as posing a threat to the USA. He argued that there was a danger that such 'rogue' states would develop chemical, biological and nuclear weapons of mass destruction for use against US targets or for supply to terrorists hostile to the USA. In response to its perception of a fundamentally changed international situation, the USA put forward a new 2002 *National Security Strategy*, including the controversial doctrine of pre-emptive self-defence. The 2006 *National Security Strategy* reaffirmed US commitment to pre-emptive self-defence.

In contrast to the broad acceptance by states of the legality of *Operation Enduring Freedom*, the right to take military action against Iraq was bitterly contested. The USA and the UK argued that Iraq was developing weapons of mass destruction, and undertook *Operation Iraqi Freedom* in

---

[7] Thus President Bush linked (Sunni) Al Qaida and (Shia) terrorists in Iraq as all part of the same global threat, Reno, Nevada, 28 August 2007; <www.whitehouse.gov/news/releases/2007/08/20070828-1.html>. See also speech by PM Blair, World Affairs Council, Los Angeles, 1 August 2006, available on <www.pm.gov.uk/output/page1.asp> under 'tony blair archive'.

[8] Secretary-General's Address to the General Assembly, 23 September 2003; Secretary-General's Message for the New Year, 2004, UN Press Release SG/SM/9095, 24 December 2003.

March 2003, leading to the overthrow of President Saddam Hussein and the occupation of Iraq. This use of force was extremely divisive and its legality was challenged not only by Russia and China, but also by close allies such as France and Germany. Even the UN Secretary-General spoke out to deny the legality of this use of force, in a departure from his normal practice. The Security Council was deeply split. Some states saw its refusal to authorize force against Iraq as a failure on the part of the Council to act in enforcement of the disarmament regime imposed on Iraq; others regarded this as the normal and successful working of the Charter system.[9] President Bush in a 2002 speech to the UN General Assembly issued a famous challenge: 'The conduct of the Iraqi regime is a threat to the authority of the United Nations, and a threat to peace. Iraq has answered a decade of UN demands with a decade of defiance. All the world now faces a test, and the United Nations a difficult and defining moment. Are Security Council resolutions to be honored and enforced, or cast aside without consequence? Will the United Nations serve the purpose of its founding, or will it be irrelevant?'[10]

After the invasion of Iraq the UN Secretary-General spoke of 'a fork in the road'; he declared dramatically that 'this may be a moment no less decisive than 1945 itself, when the UN was founded'.[11] Since then states had generally sought to deal with threats to the peace through containment and deterrence, by a system based on collective security and the UN Charter. It had been understood that when states went beyond self-defence and decided to use force to deal with broader threats to international peace and security, they needed the unique legitimacy provided by the UN. Now some said that this understanding was no longer tenable since an armed attack with weapons of mass destruction could be launched at any time, without warning; rather than wait for that to happen states have the right to use force pre-emptively, even on the territory of other states and even while weapons systems that might be used against them are still being developed. 'According to this argument, States are not obliged to wait until there is agreement in the Security Council. Instead they reserve the right to act unilaterally, or in *ad hoc* coalitions. This logic represents a fundamental challenge to the principles on which, however imperfectly, world peace and stability have rested for the last fifty-eight years.'

Accordingly the Secretary-General set up a *High-level Panel on Threats, Challenges and Change,* mandated to make a broad examination of global peace and security issues, to identify the contributions of collective action in addressing major challenges and threats, and to recommend changes

---

[9] See Falk, 'What Future for the UN Charter System of War Prevention?', 97 AJIL (2003) 590.
[10] <www.whitehouse.gov/news/releases/2002/09/20020912-1.html>.
[11] Secretary-General's Address to the General Assembly, 23 September 2003.

necessary to ensure effective collective action. In 2004 it issued its report *A More Secure World*;[12] the following year the Secretary-General issued his own report, *In Larger Freedom*,[13] in preparation for the 2005 World Summit which produced an Outcome document.[14] The consensus of all these instruments was that no change in the UN Charter provisions on the use of force was necessary. The fundamental prohibition on the use of force in Article 2(4), the right of self-defence in Article 51, and Chapter VII on collective action were all adequate to meet the new threats.[15]

Nevertheless international law on the use of force, its content and effectiveness, is now the object of more speculation than ever before. Some commentators use apocalyptic language and mourn the death of Article 2(4), the prohibition of the use of force in the UN Charter.[16] In contrast others welcome the end of the Charter system and of any international law constraint on the USA.[17] Yet others argue that international law is evolving to meet new threats, and welcome the changes they identify in the law on self-defence, intervention and regime change.[18] It remains to be seen how far the USA is deliberately posing a challenge to the whole UN system and to the existing international legal order, or whether it is operating within the system, even if manipulating the rules for its own ends. The apparently cynical manipulation of legal rules is nothing new; disingenuous rhetoric is certainly not unique to the international legal system. Thus the question arises whether US lip service to international law on the use of force is meaningless or to be welcomed as indicating continued adherence to the Charter system? Are its assertions that it is acting multilaterally and in the interests of the international community of any value? Or is the USA actually claiming special rights exercisable exclusively by it as the only remaining superpower.[19] The impact of 9/11 and of *Operation Iraqi*

---

[12] UN doc A/59/565.

[13] UN doc A/59/2005. See 11(3) Journal of Conflict and Security Law (2006) 107 for a workshop on these reports.

[14] UN doc A/60/L.70. See Gray, 'A crisis of legitimacy for the UN collective security system?', 56 ICLQ (2007) 157.

[15] UN doc A/59/565 para 192, 198; UN doc A/59/2005 para 126, 153; UN doc A/60/L.70 para 79.

[16] Franck, 'What happens now? The UN after Iraq', 97 AJIL (2003) 607. Franck had already asked 'Who killed Article 2(4)?', 64 AJIL (1970) 809.

[17] Glennon, *Limits of Law, Prerogatives of Power: Interventionism after Kosovo* (2001); 'The Fog of Law: Self-Defense, Inherence and Incoherence in Article 51 of the UN Charter', 25 Harvard Journal of Law and Public Policy (2002) 539; 'The emerging use of force paradigm', Journal of Conflict and Security Law (2006) 309; Bolton, 'Is there really "Law" in International Affairs?', 10 Transnational Journal of Law and Contemporary Problems (2000) 1.

[18] Wedgwood, 'The Fall of Saddam Hussein: Security Council mandates and pre-emptive self-defense', 97 AJIL (2003) 576; Stromseth, 'Law and Force after Iraq—A Transitional Moment', 97 AJIL (2003) 628; Yoo, 'Using Force' 71 University of Chicago LR (2004) 729.

[19] See, for example, Byers and Nolte (eds), *United States Hegemony and the Foundations of International Law* (2003); Vagts, 'Hegemonic International Law', 95 AJIL (2001) 843; Farer,

Freedom on international law on the use of force will be examined in detail in Chapters 6 and 8 below.

Even those who challenged the role of the UN Security Council with regard to the use of force against Afghanistan and Iraq subsequently turned to it for legitimacy and support in the attempts at reconstruction of those states. There is greater demand than ever before for UN peace-keeping and post-conflict peacebuilding. The problems of East Timor, Haiti and of many African states have increased awareness of the need to prevent the resurgence of conflict after the conclusion of a peace agreement or political settlement, and after the withdrawal of UN peacekeeping forces. The UN has established a new Peace-Building Commission. In 2007 the UN maintained peacekeeping forces in Africa, the Americas, Asia, Europe, and the Middle East. This major surge in peacekeeping brought with it serious difficulties in securing troops and equipment, and also calls for increased cooperation with regional organizations and for a reappraisal of peacekeeping doctrine.

Several long-lasting conflicts continue, some dating back to the establishment of the UN. Among the first conflicts ever considered by the Security Council were those between India and Pakistan and between Israel and Arab states. These disputes have continued off and on for the last fifty years and are to a large extent still unresolved. Long-lasting civil wars and separatist struggles also continue in Burma, Colombia, Georgia (Abkhazia), Indonesia, Kashmir, the Philippines and Thailand; conflict was resurgent in Sri Lanka after the government proclaimed an end to the 2002 ceasefire which had long existed in name only. The violent struggle for self-determination continued in the occupied territories of the West Bank and Gaza.

On the positive side, in 2007 the UN played a major role in ending other serious conflicts, especially in Africa where it has increasingly acted in cooperation with regional organizations. The prospects for the settlement of the complex and often interrelated conflicts in the Democratic Republic of Congo (DRC), Burundi, Uganda, Sierra Leone, Liberia, and Côte d'Ivoire were encouraging, but the situation in many of these states is far from stable. In many of these conflicts the UN played an important role in seeking a solution or in running a peacekeeping operation. But serious challenges still faced the UN in its attempts to bring peace in the interconnected conflicts in Sudan, Chad and the Central African Republic. Although the twenty-five year civil war between north and south Sudan finally ended in 2005 and a UN peacekeeping force was established, the UN had less

'The Prospect for International Law and Order in the Wake of Iraq', 97 AJIL (2003) 621; Franck, 'The power of legitimacy and the legitimacy of power', 100 AJIL (2006) 88; Krisch, 'International Law in Times of Hegemony', 16 EJIL (2005) 368.

success with regard to the humanitarian crisis in Darfur. In 2007 the government of Sudan finally agreed to the deployment of a new type of hybrid UN/AU force, marking a new era of cooperation between UN and regional organizations. The UN also cooperated with the EU in the creation of a joint peacekeeping operation in Chad and the CAR, to prevent the overspill of conflict between Darfur, Chad and the CAR, but many problems faced these two operations at the start of 2008. Again in the interconnected conflicts in the Horn of Africa the UN could make little progress in peacekeeping; the bad relations between Eritrea and Ethiopia following their 1998–2000 conflict, manifest also in the 2006 conflict in Somalia, and the serious unrest in Kenya make the region dangerously unstable. Although a small AU force was sent to Somalia after the Ethiopian invasion, the situation was too precarious for UN peacekeeping.

The rest of this chapter has two main interrelated themes: first, the problems with the identification of international law on the use of force in the light of the fundamental disagreements between states and between commentators, and second, the role of international law in this area and the complexities of any inquiry into its effectiveness.

IDENTIFICATION OF THE LAW

The starting point for any examination of the law is the prohibition of the use of force in Article 2(4) of the UN Charter.[20] Irrespective of whether the UN Charter is seen as a revolutionary departure from existing customary international law on the use of force or as a codification of rules that had already undergone a major shift in the twentieth century,[21] the Charter system was a marked departure from that of the League of Nations, and the language of Articles 2(4) and 51[22] provides a new terminology and the first expression of the basic rules in their modern form. States may still use the rhetoric of 'war', in the language of the Covenant of the League of Nations, as was apparent in the language used by Ethiopia in its recent

---

[20] Article 2(4): 'All Members shall refrain in their international relations from the threat or use of force against the territorial integrity or political independence of any state, or in any other manner inconsistent with the Purposes of the United Nations.'

[21] See, for example, the debate between Bowett, *Self-Defence in International Law* (1958) and Brownlie, *International Law and the Use of Force by States* (1963).

[22] Article 51: 'Nothing in the present Charter shall impair the inherent right of individual or collective self-defence if an armed attack occurs against a Member of the United Nations, until the Security Council has taken measures necessary to maintain international peace and security. Measures taken by Members in the exercise of this right of self-defence shall be immediately reported to the Security Council and shall not in any way affect the authority and responsibility of the Security Council under the present Charter to take at any time such action as it deems necessary in order to maintain or restore international peace and security.'

conflict, but the drafters of the UN Charter deliberately chose to use the wider term 'use of force' in the prohibition in Article 2(4).[23] This book will examine the use of force since the Charter; the focus will be on state and UN practice under the Charter.[24] The aim is to identify the areas of agreement and disagreement, to examine through practice the application and development of the law in the light of the Charter framework, and to provide enough primary material to enable the reader to decide between the sometimes radically opposed interpretations of the same practice.

The rules of the Charter on the use of force are brief and cannot constitute a comprehensive code. The provisions in Articles 2(4) and 51 are very much a response to the Second World War and are accordingly directed to inter-state conflict. It is now a commonplace that such conflict, or at any rate large scale inter-state conflicts, have proved to be the exception in the years since 1945; and that civil wars, with or without outside intervention, have outnumbered traditional inter-state wars.[25] Cross-border guerrilla incursions and limited inter-state fighting in border areas have been the norm rather than all-out wars between states. The struggles of national liberation movements for independence during the decolonization process also did not fit easily into the framework of Articles 2(4) and 51. The evolution of rules to cover these conflicts has been a complex process. Even in inter-state conflicts the apparently simple words of the Charter have given rise to fundamental differences between states.

This is one of the most controversial areas of international law; even from the early days of the UN many disagreements between states (between developed and developing, between East and West) as to the law were apparent. The prohibition of the use of force led to fundamental divisions as to whether the prohibition of the 'use of force' included economic coercion, the scope of the right of self-defence, the right to use force to further self-determination and to intervene in civil wars. These differences emerged in the context of the Cold War and the decolonization process. The end of the Cold War, the dominance of the USA as the one remaining superpower, and the virtual end of decolonization now call for a reappraisal of international law on the use of force by states and by UN forces. How far should the Charter be interpreted to allow the use of force to restore or further democracy, to restore order in a state without an effective government, to further the right to self-determination outside the decolonization context and to respond to terrorist attacks? How far should the UN Security Council exercise centralized control over these and other uses of force?

[23] Greenwood, 'The concept of war in modern international law', 36 ICLQ (1987) 283.

[24] For an authoritative account of the history of international law on the use of force, see Brownlie, *International Law and the Use of Force by States* (1963).

[25] See Human Security Report 2005, *War and Peace in the Twenty-first Century* (2005).

How, if at all, can these controversies, old and new, be resolved? A central question is whether it is possible to use state practice to arrive at an authoritative interpretation of the Charter or to supplement its brief provisions. Is it possible to find standards by which to assess the legality of states' actions and which advisers can use to give guidance to states? Given that state practice includes the actual use of force, the justification offered by states for it, the response of other states inside and outside the UN and other organizations, and their public positions in debates on general resolutions of the General Assembly on the use of force, as well as an extensive treaty practice including friendship treaties, non-aggression pacts, border treaties, mutual defence agreements and regional arrangements, how are universal rules to be extracted?[26] Questions also arise as to who speaks for a state: is it to be the US President or the more cautious US State Department Legal Adviser, the UK Prime Minister or the Attorney-General? Should the Charter be seen as open to dynamic and changing interpretation on the basis of subsequent state practice or should the prohibition of the use of force in Article 2(4) rather be seen as having a fixed meaning, established in 1945 on the basis of the meaning of the words at that date in the light of the preparatory works and the aims of the founders?[27]

The International Court of Justice in the *Nicaragua* case apparently regarded the Charter provisions as dynamic rather than fixed, and thus as capable of change over time through state practice. It said that 'The UN Charter...by no means covers the whole area of the regulation of the use of force in international relations', and went on to explain how the Charter provisions on self-defence needed to be interpreted in the light of customary international law.[28] On the fundamental principles as to the use of force contained in Article 2(4) the parties agreed that the Charter provisions represented customary law and the Court accepted this without going into the question of how far the meaning of Article 2(4) was fixed or how far it had evolved over time. The Court did, however, go into the question of what amounted to a use of force under Article 2(4) not amounting to an armed attack under Article 51.[29] It also accepted the possibility of the development of new law on forcible intervention allowing a new exception to the prohibition of the use of force in Article 2(4). That is, it seems to have accepted the possibility of a dynamic interpretation of Articles 51 and 2(4) based on the development of state practice.[30]

---

[26] See Corten, 'The controversies over the customary prohibition on the use of force', 16 EJIL (2005) 803.

[27] Ford, 'Legal Processes of Change: Article 2(4) and the Vienna Convention on the Law of Treaties', 4 Journal of Armed Conflict Law (1999) 75.

[28] *Case Concerning Military and Paramilitary Activities in and against Nicaragua* (hereafter *Nicaragua* case) ICJ Reports (1986) 14 at para 176.

[29] *Nicaragua* case para 191–5.

[30] The Court's approach to customary international law in the *Nicaragua* case, at para 183, was traditional; it stressed the need for practice and *opinio juris* and made clear that

Almost from the time of the creation of the UN the states parties have worked to elaborate on the provisions of the UN Charter on the use of force in General Assembly resolutions. Western states have often evinced some unease about this process; thus the USA has asserted that there is no lack of understanding of Article 2(4). During the Cold War the UK and the USA tended to argue that Article 2(4) should be treated as the last word, for fear that any modification would be to the advantage of the Soviet Union.[31] But the western states have come to accept the legal significance and customary international law status of certain of these resolutions. This process of elaboration on the UN Charter began with the 1949 *Resolution on the Essentials of Peace*. The ICJ in the *Nicaragua* case in 1986 singled out the 1974 *Definition of Aggression*[32] and the 1970 *Declaration on Friendly Relations*[33] to help it to identify customary international law on the non-use of force. These resolutions have since been supplemented by the 1987 *Declaration on the Non-Use of Force*.[34] But even though these resolutions adopted unanimously or by consensus may be seen as authoritative interpretations of the UN Charter or as contributing to the formation of customary international law,[35] they often leave controversial issues unresolved.

Typically the price of consensus has been ambiguity on the crucial issues that divide states. The drafting history of the resolutions reveals more about the views of states than the resolutions themselves do.[36] Thus

universal compliance was not necessary. The Court was much criticized, not so much for this traditional doctrine, but for its application of it in the pursuit of the rules of international law. It was criticized for inferring *opinio juris* from General Assembly resolutions and for not undertaking a wide survey of practice. But, as the Court said, the parties were in agreement that Article 2(4) was customary law. It is not surprising that the Court's inquiry into customary international law was relatively brief. See Gray, 'The Principle of Non-Use of Force', in Lowe and Warbrick (eds), *The United Nations and the Principle of International Law* (1994), 33.

[31] Gray, 'The Principle of Non-Use of Force', in Lowe and Warbrick (eds), *The United Nations and the Principle of International Law* (1994), 33.

[32] GA Res 3314 (1974).

[33] GA Res 2625 (1970).

[34] GA Res 42/22 (1988); see Treves, 'La Déclaration des Nations Unies sur le renforcement de l'efficacité du principe du non-recours à la force', 33 AFDI (1987) 379.

[35] *Nicaragua* case para 188; *Legality of the Threat or Use of Nuclear Weapons*, ICJ Reports (1996) 226 at para 70.

[36] Though there are problems in assessing the question how far what states say in these debates is significant. They may change their views; clearly their views at any particular time are influenced by the disputes in which they are directly involved or in which they are interested. Typically states may attack each other and set out their own justifications for force during the general debates; during the drafting of the *Declaration on the Non-Use of Force* Iran and Iraq, Cyprus and Turkey and the Arab states and Israel all criticized each other. It is important to see the statements in the context of the time in which they were made. Views expressed in debates on the adoption of declarations may be modified later in response to particular conflicts. Thus the former Soviet bloc at first opposed the inclusion of indirect aggression within the category of 'aggression and armed attack', but later apparently abandoned this view with regard to Czechoslovakia and Afghanistan.

the central question of the scope of the right of self-defence is not dealt with in the General Assembly resolutions. This issue divides states which take a wide view, such as the USA, Israel, and in the past South Africa and, to a lesser extent, the UK and France, from the vast majority of other states. These states claim a right to use force to protect nationals abroad, to take anticipatory self-defence, and to respond to terrorism as part of self-defence. The vast majority of states rejected such claims before the events of 9/11. But it seems that states preferred to avoid any substantial provision on this question of self-defence and this enabled them to maintain their opposing positions. During the debates on the 1987 *Declaration on the Non-Use of Force* only the USA and Australia spoke out expressly in favour of anticipatory self-defence; the other states were able to maintain their positions simply through the omission of any provision on self-defence apart from the general formula that 'States have the inherent right of individual or collective self-defence if an armed attack occurs, as set forth in the Charter of the UN'.[37]

Also the General Assembly resolutions could not settle the controversies that divided developed and developing states as to the meaning of 'force', as to the right to use force in the furtherance of self-determination for colonial peoples or to recover territory illegally seized by another state. Nor did the resolutions resolve the dispute as to the legality of use of nuclear weapons.[38] These differences manifested themselves during the debates on the *Declaration on Friendly Relations* from 1962; the same differences continued to divide states during the ten years' drafting of the *Declaration on the Non-Use of Force* and the end product did not constitute any real advance on the *Declaration on Friendly Relations*.[39]

And if we turn to other actions and statements of states to interpret or supplement the Charter and the General Assembly resolutions, how is the legal significance of such practice to be assessed?[40] Can state practice be used to resolve the differences between states or is it impossible to find universal standards in this context? It is important not to exaggerate these differences and to keep them in perspective, even after *Operation Iraqi Freedom*. For the vast mass of actual use of force reveals that states almost always agree on the content of the applicable law; it is on

---

[37] UN doc A/72326; see Treves, 'La Déclaration des Nations Unies sur le renforcement de l'efficacité du principe du non-recours à la force', 33 AFDI (1987) 379; Gray, 'The Principle of Non-Use of Force', in Lowe and Warbrick (eds), *The United Nations and the Principle of International Law* (1994), 33.

[38] ICJ Reports (1996) 226.

[39] The issues of economic blockade of landlocked states and environmental modification also emerged. The remaining differences between developed and developing states are summarized at UN doc A/40/41 (1985).

[40] Corten, 'The controversies over the customary prohibition on the use of force', 16 EJIL (2005) 803.

the application of the law to the particular facts or on the facts themselves that the states disagree. Of course it may be difficult to keep these three categories entirely separate, as is clear from the rather repetitive judgment of the International Court of Justice in the *Nicaragua* case. The Court made the distinction between the facts, the law and the application of the law to the facts, but it found itself unable to maintain a strict distinction, especially between the last two categories.

It is clear that in the overwhelming majority of cases of inter-state use of force both states involved invoke self-defence against an armed attack by the other state. In numerical terms, the commonest use of force since the Second World War has been the limited cross-frontier action. The only disagreement in the mass of these cases is over the questions of fact whether there was a cross-border incursion or who began the conflict. This may occur in up to a hundred minor incidents a year. The UN may receive reports from both sides but is not often in a position to assign responsibility. Thus the vast mass of state practice, even if one of the parties is breaking the law, does not lead to any need to reappraise the content of the law. Similarly, in civil wars states seem from their practice to agree that forcible intervention to help the opposition overthrow the government is unlawful whereas assistance to a government may be legal. This is the position consistently expressed by states since the Second World War.[41] The questions that divide the intervening states are questions of fact, and application of the law to those facts: who invited help; was there a genuine invitation; was it a civil war or mere internal unrest; was there already foreign intervention. State responses to forcible intervention show a lack of doubt about the law; they generally condemn if they think the intervening state was trying to interfere.

But the mass of practice on minor episodes has naturally received relatively little academic examination. The focus of writers, especially American writers, has been on US practice and, to a lesser extent, the practice of Israel; they have been less concerned with the use of force in Africa and Asia or even with the use of force in the former Soviet Union or involving China. There was also comparatively little discussion of the law on the use of force in continental European journals until 9/11 and *Operation Iraqi Freedom*; these journals also show a rather more surprising concentration on US practice and relatively little discussion of the use of force by their own states or by their own former colonies.

This focus on US practice is in part to be explained by the fact that until recently the USA often offered rather fuller articulations of its legal position than do other states using force. Also many of these episodes are unlike

---

[41] Doswald-Beck, 'The Legal Validity of Military Intervention by Invitation of the Government', 56 BYIL (1985) 189; see Chapter 3 below.

the vast mass of state practice in that they do reflect differences between states as to the applicable law; the state using force takes a controversial position as to the content of the law in order to justify its use of force. The protection of nationals, as in Iran, Grenada, and Panama, the extension of this doctrine of self-defence to cover actions in response to terrorism against Libya in 1986, against Iraq in reaction to the alleged assassination attempt on ex-President Bush in 1993, and against Afghanistan and Sudan in 1998 all produced clear divisions between states, apparent in the debates on these particular incidents and in those on the law-making resolutions. In contrast, the former-USSR generally put forward, in attempted justification of its use of force, legal doctrines that were unexceptionable in themselves; it was their application that was controversial. The USSR claimed invitation by the government and collective self-defence to justify its intervention in Hungary, Czechoslovakia and Afghanistan. In these episodes the disagreement was on the facts (had there been an invitation, who had given the invitation, was there outside intervention) rather than as to the law. The natural focus of writers on controversial episodes where the law relied on by the states using force was not generally agreed, rather than on the mass of state practice where the law was not controversial, may have the side-effect of giving a misleading overall picture. The impression that emerges may be one of greater uncertainty than the total picture would justify, even after 9/11 and *Operation Iraqi Freedom*. How far does looking at the broader picture of all states' uses of force produce a different view of the law from that produced simply on the basis of more limited practice? In any one year newspaper reports give the largest list of conflicts; many of the minor episodes reported are never referred to the UN. Some conflicts may be referred to the UN in state communications but may not be officially debated, or may be debated only in secret; some conflicts may be debated but not lead to the adoption of a resolution or a statement; if a resolution is adopted, it may be legally indeterminate.

In early years it was more common for minor incidents to be referred to the UN and debated. Higgins wrote in 1963 that even minor episodes were the subject of condemnation by the Security Council; this is no longer the case.[42] Should the episodes in which the UN has been involved be considered more important in the establishment or confirmation of legal rules? In practice it is not surprising that they tend to attract more academic discussion. But states have various motives for choosing to refer or not to refer matters to the UN and whether or not to seek a debate. In the early years the UN Yearbook specifically listed 'Matters raised but which the Security Council did not consider'; these tended to be matters dealt with

---

[42] Higgins, *The Development of International Law through the Political Organs of the United Nations* (1963) at 181.

by the OAS and this heading was later dropped.[43] The Secretary-General in his annual report has from time to time mentioned the failure of states to refer their conflicts to the UN; he has acknowledged that they may have had good reasons for this, but also has said that failure to turn to the UN may bring the organization into disrepute.[44]

It may be that willingness to refer a conflict to the UN indicates that the state taking the initiative to make the reference is acting lawfully or that it has confidence in the legality of its position, but this does not necessarily mean that the primary concern in making the reference is to secure peaceful settlement. Sometimes states try to argue that the reference to the Security Council is in itself provocative, designed to internationalize the conflict and not appropriate. Thus, for example, Yemen in 1966 said that the complaint by the UK of an air attack on its colonial territory of South Arabia by Yemen should not go to the Security Council; the issue raised by the UK was a minor matter, the alleged incursion of an aircraft, and what was really at stake was the need for the UK to allow the reunification of Yemen.[45] Again in 1946 the question of USSR involvement in Iran was referred to the Security Council by the USA, even though the question was near to peaceful resolution.[46] In 1972 Portugal and the UK argued that a use of force by Portugal against Senegal should not go to the Security Council because Portugal had admitted the violation, ordered criminal proceedings against those responsible and offered compensation. But the states voting for the resolution condemning Portugal replied that the Security Council intervention was justified because the episode was not an isolated one; it was part of Portugal's continuing illegal colonialism.[47]

The Security Council clearly has an important role, but there is controversy as to whether its findings are conclusive as to legality, illegality, and as to the content of the applicable norms.[48] How far is the law developed by institutions? That is, do states acting collectively through the UN have a more important role than they do outside the UN in the interpretation and application of the UN Charter? Does the Security Council have the

---

[43] This covered events in 1948–9 on the Costa Rica border, and between Haiti/Dominican Republic; in 1950, Dominican Republic allegations against groups in Cuba and Guatemala; in 1954, Guatemala; in 1955, Costa Rica. At this time there was a serious debate as to priority of jurisdiction between the UN and regional organizations, but this has not been a controversial issue in recent years: Simma (ed.), *The United Nations Charter: A Commentary* (2nd edn, 2002) at 840. The UN website now once more provides this information on matters brought to the attention of the SC but not discussed by it; <www.un.org/Docs/sc/annual03_pt5>.

[44] For example, 1978 UNYB 5.

[45] 1966 UNYB 190 at 192.

[46] 1946 UNYB 327; Crockett, *The Fifty Years War* (1995), 59.

[47] 1972 UNYB 136.

[48] There is also controversy as to the significance of its statements, as opposed to its resolutions: see Talmon, 'The statements by the President of the Security Council', 2 Chinese Journal of International Law (2003) 419.

final say not only as to what is an act of aggression, threat to the peace or breach of the peace under Chapter VII of the Charter, but also as to what is a threat or use of force under Article 2(4) or an armed attack and as to whether a state is acting in self-defence under Article 51? This question as to the scope of Security Council powers is important because the end of the Cold War has brought vastly increased activity by the Security Council. Whereas commentators used to discuss the problem of the inactivity of the Security Council, now they concern themselves also with difficulties over the legitimacy of its actions.[49]

The debate as to whether judicial review of the Security Council's resolutions on the use of force is possible and desirable has revived with the end of the Cold War; this issue—whether it should be the International Court of Justice rather than the Security Council that has the final word in making determinations under Article 39 and deciding on action under Chapter VII—has come up before the International Court of Justice in recent cases. Thus in the *Lockerbie* case Libya argued that a Security Council resolution was invalid because the Security Council was not entitled to find a threat to the peace under Article 39 such as to justify it in passing a binding resolution under Chapter VII.[50] And in the *Application of the Convention on the Prevention and Punishment of the Crime of Genocide* case the Court was asked to pronounce on the validity of the Security Council arms embargo on the whole of the former Yugoslavia imposed in Security Council Resolution 713 (1991), and to determine whether the embargo was invalid because it conflicted with the right of self-defence of Bosnia-Herzegovina under the UN Charter.[51] To date, the International Court of Justice has avoided a categorical answer to the sensitive question as to whether it may allow judicial review of Security Council decisions. Commentators are divided as to whether in principle judicial review should be available or whether it would be incompatible with the primary responsibility of the Security Council for the maintenance of international peace and security 'in order to ensure prompt and effective action by the United Nations' under Article 24 of the UN Charter.[52]

---

[49] Brownlie, 'The Decisions of the Political Organs of the UN and the Rule of Law', in Macdonald (ed.), *Essays in Honour of Wang Tieya* (1994), 91; Caron, 'The Legitimacy of the Collective Authority of the Security Council', 87 AJIL (1993) 552; Bedjaoui, *The New World Order and the Security Council: Testing the Legality of its Acts* (1994); Dossier: Actualité de Pouvoirs du Conseil de Securité, 37 Revue Belge de droit international (2004) 457; see also Chapter 7 below.

[50] *Cases concerning Questions of Interpretation and Application of the 1971 Montreal Convention arising from the Aerial Incident at Lockerbie, Preliminary Objections*, Libya v UK, Libya v USA, ICJ Reports (1998) 9, 115.

[51] Provisional Measures, ICJ Reports (1993) 3, 325.

[52] Gowlland-Debbas, 'The Relationship between the International Court of Justice and the Security Council in the Light of the Lockerbie case', 88 AJIL (1994) 643; Graefrath, 'Leaving to the Court what belongs to the Court', 4 EJIL (1993) 184; Franck, 'The Powers

But the Court did make clear in its discussion of admissibility in the *Nicaragua* case that it does not regard itself as excluded from deciding on cases involving ongoing armed conflict including decisions as to collective self-defence. The USA argued that

The Application was inadmissible because each of Nicaragua's allegations constitutes no more than a reformulation of a single fundamental claim that the United States is engaged in an unlawful use of armed force, or breach of the peace, or acts of aggression against Nicaragua, a matter which is committed by the Charter and by practice to the competence of other organs, in particular the United Nations Security Council. All allegations of this kind are confided to the political organs of the Organization for consideration and determination; the United States quotes Article 24 of the Charter, which confers upon the Security Council 'primary responsibility for the maintenance of international peace and security'.[53] The provisions of the Charter dealing with the ongoing use of armed force contain no recognition of the possibility of settlement by judicial, as opposed to political means.[54]

Nicaragua replied that this US argument failed to take account of the fundamental distinction between Article 2(4), which defines a legal obligation to refrain from the threat or use of force, and Article 39, which establishes a political process. The International Court of Justice chose to deal with this question together with the argument advanced by the USA that the subject matter of the Application, the ongoing exercise of the inherent right of individual or collective self-defence under Article 51 of the Charter, was outside the subject matter jurisdiction of the Court. Article 51 provides a role in such matters only for the Security Council. Nicaragua replied that Article 51 does not support the claim that the question of the legitimacy of actions assertedly taken in self-defence is committed exclusively to the Security Council. The International Court of Justice asserted the right of the Court to resolve any legal questions. But it seemed to have some sympathy with the argument that determinations of

of Appreciation: Who is the Ultimate Guardian of UN Legality', 86 AJIL (1992) 519; Alvarez, 'Judging the Security Council', 90 AJIL (1996) 1; Gray, 'The Use and Abuse of the International Court of Justice: Cases concerning the Use of Force after Nicaragua', 14 EJIL (2003) 867.

[53] Article 24 of the UN Charter provides:

1. In order to ensure prompt and effective action by the United Nations, its Members confer on the Security Council primary responsibility for the maintenance of international peace and security, and agree that in carrying out its duties under this responsibility the Security Council acts on their behalf.

2. In discharging these duties the Security Council shall act in accordance with the Purposes and Principles of the United Nations. The specific powers granted to the Security Council for the discharge of these duties are laid down in Chapters VI, VII, and XII.

3. The Security Council shall submit annual and, when necessary, special reports to the General Assembly for its consideration.

[54] *Nicaragua* case (Jurisdiction and Admissibility) ICJ Reports (1984) 551, para 89.

aggression under Article 39 of the UN Charter could be dealt with only by the Security Council. In a rather obscure passage the Court said that the USA had misrepresented the Nicaraguan case as relating to Chapter VII when in fact it concerned Article 2(4), and for this reason could properly be brought before the principal judicial organ of the UN for peaceful settlement.[55] The implication seems to be that matters under Chapter VII could not properly be entertained by the Court. It is interesting that the Court did not pronounce on the DRC's claim that Uganda was guilty of aggression in the *Case concerning Armed Activities on the Territory of the Congo*.[56]

In the *Nicaragua* case the Court said that the Security Council had only primary, not exclusive, authority under Article 24 of the UN Charter; moreover, the Court had not in the past shied away from cases merely because they had political implications or involved serious elements of the use of force. The USA itself had brought cases involving armed attacks. 'As to the inherent right of self-defence, the fact that it is referred to in the Charter as a "right" is indicative of a legal dimension; if in the present proceedings it becomes necessary for the Court to judge in this respect between the parties it cannot be debarred from doing so by the existence of a procedure for the States concerned to report to the Security Council in this connection.'

Encouraged by this reasoning, states have recently brought several cases to the Court on this sensitive subject matter of the use of force. Cameroon brought a boundary case against Nigeria, in which it also made allegations that Nigeria had illegally undertaken cross-border incursions;[57] Iran sued the USA in two cases arising out of US involvement in the 1980–88 Iran–Iraq conflict, first, the *Oil Platforms* case,[58] and, second, a case arising out of the shooting down of the Iran Airbus by a US warship;[59] Yugoslavia brought cases against ten NATO states for their bombing campaign over Kosovo;[60] Pakistan sued India for shooting down a Pakistani aircraft over Pakistani air-space;[61] DRC sued Burundi, Uganda, and Rwanda for acts of armed aggression perpetrated in flagrant violation of the UN Charter; it

---

[55] *Nicaragua* case (Jurisdiction and Admissibility) ICJ Reports (1984) 551, para 94.

[56] ICJ Reports (2005) 168. Judges Elaraby and Simma were critical of this approach in their Separate Opinions.

[57] In 1998 the Court found jurisdiction (ICJ Reports (1998) 275; it gave judgment on the merits in 2002.

[58] The Court found jurisdiction in ICJ Reports (1996) 803, and gave judgment on the merits in 2003.

[59] The *Case concerning the Aerial Incident of 3rd July, 1988* was settled: 35 ILM (1996) 550.

[60] *Legality of the Use of Force*, Yugoslavia v Belgium, ICJ Reports (1999) 124, 38 ILM (1999) 950. The Court refused provisional measures on the basis that it lacked *prima facie* jurisdiction on the merits of the case: see Chapter 2. It subsequently decided that it had no jurisdiction (ICJ Reports (2004) 279).

[61] *Aerial Incident of 10 August 1999* (Pakistan v India). The Court decided that it had no jurisdiction to decide this case: ICJ Reports (2000) 12.

claimed that the invasion by respondent state troops on 2 August 1998 in an attempt to overthrow the government and establish a Tutsi regime was a violation of the DRC's sovereignty and territorial integrity.[62] This recent trend made it possible that the Court would for the first time since the *Nicaragua* case begin to play a central role in the development of the law on the use of force.[63] As it turned out, the Court has not given decisions on the merits in many of these cases and it avoided the question of the use of force in *Cameroon v Nigeria*.[64] However, it did go out of its way to discuss the law on self-defence at some length in the *Oil Platforms* case.[65] And more recently it gave an important judgment on the use of force, intervention and self-defence in the *Case concerning Armed Activities on the Territory of the Congo (DRC v Uganda)*.[66] The Court's approach has generally been cautious in that it has avoided controversial issues such as anticipatory self-defence and the use of force against non-state actors.

The question has also arisen of the role of the General Assembly and its relationship to the Security Council in the development and application of the law in this area. Chapter IV of the UN Charter gives some guidance on the role of the General Assembly and the division of functions between the two organs of the UN. Under Article 10 the General Assembly may make recommendations to member states or to the Security Council; Article 11(1) says that the General Assembly may consider the general principles of cooperation in the maintenance of international peace and security and may make recommendations with regard to such principles; Article 11(2) sets out a division as far as *action* is concerned: any such question on which action is necessary should be referred to the Security Council; Article 11(3) authorizes the General Assembly to call the attention of the Security Council to situations likely to endanger international peace and security.[67] Article 12 is designed to avoid conflict between the two organs;

---

[62] *Armed Activities on the Territory of the Congo*. The DRC withdrew the cases against Burundi and Rwanda, but later brought a new case against Rwanda in 2002. The Court held it had no jurisdiction in this case: ICJ Reports (2006).

[63] The issue of whether the Security Council has the exclusive and final right to make determinations as to the occurrence of acts of aggression also caused problems in the work of the International Law Commission on the Draft Code of Offences against the Peace and Security of Mankind and later on the Statute of the International Criminal Court.

[64] ICJ Reports (2002) 303 para 308. For a discussion of the Court's role in cases concerning the use of force, see Gray, 'The Use and Abuse of the International Court of Justice: Cases concerning the Use of Force after *Nicaragua*', 14 EJIL (2003) 867.

[65] ICJ Reports (2003) 161. See Chapter 4 below. For a discussion of the Court's controversial assertion of its jurisdiction to consider this issue, see Chevenier, 'Oil on Troubled Waters', 63 CLJ (2004) 1. Several judges (including Judges Elaraby, Simma and Rigaux) were apparently influenced by the need to reaffirm the law on the use of force in the light of *Operation Iraqi Freedom*.

[66] ICJ Reports (2005) 168.

[67] Simma (ed.), *The UN Charter: A Commentary* (2nd edn. 2002) at 284; Bailey and Daws, *The Procedure of the UN Security Council* (3rd edn, 1998) at 281, and see Chapter 7

it provides that while the Security Council is exercising in respect of any dispute or situation the functions assigned to it in the Charter, the General Assembly shall not make any recommendation with regard to that dispute or situation unless the Security Council so requests. That is, both the General Assembly and the Security Council may discuss questions to do with the use of force and make recommendations, but the Charter scheme empowered only the Security Council to make binding decisions on action in this area under Article 25 and it was the Security Council that was to have the primary role.[68]

The question therefore arises as to how far condemnation or approval or discussion by the Security Council and by the General Assembly are of equal importance in interpreting the Charter and developing the law on the use of force by states. Both are fora in which states can set out their legal justifications for the use of force and appeal to other states for support; accordingly it does not seem appropriate to try to distinguish between the two fora with regard to the statements in debates and in explanation of votes.[69] As regards the significance of resolutions, the General Assembly may be more representative, but it was the Security Council that was expressly assigned primary responsibility for the maintenance of international peace and security. Nevertheless, the General Assembly has passed resolutions not only confirming condemnation already made by the Security Council but also condemning behaviour when a veto or threat of a veto prevented a Security Council resolution from being adopted.

At times western powers have challenged the right of the General Assembly to use terms such as 'aggression' contained in Chapter VII of the UN Charter on the ground that the General Assembly should not override the discretion of the Security Council. For example, in 1981 the UK objected to the General Assembly using the phrase in relation

---

below. On the drafting history of Articles 10–13, see also Franck, *Recourse to Force* (2002) at 31.

[68] This question arose recently in the Advisory Opinion on *Legal Consequences of the Construction of a Wall in the Occupied Palestinian Territory*, ICJ Reports (2004) 136 para 25. See Chapter 7 below. On the complex question of which Security Council resolutions are binding, see Bailey and Daws *The Procedure of the UN Security Council* (3rd edn, 1998) at 263.

[69] In more recent years since the end of the Cold War and the virtual end of decolonization General Assembly debates and Resolutions have generally become different in tone, often adopted by consensus. Also, the use of the Security Council as a mini-General Assembly, with many non-member states claiming the right to address the Council, was criticized by western states during the Cold War (for example, by Australia, SC 2620th meeting, 1985, which said that the Security Council should not be used as a forum for confrontation in this way); this practice is now much less common, see Bailey and Daws *The Procedure of the UN Security Council* (3rd edn, 1998) at 154. It is now developing states which accuse developed states of improper use of the Security Council to deal with matters properly belonging to the General Assembly: see 261 below.

to South Africa's actions against the front-line states.[70] Again Canada, speaking on the General Assembly resolution on the Israeli bombing of the Iraqi nuclear reactor, argued that the General Assembly should not use the term 'acts of aggression'; it was a matter for the Security Council to make such determinations.[71] The USA denounced the repeated condemnation of Israel for this attack as a ritualistic exercise which failed to make a positive contribution to resolving the Middle East conflict; the Security Council had itself condemned Israel for this action. Sweden opposed certain passages of General Assembly Resolution 38/180A (1983) calling for states to refrain from supplying weapons to Israel, to suspend economic and financial dealings, and to sever diplomatic, trade, and cultural links. Sweden said that these were matters for the Security Council and that the resolution could not be reconciled with the division of responsibilities between the General Assembly and the Security Council.[72] That is, western states have made it clear that they do not regard General Assembly resolutions as authoritative determinations under Chapter VII.

The assessment of Security Council and General Assembly practice may not be simple.[73] After a debate member states may choose neither to pass a resolution nor to make a statement. And in their debates states are often cautious in their language; they may not always use legal language in their assessment of the justification for a use of force. They may choose rather to express sympathy or understanding of the action taken. For example, the UK, in its reaction to controversial uses of force by the USA, has from time to time adopted forms of words that allow it to offer support or sympathy but to stop short of an unequivocal endorsement of the legal argument of the USA; to a casual observer this statement may appear to offer support for the US legal argument, but in fact it does not go so far.

The resolutions and statements of the Security Council and the resolutions of the General Assembly tend not to use the language of the Charter in Articles 2(4) and 51, nor to refer to them expressly; when they do refer to these Articles it is normally to recall them in general terms in the preamble of the resolution.[74] The Security Council in particular may

---

[70] 1981 UNYB 228.

[71] 1982 UNYB 425.

[72] 1983 UNYB 330. In the vote on GA Res 36/27 (109–2–34) condemning Israel for its attack several western states abstained on this ground.

[73] See Franck, *Recourse to Force* (2002), for an examination of Security Council practice. Franck argues that the actual practice of UN organs manifests 'a situational ethic rather than doctrinaire consistency' on self-defence and other subjects. His study leads him to conclude that certain 'unconventional justification [for the use of force] has been validated in systemic practice.' However, to the extent that he is arguing that failure by states to condemn certain controversial behaviour may lead to a change in the law and the acceptance of loopholes in the Charter allowing anticipatory self-defence and humanitarian intervention, the inferences he draws from practice are open to question: see 23 below.

[74] The *Repertoire of Practice of the Security Council* and the *Repertoire of Practice of UN Organs* list such express references. It is noteworthy that the Security Council has not expressly

not be concerned to determine legality; its role in the maintenance of international peace and security may lead it to choose to avoid any attribution of responsibility for breach of the law. Its resolutions may be indeterminate; a condemnation may be interpreted as limited to the particular facts, simply a condemnation of the particular use of force in the particular circumstances or as a pronouncement on the general law invoked by the states using force. Even when the Security Council does condemn it generally does so on the particular facts, in order to secure consensus and perhaps to secure the strongest condemnation possible. That is, the resolution makes no general pronouncement on the legality of, for example, anticipatory self-defence or the protection of nationals; it condemns the particular use of force. These episodes do not provide express confirmation that the general right invoked to justify the use of force is not part of international law, but if there is no example of a particular type of force escaping condemnation, that is persuasive evidence against that doctrine.

In contrast, the views expressed in the debates on the particular uses of force or in the general debates on law-making resolutions will be more revealing of states' views of the legal position and will reflect the doctrinal divergence behind the resolutions. A resolution condemning a particular use of force may reflect very different views of the legal position; the different states voting for the resolution may have done so for very different reasons and on the basis of different views of the law. Thus, for example, some states would reject the legality of a use of force simply because it was taken in protection of nationals abroad or was anticipatory; others would not reject all such actions in principle but would condemn the action on the particular facts because it was disproportionate or unnecessary. In the case of South Africa, Portugal, and Israel some states regarded any claim by these states to use force in self-defence against neighbouring states as defective because they were acting to further illegal policies or illegal occupation; other states accepted the possibility of self-defence by South Africa, Portugal, and Israel, but looked at each incident on its facts.

It may be argued that condemnation of a particular use of force by the Security Council or General Assembly is conclusive or at least persuasive as to illegality. Condemnation of another state by a state with whom it normally has close relations, as when the UK condemns a use of force by the USA or the USA condemns a use of force by Israel, is exceptionally strong evidence of illegality. Franck makes a convincing case with regard

---

concerned itself to identify threats of force: see Sadurska, 'Threats of Force', 82 AJIL (1988) 239. On threats of force under Article 2(4), see *Nicaragua* case, ICJ Reports (1986) 14 at para 227; *Legality of Threat of use of Nuclear Weapons*, ICJ Reports (1996) 226 at para 47. See also, Stürchler, *The Threat of Force in International Law* (2007); Roscini, 'Threats of Armed Force and Contemporary International Law', 54 Netherlands International Law Review (2007) 229.

to the General Assembly that states tended even during the Cold War to vote in a principled way in responding to a use of force by a superpower or by a third world state; there was not a double standard on the part of most states except for the superpowers themselves and their close supporters.[75] But a slight doubt arises because occasionally both the General Assembly and the Security Council seemed willing to condemn a state for a particular episode because of its past record. Examples of this can be found in the regular condemnations of Portugal and later of South Africa for particular uses of force. It seems that because these states were acting in furtherance of colonialism and apartheid there was a readiness to condemn for individual uses of force even without clear evidence with regard to the particular incident. Such doubts about the evidence led western states sometimes to abstain on certain resolutions. An example is the episode in 1969 when the UK and Spain did not join in the votes condemning Portugal for actions against Senegal, Zambia, and Guinea. The UK said that the Security Council was not dealing with Portugese policy in Africa, but with a specific incident for which it was not justified to condemn Portugal.[76] Other states argued that self-defence could not be invoked to perpetuate colonialism with regard to Guinea and Portugal.[77] Similarly in 1976 the USA refused to condemn South Africa for its use of force against Zambia on the ground that the episode needed further investigation.[78] If this apparent scrupulousness on the part of the UK and the USA is taken at face value, then condemnations may not be conclusive evidence of illegality in these cases. However, these were special cases and there are no apparent equivalents today.

The more difficult question and one that has given rise to greater controversy among writers is whether, if condemnation is evidence of illegality, the converse is true? Is failure to condemn evidence of legality? Not necessarily so, for there are many reasons for a failure to condemn.[79] Indeed, the practice of the Security Council shows a distinct reluctance to condemn; even a finding of responsibility is unusual. Even if there is an investigation of a use of force where there are conflicting claims by the

---

[75] Franck, 'Of Gnats and Camels: Is there a Double Standard at the United Nations?', 78 AJIL (1984) 811.
[76] 1969 UNYB 137.
[77] 1969 UNYB 140.
[78] 1976 UNYB 166.
[79] See Barsotti, 'Armed Reprisals', in Cassese (ed.), *Current Legal Regulation of the Use of Force* (1986), 79. For example, states on the Security Council or the General Assembly may think that, although the legality of a particular use of force is open to question, the acts should not be condemned because they were morally or politically justified. (As, for example, with the failure to condemn Israel in 1967 over the Entebbe raid, the Tanzanian invasion of Uganda to overthrow Idi Amin or the split vote on the condemnation of the US use of force against Panama.)

two sides there may be no conclusion as to responsibility and no blame.[80] Similarly the UN Secretary-General, in his many reports on conflicts to the Security Council, generally avoids the attribution of responsibility unless expressly asked to pronounce on this, as, for example, when the Security Council asked him to report on the responsibility for the start of the Iran/Iraq war in 1980.[81] He is generally very careful in his public statements not to attribute blame for breach of the law on the use of force. It is also common for the Security Council and the General Assembly's initial response to a conflict to be to avoid any finding of responsibility and simply to call for an end to all intervention.

Thus the Security Council unanimously passed Resolution 479 (1980) at the outbreak of the Iran/Iraq conflict; this called upon Iran and Iraq to refrain immediately from any further use of force and to settle their dispute by peaceful means. The resurgence of conflict in Kashmir and the outbreak of conflict between Ethiopia and Eritrea led the Security Council again simply to call for peaceful settlement. With regard to the latter conflict, the Security Council subsequently imposed an arms embargo on *both* states in Resolution 1298 (2000). In contrast the Security Council did not call for an immediate ceasefire when Israel invaded Lebanon and when Ethiopia invaded Somalia in 2006. Express findings of aggression (or of aggressive acts) are extremely unusual. It has been only states that were in some sense seen as outlaws that have been condemned for aggression by both the Security Council and the General Assembly; Portugal when it refused to relinquish its colonial possessions, Southern Rhodesia after its unilateral declaration of independence, Israel after its occupation of the West Bank, Gaza and other territory, South Africa during apartheid and its occupation of Namibia, and Indonesia after its invasion of East Timor. Express condemnation by name is also unusual, although it may nevertheless be clear which state is being criticized. For example, in 1983 the General Assembly passed Resolution 38/10 on Central America by consensus; it asserted in general terms the duty of all states to refrain from the threat of use of force, and the inalienable right of all peoples to decide on their own form of government free from all foreign intervention, coercion or limitation; it then condemned the acts of aggression against the sovereignty, independence, and territorial integrity of the states of the region, but did not name any specific state as responsible.[82] Similarly when Turkey invaded Cyprus, Iran attacked commercial shipping during the Iran/Iraq war, the USA intervened in Grenada and Nicaragua, resolutions passed by the Security Council and

---

[80] As with Iran/Iraq in 1974, 1974 UNYB 252.
[81] UN doc S/23273, 9 December 1991.
[82] 1983 UNYB 197.

the General Assembly condemned the behaviour, but did not name the state responsible.

If there is no condemnation of a particular use of force by the Security Council because a permanent member actually uses its veto, or threatens to use its veto, it would seem to be even harder to argue that the use of force is therefore legal.[83] A few writers have, however, made this argument and have asserted that failure of the Security Council to condemn (whether because of the veto or not) constitutes acquiescence by other states and helps to undermine the prohibition on the use of force or intervention and to support controversial doctrines of international law, such as a right of pro-democratic intervention or the (pre-9/11) right to use force in retaliation for terrorist attacks or the right to use force to protect nationals abroad.[84] This unusual approach to the assessment of state practice discounts the statements of states and ignores widespread condemnation; it also discounts not only general resolutions of the General Assembly on the use of force but also the massive network of treaties which reinforce the prohibitions of the use of force and of intervention; it gives decisive weight to the action of the state using force. This clearly privileges powerful states and especially the permanent members of the Security Council who, through the veto or threat of veto, can create new customary international law in reinterpretation of the Charter. In a more extreme version of this argument, some have argued that even Security Council or General Assembly condemnation of a particular use of force, if it is not followed by any action against the state condemned, also constitutes acquiescence.[85] Some, like D'Amato, have used these arguments mainly to argue that controversial US actions are lawful; others have applied it to challenge the customary status of the prohibition on force.[86] Both these approaches discount what states say in reaction to the use of force by other states; they claim that the absence of a Security Council or General Assembly resolution or of any sanctions against the state using force means that its behaviour should be seen not as a breach of international law but as the emergence of a new right to use force.

---

[83] The US government took this position with regard to regional action under Chapter VIII; failure to condemn was argued to constitute authorization by the Security Council: see Chapter 9 below.

[84] D'Amato, *International Law: Process and Prospect* (2nd edn, 1995), Chapter 6; Weisburd, *Use of Force* (1997); Arend and Beck, *International Law and the Use of Force* (1993), Chapter 10. Franck takes a similar line in *Recourse to Force* (2002). On pro-democratic invasions, see Chapter 2 below; on force against terrorist attacks and the protection of nationals, see Chapters 4 and 6 below.

[85] Weisburd, ibid.; Arend and Beck, ibid.

[86] Arangio-Ruiz, *The UN Declaration on Friendly Relations and the system of sources of international law* (1979). Franck, 'Who killed Article 2(4)?', 64 AJIL (1970) 809, and reply by Schacter, 'The Reports of the Death of Article 2(4) are Greatly Exaggerated', 65 AJIL (1971) 544; Franck, *Recourse to Force* (2002).

The effect of this argument is compounded by the fact that some of these writers also discount what the states using force actually say in justification of their use of force and try to extract new rights to use force on the basis of the actions of the states using force. That is, they ignore the fact that states generally do not claim revolutionary new rights to use force, but try to defend their use of force by claiming self-defence or other legal justifications. They say that the state practice should be reinterpreted in the light of what the state *could* or *should* have said to explain its actions. Thus, if the action could be favourably described as humanitarian intervention, or pro-democratic intervention, then this supports the emergence of such a doctrine, even though states do not invoke these new rights but base their use of force on traditional doctrines. The Court in the *Nicaragua* case refused to take this approach in its consideration of the question whether a new customary law right of forcible intervention to assist opposition forces to overthrow governments had become established. For the Court, the fact that states did not claim a new right of intervention was a decisive factor in the rejection of the emergence of any new customary law right. States in fact justified their interventions by invoking the doctrine of collective self-defence; they did not claim a new right to use force in response to invitations from opposition forces.[87]

Clearly there can be no common ground in the assessment of the significance of state practice between those writers who discount what states say and those who take the more traditional view adopted by the International Court of Justice in the *Nicaragua* case.[88] It is only a few writers who take this extreme position of treating General Assembly or Security Council condemnation as support and ignoring the actual language of states. This approach has been subjected to serious criticism,[89] but it cannot be ignored because recently with regard to Kosovo there were signs that some states were putting forward such arguments in their attempt to justify the NATO action. That is, they were arguing that past practice should be reinterpreted to support a doctrine of humanitarian intervention.[90]

---

[87] *Nicaragua* case para 207.

[88] Farer, 'Human Rights in Law's Empire: The Jurisprudence War', 85 AJIL (1991) 117; Franck, *Recourse to Force* (2002); Murphy, 'The doctrine of preemptive self-defense', 50 Villanova. LR (2005) 699 at 727; Corten, 'The controversies over the customary prohibition on the use of force', 16 EJIL (2005) 803.

[89] Mullerson, 'Sources of International Law: New Tendencies in Soviet Thinking', 83 AJIL (1989) 494 at 505; Brownlie, 'The UN Charter and the Use of Force 1945–1985', in Cassese (ed.), *The Current Legal Regulation of the Use of Force* (1986) at 491. Akehurst, 'Letter', 80 AJIL (1986) 147.

[90] See Chapter 2 below.

EFFECTIVENESS OF THE PROHIBITION OF THE USE OF FORCE

The question as to how far divergences from the prohibition on the use of force should be seen not as breaches but rather as exceptions to or modifications of the prohibition is crucial also to any assessment of the role of international law in this area. There is widespread scepticism as to the 'effectiveness' of international law on the use of force, recently intensified by *Operation Iraqi Freedom*. Is this justified? The gap between the prohibition of the use of force and the practice seems striking to some commentators, but this divergence should not necessarily be taken as proving the ineffectiveness or pointlessness of the law in this area. Conversely, international law should not be assumed to be effective in the sense of controlling or influencing state behaviour just because state behaviour is in fact in compliance with it.

As the ICJ put it in the *Nicaragua* case, in a now very well-known passage in its discussion of whether the prohibition of the use of force does represent customary international law:

It is not to be expected that in the practice of States the application of the rules in question should have been perfect, in the sense that States should have refrained, with complete consistency, from the use of force or from intervention in each other's internal affairs. The Court does not consider that, for a rule to be established as customary, the corresponding practice must be in absolutely rigorous conformity with the rule. In order to deduce the existence of customary rules, the Court deems it sufficient that the conduct of States should, in general, be consistent with such rules, and that instances of State conduct inconsistent with a given rule should generally be treated as breaches of that rule, not as indications of the recognition of a new rule. If a State acts in a way prima facie incompatible with a recognized rule, but defends its conduct by appealing to exceptions or justifications contained within the rule itself, then whether or not the State's conduct is in fact justifiable on that basis, the significance of that attitude is to confirm rather than to weaken the rule.[91]

But the insistence that breaches may be seen as strengthening rather than negating rules cannot be taken too far without losing plausibility.

In this as in other areas, it is fundamentally misguided to attribute to international law an exclusive role in controlling state behaviour; it tends to be non-lawyers rather than lawyers whose expectations are unreasonably elevated and who attack international law as having no significant role when there is anything less than perfect compliance. As in the national sphere, legal rules are only one among a variety of factors that may influence behaviour.

---

[91] *Nicaragua* case, para 186.

Questions as to whether international law does influence state behaviour involve a study of the role of international law in national decision-making; this requires empirical work on the internal decision-making processes. The focus must shift from the artificial legal entity, the state, to the politicians and officials actually making the decisions on the use of force and the response to the use of force by others. But there are all sorts of practical problems with this type of empirical work. A state is not a unitary entity; there may be a wide range of views, even diametrically opposed views, as to the content and importance of international law on the use of force within the branches of government or between those branches. This was very striking in the administration of President George W Bush where it appeared that different members of the administration deliberately expressed contradictory positions on international law. Studies such as that of Chayes on the 1962 Cuban Missile Crisis remain unusual.[92] Access to the material on national decision-making may be possible only many years after the events in question. Thus the role of the law in the UK decision-making process in the 1956 Suez Crisis came to light only thirty years later when the official papers could finally be published.[93] And generalization may not be justified; just because the officials and politicians used international law in one way in one episode it does not follow that the same approach would be adopted in different circumstances. That is, the question of the impact of international law on national decision-making is not easily resolved, if at all. In the absence of such empirical research the matter remains one for inference from public statements and actions of states. Simple conclusions as to effectiveness may not be possible. Writers differ fundamentally in their interpretation of state practice; thus some claim that 'non-intervention is preached but not practised' and that states assert a principle with which they do not comply.[94] Some have said that the prohibition on the use of force is not customary law because states had used force both before and after the Charter and the reactions of other states were often ambiguous and inadequate.[95] Others say that, broadly, states comply with the law outlawing the use of force.

One of the issues that has given rise to the most significant scepticism as to effectiveness of the prohibition of the use of force is the question of

---

[92] Chayes, *The Cuban Missile Crisis* (1987).

[93] Marston, 'Armed Intervention in the 1956 Suez Canal Crisis: The Legal Advice Tendered to the British Government', 37 ICLQ (1988) 773.

[94] Lowe, 'The Principle of Non-intervention: Use of Force', in Lowe and Warbrick (eds), *The United Nations and the Principle of International Law* (1994), 72.

[95] Arangio-Ruiz, *The UN Declaration on Friendly Relations and the system of sources of international law* (1979); Glennon, *Limits of Law, Prerogatives of Power: Interventionism after Kosovo* (2001).

whether breach of the law on the use of force is cost-free, and whether states may break the law and get away with. This question also is not susceptible of a simple answer. The UN collective security system was generally incapacitated during the Cold War, although regional organizations did impose sanctions in some cases.[96] It is notorious that the only use of Chapter VII enforcement action involving armed force was in Korea, and the legal status of even that action was controversial. The only uses of UN economic sanctions were against Southern Rhodesia and South Africa. The Security Council and the General Assembly from time to time issued condemnations of the use of force by states in their resolutions. The question as to how far a simple condemnation by the Security Council or the General Assembly or a regional organization operated as a disincentive, even in the absence of any formal collective sanction, is not a simple one. Again there can be no conclusive answer without looking behind the state facade, but it is clear from public information that states argue and negotiate to try to avoid condemnation; the price may be intangible, but it is one that states using force do not want to have to pay. The set-piece Security Council and General Assembly debates in which they repeated year after year their condemnation of earlier uses of force by certain states fulfilled a symbolic role.[97] Thus year after year the General Assembly voted to condemn the Israeli attack on the Iraqi nuclear reactor, Vietnam's intervention in Cambodia, and the USSR invasion of Afghanistan.[98] Of course a hazard of this practice is that the General Assembly is then trapped into continuing, because to stop would give the message that the behaviour is somehow now accepted.

The rules of international law in this area clearly also serve a declaratory function; they set out the goal to be aimed at, the ideal that states adhere to. This symbolic function is apparent in the *African Charter* and the 1984 General Assembly *Declaration on the Right of Peoples to Peace*, for example, when they assert the right of peoples to national and international peace and security.[99] Many resolutions of the UN General Assembly have been passed to reassert and develop the rules in the Charter. As was explained above, typically the western states have been suspicious of such resolutions and their ritual reaffirmation of existing rules. They have seen them as pointless and/or dangerous, pointless in that they add nothing to the UN Charter and dangerous in so far as they may depart from it. It is easy to be cynical about such resolutions, especially when they were advocated by

---

[96] See Chapter 9 below.

[97] Bleicher, 'The Legal Significance of Recitation of General Assembly Resolutions', 63 AJIL (1969) 444; Sloan, 'General Assembly Resolutions Revisited', 58 BYIL(1987) 41.

[98] It is interesting that after Iraq invaded Kuwait the ritual inclusion of the nuclear reactor question was dropped.

[99] 21 ILM (1981) 58.

states such as the former USSR, contemporaneously involved in aggression against others. China and Albania both regarded the proposal for the 1987 *Declaration on the Non-Use of Force* as a fraudulent abuse. Much of the debate over the 1987 Declaration was taken up by political point-scoring about breaches of the general rules that states were solemnly debating. But small and new states typically have supported the drafting of general resolutions on the use of force. They have been willing to seek consensus and not simply to use their majority in the General Assembly. Some of the suspicion of general statements of principle misses the point that many states were still colonies at the time of the adoption of the Charter by the fifty-one original member states and that they had come to want to take part in the public reaffirmation of its most important rules. Moreover, the drafting of substantive rules has from the start been accompanied by concern over the functioning of the UN system. To accompany the general resolutions on the use of force the General Assembly has worked endlessly, and often on the initiative of the western states, on resolutions with a more practical focus, such as the *Declaration on the Strengthening of International Security*, and on 'Questions concerning the UN Charter and the Strengthening of the Role of the UN', 'Good Neighbourliness' and so on.

Given the problems of any empirical investigation into 'effectiveness', it is all the more important to look at international law on the use of force in terms of the language used by states. Given that in fact they choose to use this language to explain their behaviour and to respond to that of others, anyone involved in any way in advising states or in assessing their actions will have to be able to engage in this discourse. Simple assertions that this use of language is mere cynical manipulation of the rules, and no more than *ex post facto* rationalization for actions reached on other grounds, are not justified in the absence of empirical evidence that this is in fact the case, and such assertions are no more plausible than the opposite version that states are in fact influenced by law. Of course, it is common for states to offer other justifications as well; it is rare for a state to use the language of international law exclusively. They also offer political explanations, criticisms, and justifications, but with only a tiny number of exceptions they take care to offer a legal argument for their use of force. It is very rare for them not even to try to provide a legal justification. The UK, in response to domestic pressure, gave an elaborate legal justification for its participation in *Operation Iraqi Freedom*. The USA, unconstrained by comparable domestic pressure, was nevertheless concerned to build international support for a mixture of practical and political reasons, and it also offered a legal argument, even if this was not set out in any great detail until after the event.[100]

---

[100] Taft and Buchwald, Legal Advisor and Assistant Legal Advisor, US State Department, 'Pre-emption, Iraq and International Law', 97 AJIL (2003) 557.

The rare instances when states seem to have made a deliberate decision not to give a legal explanation stand out. The absence of any real attempt at a legal justification by the USA, the UK, and France for the protection of the Kurds in 1991 and by Turkey for its incursions into Iraq in pursuit of the PKK in the 1990s and in 2007 is unusual and seems to indicate considerable doubt as to the legality of these actions.[101] Even when politicians do occasionally say that they will no longer observe international law restrictions on the use of force, as was sometimes the case during the Reagan era when the administration suggested that it was not necessary to comply with international law in response to an enemy, an evil empire that did not itself observe the law, the USA continued to offer legal argument in the Security Council.[102] Rather than not even attempt a legal justification, commonly states offer what may seem weak or unconvincing arguments. But it is always important to allow for different viewpoints; even when two opposing states both invoke self-defence they may both believe they have right on their side. Often it is a series of arguments that are offered, maybe differing over time, in order or emphasis. This combination of a series of different justifications is typical legal reasoning, often apparent in arguments in court; a whole series of arguments of differing strengths is included on the chance that one of them may appeal to one particular audience. During the Cold War a constraint on this rhetoric was the consideration that the language of states in their interpretation and application of the UN Charter could operate as a precedent and later be invoked against them.[103] The end of the Cold War has apparently weakened this constraint, at any rate as far as the USA is concerned.

---

[101] On the protection of the Kurds in Iraq, see Chapter 2 below; on Turkey's incursions into Iraq, see Chapter 4 below. On the failure of Turkey to offer reasoned legal justification for its use of force in the 1990s, see Gray and Olleson, 'The Limits of the Law on the Use of Force: Turkey, Iraq and the Kurds', 12 Finnish Yearbook of International Law (2001) 355.

[102] Kirkpatrick, the US representative to the UN, said that 'unilateral compliance with the Charter's principles of non-intervention and non-use of force may make sense in some instances but is hardly in itself a sound basis for either US policy or for international peace and security', 'Law and Reciprocity', 1986 ASIL 59.

[103] As Franck graphically illustrates in Franck and Weisband, *Word Politics* (1972).

2
The prohibition of the use of force

The central rule on the use of force, the prohibition of the threat or use of force contained in Article 2(4) of the UN Charter, is the subject of fundamental disagreement. It provides: 'All Members shall refrain in their international relations from the threat or use of force against the territorial integrity or political independence of any state, or in any other manner inconsistent with the Purposes of the United Nations.' The International Court of Justice in *Armed Activities on the Territory of Congo* proclaimed that Article 2(4) is a cornerstone of the UN Charter.[1] States and commentators generally agree that the prohibition is not only a treaty obligation but also customary law and even *ius cogens*,[2] but there is no comparable agreement on the exact scope of the prohibition.[3]

As mentioned in Chapter 1, there are disagreements between states as to the meaning of Article 2(4). There is a split between developed and developing states as to whether 'the use of force' includes not only armed force but economic coercion. There is also some debate as to what types of activities can amount to 'use of force' as opposed to intervention or mere law enforcement. The judgment in *Nicaragua* distinguished between, on the one hand, the arming and training of armed opposition forces, which could amount to an unlawful use of force, and on the other hand, the supply of funds, which could not.[4] The recent arbitral award in *Guyana v Suriname* pronounced briefly and controversially on the distinction between threat of use of force and mere law enforcement.[5] In another controversial ruling the Claims Commission held in Ethiopia's *Ius ad Bellum* Claims that Eritrea had violated Article 2(4) through its use of force in

---

[1] ICJ Reports (2005) 168 at para 148, 45 ILM (2006) 271.

[2] *Case Concerning Military and Paramilitary Activities in and against Nicaragua (Merits)*, ICJ Reports (1986) 14, para 190. See Christenson, 'The World Court and Jus Cogens', 81 AJIL (1987) 93; Ronzitti, 'Use of Force, Jus Cogens and State Consent', in Cassese (ed.) *The Current Legal Regulation of the Use of Force* (1986) 147; Weisburd, 'The emptiness of the concept of ius cogens, as illustrated by the law in Bosnia-Herzegovina', 17 Michigan Journal of International Law (1995–6) 591.

[3] This book will focus on the use of force. For an interesting discussion of the threat of force, see Stürchler, *The Threat of Force in International Law* (2007); Roscini, 'Threats of Armed Force and Contemporary International Law', 54 Netherlands International Law Review (2007) 229.

[4] *Nicaragua* case at para 228.

[5] Award of arbitral tribunal constituted pursuant to Article 287 of the UN *Convention on the Law of the Sea*, 17 September 2007, para 425–447, available on PCA website; <www.pca-cpa.org>.

defence of what a Boundary Commission subsequently decided to be its own territory.[6]

However, the most basic disagreement concerns the significance of the last part of Article 2(4). This controversy came dramatically to the fore in the use of force by NATO in Kosovo in 1999. States and commentators expressed their fundamental disagreements about the legality of this intervention in terms of Article 2(4). Some claimed that a new right to humanitarian intervention was emerging; others that the NATO action was a flagrant breach of the UN Charter.

The current debate is a reincarnation of earlier disagreements on the interpretation of Article 2(4). Here these will be set out in outline only. Writers disagreed as to whether Article 2(4) reflected existing customary international law or whether it was in 1945 a radical departure from previous customary law, to be narrowly interpreted. The controversy centred on the second part of Article 2(4): should the words 'against the territorial integrity or political independence of any state, or in any other manner inconsistent with the Purposes of the United Nations' be construed as a strict prohibition on all use of force against another state, or did they allow the use of force provided that the aim was not to overthrow the government or seize the territory of the state and provided that the action was consistent with the purposes of the UN?[7] Many US commentators argued during the Cold War that the interpretation of Article 2(4) depended on the effective functioning of the UN collective security system, and therefore that the inability of the Security Council to act because of the veto of the five permanent members meant that Article 2(4) should be read to allow the use of force to further 'world public order' or the principles and purposes of the UN.[8]

For many years this doctrinal disagreement was of limited practical significance in that states themselves rarely made any attempt to interpret Article 2(4) in this narrow fashion; they did not in fact claim that their use of force was justified because it did not aim to seize the territory or

[6] 45 ILM (2006) 430. For a critical account, see Gray, 'The Eritrea/Ethiopia Claims Commission oversteps its boundaries', 17 EJIL (2006) 699. See also the Claims Commission's subsequent Decision Number 7: Guidance Regarding *Ius ad Bellum* Liability (2007).

[7] Bowett, *Self-Defence in International Law* (1958) at 152; Brownlie, *International Law and the Use of Force by States* (1963); Cot and Pellet, *La Charte des Nations Unies* (1991) at 115; Simma (ed.) *The Charter of the United Nations: A Commentary* (2nd edn, 2002) 112; Schindler and Hailbronner *Die Grenzen des völkerrechtlichen Gewaltverbots* (1986); Waldock, 'The Regulation of the Use of Force by Individual States in International Law', 81 RCADI (1952) 415.

[8] This debate is conveniently summarized in the articles by Reisman, 'Coercion and self-determination: construing Charter Article 2(4)' and the reply by Schacter, 'The legality of pro-democratic invasion', 78 AJIL (1984) 642, 646. See also Farer, 'Human Rights in Law's Empire: the Jurisprudence War', 85 AJIL (1991) 117; Franck, 'Who killed Article 2(4)?', 64 AJIL (1970) 809; Henkin, 'The Reports of the Death of Article 2(4) are greatly exaggerated', 65 AJIL (1971) 544; Reisman, 'Kosovo's Antinomies', 93 AJIL (1999) 860.

overthrow the government of another state or because the UN system was not working. They did not rely on a narrow interpretation of Article 2(4) in order to claim a legal right to use force for humanitarian intervention or to overthrow governments in the name of democracy or some other political system. The argument of the UK in the *Corfu Channel* case remained a relatively isolated example; it claimed that its use of forcible intervention in Albanian waters to recover evidence that might indicate who was responsible for the destruction of two British warships by mines did not violate Article 2(4) because its action did not threaten the territorial integrity or the political independence of Albania. The famous rejection of this argument by the ICJ has been interpreted in fundamentally divergent ways, either as a complete rejection of the narrow interpretation of Article 2(4) or as a more limited rejection of the UK claim on the particular facts. The Court said it 'can only regard the alleged right of intervention as the manifestation of a policy of force such as has in the past given rise to most serious abuses and such as cannot find a place in international law. It is still less admissible in the particular form it would take here—it would be reserved for the most powerful states.'[9]

Similarly there were indications that Israel also took a narrow interpretation of Article 2(4) over the Entebbe incident in 1976; when hijackers diverted an aircraft bound for Tel Aviv to Uganda, Israeli forces mounted a successful rescue operation in Uganda. The main argument of Israel in the Security Council was expressly based on self-defence of its nationals, but it also put forward an interpretation of Article 2(4) by the writer O'Connell as allowing the limited use of force when UN machinery was ineffective.[10] This line was not taken up by other states in the Security Council debate, except perhaps by the USA in its passing reference to the breach of Uganda's sovereignty as only temporary.[11] The Israeli argument on Article 2(4) was expressly rejected by Sweden; it said, 'The Charter does not authorize any exception to this rule except for the right of self-defence and enforcement measures undertaken by the Council under Chapter VII of the Charter. This is no coincidence or oversight. Any formal exceptions permitting the use of force or of military intervention in order to achieve certain aims, however laudable, would be bound to be abused, especially by the big and strong, and to pose a threat, especially to the small and

---

[9] ICJ Reports (1949) 4 at 34. The ICJ, in the *Nicaragua* case para 202, construed this as a blanket condemnation of intervention. For the ongoing debate on the significance of the possibility of abuse for the existence of a doctrine of humanitarian intervention, see, for example, Hilpold, 'Humanitarian Intervention: is there a need for a legal reappraisal?', 12 EJIL (2001) 437; Kritsiotis, 'Reappraising Policy Objections to Humanitarian Intervention', 19 Michigan JIL (1998) 1005; Goodman, 'Humanitarian Intervention and Pretexts for War', 100 AJIL (2006) 107.

[10] SC 1942nd meeting (1976), para 102; 1976 UNYB 315.

[11] SC 1941st meeting (1976), para 92.

weak.'[12] The overwhelming majority of states speaking in the debate regarded Israel's action as a breach of Article 2(4). Those who did not condemn Israel did not expressly defend the legality of its action in terms of a narrow interpretation of Article 2(4).

More significantly, when the USA justified its invasion of Grenada in 1983 it suggested in the Security Council that Article 2(4) should not be seen in isolation; 'the prohibitions against the use of force in the Charter are contextual, not absolute. They provide justification for the use of force in pursuit of other values also inscribed in the Charter, such values as freedom, democracy, peace.'[13] But earlier in the debate the USA had relied on the right to protect its nationals in danger and on an invitation by the Governor-General of Grenada to justify its action. Thus in the Entebbe and Grenada incidents the narrow interpretation of Article 2(4) as a less than absolute prohibition of the use of force was not crucial to the state using force: the USA and Israel also put forward other arguments to justify their actions, and the interpretation of Article 2(4) played only a subsidiary and not a decisive role in determining the legality of the intervention. The question of the interpretation of Article 2(4) plays a more decisive role in the debate over humanitarian intervention.

HUMANITARIAN INTERVENTION

Until recently unilateral humanitarian intervention was not put forward as a legal doctrine by states. The Indian action in Bangladesh (1971) which helped the people to secure independence from Pakistan and to end repression,[14] the Tanzanian action in Uganda (1979) which led to the overthrow of Idi Amin,[15] and the Vietnamese invasion of Cambodia (1978) which led to the overthrow of Pol Pot[16] were not in fact justified by India, Tanzania and Vietnam on the basis of humanitarian action; rather, the states using force focused mainly on self-defence. The first two episodes avoided condemnation by the Security Council or the General Assembly,[17] but the last, although it was at least as persuasive a case for humanitarian

---

[12] SC 1940th meeting (1976), para 121.
[13] SC 2491st meeting (1983), para 53; 1983 UNYB 211. For a further discussion of the US intervention in Grenada, see 157 below.
[14] 1971 UNYB 144; Franck and Rodley, 'After Bangladesh: The Law of Humanitarian Intervention by Military Force', 67 AJIL (1973) 275.
[15] 1979 UNYB 262.
[16] 1979 UNYB 271.
[17] Leading some commentators to infer acquiescence and the possible development of a doctrine of humanitarian intervention. See, for example, Franck, 'Interpretation and Change in the Law of Humanitarian Intervention', in Holzgrefe and Keohane (eds), *Humanitarian Intervention* (2003) at 204. See also 23 above.

intervention, divided states partly on Cold War lines (and partly because of the regional rivalry between Vietnam and China) and was repeatedly condemned by the General Assembly.[18] Many states, including France and the UK, said that violations of human rights could not justify the use of force.[19]

During the Cold War it was writers rather than states that argued in favour of the doctrine of humanitarian intervention as a justification for the use of force by states.[20] In 1984 the UK Foreign and Commonwealth Office had expressed considerable doubt as to the existence of such a doctrine, saying that it was very controversial: the state practice to which advocates of the right of humanitarian intervention had appealed provided an uncertain base on which to rest such a right. Not least this was because history had shown that humanitarian ends were almost always mixed with other, less laudable motives for intervening, and because often the humanitarian benefits of an intervention were either not claimed by the intervening state or were only put forward as an *ex post facto* justification of the intervention. In fact 'the best case that can be made in support of humanitarian intervention is that it cannot be said to be unambiguously illegal'.[21] The absence of the express invocation of the right by states did not, however, deter some writers from arguing that all or some of the above episodes were actually part of state practice supporting a legal right to humanitarian intervention because the states using force *should have* or *could have* used this justification.[22]

These writers ignored the General Assembly resolutions on the use of force which outlawed forcible intervention in absolute terms. The *Friendly Relations Declaration* excludes the right to intervene and makes no provision for humanitarian intervention.[23] The *Definition of Aggression* provision that 'no consideration of whatever nature, whether political, economic,

---

[18] As, for example, in GA Res 34/22 (1979).

[19] 1979 UNYB 271 at 274. This intervention in Cambodia was retrospectively said by the Netherlands in the debate over NATO action in Kosovo to have been a genuine humanitarian intervention. It said that it was a shameful episode in the 1980s when the UN had been more indignant at a Vietnamese military intervention in Cambodia, which almost all Cambodians had experienced as a liberation, than at three years of Khmer Rouge genocide, UN Press Release SC/6686, 10 June 1999; SC 4011th meeting, (1999).

[20] See, for example, Lillich (ed.) *Humanitarian Intervention and the United Nations* (1973); Teson, *Humanitarian Intervention: An Inquiry into Law and Morality* (2nd edn,1997).

[21] 'UK Materials on International Law', 57 BYIL (1986) 614.

[22] See Chapter 1 above; Lillich (ed.) *Humanitarian Intervention and the United Nations* (1973); D'Amato, *International Law: Process and Prospect* (2nd edn 1995), D'Amato, 'The invasion of Panama was a lawful response to tyranny', 84 AJIL (1990) 516; Teson, *Humanitarian Intervention: An Inquiry into Law and Morality* (2nd edn,1997) at 192.

[23] GA Res 2625 (1970). For a discussion of the status of this resolution and of its provisions of the use of force, see Arangio-Ruiz *The UN Declaration on Friendly Relations and the System of the Sources in International Law* (1972); Gray, 'The principle of non-use of force', in Lowe and Warbrick (eds), *The United Nations and the Principles of International Law* (1994) 33.

military or otherwise, may serve as a justification for aggression' also supports this.[24] These writers also explained away the rejection of forcible humanitarian intervention by the ICJ in the *Nicaragua* case as either simply mistaken or limited to the particular facts.[25] The USA did not actually invoke the doctrine of humanitarian intervention to justify its support for the *contras* in their attempt to overthrow the government of Nicaragua, or to justify its direct use of force in mining Nicaraguan ports and bombing oil installations. The Court nevertheless considered whether the protection of human rights might provide a legal justification for the US use of force. The Court said, 'While the USA might form its own appraisal of the situation as to respect for human rights in Nicaragua, the use of force could not be the appropriate method to monitor or ensure such respect. With regard to the steps actually taken, the protection of human rights, a strictly humanitarian objective, cannot be compatible with the mining of ports, the destruction of oil installations, or again with the training, arming and equipping of the contras.'[26] This can be seen as either a complete rejection of any right to use force to protect human rights or as merely a finding that the particular US action did not further any humanitarian objective.[27]

Recent years have seen a shift in state practice and a polarization between NATO states on the one hand and Russia, China and the Non-Aligned Movement on the other. Certain states have now been prepared to rely more openly on a legal doctrine of humanitarian intervention. The first signs of this emerged in the UK justification of the operations which it undertook with the USA and France to protect the Kurds and Shiites in Iraq after the 1991 Iraq/Kuwait conflict.[28] During the UN-authorized operation to drive Iraqi forces out of Kuwait the Kurds and Shiites had been encouraged by the coalition states to rebel against the government, but the ceasefire resolution passed by the Security Council made no provision for the protection of the Kurds in northern Iraq and the Shiites in the south. When the operation to drive Iraqi forces out of Kuwait was over, the government of Iraq turned on the Kurds and Shiites. At first the members

---

[24] GA Res 3314 (1974).

[25] For example, Kritisiotis, 'Reappraising Policy Objections to Humanitarian Intervention', 19 Michigan Journal of International Law (1998) 1005; Teson, *Humanitarian Intervention: An Inquiry into Law and Morality* (2nd edn, 1997) at 270.

[26] *Nicaragua* case para 268.

[27] The Court drew a distinction between forcible intervention and genuine humanitarian assistance at para 242. It said, 'There can be no doubt that the provision of strictly humanitarian aid to persons or forces in another country, whatever their political affiliations or objectives, cannot be regarded as unlawful intervention, or as in any other way contrary to international law.'

[28] See Gray, 'After the Ceasefire: Iraq, the Security Council and the Use of Force', 65 BYIL (1994) 135; and 'From Unity to Polarization: International Law and the Use of Force against Iraq', 13 EJIL (2001) 1.

of the Security Council treated this as an internal question for Iraq, but under pressure from France the Security Council returned to the matter and passed Resolution 688 (1991).[29] This called on Iraq to end the repression of its civilian population and to allow access to international humanitarian organizations, but it did not authorize the use of force to help the Kurds and Shiites. The resolution was not passed under Chapter VII and it expressly recalled Article 2(7) of the UN Charter prohibiting the UN from intervention in matters within domestic jurisdiction. Even so, those states which abstained or voted against the resolution did so because they saw it as an illegitimate intervention in Iraqi internal affairs and not a matter for the Security Council.

Despite the absence of express authority from the Security Council, the USA, the UK and France nevertheless forcibly intervened to protect the Kurds and Shiites in Iraq. They proclaimed safe havens and forced Iraqi troops to leave these areas. They did not offer any explicit legal justification for their action; they did not put forward in the Security Council the doctrine of humanitarian intervention as the justification for their action. Indeed, they did not at this time seem to feel the need to put forward any legal justification. This may be seen as an indication that there was no well-established doctrine of humanitarian intervention at that time. The operation was not condemned by the Security Council or the General Assembly. The USA, the UK and France subsequently proclaimed no-fly zones over north and south Iraq and continued to patrol Iraqi airspace in order to protect the Kurds and Shiites.[30] This was also done without Security Council authority. When Iraq lodged protests with the Security Council the USA, the UK and France replied by saying that their measures were designed to prevent Iraqi repression. They also said that they were acting in support of Resolution 688 (1991). This apparent attempt to bring their action within an implied authorization by Security Resolution in the absence of any express authorization provided a pattern that was to be followed in the future.[31]

Later the UK did openly espouse the doctrine of humanitarian intervention. It modified its earlier position that the most that could be said about humanitarian intervention was that it was 'not unambiguously illegal'. From August 1992 it moved gradually towards an expression of the doctrine of humanitarian intervention as the justification for the actions in Iraq. It did so, not in the Security Council, but in response to domestic pressure, in statements and publications in the UK. The Foreign

---

[29] The resolution was passed by 10–3 (Cuba, Yemen, Zimbabwe) – 2 (China, India).

[30] France ended its participation in the operation in 1998; 1999 RGDIP 888–90.

[31] See Lobel and Ratner, 'Bypassing the Security Council: ambiguous authorization to use force, cease-fires and the Iraqi inspection regime', 93 AJIL (1999) 124; and further discussion in Chapter 8.

and Commonwealth Office said that international law develops to meet new situations. 'We believe that international intervention without the invitation of the country concerned can be justified in cases of extreme humanitarian need. This is why we were prepared to commit British forces to *Operation Haven*, mounted by the coalition in response to the refugee crisis involving the Iraqi Kurds. The deployment of these forces was entirely consistent with the objectives of SCR 688 (1991).'[32] But it did not explain *how* this alleged change in the law had come about. If Article 2(4) of the UN Charter is a dynamic provision open to changing interpretation over time, what developments in fact justified a new interpretation? The UK later elaborated on the doctrine of humanitarian intervention, putting forward conditions which could govern its use. First, there should be a compelling and urgent situation of extreme humanitarian distress which demanded immediate relief; the other state should not be able or willing to meet the distress and deal with it; there should be no practical alternative to intervening in order to relieve the stress, and also the action should be limited in time and scope.[33] This UK espousal of the doctrine of humanitarian intervention seems to have been the first open support by a state since the establishment of the UN. The USA, in contrast, did not put forward this doctrine, preferring to rely on implied authorization by the Security Council.[34]

Confrontations between Iraq and the coalition planes patrolling the no-fly zones occurred in 1991 and 1992; they escalated in 1993 when the coalition forces mounted a major operation against Iraqi missile sites and again in 1999 when a long series of confrontations occurred. The actions in 1999 went further than previous use of force in that the coalition rules of

---

[32] 'UK Materials on International Law', 63 BYIL (1992) 824.

[33] 'UK Materials on International Law', 63 BYIL (1992) at 826, 827. For later developments in the doctrine, see 70 BYIL (1999) 595; 71 BYIL (2000) 643–6; 72 BYIL (2001) 695–6. The Canadian Government established a Commission to consider this question: Report of the International Commission on Intervention and State Sovereignty, *The Responsibility to Protect* (2001). The Netherlands government also requested the Advisory Committee on Issues of Public International Law and the Advisory Council on International Affairs to produce an advisory report on the subject: *Humanitarian Intervention* (2000). Many of the writers who support a legal right to humanitarian intervention similarly have tried to produce guidelines to govern its exercise; see, for example, Lillich (ed.) *Humanitarian Intervention and the United Nations* (1973); Verwey, 'Humanitarian Intervention Under International Law', 32 Netherlands International Law Review (1985) 357; Teson, *Humanitarian Intervention: An Inquiry into Law and Morality* (2nd edn, 1997); Charney, 'Anticipatory Humanitarian Intervention in Kosovo', 93 AJIL (1999) 834; Stromseth, 'Rethinking humanitarian intervention: the case for incremental change', in Holzgrefe and Keohane (eds), *Humanitarian Intervention* (2003) at 232.

[34] Thus, for example, in 1996 when the USA intervened to protect one group of Kurds from another backed by the government of Saddam Hussein, it offered very little in the way of legal justification, leading to criticism by Russia (S/1996/711; UN docs S/1996/712; 1996 UNYB 238). See Gray, 'From Unity to Polarization: International Law and the Use of Force against Iraq', 13 EJIL (2001) at 10.

engagement were expanded to cover not only response to an armed attack, but also pre-emptive action against Iraqi missile sites and command and control centres.[35] The legal justifications put forward by the USA and the UK assumed the legality of the no-fly zones; they said that their pilots had the right of self-defence to cover action against Iraqi planes and missile sites. The protests of Iraq did not lead to condemnation by the Security Council or the General Assembly. But the escalation of activity in 1999 was discussed by the Security Council; Russia and China condemned the use of force in the no-fly zones by the US and UK aircraft.[36] The UK replied that its operations were purely reactive and not aggressive. The no-fly zones were necessary both to limit Iraq's capacity to oppress its own people and to monitor its compliance with obligations. The USA agreed with this rationale.[37] The preference of the UK and the USA not to enter into discussion of the legal basis of the no-fly zones, but to focus where possible on claims to self-defence, indicates at the least an awareness that the doctrine of humanitarian intervention remained controversial.

Further polarization of states over the no-fly zones occurred as the activities of the USA and the UK continued.[38] There was open opposition by many states; France abandoned not only its participation but also its support; there was little, if any, open support for the legality of the 'coalition' operations on the basis of humanitarian intervention. It is not clear that these actions satisfied the criteria for humanitarian intervention set out by the UK in 1992.[39] The actions could not convincingly be described as multilateral, despite the care the USA and the UK took to speak of 'coalition' action.[40] They were 'limited in time and scope' only in the sense that individual operations were so limited; the maintenance of the no-fly zones lasted for over ten years. Most important, the question was raised as to how far the USA and the UK were genuinely motivated by humanitarian concern, or whether their true aim was the overthrow of Saddam Hussein, an aim openly avowed by the USA but disavowed by the UK.[41] In the months leading up to the invasion of Iraq in March 2003 there were

[35] See Keesings (1999), 42754, 42811, 42866.

[36] SC 4008th meeting, 21 May 1999; 1999 UNYB 254.

[37] 'Contemporary Practice of the United States Relating to International Law', 93 AJIL (1999) 470 at 478.

[38] On the major operation in February 2001 see Keesings (2001), 44026; Gray, 'From Unity to Polarization: International Law and the Use of Force against Iraq', 13 EJIL (2001) 1.

[39] These criteria were subsequently modified, arguably in order to bring the operations in Iraq and Kosovo within their ambit; see 'UK Materials on International Law', 70 BYIL (1999) 595; 71 BYIL (2000) 643–6; 72 BYIL (2001) 695–6.

[40] See discussion by Minister of State, Ministry of Defence (Baroness Symons), in the House of Lords, Hansard, 19 February 2001, at columns 510–511; 'UK Materials on International Law', 73 BYIL (2002) 861.

[41] 'UK Materials on International Law', 70 BYIL (1999) 565; House of Commons, Hansard Debates for 26 February 2001, at columns 622–23.

accusations that the operations in Iraq were designed not for humanitarian protection, but to weaken Iraqi air defences to prepare for the eventual invasion of 2003.[42]

KOSOVO: A NEW ROLE FOR NATO

The NATO action in Kosovo in 1999 revealed even more clearly the fundamental split as to the legality of humanitarian intervention.[43] NATO forces undertook *Operation Allied Force* in response to the repression of ethnic Albanians in the region of Kosovo by the federal government of Yugoslavia under President Milosevic.[44] The legal arguments of states for and against this action will be discussed in detail in order to illuminate the doctrinal debate about Article 2(4), its relation to Chapter VII, and the practical importance of this debate. It was clear that this bombing campaign against Yugoslavia in protection of the Kosovo Albanians marked a new departure for NATO, which was moving away from its original role as an organization for collective self-defence. With the end of the Cold War it had sought a new role for itself; from 1990 it had begun to redefine itself.[45] It had agreed on the need to transform the Atlantic Alliance 'to reflect the new, more promising era in Europe'. It adopted a new strategic concept in 1991. This said that risks to Allied security were less likely to result from calculated aggression against the territory of the Allies, but rather from the adverse consequences of instabilities that may arise from the serious economic, social and political difficulties, including ethnic rivalries and territorial disputes which are faced by many countries in Central and Eastern Europe. These tensions could lead to crises inimical to European stability and even to armed conflicts which could involve outside powers or spill over into NATO countries, having a direct effect on the security

---

[42] 2002 UNYB 315, 2003 UNYB 370, Keesings (2002) 45005; *The Guardian*, 7, 13 September 2002, 4 December 2002, 14 January, 27 February, 3, 4 March 2003, 21, 22 June 2005.

[43] Chesterman, *Just War or Just Peace* (2001); 'Editorial Comments: NATO's Kosovo Intervention', 93 AJIL (1999) 824–60; Simma, 'NATO, the UN and the use of force: Legal Aspects', 10 EJIL (1999) 1; Cassese, '*Ex iniuria ius oritur*: are we moving towards international legitimation of forcible humanitarian countermeasures in the world community?', 10 EJIL (1999) 23, 791; Kritsiotis, 'The Kosovo Crisis and NATO's application of armed force against the Federal Republic of Yugoslavia', 49 ICLQ (2000) 330; Krisch, 'Legality, Morality and the Dilemma of Humanitarian Intervention after Kosovo', 13 EJIL (2002) 323; Kosovo Crisis Inquiry, 49 ICLQ (2000) 878.

[44] See Independent International Commission on Kosovo, *Kosovo Report* (2000); 1999 UNYB 332. For the indictment of President Milosevic for his actions in Kosovo, see Keesings (1999) 42958; (2001) 44268; 1999 UNYB 1214.

[45] On NATO's redefinition of its role up to February 1999 and on the NATO action with regard to Kosovo up to this date, see Simma, 'NATO, the UN and the use of force: Legal Aspects', 10 EJIL (1999) 1.

of the Alliance. Moreover Alliance security must also take account of the global context; security interests could be affected by other risks including proliferation of weapons of mass destruction, disruption of the flows of vital resources and actions of terrorism and sabotage. Accordingly NATO would have to be prepared to undertake management of crises. In pursuance of this new role NATO became involved in the 1991–95 conflict in the former Yugoslavia and used force other than in collective self-defence. But in that conflict its member states were specifically authorized to use force by the Security Council.[46]

After this action further changes were made to NATO's strategic concept. The 1991 new strategic concept had still emphasized that 'the Alliance is purely defensive in purpose'. This phrase has disappeared from the new strategic concept adopted in 1999. NATO was now not only to ensure the defence of its members but also to contribute to peace and security in the 'Euro-Atlantic region'. NATO would undertake new missions, including conflict prevention and crisis management. This redefinition of NATO was made specifically in response to the events in Kosovo. The member states, in announcing the 1999 strategic concept, explained that:

The continuing crisis in and around Kosovo threatens to further destabilise areas beyond the Federal Republic of Yugoslavia. The potential for wider instability underscores the need for a comprehensive approach to the stabilisation of the crisis region in South-Eastern Europe. We recognise and endorse the crucial importance of making South-Eastern Europe a region free from violence and instability. A new level of international engagement is thus needed to build security, prosperity and democratic civil society, leading in time to full integration into the wider European family.[47]

Nevertheless, when NATO resorted to force to protect ethnic Albanians in Kosovo, there was still some ambivalence in the official NATO statements as to the precise legal justification for its action against Yugoslavia. NATO did not clearly and expressly invoke humanitarian intervention as a legal doctrine; the initial authorization by the North Atlantic Council of air strikes in January 1999 said only that the crisis in Kosovo was a threat to the peace and security of the region; the NATO strategy was to halt the violence in Kosovo and thus avert a humanitarian catastrophe.[48] When *Operation Allied Force* actually began in March 1999 the NATO justification focused primarily on moral and political rather than expressly legal justifications for the action. The Secretary-General of NATO said that all efforts to achieve a negotiated, political solution to the Kosovo crisis had

---

[46] See 289 below.
[47] NATO Press Release NAC–S(99)64. On further changes to NATO's strategic concept following 9/11 see 214 below.
[48] NATO Press Release 99/12, 30 January 1999.

failed and they were taking action to support the political aims of the international community. The military aim was to disrupt the violent acts being committed by the Serb army and to weaken their ability to cause further humanitarian catastrophe. They wished thereby to support international efforts to secure Yugoslav agreement to an interim political settlement: 'We must halt the violence and bring an end to the humanitarian catastrophe now unfolding in Kosovo.'[49] Implicitly this seems to be a claim to humanitarian intervention; it also claims to be an action to further the aims of the international community. That is, NATO seemed to be relying in part on a doctrine of implied authorization by the Security Council to justify the legality of its use of force.[50] The official NATO statements left some uncertainty as to whether they were relying on an autonomous doctrine of humanitarian intervention or whether the Security Council resolutions and the doctrine of implied authorization had been a necessary part of the legal justification for the action initiated in March 1999.

In Security Council meetings a variety of arguments were put forward for and against the NATO air strikes. Those attacking the NATO action accused it of a clear violation of the UN Charter; they focused on the absolute prohibition of the use of force in Article 2(4), the primary role of the Security Council in the maintenance of international peace and security under Article 24 of the UN Charter, and the need for Security Council authorization under Chapter VII of the UN Charter rather than unilateral action. Some member states assumed NATO was a regional organization under Chapter VIII of the Charter and therefore limited also by the specific requirement in Article 53 that any enforcement action be authorized by the Security Council.[51]

The UN Secretary-General, speaking in response to the start of the NATO air strikes, reminded states of the primary responsibility of the Security Council for the maintenance of international peace and security; this was explicitly acknowledged in the NATO Treaty. Therefore the Council should be involved in any decision to resort to force.[52]

At the first emergency Security Council meeting called immediately after the start of the NATO air attacks, states supporting the action said it was taken as a last resort to prevent a humanitarian catastrophe after the failure of all diplomatic efforts to find a peaceful solution.[53] Security

---

[49] NATO Press Release 1999(040).

[50] This reflects the justification offered by NATO for its earlier threat of force against Yugoslavia in October 1998; at that time the North Atlantic Council based itself more explicitly on Security Council resolutions. See Simma, 'NATO, the UN and the use of force: Legal Aspects', 10 EJIL (1999) 1. For further discussion of the doctrine of implied authorization by the Security Council see Chapter 8 below.

[51] See Chapter 9 below.

[52] <www.un.org/News/dh/latest.htm>, 24 March 1999.

[53] SC 3988th meeting, 24 March 1999; 1999 UNYB 342.

Council resolutions had recognized that the situation in Kosovo was a threat to regional peace and security and invoked Chapter VII of the UN Charter. The USA took the line that NATO had acted to avert a humanitarian catastrophe and deter future aggression and repression in Kosovo. The UK offered a relatively extensive legal argument; it said, 'The action being taken is legal. It is justified as an exceptional measure to prevent an overwhelming humanitarian catastrophe... Every means short of force has been tried. In these circumstances, and as an exceptional measure on grounds of overwhelming humanitarian necessity, military intervention is legally justifiable. The force now being used is directed exclusively to averting a humanitarian catastrophe, and is the minimum necessary for that purpose.'

At the subsequent Security Council meeting called two days later to vote on a resolution condemning the use of force by NATO the Security Council rejected the resolution by three votes in favour (China, Namibia and Russia) to twelve against.[54] The draft resolution affirmed that the unilateral use of force by NATO constituted a violation of Article 2(4), Article 24 (on the primacy of the Security Council), and Article 53 (on the need for Security Council authorization of enforcement action by regional organizations). Those speaking against the NATO action (Cuba, India, Russia, China, Ukraine and Belarus) were clear that this was a gross violation of the Charter, whereas those defending the action concentrated on the continuing violence by the government of Yugoslavia against the people of Kosovo.

Those defending the NATO action offered a variety of legal arguments. They stressed the earlier Security Council resolutions passed under Chapter VII calling on Yugoslavia to stop its actions. Although these resolutions did not expressly authorize the use of force by NATO, several states seemed to argue that they nevertheless justified the NATO action. Thus France spoke of the fact that the Security Council had adopted three resolutions under Chapter VII. Resolution 1160 (1998) had imposed an arms embargo on Yugoslavia and called for a political solution to the issue of Kosovo; it concluded by emphasizing that failure to make constructive progress toward a peaceful resolution would lead to the consideration of additional measures. In Resolution 1199 (1998) the Council had reaffirmed that the deterioration of the situation posed a threat to regional peace and security and made a number of demands on Yugoslavia. In Resolution 1203 (1998) the Council had demanded that the agreements

---

[54] SC 3989th meeting (1999); 1999 UNYB 343. The rejection of this resolution was taken by some commentators as evidence of the legality of the NATO action; for others it was accounted for by a political reluctance to condemn an action states regarded as morally justified, even if not legal: see Chapter 1 above.

between Yugoslavia, the OSCE and NATO should be implemented. As Yugoslavia had not done so NATO's action had responded to this failure. The Netherlands took a similar approach; it said that 'the NATO action followed directly from resolution 1203 (1998), in conjunction with the flagrant non-compliance on the part of Yugoslavia. Given its complex background, the action could not be allowed to be described as unilateral use of force.' Slovenia also took a similar line; it stressed that the Security Council had declared the situation a threat to regional peace and security, had spelled out the requirements for the removal of the threat and the fact that these requirements had been flagrantly violated by Yugoslavia. The Security Council's responsibility in this area was primary but not exclusive, so NATO had been entitled to act. The USA was apparently less concerned to offer a specifically legal justification. It mentioned the violation of resolutions by Yugoslavia, and then said simply that 'NATO's actions were completely justified. They were necessary to stop the violence and to prevent a further deterioration of peace and stability in the region.'

After the end of the NATO campaign, the Security Council passed Resolution 1244 (1999) to endorse the agreement between the parties on the principles of a political solution to end the Kosovo crisis. There was controversy as to whether the adoption of this resolution marked a retrospective acceptance of the legality of the NATO action or of humanitarian intervention or merely a pragmatic acceptance of the need to provide for the future of Kosovo.[55] Many states, including some of those like Slovenia and Canada who had supported the NATO action, stressed their relief that the Security Council was again taking a central role. Those who had opposed the action took this line even more strongly. Thus Russia said that it was glad that NATO had recognized that the Security Council was the body primarily responsible for the maintenance of peace and security. China maintained its view that NATO had 'seriously violated the Charter of the United Nations and norms of international law, had undermined the authority of the Security Council, and had, hence, set an extremely dangerous precedent in the history of international relations'. Because the resolution failed fully to reflect China's principled stand China had difficulties with it, but in view of the fact that Yugoslavia had accepted the peace plan; that NATO had suspended its bombing; and that the draft resolution reaffirmed the purposes and principles of the UN Charter and the primary responsibility of the Security Council and also reaffirmed the commitment of all member states to the sovereignty and territorial

---

[55] See the debate leading up to the adoption of the resolution, SC 4011th meeting (1999). For opposing views on the significance of SC Res 1244 (1999), see Franck, 'Interpretation and Change in the Law of Humanitarian Intervention', in Holzgrefe and Keohane (eds), *Humanitarian Intervention* (2003) 204 and Hilpold, 'Humanitarian Intervention: is there a need for a legal reappraisal?', 12 EJIL (2001) 437.

integrity of Yugoslavia, China abstained rather than veto the resolution. It is noteworthy that Latin American states (Costa Rica, Brazil and Mexico) continued to express concern about the use of force by NATO without Security Council authorization.

Legality of Use of Force: the case before the International Court of Justice

As well as challenging the legality of the NATO action in the Security Council, Yugoslavia brought an action against ten NATO member states before the International Court of Justice; it alleged that by taking part in the bombing each respondent was in breach of the obligation not to use force and also that by taking part in training terrorists (the Kosovo Liberation Army) each respondent was in breach of its obligation not to intervene in the affairs of another state. During the request for provisional measures Yugoslavia set out its position on the intervention at some length.[56] Its argument was in two parts: first, there is no right to humanitarian intervention in international law and, second, even if there were such a right, the modalities chosen by NATO, the air strikes, could not constitute humanitarian intervention. In the oral argument Yugoslavia said that the prohibition in Article 2(4) was unqualified. The preparatory work of the Charter indicated that intervention for special motives was ruled out by the inclusion of the phrase 'against the territorial integrity or political independence of any State'. The subsequent practice of states had not produced a departure in international law; such a departure would be a major aberration and would require consistent and substantial evidence. Such a change in customary law had not been proved by any NATO member state. This position was confirmed in the *Friendly Relations Declaration*, which excludes the right to intervene in absolute terms; the *Definition of Aggression* provision that 'no consideration of whatever nature, whether political, economic, military or otherwise, may serve as a justification for aggression' also confirmed this. The Yugoslav argument went on to quote writers opposed to humanitarian intervention and the 1984 UK Foreign and Commonwealth Office position that humanitarian intervention was of doubtful legality.

The second stage of Yugoslavia's argument was that on the facts of the case the NATO action could not qualify as humanitarian intervention.[57]

[56] *Legality of Use of Force* (Provisional Measures) ICJ Reports (1999) 124. Yugoslavia brought actions against 10 states; for convenience reference here will be made to the case against Belgium.

[57] Simma, 'NATO, the UN and the use of force: Legal Aspects', 10 EJIL (1999) 1, argued that the NATO action could not be seen as humanitarian intervention, but was rather reprisals or countermeasures. Many commentators expressed concern that the bombing campaign

Yugoslavia claimed that there was no genuine humanitarian purpose. Moreover the modalities selected disqualified the action as a humanitarian one. Bombing populated areas of Yugoslavia from a height of 15,000 feet could not qualify. The selection of a bombing campaign was disproportionate to the declared aims of the action. In order to protect one minority in one region all the other communities in the whole of Yugoslavia were placed at risk of intensive bombing. The pattern of targets and the geographical extent of the bombing indicated broad political purposes unrelated to humanitarian issues. Finally, major considerations of international public order disqualified the bombing as a humanitarian action. NATO states had intervened in civil war in Kosovo. The threats of massive force went back seven months before the NATO action and were intended to produce a dictated result. The massive air campaign was planned in order to force Yugoslavia to accept NATO demands. There was no attempt to obtain Security Council authorization.

At the provisional measures stage most of the respondent states said that they did not want to go into the merits of the case and they limited themselves to descriptions of atrocities in Kosovo as background to their argument that Yugoslavia's claim for provisional measures should be rejected. But Belgium did go into the law on the use of force in order to offer a legal justification of the NATO action. It argued that the armed intervention was in fact 'based on' Security Council resolutions. This is another instance of the argument of implied Security Council authorization. However, Belgium said that it was necessary to go further and set out the doctrine of humanitarian intervention. There was an obligation to intervene to prevent the humanitarian catastrophe which was occurring and which had been established by the Security Council resolutions, in order to protect those essential human rights which had also achieved the status of *ius cogens*. NATO had never questioned the political independence or the territorial integrity of Yugoslavia; this was not an intervention directed against the territorial integrity or political independence of Yugoslavia. It was intended to save a population in danger and so it was compatible with Article 2(4) of the Charter, which only prohibited those interventions directed against territorial integrity or political independence. This is an express adoption of the narrow interpretation of Article 2(4).

Belgium invoked as precedents the intervention by India in Bangladesh, Tanzania in Uganda and even the intervention of Vietnam in Cambodia,

---

was not appropriate humanitarian action; the only true humanitarian action would have been a ground operation. The European Court of Human Rights found that it did not have jurisdiction to hear a case against NATO states for violations of human rights in *Bankovic*: 41 ILM (2002) 517. The ICTY Prosecutor decided that there was no case against NATO for war crimes: Keesings (2000) 43640.

despite its repeated condemnation by the General Assembly. It also invoked the ECOWAS actions in Liberia and Sierra Leone on the ground that these interventions had not been expressly condemned by the competent organs of the UN.[58] Also Belgium said that the rejection by the Security Council of the Russian draft resolution condemning the NATO action confirmed that the action was legal. The Security Council had decided that there was a humanitarian catastrophe and that the situation was a threat to the peace. It was clear from the resolutions that Yugoslavia was responsible for this state of affairs. The UN Secretary-General had said that, 'emerging slowly, but I believe surely, is an international norm against the violent repression of minorities that will and must take precedence over concerns of State sovereignty'. The intervention was also intended to safeguard the security of the whole region. These Belgian arguments, relying on what states did rather than what they said and on failure to condemn by the UN, follow the approach of those writers who had argued for a right of humanitarian intervention before this was expressly adopted by any state.

Other respondent states did not go into the legal justification for the NATO action. The USA listed a variety of justifications: that the action was to avert humanitarian catastrophe, that there was a threat to the security of the neighbouring states, that there had been serious violations of human rights by Yugoslavia and that the Security Council had determined the existence of a threat to international peace and security and had under Chapter VII demanded a halt to such violations.

The UK, in response to the Yugoslav accusation that the doctrine of humanitarian intervention had only been relied on at a late stage by NATO, and was therefore of doubtful plausibility as a justification, denied this accusation and briefly repeated the position it had put forward in the Security Council that the NATO action was designed to avert humanitarian catastrophe. In October 1998 NATO had focused primarily on implied authorization by the Security Council, but it had also included reference to the need to avert humanitarian catastrophe. The argument by Yugoslavia highlighted the (apparently deliberate) lack of clarity in the NATO position and its unwillingness expressly to rely only on the doctrine of humanitarian intervention. Yugoslavia's argument was designed to indicate that there was considerable uncertainty about the doctrine, preventing its unequivocal support by NATO.

The Court refused provisional measures in all ten cases brought by Yugoslavia against NATO member states.[59] It did not pronounce on the

---

[58] On Liberia and Sierra Leone, see Chapter 9 below.

[59] The Court refused provisional measures on the ground that it did not have *prima facie* jurisdiction on the merits of the case: *Legality of Use of Force*, ICJ Reports (1999) 124, see Gray, 49 ICLQ (2000) 730. The Court later ruled that it had no jurisdiction to decide the cases, ICJ Reports (2004) 279.

legality of NATO's use of force, but it did indicate concern. In all the cases it said:

Whereas the Court is deeply concerned with the human tragedy, the loss of life, and the enormous suffering in Kosovo which form the background of the present dispute, and with the continuing loss of life and human suffering in all parts of Yugoslavia; Whereas the Court is profoundly concerned with the use of force in Yugoslavia; Whereas under the present circumstances such use raises very serious issues of international law; Whereas the Court is mindful of the purposes and principles of the United Nations Charter and of its own responsibilities in the maintenance of peace and security under the Charter and the Statute of the Court; Whereas the Court deems it necessary to emphasize that all parties appearing before it must act in conformity with their obligations under the United Nations Charter and other rules of international law, including humanitarian law.[60]

The subsequent debate

Thus the controversy over the legality of humanitarian intervention continues. Some regard the Kosovo action as a valuable precedent for unilateral action; others regard it as a counterproductive intervention, which had the perverse effect of increasing the displacement and persecution of the Kosovan Albanians in the short term.[61] Many states in many different fora within the UN have subsequently made a point of stressing that they regard the NATO action as illegal.[62] Others such as Germany and the USA, even though they supported the operation, argued that it was not to be seen as a precedent for future action.[63] The USA has not

---

[60] ICJ Reports (1999)124, 38 ILM (1999) 950.

[61] See, for example, Van Walsum in Blokker and Schrijver, *The Security Council and the Use of Force* (2005) at 65; Kennedy, *The Dark Side of Virtue* (2005) at Chapter 8; Seybolt, *Humanitarian Military Intervention: the Conditions for Success and Failure* (2007).

[62] For example, the Non-Aligned Movement rejected humanitarian intervention as having no legal basis in the UN Charter or in the general principles of international law: UN Press Release GA/SPD/164, 18 October 1999; see also the Fourth Committee debate on peacekeeping, GA/SPD/164–6, 18–20 October 1999; Special Committee on UN Charter, UN Press Release L/2919, 12 April 1999 and the Opening Debate of the 1999 General Assembly, GA/9606, 24 September 1999. See also the NAM Comments on the High-level Panel Report, 28 February 2005, para 17; <un.int/malaysia/NAM/NAM.html>. For the Group of 77 response rejecting the legality of humanitarian intervention, see Byers and Chesterman, 'Changing the rules about rules? Unilateral humanitarian intervention and the future of international law', in Holzgrefe and Keohane (eds), *Humanitarian Intervention* (2003) 177 at 184.

[63] For the German statement in the General Assembly on 22 September 1999, see Cassese, 'A Follow-up: forcible countermeasures and *opinio necessitatis*', 10 EJIL (1999) 791 at 793; for the US statement, see Byers and Chesterman, 'Changing the rules about rules? Unilateral humanitarian intervention and the future of international law', in Holzgrefe and Keohane (eds), *Humanitarian Intervention* (2003) 177 at 199; Roth, 'Bending the Law, Breaking it or Developing it?', in Byers and Nolte (eds), *US Hegemony and the Foundations of International Law* (2003) at 232.

itself developed a doctrine of humanitarian intervention. The arguments put forward by states in the Security Council and before the International Court of Justice show vividly the fundamental differences on the law on humanitarian intervention. States are divided on treaty interpretation and on the significance of state practice. Does Article 2(4) of the UN Charter allow humanitarian intervention? The states who argued in favour of this saw humanitarian intervention as an emerging right; this indicates that they saw Article 2(4) as open to changing interpretation over time and not with a fixed meaning. They did not argue that the right of humanitarian intervention existed in 1945. But the basis for the claim that this change in meaning has taken place is not clear. Apparently it rests in part on an argument that the law of human rights has developed since 1945 to such an extent that certain human rights are now *ius cogens* just as the prohibition on the use of force is *ius cogens*. But it does not follow from the mere fact that human rights may now be *ius cogens* that this overrides the prohibition on the use of force. For this further, crucial step in the argument it would be necessary to show, not only that human rights are accepted and recognized by the international community of states as a whole as a norm from which no derogation is permitted, but also that states have accepted the right to use force to protect them.

Those who opposed the interpretation of Article 2(4) to allow humanitarian intervention saw it as a prohibition that cannot be altered without universal agreement. To confirm this view they also invoked the General Assembly resolutions on the use of force, which outlawed forcible intervention in absolute terms. They stressed the primary responsibility of the Security Council under Chapter VII in order to exclude unilateral action. This also seems to have been the final conclusion of the Secretary-General. In spite of his acceptance that human rights were not an internal matter, he wrote in his 1999 *Report on the Work of the Organization*: 'What is clear is that enforcement action without Security Council authorization threatens the very core of the international security system founded on the Charter of the UN. Only the Charter provides a universally accepted legal basis for the use of force.'[64]

Therefore it seems necessary for those states and writers supporting humanitarian intervention on the basis that it is an emerging or a new right to show how the change in the law that they rely on has come about.[65]

[64] UN doc A/54/1 (1999) at para 66; 1999 UNYB 3 at 10.

[65] There is a vast literature on this topic: for an introduction to the central arguments, see, for example, Chesterman, *Just War or Just Peace* (2001); Krisch, 'Legality, Morality and the Dilemma of Humanitarian Intervention after Kosovo', 13 EJIL (2002) 323; Hilpold, 'Humanitarian Intervention: is there a need for a legal reappraisal?', 12 EJIL (2001) 437; Holzgrefe and Keohane (eds), *Humanitarian Intervention* (2003); Franck, *Recourse to Force* (2002); Koskenniemi, 'The lady doth protest too much', 65 MLR (2002) 159; Kennedy, *The Dark Side of Virtue* (2004) Chapter 8.

Some have tried to show that state practice supports their argument as to the meaning of Article 2(4). A certain amount of revisionism in the interpretation of past practice has proved attractive to some states. The Belgian arguments on the significance of state practice in Uganda, Bangladesh and Cambodia relied on what states did rather than on what they said to justify their interventions. But the UN Secretary-General was not willing to go so far. He argued that, in all three of the cases mentioned, what justified the action in the eyes of the world was the internal character of the regimes the intervening states acted against. Yet at the time in all three cases the international community was divided and disturbed because these interventions were unilateral. The states in question had no mandate from anyone else to act as they did. He concluded that most would prefer to see such decisions taken collectively by an international institution, and surely the only institution competent to assume that role was the Security Council.[66] It is significant that only the UK invoked US and UK actions in enforcing the no-fly zones in Iraq as a precedent for humanitarian intervention in Kosovo; this clearly demonstrates the controversial nature of the US and UK actions.[67]

During the Kosovo crisis some of the states in favour of humanitarian intervention also argued that humanitarian action by the UN or authorized by the UN, as in Yugoslavia and Somalia, or taken by a regional organization and acquiesced in by the UN, as in Liberia and Sierra Leone, showed the existence of a general doctrine of humanitarian intervention and the right of states to act unilaterally.[68] This was the position of Slovenia in the Security Council and of Belgium before the International Court of Justice.[69] It is difficult to see how this argument can be sustained. The UN actions in Somalia and the former Yugoslavia were within the Charter scheme, even if such actions were not initially envisaged by the drafters of the UN Charter. Member states were specifically authorized to use force in those states for humanitarian ends by the Security Council under Chapter VII. The regional actions in Liberia and Sierra Leone were justified by ECOWAS as regional peacekeeping with the consent of the host state; the response by the Security Council was cautious. It did not authorize force except to secure compliance with an arms embargo under Article 41 of the UN Charter or on the basis of a peace agreement between

---

[66] 1998 (3) UN Chronicle 3.

[67] See Gray, 'From Unity to Polarization: International Law and the Use of Force against Iraq', 13 EJIL (2002) 1.

[68] Some states even went so far as to suggest an obligation to intervene, but the limited and selective state practice cannot support such a doctrine. As Cuba argued, there have been many other terrible violations of human rights where no humanitarian intervention was undertaken, SC 4011th meeting (1999); see also UN Press Release SC/6686, 10 June 1999.

[69] For Slovenia's argument, see SC 3989th meeting (1999).

the parties.[70] It is very doubtful whether this UN-authorized state action or regional peacekeeping could amount to a basis for a new right of humanitarian intervention not expressly authorized by the Security Council, such as the action over Kosovo.

For those states and writers which do support the legality of humanitarian intervention, the operation in Kosovo has left some basic issues as to the scope of the right unclear. The official position of NATO seemed to reflect a fundamental division as to the legal basis for the operation. It remains doubtful whether the NATO operation could be a precedent for unilateral action by one state rather than a regional organization or other group of states. The constant stress on the Security Council resolutions by certain states indicates that they were putting forward a doctrine of implied authorization by the Security Council; they were not arguing for a unilateral right of humanitarian intervention. Alternatively, a less restrictive view of the scope of the doctrine would be that, although Security Council authorization is not necessary, a determination by it under Chapter VII of the existence of a threat to international peace and security and of the imminence of humanitarian disaster is crucial to establish a plausible case that the states using force are carrying out the will of the international community. The question as to the appropriate modalities for humanitarian intervention also remains problematic.

The UK has continued to take a lead role in the development of the doctrine. In 2000 the Foreign Secretary set out a framework to guide intervention in response to massive violations of humanitarian law and crimes against humanity and submitted it to the UN Secretary-General.[71] The framework was built on six principles. First, an intervention is an admission of failure of prevention. We need a strengthened culture of conflict prevention. Second, we should maintain the principle that armed force should only be used as a last resort. Third, the immediate responsibility for halting violence rests with the state in which it occurs. Fourth, when faced with an overwhelming humanitarian catastrophe, which a government has shown it is unwilling or unable to prevent or is actively promoting, the international community should intervene. Intervention in internal affairs is a sensitive issue so there must be convincing evidence of extreme humanitarian distress on a large scale, requiring urgent relief. It must be objectively clear that there is no practicable alternative to the use of force to save lives. Fifth, any use of force should be proportionate

---

[70] For a detailed discussion of the ECOWAS action in Liberia and the Security Council response, see Nolte, 'Restoring Peace by Regional Action', 53 Zeitschrift für ausländisches öffentliches Recht und Völkerrecht (1993) 603; and Gray, 'Regional Arrangements and the UN Collective Security System', in Fox (ed.), *The Changing Constitution of the United Nations* (1997), 91.

[71] 71 BYIL (2000) 646.

to achieving the humanitarian purpose and carried out in accordance with international law. The military action must be likely to achieve its objectives. Sixth, any use of force should be collective. No individual country can reserve to itself the right to act on behalf of the international community. The Foreign Secretary said that the intervention in Kosovo was a collective decision, backed by the nineteen members of NATO; his preference would be that, wherever possible, the authority of the Security Council should be secured.

The continuing opposition of China, Russia and the Non-Aligned Movement to intervention without Security Council authority means that the doctrine is far from firmly established in international law. The decision by states not to rely on humanitarian intervention as a legal justification for *Operation Enduring Freedom* against Afghanistan in 2001 or for *Operation Iraqi Freedom* in Iraq in 2003 is another indication of its controversial status. Although UK Prime Minister Blair in the run-up to the invasion of Iraq used the language of humanitarian intervention, in response to widespread domestic opposition to the use of force, this doctrine was clearly not made part of the *legal* case for action.[72] The UK Attorney-General acknowledged in his advice on the legality of military action against Iraq that 'the doctrine remains controversial'.[73] In the USA President Bush openly called for regime change in Iraq, but even though the operation was called *Operation Iraqi Freedom* the legal basis presented by the USA was implied authorization by the Security Council rather than humanitarian intervention.[74] It seems likely that express invocation of this doctrine by states will remain exceptional and that it will continue to be writers who are its keenest proponents.

A RESPONSIBILITY TO PROTECT?

The tenth anniversary of the 1994 genocide in Rwanda prompted a reappraisal of the law in this area. As part of this process there has been much discussion of how to develop the law on humanitarian intervention and, in particular, as to whether there is now a 'responsibility to protect', that is a duty on states to intervene in certain cases of humanitarian crisis.[75] The *High-level Panel on Threats, Challenges and Change* set up by the

---

[72] See 354 below.
[73] 2005 ICLQ 767 at para 4.
[74] See Chapter 8 below.
[75] As was suggested in the Report of the International Commission on Intervention and State Sovereignty, *The Responsibility to Protect* (2001). See Stahn, 'Responsibility to Protect', 101 AJIL (2007) 99; Boisson de Chazournes and Condorelli, 'De la responsabilité de protéger', 110 RGDIP (2006) 11.

UN Secretary-General took a relatively cautious approach in its Report, *A More Secure World: Our Shared Responsibility* of December 2004.[76] It endorsed the emerging norm that there is such a collective responsibility to protect in cases of genocide and other large scale killing, ethnic cleansing or serious violation of international humanitarian law. The primary duty to protect lies with the state, but when a state fails to act to protect its own citizens the international community has a responsibility to act, by force if necessary, though only as a last resort. The responsibility to protect was exercisable by the Security Council authorizing military intervention.

The UN Secretary-General responded briefly in support of this in his 2005 Report *In Larger Freedom: towards development, security and human rights for all.*[77] He recognized that states had disagreed as to whether they had the right or even the obligation to use force protectively to rescue citizens of other states from genocide or other international crimes, but nevertheless said that they should embrace the responsibility to protect in cases where national authorities were unwilling or unable to protect their citizens. Finally, the 2005 *World Summit Outcome Document* accepted that 'we are prepared to take collective action, in a timely and decisive manner, through the Security Council in accordance with the UN Charter, including Chapter VII, on a case by case basis and in cooperation with relevant regional organizations as appropriate, should peaceful means be inadequate and national authorities manifestly failing to protect their populations from genocide, ethnic cleansing and crimes against humanity'.[78] The UN Secretary-General hailed this as a major achievement of the Summit.[79]

However, these documents leave open the crucial question as to whether there is a right of unilateral humanitarian intervention in the absence of Security Council authority. The debate on *In Larger Freedom* demonstrated that many states were suspicious of the doctrine of 'responsibility to protect', regarding it as a pretext for intervention by powerful states. The Non-Aligned Movement registered its continuing opposition to any unilateral right of humanitarian intervention.[80] And although the Security Council approved the 'responsibility to protect' in Resolution 1674 (2006)

---

[76] UN doc A/59/565 (2004) at para 199–203; see Odello, 'Commentary on the UN High-level Panel', 10 Journal of Conflict and Security Law (2005) 231.

[77] UN doc A/59/2005 at para 135.

[78] UN doc A/60/L.70 at para 139.

[79] UN docs SG/SM/10089, 13 September 2005; SG/SM/10170, 17 October 2005.

[80] UN doc GA/10337, 10338, 10339, 6–8 April 2005; NAM Comments on the High Level Panel Report, 28 February 2005; <www.un.int/malaysia/NAM/NAM.html> at para 17. See Gray, 'A Crisis of legitimacy for the UN Collective Security System?', 56 ICLQ (2007) 157 at 167.

on the Protection of Civilians in Armed Conflict it did nothing to resolve the underlying conflict as to the scope of the doctrine.[81]

The AU has apparently given its support to a regional right of humanitarian intervention in its *Constitutive Act* (2000). Article 4 set out the principles of the AU. Article 4(h) provides for 'the right of the Union to intervene in a Member State pursuant to a decision of the Assembly in respect of grave circumstances, namely: war crimes, genocide and crimes against humanity', but this follows Article 4(f) the prohibition of the use of force and (g) non interference in the internal affairs of another member state. Whatever the intent behind Article 4(h), it cannot override the UN Charter and so the interpretation of Article 2(4) of the Charter remains the critical issue.[82]

DARFUR

The problems involved in the implementation of the 'responsibility to protect', whether through the UN or, more controversially, through regional or unilateral humanitarian intervention, were all too apparent with regard to the humanitarian catastrophe in Darfur (Sudan). There were calls for military intervention, but UN action proved impossible in the absence of Sudan's consent; states were not willing to intervene through the Security Council in the absence of such consent, nor did they assert any right of unilateral action.[83] The crisis in Darfur broke out in February 2003 when conflict erupted between certain anti-government groups and government forces. Various explanations have been put forward for the escalation of violence: ethnic and religious tensions, rebellion against the government in pursuit of increased autonomy, and competition over grazing and water rights.[84] The Sudanese government employed local Arab-African militias, commonly referred to as the janjaweed, to carry

---

[81] The Security Council subsequently recalled this reference in Resolution 1706 (2006) with regard to Darfur.

[82] Article 103 of the UN Charter provides that obligations under the Charter shall prevail over other obligations. In 2005 the AU adopted a common position on the proposed reform of the UN, the Ezulwini Consensus, AU doc Ext/EX.CL/2 (VII) section B. This said that it was imperative that regional organizations should be empowered to take actions under the responsibility to protect. They agreed with the High-level Panel that intervention of regional organizations should be with the approval of the Security Council, but claimed that in certain circumstances such approval could be granted after the fact.

[83] Russia and China were reluctant to take measures against the government of Sudan; they abstained on several Security Council resolutions imposing sanctions on the government and proposing the establishment of a UN force under Chapter VII of the UN Charter: UN Press Releases SC/8191, 18 September 2004; SC/8346, 29 March 2005; SC/8821, 31 August 2006.

[84] 2004 UNYB 233. See for example, Report of Secretary-General S/2006/591.

out extreme counter-insurgency measures against the black-African rebel forces. It also conducted large-scale air bombardment of the region. The rebel groups were also responsible for atrocities and for repeated violations of cease-fires. The conflict has led to over 200,000 deaths and massive displacement of 2 million people out of a total population of 6 million.[85] The flow of 100,000 refugees into the neighbouring state of Chad created the danger of widening regional conflict.[86]

In response to calls for international action, the UN established massive humanitarian aid programmes, but left it to the AU to take the lead in seeking a political solution and in creating a force (AMIS) to monitor the succession of ineffective ceasefire agreements.[87] This force, even after its mandate was increased 'to contribute to a secure environment' and its size was repeatedly expanded, was under-resourced and proved unable to prevent the violence.[88] The AU therefore decided to support transition to a UN or hybrid AU/UN force.[89]

The Security Council itself did not pass a resolution on Darfur until July 2004, when it expressed grave concern at the ongoing humanitarian crisis. It stressed that the primary 'responsibility to protect' lay with the government of Sudan and requested the government to facilitate humanitarian relief and to disarm the janjaweed militias in accordance with its promises to the UN. It also deplored violations of ceasefires by all parties, and imposed an arms embargo on non-state groups within Sudan.[90] Later it said that it would consider further economic measures under Article 41 of the UN Charter in the event of government failure to comply with its obligations to stop the violence.[91] It subsequently imposed an arms embargo and other targeted sanctions in Resolution 1591 (2005).[92] The Security Council also turned to international criminal law.[93] For the first time it took action under the 1948 *Genocide Convention*, establishing a Commission of Inquiry to investigate reports of violations of international humanitarian law and to determine whether acts of genocide had been committed; on receipt of the Commission's

---

[85] See Report of the Secretary-General, UN doc S/2004/703, 30 August 2004, and his many subsequent reports on Darfur.

[86] See 340, 422 below.

[87] See 380 below.

[88] See, for example, Report of the Secretary-General S/2007/104, 23 February 2007 at para 41; *The Guardian* 27 January 2006, 7 June 2006.

[89] UN Press Releases SC/8628, 3 February 2006; SC/8721, 16 May 2006; Report of the Secretary-General S/2007/104, 23 February 2007.

[90] SC Res 1556 (2204) passed by 13–0–2 (China, Pakistan). It had earlier expressed concern about the situation in a series of Presidential statements.

[91] SC Res 1564 (2004) passed by 11–0–4 (Algeria, China, Pakistan and Russia).

[92] Passed by 12–0–3 (Algeria, China, Russia).

[93] SC Res 1564 (2004).

report,[94] it referred the situation in Darfur to the International Criminal Court in Resolution 1593 (2005).[95]

The UN Secretary-General repeatedly called for the Security Council to take action.[96] It held many meetings on Darfur, including one—in a rare and symbolic move—in Africa.[97] But in the absence of cooperation by Sudan the Security Council was not willing or able to take effective action to stop the violence; the government of Sudan resisted the creation of a UN rather than an AU force in Darfur. In May 2006 the *Darfur Peace Agreement* was finally concluded between the government and rebels.[98] However, two major rebel groups refused to sign and fighting continued. The government intermittently continued its air bombardments and did not take measures to establish order.[99] The implementation of Security Council proposals for a major UN force, or a hybrid AU/UN force, with the power to stop the violence and to protect civilians was seriously delayed because of lack of cooperation from the government.[100] It was only in 2007 that the government finally consented to the establishment of such a force.[101]

This failure to prevent a major humanitarian crisis demonstrates that the universal acceptance in principle of a 'responsibility to protect' in the *World Summit Outcome Document* cannot guarantee action. There was no question of the Security Council imposing humanitarian intervention by force. The AU was not willing to intervene in the absence of consent by the government of Sudan. It may be that the World Summit's acceptance of the 'responsibility to protect' has created expectations which will not be fulfilled in practice.

A RIGHT OF PRO-DEMOCRATIC INTERVENTION

Thus the debate as to the proper interpretation of Article 2(4) has proved to be of practical significance in relation to humanitarian intervention.

[94] <www.un.org/News/dh/sudan/com_inq_darfur.pdf>, 25 January 2005. The Commission reported that the government had not pursued a policy of genocide, but that grave offences such as crimes against humanity and war crimes had been committed.

[95] Passed by 11–0–4 (Algeria, Brazil, China, USA). See Happold, 'Darfur, the Security Council and the International Criminal Court', 55 ICLQ (2006) 226.

[96] See, for example, UN Press Releases SC/8196, 24 September 2004, SC/8313, 16 February 2005, SC/8823, 11 September 2006.

[97] UN Press Release SC/8248, 18 November 2004.

[98] SC Res 1679 (2006).

[99] UN Press Release SC/8833, 18 September 2006; UN Press Release SC/8993, 4 April 2007 UN doc SG/SM/10985, 9 May 2007; Report of the Secretary-General, S/2007/104, 23 February 2007.

[100] SC Res 1706 (2006), passed by 12–0–3 (China, Qatar, Russia).

[101] UN doc SG/SM/10945, 16 April 2007. On progress at the end of 2007, see Report of the Secretary-General S/2007/ 759.

In contrast, the claims by some writers that states may use force in 'pro-democratic' invasions to ensure democratic government in a foreign state have not proved attractive to states.[102] The political goals underlying the use of force may include the re-establishment of 'democratic' government, but this has not led states to espouse a legal doctrine of 'pro-democratic' invasion without UN authority.

As with humanitarian intervention before the Kosovo action, the right of pro-democratic invasion has not generally been put forward as a legal argument by states. Originally certain US commentators argued that Article 2(4) was not an absolute prohibition of the use of force, but should be interpreted in the light of the Chapter VII provisions for a collective security system. Because of the failure of the UN collective security system during the Cold War, Article 2(4) could be interpreted to allow the use of force to further 'world public order' and to justify 'pro-democratic' invasions by the USA, though not 'pro-socialist' invasions by the USSR.[103] There were indications of this approach in the US justification for its intervention in Grenada.[104] Clearly this argument has now been overtaken by events in so far as it was based on the inaction of the Security Council during the Cold War. However, the argument has not been abandoned and its proponents have chosen to shift their emphasis; the doctrine is no longer predicated on the breakdown of the UN system. They now focus on the legality of force if this is designed to further purposes of the UN such as the protection of human rights. The end of the Cold War and the collapse of communist governments in Eastern Europe brought assertions that there was now a right of peoples to democratic governance and perhaps even a right of third states to use force to help a people to assert that right.[105] Perhaps the most striking illustration of this was the claim by some in the USA that Russia could forcibly intervene in Romania to help overthrow the government that was brutally punishing demonstrators who

---

[102] For a detailed discussion of this debate, see Roth, *Governmental Illegitimacy in International Law* (1999).

[103] Reisman, 'Coercion and self-determination: construing Charter Article 2(4)', 78 AJIL (1984) 642; Reisman, 'Sovereignty and Human Rights in Contemporary International Law', 84 AJIL (1990) 866; D'Amato, 'The invasion of Panama was a lawful response to tyranny', 84 AJIL (1990) 516; Teson, *Humanitarian Intervention: An Inquiry into Law and Morality* (2nd edn, 1997).

[104] See 33 above.

[105] Franck, 'The Emerging Right to Democratic Governance', 86 AJIL (1992); Franck, *Fairness in International Law and Institutions* (1995); Crawford, 'Democracy and International Law', 44 BYIL (1993) 113; Fox, 'The Right to Political Participation in International Law', 17 Yale Journal of International Law (1992); Roth, *Governmental Illegitimacy in International Law* (1999); Murphy, 'Democratic Legitimacy and the Recognition of States and Governments', 48 ICLQ (1999) 545.

were trying to secure a change of government, and to install democratic government in 1989.[106]

But it is clear that state practice cannot support such a new right. The 2006 *US National Security Strategy* devotes many pages to the promotion of freedom, but it does not openly propound a legal right to use force in order to implement democracy.[107] This follows earlier US doctrine. In its intervention in Panama at the end of 1989 the USA deliberately did not offer the restoration of democracy as a legal justification. In Panama former President Noriega had refused to accept the results of elections held in the middle of 1989 in which Endara was elected President. In December 1989 the USA forcibly intervened. Its legal argument, expressed in a letter to the Security Council, was that it was acting in self-defence in protection of US nationals in Panama.[108] The USA distinguished between its legal justification and its goals; the latter ostensibly included the defence of democracy in Panama. In the Security Council debate on the US intervention no state put forward a legal right to use force to restore democratic government. The USA itself expressly distinguished between its legal justification for the intervention, which was self-defence of its nationals, and its political interest in the protection of democracy. Its representative said, 'I am not here today to claim a right on behalf of the United States to enforce the will of history by intervening in favour of democracy where we are not welcomed. We are supporters of democracy but not the gendarmes of democracy, not in this hemisphere or anywhere else...We acted in Panama for legitimate reasons of self-defence and to protect the integrity of the Canal Treaties.'[109] Other states in the Security Council debate did not offer any support for a doctrine of pro-democratic intervention. Thus commentators wishing to assert a legal right of pro-democratic intervention have to discount not only the condemnation by the General Assembly and the OAS but also the express words of the US

---

[106] Reisman, 'Allocating Competences to Use Coercion in the Post-Cold War World', in Damrosch and Fischer (eds) *Law and Force in the New International Order* (1991), 26 at 36.

[107] The 2006 US *National Security Strategy* is available on the White House website; <www.whitehouse.gov>. See Gray, 'The Bush Doctrine Revisited: the 2006 National Security Strategy of the USA', 5 Chinese Journal of International Law (2006) 555.

[108] UN doc S/21035, 20 December 1989; 1989 UNYB 172.

[109] SC 2902nd meeting (1989). In its intervention in the Dominican Republic in 1965 the USA had similarly offered a mixture of legal and political justifications. It said that the aim of its action was to make the Dominican Republic safe for democracy and to prevent the formation of another communist government in the western hemisphere. But it also put forward legal justifications for this, its first overt military intervention since the Second World War. The invocation of regional action by the OAS did not serve to legitimate the intervention. As later in the Nigerian intervention in the name of ECOWAS in Sierra Leone, so here military dictatorships intervened in the name of democracy. For a fuller discussion of the US intervention in the Dominican Republic, see Franck and Weisband, *Word Politics* (1972), 96.

government and its deliberate choice not to put this argument forward as a legal justification for its intervention.[110]

In contrast, the forcible intervention to restore democratic government in Haiti was authorized by the UN. After the overthrow of Haiti's first democratically elected government in a coup in 1991 the Security Council declared that the situation constituted a threat to international peace and security under the UN Charter.[111] This was a radical step, but the Security Council showed distinct caution; it referred expressly to the unique and exceptional circumstances in making this determination. The subsequent resolutions authorizing sanctions and authorizing member states to create a multinational force to facilitate the departure of the junta and the prompt return of the legitimately elected President Aristide also recognized 'the unique character of the present situation in Haiti and its deteriorating, complex and extraordinary nature requiring an exceptional response'.[112] It may be inferred that the Security Council was anxious that its action should not be seen as setting a precedent, even for future UN action, let alone for unilateral intervention. However, the UN intervened again in Haiti in 2004 when President Aristide was forced out of power with the acquiescence of France and the USA.[113] The UN authorized further military intervention, first by a multinational force and then by a UN stabilization force to ensure a secure and stable environment, to restore law and order and to foster democratic governance. Although new elections were eventually held in 2006, the UN force remains in Haiti and the situation is determined by the Security Council to remain a threat to international peace and security in the region. The UN has also authorized what might be described as pro-democratic intervention in the Central African Republic, Côte D'Ivoire and Chad.

Another episode which has been argued to support a right to humanitarian action or forcible action to restore a democratically elected government is that of Sierra Leone. The government elected under UN supervision after a prolonged civil war was overthrown by a coup in 1997. Nigeria, acting in the name of ECOWAS, used force to restore the legitimate government. The basis for the legality of the ECOWAS action was the express consent of the democratically elected President both before

---

[110] D'Amato, 'The invasion of Panama was a lawful response to tyranny', 84 AJIL (1990) 516. Against this, Henkin, 'The Invasion of Panama under International Law: A Gross Violation', 29 Columbia Journal of Transnational Law (1991) 293; Nanda, 'The validity of UN Intervention in Panama under International Law', 84 AJIL (1990) 494.

[111] SC Res 841 (1993); 1991 UNYB 151; Agora, 'The 1994 US Action in Haiti', 89 AJIL (1995) 58.

[112] SC Res 940 (1994); UN Publications, Blue Book Series Vol 11, *Les Nations Unies et Haiti* (1996).

[113] 2004 UNYB 288; UN doc S/2004/145; Keesings (2004) 45841, 45895, *The Guardian* 26, 28 February; 3, 9 March 2004.

and after the coup in May 1997. ECOWAS itself based its use of force on specific authorization by the Security Council of force to implement an arms embargo and on the limited right of self defence of the peacekeeping force. The Security Council did not condemn the use of force, but it did not give any express approval until after the presence of ECOMOG was legitimised by a peace agreement.[114] In contrast, the overthrow of democratic rule or the annulment of democratic elections in, for example, Burma (1990), Algeria (1991), Nigeria (1993), Niger (1996), Pakistan (1999), Côte D'Ivoire (1999), Fiji (2000, 2006), Central African Republic (2003) and Thailand (2006) did not produce any UN authorization of the use of force or even of sanctions.

It seems to go too far to argue that these instances of UN and regional action show a right for states unilaterally to use force to restore democratic government. And, as a practical matter, the crucial question that arises after *Operation Enduring Freedom* in Afghanistan and *Operation Iraqi Freedom* in Iraq is whether democracy can ever be established by force.

FORCE AND SELF-DETERMINATION

The argument over whether Article 2(4) allows pro-democratic invasion mirrors the earlier debate as to whether it allows the use of force to further the right of a people to self-determination. This issue produced bitter divisions between states during the decolonization period, but is now of considerably reduced practical importance[115] and will be discussed only briefly. The debate was over the right of national liberation movements in pursuit of self-determination to use force and, more controversially, over the right of other states to assist them in their forcible pursuit of independence.

After the Second World War those states that resisted decolonization were met by force. France encountered violent independence movements in Tunisia, Morocco and Algeria and recognized their independence; similarly the UK was hastened out of Malaya, Kenya and Cyprus and the Netherlands out of Indonesia. When India forcibly drove Portugal out of its colony, Goa, in 1961 and itself annexed the territory, the outlines of the legal argument over the right to use force against colonial powers emerged in the Security Council debates. States divided as to whether Portugal's continued occupation of Goa amounted to aggression

---

[114] See 44 above.
[115] Although this is still a divisive issue whenever the definition of terrorism is discussed in the UN.

and a breach of Article 2(4) because the territory formed an integral part of India or whether India's use of force to seize the territory was itself a violation of Article 2(4).[116] Some states argued that the issue should be seen as one of colonialism; this was the position of India, the USSR, Ceylon (now Sri Lanka), Liberia and the UAR. Other states—the colonial powers Portugal, the UK and France, and the USA—said that the issue was one of the illegal use of force to settle territorial disputes. The divisions within the Security Council prevented the adoption of any decisive resolution.

Later in the 1960s, in response to Portugal's refusal to give independence to Guinea-Bissau, Angola and Mozambique, South Africa's occupation of Namibia and perpetuation of apartheid, and the declaration of independence by a white minority government in Rhodesia, certain newly independent and socialist states began more clearly to claim a legal right not only to self-determination but also for national liberation movements to use force under international law, and for third states to use force to help them. The colonial powers and western states resisted such claims.

The first major General Assembly resolution on the right to decolonization, Resolution 1514 (1960), the *Declaration on the Granting of Independence to Colonial Peoples*, made no mention of force. The first General Assembly resolution claimed to assert a right to use force was passed, 74–6–27, in 1964 in response to the denial of self-determination by Portugal, South Africa and Rhodesia; Resolution 2105 (1965) 'recognizes the legitimacy of the struggle by the peoples under colonial rule to exercise their right to self-determination and independence and invites all states to provide material and moral assistance to the national liberation movements in colonial territories'. But there was a deliberate ambiguity here, repeated in many subsequent resolutions: the word 'struggle' was taken by some states to mean armed struggle and by other states to mean peaceful struggle. The colonial powers and the USA opposed any express assertion of the right of a people in international law to use force to pursue self-determination, let alone the right of third states to intervene in support of national liberation movements.

The drafting history of the general 'law-making' resolutions on the use of force reveals the continuing disagreement between states; consensus was attained only at the price of ambiguity. Resolutions deliberately masked the differences between states. The arguments as to the legality of the use of force in pursuit of self-determination took different forms; there was no clear focus to the legal debate leading to this or to other

---

[116] 1961 UNYB 129; see Higgins, *The Development of International Law Through the Political Organs of the United Nations* (1963), 187.

resolutions.[117] Sometimes the issue was framed in terms of Article 2(4): the use of force by a people with the right of self-determination was not covered by the prohibition in Article 2(4) and states had the right to assist them in their struggles. An alternative focus was that colonialism was in itself an unlawful use of force, amounting to aggression and a breach of Article 2(4); if so, the people were said to have the right to use force in self-defence, not just in response to violent repression but in order to drive out the colonial power.[118] Related debates concerned the international nature of self-determination conflict and the applicability of Chapter VII of the UN Charter and of the humanitarian law on international rather than internal armed conflict.[119]

The *Friendly Relations Resolution* (1970) avoided a direct statement of the right of a people to use force and of states to assist them; it did this in order to achieve consensus. Rather it focused on the duty of states not to use force against a people with the right of self-determination, a simple corollary of the right of the people. It said, 'Every State has the duty to refrain from any forcible action which deprives peoples...of their right to self-determination and freedom and independence. In their actions against, and resistance to, such forcible action in pursuit of the exercise of the right to self-determination, such people are entitled to seek and to receive support in accordance with the purposes and principles of the Charter.' Again this deliberately does not unequivocally set out any right of national liberation movements or of sympathetic states to use force.

This focus on the prohibition of the use of force against a people with the right of self-determination, rather than on the more controversial right of a national liberation movement to use force, enabled states to join in condemnation of the use of force by colonial powers to deprive people of their right of self-determination. Those supporting the use of force by colonial peoples condemned any use of force by Portugal, South Africa and Israel against those seeking self-determination; the former colonial powers and western states tended to condemn the particular use of force by a colonial power as unnecessary and disproportionate rather than deny it any right to use force in self- defence.[120]

---

[117] See Wilson, *International Law and the Use of Force by National Liberation Movements* (1988), 130; Abi-Saab, 'Wars of National Liberation and the Geneva Conventions and Protocols', 165 RCADI (1979–IV) 363; Grahl-Madsen, 'Decolonization: The Modern Version of a Just War', 22 German Yearbook of International Law (1979) 255; Falk, 'Intervention and National Liberation', in Bull (ed.), *Intervention in World Politics*, (1984) 119.

[118] Dugard, 'The OAU and Colonialism: An Inquiry into the plea of self-defence as a justification for the use of force in the eradication of colonialism', 16 ICLQ (1967) 157; Rosenstock, 'The Declaration of Principles of International Law Concerning Friendly Relations: A Survey', 65 AJIL (1971) 713.

[119] See Wilson, *International Law and the Use of Force by National Liberation Movements* (1988).

[120] See 136 below.

Other law-making resolutions were also drafted in ambiguous terms in order to secure consensus. The best known is the provision in the 1974 *Definition of Aggression* Article 7 that:

Nothing in this Definition...could in any way prejudice the right to self-determination, freedom and independence, as derived from the Charter, of peoples forcibly deprived of that right and referred to in the Declaration on Principles of International Law concerning Friendly Relations and Cooperation among States in accordance with the Charter of the United Nations, particularly peoples under colonial and racist regimes or other forms of alien domination; nor the right of these peoples to *struggle* to that end and to seek and receive support, in accordance with the principles of the Charter and in conformity with the above-mentioned Declaration.[121]

The Security Council passed many resolutions on situations in colonies using this ambiguous term.[122]

Early General Assembly resolutions on Portuguese colonies and on the situation in Namibia affirmed the legitimacy of the struggle of the peoples in these territories 'by all means at their disposal'.[123] It is interesting that here and elsewhere the word 'legitimacy' is used rather than 'legality'. This resolution was still sufficiently ambiguous to allow abstention rather than opposition by western states. In contrast, those resolutions, whether general or passed in response to specific conflicts, which did expressly spell out the right to use armed force in pursuit of self-determination met with opposition from colonial powers and other western states.[124] Thus from 1973 the annual resolution on 'The importance of the universal realization of the right of peoples to self-determination and of the speedy granting of independence to colonial countries and peoples for the effective guarantee and observance of human rights' contained in paragraph 2 an affirmation of support for 'armed struggle'. This formula was finally abandoned in 1991 when the resolution reverted to the formula 'all available means'.[125] Similarly the 1981 *Declaration on the Inadmissibility of Intervention*, Resolution 36/103, said that the right and duty of states to support self-determination included the right of these people to wage both political and armed struggle. Such resolutions did not secure consensus.[126]

---

[121] See 1974 UNYB 845 for an account of the debate on this point.

[122] For example, SC Res 386 (1976), 392 (1976), 428 (1978), 445 (1979).

[123] GA Res 2708 (1970), 2652 (1970); 3295 (1974); in the debates many states spoke in favour of the armed struggle (1974 UNYB 156).

[124] GA Res 3070 (1973), 97–5–28; South Africa GA Res 39/72 (1984), 1984 UNYB 128 at 130.

[125] GA Res 46/87 (1991); 47/82 (1992); GA Res 48/94 (1993). The last such resolution, 49/151, was passed in 1994.

[126] 1981 UNYB 145; GA Res 36/103 (1981) , 120–22–6.

There has been less discussion of the theoretically even more controversial right of states to provide forcible help to peoples with the right of self-determination. States were divided on this issue on the same lines as on the question whether a people with the right of self-determination had a right in international law to use force.[127] The resolutions adopted by consensus assert a right to help peoples and urge such help for states involved in the struggle against colonial, alien and racist domination without specifying the right to use force. For example, the Security Council resolutions commending Angola and Mozambique for their support to the people of Zimbabwe in their 'struggle' deliberately used this ambiguous term.[128]

But in practice the southern African front-line states, those neighbouring Portuguese colonies and the neighbours of Israel were not willing openly to assert such a right to use force to assist the national liberation movements operating from their territories. Such states typically denied that they were helping liberation movements; this was clearly because Portugal, South Africa and Israel used force against neighbouring states from which national liberation movements were operating. In doing so they claimed to be acting in self-defence against attacks for which neighbouring states were responsible on the ground that states were providing assistance to national liberation movements or were tolerating their presence. Such claims were rejected in principle by developing and communist states on the basis that Portugal, South Africa and Israel could not lawfully invoke self-defence because they were using force to maintain their illegal possessions against people with the right of self-determination. Colonial powers and western states did not go so far.[129] The Court in the *Nicaragua* case deliberately and expressly left this question out of its consideration of the law on the prohibition of intervention to assist opposition forces. It said that 'the Court is not here concerned with the process of decolonization; this question is not in issue in the present case'.[130] Judge Schwebel was critical of this express disclaimer; he said that the implication was that the Court had endorsed a special exception for wars of national liberation.[131]

Now that the decolonization process is almost complete, and now that South Africa has given up apartheid and its occupation of Namibia, the debate over the right of a people to seek self-determination through the

[127] Zambia, Senegal and Guinea asserted the right to use force in support of national liberation movements under Article 2(4) of the UN Charter, *Repertoire of the Practice of UN Organs*, No. 4, 45; China called on all states to help National Liberation Movements, *Repertoire of the Practice of the Security Council 1972–74*, 172.

[128] SC Res 445 (1979). Also SC Res 428 (1978) affirmed the right of Angola to help the people of Namibia in similar terms.

[129] See 139 below.

[130] *Nicaragua* case para 206.

[131] Dissenting Opinion para 179–80.

use of force, with the help of third states, has lost much of its significance. The issue is still important in the context of the Palestinian struggle for self-determination in the territories of the West Bank and Gaza occupied by Israel since 1967. The states that support the Palestinian intifada generally prefer to make their case in terms of the violations by Israel of the law of belligerent occupation; they are reluctant openly to argue for a legal right to use force for self-determination.[132] This was the approach they took in their statements to the International Court of Justice in the *Wall* Advisory Opinion.[133] However, some limited support for this doctrine of the right of a people to seek self-determination against alien occupation by force may be seen in regard to Lebanon. Syria and Iran repeatedly distinguish between terrorism and legitimate resistance to foreign occupation, and they refused to condemn Hezbollah as a terrorist organization on the ground that it was struggling against Israel's continued occupation of Lebanese territory it had occupied by force in 1982.[134]

In general the extension of the right of self-determination outside the colonial context in the break up of the USSR, Yugoslavia and Czechoslovakia has not brought with it any state support for the use of force for this end.[135] There is no support for the right to use force to attain self-determination outside the context of decolonization or illegal occupation. Still less is there any support by states for the right of ethnic groups to use force to secede from existing states. But when claims to secession, or even to more limited autonomy, are met with forcible repression, as in the cases of Kosovo, the Chechens and the Kurds, the use of force against a people may strengthen its case for self-determination.[136]

---

[132] For a reaffirmation of the right of the Palestinians to self-determination see 2004 UNYB 710. GA Res 59/502 on 'The right of the Palestinian people to self-determination' (179–5–3) deliberately omitted any reference to the divisive issue of the use of force. Compare this with earlier resolutions, such as GA Res 41/101 (1986 UNYB 694 at 697), which in paragraph 33 urged states to extend their support to the Palestinian people in its struggle to regain its right to self-determination. The main focus of the current debate on the rights of Palestinians in the Security Council and the General Assembly is on issues of the law of occupation. The response to the Palestinian *intifada* (uprising) since September 2000 has been to call on Israel to comply with the Fourth Geneva Convention and relevant Security Council resolutions on the duties of an occupying power and to focus on the use of force by Israel against the Palestinians, rather than directly to address any possible right of the Palestinians to use force; see, for example, 2000 UNYB 414.

[133] ICJ Reports (2004) 3.

[134] See, for example, Report of the Secretary-General S/2004/777 para 19. See also 234 below.

[135] The Yugoslavia Arbitration Commission in Opinion 2 (31 ILM (1992) 1497) affirmed the right of self-determination of the Bosnian Serbs, but denied that this gave them the right to use force to alter existing boundaries.

[136] See Supreme Court of Canada, *Reference re Secession of Quebec*, 37 ILM (1998) 1340 at 1372. There are clear dangers that this will encourage those seeking independence to use violence to provoke a repressive response: see Roth, 'Bending the Law, Breaking it or Developing it?', in Byers and Nolte, *US Hegemony and the Foundations of International Law* (2003) 232 at 257.

OTHER CLAIMS UNDER ARTICLE 2(4)

In contrast to this division between states over the right of national lib-eration movements and states to use force to further self-determina-tion, there has been general agreement that irredentist claims did not justify the use of force. That is, the use of force to recover pre-colonial title (on the basis that the colonial title is invalid and that therefore the use of force does not violate Article 2(4) because the state using force has title to the territory) is not generally accepted. India's annexation of Goa is the only instance where the UN has eventually acquiesced in the 'recovery' of territory by force, despite its initial condemnation by a majority of states in the Security Council—apparently on the basis that the Indian action in fact furthered the self-determination of the inhabitants.[137] Subsequent use of this argument based on pre-colonial title has been rejected by the UN. Morocco's claim to Western Sahara on the basis of a title preceding that of Spain, the colonial power, and Indonesia's claim to East Timor on the basis of pre-colonial title preceding that of Portugal were not regarded as justi-fication for the forcible seizures of these territories in 1976.[138] Argentina's use of force in 1982 to terminate the colonial occupation of the Falklands (Malvinas) by the UK did not meet with support. Even those who backed Argentina's claim to the Falklands said that it should have used peaceful means to resolve the dispute. Iraq's invasion of Kuwait in 1990 on the pre-text that it had pre-colonial title was even more strongly condemned.[139] That is, such claims are not treated as a special case; they have not been treated differently from other claims by states using force that they are not in breach of Article 2(4) as they are not using force against the territorial integrity of another state because it is in fact their own territory.

Perhaps the most serious disagreement about the application of Article 2(4) arises out of the claims by China with regard to Taiwan.[140] In 2005 China passed the Anti-Secession Law reaffirming in a formal manner its longstanding policy not to rule out or renounce the use of force to recover Taiwan.[141] This policy seems inconsistent with the duty to

---

[137] See Korman, *The Right of Conquest* (1996), 267.

[138] Ibid., at 281 on East Timor. On Western Sahara, see Franck, 'The Stealing of the Sahara', 70 AJIL (1976) 694. For further discussion of East Timor, see Chapter 7 below.

[139] See Korman, *The Right of Conquest* (1996) at 275, 292.

[140] After the 1945–1949 civil war in China leading to the establishment of the PRC the defeated party retreated to the island of Taiwan; the governments of the PRC and of Taiwan both claimed to be the legitimate government of the whole of China and both sought the reunification of China (see Crawford, *The Creation of States in International Law* (2nd edn, 2006) at 197.

[141] Keesings (2005) 46251. Article 8 provides 'In the event that the "Taiwan independ-ence" secessionist forces should act under any name or by any means to cause the fact of Taiwan's secession from China, or that major incidents entailing Taiwan's secession from China should occur, or that possibilities for a peaceful reunification should be completely

settle disputes, including territorial and boundary disputes, by peaceful means established in Article 2(3) of the UN Charter, and elaborated on in the *Friendly Relations Resolution* and the *Definition of Aggression*. But China argues that the Taiwan question is an internal affair of China.[142] The USA while accepting the one-China policy that Taiwan has no claim to be an independent state, nevertheless maintains the *Taiwan Relations Act* (1979) which stipulates that any effort to determine the future of Taiwan by other than peaceful means would be a matter of grave concern to the USA.

exhausted, the state shall employ non-peaceful means and other necessary measures to protect China's sovereignty and territorial integrity.'

[142] See protest letter by Taiwan, UN doc A/59/877 (2005) and Chinese communications, UN doc A/59/879, A/60/255, A/60/390 (2005).

3

Invitation and intervention: civil wars and the use of force

It is notorious that Article 2(4), drafted in response to the Second World War, was addressed to inter-state conflicts. It says, 'all Member States shall refrain in their *international relations* from the threat or use of force'. Internal conflicts were seen as a domestic matter except in so far as they might constitute a threat to international peace and security under Chapter VII of the UN Charter.[1] But in fact large scale inter-state conflicts have been exceptional since 1945; most inter-state conflicts have been limited to border actions. More common have been civil wars, whether purely civil or fuelled by outside involvement or which have spilled over into neighbouring states.[2] As well as direct intervention in civil wars through their regular armies, states have used indirect intervention through support to irregular forces, and also more limited forms of intervention. This chapter will focus on the law applicable to the use of force and intervention in such conflicts.

The rules prohibiting forcible intervention in civil conflict have been developed through General Assembly resolutions designed to elaborate on the UN Charter rules on the use of force and to supplement the express prohibitions of intervention in the constituent instruments of the major regional organizations.[3] An early general provision was included in General Assembly Resolution 375 (1949) on the *Rights and Duties of States*; this said that every state has the duty to refrain from intervention in the internal or external affairs of any other state and that every state has the duty to refrain from fomenting civil strife in the territory of another state and to prevent the organization within its territory of activities calculated to foment such civil strife. Similar provision was included in Resolution 2131 (1965) on the *Inadmissibility of Intervention*; this said, 'No state has the right to intervene, directly or indirectly, *for any reason whatever*, in the internal or external affairs of any other state. Consequently, armed intervention and all other forms of interference or attempted threats against the personality of the state or against its political, economic, and cultural elements, are

---

[1] See Chapter 7 below.

[2] Human Security Report 2005, *War and Peace in the 21st Century* (2005) at 22–23.

[3] Arab League Pact (70 UNTS 237) Article 8; OAS Charter (119 UNTS 48) Article 15; OAU Charter (479 UNTS 70) Article 3; AU Charter Article 4(g); <www.africa-union.org/About_AU/AbCopnstitutive_Act.htm>, 12 African Journal of International and Comparative Law (2000) 629).

condemned.' The 1970 *Declaration on Friendly Relations* (Resolution 2625) followed the same approach. It spelled out the content of the prohibition of the use of force as regards civil conflict: 'Every state has the duty to refrain from organizing, instigating, assisting or participating in acts of civil strife or terrorist acts in another State or acquiescing in organized activities within its territory directed towards the commission of such acts, when the acts referred to in the present paragraph involve a threat or use of force.' The duty of non-intervention added to this the duty not to foment, finance, incite or tolerate subversive, terrorist or armed activities directed towards the violent overthrow of the regime of another state and the duty not to interfere in civil strife in another state.

The International Court of Justice in the *Nicaragua* case and in *Armed Activities on the Territory of Congo* confirmed that these provisions of the *Declaration on Friendly Relations* were declaratory of customary international law.[4] Thus, the status of the rules on forcible intervention in civil wars is not controversial; it was their application that led to fundamental divisions during the Cold War when the superpowers and others waged proxy wars in Africa, Latin America, and Asia. The previous chapter centred on the debate as to the proper interpretation of Article 2(4); this chapter will show that in the vast majority of cases of forcible intervention in a civil war it is not the interpretation but the application of the law that leads to difficulty. That is, there is a general consensus between states as to the principles to be applied to forcible intervention in civil conflicts, but in practice the disagreements as to the facts and as to the application of the law to those facts can fundamentally divide states, as can be seen clearly in the accusations and counter-accusations between Chad and Sudan; the DRC, Rwanda and Uganda; Ethiopia, Eritrea and Somalia; the USA, Iran and Syria; Pakistan and Afghanistan; Georgia and Russia.

RECENT APPLICATION OF THE LAW ON INTERVENTION IN
CIVIL WARS: AFRICA AFTER THE COLD WAR

The conflict which started in the vast, mineral-rich Democratic Republic of Congo (DRC, formerly Zaire) in 1998 serves as an example, though perhaps an unusually complex example, illustrating the type of conflict that has been common since the Second World War.[5] After thirty-two years in power President Mobutu, supported by France throughout the Cold War,

---

[4] ICJ Reports (1986) 14 at para 191; ICJ Reports (2005) 168 at para 162.
[5] For an account of events in the DRC, see UN Press Release SC/7507, 19 September 2002; 1998 UNYB 82, 1999 UNYB 81, 2000 UNYB 119, 2001 UNYB 116, 2002 UNYB 102, 2003 UNYB 113, 2004 UNYB 119, and the Reports of the Secretary-General. See also Okowa, 'Congo's war', 77 BYIL (2006) 203.

was overthrown by Laurent Kabila in May 1997 with the help of forces from some of the nine neighbouring states. Uganda and Rwanda helped Kabila to seize power partly because they were concerned to stop insurgents operating from the territory of the DRC challenging their governments. But when President Kabila came to power he himself used these insurgent forces and was seen as betraying his former allies; Uganda and Rwanda turned against him and undertook extensive military activities on the territory of the DCR against the government, against rebel groups and even against each other.[6] President Kabila sought help from Zimbabwe, Namibia, and Angola and they sent forces to support him in August 1998. They were apparently motivated in part by hostility to ex-President Mobutu; he had for many years supported UNITA opposition forces which had operated against their governments. Mobutu had continued to back UNITA even after the USA and South Africa had abandoned it. Congo (Brazzaville), Central African Republic, Sudan, Chad, and Gabon also promised help to Kabila. Thus a civil conflict in the DRC was fuelled by outside involvement from many states because conflicts in their states had spilled over into the DRC and because the DRC had played a role in the conflicts in other states.[7] This conflict gave rise to the *Case concerning Armed Activities on the Territory of the Congo (DRC v Uganda)* before the ICJ.[8]

The Security Council, in Resolution 1234 (1999), expressed its concern at the continuation of hostilities and stressed its firm commitment to preserving the national sovereignty, territorial integrity, and political independence of the DRC. In particular it was concerned at reports of measures by forces opposing the government of President Kabila in violation of the national sovereignty and territorial integrity of the country; in the preamble it recalled the inherent right of individual or collective self-defence in accordance with Article 51 of the UN Charter. It also deplored the continuing fighting and the presence of foreign troops in a manner inconsistent with the principles of the Charter of the UN and called upon those states to bring to an end the presence of the uninvited forces.

This resolution is stronger than the earlier reaction of the Security Council when President Mobutu was overthrown by Laurent Kabila with the help of Rwanda and Uganda in 1997; the Security Council then simply

---

[6] On 23 June 1999 the DRC brought three cases before the International Court of Justice against Burundi, Uganda, and Rwanda for acts of armed aggression in August 1998. It subsequently withdrew the cases against Rwanda and Burundi, but the case against Uganda continued and was decided in 2005. The DRC brought a new case against Rwanda in 2002; in 2006 the Court held that it had no jurisdiction in that case.

[7] As a reflection of their involvement six states signed the *Lusaka Ceasefire Agreement* for the DRC on 15 July 1999: 1999 UNYB 87; Keesings (1999) 43051.

[8] ICJ Reports (2005) 168, noted by Gathii, 101 AJIL (2007) 142.

expressed concern at the deteriorating situation in the region and called on the revolutionary forces led by Kabila to accept an immediate cessation of hostilities and the implementation of a peace plan.[9] The Security Council subsequently expressed its support for the people of the DRC as they began a new period in their history. However, it also rejected outside intervention. It said that the Council respected the legitimate national aspirations of the people of the DRC to achieve peace, national reconciliation and progress in the political, economic, and social fields to the benefit of all, and opposed any interference in its internal affairs. It called for the withdrawal of all external forces.[10]

Resolution 1234(1999) clearly reflects the duty not to use force against another state and also the duty not to intervene in its internal affairs. It is based on the legal right of the government of the DRC to seek help and the illegality of the behaviour of the foreign states using force to overthrow that government. It shows that the Security Council regarded the conflict as a mixture of civil war and inter-state conflict and that it took a clear position: aid to the government was permissible, intervention or force to overthrow the government was not.

However, the Security Council subsequently took a more ambiguous position as the war continued. After the *Lusaka Ceasefire Agreement* between the DRC and the five regional states involved in the conflict was concluded in July 1999 the Security Council's main concern was to secure implementation of that Agreement and the deployment of a peacekeeping force, MONUC.[11] The government of Laurent Kabila proved reluctant to cooperate with the peace process.[12] The Security Council accordingly stressed the mutual obligations of all the states under the *Lusaka Ceasefire Agreement*, and the duty of all foreign forces to withdraw from the DRC; it did not again refer to the rights of individual and collective self-defence.[13] The DRC repeatedly wrote to the Security Council objecting that it was necessary to distinguish between the aggressor states—Uganda and Rwanda—and those aiding the legitimate government.[14] Rwanda and Uganda continued to maintain that they had no territorial interests or economic interests in the DRC, but that they were concerned only to protect

[9] S/PRST/1997/11.
[10] S/PRST/1997/31.
[11] See 316 below.
[12] *The Annual Register* (1999) 275, (2000) 259; Keesings (2001) 43932, 43988.
[13] SC Res 1258, 1273, 1279 (1999), 1291 (2000). Uganda in *Armed Activities on the Territory of the Congo (DRC v Uganda)*, Provisional Measures, ICJ Reports (2000) argued that the *Lusaka Ceasefire Agreement* now governed the relations between the parties and that it was therefore not under any immediate and unconditional duty to leave the DRC. The ICJ avoided the issue of the relation of the *Lusaka Ceasefire Agreement* and general international law on the use of force. See note by Sagrado, 72 BYIL (2001) 357.
[14] 1999 UNYB 81, 2000 UNYB 119–4, 2001 UNYB 116–36.

themselves against rebel forces operating from the DRC.[15] However, there were armed clashes between the forces of Rwanda and Uganda in Kisangani in August 1999.[16] And the Expert Panel created by the Security Council to report on the 'Illegal Exploitation of Natural Resources of the DRC' reported that the armies of Uganda and Rwanda had carried out, first, mass-scale looting and then systematic exploitation of the DRC's rich mineral resources.[17]

The Security Council started to distinguish between invited and uninvited forces again after the events of June 2000, when Ugandan and Rwandan forces fought over the diamond trade centred on the town of Kisangani—the first time since the Second World War that two foreign regular armies had engaged with each other in the territory of a third state with a view to appropriating that state's wealth.[18] The Security Council used unusually strong language in Resolution 1304 (2000). In the preamble it expressed its 'outrage at renewed fighting between Ugandan and Rwandan forces in Kisangani'. It unreservedly condemned the fighting and expressly demanded that Uganda and Rwanda 'as well as forces of the Congolese armed opposition and other armed groups' withdraw their forces from Kisangani. It demanded that Uganda and Rwanda 'which had violated the sovereignty and territorial integrity of the DRC' withdraw all their forces from its territory without delay, in conformity with the timetable of the *Ceasefire Agreement*. In its subsequent resolutions, although it called for the withdrawal of all foreign forces, the Security Council continued expressly to single out Uganda and Rwanda.[19] It did, however, also address the security concerns of Rwanda with regard to opposition forces operating from the DRC[20] and condemn incursions into Rwanda and Burundi by armed bands from the DRC.[21]

After Laurent Kabila was assassinated in January 2001 he was succeeded as President by his son, Joseph Kabila, who was more willing to participate

---

[15] See, for example, UN Press Release SC/7507, 19 September 2002, SC/7561, 5 November 2002, 1999 UNYB 84, 2000 UNYB 122, 2001 UNYB 122.

[16] 1999 UNYB 90.

[17] 2001 UNYB 140–5. Uganda, Rwanda and Burundi objected to the April 2001 report, and the initial accusations against Burundi were dropped. The Expert Panel issued additional reports on the self-financing nature of the conflict and the continuing illegal exploitation of the DRC's natural resources by state and non-state actors (UN docs S/2001/1072, S/2002/1146). Rwanda rejected the accusations that it was involved in the DRC for purely economic reasons; it maintained that it was concerned to prevented Rwandan opposition forces crossing into its territory; Uganda also said that the Final Report of the Panel ignored the fact that its forces were in the DRC for genuine security reasons; Zimbabwe and Angola drew a distinction between their position and that of the uninvited forces, UN Press Release SC/7561, 5 November 2002.

[18] 2000 UNYB 126, 129.

[19] SC Res 1332 (2000), 1341 (2001), 1355 (2002).

[20] SC Res 1417 (2002) paras 10, 12.

[21] SC Res 1355 (2001) para 10.

in the peace-making process.[22] Bilateral peace agreements between the DRC and Uganda and Rwanda in 2002 led finally to major withdrawals of troops.[23] The states assisting the government of the DRC also began to pull out their troops.[24] A final peace agreement was reached at the end of 2002 and a new government was installed.[25] But the government found it difficult to assert control over its vast territory and fighting between armed militias continued, especially in the east of the country, despite the deployment of a large UN force in 2003. In 2004 the DRC accused Rwanda of continued intervention and requested the Security Council to impose sanctions on it.[26] The Security Council took a cautious approach and in its resolutions it urged not only Rwanda but also Burundi, Uganda and the DRC to ensure that their territory was not used in support of activities of armed groups or to infringe the sovereignty of others.[27] At the end of 2004 when Rwanda openly threatened to send its armed forces back into the DRC to take action against Rwandan rebel forces operating from the DRC, the Security Council went slightly further: in a statement it expressed very deep concern at the multiple reports of military operations by the Rwandan army in the eastern part of the DRC; underlined that the threat or use of force was contrary to the UN Charter; strongly condemned any such military action; and demanded that Rwanda withdraw without delay any troops it may have on the territory of the DRC.[28] Although this stopped short of any formal finding of unlawful intervention by Rwanda it clearly comes near to such a finding.

The situation in eastern DRC gradually improved, but there was still intermittent fighting between militias. In 2005 the Secretary-General said that it was difficult to assess whether direct support to the militia groups in Ituri was being provided from neighbouring countries, but reports indicated that representatives of the groups moved freely between the DRC, Uganda and Rwanda. He urged neighbouring states to ensure

---

[22] Keesings (2001) 43932.

[23] In these Rwanda (UN Press Release SC/7483,15 August 2002, 41 ILM (2002) 1053) and Uganda (UN Press Release SC/7498, 6 September 2002) undertook to withdraw their forces and the DRC agreed to deal with the rebel groups operating from its territory (Keesings (2002) 44886, 44970; 2002 UNYB 98, 102).

[24] SC Res 1376 (2001) 1445 (2002); 2001 UNYB 116; UN Press Release SC/7622, 13 February 2003; Report of the Secretary-General S/2002/1180; Keesings (2002) 44970, 45025, 45230; 2002 UNYB 102.

[25] 2003 UNYB 129; Keesings (2003) 45331; UN Press Release SG/SM/8785, 18 July 2003.

[26] 2004 UNYB 123, 133; The Security Council Committee established pursuant to SC Res 1533 (2007) found in its Report that Rwanda was responsible for support to rebel armed groups in the DRC, S/2004/551 at para 65–66.

[27] SC Res 1565 (2004), 1592 (2005), 1649 (2005), 1653 (2006), 1756 (2007).

[28] S/PRST/2004/45, 7 December 2004; see also the SC debate, SC 5096th meeting, 8 December 2004; 2004 UNYB 133, Report of the Secretary-General on the MONUC, S/2004/1034, at para 16–21.

that remaining militia groups were not allowed to use their territories as rear bases, safe havens or as a supply route for illegal arms trafficking.[29] There were still tensions between the DRC and Uganda because of the operation of the Ugandan rebels, the Lord's Resistance Army, on the territory of the DRC.[30] There were also incursions on the border with Burundi,[31] and continuing problems with Rwanda.[32] Relations between the states of the region nevertheless improved and the signing of the *Pact on Security, Stability and Development in the Great Lakes Region* by eleven regional states on 15 December 2006 was an 'historic development' bringing hope for the future.[33] This Pact includes a *Protocol on Non-aggression and Mutual Defence* in which the parties undertake 'to abstain from sending or supporting armed opposition forces or armed groups or insurgents onto the territory of other states or from tolerating the presence on their territories of armed groups or insurgents engaged in armed conflicts or involved in acts of violence or subversion against the Government of another state'.

However, the security situation in the east deteriorated in 2007, and serious fighting between dissident militias and government forces broke out.[34] The Security Council expressed its grave concern at the continued presence of foreign armed groups in the east. It commended the joint efforts of the DRC and Rwanda to address their common security concerns through dialogue and cooperation and welcomed their November 2007 agreement on a common approach to end the threat posed to peace and stability to both countries.[35]

Just as the Security Council with regard to the conflict in the DRC drew a distinction between outside forces invited by the government and those of Uganda and Rwanda, so with regard to other conflicts the Security Council has taken the same approach. When civil war broke out in Congo (Brazzaville) in 1997, Angola intervened and sent troops to support the opposition forces, which then secured victory. The Security Council, in a Presidential Statement, condemned outside intervention; it expressed concern about the grave situation and called for an end to hostilities. It condemned all external interference, including the intervention of foreign

---

[29] Report of the Secretary-General on MONUC, S/2005/506, at para 27.
[30] Report of the Secretary-General on MONUC, S/2006/390, at para 31; S/PRST/2005/46; S/PRST/2006/4; Keesings (2007) 48070. However, in September 2007 Uganda and the DRC agreed on joint action to secure the stability of their border, Report of the Secretary-General on MONUC, S/2007/671.
[31] Report of the Secretary-General on MONUC, S/2005/506, at para 20.
[32] Report of the Secretary-General on MONUC, S/2007/156, at para 16.
[33] 46 ILM (2007) 173; Report of the Secretary-General on MONUC, S/2007/156, at para 21; SC 5603rd meeting, 20 December 2006.
[34] Report of the Secretary-General on MONUC, S/2007/671 at para 12.
[35] SC Res 1794 (2007).

forces, in violation of the Charter of the UN and called for the immediate withdrawal of all foreign forces.[36]

The traditional position was again adopted with regard to intervention in the conflict in Sierra Leone. A civil war started in 1991 when opposition forces of the Revolutionary United Front (RUF) tried to overthrow the government. The RUF refused to accept the settlement ending the conflict and did not participate in the 1996 elections. It seized power in a military coup in 1997, but the UN refused to accept the overthrow of the democratically elected government under President Kabbah and this government was restored in 1998. The RUF continued their armed struggle. There were accusations that President Charles Taylor of Liberia was intervening to assist them to overthrow the government of Sierra Leone.[37] Many states in West Africa, including Sierra Leone, Liberia, Guinea and Côte d'Ivoire, were involved in a series of interconnected conflicts.[38] Armed elements and criminal gangs operated across the borders; massive refugee flows aggravated the situation; the states in the region made accusations and counter-accusations of unlawful intervention.[39] The Security Council called on all states in the region to take action to prevent armed groups from using their territory to prepare and commit attacks on neighbouring countries, but it singled out Liberia for express condemnation and sanctions. In Resolution 1343 (2001) it demanded that the government of Liberia immediately cease its support for the RUF in Sierra Leone and for other armed rebel groups in the region; called on it to expel RUF members from Liberia and to prohibit all RUF activities on its territory; to cease all financial and military support to the RUF, including all transfers of arms and all military training; and it imposed measures under Article 41 on Liberia and individual members of its government.[40] Later it called on Liberian forces to refrain from unlawful incursions into Sierra Leone, and expressly determined that the active support by the Government of Liberia to armed rebel groups in the region, including to rebels in Côte d'Ivoire and former RUF combatants who continued to destabilize the

---

[36] S/PRST/1997/47; 1997 UNYB 112.

[37] In 2003 Charles Taylor was indicted for war crimes and crimes against humanity for his part in the conflict in Sierra Leone; he is facing trial before the Special Court for Sierra Leone. On UN and regional peacekeeping in Sierra Leone, see Chapters 7 and 9 below.

[38] 2001 UNYB 159; SC Res 1470 (2003); Reports of the Secretary-General S/2001/228, S/2002/679; UN Press Release SC/7702, 21 March 2003; 2002 UNYB 147, 2003 UNYB 159, 2004 UNYB 164.

[39] Guinea accused Liberia and Burkina Faso of support for armed opposition to its government; Liberia accused Guinea and Côte d'Ivoire (2000) (UNYB 180, 182; 2001 UNYB 180, 2002 UNYB 186–7; Reports of the Secretary-General S/2003/466, S/2002/494; UN Press Release SC/7196, 5 November 2001; Keesings (2000) 43737, 43781, (2001) 43933, 43985, 44041, 44141, (2002) 44605).

[40] See Secretary-General's Reports on whether Liberia had complied with these demands: S/2002/494; 2001 UNYB 184, 186, 2002 UNYB 168.

region, constituted a threat to international peace and security in the region.[41]

The Security Council reaction to these interventions in civil conflict constitutes a clear reaffirmation of the prohibition of forcible intervention.[42] Resolution 1234 on the DRC used the language both of Article 2(4) and of the rules on intervention. This and the other statements of the applicable rules by the Security Council reflect the reasoning of the Court in the *Nicaragua* case, of paramount importance in this area. The Court has recently reaffirmed its commitment to this approach in the *Case Concerning Armed Activities on the Territory of Congo (DRC v Uganda)*.

THE *NICARAGUA* CASE[43]

This case was brought by Nicaragua against the USA both for the unlawful use of force against the government of Nicaragua and for its intervention through its support for military and paramilitary activities of the opposition *contra* forces. The part of the judgment which deals with the use of force and non-intervention provides an authoritative statement of the law on this area; it has proved relatively uncontroversial among commentators, in contrast to the critical response from many US writers to the Court's reasoning on collective self-defence.[44] Indeed, there was consensus between the USA and Nicaragua as to the applicable law.[45]

Issues of classification played a central role in this case. Did the actions of the USA constitute an illegal use of force against Nicaragua under the customary international law rule codified in Article 2(4)? Were its actions an unlawful intervention against the government of Nicaragua? If so, could they be justified as collective self-defence or collective countermeasures in protection of Costa Rica, Honduras and El Salvador against an armed attack or unlawful intervention by Nicaragua?[46] The Court undertook an examination of the prohibition of intervention and of the scope of the prohibition of the use of force; it elaborated on the content of these

---

[41] SC Res 1408, 1436 (2002) para 13; SC Res 1478 (2003).

[42] More commonly the SC does not expressly attribute responsibility for intervention, but calls in general terms for an end to such activity. Thus, when the Darfur conflict in Sudan spilled over into neighbouring states and threatened to destabilize their governments, the DRC, Chad, CAR, Uganda, Eritrea and Sudan made accusations and counter-accusations of unlawful support for rebel groups. Each state denied such accusations. The SC typically reaffirmed the duty of non-intervention in general terms. See, for example, 2004 UNYB 256, UN docs S/2005/80, 26 January 2005, S/2005/821, 21 December 2005, S/2006/256, 21 April 2006, S/2006/433, 22 June 2006, S/2006/770, 21 September 2006, S/2007/97, 23 February 2007.

[43] ICJ Reports (1986) 14.

[44] See Chapter 5 below.

[45] *Nicaragua* case para 184.

[46] On collective self-defence, see Chapter 5 below.

two sets of rules and on the relationship between them. As regards the identification of the customary law on the prohibition of the use of force codified in Article 2(4), the Court used the *Declaration on Friendly Relations* principles on the use of force quoted at the start of this chapter on the duty not to organize civil strife in another state in support of an opposition party.[47] It also set out the basic law on intervention at some length: 'The principle of non-intervention involves the right of every sovereign state to conduct its affairs without outside interference; though examples of trespass against this principle are not infrequent, the Court considers that it is part and parcel of customary international law.'[48] It invoked the *Corfu Channel* case, General Assembly resolutions and inter-American practice as authority for the principle of non-intervention.

The Court then went on to consider the exact content of the principle as far as was relevant to the resolution of the dispute:

The principle forbids all states or groups of states to intervene directly or indirectly in internal or external affairs of other states. A prohibited intervention must accordingly be one bearing on matters in which each state is permitted, by the principle of state sovereignty, to decide freely. One of these is the choice of a political, economic, social and cultural system, and the formulation of foreign policy. Intervention is wrongful when it uses methods of coercion in regard to such choices, which must remain free ones. The element of coercion, which defines, and indeed forms the very essence of, prohibited intervention, is particularly obvious in the case of an intervention which uses force, whether in the direct form of military action, or in the indirect form of support for subversive or terrorist armed activities within another state. General Assembly resolution 2625 (XXV) equates assistance of this kind with the use of force by the assisting state when the acts committed in another state involve a threat or use of force. These forms of action are therefore wrongful in the light of both the principle of the non-use of force and that of non-intervention.[49]

The *Nicaragua* case thus made clear the considerable overlap between the rules on forcible intervention and the customary law codified in Article 2(4).

After its statement of the general prohibition of forcible intervention the Court had to consider whether any fundamental modification of the principle of non-intervention had taken place. Significantly, the USA did not itself put forward any argument that there had been such a fundamental shift in the law. It did not advance the argument that it had a legal right to help the opposition *contras* to use force to overthrow a government; it based its right to use force on collective self-defence. Nevertheless,

---

[47] *Nicaragua* case para 191.
[48] Ibid., para 202.
[49] Ibid., para 205.

the Court examined the possible argument that the USA was justified in using force against Nicaragua to help the *contras* in their forcible opposition to the government. The International Court of Justice said that a government may invite outside help, but a third state may not forcibly help the opposition to overthrow the government. Although there had been in recent years a number of instances of foreign intervention for the benefit of forces opposed to the government of another state this did not in itself change the law. The Court had to consider whether there were indications of a practice illustrative of a belief in a kind of general right for states to intervene in support of internal opposition in another state, whose cause appeared particularly worthy by reason of the political and moral values with which it was identified. For such a general right to come into existence, a fundamental modification of the customary principle of non-intervention would be involved.

The Court, in considering whether there was *opinio juris* to support such a change, said it had to take account of the grounds offered by states to justify their interventions in support of opposition; states had not in fact justified their conduct by reference to a new right of intervention or a new exception to the principle of its prohibition. The United States authorities had on some occasions stated their grounds for intervening in the affairs of a foreign state for reasons connected with the domestic policies of that country or its ideology, the level of its armaments or the direction of its foreign policy. But these were statements of international policy and not an assertion of rules of existing international law. Accordingly, 'The Court therefore finds that no such general right of intervention in support of an opposition within another State exists in contemporary international law. The Court concludes that acts constituting a breach of the customary principle of non-intervention will also, if they directly or indirectly involve the use of force, constitute a breach of the principle of non-use of force in international relations.'[50] It later said that the principle of non-intervention would certainly lose its effectiveness as a principle of law if intervention 'which is already allowable at the request of the government of a State' were also to be allowed at the request of the opposition. This would permit any state to intervene at any moment in the internal affairs of another state.[51]

On the facts of the case the Court found that the US aid to the *contras* in Nicaragua in 'recruiting, training, arming, equipping, financing, supplying and otherwise encouraging, supporting, aiding and directing military and paramilitary actions in and against Nicaragua' was a breach

---

[50] Ibid., paras 206–9. The ICJ deliberately left on one side the question of the use of force by national liberation movements. Judge Schwebel, in his Dissenting Opinion, para 179–80, was critical of this in so far as it indicated an exception to the principle of non-intervention.

[51] *Nicaragua* case para 246.

of the prohibition of the use of force. The Court found that the USA had committed a *prima facie* violation of the principle of the non-use of force by 'organizing or encouraging the organization of irregular forces or armed bands... for incursion into the territory of another state' and 'participating in acts of civil strife in another state' in the terms of the *Declaration on Friendly Relations*. The arming and training of the *contras* could be said to involve the threat or use of force against Nicaragua, but the mere supply of funds to the *contras*, while undoubtedly an act of intervention in the internal affairs of Nicaragua, did not in itself amount to a use of force.[52]

The Court made it clear that it was not necessary to show that the intent behind the US intervention was actually to overthrow the government of Nicaragua. Nicaragua had claimed that this was the aim of the USA. But the Court said that in international law, if one state, with a view to the coercion of another state, supports and assists armed bands in that state whose purpose is to overthrow the government, that amounts to an intervention, whether or not the political objective of the state giving such support and assistance is equally far-reaching.[53]

ARMED ACTIVITIES ON THE TERRITORY OF THE CONGO (*DRC V UGANDA*)[54]

In 2005 the Court followed the *Nicaragua* case in its judgment on the case brought by the DRC against Uganda. The DRC in its Application accused Uganda of aggression, and of violation of the principle of unlawful use of force and also of 'the principle of non-interference in matters within the domestic jurisdiction of states which includes refraining from extending any assistance to the parties to a civil war operating on the territory of another state'. Uganda admitted its assistance to an armed opposition group, the MLC, but claimed that this was limited to what was justified in self-defence.[55] Like the USA in the *Nicaragua* case, Uganda did not claim a right to support armed opposition groups in their military campaign to overthrow a government, but rather a right to self-defence. It said that it was not acting unlawfully in supporting the armed opposition groups as it had refrained from providing the rebels with the kind or amount of support they would have required to achieve such far-reaching purposes as the conquest of territory or the overthrow of the Congolese government.[56]

---

[52] *Nicaragua* case para 228. See 30 above.
[53] Ibid., para 241.
[54] ICJ Reports (2005) 168.
[55] It also claimed that its troops were in the DRC with the consent of the government for part of the time, ICJ Reports (2005) 168 para 92–105. The Court rejected this claim: see Christakis and Bannelier, 'Volenti non fit injuria', 50 AFDI (2004) 102.
[56] ICJ Reports (2005) 168 para 41.

The Court confirmed that the provisions of the 1970 *Declaration on Friendly Relations* on non-intervention were declaratory of customary international law.[57] It held that Uganda's actions were not justified self-defence,[58] and since Uganda had admitted its training and military support for the MLC it was guilty of unlawful intervention. As in the *Nicaragua* case, Uganda could be held to have violated the prohibition on intervention even if its objective was not actually to overthrow President Kabila.[59] 'The Court accordingly concludes that Uganda has violated the sovereignty and also the territorial integrity of the DRC. Uganda's actions equally constituted an interference in the internal affairs of the DRC and in the civil war there raging. The unlawful military intervention by Uganda was of such a magnitude and duration that the Court considers it to be a grave violation of the prohibition on the use of force expressed in Article 2, paragraph 4, of the Charter.'[60]

The Court considered another aspect of the law on intervention in regard to Uganda's first Counterclaim against the DRC.[61] Uganda claimed that the DRC had violated the principles of non-use of force and non-intervention because it had not only actively supported anti-Ugandan rebels operating from the DRC against the government of Uganda, but had also tolerated the activities of the rebels on its territory. This argument invokes a different aspect of the duty of non-intervention from that alleged by the DRC, and from that involved in the *Nicaragua* case. Uganda said that the duty of non-intervention involved not only the duty not to provide support to groups carrying out subversive or terrorist activities against another state, but also a 'duty of vigilance' to ensure that such activities were not tolerated. It argued that the DRC was guilty of intervention not only because of its active support for the anti-Ugandan rebels, but also because it had tolerated their activities on the territory of the DRC. According to the decision of the Court in the *Corfu Channel* case, every state had an obligation not to allow knowingly its territory to be used for acts contrary to the rights of other states.

The Court accepted that the prohibition of intervention as set out in the *Declaration on Friendly Relations* includes a 'duty of vigilance': the Declaration provides that 'every State has the duty to refrain from... acquiescing in organized activities within its territory directed towards the commission of such acts' (e.g., terrorist acts, acts of internal strife) and also that 'no State shall... tolerate subversive, terrorist or armed activities directed towards the violent overthrow of the regime of another State'.

---

[57] Ibid., para 162.
[58] For further discussion of the Court's treatment of self-defence in this case, see 133 below.
[59] ICJ Reports (2005) 168 paras 148–165.
[60] Ibid., para 165.
[61] Ibid., paras 276–305.

However, Uganda failed to prove its allegations of intervention. It did not show active support by the DRC for attacks on Ugandan territory.[62] Nor did it show acquiescence or toleration of anti-Ugandan rebels on its territory. The parties did not dispute the presence of the rebels on the territory of the DRC. Uganda argued that before 1997 the rebel groups were able to act unimpeded in the border region because of its mountainous terrain, its remoteness from the capital and the almost complete absence of central governmental presence in the region. The Court did not accept that the absence of action by the government of the DRC (then known as Zaire) against the rebel groups in the border area was tantamount to 'tolerating' or 'acquiescing' in their activities.[63] At first the DRC had not been capable of stopping the actions of the rebels; subsequently it had in fact taken clear action.[64] This is an important decision on the scope of the duty of non-intervention. The Court took a strict approach and was not willing to accept that inability to act against rebels or ineffective action make a state guilty of intervention. There must be actual toleration or acquiescence.[65] Clearly this may be difficult to prove. Hence the dissenting judges in this case argued it was for the state accused of unlawful intervention to show that it had discharged its 'duty of vigilance', but the Court did not agree.[66] The practical difficulties in proving violation of this duty may be seen arising from the accusations and counteraccusations of the governments of Afghanistan and Pakistan, each accusing the other of toleration of Taliban and Al Qaeda forces operating from their territories in 2006–7.[67]

THE RIGHT OF A GOVERNMENT TO INVITE OUTSIDE INTERVENTION

The reference by the Court in the *Nicaragua* case to the legality of intervention in response to an invitation by the government was very brief; this brevity masks the complexity that may arise in the interpretation

---

[62] ICJ Reports (2005) 168 para 297–299.

[63] Ibid., para 300–301. Three judges (Tomka, Kooijmans and Kateka) disagreed with the Court on this point. They argued that it was for the DRC to show that it had fulfilled its duty of vigilance and that in the absence of such evidence it was guilty of tolerating the activities of the rebels.

[64] Ibid., para 302–303. The Court divided its consideration of Uganda's first Counterclaim into three periods as suggested by the DRC.

[65] This issue arises again with regard to the question whether there can be an armed attack by non-state actors in the absence of state involvement in that attack: see below at Chapter 4.

[66] See note 63 above.

[67] See, for example, Keesings (2006) 47149–50, 47464–5, 47641, (2007) 47694–5, 47755.

and application of this rule. The basic principle of the right of a government to invite a third state to use force and the absence of any such right for an opposition may be accepted in theory, but its application in practice has not been simple.[68] The previous chapter examined the debates as to humanitarian intervention, national liberation movements, and pro-democratic intervention; the law on all these may affect the legality of help to the opposition in a state. Various other limits on the right of a government to seek and receive outside assistance have been suggested as evolving through practice since the inception of the UN. The duty of non-intervention and the inalienable right of every state to choose its political, economic, social, and cultural systems have brought with them the duty not to intervene to help a government in a civil war. However, if there has been outside subversion against the government, then help to the government becomes permissible, whether or not there is a pre-existing treaty provision for this. And if the conflict is limited then it will not be characterised as a civil war, but merely as domestic unrest, and so help will be permissible.

This generally agreed position was put forward by the UK in a *Foreign Policy Document* in 1984 which set out the general prohibition of forcible intervention and the possible exceptions to this.[69] It said that normally if one state requested assistance from another, then clearly that intervention could not be dictatorial and therefore unlawful. But a major restriction on the lawfulness of states providing outside assistance to other states was that any form of interference or assistance was prohibited when a civil war was taking place and control of the state's territory was divided between warring parties.[70] However, it was widely accepted that outside interference in favour of one party to the struggle permitted counter-intervention on behalf of the other.[71]

---

[68] See Nolte, *Eingrefen auf Einladung* (1999).
[69] 'UK Materials on International Law', 57 BYIL (1986) 614.
[70] This relatively narrow conception of a civil war requires that the opposing forces control territory; this mirrors the provision in the laws of armed conflict set out in the 1977 *Additional Protocol II to the 1949 Geneva Conventions Relating to the Protection of Victims of Non-International Armed Conflicts.* Article 1 sets the threshold for the existence of a non-international armed conflict and the application of the Protocol at a high level, requiring that dissident armed forces or other organized armed groups exercise such control over part of its territory as to enable them to carry out sustained and concerted military operations and to implement this Protocol. The Protocol does not apply to internal disturbances and tensions such as riots, isolated and sporadic acts of violence, and other acts of a similar nature. This threshold is higher than that set in Common Article 3 of the 1949 *Geneva Conventions.* Article 1(4) of *Additional Protocol I* provided that conflicts involving national liberation movements should be categorized as international. See Fleck (ed.), *The Handbook of Humanitarian Law in Armed Conflicts* (2nd edn, 2008), 45; Rogers, *Law on the Battlefield* (2nd edn, 2004) 218.
[71] The UK cited Angola as an example of this; see 107 below.

Classification of conflicts

The categorization of a conflict may therefore be crucial in the determination of the legality of forcible intervention. The question arises first as to whether a conflict is actually a civil war or whether it is merely limited local unrest. Are opposition forces in control of territory? This line between unrest and civil war has proved controversial. States have not on the whole been willing to admit that the threshold of a civil war has been reached; they see such an acknowledgement as legitimating opposition forces. This has proved a fundamental obstacle to the effective implementation of humanitarian law in non-international armed conflicts. Second, if the conflict is a civil war, is it a purely civil war or has there been outside intervention? What has been the scope of the outside intervention: does it amount to an armed attack allowing collective self-defence or is it merely a lesser intervention allowing aid short of collective self-defence to the government? Is the government using force against a people with the right of self-determination? All these issues affect the rights of third states to intervene to assist the government.

Even the determination as to whether a conflict is an inter-state conflict or a civil war may be far from straightforward. Questions as to classification—is the conflict civil or international?—may be decisive as to the applicable law and as to the legality of the use of force. In the past this issue came up dramatically over the 1961–75 war in Vietnam. The competing parties fundamentally disagreed as to the nature of the conflict. The USA and South Vietnam argued that the conflict was an inter-state war begun by the invasion of South Vietnam by North Vietnam, a Cold War conflict in which the USA was operating in collective self-defence of its ally against a Chinese-aided invasion by North Vietnam, and later also against forces in Cambodia and Laos. North Vietnam argued that the conflict was one of decolonization; the people of the whole of Vietnam were resisting the perpetuation of colonial rule.[72] If the former was accurate, then the rules applicable were those in Article 51 on inter-state conflict; if the latter view was correct, then the conflict was one in which the USA was intervening in a struggle for decolonization by the people of the whole of Vietnam. The Security Council did not play an active role in this conflict and did not pronounce on the issue.[73] Conflicts in other divided

---

[72] See Wright, 'Legal Aspects of the Viet-Nam Situation', 60 AJIL (1966) 750; Falk (ed.), *The Vietnam War and International Law*, 4 volumes (1968, 1969, 1972, 1978).

[73] 1965 UNYB 185. The UN Secretary-General said: The escalation of the conflict in Vietnam was perhaps the most important of developments on the international scene which had repercussion on the UN. Paradoxically the problem was one in regard to which the Organization had not been able to take any constructive action, as was to some extent understandable since the settlement reached at Geneva in 1954 prescribed no role for the UN. Moreover, neither North Vietnam nor South Vietnam was a Member of the UN and

states such as Korea, Yemen, and Ireland have given rise to similar issues of classification.

More recently the question of classification came up in the 1991–95 conflict in Bosnia-Herzegovina.[74] The states involved took radically opposing views on the nature of the conflict; Bosnia-Herzegovina said that it was the victim of aggression by Yugoslavia (Serbia and Montenegro) whereas Yugoslavia claimed that the conflict in Bosnia was a civil war. This issue of classification arose in many different contexts; it was central to the case brought by Bosnia against Yugoslavia before the International Court of Justice; it affected Yugoslavia's claim to be treated as the successor state to the former Yugoslavia; it was important in the debate over the lifting of the arms embargo on Bosnia and on Bosnia's right to self-defence. The issue of classification was also central to the application of the laws of war. This question had arisen earlier in the *Nicaragua* case when the Court said that the conflict between the *contras'* forces and those of the government of Nicaragua was an armed conflict which was not of an international character and the acts of the *contras* towards the Nicaraguan government were therefore governed by the law applicable to conflicts of that character, whereas the actions of the USA in and against Nicaragua fell under the legal rules relating to international conflicts.[75] In Yugoslavia this question came up in several cases before the International Tribunal for the Former Yugoslavia with regard to the scope of the jurisdiction of the Tribunal and as to the availability of charges of 'grave breaches' of the laws of war in international armed conflict.[76]

The classification of the conflict was also an issue in the complex and prolonged conflict in the DRC. The DRC accused Uganda and Rwanda of aggression in August 1998; it wrote to the Security Council setting out the actions of the Rwandan/Ugandan coalition and justifying its invitation to Angola, Namibia and Zimbabwe as a response to foreign intervention and collective self-defence.[77] In reply Rwanda initially denied any involvement in what it said was an internal matter, an army rebellion in the DRC.[78] Uganda also claimed that the conflict in the DRC was an internal matter

---

parties directly interested in the conflict had openly voiced the view that the UN as such had no place in the search for a solution to the problem. This, of course, could not in itself prevent the UN from discussing the problem, but it did militate against the Organization being able to play a constructive role at the present stage.

[74] See Gray, 'Bosnia and Herzegovina: Civil War or Inter-State Conflict?', 67 BYIL (1996) 155.

[75] *Nicaragua* case, para 216, 219.

[76] This issue has arisen in several cases, including *Tadic Jurisdiction*, 35 ILM (1996) 132; *Judgment*, 36 ILM (1997) 908; *Appeal*, 38 ILM (1999) 1518; *Celebici*, 38 ILM (1999) 57; *Rajic*, 91 AJIL (1997) 523.

[77] 1998 UNYB 82–88; UN doc S/1998/827. It made several later allegations of aggression by Uganda and Rwanda (UN docs S/2000/466, S/2000/548, S/2000/1237, S/2000/1245).

[78] UN doc S/1998/784.

and denied that it was responsible for any invasion.[79] Both later said that for their own security reasons they had an interest in the DRC; rebel forces threatening their governments were allowed to operate from the DRC against their territories. In reply Zimbabwe described the conflict as a war between Namibia and Angola and itself on one side, assisting the government of the DRC, against Rwanda and Uganda on the other; the former group of states had responded to an appeal from President Kabila to assist his government against the foreign invaders.[80] In passing Resolution 1234 the Security Council implicitly accepted the DRC version of events: this was not a purely internal conflict but one in which outside states were threatening the territorial integrity and political independence of the DRC. The International Court of Justice agreed: in the dispositive part of its judgment it found that Uganda 'by engaging in military activities against the DRC on the latter's territory, and by...actively extending military, logistic, economic and financial support to irregular forces having operated on the territory of the DRC, violated the principle of the non-use of force in international relations and the principle of non-intervention.'[81]

Invitation by governments in practice

Many states have relied on an invitation by a government to justify their use of force; they have claimed that their intervention was lawful because they were merely dealing with limited internal unrest or, at the other end of the spectrum, because they were helping the government respond to prior intervention by other states. In many cases a government has been maintained in power not by the actual use of force by foreign troops, but by less dramatic means. A foreign government may provide financial support or arms or training for the armed forces or police. Foreign military bases or other forms of foreign military presence may also provide stability.[82] During the Cold War the superpowers and other states used these means to help maintain friendly governments in power. US support for the governments that it helped to instal by coups in Guatemala (1954), Chile (1973), and Iran (1953) and for pro-western governments all over the world, and USSR support for governments such as those of Cuba, Angola, Vietnam, and Ethiopia was well known. Similarly France supported

---

[79] UN doc S/1998/784 and UN doc S/1998/755.
[80] UN doc S/1998/891.
[81] ICJ Reports (2005) 168, para 345.
[82] The impact of such facilities was indicated by the General Assembly in, for example, Resolution 51/427 (1996) on Bases and Installations on Non-Self Governing Territories, passed by 109–47–5. This expressed the strong conviction that military bases and installations in the territories could constitute an obstacle to the exercise by the people of those territories of their right to self-determination.

certain regimes in Africa in order to maintain its influence; it concluded defence treaties and retained bases in many of its former colonies. Also its aid and support for rulers in francophone Africa such as President Mobutu in Zaire, Emperor Bokassa in the Central African Republic, the Hutu regime in Rwanda, and President Eyadema in Togo helped them to remain in power for many years.[83] It currently maintains troops in the CAR and Chad in support of the governments and military bases in Djibouti, Senegal and Gabon.

The right of a third state actually to use force at the invitation of a government in order to keep that government in power or to maintain domestic order has apparently been taken for granted by states since 1945 if the domestic unrest falls below the threshold of civil war. It is commonly said that the *Definition of Aggression* implicitly acknowledges the right of a state to invite a foreign army because it spells out that failure of that foreign army to leave or actions in excess of the invitation will constitute aggression.[84] Interventions limited to action to help governments to repress local protests or army mutinies have generally attracted relatively little international attention. Thus France intervened at the request of the government of Gabon to protect it against an army mutiny in 1964; it invoked a defence treaty which allowed force not only against external attack but also against domestic unrest, and sent extra troops to supplement those French forces already in Gabon.[85] Its justification was that it had been invited to re-establish the elected government and to prevent disorder. There was no discussion in the UN. France also used this justification in 1968 when its troops in Chad were strengthened by reinforcements from outside to 're-establish order' at the request of the government under a 1960 defence treaty. Its troops remained until 1972.[86] Again when France intervened to overthrow Emperor Bokassa in the Central African Republic in 1979 it claimed that it had been invited in by the new ruler to ensure

---

[83] Moisi, 'Intervention in French Foreign Policy', in Bull (ed.), *Intervention in World Politics* (1984), 67.

[84] The *Definition of Aggression* Article 3(e) provides: 'The use of armed forces of one state which are within the territory of another state with the agreement of the receiving state, in contravention of the conditions provided for in the agreement or any extension of their presence in such territory beyond the termination of the agreement.' The delay by Russia in withdrawing their forces from the Baltic states (1994 UNYB 58, 576); by the UK in leaving Egypt (1947 UNYB 356); and by France in leaving Tunisia (1961 UNYB 101) were all the subject of complaint on this basis. Also the DRC claimed that Uganda's continued use of force on its territory after its consent to the presence of the Ugandan forces had ended constituted aggression. The ICJ avoided any specific finding of aggression, but it did hold that Uganda was guilty of a violation of Article 2(4): ICJ Reports (2005) 168 at para 42–54, 92–105, 110–111, 165.

[85] Keesings (1964) 20024.

[86] 1969 RGDIP 469.

order; in fact the French forces and the new President arrived together.[87] In 2002 when French troops were ostensibly supporting the democratically elected government of Côte d'Ivoire against a military threat there were suspicions that France was actually putting pressure on the government to come to terms with the rebels. The Security Council nevertheless welcomed its intervention.[88]

The UK provision of troops to use force in support of the governments of Tanganyika, Uganda and Kenya against army mutinies in 1964 similarly did not meet with any adverse response.[89] A more recent example is the intervention by Senegal when it sent troops into Guinea-Bissau in 1998 to protect the government against an army rebellion.[90]

The case of Sri Lanka demonstrates the reluctance of states to acknowledge the existence of a civil war; states may continue to claim that a conflict is mere internal unrest even when rebels have in fact gained control of territory.[91] The Tamil Tigers sought a separate state for the minority Tamil population; the government of Sri Lanka regarded the Tamil Tigers as a terrorist force without legitimacy. India, which has a large Tamil population in Tamil Nadu, and which was accused of allowing support to the Tamil Tigers from its territory, put pressure on Sri Lanka to negotiate a political settlement with the Tamil Tigers. But in 1987 Sri Lankan government troops responded to the increasing attacks by the Tamil Tigers by resorting to large-scale force against them; the government attempted to reassert control of the Jaffna peninsula from which the Tigers operated and which they effectively controlled. India then intervened. It sent humanitarian supplies to Sri Lanka destined for the Tamils; the ships carrying these were turned back by the Sri Lankan navy. India then made airdrops over Sri Lanka; Sri Lanka protested.[92] Under pressure from India the government of Sri Lanka entered into negotiations with the Tamil Tigers and with India and arranged a far-reaching ceasefire agreement. This agreement included a provision that Sri Lanka could request India to send troops to police the ceasefire.[93] Sri Lanka immediately made such a request.

Both states insisted on the legality of the Indian presence. Sri Lanka said that India was there at its invitation and would leave when requested.[94]

---

[87] 1979 AFDI 908.
[88] See 334 below.
[89] Keesings (1964) 19963.
[90] Keesings (1998) 42323. It was subsequently replaced by a regional force established by ECOWAS, see 390 below.
[91] Alam, 'Indian intervention in Sri Lanka and International Law', 38 Netherlands International Law Review (1991) 346.
[92] Keesings (1987) 35315.
[93] 26 ILM (1987) 1175.
[94] India UN doc S/19354, Sri Lanka UN doc S/19355.

The ceasefire agreement broke down and India sent a total of 65,000 troops to try to stop the disorder; they operated against the Tamil Tigers in the north. Just as there was room for doubt about the free nature of the original invitation to India to intervene, so the voluntary nature of the continuation of that consent was also doubtful. India proved reluctant to withdraw its troops even when asked to do so by Sri Lanka in June 1989. The Indian forces finally left in March 1990. The Indian intervention did not meet with any UN response.

Another example of a state denying intervention in a civil war can be seen in the US insistence that it was not interfering in the long-running (since the 1960s) civil war in Colombia but was merely helping the government to fight the drugs trade. The USA funded and trained a Colombian anti-narcotics army battalion and shared intelligence with the Colombian army, but denied any intent to intervene militarily in the conflict. The theoretical distinction that the USA drew between the anti-drugs efforts and involvement in the civil war was difficult to maintain in practice.[95] The USA now justifies its continuing large-scale assistance to the government on the basis of what it describes as the unified war against narcotics and terrorism.[96]

In contrast to the above examples of intervention that have escaped international condemnation, there have been dramatic abuses of the right to assist a government. The USSR intervention in Hungary in 1956 to repress the move away from one-party rule was justified by the USSR as a response to a request from the former Prime Minister. It was 'an internal matter' for Hungary to invite the Soviet forces already present in Hungary to suppress an armed rebellion by a 'reactionary underground movement'. This intervention was condemned by the General Assembly by 50–8–15, and condemnation by the Security Council was avoided only by a USSR veto.[97] It is striking that when the USSR later intervened in Czechoslovakia in 1968 to deal with a similar attempt to move away from one-party rule it did not again base its justification on an invitation to deal with internal unrest; rather, it sought to portray the events in Czechoslovakia as an international conflict. The move for change in Czechoslovakia was portrayed as the result of foreign subversion which justified intervention to assist the government.[98]

The maintenance of order was also one of the justifications that was claimed by Iraq for its invasion of Kuwait in August 1991; it said that its

---

[95] *The Guardian*, 15 September 1999; Keesings (2000) 43352, 43454, 43616, 43699, 43789, 43940.
[96] Keesings (2001) 44339, (2002) 44606, 44609, 44931, (2003) 45234, (2005) 46938. See Chapter 6 below.
[97] 1956 UNYB 67. The only states defending the USSR were from the socialist bloc.
[98] 1968 UNYB 298.

forces had responded to a request from the Free Provisional Government of Kuwait to assist it 'to establish security and order so that Kuwaitis would not have to suffer'. Iraqi troops would withdraw as soon as order had been restored.[99] This specious claim was unanimously rejected by the Security Council in Resolution 660, (1990) which condemned the invasion and called for the immediate and unconditional withdrawal of Iraqi forces. In both these cases claims to be using force to help a government maintain order were mere pretexts for much more far-reaching intervention and as such were rejected by the Security Council in the case of Kuwait and by the General Assembly in the case of Hungary.

INTERVENTION AND PROTECTION OF NATIONALS

Because intervention to prop up unpopular governments has often proved controversial, foreign states in some instances have not openly said that they were using force to quell unrest at the request of the government. Rather, they have chosen to say that their role was limited to the protection of foreign nationals with the consent of the government, or to claim this as an additional justification to strengthen the other.[100] The USA in particular has sometimes chosen to offer a variety of legal arguments in justification of its interventions. In 1964 US and Belgian forces went into the Congo (as it then was) at the request of President Tshombe, who was faced with rebel seizure of Stanleyville; they reported to the Security Council that they had been invited by the government and were also acting to protect US nationals. Twenty-two states called for a meeting of the Security Council and condemned the intervention; they said that the intervention was a dangerous precedent which might threaten the independence of African states. They also questioned the legality of the government. The USSR claimed that President Tshombe had not taken the initiative of requesting the Stanleyville operation, but had rather given his agreement only after such an agreement had been sought from him. The Congo in turn accused Algeria, Sudan, Ghana, UAR, China, and the USSR of assisting the rebels. The Security Council passed Resolution 199 (1964) in general terms requesting all states to refrain from intervention and appealing for a ceasefire.[101]

Again France (with logistic support from the USA) and Belgium used force in Zaire in 1978 when rebels threatened to bring down President

[99] SC 2932nd meeting (1990).
[100] See Chapter 4 below on the use for force in protection of nationals abroad without the consent of the territorial state.
[101] 1964 UNYB 95; see Virally, 'Les Nations Unies et L'Affaire du Congo', 1960 AFDI 557; Abi-Saab, *The United Nations Operation in the Congo 1960–1964* (1978).

Mobutu; Belgium was careful to emphasize that its action was limited to the evacuation of nationals, whereas the mission of France was also to re-establish security.[102] In other cases France claimed that its action was limited, but in Mauritania in 1977 and in Gabon in 1990 there were doubts as to whether the French intervention was really just to protect nationals.[103] In the Central African Republic (CAR) in 1996 France used force ostensibly to protect its nationals but in fact to prop up the government.[104] A further mutiny was defeated by French troops protecting the palace. But when yet another mutiny occurred in 1997 French troops left and were replaced by an African force (MISAB) and then a UN force (MINURCA). After another coup in March 2003 (supported by Chad) France did limit itself to the evacuation of its nationals.[105] However, the situation remained unstable. The crisis in Darfur in Sudan affected the security of the CAR (and of Chad);[106] in 2006 the CAR accused the government of Sudan of support for armed rebels against it.[107] When these rebels threatened the government French ground and air forces took action to assist the government.[108] France kept its troops in the country and they were involved in further clashes with rebel forces in March 2007.[109]

France's intervention in Chad in 1992 was similarly claimed to be limited to the protection of nationals, although in fact it seems to have gone beyond this to protect the government of President Deby.[110] Subsequently France kept 1,000 troops in Chad in support of the government, and in 2004 it also stationed a small number of troops on the border with Sudan to prevent the conflict in Darfur from undermining the security of Chad.[111] Chad repeatedly accused the government of Sudan of support for rebel

---

[102] Keesings (1978) 29125.
[103] Keesings (1977) 28573, (1990) 37444.
[104] Keesings (1996) 41080, 41353. France also put pressure on the government; when a settlement was negotiated after the army mutinies had been suppressed France secured the appointment of a new Prime Minister of its choice.
[105] Keesings (2003) 45276. Earlier in the year Chad was accused of attempting to overthrow the government of President Patasse. It maintained that it had sent in troops only in reaction to the massacre of its nationals (Report of the Secretary-General S/2003/5; *The Guardian* 17 and 20 March 2003). Its troops remained as part of a regional force. After the successful coup in March the regional force was invited to stay by the new government (Report of the Secretary-General S/2003/661). France provided logistical and financial support to this force (UN Press Release SC/7593, 10 December 2002, SC/7626, 8 January 2003).
[106] SC 5572nd meeting (2006).
[107] Report of the Secretary-General on the situation in the CAR, S/2006/1034; Report of the Secretary-General on Chad and the CAR, S/2007/97, at para 5.
[108] Ibid., at para 5; *The Independent*, 15 December 2006; Keesings (2006) 47622.
[109] Report of the Secretary-General on the situation in the CAR, S/2007/376, 22 June 2007; *The New York Times*, 5 March 2007, Keesings (2007) 47793.
[110] Keesings (1992) 38710.
[111] Keesings (2004) 46148.

forces.[112] When rebels again threatened the government in 2006 France acknowledged that it was reinforcing its troops to evacuate its nationals, but denied actual involvement in the conflict.[113] Chad accused 'mercenaries acting on behalf of the government of Sudan' of involvement in the attempt to destabilize the government.[114] The Security Council expressed concern, but did not expressly hold the government of Sudan responsible. It condemned the rebel attacks and said that any attempt to seize power by the use of force would be regarded as unacceptable.[115] Again the intervention by France, Belgium, and Zaire in Rwanda in 1990 was in fact to protect the Hutu government threatened by a Tutsi invasion rather than merely to protect nationals as claimed.[116]

Also France repeatedly claimed that its role in Côte d'Ivoire was simply to protect its nationals after a coup attempt in September 2002.[117] Even when it subsequently increased the number of its forces it still maintained that it was concerned only to evacuate its nationals.[118] The French troops later took on the monitoring of the 2003 ceasefire agreement. Even though this agreement was endorsed by the Security Council in Resolution 1464 (2003) which welcomed the French contribution, there were significant anti-French riots which reflected the suspicion that France was not neutral in the civil war, but rather had pursued its own agenda in putting undue pressure on the government to accommodate the rebels.[119] In 2004 the Security Council authorized the French troops to use force in support of peacekeeping forces.[120] It then approved the significant anti-government action taken by the French forces when they destroyed the national air force in retaliation for a breach of the ceasefire by government forces which had caused the death of nine French soldiers.[121]

The UK intervention in Sierra Leone in 2000 was initially claimed to be an action undertaken to allow its nationals to leave the country, but it was clear that there was also an intention to prop up the government against rebel forces at a critical time. The UK forces took action to secure the

---

[112] Keesings (2005) 46974, (2006) 47188, 47242, 47504, 47563; Reports of the SC Mission to the Sudan and Chad, S/2006/433, 22 June 2006 at para 51, Report of the Secretary-General S/2006/1019, at para 11–12.

[113] Keesings (2006) 47188, 47445, 47563; *The Guardian* 13, 14 April 2006.

[114] UN Doc S/2006/256, 21 April 2006.

[115] S/PRST/2005/48, S/PRST/2006/19, S/PRST/2006/53, SC Res 1679 (2006), 1706 (2006). In May 2007 Chad and Sudan concluded an agreement to strengthen their relations, UN Press Release SG/SM/10977, 7 May 2007; Report of the Secretary-General S/2007/488 at para 12.

[116] Keesings (1990) 37766.

[117] Keesings (2002) 44968); <www.diplomatie.gouv.fr/actu/impression.gb.asp?ART=30120>; <www.diplomatie.gouv.fr/actu/impression.gb.asp?ART=30929>.

[118] Keesings (2002) 45026, 45131, (2003) 45230.

[119] Keesings (2003) 45175, 45230.

[120] SC Res 1527 (2004), 1528 (2004).

[121] SC Res 1572 (2004), 2004 UNYB 185–186, 2004 AFDI 943.

airport and the capital against rebel forces.[122] In September 2000 the Foreign Secretary said that British troops were in Sierra Leone for three reasons: to protect the people, to assist the democratically elected government and to provide support to the UN peacekeeping force.[123] The UK subsequently offered training and equipment to the Sierra Leone army and helped to fund the disarmament of the rebel forces.[124]

More attention has been paid to the instances when the USA used force claiming to be acting both at the invitation of a government and in protection of nationals. The USA, in its forcible interventions in the Dominican Republic (1965) and Grenada (1983), used the justification that it was invited by the legitimate government as part of a regional peacekeeping operation and also that it was acting to protect US nationals in self-defence; in both operations it actually overthrew the old government and installed new governments. Controversy about the existence of the invitation and its constitutional propriety was strong in both cases; in the former the invitation came from unspecified 'government officials' and in the latter from the Governor-General, a post without executive powers. The intervention in the Dominican Republic was the first overt military intervention by the USA after the Second World War, designed to prevent the establishment of another communist government in the western hemisphere; its legality was supported in the Security Council only by the UK. There was also criticism in the General Assembly, but no condemnation by either body.[125] The intervention in Grenada was condemned by the UN General Assembly which said it 'deeply deplores the armed intervention in Grenada, which constitutes a flagrant violation of international law and of the independence, sovereignty and territorial integrity of that state'.[126]

It is significant that when the USA intervened in Panama in 1989 it chose not to rely on invitation by a government. Although it noted that Guillermo Endara (who had a clear claim to the presidency because he had been elected to replace General Noriega, but had been prevented by him from taking power[127]) had welcomed the intervention, the US legal

---

[122] 2000 UNYB 195. Statement by the Secretary of State for Defence in the House of Commons, 15 May 2000; UN Press Release SC/6857, 11 May 2000. See Chapters 7 and 9 on peacekeeping in Sierra Leone.

[123] <www.fco.gov.uk/news/newstext.asp?4130>.

[124] Keesings (2000) 43552, (2001) 44330, 2000 UNYB 195, 207. The UK forces remained until July 2002 (Keesings (2002) 44888); they returned briefly in February 2003 because of concern about possible destabilization as a result of the conflict in Liberia (Keesings (2003) 45231, UN Press Release SC/7456, 18 July 2002).

[125] 1965 UNYB 140; Meeker, 'The Dominican Situation in the Perspective of International Law', 53 Department of State Bulletin (1965) 60.

[126] The GA condemned the intervention in GA Res 38/7 (1983) (108–9–27). The condemnation by the Security Council was vetoed by the USA: 1983 UNYB 211. See Gilmore, *The Grenada Intervention* (1984).

[127] 1989 UNYB 172.

justification as reported to the Security Council was self-defence in protection of its nationals and defence of the Panama Canal under the 1977 Canal Treaty. This reluctance to rely on invitation may indicate a new caution about using invitation by a 'legitimate' rather than an effective government. The Security Council resolution denouncing the US intervention was vetoed by the USA, the UK and France on the ground that it was unbalanced in that it did not address the illegal nature of the Noriega regime. The General Assembly condemned the intervention in Resolution 44/240 by 75–20–40. This less than overwhelming vote is usually explained as attributable to the hostility to Noriega and the special relation of the USA to Panama. The OAS, however, overwhelmingly condemned the intervention.[128]

In all these cases of US intervention the defence of nationals was used to mask the use of force to overthrow the government; the motive of the USA was to install a new government more ideologically appealing to it. The claim of invitation was controversial in the case of the Dominican Republic, was not accepted as a justification in the case of Grenada, and was abandoned in Panama. The US interventions clearly went beyond the protection of nationals that was claimed as one of the justifications for the intervention and the invitation was not enough to legitimate the intervention as far as a majority of states were concerned.[129]

INTERVENTION IN RESPONSE TO PRIOR
FOREIGN INTERVENTION

If there is a civil war rather than mere internal unrest, it has come to be accepted that there is a duty not to intervene, even at the request of the government, in the absence of UN or regional authorization. But even if there is a civil war, states may justify forcible intervention at the request of the government on the ground that there has been prior foreign intervention against the government. This is the best established exception to the prohibition of intervention and possibly the most abused. The USSR interventions in Czechoslovakia (1968) and Afghanistan (1979) are the most infamous examples of abuse of the doctrine that prior foreign intervention justifies counter-intervention at the request of the

---

[128] Keesings (1989) 37113; D'Amato, 'The Invasion of Panama was a Lawful Response to Tyranny', 84 AJIL (1990) 516; Henkin, 'The Invasion of Panama under International Law: A Gross Violation', 29 Columbia Journal of Transnational Law (1991) 293.

[129] On the regional peacekeeping justification also used in the Dominican Republic and Grenada, see Chapter 9 below.

government.[130] In both the invitation was a fiction. In the former the USSR first claimed invitation by the existing government, but Czechoslovakia appeared before the Security Council to deny this.[131] In Afghanistan the USSR installed a new government and then said that it had invited in their forces.

The intervention in Czechoslovakia was explained by the USSR in terms of the 'Brezhnev doctrine' of limited sovereignty for socialist bloc states: this portrayed the movement away from one-party socialism in Czechoslovakia as necessarily the result of foreign subversion and thus as justifying a forcible response by the USSR in collective self-defence.[132] Inconsistently with this, the USSR also argued that the matter was a purely internal affair for Czechoslovakia and so not appropriate for discussion in the Security Council.[133] Under President Gorbachev the USSR later expressly disavowed the Brezhnev doctrine; the USSR and the four other Warsaw Pact states which had participated in the invasion and occupation made a statement condemning the invasion of Czechoslovakia as an unlawful interference in an internal dispute and an intervention in a friendly state. They also acknowledged that the intervention in Hungary had been unjustified.[134] The 75,000 Soviet troops remaining in Czechoslovakia were withdrawn by May 1991. The USSR and Czechoslovakia, and later Russia and Czechoslovakia, concluded Friendship Treaties confirming the denunciation of the 1968 invasion.[135]

In Afghanistan the new government installed by the USSR said that it had requested Soviet military aid because of foreign threats. The USSR claimed that it was responding to a request from the government to repel armed intervention from outside on the basis of a treaty of December 1978. In the Security Council debate the USSR said that it was responding to US and other western intervention and China's intervention in Afghanistan's internal affairs to foment counter-revolution; in the General Assembly it invoked instead collective self-defence.[136] This intervention, unlike that in Czechoslovakia, was condemned by a resolution of the General

---

[130] Both these episodes show the absence of a clear line between helping a government to deal with outside subversion and collective self-defence; it was not always obvious which argument the government was relying on. But the distinction does not affect the right to send troops into the state to help the government; it only affects the scope of the right to use force. See Chapter 5 on collective self-defence.

[131] SC 1441st meeting (1968), para 133; 1968 UNYB 299.

[132] On the relationship between the Brezhnev doctrine and earlier US justification for its intervention in the Dominican Republic, see Franck and Weisband, *Word Politics* (1972).

[133] 1968 UNYB 299.

[134] Keesings (1991) 38687.

[135] Keesings (1989) 36982; see Gray, 'Self-Determination and the Break-Up of the Soviet Union', 12 European Yearbook of International Law (1992) 465.

[136] 1980 UNYB 296 at 298, 299.

Assembly.[137] The Soviet forces remained until 1989.[138] In both these cases, Czechoslovakia and Afghanistan, the claim of an invitation masked an invasion to overthrow the government.

Turkey also invoked a prior intervention to justify its invasion of Cyprus in 1974 and again this justification was overwhelmingly rejected by the UN. In July 1974 a coup was instigated against the President of Cyprus, apparently with the support of the government of Greece, in order to destroy the constitution created for Cyprus on independence and to secure the union of Greece and Cyprus. The constitution had been designed to protect the interests of both Greek Cypriot and Turkish Cypriot communities. Turkey argued that this was equivalent to a Greek intervention in Cyprus and therefore that it was justified in using force under the 1960 *Treaty of Guarantee* to secure the independence and constitution of Cyprus. Article IV provided that, 'In the event of a breach of the provisions of the present Treaty, Greece, Turkey and the United Kingdom undertake to consult together with respect to the representations or measures necessary to ensure observance of those provisions. In so far as common or concerted action may not prove possible, each of the three guaranteeing powers reserves the right to take action with the sole aim of reestablishing the state of affairs created by the present Treaty.' Turkey seized control of about a third of Cyprus and in 1983 Turkish Cyprus proclaimed itself a state.[139]

The Security Council passed a series of resolutions deeply deploring the outbreak of violence and calling for a ceasefire and an immediate end to foreign military intervention in Cyprus; Resolution 360 (1974) expressed formal disapproval of the unilateral military actions against Cyprus and called for the withdrawal of foreign military personnel.[140] The General Assembly also condemned the intervention in Resolution 3213 (1974) by 117–0. The Turkish use of the *Treaty of Guarantee* was apparently not accepted as justifying unilateral forcible intervention, although there was no extended discussion of this in 1974.

Other states making forcible interventions in civil wars have almost invariably argued that they did so in response to a prior outside intervention against the government.[141] Those rejecting these claims have denied the existence of such prior intervention, or denied that there was any

---

[137] GA Res 35/37 (1980) (111–22–12), 1980 UNYB 296, 308.

[138] Keesings (1991) 38437; (1992) 38725.

[139] For a discussion of the Cyprus intervention and the interpretation of the Treaty of Guarantee, see Ronzitti, *Rescuing Nationals Abroad* (1985) at 117–34; Necatigil, *The Cyprus Question and the Turkish Position in International Law* (1989); 1974 UNYB 256.

[140] SC Res 351, 353, 355, 356, 358, 359, 360, 361 (1974), etc.

[141] This was the position of Angola, Namibia and Zimbabwe as regards their intervention to assist the government of the DRC against Rwanda and Uganda: see 68 above.

invitation from the government. Intervention in response to government request has met with protest when it was seen as support for an unacceptable government or for an outdated monarchy. In the 1950s and 1960s the UK in the Middle East claimed to be responding to government requests to deal with outside subversion or even threatened armed attacks, but it encountered criticism that it was hiding its true motives. The Security Council in these cases was called on to take a view as to whether an intervention was a lawful response to an invitation by a ruler to an outside threat, even amounting to collective self-defence, or whether it was an interference with a popular movement to overthrow a hereditary ruler, an attempt to keep in power a ruler sympathetic to a former colonial power. As with the USA in Vietnam, the UK description of its role as support at the invitation of a government to resist outside subversion or attack was rejected by others who saw it as the perpetuation of colonial rule.

Thus, when the UK forcibly intervened in 1958 to protect the ruler of Jordan, it argued that its intervention was lawful because it was in response to an invitation and was a response to external subversion by the UAR. Jordan invoked Article 51 of the UN Charter and called a meeting of the Security Council. This intervention met with criticism by the USSR that the UK was intervening in an internal struggle; it cast doubt on the free nature of the invitation by pointing out that the invitation by Jordan and the UK response took place on the same day.[142] In the debate in the Security Council states who were opposed to the continued British presence denied that there had really been outside intervention. The intervention took place against the background of the rise of Arab nationalism and a successful revolution in Iraq overthrowing the royal family; it was claimed that the true motive of the UK was to repress the rise of Arab nationalism.[143] The General Assembly unanimously passed a resolution calling for the withdrawal of all foreign forces from Jordan.[144]

Again in Oman from 1957 to 1962 the UK said that it was helping the Sultan against rebels from outside; others said that it was a purely civil conflict and the UK was intervening to maintain the Sultan in power and to perpetuate its influence in the region. They called on the UK to give independence to Oman, although the UK said that it was already independent. The Arab League referred the question to the Security Council, but the item was not included on its agenda.[145] Also from 1965 to 1976 there was civil war in Oman when rebels rose against the Sultan and subsequently his son; the UK provided help to the rulers and said that the

---

[142] SC 831st meeting (1958), para 3; 1958 UNYB 41.
[143] SC 831st meeting (1958), para 32, 33.
[144] 1958 UNYB 36, 41.
[145] 1957 UNYB 57, 1960 UNYB 194, 1961 UNYB 149.

rebels were helped by South Yemen and the USSR.[146] And in North Yemen when the UAR organized a republican coup against the monarchist rulers in 1962 the UK and Saudi Arabia supported the royalist government.[147] In all these cases the legality of the UK intervention was challenged by those who were suspicious of its motives.

Chad 1975–1993

The problems with the application of the doctrine that a government may invite outside intervention in a civil war if there has been foreign interference were also apparent in the 1975–1993 civil war in Chad. Thus when France and Libya intervened in the prolonged civil war each supported a different faction and claimed that it was the true government of Chad.[148] The complexities of the long civil war in which leaders repeatedly shifted allegiance made any objective assessment of the validity of these claims problematic at times. France maintained a military presence in Chad almost continuously from its independence in 1960; the French position when it actually used force was that it was helping the government against Libyan intervention. In 1978 France was accused of sending combat troops to Chad to intervene in the civil war, but it denied this, saying that its soldiers were there only to ensure the safety of French nationals and to train the army of Chad.[149] In 1983 and 1986–7 French troops intervened on the basis that they were helping the government because of prior Libyan intervention. In some of these episodes the French response was expressed to be collective self-defence, in others it was said to be a response to foreign intervention and Article 51 was not invoked. Libya generally denied intervention; it said that the conflict in Chad was internal. When it occupied the Aouzou strip on the border of Libya and Chad in 1973 it claimed that this was part of its own territory. It also denied the legitimacy of the government which had invited France.

When a pro-Libyan government came to power in Chad in 1979 the positions were reversed and Libya claimed invitation by the government.[150] The OAU expressed concern when Libya subsequently announced a union with Chad. Libyan troops withdrew in 1981 and were replaced by an OAU peacekeeping force in 1981–2, but the civil war continued. By 1988 all parties were ready for peace; Libya recognized the Habré government against which it had been fighting for much of the past ten years.

---

[146] Weisburd, *Use of Force* (1997), 187.
[147] Ibid., 184.
[148] For a general account of the conflict in Chad, see Weisburd, *Use of Force* (1997), 188; Alibert, 'L'affaire du Tchad', 90 RGDIP (1986) 368.
[149] Keesings (1978) 28976.
[150] 1981 UNYB 222.

Libya and Chad agreed to submit the dispute about sovereignty over the Aouzou strip to the International Court of Justice. But France finally ended its support for Habré, and when there was a coup against him in 1990 the French troops stationed in Chad did not intervene; in 1991, when Habré supporters attacked the capital, France sent more troops to protect the new government of President Deby. Again in 1992 French troops intervened in response to repeated incursions by rebels; France claimed that it was acting merely to protect its nationals, but it was actually seen to be helping the government.[151] The new government remained in power and maintained good relations with France and Libya. Libya accepted the judgment of the International Court of Justice when it determined that Chad had title to the Aouzou strip and withdrew its troops. In 1997 the first multi-party elections were held and in 1999 precarious peace continued until security in Chad was threatened by the crisis in Darfur.

Generally the international response to foreign intervention in Chad was limited. In 1978 Chad made a complaint about Libyan aggression; Libya denied that it was involved in the internal struggle in Chad and said that any frontier dispute should be handled within the OAU.[152] When a ceasefire was agreed Chad withdrew its complaint to the Security Council. Again in 1983 Chad took two complaints of Libyan intervention to the Security Council in March and August. Libya again denied unlawful intervention in the affairs of Chad; it underlined that it did not recognize the Habré government of Chad and said that it had been invited to send its army to help the legitimate government of Oueddei. Few states spoke in favour of Libya, but equally it was condemned only by those who were hostile to it. The split was clearly on Cold War lines. A significant number of states limited themselves to calling for peaceful settlement or, like the Netherlands, for an end to all foreign intervention. The Security Council issued a statement simply expressing concern and calling for peaceful settlement.[153]

In its second complaint in August 1983 Chad accused Libya of escalating aggression. Libya again denied intervention and said that the cause of instability was the intervention by the USA, France, Sudan, and Zaire to help Habré; they were intervening in a civil war. Zaire and France replied that their forces were in Chad at the request of the legitimate government because there had been external aggression. France said that it was pursuing no other goal but that of allowing Chad to exercise fully its right of self-defence as enshrined in Article 51 of the Charter. Some states called for an end to all external involvement, but the Netherlands now said that

[151] Keesings (1992) 38710.
[152] 1978 UNYB 235.
[153] SC 2419th meeting, 2428–2430th meetings (1983); 1983 UNYB 180.

it was necessary to distinguish between the provision at the request of the legitimate government of military assistance to a country acting in self-defence on the one hand and an instance of armed intervention in the affairs of a neighbouring state in clear violation of the Charter on the other hand. The UK took the same line. Sudan argued that no dispute over the legitimacy of governments could serve as a pretext for occupation or aggression. Despite the calls for Security Council action or at least condemnation of Libyan intervention, the Council was not able to agree on a resolution; the NAM member states were not willing to pass a resolution to condemn Libya.[154] Again in 1986–7 the parties characterized the dispute in radically different ways. Chad and France accused Libya of intervention and invoked collective self-defence; Libya maintained that the dispute was a civil war going back to 1965, and an internal problem arising from French colonialism. It had withdrawn when requested by the legitimate government and had returned to assist that government when requested. It called on other states to end their intervention. It also claimed that it was acting in self-defence of the Aouzou strip, under attack from Chad and France.[155] Thus the states involved agreed on the applicable rules on intervention, but disagreed fundamentally on which was the legitimate government and on the characterization of the conflict.

The identification of the government entitled to invite intervention

As well as its long involvement in Chad, France repeatedly justified its interventions in other African states by claiming that it was responding to prior foreign intervention. For example, it used force to help the government of Tunisia in 1980, saying that it was threatened by insurgents supported by Libya.[156] In 1986 it helped Togo to keep the dictator Eyadema in power, saying that Ghana and Burkina Faso had intervened against the government.[157] It helped the government of Djibouti in 1991 against an alleged Ethiopian intervention; the defence treaty between France and Djibouti did not allow intervention to restore domestic order but did allow the use of force if there was a foreign threat.[158] Other states have also used this justification. Senegal helped the government of Gambia against alleged Libyan opposition in 1981 under their 1965 mutual defence agreement.[159] From 1986 Tanzania and Zimbabwe used force to help the

---

[154] SC 2462–3, 2465, 2467, 2469th meetings (1983); 1983 UNYB 184.
[155] 1986 UNYB 168; 1987 UNYB 176.
[156] Keesings (1980) 30261.
[157] Keesings (1987) 35110.
[158] Keesings (1991) 38564, (1992) 38755.
[159] Keesings (1981) 30687, 31165.

government of Mozambique in its battle against subversion by South African-backed RENAMO rebels.[160]

It is apparent that in many of these cases there has been controversy as to the right of the government to invite outside intervention. This question as to who may invite outside help arises not only in this context of civil wars but also with regard to collective self-defence, invitation to UN and regional peacekeeping forces and rescue of foreign nationals. Academic debates about effectiveness and legitimacy of governments have been common; writers have divided on the question whether an invitation can only justify intervention if it comes from the effective government or whether it is the legitimate government that has the right to invite assistance to maintain itself in power or to restore it to power when it has been overthrown. Such academic debate has been inconclusive in the light of the diversity of state practice. Roth's exhaustive study demonstrates persuasively that state practice has not produced uniform doctrine as to who counts as the government with the right to invite outside intervention in this context. Cold War divisions meant that, although there was agreement as to the principles governing non-intervention, states often divided on political lines in their determination of who was the government or whether there was a government, whether there actually was an invitation and, if so, whether it was freely given.[161] The disagreements as to who was the government in Chad and Angola are among the most dramatic examples of splits along Cold War lines; the question also arose with regard to Hungary, Afghanistan, Czechoslovakia, the Dominican Republic, and Grenada. In all these cases the claims of invitation were not accepted as a justification for the use of force and the intervention led to condemnation. But in Security Council and General Assembly debates on the use of force, although there has been discussion of the reality of the invitation and of the effectiveness or legitimacy of the government concerned, the main focus has been on the substantial issue of whether the invitation was a mere pretext for intervention.[162]

In contrast, India's intervention in Sri Lanka in 1987 met with no General Assembly or Security Council condemnation. The prolonged Syrian intervention in Lebanon since 1976 also escaped condemnation for many years.[163] In both cases there was a serious conflict; in both the government

---

[160] The United Nations Blue Book Series, Vol V, *The United Nations and Mozambique 1992–1995* (1995), 11.

[161] See Roth, *Governmental Illegitimacy in International Law* (1998).

[162] Doswald Beck, 'The Legal Validity of Military Intervention by Invitation of the Government', 56 BYIL (1985), 189; Mullerson, 'Intervention by invitation' in Damrosch and Scheffer (eds), *Law and Force in the New International Order* (1991), 13; Nolte, *Eingreifen auf Einladung* (1999).

[163] For an account of Syria's presence in Lebanon, see *Report of the Secretary-General pursuant to SC Resolution 1559 (2004)*, S/2004/777.

did not control the whole of its territory. In both cases the voluntary nature of the invitation by the government and the motives of the intervening state were at least open to doubt. Syria kept a substantial number of troops in Lebanon for almost thirty years after 1976; it maintained that it had a special 'fraternal' relation with Lebanon, deriving from their early unity under the Ottoman Empire until the territory was divided by France during the mandate.[164] The need to balance Muslim and Christian interests led to instability and Lebanon was further destabilized by its involvement in the conflict between Palestinians and Israel, and between Syria and Israel. In 1975 civil war broke out between the Maronite Christians on one side and the Muslims and Palestinians on the other.[165] Israel secretly supplied weapons to the Christians[166] and Syria sent troops to Lebanon, at the invitation of President Franjieh.[167] Israel and the USA initially acquiesced in the Syrian intervention; Iraq and Libya protested. But in June 1976 the Syrian intervention acquired greater legitimacy through its official absorption into a regional peacekeeping force of the Arab League, the Arab Security Force, later to become the Arab Deterrent Force of about 30,000 soldiers. This remained in Lebanon until 1983, and was dominated by the Syrians. From 1979 this force was intermittently involved in clashes with Israeli forces in Lebanon. Israel had invaded Lebanon in 1978 in response to a terrorist attack (for which Lebanon denied responsibility); the Security Council in Resolution 425 (1978) called on Israel to withdraw and also called for a strict respect for the territorial integrity, sovereignty and political independence of Lebanon.[168] In contrast the legality of Syria's presence was not challenged in the UN.

After 1982 the situation changed and the USA and Israel took a different line with regard to the Syrian presence in Lebanon. Israel carried out a major invasion of Lebanon in 1982 in response to minor border incidents and to a terrorist attack on the Israeli ambassador to the UK; it subsequently carried out a prolonged siege of Beirut.[169] The Security Council again called on Israel to withdraw its forces in Resolution 520 (1982). Israel continued to occupy southern Lebanon until 2000. A multinational force of western states was established in Beirut and remained until February 1984. Elements of this force became involved in the civil war and in clashes

---

[164] An indication of this special relationship was that there were no diplomatic relations between the two states; they did not maintain embassies on each other's territory. The Security Council later called for the establishment of normal diplomatic relations in Resolution 1680 (2006).

[165] For an account of the conflict in Lebanon, see Weisburd, *Use of Force* (1997), 155.

[166] Bregman and El-Tahri, *The Fifty Years War* (1998), 157–60.

[167] Keesings (1976) 27765; *Report of the Secretary-General pursuant to SC Resolution 1559* (2004), S/2004/777 at para 4, 13.

[168] 1978 UNYB 371.

[169] 1982 UNYB 428.

with Syrian forces. In September 1982 the President of Lebanon requested an end to the ADF mandate and in March 1983 he formally dissolved it, but he did not ask the Syrian forces to leave.[170] From 1984 (after the peace treaty negotiated in May 1983 between Israel and Lebanon was rejected by Lebanon) Israel and the USA protested at the Syrian presence. They complained of double standards in Security Council debates on Israel and the Lebanon; they said that, in contrast to the repeated calls for Israeli troops to leave the 'security zone' that they occupied in south Lebanon, little had been said by other states about the presence of 50,000 Syrian troops in Lebanon.[171] The USA vetoed resolutions calling for Israeli withdrawal, saying that it was necessary that all foreign forces should leave. Syria replied that its presence was based on a legitimate Lebanese request: Israel tried to give the impression that the Syrian presence was an occupation imposed on Lebanon, but in fact it was there at the request of the legitimate Lebanon government. The Arab League said that whatever might have been the circumstances of the Syrian presence it could not be equated with that of Israel.[172] In December 1985 the position was formalized in the 1985 *Damascus Accord;* Lebanon and Syria both referred to this as an invitation justifying the continued Syrian presence. Israel challenged this, saying that the agreement simply formalized Syrian control of Lebanon.[173]

There were occasional challenges from Lebanon to the presence or activity of the Syrian troops; in 1987 the Lebanese President challenged the constitutionality of 7,000 Syrian troops going into Beirut, but he later reversed his position. In 1989 the Maronite commander, General Aoun, with some backing from France, called for the Syrians to leave and tried to drive them out, but the Arab League negotiated a ceasefire and a new constitutional settlement was accepted by all but Aoun under the 1989 Taif Agreement ending the civil war. The Syrians supported the new government and helped it to reassert control over its territory and to ensure stability against the militias. In 1991 Lebanon and Syria concluded two treaties. The first in May was on coordination and cooperation; Lebanon would not allow forces hostile to Syria to operate from its territory and joint councils would coordinate policy. The second agreement in September was a mutual defence treaty. These agreements formally recognized the special position of Syria.[174] Lebanon gradually returned to peace, apart from the repeated confrontations arising out of the continued occupation

---

[170] Keesings (1983) 31905.
[171] 1984 UNYB 285.
[172] 1984 UNYB 285; SC 2556th meeting (1984), UN doc S/17694 (1985).
[173] SC 2640th meeting (1986).
[174] 1991 *Annual Register* 215.

of the southern 'security zone' by Israel until May 2000.[175] That is, there were occasions when the Syrian presence in Lebanon was challenged, but on the whole it was only Israel and the USA which did so without support from other states. In 2001, when Israel used force against Syrian targets in Lebanon, Israel again challenged the legitimacy of the Syrian presence in Lebanon. Both Syria and Lebanon reasserted their established position. According to Syria, the two states have a pact of brotherhood and 'Syria provides Lebanon with everything it needs to defend its territory and achieve security and stability'.[176] Lebanon said that Syrian forces were stationed inside Lebanon at the request of and with the agreement of the Lebanese government. Their presence was necessary, legitimate and temporary (even after nearly 30 years) and not Israel's concern.[177]

However, the situation changed after 9/11, and especially after *Operation Iraqi Freedom* in 2003. The USA increasingly accused Syria of support for terrorism against Israel and against Iraq; it began a campaign to secure the withdrawal of Syria's troops from Lebanon. Thus, for example, in December 2003 the USA passed the *Syria Accountability and Lebanese Sovereignty Restoration Act*. This proclaimed that Syria was a 'state sponsor of terror' responsible for support for international terrorism by its provision of safe haven for organizations such as Hezbollah and various Palestinian groups including Hamas. Syria exerted undue influence on Lebanon, through the presence of its 20,000 troops; it was preventing Lebanon from complying with the requirement of Security Council Resolution 425 (1978) to deploy its troops to the southern border, and it was allowing Hezbollah to operate against Israel from southern Lebanon. The Act also accused Syria of pursuing WMD, and of allowing the transfer of weapons to insurgents in Iraq. Therefore the Act demanded that Syria should *inter alia* immediately halt support for terrorism, and announce its commitment completely to withdraw its armed forces from Lebanon. It imposed sweeping sanctions on Syria until it should comply with these demands.

In 2004 there was a major change in the approach of the Security Council with regard to the Syrian presence in Lebanon. The government of Lebanon unconstitutionally extended the term of office of the President by three years, allegedly under pressure from Syria.[178] The Security Council

---

[175] In April 2000 Israel notified the UN Security Council of its intent to withdraw from Lebanon (UN doc S/PRST/2000/13). The Secretary-General put forward the requirements for the implementation of SC Res 425 (1978) regarding withdrawal (Report of the Secretary-General S/2000/460) and this was endorsed by the Security Council (UN Press Release SC/6865, 23 May 2000). In June 2000 the Security Council endorsed the Secretary-General's conclusion that Israel had withdrawn in accordance with SC Res 425(1978) (SC 4160th meeting (2000), UN Press Release SC/6878, 23 May 2000).

[176] UN doc S/2001/438.

[177] 2001 UNYB 448 at 450.

[178] 2004 UNYB 505.

then passed Resolution 1559 (2004) by 9–0–6 (Algeria, Brazil, China, Pakistan, Philippines, Russia) to bring an end to the Syrian military presence in Lebanon. This 'noted the determination of Lebanon to ensure the withdrawal of all non-Lebanese forces from Lebanon'; it expressed grave concern at the continued presence of armed militias in Lebanon which prevented the government from exercising its full sovereignty over the Lebanese territory; it reaffirmed its call for the strict respect of the sovereignty, territorial integrity, unity and political independence of Lebanon under the sole and exclusive authority of the Government of Lebanon throughout Lebanon; it called for all remaining foreign forces to leave and for the disarmament of all militias; and it declared its support for a free and fair electoral process in the upcoming presidential election.

This was an extremely controversial resolution; it was not passed under Chapter VII of the UN Charter. It seemed that the Security Council was no longer willing to take at face value the argument that the Syrian troops were lawfully in Lebanon with the consent of the government. The USA and France, co-sponsors of the resolution, accused Syria of serious interference in the political life of Lebanon.[179] However, Lebanon itself spoke in opposition to the consideration of the resolution and called for its withdrawal: 'Friendly Syria has helped Lebanon to maintain stability and security within its borders. It has fended off the radicalism and violence that are fed by Israel's extremism and violence against the Palestinians.' Syrian troops came to Lebanon in accordance with legitimate requests. There were no militias in Lebanon, but only the Lebanese national resistance which would remain as long as Israel occupied parts of Lebanon. Syria supported this Lebanese national resistance. 'The draft resolution also discusses bilateral relations between two friendly countries, neither of which has filed any complaint with regard to those relations.' Lebanon also argued that the presidential electoral process was purely internal, and therefore not a matter for the Security Council.

China abstained on the ground that the presidential elections were an internal matter for Lebanon. Russia abstained because the resolution was one-sided in that it dealt with only one part of the situation in the Middle East. Pakistan, Algeria, Brazil and the Philippines all said that the resolution was not consistent with the Security Council's functions and responsibilities. This was an internal matter; there was no evidence of any urgent threat to the peace. There had been no complaint from the country whose sovereignty and integrity the resolution purported to uphold. Besides, the text addressed the wrong threat: any threat to Lebanon did not arise from Syria but rather from Israel which continued to occupy the Lebanese Shab'a farms, the Syrian Golan, and the West Bank and Gaza.

---

[179] SC 5028th meeting (2004).

Initially there were delays in the implementation of Resolution 1559 (2004) by Syria and Lebanon. Both said that the withdrawal of Syrian troops was a matter for bilateral agreement depending on defence requirements and the threat from Israel.[180] But international pressure grew after February 2005; the catalyst for revolutionary change in Lebanon was the assassination of former Prime Minister Rafik Hariri on 14 February 2005.[181] Suspicion fell on Syria and the pressure on it mounted.[182] It finally agreed to withdraw its troops and completed this process by the end of April 2005.[183] Elections followed and a broadly anti-Syrian government was elected, but the situation was far from stable. The Secretary-General in his reports on the implementation of Resolution 1559 (2004) accepted that Syrian troops had withdrawn.[184] However, there were problems with the disbanding of militias, especially with regard to Hezbollah, and with the extension of the control of the government of Lebanon over all its territory. The Security Council accordingly called for the full implementation of Resolution 1559 in a series of resolutions.[185] Lebanon's position on Hezbollah was that it was not a militia but a national resistance group with the goal of defending Lebanon from Israel, and the removal of Israeli forces from Lebanon. It had first been established in response to Israel's occupation of Lebanon in 1982. Lebanon now claimed that its concern was to recover the Shab'a farms from Israeli occupation.[186] But the border which had been established by the UN at the time of the withdrawal by Israel in 2000—the Blue Line—put the Shab'a farms on the Israeli side of the border, treating it as Israeli-occupied Syrian territory.[187] This was only a provisional delimitation for the purpose of confirming Israel's withdrawal under Resolution 425, without prejudice to the final determination of the boundary between Lebanon and Syria, but both Israel and Lebanon had said that they would respect this line.[188] The Security Council repeatedly called for respect for the Blue Line.[189] The Secretary-General reported that there were recurring violations of the Blue Line by Hezbollah and

---

[180] SC 5058th meeting (2004).

[181] SC 5122nd meeting (2005).

[182] The UN SC established an International Commission of Inquiry into the assassination by Resolution 1595 (2005). In SC Res 1757 (2005) the SC provided for the establishment of an international tribunal to try those found responsible for any terrorist crime.

[183] UN Press Release SC/5172, 29 April 2005.

[184] Secretary-General's Reports S/2004/777; S/2005/272; S/2005/673; S/2006/248; S/2006/832.

[185] SC Res 1614 (2005), SC Res 1655 (2006), SC Res 1680 (2006).

[186] Report of the Secretary-General S/2004/777 at para 18–21.

[187] Report of the Secretary-General S/2000/460. Both Syria and Lebanon said that they regarded the territory as part of Lebanon.

[188] Report of the Secretary-General S/2000/460; UN doc S/2000/564, 12 June 2000; UN Press Releases SC/6865, 23 May 2000, SC/6878, 18 June 2000.

[189] S/PRST/2000/21, 18 June 2000; SC Res 1583 (2005), 1614 (2005);

by Israel.[190] These continued until a more serious conflict broke out in 2006.[191]

FORCIBLE INTERVENTION TO ASSIST THE OPPOSITION

It is apparent from all the above cases that states will seek to invoke an invitation by a government to justify their invasion where this is even remotely plausible. They do not generally claim a legal right to use force to help the opposition forcibly to overthrow the government except in cases of national liberation movements seeking decolonization, as the International Court of Justice made clear in the *Nicaragua* case. Some writers have doubted the legal force of the prohibition of intervention to assist the opposition against the government because practice since the Second World War shows such extensive intervention to help oppositions.[192] But they acknowledge that in fact those states helping the opposition have generally done so without direct use of their own troops. Nor have they openly assisted opposition forces to operate from their territory; often a civil war is internationalized when opposition forces operate from a neighbouring state against their government. If the neighbouring state supports this action, then it is intervening in the civil war. Such support could constitute aggression, use of force or armed attack. But almost invariably states deny any such support for the rebels on their territory for fear of a forceful response.

The open use of a state's own troops against a foreign government involved in civil conflict was rare. Covert action was much more common even in cases where the intervening state challenged the legitimacy of the government of the state involved in civil war. The US intervention in Laos illustrates this clearly. From 1958 to 1960 the USA was trying to secure the removal of a government it saw as ideologically unsound; its intervention was covert. But when a government friendly to the USA came to power in 1961 the USA was willing to use force openly in its support. It undertook bombing against opposition forces which it said were supported from outside.[193]

---

[190] Secretary-General's Reports S/2004/777; S/2005/272; S/2005/673; S/2006/248; S/2006/832; UN Press Release SC/8465, 29 July 2005; SC 5175th meeting (2005); SC 5352nd meeting (2006).
[191] See 237 below.
[192] Lowe, 'The Principle of Non-intervention: Use of Force', in Lowe and Warbrick (eds), *The United Nations and the Principles of International Law* (1994), 66; Weisburd, *Use of Force* (1997), 1–27. See *contra*, Mullerson, 'Sources of International Law: New Tendencies in Soviet Thinking', 83 AJIL (1989) 494.
[193] Weisburd, *Use of Force* (1997), 179.

The USA, although it gave support to opposition groups in Angola, Cambodia, and Afghanistan, did not openly go beyond this to direct forcible intervention. Any direct use of force was generally, as in the *Nicaragua* case, carried out covertly through the CIA. The supply of arms or training to opposition forces was generally covert and thus did not involve a need for legal justification. But it was in the massive financial support for opposition groups in Angola, Cambodia, Afghanistan and Nicaragua under President Reagan that the USA seemed to come close to blatant disregard, if not rejection, of the legal principle of non-intervention. The President's development of the 'Reagan doctrine' for the containment of the spread of socialism, with its rhetoric of the duty to help 'freedom fighters' against socialist governments, seemed to indicate that the USA was applying a new doctrine of national liberation; it was apparently adopting the doctrine developed by former colonies and socialist states during decolonization, the doctrine that it was legal for national liberation movements to use force in self-determination, to justify intervention in civil wars.[194] But the Reagan doctrine was, like the Brezhnev doctrine, not put forward as a legal justification of the use of force; the right to use force was still based on self-defence.[195] The aid was ostensibly limited to financial assistance, sometimes portrayed as 'non-lethal' or 'humanitarian' aid.[196]

In the case of Cambodia after the Vietnamese invasion of 1978 the government installed by the Vietnamese forces was not accepted in the UN as the legitimate representative of the state and the invasion was repeatedly condemned by the General Assembly by increasing majorities.[197] But even though the General Assembly deplored the foreign armed intervention and occupation and noted 'the continued and effective struggle waged against foreign occupation by the Kampuchean forces' under the leadership of Sihanouk, it did not expressly call for aid to the Sihanouk forces

---

[194] Reisman, 'Old Wine in New Bottles: The Reagan and Brezhnev Doctrines in Contemporary International Law and Practice', 13 Yale Journal of International Law (1988) 171; Reisman, 'The Resistance in Afghanistan is Engaged in a War of National Liberation', 81 AJIL (1987), 906 and (1988), 82. Reisman seems to go further than the US government in his argument. Vertzberger, *Risk Taking and Decisionmaking; Foreign Military Intervention Decisions* (1998), demonstrates that despite the belligerent rhetoric, President Reagan's administration in fact took a cautious attitude to intervention.

[195] Kirkpatrick and Gerson, 'The Reagan Doctrine, Human Rights and International Law', in Henkin (ed.), *Right v Might* (1991), 19. D'Amato also was insistent that the doctrine did not involve the forcible overthrow of the government: 'The Secret War in Central America and the Future of World Order', 80 AJIL (1986) 43 at 111.

[196] Keesings (1986) 34426; (1987) 35121, 35174; (1988) 35896. This pretence seems to have come near to being abandoned in 1987 with reports of the *direct* supply of Stinger missiles to the opposition forces in Angola and Afghanistan: Keesings (1987) 34864; (1988) 35786. Some of these weapons ended up in the hands of the Iranian opposition and of Qatar: Keesings (1998) 36220, 36313.

[197] UN Publications, Blue Book Series, Vol II, *The United Nations and Cambodia 1991–1995* (1995).

in the way that it called for assistance to Angola against South Africa.[198] However, the repeated accusations by Vietnam that China, Thailand and the USA were helping Pol Pot opposition forces against the government of Cambodia did not elicit any Security Council action or General Assembly response. In all these cases the USA challenged the legitimacy of the government it was attempting to subvert. Even in the middle of the Reagan era, however, the USA was not willing to try to justify its support for the *contras* in Nicaragua as based on the right to support oppositions forcibly to overthrow the government. In the *Nicaragua* case, as was discussed above, the USA did not rely on a legal right to intervene in support of 'freedom fighters', but rather on collective self-defence; this was clearly regarded as important by the Court.

INTERVENTION AND COUNTER-INTERVENTION IN ANGOLA AND MOZAMBIQUE

The civil war in Angola was fuelled by outside intervention; states divided on Cold War lines.[199] But all were in agreement as to the governing principle that forcible assistance to opposition forces is illegal. When South Africa intervened in Angola it did not openly claim the right to use force to help the opposition against the government, even though it did challenge the legitimacy of the government. In the period leading to independence in Angola (before Portugal finally abandoned its long opposition to independence for its colonies) there was conflict between the different liberation movements in Angola. Both the MPLA and the FNLA had been recognized by the UN as representatives of the people of Angola.[200] Portugal recognized the MPLA, the FNLA, and UNITA as the sole and legitimate representatives of the people of Angola.[201] All received support from other states: the FNLA received aid from the USA, China and Zaire; the USSR supported the MPLA; and South Africa supported UNITA.

At the start of 1975 the three movements made an agreement to form a coalition government, but on the day after it was formed fighting broke out again. South Africa provided training and leaders to UNITA; Cuba sent military advisers to assist the MPLA. In August 1975 South African forces went into Angola in support of UNITA and the FNLA; the justification that South Africa put forward was that it had acted to protect a hydroelectric project. It claimed that it had expressed a readiness to withdraw from

---

[198] GA Res 43/19 (1988).
[199] For a general account of the conflict in Angola, see Brogan, *World Conflicts* (1998), 13; UN Publications, *The Blue Helmets: A Review of UN Peace-Keeping* (3rd edn, 1996) at 231.
[200] 1974 UNYB 820.
[201] 1975 UNYB 863.

Angolan soil in September 1995, long before the date set for independence. However, because of the Portuguese government's inability to provide the necessary protection South Africa had no choice but to protect the project. South Africa claimed that Portugal had said that it would like its troops to stay until the takeover of the next government; Portugal denied this claim.[202] In November Cuba sent armed forces, airlifted in by the USSR, and with their help the MPLA repelled the attack and drove the South African forces out. Some states in the UN General Assembly expressed concern over the direct intervention by South African forces in Angola.[203] The USA accused the USSR of expansionism and said that Angola had been invaded by two other countries as well as South Africa.[204]

The MPLA gained control of most of the territory of Angola and was accepted by the OAU as the government of Angola when it came to independence on 11 November 1975. In 1976 Angola became a member of the UN even though the USA and China wanted to defer this because of the presence of Cuban troops in Angola. The MPLA government answered that the troops were present at the request of the government and would be withdrawn when Angola could defend itself.[205]

The Security Council debates in 1976 set the pattern that was to be followed for the next twelve years. Western states like the USA and the UK said that all foreign intervention should end, but did not actually challenge the *legality* of the Cuban presence. Other states expressly affirmed the right of the MPLA government to invite outside help; they rejected any linkage between the withdrawal of South African forces illegally in Angola and those of Cuba present at the invitation of the government.[206] The Security Council passed Resolution 387 (1976) by 9–0–5; this condemned South Africa's acts of aggression against Angola. The USA, France, Italy, Japan and the UK abstained because, while the intervention of South Africa was condemned, they would also have liked to have seen that condemnation extended to all foreign military intervention in Angola. Later Security Council resolutions, when not vetoed as one-sided by the USA, condemned South African incursions into Angola and also warned South Africa against destabilization of independent African states. For example, Resolution 581 (1986) deplored any form of assistance which could be used to destabilize states in southern Africa.

In 1975 the US Congress passed the Clark Amendment barring covert aid to UNITA by the US government, but South Africa continued to

---

[202] 1976 UNYB 175.
[203] 1975 UNYB 147.
[204] Ibid.
[205] 1976 UNYB 305.
[206] The Security Council later rejected linkage in SC Res 539 (1983).

support UNITA and to deny the legitimacy of the government.[207] It said that it did not recognize the government because it did not control the whole territory and was incapable of maintaining itself without foreign troops.[208] But when South Africa made incursions into Angola after independence it invoked self-defence of Namibia against SWAPO guerrillas operating from Angola. In fact its aim was not limited to this; it was dedicated to the destabilization of Angola and the overthrow of the government. Accordingly it helped UNITA covertly, but also intervened with its own forces to help UNITA in 1985 and 1987. Even so, when Angola then accused it of aggression, South Africa continued to use self-defence as the main justification of this use of force; it said that the sources of the conflict were the civil war in Angola between the MPLA and UNITA and the presence of Cuban forces and SWAPO. South Africa claimed to be protecting the people of Namibia against incursions from Angola.[209]

South Africa also referred to the support by the USA for UNITA to back its claim of the lack of legitimacy of the government. Under President Reagan Congress had repealed the Clark Amendment in 1985 and the government gave massive aid to UNITA.[210] The NAM expressed concern at this as the repeal indicated that the USA was contemplating assistance to rebels in Angola. The Security Council passed several resolutions condemning South Africa for its acts of aggression against Angola in 1985; Resolutions 574 (1985) and 577 (1985) affirmed the right of Angola to self-defence under Article 51. The USA was critical of this as it 'incorrectly implies' that outside intervention was the main cause of destabilization in Angola.[211] The USA went on covertly assisting UNITA, mainly through Zaire with the assistance of the government of President Mobutu.

Even after the tripartite agreement between Angola, Cuba, and South Africa in 1988 whereby South Africa would leave Namibia and Cuban forces would leave Angola, the USA went on helping UNITA, although South Africa terminated its aid.[212] After peace was agreed between the MPLA government and UNITA in 1991, the USA later ended its aid in 1993 when it finally recognized the MPLA government of Angola in response to UNITA's failure to comply with the peace agreement.[213] Thus from the moment of Angola's independence the USA and South Africa challenged the legitimacy of its government, but even so they did not claim a legal right forcibly to overthrow that government.

[207] 1985 UNYB 178.
[208] 1985 UNYB 180.
[209] 1985 UNYB 181, 1987 UNYB 167.
[210] 1985 UNYB 183, 1986 UNYB 162.
[211] SC 2662nd meeting (1986).
[212] Keesings (1989) 36388, 36453.
[213] Keesings (1992) 38752, (1993) 39447.

South Africa played a similar role in Mozambique, and here again it did not openly claim a right to help the opposition RENAMO forces.[214] The Frelimo government came to power in Mozambique on its independence from Portugal in 1975; Frelimo had been supported in its struggle for independence by the USSR and Cuba. On achieving independence it supported the opposition to the white minority government in Rhodesia; Rhodesia responded by fighting against the government of Mozambique through RENAMO. When Rhodesia reached majority rule and came to independence as Zimbabwe in 1980, South Africa took over the support for RENAMO. Malawi also allowed RENAMO to operate from its territory. But South Africa denied that it was aiding RENAMO. It justified its incursions into Mozambique as self-defence against ANC forces; it did not claim a legal right to support an opposition to overthrow a government. Nevertheless, it concluded the *Nkomati Accord* with Mozambique in 1984: Mozambique would end its support for the ANC and South Africa would not support RENAMO.[215] This may be seen as an implicit admission of intervention in that both parties undertook not to allow their territory to be used to launch acts of aggression against the other. Mozambique made repeated complaints that South Africa did not comply with this commitment and that it continued to help RENAMO.[216] Mozambique turned to Zimbabwe for assistance; its forces remained until 1993.[217] The UN General Assembly condemned covert and overt aggression aimed at the destabilization of the front-line states.[218] In 1986 the Security Council also condemned the destabilization in general terms in Resolution 581. After the reactivation of the *Nkomati Accord* in 1988 South Africa claimed that the continued fighting in Mozambique was between Frelimo and RENAMO when Mozambique accused it of further attacks.[219]

THE END OF THE COLD WAR AND THE START OF THE 'WAR ON TERROR'

The end of the Cold War brought an end to many of these conflicts as the USSR and USA abandoned their expensive support for sympathetic governments or opposition forces. South Africa left Namibia and Cuba pulled

---

[214] The United Nations Blue Book Series, Vol V, *The United Nations and Mozambique 1992–1995* (1995).

[215] 1984 UNYB 178.

[216] 1985 UNYB 178, 196; 1986 UNYB 156. In 1985 South Africa admitted involvement but only a technical violation of the accord.

[217] The United Nations Blue Book Series, Vol V, *The United Nations and Mozambique 1992–1995* (1995) at 11.

[218] 1984 UNYB 180; also GA Res 39/17, 39/43, 39/72.

[219] 1988 UNYB 161.

out of Angola; Vietnam left Cambodia; France has repeatedly announced an end to its intervention in Africa. Agreements were made to end the conflicts in Angola, Namibia, Mozambique, Cambodia, Afghanistan, and Central America with UN help. Some of these agreements clearly reflected the foreign involvement that had occurred in the conflicts.[220] As regards Afghanistan, a series of four *Agreements on the Settlement of the Situation Relating to Afghanistan* were concluded on 14 April 1988: first, a bilateral agreement between Afghanistan and Pakistan on the principles of mutual relations, in particular on non-interference and non-intervention. This expressly referred to the obligations in the 1970 *Declaration on Friendly Relations* and the 1981 *Declaration on the Inadmissibility of Intervention*. Second, a declaration on international guarantees was agreed between the USA and the USSR; in this the parties agreed to refrain from any form of interference in Afghanistan or Pakistan internal affairs. Third, a bilateral agreement between Afghanistan and Pakistan on the return of refugees and, fourth, an agreement between all four states providing for the withdrawal of Soviet forces.[221]

The agreement to end the conflict in Angola was tripartite; Angola, Cuba. and South Africa made an agreement on 22 December 1988 after South Africa agreed to accept the implementation of Security Council Resolution 435 (1987) on Namibia; Angola and Cuba accordingly agreed on the withdrawal of Cuban troops.[222] South Africa ended its support for UNITA. At first the USA did not follow suit, but when UNITA did not cooperate with the UN peace process the USA finally terminated its aid in 1993.[223]

In contrast, the Mozambique peace agreement was bilateral, although intervention by South Africa directly and through RENAMO had profoundly destabilized Mozambique.[224] In 1990 there was a partial ceasefire and in October 1992 a General Peace Agreement, a bilateral agreement between the government and RENAMO. But the UN account said that the regional dimension was a crucial factor in the peace process: 'A key element in this success was the active participation of governments in the region in bringing peace negotiations to a fruitful conclusion.'[225]

---

[220] But contrary to the reasoning in the *Tadic appeal*, 38 ILM (1999) 1518 at para 157, such agreements do not necessarily demonstrate control or responsibility by the intervening state for all the acts of the opposition forces.

[221] 1988 UNYB 184; 27 ILM (1988) 577. After 9/11 and *Operation Enduring Freedom* in Afghanistan, a non-aggression agreement was concluded between Afghanistan and six neighbouring states (Keesings (2001) 45142). The *Kabul Declaration* committed the parties to respect for territorial sovereignty and non-intervention.

[222] 1988 UNYB 159.

[223] Keesings (1993) 39447.

[224] 1988 UNYB 158.

[225] 1992 UNYB 193; UN Publications, Blue Book Series, Vol V, *The United Nations and Mozambique 1992–1995* (1995).

In Cambodia Vietnam withdrew the last of its forces in 1988.[226] The *Paris Peace Agreements* followed in October 1991; the peace conference was attended by nineteen states and the four Cambodian factions. There were nineteen signatory states to the peace agreements, a symbol of the manifold ramifications of the conflict.[227] Article 10 of the UN-sponsored peace agreement provided that 'Upon entry into force of this Agreement, there shall be an immediate cessation of all outside military assistance to all Cambodian parties'. Thailand and China claimed to end their support for the Khmer Rouge and they gradually lost influence, but it was not until 1990 that the USA ended its aid to the opposition.[228]

But some of the conflicts continued, despite the peace settlements; in Angola, Afghanistan, and Cambodia fighting broke out again. The massive assistance that the parties had received during the Cold War helped them to continue the conflict. Thus in Afghanistan the withdrawal of Soviet troops did not end the conflict; Afghanistan accused the USA and Pakistan of continuing to help the rebels. In 1991 the USA and the USSR agreed to halt arms supplies to Afghanistan from 1 January 1992; they also called on Saudi Arabia and Pakistan to follow suit.[229] But intervention from Pakistan in support of Taliban opposition forces continued. The government of Afghanistan complained to the Security Council, saying that the objective of Pakistan was strategic, to be secured through a subservient Taliban government. Pakistan said that the Taliban believed that they were being unjustly treated by the international community, despite the fact that they controlled 90 per cent of the territory, including the capital.[230] The Security Council had repeatedly called for an end to foreign intervention, directed at Pakistan.[231] After 9/11 Pakistan ended its support for the Taliban regime and declared that it was joining the war on terrorism.[232] But the USA has accused its government of a failure to prevent Al Qaeda and Taliban forces from operating on its territory.[233]

---

[226] 1988 UNYB 179.

[227] UN Publications, Blue Book Series, Vol II, *The United Nations and Cambodia 1991–1995* (1995), 5–8. The parties were Cambodia (represented by a coalition government, the Supreme National Council formed in 1990 by the warring parties), the five permanent members of the Security Council, the six members of ASEAN, Laos and Vietnam, Australia, Canada, India, Japan, and Yugoslavia.

[228] Keesings (1990) 37598. Other civil wars also ended. In Central America settlements were reached in Nicaragua in 1988, El Salvador in 1992, and Guatemala in 1996 when an *Agreement on a Firm and Lasting Peace* was concluded (1995 UNYB 419, 1996 UNYB 152). With regard to the thirty-year civil war in Guatemala, President Clinton acknowledged in 1999 that the USA had been wrong to interfere (Keesings (1999) 42828). In Chad, Libya pulled out of the Aouzou strip which it had occupied since 1973 after the decision of the ICJ in 1994.

[229] Keesings (1991) 38437; 1991 UNYB 161.

[230] SC 4039th meeting (1999), UN Press Release SC/6718, 27 August 1999.

[231] S/PRST/1996/6 and 40; 1995 UNYB 472. The Security Council has called for an end to intervention in a series of resolutions: SC Res 1076 (1996), 1193 (1998), 1214 (1998).

[232] Keesings (2003) 44343.

[233] Keesings (2007) 47694–5.

The Cold War conflicts demonstrated irreconcilable divisions between states on the question as to who was the legitimate government, but they also show an impressive uniformity among states as to the law on intervention. States did not claim the legal right forcibly to overthrow a government; when they did aid the opposition they challenged the legitimacy of the government. The end of the Cold War has not brought an end to foreign intervention in civil wars, but it has made it easier for the UN to play a much greater role in this area. The Security Council may now find it easier to pronounce on who is the government, partly because the UN increasingly plays a role in monitoring or supervising the conduct of elections as part of post-conflict peace-building. Thus in Sierra Leone and Côte d'Ivoire, Burundi and Somalia[234] the Security Council took a clear view on the identification of the government and the right of states to support that government in a civil war. In recent years when the Security Council has imposed an arms embargo on a state on the outbreak of civil war it has sometimes subsequently made an express exception for the supply of arms to the government it regards as legitimate and also to states assisting that government.[235] However, the international consensus on the prohibition on forcible intervention to overthrow a government has apparently come under pressure from the actions and the rhetoric of the USA with regard to the regime change in Afghanistan after 9/11 and in Iraq in 2003. The USA nevertheless continued to accuse other states—in particular, Syria and Iran – of unlawful intervention against the new governments of Afghanistan and Iraq.[236] The impact of the 'war on terror' on the law on intervention is considered further in Chapter 6.

---

[234] It is striking that in so far as Ethiopia offered a legal justification for its 2006 invasion of Somalia it chose to rely on self-defence rather than on invitation by the government: see 244 below. See Corten, 'La licéité douteuse de l'action militaire de l'Ethiopie en Somalie', 111 RGDIP (2007) 513.

[235] See 267 below.

[236] For accusations against Syria, see, for example, Keesings (2005) 46651,46714; *The Guardian*, 24 June, 18 August 2005; for accusations against Iran, see, for example, Keesings (2005) 46905, (2007) 47679, 47780, 47867, (2007) 47679, 47722, 47780, 48063, 48102; *The Guardian*, 30 January, 12, 15 February, 1 March, 19 April, 22, 29 May, 3, 16 July 2007. Some of these accusations expressly allege government responsibility for intervention; others are more general claims that there is intervention by Syrian or Iranian groups or from the territory of Syria and Iran.

4
Self-defence

INTRODUCTION

The law on self-defence is the subject of the most fundamental disagreement between states and between writers. The divisions over the scope of the right of self-defence, especially as to whether anticipatory or 'pre-emptive' self-defence and protection of nationals are lawful, are much discussed and date back to the creation of the United Nations.[1] These issues have recently acquired new prominence in the light of the development of a possible new 'Bush doctrine' of pre-emptive self-defence.[2] Other divisions centre on the right to use force in self-defence in response to colonial occupation, to terrorist attacks, and to other attacks by non-state actors. The events of 9/11 and their aftermath have brought a fundamental reappraisal of the law on the use of force against terrorism. Chapter 6 will examine the impact of the 'war against terror' on international law; this chapter focuses on the general law of self-defence.

Differences over the scope of self-defence prevented any substantive provision on this being included in General Assembly resolutions designed to codify the law on the use of force. States negotiating the 1970 *Declaration on Friendly Relations* and the 1974 *Definition of Aggression* did not include any provision on self-defence; in the 1987 *Declaration on the Non-Use of Force* they could not go beyond the statement that 'States have the inherent right of individual or collective self-defence if an armed attack occurs, as set forth in the Charter of the United Nations'.[3]

However, in practice these fundamental doctrinal differences were not (until recently) of decisive significance as to the legality of the use of force except in a few isolated, though much discussed, instances. States using force against another state almost invariably invoke self-defence; in the vast majority of such claims this has not given rise to any doctrinal issues or to any divisions between states as to the applicable law. Whether the

---

[1] Cot and Pellet, *La Charte des Nations Unies* (1991), 771; Simma, *The Charter of the United Nations: a Commentary* (2nd edn 2002) 788; Alexandrov, *Self-Defense Against the Use of Force in International Law* (1996); Bowett, *Self-Defence in International Law* (1958); Brownlie, *International Law and the Use of Force by States* (1963); Zourek, 'La notion de légitime défense en droit international', 56 Annuaire de l'Institut de Droit International (1975) 1.

[2] See Chapter 6 below.

[3] See Treves, 'La Déclaration des Nations Unies sur le renforcement de l'efficacité du principe du non recours à la force', 1987 AFDI 379; Gray, 'The Principle of Non-use of Force' in Lowe and Warbrick (eds), *The United Nations and the Principles of International Law* (1994), 33 at 38.

use of force is a one-off minor incident (either involving an attack on a state's territory or on its land, sea or air forces outside its territorial limits[4]) or an ongoing conflict, typically one or both states involved asserts that it has been the victim of an armed attack and claims the right to self-defence; the controversy centres on the questions of fact as to whether there has actually been an armed attack of the type claimed and, if so, which state was the victim. In theory it should always be possible to determine whether there was an armed attack and who is acting in self-defence. But in practice the situation is more complex.[5] The difficulties in establishing the facts in cases involving self-defence and the legality of use of force were very obvious in the recent ICJ cases, *Cameroon v Nigeria* (2002),[6] *Iranian Oil Platforms* (2003),[7] and *Armed Activities on the Territory of the Congo (DRC v Uganda)* (2005).[8] The issue is left unresolved in the vast

---

[4] On the inclusion of such attacks as self-defence, see Simma, *The Charter of the United Nations: a Commentary* (2nd edn 2002) 797. In the *Oil Platforms* case *(Iran v USA)* the Court said that it 'does not exclude the possibility that the mining of a single military vessel might be sufficient to bring into play the "inherent right of self-defence"', ICJ Reports (2003) 161 at para 72.

[5] For further discussion of the concept of 'armed attack' see 128 below.

[6] ICJ Reports (2002) 303 para 308–324. This was predominantly a boundary dispute between Cameroon and Nigeria, but Cameroon also claimed that Nigeria had illegally used force against it, including a full-scale invasion of the Lake Chad area in 1987 and a series of attacks into the Bakassi peninsula. Cameroon argued that in thus invading and occupying its territory Nigeria had violated Article 2(4) of the UN Charter and the principle of non-intervention. Nigeria replied that it was in peaceful possession of the disputed territory and that any use of force had been in self-defence. Although the parties had produced very extensive arguments on the use of force, the Court dealt with this part of the case only briefly. It simply noted that its decision on the location of the boundary meant that Nigerian forces and administration were in place in areas which the Court had determined were Cameroonian territory. Therefore Nigeria was under an obligation expeditiously and without condition to withdraw its administration and forces from those areas. The Court refused to order Nigeria to make guarantees of non-repetition as it 'cannot envisage a situation' where either party would fail to respect the territorial sovereignty of the other (para 318–9). Thus the Court effectively avoided a decision on the use of force in self-defence in this case. For further discussion, see Gray, 'The Use and Abuse of the International Court of Justice: Cases concerning the Use of Force after *Nicaragua*', 14 EJIL (2003) 467.

[7] ICJ Reports (2003) 161. In this case the parties again produced very extensive argument on the use of force during the 1980–88 Iran/Iraq war. But the Court held that the USA had failed to establish that Iran was responsible for armed attacks on US-flagged vessels and aircraft entitling the USA the right to use force in self-defence: see 143 below.

[8] ICJ Reports (2005) 168. In this case, as regards a large part of the DRC claims against Uganda for unlawful use of force, the Court was able to avoid the problematic task of establishing the facts because they were relatively uncontested between the parties; the crucial issue was how the facts should be characterized (para 55, 72). Uganda admitted that its troops were present in the DRC and that they had carried out certain operations, but it justified these actions on the basis of consent by the DRC and self-defence. The Court rejected these justifications, and so it followed that Uganda had acted unlawfully. However, in some instances Uganda denied the presence of its troops and the Court had to set out its approach to the facts (para 55–71) and to try to establish what had happened. See Teitelbaum, 'Recent Fact-finding Developments at the ICJ', 6 The Law and Practice of International Courts and Tribunals (2007) 129. In contrast the Eritrea/Ethiopia Claims Commission in Ethiopia's

majority of cases; certainly the Security Council does not generally make express pronouncements determining this crucial legal issue. The parties may register their positions with the Security Council, but often there may be no debate and no resolution or statement. Even if there is a resolution or statement, it is far more common for this to take the form of a call for a ceasefire rather than any attribution of responsibility.[9] This can be seen in the 1998–2000 conflict between Ethiopia and Eritrea; the Security Council did not condemn one or the other of the two states involved in the conflict, but repeatedly called for an end to the hostilities and peaceful settlement of the territorial dispute which was at the root of what the Secretary-General called an 'incomprehensible war'.[10]

The 1980–88 Iran/Iraq conflict was unusual in that the Security Council asked the UN Secretary-General to investigate responsibility for the conflict and the latter did make an express finding on the facts of the case after the conflict had ended. Iran persistently claimed that Iraq bore responsibility for initiation of the conflict and eventually secured an inquiry into the origin of the conflict by the UN Secretary-General and vindication of its position. The Secretary-General reported that the conflict was begun in contravention of international law through the illegal use of force and disregard for a state's territorial integrity; Iraq was responsible for the conflict because of its armed attack against Iran on 22 September 1980.[11] This willingness to identify the outbreak of a conflict and to determine responsibility was more common in the early days of the UN.[12] It is rare for the Security Council today to enter into this question; members clearly see its role as the promotion of the restoration of peace rather than as the assignment of responsibility. The 1990 Iraq/Kuwait conflict was another exceptional case, seen by many as marking a new role for the Security Council and the start of a new legal order; in this case the Security Council did

---

Ius ad Bellum Claims 1–8, 45 ILM (2006) 430, did not include any detailed discussion of the crucial issue of the establishment of the facts: see Gray, 'The Eritrea/Ethiopia Claims Commission oversteps its boundaries: a Partial Award', 17 EJIL (2006) 699.

[9] The failure of the SC to call for an immediate ceasefire in the 2006 Israel/Lebanon conflict was the subject of much controversy, see 237 below.

[10] UN Press Release SG/SM/7410, 22 May 2000; SC Res 1171 (1998), 1226 (1999), 1297 (2000). The Eritrea/Ethiopia Claims Commission in Ethiopia's *Ius ad Bellum* Claims 1–8, 45 ILM (2006) 430, nevertheless showed no hesitation in asserting jurisdiction to decide this controversial questions, and in finding that it was Eritrea which was responsible for a violation of Article 2(4).

[11] 1991 UNYB 165; UN doc S/23273, 9 December 1991. After the overthrow of Saddam Hussein the new government of Iraq announced that it had been the aggressor in the 1980–88 conflict, Keesings (2005) 46656.

[12] For example, Greece 1947–8 UNYB 63, 337; 1948–9 UNYB 238; Indonesia/Netherlands 1947–8 UNYB 369; 1948–9 UNYB 212; Korea 1950 UNYB 245, 251–1; Laos 1959 UNYB 62; Cambodia/Thailand 1959 UNYB 80. On the early practice of the UN in establishing responsibility, see Higgins, *The Development of International Law through the Political Organs of the United Nations* (1963), 166.

explicitly uphold the right of Kuwait to self-defence.[13] But more typical have been the many, relatively minor, limited conflicts where the Security Council did not involve itself in any pronouncements on self-defence. There is a striking contrast between the hundreds of communications to the Security Council in which states claim to be the victims of armed attacks and the few conflicts discussed by the Council. The vast mass of use of force passes unmarked by any debate or resolution, let alone by any formal finding as to who was the victim. And in the vast mass of cases – both before and after 9/11 – there is no controversy as to the applicable law.

Thus the natural focus of writers on controversial cases where states invoke self-defence in protection of nationals, anticipatory or pre-emptive self-defence, and response to terrorism inevitably gives an unbalanced picture and distorts our perception of state practice; it helps to give the impression that the far-reaching claims of states like the USA and Israel are normal rather than exceptional.

THE ACADEMIC DEBATE

As far as writers are concerned, the disagreement as to the scope of self-defence generally turns on the interpretation of Article 51. This provides:

> Nothing in the present Charter shall impair the inherent right of individual or collective self-defence if an armed attack occurs against a member of the United Nations, until the Security Council has taken measures necessary to maintain international peace and security. Measures taken by Members in the exercise of the right of self-defence shall be immediately reported to the Security Council and shall not in any way affect the authority and responsibility of the Security Council under the present Charter to take at any time such action as it deems necessary to maintain or restore international peace and security.

There is no need here to do more than set out the basic arguments of the two main groups of writers whose opposing positions have become well entrenched in the last fifty years. Those who support a wide right of self-defence going beyond the right to respond to an armed attack on a state's territory argue, first, that Article 51 of the UN Charter, through its reference to 'inherent' right of self-defence, preserves the earlier customary international law right to self-defence. The Charter does not take away pre-existing rights of states without express provision. Second, they argue that at the time of the conclusion of the Charter there was a wide customary international law right of self-defence, allowing the protection

---

[13] SC Res 661 (1990) (13–0–2).

of nationals and anticipatory self-defence.[14] The opposing side argues that the meaning of Article 51 is clear; the right of self-defence arises only if an armed attack (French: *agression armée*) occurs. This right is an exception to the prohibition of the use of force in Article 2(4) and therefore should be narrowly construed. The limits imposed on self-defence in Article 51 would be meaningless if a wider customary law right to self-defence survives unfettered by these restrictions. Moreover, they claim that by the time of the Charter customary law allowed only a narrow right of self-defence.[15] These early arguments turned, first, on treaty interpretation and, second, on an assessment of the state of customary international law in 1945. Policy considerations as to the realism of taking a wide or narrow view also played a crucial role.

Those still supporting the wide right of self-defence today – in contexts outside the war against terror – discount the rejection of their position by the large majority of states in practice since 1945; for these writers the Charter preserves customary law as it allegedly was in 1945. Thus the term 'inherent right of self-defence' in Article 51 is not for them a dynamic term capable of shifting in meaning over time; the scope of the right was fixed in customary international law in 1945 and was apparently not susceptible of restriction in the light of subsequent state practice.[16] An alternative approach invokes the breakdown of the UN collective security system during the Cold War in order to justify a wide right to self-defence in the same way that some argue for a narrow interpretation of the prohibition of the use of force in Article 2(4).[17] Again this argument is at variance with the mass of state practice and has to discount the views of the vast majority of states.

In practice, states making their claims to self-defence try to put forward arguments that will avoid doctrinal controversy and appeal to the widest possible range of states. Especially since the *Nicaragua* case, states have taken care to invoke Article 51 to justify their use of force. They do so even when this seems entirely implausible and to involve the stretching of Article 51 beyond all measure. Even when relying on a wide right of self-defence in the absence of an armed attack on their territory, or on their armed forces outside their territory, states invoke Article 51. Either

---

[14] For example, Bowett, *Self-Defence in International Law* (1958); Schwebel, 'Aggression, Intervention and Self-Defense in Modern International Law' 136 RCADI (1972–II) 463; McDougal and Feliciano, *Law and Minimum World Public Order* (1961).

[15] For example, Brownlie, *International Law and the Use of Force by States* (1963); Rifaat *International Aggression: A Study of the Legal Concept* (1979).

[16] However, these states are not consistent in their approach. After 9/11 they apparently assumed that the right of self-defence in Article 51 is susceptible of expansion in the context of the 'war on terror' and thus not frozen as it had been in 1945: see Chapter 6 below.

[17] This argument was adopted by Judge Jennings in his Dissenting Opinion in the *Nicaragua* case, at 543–4.

this is just ritual incantation of a magic formula, not expected to be taken seriously, or their case is implicitly that Article 51 allows a wider customary right, including anticipatory self-defence or forcible response to terrorism.

States, in making their own justification or in responding to the claims of others, on the whole and not surprisingly do not enter into extended doctrinal debate in their communications to the Security Council. And even in Security Council debates or in negotiation of General Assembly 'law-making' resolutions on the use of force, they tend simply to assert a wide or narrow view of self-defence without going into the theoretical justifications for their view. Generally more time is devoted to expounding their own version of the facts and their political justifications. It is only in the most controversial cases where there is a doctrinal division that states do enter into protracted legal justification. Israel's arguments in defence of its 1976 rescue operation at Entebbe and of its attack on the Iraqi nuclear reactor in 1981 are unusual in that they are protracted.[18] There was a similarly protracted discussion of the US 1983 intervention in Grenada and its 1986 bombing of Tripoli.[19]

THE ROLE OF THE SECURITY COUNCIL

Article 51 assigns a central role to the Security Council: states are under a duty to report measures taken in the exercise of the right of self-defence to the Security Council and the right to self-defence is temporary until the Security Council 'takes measures necessary to maintain international peace and security'. The USA in the *Nicaragua* case argued that the International Court of Justice should not pronounce on claims of self-defence because Article 51 provides a role in such matters only for the Security Council.[20]

---

[18] On Entebbe, see SC 1939th–1943rd meetings (1976); on the Iraqi nuclear reactor, see 1981 UNYB 275.

[19] On Grenada, SC 2677th meeting (1987); on Tripoli, 1986 UNYB 247. In contrast, there was little discussion in the Security Council of the US action against sites in Afghanistan and Sudan in response to the terrorist attacks on its embassies in Kenya and Ethiopia in August 1998: 'Contemporary Practice of the US', 93 AJIL (1999) 161. There was also relatively little discussion of the legality of the 2006 conflict in the Lebanon and of the 2006 Ethiopian intervention in Somalia: see 237 below.

[20] *Nicaragua case, Jurisdiction and Admissibility*, ICJ Reports (1984) 551 para 92–3; the Court rejected this argument, saying that the USA was attempting to transfer municipal law concepts of separation of powers to the international plane, whereas these concepts are not applicable to the relations among international institutions for the settlement of disputes. Also the fact that a matter is before the Security Council should not prevent it being dealt with by the Court.

Although Article 51 envisages a crucial role for the Security Council, it does not necessarily require the Council to pronounce on the legality of any claim to self-defence. In practice the Security Council has generally not made such express pronouncements. Some French writers have therefore claimed that it has not done enough to give self-defence a clear content or indeed any real meaning: the right of self-defence is 'indeterminate' or even obsolescent.[21] Thus Combacau takes a rather formalistic approach. He argues that the Security Council can only contribute to the crystallization of the law in this area when a state *expressly* makes a claim to be acting in self-defence to the Council and the Council makes an express response; on the basis of the *Repertoire of the Practice of the Security Council* up to 1974 Combacau claimed that states rarely made such claims. First, this approach seems too rigid. Security Council resolutions and statements may be of significance in the development of the law if in substance they deal with state behaviour and implicitly or expressly accept or reject claims of self-defence. Second, his argument was based on the *Repertoire of the Practice of the Security Council* up to 1974. This does not give a complete picture and, moreover, is based on practice before the decision in the *Nicaragua* case which led to a clear change in state behaviour.

It is true that only a very few Security Council resolutions have made express reference to Article 51. Typically these assert in general terms the right of a particular state to take action in self-defence. Such resolutions have generally not been passed in recent years. They were passed in response to South Africa's attacks on the front-line states during the apartheid era, and in response to the use of force by Portugal and Israel. For example, Angola's right to take measures in accordance with Article 51 when it had been subject to attacks by South Africa was affirmed by the Security Council; these resolutions also condemned South Africa's use of force.[22] More recently, and exceptionally, Kuwait's right to self-defence was affirmed by the Security Council after the Iraqi invasion.[23] And Resolution 1234 on the conflict in the DRC affirmed in general terms the right of individual or collective self-defence in accordance with Article 51.[24]

Other resolutions respond to the use of force by states; in so far as they condemn particular actions they may be taken as rejections of a state's claim to self-defence even if this is not express in the resolution. Thus the attempt to deny any clear content to the right of self-defence because of

---

[21] Combacau, 'The exception of self-defence in UN practice', in Cassese (ed.), *The Current Legal Regulation of the Use of Force* (1986), Chapter 13; Delivanis, *La légitime défense en droit international public moderne* (1971).

[22] SC Res 546 (1984); 1984 UNYB 180–3, SC Res 574 (1985); 1985 UNYB 178 at 187, GA Res 38/39 (1983); 1983 UNYB 173 at 174.

[23] See 125 below.

[24] On the conflict in the DRC, see Chapter 3 above.

the nature of the decision-making of the Security Council underestimates the significance of the vast mass of state practice, and especially of the many state communications to the Security Council. The core content of self-defence is universally accepted.[25]

However, the approach of Combacau and Delivanis, although formalistic, has some justification. The Security Council resolutions and statements, although they may be authoritative as to the *legality* of particular uses of force, cannot do much to resolve the doctrinal controversies as to the *scope* of the right of self-defence. Any condemnation of controversial use of force such as protection of nationals, anticipatory self-defence, and action against irregulars and terrorists may be limited to the particular facts. Rather than condemn protection of nationals or anticipatory self-defence in general, the Security Council condemns the particular use of force. The Security Council debates will usually reveal the doctrinal divisions between states; it is clear that in order to secure agreement on a resolution the Security Council may have to avoid any pronouncement on the underlying doctrine. Therefore, the resolutions may provide only indirect evidence as to the state of the law. They do not contain general statements of the law. Pronouncements on individual breaches may do no more than make it possible to argue, for example, that the fact that almost all uses of anticipatory self-defence have been condemned suggests the weakness of such a doctrine.

The duty to report to the Security Council

Since the judgment in the *Nicaragua* case it is noticeable that states on the whole do comply with the Article 51 requirement that 'measures taken by Members in the exercise of the right of self-defence shall be immediately reported to the Security Council'; it is clear that states have taken seriously the Court's message that failure to do this will weaken any claim to be acting in self-defence. The Court held that 'the absence of a report may be one of the factors indicating whether the State in question was itself convinced that it was acting in self-defence'.[26] Judge Schwebel, in his Dissenting Opinion, strongly criticized this as unacceptable in the case of covert self-defence.[27] But any attempt to attack this finding by the Court as an objectionable innovation is fundamentally misconceived.

The argument that failure to report was evidence against a claim to self-defence had been made many times even before the case. For example, the UK during the Vietnam conflict said that the fact that the USA had

---

[25] Schacter, 'Self-Defense and the Rule of Law', 83 AJIL (1989) 259.
[26] *Nicaragua* case, ICJ Reports (1986) 14, para 200.
[27] Dissenting Opinion, paras 7, 221–30.

reported to the Security Council in 1964 its actions in response to alleged attacks by North Vietnamese naval vessels in the Gulf of Tonkin was an indication that it was actually acting in self-defence.[28] And after the USSR intervention in Afghanistan the UK asked in the General Assembly debate why, if there had really been attacks on Afghanistan, it had not raised the matter before the Security Council.[29] Failure to report was also used as a sign of bad faith by the USA itself. After the clashes between the USA and Libya in the Gulf of Sirte in March and April 1986 (that is, during the *Nicaragua* case proceedings) the USA used the argument that Libya had not reported its actions to the Security Council as evidence that it was not acting in self-defence. Conversely, the UK said that the US report of these episodes to the Security Council under Article 51 was a sign of good faith.[30] However, it is clear that the reporting requirement is merely procedural; failure to comply does not of itself destroy a claim to self-defence.[31]

After its decision in the *Nicaragua* case the Court in *Armed Activities on the Territory of the Congo (DRC v Uganda)* simply 'noted' Uganda's failure to report the use of force it claimed as self-defence. The Court did not discuss this further, but the clear implication was that this was another factor indicating that Uganda had not been acting lawfully. And in the Eritrea/Ethiopia Claims Commission award on Ethiopia's *Ius ad Bellum* Claims 1–8 the tribunal in making its controversial finding that Eritrea was not acting in self-defence (even though it was using force against Ethiopian troops on Eritrean territory) took account of the fact that Eritrea, unlike Ethiopia, had not reported its actions to the Security Council under Article 51.[32] It is therefore surprising that Ethiopia did not report its 2006 intervention in Somalia to the Security Council under Article 51, even though it claimed that it was acting in self-defence.[33]

Before the *Nicaragua* case the reporting requirement was not always strictly observed in cases of individual self-defence (in marked contrast to the practice with regard to collective self-defence). But, even before the *Nicaragua* decision, reporting by states was more common than the *Repertoire of the Practice of the Security Council* indicates; a study of the communications of states to the Security Council gives a fuller picture of state

---

[28] 1964 UNYB 147.
[29] 1980 UNYB 296 at 300; see also Higgins, *Development of International Law through the Political Organs of the United Nations* (1963) at 207.
[30] SC 2671st meeting (1986); UN doc S/17938, 25 March 1986; SC 2668th meeting (1986). Here again self-defence is being invoked with regard to the protection of armed forces outside a state's territory.
[31] Greig, 'Self-Defence and the Security Council: What does Article 51 require?', 40 ICLQ (1991) 366.
[32] Ethiopia's *Ius ad Bellum* Claims 1–8, 45 ILM (2006) 430 at para 11.
[33] See 244 below.

practice in this regard.[34] After *Nicaragua* it can no longer be maintained that the reporting requirement is rarely observed.[35]

Indeed, there is now a tendency to over-report claims to individual self-defence, if anything. It seems clear that a state involved in a one-off episode should report if relying on self-defence. Also states parties to a prolonged conflict should, if relying on self-defence, go to the Security Council at the start of that conflict. However, when there is a prolonged conflict the states parties tend not simply to make their claims to self-defence at the start of the conflict, but often to report each episode separately. That is, they apparently interpret the reporting requirement in Article 51 that 'Measures taken by Members in the exercise of this right of self-defence shall be immediately reported to the Security Council' as requiring continuing reports. This may significantly increase the burden on the state claiming self-defence in that it has to show that each episode in isolation constitutes necessary and proportionate self-defence, rather than simply the campaign taken as a whole. This repeated reporting was marked in the practice of Iran and Iraq during their 1980–8 conflict[36] and in the practice of the UK and Argentina in the Falklands conflict.[37] Similarly in the 1998–2000 conflict between Eritrea and Ethiopia both parties repeatedly invoked self-defence.[38]

It was also the practice of the USA with regard to its involvement in the 1980–8 Iran/Iraq conflict, when the US navy was providing convoys for US-flagged ships through the Gulf to protect them against attack by the belligerent parties. Instead of making a blanket statement at the start of its involvement, the USA sought to justify each episode of the use of force against Iran.[39] Here we see self-defence being invoked with reference to

---

[34] There was, however, some genuine concern about the issue; the UN Secretary-General in *The Report of the Special Committee on Enhancing the Effectiveness of the Principle of the Non-Use of Force in International Relations* (1986), A/41/41, called for consideration of the possibility that the Security Council might inquire into episodes when the states involved had not reported.

[35] This is apparent from any search of communications to the Security Council (S/documents). A misleading impression has been given by writers who still rely on an earlier, pre-*Nicaragua* account: Simma, *The Charter of the United Nations: A Commentary* (1st edn 1994), 677, note 148, (2nd edn, 2002) 804, note 152; Schacter, 'Self-Defense and the Rule of Law', 83 AJIL (1989) 259, Greig, 'Self-Defence and the Security Council', 40 ICLQ (1991) 366, and Ronzitti, 'The expanding law of self-defence', 11 Journal of Conflict and Security Law (2006) 343 at 356 all rely on Combacau's earlier, pre-*Nicaragua* account based on *The Repertoire of Practice of the Security Council* up to 1974. Combacau, 'The Exception of Self-defense in UN Practice', in Cassese (ed.), *The Current Legal Regulation of the Use of Force* (1986), Chapter 13, also took a formalistic approach in that he distinguished between a special report and ordinary communications to the Security Council or statements in debates. Thus there is a danger that a myth of non-reporting will be perpetuated.

[36] *Repertoire of the Practice of the Security Council* 1985–88, Part XI note 141.

[37] *Repertoire of the Practice of the Security Council* 1981–84, Part XI note 73.

[38] 1998 UNYB 144, 1999 UNYB 130.

[39] UN docs S/19149, 22 September 1987, S/19194, 9 October 1987, S/19219, 19 October 1987, S/19791, 18 April 1988, S/19989, 6 July 1988.

the protection of US ships and aircraft; this is sometimes referred to as 'unit self-defence' as opposed to 'national self-defence' of a state's territory. This choice to report individual episodes led the USA into some difficulties when it had to justify its actions against Iranian oil platforms and its shooting down of the Iran Airbus in 1988 as self-defence.[40]

Such repeated reporting may seem to play partly a propaganda role.[41] Given that the Security Council does not usually pronounce on the legality of a claim to self-defence at the start of a conflict, it may be understandable that the states refer each individual episode to the Security Council in an attempt to portray themselves as victims, as in the Iran/Iraq conflict when Iran and Iraq repeatedly reported particular incidents to the Security Council. Because the Security Council made no initial determination that Iraq was the aggressor, it could seek to portray itself as the victim, especially when Iran later refused to accept the 1987 mandatory ceasefire resolution. Also controversially, such reporting of individual episodes as self-defence may represent an attempt to rely on Article 51 rather than the laws of war where an action's legality is doubtful as a matter of international humanitarian law. Thus in the Vietnam war the USA justified its use of force generally as collective self-defence of South Vietnam. It also subsequently reported individual episodes such as its mining of the ports of North Vietnam and its bombing of neutral Cambodia as constituting self-defence.[42] Again in the Falklands conflict the UK reporting of individual episodes as self-defence may reflect its doubts as to the adequacy of the laws of war at sea.[43]

Self-defence as a temporary right

The Security Council also has a role in the control of the right of self-defence through the stipulation in Article 51 that the right of self-defence continues 'until the Security Council has taken measures necessary to maintain international peace and security'. Given that the UN Charter aims not only to limit, but also to centralize, the use of force under UN control, it seems clear that the intention was to give the Security Council itself the right to

---

[40] Iran took both these cases to the ICJ. In the first, the *Oil Platforms* case, the Court held that the USA had not acted in self-defence (ICJ Reports (2003) 161 at paras 38–78); see 143 below. The second case, *Aerial Incident of 3 July 1988,* was withdrawn in 1996 after a settlement between the parties and the payment by the USA of *ex gratia* compensation; see 162 below.

[41] Combacau, 'The exception of self-defence in the practice of the United Nations', in Cassese (ed.), *The Current Legal Regulation of the Use of Force* (1986), 21.

[42] On the US mining, see 1972 UNYB 153; on the US actions in Cambodia, see Falk (ed.) *The Vietnam War and International Law,* Vol 3 (1972), 23–148.

[43] 1982 UNYB 1320 at 1325; see also Gray, 'The British Position in regard to the Gulf Conflict, Part 1', 37 ICLQ (1988) 420.

decide whether such measures terminating the right to self-defence had been taken. But, in the absence of express determination of the existence or continuation of the right to self-defence, this provision has in the past given rise to some controversy.[44] The Falklands (Malvinas) conflict is a famous example; after the Argentine invasion of the UK colonial territory in 1982 the Security Council, in Resolution 502 (10–1–4), determined that there had been a breach of the peace, demanded an immediate cessation of hostilities, demanded an immediate withdrawal of all Argentine forces, and called on the governments of Argentina and the UK to seek a diplomatic solution to their difficulties. Did this amount to 'necessary measures to maintain international peace and security' which terminated any UK right to use force in defence of the Falklands? The UK argued that it did not, since Argentina, the aggressor, remained in occupation of the islands.[45] The question came up again in the 1980–8 Iran/Iraq conflict. After the mandatory Security Council Resolution 598 (1987) calling for a ceasefire, was Iran subsequently exceeding its right to self-defence in its refusal to accept the ceasefire, given that it had already by mid-1982 recovered the territory earlier occupied by Iraq? Although the USA and the UK did not expressly make this argument in the Security Council, they came close to it.[46]

The UK apparently learned its lesson from the controversy over the Falklands. When the Security Council responded to Iraq's 1990 invasion of Kuwait it imposed sanctions on Iraq; in the same resolution it included an affirmation of 'the inherent right of individual or collective self-defence, in response to the armed attack by Iraq against Kuwait, in accordance with Article 51 of the Charter'. Thus no problem could arise as to whether the imposition of economic sanctions by the Security Council had terminated any right of states to use collective self-defence to help Kuwait. The USA and the UK could act in collective self-defence of Kuwait even before specific authorization for the interception of ships and aircraft bound for Iraq and Kuwait was given by the Security Council.[47]

---

[44] Higgins, *The Development of International Law through the Political Organs of the United Nations* (1963) at 198, 206; Waldock, 'The Regulation of the Use of Force by Individual States in International Law', 81 RCADI (1952–II) 496. On drafting history, see Halberstam, 'The Right to Self-Defense once the Security Council takes action', 17 Michigan JIL (1995–6) 229; see also Chayes, Reisman, and Schacter in Damrosch and Fisher (eds), *Law and Force in the New International Order* (1991), 1, 26, 65; Franck and Patel, 'UN Police Action in Lieu of War', 85 AJIL (1991) 63; Rostow, 'Until What? Enforcement Action or Collective Self-Defense?', 85 AJIL (1991) 506.

[45] 1982 UNYB 1320; SC 2360th meeting (1982), SC 2362nd meeting, (1982).

[46] See De Guttry and Ronzitti (eds), *The Iran-Iraq War (1980–1988) and the Law of Naval Warfare* (1993) at 219, 226; Gray, 'The British Position with regard to the Gulf Conflict', 37 ICLQ (1988) 420 at 427, 40 ICLQ (1991) 464 at 466.

[47] SC Res 661 (1990). Greenwood, 'New World Order or Old?', 55 MLR (1992) 153; Warbrick, 'The Invasion of Kuwait by Iraq', 40 ICLQ (1991) 482; UN Blues Book Series Vol IX, *The UN and the Iraq/Kuwait Conflict 1990–1996* (1996) at 16.

Security Council measures and self-defence

The question has also arisen of the relationship between the state's right to self-defence and the powers of the Security Council: are the powers of the Security Council under Chapter VII of the Charter limited by the requirement that such measures do not undermine the right of self-defence under Article 51? This question came up first in 1977 when France argued that an arms embargo on South Africa might violate its right to self-defence. However, France said, the intention here, in the aftermath of the recent crackdown by the South African government, was to protest against the stockpiling of weapons intended for purposes of internal repression; therefore it had decided to vote in favour of a mandatory arms embargo on South Africa.[48] This issue arose again in the debate over the compatibility of the arms embargo on the whole of the former Yugoslavia with the right of self-defence under Article 51.[49] At the outbreak of the conflict in Yugoslavia in 1991 the Security Council imposed an arms embargo on the whole of Yugoslavia. Resolution 713 (1991) was passed unanimously and the arms embargo was imposed with the consent of the federal government of Yugoslavia. When Yugoslavia split up and Bosnia-Herzegovina became a member state of the UN in May 1992 it argued that the arms embargo should not be applied to it. It sought the lifting of the embargo by the Security Council from September 1992. It claimed that its inherent right to self-defence under Article 51 took priority over the embargo, and that in order to exercise this right against Yugoslavia (Serbia and Montenegro) the embargo must be lifted. In the Security Council debates those in favour of lifting the embargo argued either that Resolution 713 (1991) had been superseded when Bosnia became a member of the United Nations or that the resolution should be interpreted as not applying to Bosnia or, more radically, that if the resolution did impose an embargo on it, then the resolution was invalid as outside the powers of the Security Council because it violated Bosnia's inherent right to self-defence. The Security Council refused to accept this argument and did not lift the embargo even though the General Assembly repeatedly urged it to consider this.[50]

---

[48] *Repertoire of Practice of the Security Council 1975–1980*, 311. This question also came up over Sierra Leone when those who wanted to defend the supply of arms to the legitimate government claimed that the arms embargo applied only to those who had seized power in a coup. However, this was not express in SC Res 1132 (1997). See UK *Parliamentary Report of the Sierra Leone Arms Investigation* (1998).

[49] Gray, 'Bosnia and Herzegovina: Civil War or Inter-State Conflict? Characterization and Consequences', 67 BYIL (1996) 155; Report of the Secretary-General pursuant to GA Resolution 53/35 (1998), 'Srebrenica' Report.

[50] The International Court of Justice, in *Application of the Convention on the Prevention and Punishment of the Crime of Genocide (Provisional Measures)* ICJ Reports 1993, 3, 325, was also faced with a claim by Bosnia for the lifting of the arms embargo, but it decided that this was

It is clear that there are strong arguments against a claim that an arms embargo violates Article 51 of the UN Charter. If every arms embargo is automatically inconsistent with Article 51 this would restrict the Security Council's discretion to take measures under Article 41 and deprive it of a useful tool to put pressure on a wrongdoing state or to try to limit the escalation of a conflict. All states subject to an arms embargo could claim that their rights under the Charter prevailed over the arms embargo. It seems unlikely that Bosnia-Herzegovina, in putting its claim for the lifting of the embargo, was really making the argument that every arms embargo violated Article 51.

Even if Bosnia-Herzegovina was putting forward a less fundamental argument and was claiming merely that in the particular circumstances the arms embargo in Resolution 713 (1991) violated its right to self-defence, this seems a dangerous precedent and one that would undermine the freedom of the Security Council to maintain an arms embargo. States suffering civil wars and subject to arms embargoes could make plausible cases that they were under outside threat and needed to exercise their rights to self-defence. The better position is that an arms embargo may affect the right to self-defence but does not actually deny that right.

This question came up again with regard to Rwanda.[51] The Security Council imposed an arms embargo in 1994, against the wishes of the government then in power, to try to prevent the escalation of violence. Following Bosnia's claims, Rwanda pursued a similar line of argument, that the arms embargo imposed on it after large-scale massacres in 1994 should be lifted because there was a threat to it from outside. This time the Security Council did respond, noting with concern the reports of military preparations and incursions into Rwanda by supporters of the former government. It recalled that the original prohibition on the delivery of arms was aimed at preventing their use in the massacre of innocent citizens. The embargo was lifted as far as arms destined for the government were concerned, but otherwise remained in place.[52] This precedent may have made it more difficult for the Security Council to keep in place against the wishes of the government of the state concerned an arms embargo imposed during a civil war. The modification of the total arms embargo on Sierra Leone to allow arms to be supplied to the government

not within its jurisdiction; see Gray, 43 ICLQ (1994) 704; Report of the Secretary-General pursuant to GA Resolution 53/35 (1998), '*Srebrenica*' *Report* para 99–102.

[51] Rwanda successfully campaigned for the lifting of the arms embargo imposed on it because of the internal conflict on the grounds that this made it vulnerable to outside interference: 1995 UNYB 347.

[52] 1994 UNYB 281; 1995 UNYB 370 at 380; SC Res 1011 (1995); UN Publications Blue Book Series, Vol 10, *The United Nations and Rwanda 1993–1996* (1996).

and those supporting it reinforces this view.[53] But the argument for the lifting of an arms embargo is less attractive where the embargo has been imposed as a sanction, as in the case of Liberia and, arguably, in the case of the Ethiopia/Eritrea conflict. In the former Liberia was subjected to an arms embargo for its intervention in the conflict in Sierra Leone. In the latter the Security Council simply urged member states not to supply arms to either side: the arms embargo was designed to help to bring an end to a 'senseless war'.[54] The claims by Liberia and Ethiopia that the embargoes were unlawful as they denied the states concerned the right to defend themselves were not successful.[55]

THE SCOPE OF SELF-DEFENCE

Armed attack

All states agree that if there is an armed attack the right to self-defence arises, but there are controversies as to what constitutes an armed attack. The paradigm case is obviously an invasion by the regular armed forces of one state into the territory of another state. However, questions concerning the definition of the concept and the identification of the start of an armed attack may arise out of the special characteristics of particular weapons.[56] Thus the concept of armed attack by modern missiles[57] and naval mines[58] has given rise to special questions. Questions as to the regulation

---

[53] SC Res 1132 (1997), 1171 (1998), 1299 (2000).

[54] SC Res 1227 (1999) See 267 below.

[55] Liberia – 2001 UNYB 185, 202; Reports of the Secretary-General S/2002/1183, S/2003/466 para 28–30; UN docs S/2003/498, para 5, 69; S/2001/474; S/2001/851. Ethiopia—UN doc S/1999/154.

[56] On the special question of nuclear weapons, see Boisson de Chazournes and Sands (eds), *International Law, the International Court of Justice and Nuclear Weapons* (1999). For an early discussion of naval mines and modern missiles, see O'Connell, *The Influence of Law on Sea Power* (1975), 70.

[57] As regards modern radar-guided missiles, some states argue that an armed attack begins when the radar guiding the missile is locked on ready to fire. The rules of engagement of their armed forces reflect this approach. For example, in 1998 US aircraft in the no-fly zone over Iraq fired at a missile battery when its radar had locked on to planes patrolling the zone. There was controversy over whether the radar had actually locked on (and over the right of the planes to fly over Iraq), but the idea that an armed attack started when the radar locked on was apparently accepted by Iraq and other states: Keesings (1998) 42368. This contrasts with the hostile reaction that the USA and the UK met later when they further extended their rules of engagement to allow a wider range of targets (see 163 below).

[58] With regard to naval mines, the difficulty of fitting these into the traditional conception of self-defence became apparent during the Iran/Iraq war. The USA provided convoys for US-flagged vessels through the Gulf, and some of its vessels were harmed by mines. The USA held Iran responsible and used force in response, claiming self-defence. Also the *Iran Ajr* was detected laying mines; the USA boarded and seized the Iranian vessel.

of cyber-attacks have also arisen in recent years.[59] There are also disagreements as to the degree of gravity necessary for an armed attack, as to whether it is possible for a cumulative series of minor attacks to constitute an armed attack, and as to whether any specific intent on the part of the attacking state must be shown. Other questions centre on cross-border activity by irregular forces: what degree of state involvement, if any, is necessary for the existence of an armed attack?

The International Court of Justice has considered the concept of armed attack in a series of cases, starting with the *Nicaragua* case. In that case, *Oil Platforms*,[60] *Armed Activities on the Territory of the Congo (DRC v Uganda)*[61] and in the brief and obscure passage in its Advisory Opinion on *The Legal Consequences of the Construction of a Wall on the Occupied Palestinian Territory*[62] it generally took a cautious approach to the right of self-defence and was careful to avoid pronouncing on the most contentious issues where this was not necessary for its decision.[63]

Because the USA claimed not to be a party to the conflict, it had to justify its actions in protection of US-flagged vessels incident by incident rather than invoke self-defence once to cover its entire operation. It had to explain its actions against Iranian minelayers in terms of Article 51 rather than just the laws of war. Accordingly it argued that its actions taken to intercept minelaying vessels were in self-defence. See Gray, 'The British Position in Regard to the Gulf Conflict', 37 ICLQ (1988) 420 at 427; Thorpe, 'Mine Warfare at Sea', 18 Ocean Development and International Law (1987) 255; Nordquist and Wachenfeld, 'Legal Aspects of Reflagging Kuwaiti Tankers and the Laying of Mines in the Persian Gulf', 31 German Yearbook of International Law (1988) 138.

Also, in response to mine damage to the *USS Samuel B. Roberts* in 1988, the USA attacked and destroyed Iranian oil platforms which it said had been used as a base for Iranian military operations. The USA reported its actions to the Security Council under Article 51 as self-defence, but the justification that it offered made the action appear more like a reprisal; it said that its actions were designed to deter further unlawful use of force against the USA: Gray, 'The British Position in Regard to the Gulf Conflict, Part II', 40 ICLQ (1991) 464; 1987 UNYB 235, UN doc S/19149, 22 September 1987; see also De Guttry and Ronzitti (eds), *The Iran–Iraq War (1980–1988) and the Law of Naval Warfare* (1993) at 195–7, 222–3. The legality of the US actions was considered by the International Court of Justice in the *Case Concerning Oil Platforms*. The Court said that it 'does not exclude the possibility that the mining of a single military vessel might be sufficient to bring into play the "inherent right of self-defence"', but on the facts the US use of force was held not to be lawful self-defence, ICJ Reports (2003) 161 para 72, 38–78).

[59] On computer warfare, see Schmitt and O'Donnell (eds), *Computer Network Attack and International Law* (2001); Schmitt, 'Computer Network Attack and the Use of Force in International Law: Thoughts on a Normative Framework', 37 Columbia Journal of Transnational Law (1998–9) 885. In 2007 there was a network attack on Estonia, called by some the world's first cyberspace war. There was some discussion as to whether Russia was responsible for the attack: Keesings (2007) 47944. Later there were further attacks on US, German and UK computer networks which were said to have originated in China: Keesings (2007) 48095, 48139.

[60] *Iran v USA*, ICJ Reports (2003) 161.

[61] ICJ Reports (2005) 168.

[62] ICJ Reports (2004) 3.

[63] The Eritrea/Ethiopia Claims Commission in Ethiopia's *Ius ad Bellum* claims 1–8 , 45 ILM (2006) 430 also took a restrictive approach.

The concept of armed attack was central to the International Court of Justice's judgment on collective self-defence in the *Nicaragua* case; the USA claimed that its use of force against Nicaragua was justified as collective self-defence of Costa Rica, Honduras, and El Salvador in response to armed attacks on those states by Nicaragua, but the Court rejected this as it found that there was no armed attack by Nicaragua. The Court's view of armed attack has been severely attacked, especially by US writers.[64] However, the Court's description of the scope of armed attack was consistent with state practice and with the practice of the Security Council.

The Court first considered whether an armed attack had to be by a regular army. It used the *Definition of Aggression* to support its view that 'the sending by or on behalf of a state of armed bands, groups, irregulars or mercenaries, which carry out acts of armed force against another state of such gravity as to amount to (*inter alia*) an actual armed attack conducted by regular forces, or its substantial involvement therein' could be an armed attack. This limited reliance on the *Definition of Aggression* (stopping short of a complete identification of the two concepts) to elucidate the meaning of armed attack seems justified in the light of state practice.[65] States do not today challenge the view that actions by irregulars can constitute armed attack; the controversy centres on the degree of state involvement that is necessary to make the actions attributable to the state and to justify action in self-defence in particular cases. This question has attracted a large amount of academic discussion since the terrorist attacks of 9/11.[66]

The Court then held that assistance to rebels in the form of the provision of weapons or logistical or other support did not amount to an armed attack, although it could be illegal intervention.[67] This was strongly criticized by Judges Schwebel (USA) and Jennings (UK) in their Dissenting Opinions. Judge Schwebel said that the reference in the *Definition of Aggression* to 'substantial involvement' in the sending of armed bands meant that an armed attack could include financial and logistical support for armed bands. However, the drafting history of the resolution

---

[64] For example, Franck, 'Some Observations on the ICJ's Procedural and Substantive Innovations', 81 AJIL (1987) 116; Norton Moore, 'The *Nicaragua* case and the Deterioration of World Order', 81 AJIL (1987) 151; Macdonald, 'The Nicaragua case: New Answers to Old Questions', 1986 Canadian Yearbook of International Law 127; Higgins, *Problems and Process* (1994), 251.

[65] Judge Ago, in his Separate Opinion, 181 para 7, expressed reservations about the legal significance of General Assembly resolutions. In contrast, Judge Schwebel was prepared to accept the *Definition of Aggression* as reflecting customary international law (Dissenting Opinion para 168). See Gray, 'The Principle of Non-Use of Force', in Lowe and Warbrick (eds), *The United Nations and the Principles of International Law* (1994), 33.

[66] See Chapter 6 below

[67] *Nicaragua* case, ICJ Reports (1986) 14 at para 195.

does not support this construction and it is not consistent with Schwebel's own earlier recognition of a distinction between the wider conception of aggression and the narrower conception of armed attack.[68] Schwebel argued that the Court's narrow definition of armed attack and consequent limit of the right of self-defence offered a prescription for overthrow of weaker governments by predatory governments while denying potential victims what in some cases may be their only hope of survival.

Judge Jennings similarly argued that the Court's approach was not realistic, given that power struggles are in every continent carried on by destabilization, interference in civil strife, comfort, aid and encouragement to rebels, and the like. Because Chapter VII of the UN Charter was not working it was dangerous to define unnecessarily strictly the conditions for lawful self-defence.[69] The converse argument could equally well be made; because Chapter VII was not working it was important not to allow the abuse of the right of self-defence. Jennings said that 'It may readily be agreed that the mere provision of arms cannot be said to amount to an armed attack. But the provision of arms may nevertheless be an important element in what might be thought to amount to an armed attack where it is coupled with other kinds of involvement.'[70]

The focus for both dissenting judges was on the question of fact: did the particular actions of Nicaragua taken as a whole amount to an armed attack? They were also making policy arguments as to what the law ought to be. Neither Schwebel nor Jennings adduced any evidence that in state practice mere provision of weapons and logistical support in isolation had been treated as armed attack (as opposed to unlawful intervention) in cases of self-defence.

A few commentators accepted the arguments of the dissenting judges on the facts, but also went further and made strong criticisms of the Court's conception of armed attack. That is, they did not just reject the Court's interpretation of the facts, they also said that it was mistaken on the law.[71] They did not go so far as to say that a mere supply of arms could alone amount to an armed attack, but they argued that arms supply combined with financial and logistical support could in principle be an armed attack. However, their criticisms were based on policy considerations; they did not give any examples of state practice or Security Council

---

[68] Schwebel, 'Aggression, Intervention and Self-Defense in Modern International Law', 136 RCADI (1972–II) 463.

[69] Dissenting Opinion 543–4; Jennings' argument echoes that of Reisman, 'Coercion and self-determination: construing Charter Article 2(4)', and is open to the rebuttal by Schachter, 'The legality of pro-democratic invasion', 78 AJIL (1984) 642, 646.

[70] Jennings, Dissenting Opinion 543.

[71] Franck, 'Some observations on the ICJ's Procedural and Substantive Innovations', 81 AJIL (1987) 116 at 120; Norton Moore, 'The *Nicaragua* case and the deterioration of World Order', 81 AJIL (1987) 151 at 154.

practice to support their arguments. Nor do they apply such principles to US interventions. In contrast, the Court's judgment is consistent with state practice. The Security Council, in its many calls for an end to the supply of arms or other outside support to opposition forces in situations such as those in Afghanistan, Yugoslavia, and Rwanda, has never identified such interventions as an armed attack.

In *Armed Activities on the Territory of the Congo (DRC v Uganda)* the DRC brought an action against Uganda for unlawful use of force. Uganda sought to justify its use of force partly on the basis of self-defence. In order to do so it took a wide view of armed attack to support its claim that the DRC was responsible for attacks by the irregular forces of the Allied Democratic Forces (ADF) operating from the DRC against Uganda. Uganda 'recalled the existence of a powerfully expressed alternative view according to which the formulation of the majority of the Court in the *Nicaragua* case was excessively narrow in its approach to the interpretation of the phrase "armed attack"'. Uganda said that the alternative view could be expressed: the giving of logistical support to armed bands with knowledge of their objectives may constitute an armed attack.[72] But the support Uganda offered for this argument in its Pleadings was extremely weak and the Court did not change its view.[73]

Cross-border action by irregular forces

The issue of cross-border action by irregular forces has given rise to much difficulty. If these forces are acting on behalf of the state from whose territory they are operating and their actions are of such gravity as to amount to an armed attack, the situation is clear.[74] However, the question of what degree of state involvement is necessary to allow the use of force against the territory of the host state in self-defence has proved an intractable issue. In the *Nicaragua* case the Court treated the *Definition of Aggression* with its provision 'sending by or on behalf of a state…or its substantial involvement therein' as definitive as to what amounted to an armed attack. It did not expressly go into the issue of whether a lesser degree of state involvement, such as acquiescence or even inability to control armed bands operating on its territory, could ever be enough to constitute an armed attack,

---

[72] Uganda, Counter-Memorial at 350; Rejoinder at 268–270.

[73] Judge *ad hoc* Kateka in his Dissenting Opinion, para 13–34, criticized this narrow approach and said that the Court should not have followed the decision of the Court in the *Nicaragua* case, but should have adopted that of Judge Jennings.

[74] Brownlie, 'International Law and the Activities of Armed Bands', 7 ICLQ (1958) 731; Cot and Pellet (eds) *La Charte des Nations Unies* (1991) 780; Rifaat, *International Aggression: A Study of the Legal Concept* (1979) Chapter 15; Lamberti-Zanardi, 'Indirect Military Aggression', in Cassese (ed.), *Current Legal Regulation of the Use of Force* (1986), 111.

but it seems implicit in its judgment that armed attack is narrower than this.[75]

The Court followed the same approach in *Armed Activities on the Territory of the Congo (DRC v Uganda)* in considering Uganda's claim that it was using force in self-defence against armed attacks by non-state actors from the territory of the DRC in the period from August 1998 till June 2003.[76] The Court first examined the nature of the Ugandan operations in the DRC in order to determine whether they could qualify as self-defence. Uganda had claimed that its Operation *Safe Haven* was conducted on this basis. However, the Ugandan forces in a very short space of time moved rapidly beyond the border area. The Court examined whether, throughout the period when its forces were rapidly advancing across the DRC, Uganda was entitled to engage in military action in self-defence against the DRC. It held, first, that the objectives of Operation *Safe Haven* were not consonant with the concept of self-defence as understood in international law. Second, Uganda did not argue that the regular army of the DRC was making attacks; it claimed that the ADF, a rebel group operating against Uganda from Congolese territory, was being supplied and equipped by the Sudan and the DRC government. But the Court found no evidence of a tripartite conspiracy between the DRC, the ADF and the Sudan. The Court accepted that there was evidence of a series of cross-border attacks by the ADF from May 1998. However, Uganda had not shown any involvement of the DRC in these attacks. Moreover, third, Operation *Safe Haven* seemed to be essentially preventative in nature—to secure Uganda's legitimate security interests—but Uganda was not claiming any right to anticipatory self-defence; Uganda was relying on self-defence against attacks that had occurred. However, it had not reported its use of force to the Security Council under Article 51.

---

[75] This question of state involvement in irregular actions arises in several different contexts: the definition of intervention, aggression, armed attack, and use of force. The drafting of the GA resolutions on *Friendly Relations*, *Definition of Aggression*, and *Non-Use of Force* reflected differences between states on these issues. There are also questions about the degree of state involvement necessary for the acts of armed bands to give rise to state responsibility. Since 9/11 much has been written on the relationship between issues of state responsibility and the definition of armed attack: see Becker, *Terrorism and the State* (2006). Questions about the relationship between state responsibility for the actions of irregular forces and the international nature of a conflict arose before the ICTY; see Meron, 'Classification of Armed Conflict in the former Yugoslavia: Nicaragua's Fallout', 92 AJIL (1998) 236; *Tadic Appeal*, 38 ILM (1999) 1518. The ICJ in the *Application of the Convention on the Prevention and Punishment of the Crime of Genocide* (Bosnia and Herzegovina v Serbia and Montenegro), ICJ Reports (2007) para 402 recently rejected the ICTY's approach to state responsibility in the *Tadic* case.

[76] *Armed Activities on the Territory of the Congo, (DRC v Uganda)*, ICJ Reports (2005) 168 para 106–147.

It was after its recital of all these factors (which would in themselves cumulatively go a long way towards the undermining of Uganda's claim to self-defence) that the Court then considered the question as to whether the DRC was responsible for the cross-border attacks by the ADF.[77] Uganda did not claim that it had been subjected to an armed attack by the armed forces of the DRC. The armed attacks to which reference was made came from the ADF. The Court found that there was no satisfactory proof of the involvement in these attacks, direct or indirect, of the government of the DRC. It invoked the *Definition of Aggression* Article 3(g) to conclude that on the evidence before it the attacks were not attributable to the DRC.[78] For all these reasons it found that the legal and factual circumstances for the exercise of a right of self-defence by Uganda against the DRC were not present. This is a clear reaffirmation of the Court's position in the *Nicaragua* case.

Then follows what has proved to be the most controversial part of the judgment: 'Accordingly, the Court has no need to respond to the contentions of the Parties as to whether and under what conditions contemporary international law provides for a right of self-defence against large-scale attacks by irregular forces.'[79] That is, the Court avoided the questions whether there may be an armed attack by non-state actors in the absence of state involvement, and what measures a state may take against such an attack.[80]

---

[77] *Armed Activities on the Territory of the Congo, (DRC v Uganda)*, ICJ Reports (2005) 168 para 146.

[78] In its discussion of the prohibition of intervention, the Court rejected the argument that absence of action against rebel groups operating against another state amounted to tolerating or acquiescing in their activities. Inability to act against rebels or ineffective action did not make a state guilty of intervention. A priori it would seem that mere inaction cannot amount to an armed attack. See 79 above.

[79] *Armed Activities on the Territory of the Congo (DRC v Uganda)*, ICJ Reports (2005) 168 para 147.

[80] The Court was able to do so because Uganda had not clearly argued for such a wide view of armed attack. In its written pleadings Uganda did not justify its use of force against the DRC on the basis that self-defence extended to action against non-state actors in a third state in the absence of substantial involvement of that state in the sending of the armed bands. Rather it argued for a wide, four-fold concept of armed attack by a state, to include (1) sending by a state, (2) provision of logistical support in the form of arms, training or financial assistance by a state, (3) the operation of armed groups forming part of the command structure of the state, and (4) a conspiracy between the state and the armed bands (Counter-Memorial, para 359). Uganda went further in its oral pleadings, arguing that 'toleration of armed bands by the territorial state generates responsibility and *therefore* constitute armed attacks for the purpose of Article 51. Failure to control the activities of armed bands creates a susceptibility of action in self-defence by neighbouring states': Ugandan Oral Pleadings, CR 2005/7, para 80, quoted by Judge Kooijmans in his Separate Opinion para 21. This conflation of state responsibility for unlawful intervention by irregular forces and armed attack has proved attractive to some commentators, but it confuses primary rules (the definition of armed attack) and secondary rules (the attribution of state responsibility for the breach of those primary rules). The Ugandan oral argument was also implicitly rejected by the Court in this case in its finding that failure to control does not amount to toleration of armed

The Court was criticised by some judges and commentators for not taking a more radical approach.[81] Judge Simma and Judge Kooijmans both said that the Court should have taken the opportunity presented by the case to clarify the state of the law on a matter which is marked by great controversy and confusion: self-defence against armed attacks by non-state actors. In their Separate Opinions they argued that if armed attacks are carried out by irregular forces from a state which does not exercise effective authority over its territory these activities are still armed attacks, even if they cannot be attributed to the territorial state, and that it would be unreasonable to deny the attacked state the right to self-defence.[82] In support of their argument they claimed that the events of 9/11 had brought about a change in the law. However, the significance of 9/11 and its aftermath for the general law of self-defence remains an extremely controversial question, and it is not surprising that the Court chose to avoid it.[83]

It is interesting that Judges Buergenthal and Higgins did not give Separate Opinions in this case, and did not here raise the question of armed attacks by non-state actors, as they had done earlier in the Court's Advisory Opinion on *Legal Consequences of the Construction of a Wall on Occupied Palestinian Territory*.[84] The Court in that case avoided any pronouncement on the possibility of self-defence against an armed attack by non-state actors. However, its discussion of self-defence was so brief and opaque that many have interpreted it as an express rejection of this doctrine.[85] In the relevant paragraph on self-defence the Court said: 'Article 51 of the Charter thus recognizes the existence of an inherent right of self-defence in the case of armed attack by one State against another State.'[86] This is simply a statement of the basic central right of self-defence. The Court does not say there is a right of self-defence *only* in the case of an armed attack by one state against another.[87] However, in their Separate

---

bands in violation of the duty of vigilance (*DRC v Uganda*, ICJ Reports (2005) 168 para 277, 300–301; see Chapter 3 above).

[81] See, for example, Okowa, 'Congo's War: the legal dimensions of a protracted conflict', 72 BYIL (2006) 203.

[82] Judge Simma, Separate Opinion, para 4–15; Judge Kooijmans, Separate Opinion, para 16–31. Judge Kooijmans went on to suggest that such a reaction by the attacked state might be called an act under the state of necessity or 'extra-territorial law enforcement', but he gave no detailed discussion of the significance of these terms.

[83] See Chapter 6 below.

[84] ICJ Reports (2004) 3, Judge Buergenthal Declaration; Judge Higgins Separate Opinion.

[85] See, for example, Murphy, 'Self-defense and the Wall Opinion', 99 AJIL (2005) 62; Wedgwood, 'The ICJ Advisory Opinion on the Israeli security fence and the limits of self-defense', 99 AJIL (2005) 52, Tams, 'Light treatment of a complex problem: the law of self-defence in the Wall case', 16 EJIL (2005) 963.

[86] ICJ Reports (2004) 3, para 139.

[87] As Tams seems to have assumed in 'Light treatment of a complex problem: the law of self-defence in the Wall case', 16 EJIL (2005) 963. He is more cautious in 'Note Analytique: Swimming with the tide or seeking to stem it', 18 Revue québécoise de droit int (2005) 275.

Opinions Judges Higgins and Buergenthal seem to interpret it in this way;[88] in contrast Judge Koojmans said that the Court had bypassed the issue.[89] Israel was not claiming a right of self-defence against another state in this case. The Court then went on, 'The Court also notes that Israel exercises control in the Occupied Palestinian Territory and that, as Israel itself states, the threat which it regards as justifying the construction of the wall originates within, and not outside, that territory. The situation is thus different from that contemplated by Security Council Resolutions 1368 (2001) and 1373 (2001), and therefore Israel could not in any event invoke those resolutions in support of its claim to be exercising a right of self-defence. Consequently, the Court concludes that Article 51 of the Charter has no relevance in this case.' This could be interpreted as leaving open the possibility of self-defence against non-state actors in situations like those contemplated in Security Council Resolutions 1368 and 1373 and as avoiding taking a position on the issue of principle.[90] This question will be discussed further in Chapter 6.

'Victim' states have tended to blame the host state for incursions by armed bands operating from their territory and to hold it responsible in order to justify their invocation of self-defence; that is, they seem implicitly to take the view that if there is no state involvement in the actions of the irregular forces there can be no self-defence against that state but only lesser action not going beyond the territory of the victim state. The best known practice is that of Israel, South Africa, and Portugal: they all took extensive action against irregular forces in neighbouring states.

Portugal's reluctance to give up its colonial possessions in Africa led it into conflict with national liberation movements and newly independent African states. In the 1960s and 1970s Guinea, Senegal, and Zambia repeatedly complained of armed invasions by Portugal from its colonies. Portugal argued in response that it was acting in self-defence because these states were responsible for the acts of terrorists operating from their

---

[88] Judge Buergenthal, Separate Opinion, para 6. Judge Higgins, Separate Opinion, para 33–35. Judge Higgins made the important point that the invocation of Article 51 was not appropriate in this situation as the construction of the wall was not a forcible action. Both judges were unhappy with the Court's view that there could not be self-defence where the attacks emanate from occupied territory.

[89] Kooijmans Separate Opinion para 35.

[90] On self-defence against non-state actors, see Becker, *Terrorism and the State* (2006); Jinks, 'State responsibility for the acts of private armed groups', 4 Chicago JIL (2003) 83; Kammerhofer, 'The Armed Activities case and non-state actors in self-defence law', 20 Leiden JIL (2007) 89; Murphy, 'Terrorism and the concept of armed attack in Article 51 of the UN Charter', 43 Harvard JIL (2002) 41; Ruys and Verhoeven, 'Attacks by private actors and the right of self-defence', 10 Journal of Conflict and Security law (2005) 289; Travalio and Altenburg, 'Terrorism, State responsibility and the use of military force', 4 Chicago JIL (2003) 97; Tams, 'Note Analytique: Swimming with the tide or seeking to stem it', 18 Revue québécoise de droit int (2005) 275.

territories against its colonies.[91] Similarly South Africa's apartheid regime and illegal occupation of Namibia led to conflict; also on the independence of Angola and Mozambique, South Africa intervened in the Cold War-fuelled conflicts in those states. It said in justification of its invasions of the frontline states, Angola, Botswana, Mozambique, and Zambia, that these states had been supporting terrorist operations by the ANC and SWAPO, or acquiescing in their operations, or allowing their territory to be used by them.[92] Israel had been involved in cross-border actions against irregular forces operating from neighbouring states since 1948; in particular, it undertook operations against forces in Lebanon from 1967. It held Lebanon responsible for not preventing armed action against Israel and claimed the right to take action in self-defence.[93] The precise degree of host state involvement alleged has varied, but Portugal and Israel seemed to feel the need to assert some degree of state involvement in the cross-border activities of the armed bands. At the widest, failure to prevent, or mere acquiescence in, the activities of armed bands was claimed not only to cause state responsibility but also to justify self-defence.

In contrast, South Africa sometimes did not allege state complicity to justify its use of force, but rather relied on a novel doctrine of 'hot pursuit'. This is a law of the sea doctrine whereby coastal states have the right to pursue ships guilty of offences in territorial waters into areas of the sea beyond national jurisdiction; by analogy with this South Africa claimed the right to pursue alleged terrorists into neighbouring states.[94] But this doctrine was not well received; in Resolution 568 (1985) the Security Council said that it 'denounces and rejects racist South Africa's practice of "hot pursuit" to terrorize and destabilize Botswana and other countries in southern Africa'. South Africa later abandoned this argument and returned to asserting the responsibility of the state from whose territory the guerrillas were operating.[95]

---

[91] For example, 1966 UNYB 117, 122; 1967 UNYB 123, 131; 1968 UNYB 159; 1969 UNYB 135, 137, 140; 1970 UNYB 187, 191, 192; 1971 UNYB 113, 116, 119, 121; 1972 UNYB 136; 1973 UNYB 109. See Alexandrov, *Self-Defence against the Use of Force in International Law* (1996), 179.

[92] For example, South Africa argued host state support by Angola: 1981 UNYB 217, Mozambique, 1981 UNYB 228, Botswana, 1985 UNYB 189, Zambia, 1980 UNYB 263. See Alexandrov, *Self-Defense against the Use of Force in International Law* (1996), 180.

[93] For example, 1969 UNYB 200, 1970 UNYB 227, 1978 UNYB 295, 1982 UNYB 428 at 431. See Alexandrov, *Self-Defense against the Use of Force in International Law* (1996), 174. For more recent cross border action by Israel, see Chapter 6 below. In recent years Israel has responded forcibly to attacks by Hezbollah across its border with Lebanon; it has claimed to be acting in self-defence. It has taken care to attribute responsibility for the Hezbollah attacks to Lebanon because of its alleged collusion and support for Hezbollah.

[94] SC 1944th meeting (1976).

[95] SC 1944th meeting (1976); 1985 UNYB 180 at 184. Hot pursuit was rejected by India and Nigeria (SC 2606th meeting 1985), by Trinidad (SC 2607th meeting 1985). In SC 2616th meeting (1985) Mozambique said South Africa has abandoned hot pursuit. See Kwakwa, 'South Africa's May 1985 Military Incursions into Neighbouring African States', 12 Yale JIL (1987)

The Court in the *Nicaragua* case, in its discussions as to whether the actions of irregular forces could constitute an armed attack, said that customary international law required that the actions be of such gravity that they would amount to an armed attack if committed by regular troops. This distinction between armed attack and acts of lesser gravity was later elaborated on by the Court and will be discussed further in Chapter 5 in the context of collective self-defence.

Although, as the Court recognized in the *Nicaragua* case, in principle self-defence is permissible against attacks by irregular forces where there is substantial state involvement in the sending of those forces, in practice the claims by Portugal, South Africa, and Israel to be acting in self-defence were generally not accepted by the Security Council. These claims to self-defence were undermined by the fact that the states invoking self-defence were regarded as being in illegal occupation of the territory they were purporting to defend. Portugal's defence of its colonial possessions in Africa led it into conflict with forces fighting for decolonization; its attacks on states such as Guinea, Zambia, and Senegal were condemned by the Security Council. Many of the states arguing for condemnation did so because Portugal was using force to maintain its illegal colonial power. The right of self-defence could not be invoked to perpetuate colonialism and to flout the right to self-determination and independence.[96] South Africa was in illegal occupation of Namibia and therefore many states were not willing to accept that it could use force in self-defence to protect the regime in Namibia.[97] South Africa's claims to be acting in self-defence against incursions by SWAPO fighters seeking the liberation of Namibia were not valid. South African territory was not in danger; the cause of the dangerous situation was the illegal presence of South Africa in Namibia. Even France and the USA sometimes took this line; they continued to make this argument even when they later vetoed condemnations of South Africa in pursuit of their policy of constructive engagement or seeking a negotiated solution.[98] Very unusually, in its resolutions rejecting South Africa's justifications for its use of force against Angola and condemning this use of force the Security Council expressly asserted the right of Angola to self-defence under Article 51 of the UN Charter in Resolutions 546 (1984) and 574 (1985). Again the mere fact that many states regarded Israel's occupation of the West Bank and Gaza, the Golan, and (until 2000) areas of South Lebanon as illegal was enough for them to condemn Israel's

---

421. The white minority government in Rhodesia also espoused hot pursuit; see Luttig, 'The legality of the Rhodesian military operations inside Mozambique—the problem of hot pursuit on land', 1977 SA Yearbook 136.

[96] 1969 UNYB 137, 140, 143.
[97] *Namibia* Advisory Opinion, ICJ Reports (1971) 16.
[98] 1980 UNYB 252; 1981 UNYB 220; SC 2607th meeting (1985).

use of force against cross-border attacks by irregulars. They say that Israel has no right to be in these territories and so no right to invoke self-defence against attacks on their forces in these territories or against attacks on Israel designed to secure its withdrawal from the territories it occupied illegally.[99]

The use of force against neighbouring states by Portugal, South Africa, and Israel was condemned on many different grounds. States in the Security Council debates on the use of force by these states mentioned many factors as contributing to the illegality of their actions in different cases: the neighbouring states were not responsible for any armed attack; the response to cross-border incursions was disproportionate; the use of force was not necessary. All three grounds for condemnation were invoked in the responses to the massive invasions and lengthy occupations of Lebanon by Israel in 1978 and 1982, and the South African operations in Angola from 1981.[100] Also in some cases actions by South Africa and Israel were seen as unlawful reprisals rather than self-defence; the states using force regularly said that their aim was to prevent future attacks.[101] And for many states the use of force by Portugal, South Africa and Israel was illegal because it was directed against the legitimate struggle of a people with the right to self-determination.

Even when western states on the Security Council abstained or vetoed a resolution condemning the use of force by Portugal, South Africa, and Israel, they did not necessarily do so because they defended the legality of the actions of those states. In the early days of the decolonization struggle against Portugal the USA and the UK sometimes abstained on the grounds that the facts of the particular case had not been properly established or there were extenuating circumstances.[102] As regards South Africa, the USA and UK sometimes abstained as part of their policy of seeking a negotiated solution.[103] Occasionally they said that they regarded the resolution as one-sided because they wanted an end to all foreign

---

[99] Barsotti, 'Armed Reprisals', in Cassese (ed.), *The Current Legal Regulation of the Use of Force* (1986), 79. On cross border attacks by Israel against Lebanon in response to actions by Hezbollah against Israeli armed forces and civilians, see 234 below.

[100] 1978 UNYB 295, 1981 UNYB 217, 1982 UNYB 312, 428.

[101] On pre-emptive action by South Africa against the ANC, see, for example, SC 2598th meeting (1985); against SWAPO, SC 2606th meeting (1985), Botha, 'Anticipatory Self-Defence and Reprisals Re-examined', 11 South African Yearbook of International Law (1985–86) 138. On pre-emptive action by Israel, see, for example, 1982 UNYB 428 at 435, O'Brien, 'Reprisals, Deterrence and Self-Defense in Counterterror Operations', 30 Virginia Journal of International Law (1990) 421, Alexandrov, *Self-Defense against the Use of Force in International Law* (1996), 174, 180.

[102] 1969 UNYB 134, 137, 140; 1971 UNYB 116; 1972 UNYB 136.

[103] SC Res 447 (1979) and 454 (1979) on Angola, 1979 UNYB 225; SC Res 475 (1980), 1980 UNYB 252; SC Res 545 (1983), 1983 UNYB 169; SC Res 546 (1984), 1984 UNYB 177.

intervention in Angola.[104] They used the veto to prevent the imposition of mandatory economic sanctions. As regards Israel, they sometimes said that they would abstain or veto a resolution because it was one-sided in that it did not condemn terrorist attacks against Israel.[105] But for the most part, Portugal, South Africa, and Israel were regarded as not able to invoke self-defence because of their illegal occupation of territory. Issues of the precise involvement of states in the actions of armed bands thus did not have to be determined.

Other more straightforward claims to self-defence against irregular forces operating from neighbouring states have also been made. These have generally been more limited operations than the long-term and extensive action by the three states discussed above. For example, Thailand pursued guerrillas into Burma in 1995 after warning Burma to control the cross-border attacks by the guerrillas.[106] Senegal similarly went into Guinea-Bissau in operations against opposition forces based in Guinea-Bissau in 1992 and 1995. In the latter case it is interesting that in 1992, when Guinea-Bissau protested that it had not supported the rebel incursions into Senegal, Senegal apologized for its action.[107] Tajikistan was involved in more extensive actions against irregular forces operating from Afghanistan. On attaining independence in 1991 Tajikistan became involved in a civil war which continued until the 1997 *General Agreement on the Establishment of Peace and National Accord in Tajikistan*; forces opposing the government made cross-border attacks from Afghanistan. Tajikistan blamed Afghanistan for supporting the opposition forces and claimed the right to act in self-defence against the armed bands in Afghanistan.[108]

Turkey, Iraq and the Kurds

Special problems over responses to cross-border attacks by irregular forces arose with regard to Turkey's actions against the Kurds in Iraq.[109]

---

[104] SC Res 387 (1976), 1976 UNYB 171. Most extreme was the US statement in 1981 when it vetoed a draft resolution condemning the large scale invasion by South Africa into Angola. The USA said that the draft blamed South Africa alone for the escalation of violence, but the presence of Cuban troops and USSR military advisers in Angola had fuelled the explosive atmosphere: 1981 UNYB 217. The USA made a similar statement in 1987, but was nevertheless prepared to vote for the resolution condemning South Africa's invasion of Angola: 1987 UNYB 167.

[105] 1984 UNYB 289, 1985 UNYB 299, 1986 UNYB 286, 1988 UNYB 218; see Patil, *The UN Veto in World Affairs* (1992), 287.

[106] Keesings (1995) 40554.

[107] Keesings (1992) 39228; (1995) 40396.

[108] 1993 UNYB 382. Tajikistan said that *mujahedin* and sub-units under the ministry of defence of Afghanistan were responsible for a major incursion into Tajikistan on 13 July 1993: Russia UN doc S/26110, 19 July 1993; Tajikistan UN doc S/26092, 16 July 1993; Afghanistan UN doc S/1994/310.

[109] See Gray and Olleson, 'The Limits of the Law on the Use of Force: Turkey, Iraq and the Kurds', 12 *Finnish Yearbook of International Law* (2001) 387.

As part of its domestic campaign against the Kurdish Workers Party (PKK), a Kurdish separatist organization involved in terrorism since the 1970s,[110] Turkey has undertaken cross-border operations against Kurdish bases in northern Iraq. These operations escalated after the Iraqi invasion of Kuwait in 1990, the imposition of the ceasefire on Iraq under Resolution 687, and the creation of 'safe havens' for the Iraqi Kurds in northern Iraq patrolled by US and British aircraft operating from Turkey. As long as Iraq acquiesced in or even formally consented to Turkey's operations on its territory, and in the absence of any international support for the right of the Kurds to independent statehood, Turkey at first offered little in the way of legal justification for its cross-border operations against Kurds.[111]

Since 1991 Iraq repeatedly protested at Turkey's incursions. It complained of the penetration by Turkish armed forces inside Iraqi territory on the pretext that they were in pursuit of separatist terrorists; this was a violation of the UN Charter and of international law.[112] Like Turkey, Iran also occasionally pursued Kurds over the border into Iraq; when it did so, it did not directly accuse Iraq of supporting the 'bands of armed and organised terrorist mercenaries' engaged in trans-border military attacks against and sabotage in Iranian border provinces. However, Iran did expressly invoke self-defence as a justification for its operations. It said that 'in response to these armed attacks from inside Iraq and in accordance with Article 51 of the Charter of the United Nations, the fighter jets of the Islamic Republic Air Force carried out a brief, necessary and proportionate operation against the military bases of the terrorist group where the recent armed attacks had originated'.[113]

In contrast, Turkey has not expressly invoked Article 51; it did not itself report its operations in Iraq to the Security Council. It normally only responded (usually belatedly) to Iraq's allegations; even then it did not clearly rely on self-defence. Thus Turkey avoided the issue as to how far Iraq was responsible for the actions of the Kurds and whether it was guilty of an armed attack, but left the legal basis for Turkey's actions unclear. After a major operation in 1995 Turkey said:

As Iraq has not been able to exercise its authority over the northern part of its country since 1991 for reasons well known, Turkey cannot ask the Government of Iraq to fulfil its obligation, under international law, to prevent the use of its territory for the staging of terrorist acts against Turkey. Under these circumstances, Turkey's resorting to legitimate measures which are imperative to its own

---

[110] The EU and the USA have both designated the PKK (which has changed its names several times) as a terrorist organization, Keesings (2004) 45820, 45974, 46026, 46175.
[111] Bothe and Lohmann, 'Der türkische Einmarsch im Nordirak', 5 *Schweizerische Zeitschrift für internationales und europäisches Recht* (1995) 441.
[112] For example, UN docs S/23141, 14 October 1991, S/23152, 17 October 1991.
[113] UN doc S/25843, 26 May 1993.

security cannot be regarded as a violation of Iraq's sovereignty. No country could be expected to stand idle when its own territorial integrity is incessantly threatened by blatant cross-border attacks of a terrorist organization based and operating from a neighbouring country, if that country is unable to put an end to such attacks. The recent operations of limited time and scope were carried out within this framework.[114]

It is very striking that the USA, in defending the Turkish action, apparently took the view that it was acting in self-defence,[115] whereas Turkey itself did not make this claim. And in other letters to the Security Council, in response to Iraqi protests about its cross-border actions in 1996 and 1997, Turkey again did not mention Article 51 or self-defence; it referred to the duty in the *Friendly Relations Resolution* to refrain from acquiescing in organized activities within its territory directed towards the commission of terrorist acts in another state. It relied on the principles of necessity and self-preservation. It also referred to its determination to take measures to safeguard its legitimate security interests, defending its borders and protecting its people against terrorism.[116] This may come nearer to the language of self-defence, but it falls short of an express claim. Nor did Turkey offer a clear legal justification of its occupation of a 'buffer zone' in northern Iraq.[117]

Iraq claimed, with some plausibility, that there was a double standard: while the UN claimed that it was protecting the Kurds in Iraq against the Iraqi government, it closed its eyes to persecution by Turkey of its own Kurds. Iraq said that it could not be held responsible for the incursions by Kurds from its territory into Turkey because of the abnormal situation in northern Iraq, created particularly by the USA. It said that the US policy of interference and the deployment of US and British forces in Turkey in order to intervene militarily in northern Iraq prevented Iraq from exercising its sovereignty there. Iraq complained of the inaction of the Security Council.[118] For, in spite of the absence of a clear legal justification for its use of force, Turkey avoided condemnation by the Security Council; the apparent support of the USA helped it to escape discussion of its actions. But condemnation was expressed by the Arab League, the Gulf Cooperation Council and the NAM.[119]

In 2003 *Operation Iraqi Freedom* brought about the overthrow of Saddam Hussein and the installation of a new regime in Iraq which provided for the establishment of an autonomous Kurdish region in northern

---

[114] UN doc S/1995/605.
[115] UN doc S/1995/566.
[116] UN docs S/1996/479, S/1997/7, S/1997/552.
[117] UN docs S/1996/731, S/1996/796.
[118] UN docs S/1995/566, S/1997/393, S/1997/420; Keesings (1997) 41652.
[119] UN doc S/1997/461.

Iraq. Turkey is concerned that this will strengthen claims by the PKK to autonomy for the Turkish Kurds; it has alleged that the Kurdish regional government in Iraq provides aid to the PKK and turns a blind eye to its cross-border incursions into Turkey. It has deployed troops to the border area; there were reports of Turkish shelling of PKK positions in Iraq and of small-scale incursions into Iraq in 2006. At first the USA made it clear that it opposed any military action by Turkey against the PKK in Iraq as this could threaten order in the one stable area of Iraq. It warned Turkey against such action.[120] Turkey and Iraq made an agreement to cooperate against the PKK, but this did not include any acceptance by Iraq of cross-border action.[121] Nevertheless the Turkish Parliament passed a resolution on 17 October 2007 authorizing cross-border operations against the PKK.[122] And at the end of 2007 Turkey mounted a series of cross-border air and ground raids into Iraq in pursuit of the PKK, with the apparent acquiescence of the USA.[123] There were newspaper reports that the USA had agreed to provide intelligence to Turkey as to the movements of the PKK in Iraq in the hope that by allowing limited cross-border operations it might avoid a full-scale invasion.[124] At a meeting with the Prime Minister of Turkey, President Bush said: 'PKK is a terrorist organization. They're an enemy of Turkey, they're an enemy of Iraq, and they're an enemy of the United States.'[125] Turkey did not report its 2006 and 2007 cross-border operations to the Security Council under Article 51, and it has not offered any detailed legal justification for its use of force. This may be taken as an indication that it is unsure as to the adequacy of its legal case, and that states using force in what they see as a 'war on terror' may feel less constrained to offer such legal justification.[126]

Iranian Oil Platforms case

A different set of questions with regard to 'armed attack' came up in the *Iranian Oil Platforms* case.[127] Could an attack on a single US-flagged or US-owned merchant vessel amount to an armed attack under Article 51? Could an attack on a single naval vessel? What degree of gravity was necessary for an attack to constitute an armed attack; could a series of

---

[120] Keesings (2006) 47377–8, (2007) 47706, 47831, 47949, 48009; *The Guardian* 23 March, 13 April, 1, 30 June 2007.
[121] Keesings (2007) 48151, 48094.
[122] Keesings (2007) 48219, 48223.
[123] *The Guardian*, 2, 17, 19, 24 December 2007. Iran has also been involved in military action against Iraqi Kurds on the Iran/Iraq border: *The Guardian*, 20 August 2007.
[124] Keesings (2007) 48265. See also, US Department of Defense News Briefing, 14 December 2007; <www.defenselink.mil.transcripts.aspx?transcriptid=4106>.
[125] <www.whitehouse.gov/news/releases/2007/11/20071105–3.html>.
[126] See Chapter 6 below.
[127] ICJ reports (2003) 161, noted by Raab, 17 Leiden JIL (2004) 719.

minor attacks cumulatively amount to an armed attack? Was it necessary that the attacking state have an intent to attack the particular victim state? This case arose out of the 1980–88 conflict between Iran and Iraq. After Iraq invaded Iran, the conflict spread beyond the land to the waters of the Gulf and affected commerce and navigation in the region. In 1984 Iraq initiated the 'Tanker War', attacking ships in the Gulf, particularly tankers carrying Iranian oil; Iran responded against vessels trading with Iraq. In order to ensure the safety of its merchant vessels in the Gulf Kuwait turned to the USA, the UK, and the Soviet Union to re-flag some of its vessels and thus to ensure their naval protection. The USA agreed to provide all US-flagged ships with a naval escort through the Gulf; these convoys began in July 1987. Other foreign powers took parallel action. But a number of ships suffered attack or struck mines in the Gulf.[128]

Two specific attacks were central to this case. First, on 16 October 1987 the Kuwaiti tanker *Sea Isle City*, re-flagged by the USA, was hit by a missile. The USA blamed Iran for this attack, and three days later it attacked Iranian offshore oil installations, claiming to be acting in self-defence on the basis that the oil platforms had been engaged in a variety of actions directed against US vessels and other non-belligerent vessels and aircraft. Second, on 14 April 1988 the US warship *Samuel B Roberts* struck a mine in international waters in the Gulf; four days later the USA attacked and destroyed further Iranian oil platforms.[129]

Iran brought a case to the International Court of Justice, saying that the USA had violated Article X of the 1955 *Treaty of Amity* guaranteeing freedom of commerce and navigation between the two states. The USA counterclaimed that Iran had also broken the treaty 'in attacking vessels in the Gulf with mines and missiles and otherwise engaging in military actions that were dangerous and detrimental to commerce and navigation between the territories of the two states'. Iran denied responsibility for these attacks, suggesting that they were committed by Iraq, and claiming that Iran's attitude was purely defensive. The Court examined the question whether the USA had demonstrated that it had been the victim of an armed attack by Iran such as to justify its using armed force in self-defence; it held that the burden of proof rested on the USA.[130] The Court first dealt with the missile attack on the *Sea Isle City*; it examined in detail

---

[128] ICJ Reports (2003) 161 para 23–6.

[129] Ibid., para 25.

[130] Ibid., para 51. Some judges—Judges Buergenthal, Higgins, Kooijmans, Owada and Parra-Aranguren – argued that the Court had acted outside its jurisdiction in considering this question of self-defence. The Court had decided that there was no violation of the 1955 *Treaty of Amity* because there was no actual interference with commerce between the territories of the two parties; there was therefore no need for the Court to consider whether the US use of force had been justified under Article XX of the Treaty of Amity as action necessary to protect its essential security interests.

the evidence relating to that incident and concluded that the USA had not produced sufficient evidence to support its contentions that Iran was responsible for the missile attack. 'The burden of proof of the existence of an armed attack by Iran on the United States, in the form of the missile attack on the Sea Isle City, has not been discharged.'[131]

The USA had not relied solely on the *Sea Isle City* incident as constituting the 'armed attack' to which it claimed to be responding in self-defence. There is considerable doubt as to whether a single attack on a merchant vessel (as opposed to a military vessel) could constitute an armed attack on a state and the Court itself did not directly address this issue.[132] The USA asserted that this was the latest in a series of such missile attacks against US-flagged and other non-belligerent vessels in Kuwaiti waters. The alleged pattern of Iranian use of force 'added to the gravity of the specific attacks, reinforced the necessity of action in self-defence, and helped to shape the appropriate response.' The USA is clearly trying to address the argument that a single episode could not be serious enough to amount to an armed attack and that its response was disproportionate. The USA set out a series of incidents involving US-flagged or US-owned vessels and aircraft in the period up to the end of the conflict: the mining of the US-flagged *Bridgeton*, and of the US-owned *Texaco Caribbean*, the firing on US navy helicopters and the minelaying by an Iranian vessel, the *Iran Ajr*.[133]

However, even assuming that all these events were attributable to Iran, the Court held that the USA had not shown that the series of incidents could be categorized as an armed attack. Attacks on US-owned (as opposed to US-flagged) vessels did not amount to an attack on the state.[134] There was no evidence that the minelaying alleged to have been carried out by the *Iran Ajr*, at a time when Iran was at war with Iraq, was aimed specifically at the USA; similarly it had not been established that the mine which struck the *Bridgeton* had been laid with the specific intention of harming that ship or other US vessels. That is, it had not been established that the incidents were aimed at the USA (as opposed to Iraq). The Court apparently decided that harm by a mine or a missile constitutes an armed attack on a third state during a conflict between two other states only if the attack was specifically aimed at that third state. This is a brief and rather obscure discussion of a difficult issue; the Court does not go into

---

[131] ICJ Reports (2003) 161 para 51–61. Some judges were critical of the Court's approach to the burden of proof and the standard of evidence: Higgins para 30–9; Buergenthal para 33–46; Owada para 41–52.
[132] For the debate (and useful references) on this issue see ICJ Pleadings, Iran *Reply* para 7.36; US *Rejoinder* para 5.16, 5.19.
[133] ICJ Reports (2003) 161 para 50, 62.
[134] Ibid., para 64.

any greater detail as to the element of intent apparently required by the notion of armed attack in this particular context or as to the general significance (if any) of its approach.[135]

The US State Department Legal Adviser was very critical of the Court's judgment on this point.[136] He claimed that the need to prove a specific intent would undermine international peace and security; a requirement of specific intent would encourage intentionally indiscriminate attacks, since no victim would have the right to defend against them. However, this does not seem convincing, especially given the prohibitions on indiscriminate attacks in international humanitarian law. And it is not clear whether the Court was trying to establish a general requirement for all armed attacks or whether its brief statements on the intent requirement should be limited to the particular and unusual facts of the case where there was US involvement in a conflict between two other states. The Court concluded that even taken cumulatively these incidents did not constitute an armed attack on the USA of the kind which met the *Nicaragua* test of constituting a 'most grave' form of the use of force.[137] This left open the question whether an accumulation of events can amount to an armed attack.[138]

The second US attack on Iranian oil installations took place on 18 April 1988 after the *Samuel B Roberts* was blown up by a mine in international waters; again the USA claimed to be acting in self-defence.[139] The Court noted that the attacks on the oil platforms were not an isolated operation aimed simply at the oil installations, as had been the case with the attacks of 19 October 1987; rather the US attacks of 18 April 1988 formed part of a much more extensive military action, designated *Operation Praying Mantis*, and directed against a number of targets, including two Iranian frigates and other Iranian naval vessels and aircraft. The USA had discovered several mines bearing Iranian serial numbers in the vicinity in the days following the attack, and it also adduced other evidence of Iranian minelaying activity. But Iran denied that it had systematic recourse to minelaying in the Persian Gulf, and suggested that the mine that hit the *Samuel B Roberts* might have been laid by Iraq. The Court held that because mines were being laid by both Iraq and Iran at the relevant time evidence of other minelaying operations by Iran was not conclusive as to responsibility of

---

[135] The USA addressed the Iranian arguments on intent which were accepted by the Court in its ICJ Pleadings (US *Rejoinder* para 5.23, 5.26). However, the US argument focused on the laws of naval warfare rather than the concept of armed attack.

[136] Taft, 'Self-Defense and the *Oil Platforms* Decision', 29 Yale Journal of International law (2004) 295.

[137] ICJ Reports (2003) 161 para 62–4. See Chapter 5 below.

[138] See 146–7 below.

[139] ICJ Reports (2003) 161 para 67.

Iran for the particular mine which had hit the *Samuel B Roberts*. The evidence produced by the USA was highly suggestive but not conclusive.[140] The USA in its communications to the Security Council had linked the attack on the *Sea Isle City* with a series of offensive acts and provocations by Iranian naval forces against neutral shipping in the Gulf. Before the Court the USA argued (as it had with regard to the *Sea Isle City*) that the pattern of Iranian use of force 'added to the gravity of the specific attacks, reinforced the necessity of action in self-defense and helped to shape the appropriate response'. The Court did not exclude the possibility that the mining of a single military vessel might alone be sufficient to bring into play the inherent right of self-defence, but in view of all the circumstances, including the inconclusiveness of the evidence of Iran's responsibility for the mining of the *Samuel B Roberts*, the Court was unable to find that the attacks on the oil platforms were justifiably made in response to an armed attack on the US by Iran.[141]

Gravity of attack

The *Oil Platforms* judgment raised the question of the gravity of an armed attack. It quoted the passage of the *Nicaragua* case in which the Court famously and controversially said that 'It is necessary to distinguish the most grave forms of the use of force (those constituting an armed attack) from other less grave forms.'[142] In the *Nicaragua* case this distinction was made in the context of collective self-defence and this issue will be discussed in the next chapter. The distinction attracted much criticism; many argued that it was not necessary to limit the right to self-defence in this way and that the doctrines of necessity and proportionality would be sufficient to prevent the unnecessary use of force.[143] However, in the *Oil Platforms* case the Court reaffirmed the gravity requirement in the context of the US involvement in the Iran/Iraq conflict.[144] The US State Department Legal Adviser was again critical of the Court's judgment on this point.[145] He argued that the gravity requirement should be limited to its original context in the *Nicaragua* case, that of the sending by a state of irregular armed bands; he rejected the proposition that the use of deadly force by a state's regular armed forces, such as the attacks by Iran in this case, does not qualify as an armed attack unless it reaches a certain level of gravity. Like the earlier critics of the *Nicaragua* case on this point, he claimed that the

---

[140] Ibid., para 65–71.
[141] Ibid., para 72.
[142] ICJ Reports (1986) 14 para 191
[143] See 147–8 below.
[144] ICJ Reports (2003) 161 para 51, 62
[145] Taft, 'Self-Defense and the Oil Platforms Decision', 29 Yale Journal of International law (2004) 295.

requirement that an attack reach a certain level of gravity before triggering a right of self-defence would make the use of force more rather than less likely, because it would encourage states to engage in a series of small-scale military attacks, in the hope that they could do so without being subject to defensive responses. This implausible empirical claim has not been borne out by practice since the *Nicaragua* case. The counter-argument could be made that the presumption should always be against the use of force and in favour of peaceful settlement. If there is no gravity requirement for an armed attack and self-defence, then an inter-state conflict could arise out of minor cross-border incidents or other minor uses of force.

The distinction between armed attack and other less grave use of force played a crucial role in the Eritrea/Ethiopia Claims Commission Award on Ethiopia's *Ius ad Bellum* Claims 1–8.[146] This decision was made in the context of a traditional inter-state conflict. The crucial issue before the tribunal was whether Ertirea had started the 1998–2000 conflict and should be held responsible for all the harm to Ethiopia caused by that conflict. The parties disagreed as to the starting point of the conflict. Ethiopia said it began with armed attacks by Eritrea on 12 May 1998; Eritrea said that those actions were taken in self-defence against Ethiopian forces in illegal occupation of its territory; it also claimed that the 1998 conflict had originated earlier on 6 May. The Commission said that the parties had given very different accounts as to the location of the incidents on 6 and 7 May and of the numbers and types of forces involved. However, it had no need to resolve these differences because it was clear that these incidents were 'geographically limited clashes' between small Eritrean and Ethiopian patrols along a remote, unmarked and disputed border. The Commission was satisfied that these relatively minor incidents were not of a magnitude to constitute an armed attack by either state within the meaning of Article 51. This is a clear affirmation of the need for a use of force to reach a certain level of gravity before it constitutes an armed attack.

Necessity and proportionality

As part of the basic core of self-defence all states agree that self-defence must be necessary and proportionate.[147] The requirements of necessity and proportionality are often traced back to the 1837 *Caroline* incident,

---

[146] 45 ILM (2006) 430.

[147] A few writers have rejected these limits on self-defence as not established in customary international law: Kunz, 'Individual and Collective Self-defence in Article 51 of the Charter of the UN', 41 AJIL (1947) 872; Delivanis, *La légitime défense en droit international public moderne* (1971) Chapter 2. See also, Gardam, 'Proportionality and Force in International Law', 87 AJIL (1993) 391 and Gardam, *Necessity, Proportionality and the Use of Force by States* (2004).

involving a pre-emptive attack by the British forces in Canada on a ship manned by Canadian rebels, planning an attack from the USA.[148] This episode has attained a mythical authority. States and writers still refer to it, generally to support their own wide claims to self-defence, but also to support the necessity and proportionality limitation.[149] They invoke the famous formula that there must be a 'necessity of self-defence, instant, overwhelming, leaving no choice of means and no moment of deliberation'. Others challenge the authority of this episode for the modern doctrine of self-defence, seeing it rather as an episode of self-help pre-dating the modern law on the use of force and as a one-off episode of pre-emptive action not of relevance to the conduct of wider-scale conflict.[150] But, irrespective of the status of the *Caroline* incident as a precedent, necessity and proportionality have played a crucial role in state justification of the use of force in self-defence and in international response.

The *Nicaragua* case,[151] the Advisory Opinion on the *Legality of the Threat or Use of Nuclear Weapons*,[152] the *Oil Platforms* case,[153] and *Armed Activities*

---

[148] See Jennings, 'The Caroline and McLeod cases', 32 AJIL (1938) 86.

[149] For example, the UAE referred to the *Caroline* case in SC 2616th meeting (1985); the GDR invoked it over the clashes between the USA and Libya (SC 2677th meeting 1986). When an advisory report to the Dutch government recommended use of the Caroline case to determine whether an armed attack was imminent (*Pre-emptive Action*, No. 36, AIV/No. 15, CAVV, July 2004) the government response was, 'Whether the Caroline criteria are adequate today for deciding whether a threat is sufficiently imminent to justify exercising the right of self-defence, only experience will tell. While these criteria are a useful tool, one cannot exclude the possibility that they will have to be refined at some point.' (Government Letter to the House of Representatives, 29800 V, No.56, 29 October 2004)

[150] Cot and Pellet (eds), *La Charte des Nations Unies* (1991) 772; Brownlie in Butler (ed.), *The Non-Use of Force in International Law* (1989), 17; Kearley, 'Raising the Caroline,' 17 Wisconsin International Law Journal (1999) 325. Judge Schwebel, in the *Nicaragua* case, Dissenting Opinion, para 200, argued that the narrow criteria of the *Caroline* case concerned anticipatory self-defence only. This issue also came up in the *Oil Platforms* case, where Iran invoked the Caroline case as imposing limits on the right of self-defence and the USA argued that it was not relevant to the use of force in a continuing engagement: ICJ Pleadings US *Rejoinder* para 5.32, *Counter Memorial* para 4.44.

[151] ICJ Reports (1986) 14 para 194.

[152] ICJ Reports (1996) 226 para 141; the Court went on at para 143 to refuse to decide the issue whether the effects of any use of nuclear weapons would be so serious that it could not constitute a necessary and proportionate measure. It said, 'Certain states have in their written and oral pleadings suggested that in the case of nuclear weapons, the condition of proportionality must be evaluated in the light of still further factors. They contend that the very nature of nuclear weapons, and the high probability of an escalation of nuclear exchanges, mean that there is an extremely strong risk of devastation. The risk factor is said to negate the possibility of the condition of proportionality being complied with. The Court does not find it necessary to embark upon the quantification of such risks; nor does it need to enquire into the question whether tactical nuclear weapons exist which are sufficiently precise to limit those risks: it suffices for the Court to note that the very nature of all nuclear weapons and the profound risks associated therewith are further considerations to be borne in mind by States believing they can exercise a nuclear response in self-defence in accordance with the requirements of proportionality.'

[153] ICJ Reports (2003) 161 para 43.

on the Territory of the Congo (DRC v Uganda)[154] reaffirmed that necessity and proportionality are limits on all self-defence, individual and collective. These requirements are not express in the UN Charter, but are part of customary international law. There has been relatively little general academic discussion of these essential characteristics of self-defence, as opposed to discussion in application to particular incidents.[155] The question whether self-defence lives up to these requirements is often treated as almost exclusively one of fact. However, there are issues of principle involved: most basically, the different views of the scope of the right of self-defence will affect the scope of proportionality. Thus those who accept a right of anticipatory self-defence or self-defence against an accumulation of events will assert a much wider concept of proportionality.[156] The recent conflicts in Lebanon and Somalia have given rise to important issues of principle: some states have argued that the 'war on terror' justifies a very wide interpretation of necessity and proportionality.[157]

In theory it is possible to draw a distinction between necessity and proportionality, and the International Court of Justice typically applies the two requirements separately. Necessity is commonly interpreted as the requirement that no alternative response be possible.[158] Proportionality relates to the size, duration and target of the response, but clearly these factors are also relevant to necessity. It is not clear how far the two concepts can operate separately. If a use of force is not necessary, it cannot be proportionate and, if it is not proportionate, it is difficult to see how it can be necessary. Commentators agree on a few, basic, uncontroversial principles: necessity and proportionality mean that self-defence must not be retaliatory or punitive; the aim should be to halt and repel an attack. This does not mean that the defending state is restricted to the same weapons or the same numbers of armed forces as the attacking state; nor is it necessarily limited to action on its own territory. Reprisals are generally agreed

---

[154] ICJ Reports (2005) 168 para 147.

[155] See Gardam, *Necessity, Proportionality and the Use of Force by States* (2004), Okimoto, *The Distinction and Relationship between Ius ad Bellum and Ius in Bello* (University of Cambridge, PhD thesis, 2007) at 128, 153.

[156] See, for example, the wide views of the US State Department Legal Adviser, Taft 'Self-Defense and the Oil Platforms Decision', 29 Yale Journal of International law (2004) 295. and of the UK Attorney-General, House of Lords debates, 21 April 2004, Hansard Column 370. The latter said that where use of force is used in self-defence in anticipation of an imminent armed attack, 'First, military action should be used only as a last resort. It must be necessary to use force to deal with the particular threat that is faced. Secondly, the force used must be proportionate to the threat faced and must be limited to what is necessary to deal with the threat.'

[157] See 241, 252 below.

[158] There is controversy as to whether self-defence should be immediate, as in the Caroline incident: see Gardam, *Necessity, Proportionality and the Use of Force by States* (2004), at 149–153.

to be unlawful. The General Assembly made this clear in the *Declaration on Friendly Relations* and the *Resolution on the Inadmissibility of Intervention.* The Security Council also passed Resolution 188 in 1964, in response to a British attack on Yemen, but declaring in absolute terms that it condemned reprisals as incompatible with the purposes and principles of the UN. But the distinction between reprisals and self-defence is sometimes problematic in practice.[159]

In the *Nicaragua* case the Court treated these limitations of necessity and proportionality as marginal considerations. That is, the use of force by the USA was first held not to qualify as lawful self-defence on other grounds, then its illegality was confirmed because the actions were not necessary or proportionate. The Court applied the requirements in turn. Even if the supply of arms from Nicaragua to opposition forces in El Salvador had amounted to an armed attack, the measures taken by the USA against Nicaragua were not necessary because they were taken months after the major offensive of the opposition against the government of El Salvador had been completely repulsed. Nor were the US activities relating to the mining of the Nicaraguan ports and attacking oil installations proportionate to the aid received by the Salvadoran opposition from Nicaragua.[160] Thus the questions of necessity and proportionality are dependent on the facts of the particular case.

The inquiry into necessity and proportionality in the *Nicaragua* case was not necessary for the Court's judgment on the merits; the US use of force had already been found to be illegal on other grounds. These criteria of necessity and proportionality were said by the Court to be an additional ground of wrongfulness. The same approach was taken in the *Iranian Oil Platforms* case; having held that the USA had failed to establish that Iran was responsible for an armed attack, the Court also went on to add that the US response was not necessary and proportionate. One aspect to be taken into account in assessing this (as the Court had implicitly done in the *Nicaragua* case) was the nature of the target. In its communications to the Security Council the USA had indicated the grounds on which it regarded the Iranian platforms as legitimate targets for armed action in self-defence. The USA maintained that the platforms were used for collecting intelligence concerning passing vessels and that they acted as a military communication link co-ordinating Iranian naval forces and served as staging bases to launch helicopters and small boat attacks on neutral shipping. Iran acknowledged the presence of military personnel and equipment on some of the platforms, but said that their purpose was exclusively defensive and justified by previous Iraqi attacks on the oil

---

[159] See 153 below.
[160] *Nicaragua* case para 237.

platforms. The Court said that it was not sufficiently convinced that the evidence supported the contentions of the USA, and even if those contentions were accepted the Court was unable to find that the attacks on the platforms could have been justified as acts of self-defence. In the case of the attack on the *Sea Isle City* and the mining of the *Samuel B Roberts* the Court was not satisfied that the attacks on the platforms were necessary to respond to these incidents. There was no evidence that the USA had complained to Iran of the military activities of the platforms, which suggested that the targeting of the platforms was not seen as a necessary act.[161]

The Court gave separate, though brief, consideration to proportionality. It held that the attack of 19 October 1987 might have been proportionate if it had been found to be necessary, but the attacks of 18 April 1988 were conceived and executed as part of a more extensive operation. The Court could not close its eyes to the scale of the whole operation.[162] As a response to a mining by an unidentified agency of a single US warship which was severely damaged but not sunk and without loss of life the operation was not a proportionate use of force in self-defence.[163]

Although the Court found in the operative part of its judgment that there had been no armed attack on the USA and that it had not acted in self-defence when it attacked the oil platforms, the Court did not spell out consequences as some judges would have preferred.[164] It limited itself to concluding that the actions carried out by the USA against Iranian oil installations on 19 October 1987 and 18 April 1988 could not be justified as 'measures necessary to protect the essential security interests' of the USA under Article XX of the Treaty of Amity since those actions constituted recourse to armed force not qualifying under international law as acts of self-defence. As the Court went on to determine that these actions did not in fact interfere with commerce between Iran and the USA it therefore did not specify consequences.

---

[161] ICJ Reports (2003) 161 para 73–6. The US State Department Legal Adviser criticized this statement as unduly restrictive and without basis in international law or practice, Taft, 'Self-Defense and the Oil Platforms Decision', 29 Yale Journal of International law (2004) 295. But it is not clear that the ICJ was laying down a mandatory requirement for all self-defence; rather the fact that the USA had not complained was part of the evidence that it was not necessary to use force against the oil platforms in response to the attacks on the US ships.

[162] ICJ Reports (2003) 161 para 77.

[163] Again the US State Department Legal Adviser was critical, Taft, 'Self-Defense and the Oil Platforms Decision', 29 Yale Journal of International law (2004) 295 at 305. He said that there is no requirement that a state exercising the right of self-defence must use the same degree or type of force used by the attacking state in its most recent attack. Rather the proportionality of the measures is to be judged according to the *threat* being addressed. This is a very wide and controversial view of proportionality and one which will be examined in more detail in Chapter 6.

[164] Those calling for a fuller exposition of the law on the use of force included Judges Simma, Elaraby and Rigaux.

Some judges went further than the Court in holding that these US actions were actually unlawful reprisals as they were not necessary and proportionate.[165] The parties had produced radically opposed arguments on the scope of self-defence and its relation to reprisals. The crucial issue was the characterization of the clashes between Iran and the USA: were they a series of individual incidents or should they be seen as an ongoing conflict? Iran argued that as the USA was not a party in the Iran/Iraq conflict it was necessary to determine whether each single incident of the use of force could be justified as self-defence.[166] It also took a narrow view of self-defence, arguing that it was only available against an armed attack and could not be anticipatory or preventive. Iran set out a four-fold test to determine whether a particular use of force was lawful self-defence or unlawful reprisals;[167] the use of force should be timely, not disproportionate, not premeditated and should be directed against the correct target. Therefore it argued that the US actions were unlawful reprisals because their attacks on the oil platforms took place after the missile and mine had damaged the two ships, involved disproportionate force, were premeditated and because the missile and mine attacks had not originated from the oil platforms.

The USA's official position was that it was neutral in the Iran/Iraq conflict and not itself involved in an ongoing armed conflict with Iran. It was therefore more difficult for it to argue that its use of force was lawful self-defence rather than reprisals. It accordingly tried to argue that the overall pattern of Iran's continuing deadly and illegal use of force must be taken into account in applying the elements of the law of self-defence.[168] It said that the right to self-defence was not limited to repelling an attack while it was in progress. The USA argued that Iran's conception of self-defence was too limited and would embolden aggressor states. A state could also use force to remove continuing threats to future security.[169] But the US position—even if acceptable as between two parties involved in an ongoing conflict—is difficult to maintain where the state claiming such a right is not itself a party. The Court did not have to pronounce on this

---

[165] Judge Simma (Separate Opinion para 15) concluded that the USA used these two incidents to teach Iran a broader lesson: 'nowhere in these materials do we find any trace of the considerations that an international lawyer would regard as necessary in order to justify action taken in self-defence.' Kooijmans (Separate Opinion para 52, 55, 62) found it hard to avoid the impression that in reality a punitive intent prevailed; Judge Elaraby (Dissenting Opinion para 1.2) said that the USA's aim was punitive and that its actions were reprisals; it would have been advisable for the Court to insert a decisive and straightforward statement that defined the legal character of the US use of armed force.
[166] ICJ Pleadings, Iran *Reply* para 7.13–7.22.
[167] ICJ Pleadings, Iran *Memorial*, Part IV at para 4.29.
[168] ICJ Pleadings, US *Counter Memorial* para 4.09.
[169] ICJ Pleadings, US *Counter Memorial* Part IV para 4.21; *Rejoinder* para 5.06.

issue as it found that there was no armed attack by Iran; nevertheless it may be argued that it is implicit in the Court's finding that the US use of force was not necessary that its actions were in fact reprisals.

Most recently the Court in *DRC v Uganda* followed the same approach. After its rejection of Uganda's claim to be acting in self-defence, it said that there was no need for it to inquire into necessity and proportionality. It said only that 'The Court cannot fail to observe that the taking of airports and towns many hundreds of kilometres from Uganda's border would not seem proportionate to the series of transborder attacks it claimed had given rise to the right of self-defence, nor to be necessary to that end.'[170]

The International Court of Justice's approach in these cases – that of treating necessity and proportionality as marginal considerations, to be considered after the legality or otherwise of the use of force had already been established on other grounds – may seem a logical approach, but in state practice generally these factors of necessity and proportionality are often the *only* factors relied on in deciding the legality of particular actions. They constitute a minimum test by which to determine that a use of force does not constitute self-defence. In Security Council debates states have thus been able to avoid going into doctrinal disputes as to whether self-defence is wide or narrow; they can simply say that the use of force was not necessary or proportionate and therefore illegal. Thus, recently, some states were willing to condemn Israel for disproportionate use of force in Lebanon in 2006, even though they did not want to go into the controversial issue as to whether the actions of Hezbollah could constitute an armed attack.[171] Moreover, those states which maintain a controversially wide view of self-defence allowing protection of nationals or anticipatory self-defence are able to make an argument rejecting wide claims to self-defence by other states without undermining their doctrinal position. For example, condemnation of Israel and South Africa for pre-emptive action was possible for states supporting the legality of anticipatory self-defence on the basis that the use of force was not necessary or proportionate on the particular facts.[172]

Necessity and proportionality are also crucial in the rejection by states of the legality of prolonged occupation of territory in the name of

---

[170] ICJ Reports (2005) 168 para 147. Judge Kooijmans partly dissented on this point in his Separate Opinion, para 33–34. He said that the seizure of towns and airports in an area contiguous to the border zone was not unnecessary or disproportionate to the purpose of repelling the persistent attacks of the Ugandan rebel movements.

[171] See 237 below.

[172] See, for example, the US statement with regard to South Africa's pre-emptive action against Angola in 1985, that there is no inherent right to engage in military activity across one's border on the basis that it is a pre-emptive strike. The question is whether it is self-defence, a necessary, reasonable, and proportionate response to the danger posed. In this instance the USA said that it was not: SC 2616th meeting (1985).

self-defence. Thus Israel's presence in South Lebanon from 1978 to 2000 and South Africa's occupation of a buffer zone in Angola from 1981 to 1988 were both claimed to be justified as self-defence and both repeatedly and universally condemned as not necessary or proportionate self-defence.[173] And similarly the use of force in self-defence has not been accepted as a valid root of title to territory.[174]

Accumulation of events

Questions of necessity and proportionality also help states to distinguish unlawful reprisals from lawful self-defence. In cases of repeated cross-border incursions commentators have spoken of the 'accumulation of events' or 'pin prick' theory of armed attack in order to justify an other-wise disproportionate response.[175] That is, they claim that states may use force not in response to each incursion in isolation but to the whole series of incursions as collectively amounting to an armed attack. Such arguments were made by the USA with regard to Vietnam and by Israel, South Africa, and Portugal. Some have claimed that the Security Council has rejected this doctrine of accumulation of events and have criticized it for this.[176] In fact the Security Council has not gone so far. It has certainly condemned disproportionate responses by Israel, Portugal, and South Africa, but as usual the condemnation did not address the doctrinal issue of the scope of self-defence; it could be interpreted as based strictly on the special facts of these cases.[177] The International Court of Justice in the *Nicaragua* case seemed to leave open the possibility of an accumulation of events amounting to an armed attack when it said of the trans-border incursions into Honduras and Costa Rica that 'Very little information is available to the Court as to the circumstances of these incursions or their possible motivations, which renders it difficult to decide whether they may be treated for legal purposes as amounting, singly or collectively, to an armed attack by Nicaragua on either or both States.'[178] Similarly in

[173] On Israel, see 1978 UNYB 295, 306. The Security Council called for Israel to end its occupation in SC Res 425 (1978). On South Africa, see 1982 UNYB 312; the Security Council called for it to withdraw in SC Res 545 (1983); the General Assembly also called for this in GA Res 36/9 (1981).

[174] Jennings, The *Acquisition of Territory in International Law* (1963), 55; Korman, *The Right of Conquest* (1996), 203; Gerson, *Israel, the West Bank and International Law* (1978).

[175] Feder, 'Reading the UN Charter connotatively: toward a new definition of armed attack', 19 New York University Journal of International Law and Politics (1987) 395; Higgins, *The Development of International Law through the Political Organs of the United Nations* (1963), 201.

[176] Levenfeld, 'Israeli counter-fedayeen tactics in Lebanon: Self-Defense and Reprisal under Modern International Law', 21 Columbia Journal of Transnational Law (1982–3) 1.

[177] Higginbottom, 'International Law and the use of force in self-defence and the Southern Africa Conflict', 25 Columbia Journal of Transnational Law (1986–7) 529.

[178] *Nicaragua* case para 231.

Cameroon/Nigeria, Iranian Oil Platforms and *DRC v Uganda* the Court apparently contemplated the possibility of an 'accumulation of events' model of armed attack, but did not discuss this controversial question.

In the first case Cameroon argued that Nigeria was responsible for several frontier incidents; it did not seek a ruling on each individual violation but on the incidents collectively. Nigeria replied that the Court must consider the incidents one by one. It was clear that Cameroon feared that each individual incident would be regarded by the Court as a mere frontier incident not amounting to an armed attack for which Nigeria was responsible. The Court avoided any ruling on the principle; it held that Cameroon had not sufficiently proved the facts or the imputability of the alleged incursions to Nigeria.[179] In the *Iranian Oil Platforms* case the USA also invoked a series of incidents rather than just the attacks on the *Sea Isle City* and the *Samuel B Roberts* in order to justify its use of force against the oil platforms as self-defence. Iran specifically challenged the accumulation of events model of armed attack in its Pleadings,[180] but the Court did not have to address the issue as it found that the USA had not shown that the events amounted to an armed attack on the USA or that they were imputable to Iran.[181] The question also came up in passing in *DRC v Uganda*, but was not investigated by the Court.[182]

Protection of nationals

The use of force to rescue nationals in a foreign state without the consent of that state is uncommon and has been practised by only a few states since the Second World War.[183] Nevertheless, it attracted a vast amount of academic debate. The interventions in Suez (1956), Lebanon (1958), Congo (1960), Dominican Republic (1965), in the *Mayaguez* incident (1975), Entebbe (1976), Iran (1980), Grenada (1983), and Panama (1989) have all been exhaustively discussed.[184] In these episodes all the states using force

---

[179] *Land and Maritime Boundaries between Cameroon and Nigeria*, ICJ Reports (2002) 303 para 323.

[180] ICJ Pleadings, Iran *Reply* para 7.2.

[181] Judge Simma rejected the accumulation of events doctrine: 'Also, there is in international law on the use of force no "qualitative jump" from iterative activities remaining below the threshold of Article 51 of the Charter to the type of "armed attack" envisaged there.' ICJ Reports (2003) 161, Separate Opinion para 14.

[182] ICJ Reports (2005) 168 at para 146.

[183] See Chapter 3 above for further practice where the state using force in protection of nationals claimed consent by the host state.

[184] For early practice on protection of nationals, see Bowett, 'The Use of Force for the Protection of Nationals Abroad', in Cassese (ed.), *The Current Legal Regulation of the Use of Force* (1986), 39; Schweisfurth, 'Operations to Rescue Nationals in Third States', 23 German Yearbook of International Law (1980); Ronzitti, *Rescuing Nationals Abroad* (1985). On Suez see Marston, 'Armed Intervention in the 1956 Suez Canal Crisis: the Legal Advice tendered

invoked self-defence as at least a partial justification for their action. For the most part they expressly referred to Article 51 as covering their operation.[185] That is, these states and those who expressly support them interpret the Charter as allowing the forcible protection not only of a state's territory but also of its nationals abroad. The UK view is typical; it says that 'the better view' is that the justification comes from Article 51 as a form of self-defence: 'An alternative, less satisfactory view is to seek to derive from customary international law a right of intervention to protect nationals.'[186]

The international response to these interventions shows a clear division between states, with few states accepting a legal right to protect nationals abroad. The legal arguments of Belgium, the USA, Israel, and the UK in favour of such a wide right to self-defence have attracted few adherents.[187] The Security Council has generally not taken a collective view or has been prevented by the veto from condemnation.[188] Its debates show the radical divisions between states on the doctrinal issue of the permissibility of the use of force to protect nationals. In the most recent cases the General Assembly condemned the US interventions in Grenada and Panama, but these condemnations were not unequivocal. First, in these particular episodes the US action went far beyond the protection of nationals and the USA offered other justifications for its intervention. In Grenada the US forces argued that US nationals were in danger after a socialist coup, but there was considerable controversy as to the reality of this danger. Moreover, the US forces did not simply rescue the nationals; they remained and oversaw the installation of a new government. To justify its

---

to the British Government' 37 ICLQ (1988) 773; on Entebbe, see *Repertoire of Practice of the Security Council 1975–80*, 286; on the attempted rescue of the Iranian hostages, see Stein, 'Contempt, Crisis and the Court', 76 AJIL (1982) 499; on Grenada, 'Contemporary Practice of the US', 78 AJIL (1984) 200; on Panama, 'Contemporary Practice of the US', 84 AJIL (1990) 545.

[185] With regard to Iran, the USA reported its action to the Security Council under Article 51, *Case concerning United States Diplomatic and Consular Staff in Tehran*, ICJ Reports 1979, at 18. The ICJ did not pronounce on the legality of the US action; Judges Morozov and Tarazi, in their Dissenting Opinions, ICJ Reports 1980, 57, 64, said that the US action was not lawful self-defence. With regard to Grenada, the USA invoked Article 51 (UN doc S/16076, 25 October 1983). With regard to Panama, it invoked Article 51 as giving an inherent right of self-defence to protect American lives (UN doc S/21035, 20 December 1989).

[186] 'UK Materials on International Law', 57 BYIL (1986) 614.

[187] The statements by certain Russian government ministers after the break-up of the former Soviet Union that Russia would intervene using force in the former republics to protect ethnic Russians gave rise to concern rather than support, even from the states that have themselves used force to protect their nationals. It led to concern in the Baltic states and the claim has not been publicly pursued: Keesings (1993) 40513.

[188] On Grenada the draft resolution was defeated by 11–1 (USA) –3 (France, Canada, UK), 1983 UNYB 211. On Panama the draft resolution was defeated by 10–4 (France, UK, USA, Canada) – 1, 1989 UNYB 172 at 174.

intervention the USA used not only protection of nationals but also relied on an invitation by the Governor-General of Grenada and the claim that its action was regional peacekeeping under Chapter VIII of the Charter.[189] In justification of its use of force in Panama the USA put more stress on protection of nationals than it had with regard to Grenada, but its actions clearly went far beyond this. The US forces again installed a new government. Moreover, just as in Grenada, there was controversy as to the existence of actual danger to US nationals. Its other main legal argument was that it was acting to defend the integrity of the Panama Canal Treaties. Therefore the grounds for condemnation of the US use of force were not necessarily based on the rejection of a wide doctrine of self-defence that covered protection of nationals.[190] Second, the condemnations by the General Assembly in these two cases, especially in the case of Panama, were less than overwhelming.[191]

Some writers who seek to justify the use of force in protection of nationals seize on this failure to condemn by the Security Council and the failure to take any action against the state using force.[192] They discount the General Assembly votes and the rejection by a majority of states of such a doctrine. There is a clear division between writers on this question; some see intervention as furthering the purposes of the United Nations and attempt to derive from state practice conditions under which the right may be exercised.[193] Essentially these are all variations on the early version offered by the UK over its intervention in Suez in 1956. It said that the relevant conditions were: (a) whether there is an imminent threat of injury to nationals; (b) whether there is a failure or inability on the part of the territorial sovereign to protect the nationals in question; and (c) whether the measures of protection are strictly confined to the object of protecting them against injury.[194] On the other side are those writers who regard

---

[189] For the USA justification for Grenada, see 1983 UNYB 211, UN doc S/16076, 25 October 1983; SC 2487th, 2489th, 2491st meetings (1983). Gilmore, *The Grenada Intervention* (1984); Weiler, 'Armed Intervention in a Dichotomized World: The Case of Grenada', in Cassese (ed.), *Current Legal Regulation of the Use of Force* (1986), 241.

[190] For the USA justification for Panama, see UN doc S/21035, 20 December 1989; 84 AJIL (1990) 545. Contrasting assessments of the intervention are given by Henkin, 'The Invasion of Panama under International Law: a Gross Violation', 29 Columbia Journal of Transnational Law (1991) 293 and D'Amato, 'The Invasion of Panama was a Lawful Response to Tyranny,' 84 AJIL (1990) 516.

[191] GA Res 38/7 on Grenada was passed by 108–9–27, 1983 UNYB at 214; GA Res 44/240 on Panama was passed by 75–20–40, 1989 UNYB 175.

[192] Arend and Beck, *International Law and the Use of Force: Beyond the UN Charter Paradigm* (1993), 107–110; Franck, *Recourse to Force* (2002) 76–96.

[193] Bowett, 'The Use of Force for the Protection of Nationals Abroad', in Cassese (ed.), *The Current Legal Regulation of the Use of Force* (1986), 39; Dinstein, (4th edn, 2005) 231 *War, Aggression and Self-Defense* (3rd edn 2001), 203.

[194] Marston, 'Armed Intervention in the 1956 Suez Canal Crisis: the Legal Advice tendered to the British Government', 37 ICLQ (1988) 773 at 795, 800.

intervention to protect nationals as of doubtful value in furthering the purposes of the United Nations as it may be a pretext for intervention and cause more harm than it prevents.[195]

Irrespective of the doctrinal divide, most of the above interventions clearly could not be justified as protection of nationals because the action was not necessary or proportionate and was really a pretext for intervention. Only the rescue operation of the *Mayaguez*, and those in Iran and Entebbe were limited actions; in Suez, the Dominican Republic, Grenada, and Panama the interventions were prolonged and the states using force added further justifications.

In recent practice there have been various instances of states sending in troops to extract nationals and others from dangerous situations where a state was involved in a civil war or domestic unrest. The USA sent troops into Liberia in 1990,[196] the Central African Republic in 1996,[197] Sierra Leone in 1997,[198] Côte d'Ivoire in 2002[199] and Haiti in 2004;[200] France and Belgium intervened in Rwanda in 1990, 1993, and 1994;[201] France intervened in the Central African Republic,[202] Côte d'Ivoire[203] and Liberia in 2002-3,[204] and in Chad in 2006.[205] Many states evacuated their nationals from Lebanon after the Israeli invasion in 2006.[206] However, with regard to these recent episodes, issues of legality have not been raised in the United Nations. The state using force has not reported it to the Security Council under Article 51 and the state where the intervention took place did not raise the matter. Nor did other states protest about the use of force. These can therefore be seen as cases of consent or perhaps implied consent by the government to the rescue operation. But many of these cases occurred when there was no effective government: the previous government had been overthrown and the state was in confusion. It seems that third states were willing to acquiesce in the forcible evacuation of nationals; their concern is roused only with regard to those rescue missions where the

---

[195] Brownlie, *International Law and the Use of Force by States* (1963), 432; Akehurst, 'Humanitarian Intervention', in Bull (ed.), *Intervention in World Politics* (1984), 95; Ronzitti, *Rescuing Nationals Abroad* (1985).

[196] Lillich, 'Forcible protection of nationals abroad: the Liberian incident of 1990', 35 German YIL (1992) 205; Weller, *Regional Peace-Keeping and International Enforcement: The Liberian Crisis* (1994), 63-5, 85.

[197] Keesings (1996) 41080.

[198] Keesings (1997) 41626.

[199] *The Guardian*, 25 and 26 September 2002.

[200] *The Guardian*, 26 February 2004.

[201] Keesings (1990) 37765-6, (1993) 39304, (1994) 39943-4.

[202] Keesings (2003) 45276; Chad also rescued its nationals, *The Guardian*, 17, 20 March 2003.

[203] Keesings (2002) 44968, 45026, 45131, (2003) 45230; UN doc S/2003/374.

[204] Keesings (2003) 45452.

[205] Keesings (2006) 47188, 47445, 47563.

[206] Keesings (2006) 47389.

territorial state objects to the intervention or where the protection of the nationals was just a pretext for an invasion with wider objectives.

Moreover, this may be a topic of mainly historical interest. There have been no significant instances of use of force to rescue nationals in the last ten years.[207] The underlying question as to whether an attack on nationals abroad can constitute an attack on a state remains important in the context of the 'war on terror'.[208]

Anticipatory self-defence before the 'Bush doctrine'

The same states – the USA, Israel and the UK – that claim a right under Article 51 to protect their nationals abroad also claim or defend the right to use force, even before their territory or units of their armed forces abroad are actually attacked, if an attack is imminent.[209] The majority of states reject anticipatory self-defence. The divisions between states as to the scope of the right of self-defence meant that no detailed provisions on self-defence could be included in General Assembly resolutions such as the *Declaration on Friendly Relations*, the *Definition of Aggression*, and the *Declaration on the Non-Use of Force*. It is interesting that those states which argued that self-defence is permissible only against an armed attack made this argument expressly, whereas those states who took a wider view of self-defence adopted a low profile and simply resisted the inclusion of any detailed provisions.[210] Also in the ILC work on state responsibility when self-defence was considered as a circumstance precluding wrongfulness, the states taking a wide view of self-defence argued that the ILC should not try to define the scope of self-defence; they did not actually send in comments in favour of anticipatory self-defence.[211] These differences persist today, as was apparent in the debates leading up to the 2005 World Summit.[212]

---

[207] Though this doctrine has been invoked in rather bizarre form in the *American Servicemembers' Protection Act* (2002) para 3008 (popularly called the Hague Invasion Act); this authorized the US President to use all necessary means to bring about the release of American nationals detained by the International Criminal Court at the Hague. The US government's hostility to the ICC apparently led it to claim a right to use force in protection of nationals, 96 AJIL (2002) 975; *The Washington Times*, 5 July 2002.

[208] See Chapter 6 below.

[209] The UK Attorney-General formally reasserted the longstanding UK support for this position in 54 ICLQ (2005) 767; see also his recent statement to the House of Lords, Hansard House of Lords Debate, 21 April 2004, Columns 369–370. The US position is set out in the 2002 US *National Security Strategy* at 15.

[210] Ferencz, 'Defining Aggression: Where it stands and where it's going', 66 AJIL (1972) 491; Gray, 'The Principle of Non-Use of Force', in Lowe and Warbrick (eds), *The United Nations and the Principles of International Law* (1994, 33.

[211] Cot and Pellet, *La Charte des Nations Unies* (1991), 779.

[212] See Ghafur Hamid, 'The legality of anticipatory self-defence in the 21st century world order', 54 Netherlands International Law Review (2007) 441; Gray, 'A Crisis of Legitimacy for the UN Collective Security System?', 56 ICLQ (2007) 157.

Moreover, the actual invocation of the right to anticipatory self-defence in practice is rare. States clearly prefer to rely on self-defence in response to an armed attack if they possibly can. They prefer to take a wide view of armed attack rather than openly claim anticipatory self-defence. It is only where no conceivable case can be made that there has been an armed attack that they resort to anticipatory self-defence. This reluctance expressly to invoke anticipatory self-defence is in itself a clear indication of the doubtful status of this justification for the use of force. States take care to try to secure the widest possible support; they do not invoke a doctrine that they know will be unacceptable to the vast majority of states. Certain writers, however, ignore this choice by states and argue that if states in fact act in anticipation of an armed attack this should count as anticipatory self-defence in state practice. This is another example of certain writers going beyond what states themselves say in justification of their action in order to try to argue for a wide right of self-defence.[213]

Thus in 1967 Israel launched what was apparently a pre-emptive strike against Egypt, Jordan, and Syria, but it did not seek to rely on anticipatory self-defence. It argued that the actions of the Arab states in fact amounted to prior armed attack. For example, in the Security Council debates Israel claimed that the blocking by Egypt of the Straits of Tiran to passage by Israeli vessels amounted to an act of war; it was an armed attack justifying self-defence under Article 51. Some states rejected this claim and ruled out the legality of anticipatory use of force; some said that it was not productive to apportion blame; even those supporting the Israeli action did not expressly give their backing to its claim that it had been the victim of a prior attack.[214] But, whatever position is taken on the facts of the outbreak of the Six Day War,[215] the point of importance here is that Israel did not rely on anticipatory self-defence to justify its actions.

Again in the 1962 Cuban missile crisis, when Cuba was proposing to import nuclear missiles from the USSR, the USA did not rely on anticipatory self-defence to justify its forcible interception of the missiles on the high seas; rather, it relied on regional peacekeeping under

---

[213] Both Alexandrov, *Self-Defense against the Use of Force in International Law* (1996) and Arend and Beck, *International Law and the Use of Force: Beyond the UN Charter Paradigm* (1993), include a very wide range of incidents under the heading collective self-defence; they do not restrict themselves to those episodes where states actually invoked the doctrine. The latter make the unusual argument that a great many states are for anticipatory self-defence. They base this on the states using force and are extremely selective in their choice of practice; they do not refer to all the statements of states against their position.

[214] 1967 UNYB 166, 174, 196; Pogany, *The Security Council and the Arab-Israeli Conflict* (1984).

[215] It is the subject of much controversy whether the government of Israel genuinely believed that Arab states were about to mount an imminent attack: see, for example, Shlaim, *The Iron Wall: Israel and the Arab World* (2001) and Oren, *Six Days of War* (2002) for contrasting accounts.

Chapter VIII of the UN Charter.[216] And in the Iran/Iraq war Iraq first began its justification for its invasion of Iran in 1980 by relying on preventive self-defence, but quickly shifted its position and claimed to be acting in response to a prior armed attack by Iran; this remained its position and this was the view that it put in response to the Secretary-General's report on the responsibility for the conflict.[217]

The USA, in its attempt to justify the shooting down by the *USS Vincennes* of the civilian Iran Airbus Flight 655 in July 1988 during the Iran/Iraq war, made elaborate argument that its action had been part of an ongoing battle and that it was engaged in a response to an armed attack by Iran.[218] It said that its forces had exercised self-defence under international law by responding to an attack by Iran: Iranian aircraft had fired on a helicopter from the *USS Vincennes*, then Iranian patrol boats had closed in. In the course of exercising its right to self-defence the *USS Vincennes* fired at what it believed to be a hostile Iranian military aircraft after sending repeated warnings. It is very striking that the USA did not expressly rely on anticipatory self-defence, even though its rules of engagement had been altered to allow its forces to take action against enemy ships and aircraft displaying 'hostile intent'.[219] The USA maintained the same position in its arguments to the International Court of Justice in the *Aerial Incident* case arising out of the shooting down of the Iran Airbus.[220] Iran argued that Article 51 does not allow pre-emptive self-defence and that the US action amounted to aggression.[221] Many other states also took this approach. The UK offered support for the US action in general terms, but did not expressly support anticipatory self-defence.[222]

The USA and the UK (and France until 1996), in patrolling the 'no-fly' zones over Iraq, claimed the right to use force in self-defence. After the establishment of the northern zone in 1991 and the southern zone in 1993 there were many clashes between US and UK aircraft and Iraqi aircraft and ground defences. Iraq denied the legality of the 'no-fly' zones; in this it was supported by Russia and China and other states who said that the USA and

---

[216] Alexandrov, *Self-Defense against the Use of Force in International Law* (1996) at 154 uses these as examples of anticipatory self-defence despite the choice of the USA and Israel not to invoke this doctrine. Chayes, 'Law and the Quarantine of Cuba', 41 Foreign Affairs (1963) 550.

[217] 1980 UNYB 312. For Iraq's reaction to the Secretary-General's Report, see 1991 UNYB 165.

[218] SC 2818th meeting (1988); UN doc S/19989, 6 July 1988; 1988 UNYB 199; see also Gray, 'The British Position with regard to the Gulf Conflict', 37 ICLQ (1988) 464.

[219] 26 ILM (1987) 1422 at 1454.

[220] ICJ Pleadings, *Aerial Incident* case, Vol II. The USA argued that the incident of Iran Air Flight 655 could not be separated from the events that preceded it. The case was settled in 1996.

[221] ICJ Pleadings, *Aerial Incident* case, Vol I, 91, 212.

[222] SC 2818th meeting (1988).

the UK acted unilaterally and without Security Council authorization in establishing the zones. In 1999 the USA and the UK significantly extended the rules of engagement for their aircraft; they were now to take pre-emptive action against Iraq's air defences. Not only the direct source of an attack, such as a missile site, but any threat to aircraft, such as a command centre, could be targeted.[223] However, the USA and the UK continued to insist that their actions were purely defensive. Their legal position remained that the military actions were taken to ensure the safety of aircraft patrolling the zone in support of Security Council Resolution 688; once a no-fly zone was authorized in accordance with international law it was entirely appropriate to act in self-defence to ensure the safety of those who were imposing the no-fly zone.[224] In Security Council debates on Iraq discussion focused on the legality of the no-fly zones; Russia, China, and Iraq condemned the US and UK actions on the fundamental basis that there was no legal basis for the no-fly zones and therefore no justification for the presence of US and UK aircraft and no right for them to act in self-defence.[225]

Very occasionally states have expressly used anticipatory self-defence. As was mentioned above, Israel and South Africa both claimed the right to take 'pre-emptive action' against incursions from neighbouring states. These claims were expressly rejected by some states on the ground that anticipatory self-defence was unlawful. Other states used other grounds for condemnation. Therefore authoritative pronouncements on the issue of principle—the legality of anticipatory self-defence—were avoided in these cases by the Security Council and the General Assembly.

Israel, in its 1981 attack on the Iraqi nuclear reactor, claimed anticipatory self-defence. It said that it had acted to remove a nuclear threat to its existence; the Iraqi reactor under construction was designed to produce nuclear bombs whose target would have been Israel. Under no circumstances would Israel allow an enemy to develop weapons of mass destruction against it. In the Security Council debate it relied on a series of writers to support its position that anticipatory defence was lawful. But significantly Israel was not able to rely on any clear state practice to support its position.[226] In none of these cases did the Security Council make any

---

[223] Keesings (1999) 42754, 42811, 42866, 42917, 42972, 43036; (2000) 43492, 43542.

[224] For an early statement of this position, see 'UK Materials on International Law', 64 BYIL (1993) 728; more recently, 'Contemporary Practice of the United States Relating to International Law', 94 AJIL (2000) 102; 'UK Materials on International Law', 73 BYIL (2002) 861 at 867.

[225] SC 4084th meeting (1999). For more recent practice, see Gray, 'From Unity to Polarization: International Law and the Use of Force against Iraq', 13 EJIL (2002) 1 at 16.

[226] 1981 UNYB 275; Israel explained its action in UN doc S/14510, 8 June 1981; in the Security Council debates Israel referred to writers in support of the doctrine of anticipatory self-defence: SC 2280th meeting (1981) at para 98, 99, 100; SC 2288th meeting (1981) at para 38. The General Assembly voted to condemn Israel's action as a premeditated and

pronouncement on doctrine; the debates again revealed the divisions between states on the law in this area. The USA, in allowing the condemnation of Israel by the Security Council, said that its judgment that Israel's actions violated the Charter was based solely on the conviction that Israel had failed to exhaust peaceful means for the resolution of the dispute. Others said that the action was not justified on the particular facts, given that the IAEA said that there was no evidence that Iraq was planning to use the reactor for the development of nuclear weapons. Other states rejected anticipatory self-defence in principle.[227]

This reluctance to rely on anticipatory self-defence even by the USA and Israel is not conclusive that they did not believe that it was legal, as it is natural for states to choose the strongest grounds to justify their claims, but it is convincing evidence of the controversial status of this justification for the use of force, as is the deliberate avoidance of the issue of the legality of anticipatory self-defence by the International Court of Justice in the *Nicaragua* case and more recently in *Armed Activities on the Territory of the Congo (DRC v Uganda)*. In *DRC v Uganda* the Court recalled that Uganda had insisted that Operation Safe Haven was not a use of force against an anticipated attack. The Court therefore expressed no view on that issue.[228] However, some of its subsequent reasoning seems to indicate a narrow view of self-defence which would exclude pre-emptive action. Thus, the Court observed that the official Ugandan document on the conflict made no reference whatever to armed attacks which had already occurred against Uganda. Rather the position of the Ugandan High Command was that it was necessary to 'secure Uganda's legitimate security interests'. The specified security interests were essentially preventative—to ensure that the political vacuum in the DRC did not adversely affect Uganda, to prevent attacks from genocidal elements, to be in a position to safeguard Uganda from irresponsible threats of invasion and to deny the Sudan the opportunity to use the territory of the DRC to destabilize Uganda.[229] The Court said that Article 51 may justify a use of force in self-defence only within the strict confines there laid down. It does not allow the use of force by a state to protect perceived security interests beyond these parameters. Other means are available to a concerned state, including, in particular, recourse to the Security Council.[230]

---

unprecedented act of aggression in GA Res 36/27 (1981) (109–2–34). Many of those who abstained said that they did so because it was for the Security Council rather than the General Assembly to act. D'Amato defended the legality of the use of force: 'Israel's Air Strike upon the Iraqi Nuclear Reactor', 77 AJIL (1983) 584.

[227] SC 2288th meeting (1981) para 156.
[228] *Nicaragua* case para 194; *DRC v Uganda*, ICJ Reports (2005) 168 para 143.
[229] ICJ Reports (2005) 168 para 143.
[230] Ibid., at para 148. For further discussion of the debate on pre-emptive self-defence, see Chapter 6.

In practice states prefer to argue for an extended interpretation of armed attack and to avoid the fundamental doctrinal debate. The clear trend in state practice before 9/11 was to try to bring their use of force within Article 51 and to claim the existence of an armed attack rather than to argue expressly for a wider right under customary international law. This practice, the cautious approach of the ICJ and the clear and long-standing divisions between states on this issue make it all the more surprising that the High-level Panel set up by the UN Secretary-General[231] proclaimed in its December 2004 Report that 'Long-established customary international law makes it clear that States can take military action as long as the threatened attack is imminent, no other means would deflect it, and the action is proportionate.'[232] As we have seen, this is actually an extremely controversial assertion. Nevertheless the Secretary-General in his own subsequent report of March 2005, *In Larger Freedom*, asserted that imminent threats are fully covered by Article 51: 'lawyers have long accepted that this covers an imminent attack as well as one that has already happened'.[233] The Secretary-General's statement is marginally less controversial in that he refers to 'lawyers' rather than 'customary international law' as accepting the doctrine of anticipatory self-defence. He also tries to argue that self-defence against an imminent attack comes within the words of Article 51, rather than accepting the High-level Panel's more controversial position that a wider customary international law right survives. These statements did not attract wide support from states: the Non-Aligned Movement (now with 118 member states) rejected this position.[234] And the 2005 World Summit for which the two reports had been prepared not surprisingly avoided the issue in its Outcome Document.[235] It is clear that states remain fundamentally divided on this question.

CONCLUSION

The picture that emerges is one of polarization. Before 9/11 few states claimed very wide rights of self-defence to protect nationals, anticipate attack, or to respond to terrorist and other past attacks.[236] It seems that the lesson they learned from the judgment in the *Nicaragua* case was that

---

[231] See 3 above.
[232] UN doc A/59/565 (2004) at 188–92.
[233] UN doc A/59/2005, 21 March 2005, para 124.
[234] NAM Comments on the High-level Panel Report, 28 February 2005; <www.un.int/malaysia/NAM/NAM/html> para 26–28, UN doc A/59/PV.85, 14–15. The NAM repeated its view that Article 51 is a restrictive provision at its 2006 Havana Conference, UN doc S/2006/780, 29 September 2006, para 19.
[235] UN doc A/60/L.70, 15 September 2005.
[236] See Chapter 6 below.

form is more important than substance. As long as they pay lip-service to the need to act in self-defence, and as long as they report to the Security Council invoking the magical reference to Article 51, somehow their action acquires a veneer of legality and their argument will be treated seriously by commentators. A few of these commentators seem prepared to treat any US action as a precedent creating new legal justification for the use of force.[237] Thus they use the US actions as shifting the Charter paradigm and extending the right of self-defence. The lack of effective action against the USA as a sanction confirms them in this view. But the vast majority of other states remained firmly attached to a narrow conception of self-defence. This long-standing disagreement between states on interpretation of the UN Charter seemed beyond resolution, and states accordingly sought to avoid doctrinal dispute by appealing to doctrines, such as necessity and proportionality, on which there was universal agreement where at all possible. It is likely that this approach will survive the impact of 9/11.[238]

---

[237] Arend and Beck, *International Law and the Use of Force* (1993); Weisburd, *The Use of Force* (1997); D'Amato, *Prospect and Process* (2nd edn 1995).
[238] See Chapter 6 below.

5

Collective self-defence

It is well known that there is comparatively little practice on the use of force in collective self-defence; states have generally avoided direct and open military participation by their armed forces in conflicts between other states. The relatively large number of treaties on collective self-defence is not matched by extensive state practice.[1] Commentators list the following instances where states have actually invoked collective self-defence: USA and Lebanon (1958), UK and Jordan (1958), UK and South Arabian Federation (1964), USA and Vietnam (1961–75), USSR and Hungary (1956),[2] Czechoslovakia (1968), Afghanistan (1979), France and Chad (1983–4, 1986), USA and others and Kuwait (1990). More recently, the right was invoked by the government of the DRC in support of its request to Angola, Namibia and Zimbabwe for military assistance against Rwanda and Uganda in 1998.[3] It was also invoked to justify *Operation Enduring Freedom* in Afghanistan.[4] But this cannot be taken as a definitive list; different commentators produce different lists.[5] Controversially, some

---

[1] The main multilateral treaties are the NATO Treaty (1949) 34 UNTS 243; the (now defunct) Warsaw Pact (1955) 219 UNTS 24; the Rio Treaty (1947) 21 UNTS 77; the Security Treaty between Australia/New Zealand/USA (1951) 131 UNTS 83; South East Asia Collective Defense Treaty (1954) 209 UNTS 20; the Baghdad Pact (1955) 233 UNTS 199; Pact of the Arab League (1945) 70 UNTS 237; Arab League Treaty of Joint Defence (1955) 49 AJIL Supplement (1955) 51; Commonwealth of Independent States Collective Security Treaty (1992); African Union Non-Aggression and Common Defence pact (2005), not yet in force; EU Treaty of Lisbon (2007) Article 28A7. There are also hundreds of bilateral treaties which provide for collective self-defence. On the more than 60 Soviet bloc treaties made in the 1970s, see Zipfel, *Die Freundschafts und Kooperationsverträge der Kommunistischen Staaten* (1983). The USA, the UK and France each have an extensive network of treaties. On French treaties, see Keesings (1996) 41402. For a discussion of the different types of collective self-defence treaty, see Dinstein, *War, Aggression and Self-Defence* (4th edn, 2005) 256.

[2] The inclusion of the Soviet intervention in Hungary as an instance of collective self-defence being invoked by a state is very doubtful; apart from a reference to the intervention being in accordance with the Warsaw Treaty, the USSR did not refer to collective self-defence to justify its action (1956 UNYB 67).

[3] See 68 above.

[4] See 203 below.

[5] Cot and Pellet (eds), *La Charte des Nations Unies* (1991), 787; Alexandrov, *Self-Defence Against the Use of Force in International Law* (1996), 216. It is noteworthy that this list is exclusively collective self-defence of territory. The issue of collective self-defence of ships at sea came up in the Iran–Iraq conflict when the USA, on 29 April 1988, decided to extend the protection offered by its naval forces in the Gulf to friendly neutral vessels. It announced that, following a request from the vessel under attack, assistance would be rendered by a US warship or aircraft. It used this power twice in 1988 to protect a Danish and a Panamanian vessel, but apparently did not expressly rely on collective self-defence; it spoke of assistance to vessels in distress, following a request from the vessel under attack: Gray, 'The British

add the UN-authorized actions in Korea and Iraq as further examples of collective self-defence.[6]

The above list includes some episodes where collective self-defence was invoked and foreign troops were introduced into the 'victim' state requesting assistance, but force was not used in actual conflict, or was not used beyond the national border of the victim state. States have invoked collective self-defence as a justification for inviting in foreign troops before any armed attack has occurred, in case collective self-defence is needed in the future; that is, as a deterrent or as a precaution. The sending of troops and the provision of other aid has been much more common than the use of those troops in actual fighting against an attacking state. The US use of force against North Vietnam, Cambodia, and Laos in the name of the collective self-defence of South Vietnam and the US use of force against Nicaragua (in the name of collective self-defence of El Salvador, Costa Rica, and Honduras) are exceptional in that the USA used force outside the 'victim' state.

That is, although in theory there is a distinction between collective self-defence and assistance in reply to an invitation by a government to respond to external intervention against that government, in practice the line may not be a clear one.[7] The states sending in their troops make choices as to the justification they offer. They may invoke collective self-defence before it is actually necessary and conversely they do not always expressly invoke collective self-defence even when a case could be made for it on the basis that there has been or might be an armed attack.

Thus, for example, Ethiopia, the USSR and Cuba all tended to play down the presence of Soviet and Cuban troops in Ethiopia (1977–78) even though there had been an armed attack by Somalia into the Ogaden region of Ethiopia after the overthrow of Emperor Haile Selassie, and the armed response by Ethiopia was limited to driving out the invading forces.[8] Also with regard to the collective self-defence of Angola against attacks by South Africa, Cuba at first simply stressed that it had been invited in by the MPLA, which subsequently formed the government on the coming to

Position with regard to the Gulf Conflict (Iran–Iraq): Part 2', 40 ICLQ (1991) 465 at 468. See de Guttry and Ronzitti, *The Iran–Iraq War (1980–1988) and the Law of Naval Warfare* (1993), 196, 304. When this case went to the ICJ the USA did not invoke collective self-defence as justification for its use of force (*Case Concerning Oil Platforms*, ICJ Reports (2003) 161, para 51).

[6] Alexandrov, *Self-Defense Against the Use of Force in International Law* (1996) at 252; he also includes regional action under this heading of collective self-defence. See also Dinstein, *War, Aggression and Self-defence* (4th edn, 2005) 273.

[7] Mullerson, 'Intervention by Invitation', in Damrosch and Scheffer (eds), *Law and Force in the New International Order* (1991), 127; Diaz Barrado, *El Consentimiento, Causa de Exclusion de la Ilicitud del Uso de la Fuerza en Derecho Internacional* (1989), 78.

[8] Keesings (1978) 28760, 28989. A Friendship Treaty was concluded between the USSR and Ethiopia in November 1978: Keesings (1979) 29435.

independence of Angola in 1975. Angola referred to Article 51 in relation to the presence of the Cuban troops only from 1983, after the issue of 'linkage' had become more prominent. On the basis of 'linkage', South Africa argued that its withdrawal from Namibia was linked to that of Cuba from Angola, thus implying an equivalence between the two situations. Angola replied that the Cuban presence had been requested by the legitimate government of Angola for the clear and express objective of repulsing the open and flagrant invasion by South Africa. The first invasion (in 1975) was repulsed by the Angolan people with the assistance of Cuban troops, but South African aggression had continued. There was a continued need for the assistance of Cuban forces in full conformity with Article 51, as every state has the right to individual or collective self-defence.[9]

All the episodes listed above pre-date the judgment in the *Nicaragua* case.[10] After the judgment the USA occasionally again invoked collective self-defence against Nicaragua in Central America.[11] And subsequently claims to collective self-defence to justify the use of force in defence of Kuwait,[12] Tajikistan,[13] and the DRC[14] again reveal the complexity of such claims. The legality of the third state use of force was controversial in almost all these cases, both those before and those after the *Nicaragua* case, but the disagreements between states on the legality of these uses of force have generally centred on the facts rather than the law. In almost all these cases the controversy concerned the question whether there had been an armed attack and also whether there had been a genuine request for help by the victim state. In contrast, *Operation Enduring Freedom* in Afghanistan did raise fundamental legal questions about the concept of 'armed attack'.[15]

[9] For example, SC 2481st meeting (1983), 2565th meeting (1984). On the history of Cuban involvement in Angola, see *Repertoire of the Practice of the Security Council 1975–1980*, 260. The Security Council expressly rejected the doctrine of linkage; see, for example, SC Res 539 (1983).

[10] *Case concerning Military and Paramilitary Activities in and against Nicaragua*, 1986 ICJ Reports 14 (hereafter *Nicaragua* case).

[11] For example, 1988 UNYB 170; SC 2800th, SC 2802nd meetings (1988), UN doc A/42/931.

[12] The USA and the UK invoked collective self-defence after the Iraqi invasion of Kuwait in 1990 to justify their naval operations undertaken after the imposition of an economic embargo on Iraq but before the specific authorization of force by the Security Council. Kuwait and other states in the region requested third state assistance, and Kuwait reported its action under Article 51 to the Security Council (UN Publications, *The UN and the Iraq–Kuwait Conflict 1990–1996* at 16.) The USA and the UK imposed a 'naval interdiction' to stop ships violating the embargo. In this instance controversy over legality centred on the question whether the USA and the UK were entitled to act after the imposition of an economic embargo without Security Council authority. See Warbrick, 'The invasion of Kuwait by Iraq', 40 ICLQ (1991) 482, 964; Greenwood, 'New World Order or Old?', 55 MLR (1992) 153 at 161, 164–5.

[13] On Tajikistan, see 175 below.

[14] See 68 above.

[15] See 199 below.

On the whole, however, the states directly involved and those responding to their use of force through international organizations have not disagreed as to the *content* of the applicable law. This may seem surprising, given that the theory of collective self-defence has been controversial since the debate over its express inclusion in the UN Charter. Collective self-defence was included at the instance of the Latin American states to make clear the compatibility of the existing American system and the new UN system. After prolonged debate, collective self-defence was included in Chapter VII on the powers of the Security Council rather than in Chapter VIII on regional arrangements.[16] There has subsequently been controversy as to whether collective self-defence was a new concept when it was included in the Charter in 1945.[17] Some of the judges in the *Nicaragua* case took the view that it was an innovation. Thus, for example, Judge Oda said that the term 'collective self-defence' was unknown before 1945 and therefore expressed doubt as to whether it was an inherent right.[18] Judge Jennings agreed that it was a novel concept.[19] Whether or not collective self-defence was a totally new concept, the post-1945 practice has been crucial in the crystallization of the concept.

Early debates on Article 51 of the UN Charter focused on whether collective self-defence was an autonomous right allowing any third state to use force in defence of the victim of an armed attack, or whether it was a collection of rights to individual self-defence only to be exercised if the third state was itself a victim or if the interests of the third state were somehow engaged.[20] What were the conditions for its exercise: did it require a pre-existing treaty arrangement for collective action? Some argued that there was a need of prior agreement for collective self-defence, otherwise the use of force would be contrary to the spirit of Article 51;[21]

---

[16] Judge Oda and Judge Schwebel go into the history of the drafting of the UN Charter provisions on collective self-defence in their Dissenting Opinions, 1986 ICJ Reports 212 at para 91–6; 266 at para 194. See also Alexandrov, *Self-Defense Against the Use of Force in International Law* (1996) at 90; Franck, *Recourse to Force* (2002) at 48.

[17] Brownlie, *International Law and the Use of Force by States* (1963), 328, 229–30; Higgins, *The Development of International Law through the Political Organs of the United Nations* (1963), 208; Kelsen, *Law of the United Nations* (1950) at 793, Delivanis, *La légitime défense en droit international public moderne* (1971), Chapter 2; Macdonald, 'The Nicaragua case: New Answers to Old Questions', 1986 Canadian Yearbook of International Law 127 at 143.

[18] Oda, Dissenting Opinion at 253, paras. 90–7.

[19] Jennings, Dissenting Opinion at 530–1.

[20] Alexandrov, *Self-Defense Against the Use of Force in International Law* (1996) at 101; Higgins, *The Development of International Law through the Political Organs of the United Nations* (1963) at 208; see also *Nicaragua* case, Jennings, Dissenting Opinion at 544–6.

[21] Delivanis, *La légitime défense en droit international public moderne* (1971), Part II, Chapter 2; Kulski, 'The Soviet System of Collective Security compared with the Western System', 1950 (44) AJIL 453.

other writers like McDougal insisted on a common interest rather than a pre-existing treaty.[22]

THE *NICARAGUA* CASE

The ICJ decision in the *Nicaragua* case on the legality of the US use of force and intervention in Nicaragua renewed the passion of the debate on the scope of collective self-defence. The judgment has been much attacked and much misinterpreted. It plays a crucial role in this area. The Court's decision, its first extended discussion of the law on the use of force, was based on customary international law because of the US reservation to its Optional Clause acceptance. The Court found that the US multilateral treaty reservation prevented it from applying the UN Charter and other multilateral treaties, such as the OAS Charter and the Rio Treaty, which in fact bound the parties. However, the reservation did not stop the Court from deciding the case on the basis of customary international law, which continued to exist alongside treaty law.[23] Moreover, the Court could properly adjudicate because the provisions of multilateral treaties did not diverge from customary international law to such an extent that a judgment of the Court on custom would be a wholly pointless exercise. The Court went on to say that, although it had no jurisdiction to determine whether the conduct of the USA constituted a breach of the Charter of the UN and that of the OAS, it could and must take them into account in ascertaining the content of customary international law.[24]

The Court's exposition of the law on collective self-defence, the justification used by the USA to support its use of force and intervention in and against Nicaragua, was relatively brief. The parties, in view of the circumstances in which the dispute had arisen, had relied only on the right of self-defence in the case of an armed attack which had already occurred;

---

[22] McDougal and Feliciano, *Law and Minimum World Public Order* (1961); Bowett, *Self-Defence in International Law* (1958), 216.

[23] *Nicaragua* case paras 172–6.

[24] Ibid., para 183. Judge Ago expressed 'serious reservations with regard to the seeming facility with which the Court – while expressly denying that all the customary rules are identical in content to the rules in the treaties – has nevertheless concluded in respect of certain key matters that there is a virtual identity of content as between customary international law and the law enshrined in certain major multilateral treaties' (Separate Opinion at 183, para 6). Judge Jennings was similarly sceptical as to whether custom could have developed since the adoption of the UN Charter on the basis of the rules in the Charter (Dissenting Opinion at 531). Other judges in their Separate Opinions argued that the US multilateral treaty reservation should not be given any effect and that the Court could apply the UN Charter and other multilateral treaties (Judge Sette Camara, Separate Opinion 192; Judge Ni, Separate Opinion 201).

the lawfulness of a response to the imminent threat of armed attack was not raised.[25] Also the parties agreed that any exercise of self-defence must be necessary and proportionate. The Court accordingly went on to define the other specific conditions which had to be met for the exercise of collective self-defence.[26]

First, the Court considered what constituted an armed attack: the sending of armed bands rather than regular army could constitute an armed attack, provided that the scale and effects of the operation were such as to be classified as an armed attack and not a mere frontier incident. Assistance to rebels in the form of the provision of weapons or logistical or other support could amount to a threat or use of force or intervention, but did not constitute an armed attack.[27] Second, 'it is also clear that it is the State which is the victim of the armed attack which must form and declare the view that it has been so attacked. There is no rule in customary international law permitting another state to exercise the right of collective self-defence on the basis of its own assessment of the situation. Where collective self-defence is invoked, it is to be expected that the State for whose benefit this right is used will have declared itself to be the victim of an armed attack.'[28] Third, the Court held that 'there is no rule permitting the exercise of collective self-defence in the absence of a request by the State which regards itself as the victim of an armed attack'.[29] The Court also held that the requirement in Article 51 of the UN Charter that the state claiming to use the right of individual or collective self-defence must report to the Security Council was not a customary law requirement, although 'the absence of a report may be one of the factors indicating whether the state in question was itself convinced that it was acting in self-defence'.[30]

The Court was criticized for its treatment of collective self-defence in the separate and dissenting opinions on contrasting grounds. Judge Ruda

---

[25] *Nicaragua* case para 194. The *Rio Treaty*, by which the parties were in fact bound, requires an armed attack in its express provision for collective self-defence in Article 3 (see *Nicaragua* case paras 196–7). There is an important distinction between Article 3 which allows collective self-defence in cases of armed attack, and Article 6, which provides for cooperation in response to other types of outside intervention. Many other collective self-defence treaties make the same distinction. Judge Schwebel, in his Dissenting Opinion, blurred this distinction.

In state practice there are no instances of anticipatory collective self-defence being expressly invoked to justify the actual use of force, except perhaps in the Harib fort incident, 1964 UNYB 181; this use of force by the UK was condemned by the Security Council as a reprisal. Judge Schwebel (Dissenting Opinion para 172–173) apparently argued that there is a right of anticipatory self-defence, but he did not support this by reference to any state practice on collective self-defence.

[26] *Nicaragua* case para 194.
[27] Ibid., para 195.
[28] Ibid.
[29] Ibid., paras 196–8.
[30] Ibid., para 200.

said that the Court should not have gone into the topic at all, given that it had held that there was no armed attack.[31] Judge Oda said that if it was going to consider collective self-defence, it had been far too brief on this controversial topic.[32]

The judgment on the merits in *Nicaragua* attracted strong criticism, especially from US writers.[33] They were unhappy at the brevity of the Court's reasoning on collective self-defence and at its approach to customary international law. Or it may be more accurate to say that, because some of the writers were unhappy with the substantive conclusions of the Court that the USA had illegally used force and intervened in Nicaragua, they therefore attacked its legal reasoning. How far were the Court's conclusions on collective self-defence justified on the basis of customary international law and compatible with treaty law? To what extent were they based on sound policy considerations?

THE MEANING OF ARMED ATTACK

The actions of armed bands and irregular forces

As was discussed in the previous chapter, the Court asserted that on the central question of what constitutes an armed attack the *Definition of Aggression* gave guidance. An armed attack included the actions of armed bands where these were imputable to a state.[34] This limited use of the *Definition of Aggression* seems justified in the light of state practice.[35]

A central issue in all the episodes where collective self-defence was expressly invoked by states was whether there had been an armed attack

---

[31] Judge Ruda (Separate Opinion, 174 at 176, para 12) was critical of this.

[32] Judge Oda, Dissenting Opinion at 212, paras 90, 97.

[33] For criticism of the Court's doctrine of collective self-defence, see, for example, Franck, 'Some Observations on the ICJ's Procedural and Substantive Innovations', 81 AJIL (1987) 116; D'Amato, 'Trashing Customary International Law', 81 AJIL (1987) 101; Hargrove, 'The *Nicaragua* Judgment and the Future of the Law of Force and Self-defense', 81 AJIL (1987) 135; Norton Moore, 'The *Nicaragua* case and the Deterioration of World Order', 81 AJIL (1987) 151; see also Macdonald, 'The *Nicaragua* case: New Answers to Old Questions', 1986 Canadian Yearbook of International Law 127 at 149.

[34] *Nicaragua* case para 195.

[35] Judge Ago, in his Separate Opinion 181, para 7, expressed reservations about the legal significance of General Assembly resolutions. In contrast, Judge Schwebel was prepared to accept the *Definition of Aggression* as reflecting customary international law (Dissenting Opinion, para 168). See Gray, 'The Principle of Non-use of Force', in Lowe and Warbrick (eds), *The United Nations and the Principles of International Law* (1994), 33. In the *Oil Platforms* case (ICJ Reports (2003) the USA argued that the *Definition of Aggression* should not be treated as authoritative as to the meaning of armed attack, at least as regards the question whether an attack on a merchant ship could constitute an 'armed attack' under Article 51 of the UN Charter (ICJ Pleadings, US *Rejoinder*, para 5.19).

such as to justify the third state assistance to the victim state. In state prac-tice it has been accepted since the early days of the UN that the actions of armed bands and irregular forces could constitute an armed attack by a state. This has been accepted in the context of collective self-defence as well as individual self-defence.[36] During the US intervention in Lebanon in the name of collective self-defence in 1958 there was initially some uncertainty on this issue.[37] The USA and Lebanon did not at first mention armed attack, although they both reported to the Security Council that the US intervention was in response to a request by Lebanon under Article 51 of the UN Charter. But subsequently Lebanon expressly argued that there was an armed attack by the United Arab Republic (Egypt and Syria) and that there was no difference between a regular army and irregular forces for the purposes of Article 51.[38] China also took this position and no state challenged it.[39] The reason why the claim to collective self-defence was controversial in Security Council and General Assembly debates was that states were sceptical as to whether there had in fact been any armed attack, whether by regular or irregular troops; they claimed that the USA was simply trying to protect an unpopular leader from internal unrest at a time of growing Arab nationalism and republicanism.

Again, in the case of Vietnam, the USA argued that the infiltration from North Vietnam amounted to an armed attack justifying collective self-defence of South Vietnam. It famously asserted that from 1959 until 1964 the North infiltrated over 40,000 men into the South. It said that in these circum-stances armed attack was not as easily fixed by date and hour as in the case of traditional warfare, but the infiltration of thousands of men clearly con-stituted an armed attack under any reasonable definition.[40] States did not deny that the actions of irregular troops could be attributed to a state, but they doubted whether in fact there was an invasion of one state by armed bands from another rather than an uprising throughout Vietnam.[41] Similarly, with regard to its intervention in Afghanistan in 1979 the USSR claimed collective self-defence against at first unspecified 'foreign intervention'; it was not controversial that the actions of armed bands could constitute an armed attack, but there was doubt as to the existence of such an attack.[42]

---

[36] Judge Schwebel, Dissenting Opinion para 157–8; Brownlie, 'International Law and the Activities of Armed Bands', 7 ICLQ (1958) 712; Gill, 'The Law of Armed Attack in the Context of the *Nicaragua* case', 1 Hague Yearbook of International Law (1988) 30.

[37] 1958 UNYB 36.

[38] SC 833rd meeting (1958).

[39] SC 831st meeting (1958) para 99.

[40] Department of State Bulletin, 28 March 1966, see 60 AJIL (1966) 565.

[41] Wright, 'Legal Aspects of the Vietnam Situation', 60 AJIL (1966) 750; see also Falk (ed.), *The Vietnam War and International Law* (1968).

[42] Cot and Pellet (eds) *La Charte des Nations Unies* (1991) 787; Doswald-Beck, 'The Legal Validity of Military Intervention by Invitation of the Government', 56 BYIL (1985) 189.

More recently, in Tajikistan there was controversy as to the existence of armed attacks from Afghanistan against Tajikistan.[43] After Tajikistan attained independence in 1991 civil war broke out and opposition forces operated against the government from Afghanistan. Russia argued that it was justified in using force in collective self-defence of Tajikistan against these incursions. In 1993–5 Russia and Tajikistan repeatedly accused Afghanistan of involvement in the attacks; Afghanistan denied these claims. This continued even after the conclusion of a border agreement between Afghanistan and Tajikistan, an *Agreement on a Temporary Ceasefire and the Cessation of Other Hostile Acts on the Tajikistan/Afghanistan Border and within the Country* between the warring parties in Tajikistan, and the creation of a UN observer force (UNMOT) to monitor the border/ceasefire. The UN Secretary-General made various reports on the situation, but did not come to any public conclusions as to the occurrence of armed attacks and the right of Tajikistan and Russia to act in collective self-defence against Afghanistan.

The supply of arms

What proved more controversial than the attribution of the actions of armed bands to a state was the ICJ's assertion in the *Nicaragua* case that the supply of arms, financial and logistic support could not amount to an armed attack. The USA contended that Nicaragua had intervened in El Salvador and other neighbouring states in order to foment and sustain armed attacks upon the governments of those states, and that its subversive intervention in the governing circumstances was tantamount to an armed attack. The Court said that such assistance as the supply of arms, financial and logistic support could be regarded as a threat or use of force, or amount to intervention in the internal or external affairs of other states, but that it did not amount to an armed attack.[44] The Court gave no authority for this statement and was criticized for its failure to do so by some commentators. But the Court's choice not to elaborate on the basis for its finding may be explained by the fact that the parties had not disagreed about the meaning of armed attack.[45] Rather, the central disagreement was whether, on the application of the law to the particular facts, the actions of the Nicaraguan government amounted to an armed attack. On the facts of the case the Court found that there had been no significant assistance to the opposition in El Salvador since 1981 and that Nicaragua could not be

---

[43] 1993 UNYB 383, 514; 1994 UNYB 454, 591; 1995 UNYB 495.
[44] *Nicaragua* case para 195.
[45] This was accepted by Schwebel (Dissenting Opinion para 160,172); see also Rostow, 'Nicaragua and the Law of Self-Defense Revisited', 11 Yale JIL (1987) 437.

held responsible for the limited assistance that had been given.[46] Therefore there was actually no need for the Court to go into the question of the definition of armed attack; the decision on the general question of what counted as an armed attack was not decisive.

In state practice the supply of arms, money, and logistic support have not generally been treated as armed attacks in the context of collective self-defence. Occasionally there have been hints of such a position. For example, in Lebanon in 1958 the USA and Lebanon at first simply said that the infiltration of armed men, arms, and supplies from Syria in the UAR threatened the independence of Lebanon and that this gave the right of collective self-defence. They did not expressly mention armed attack at this stage; they invoked Article 51 as a precaution, saying that their forces were not there to engage in hostilities.[47] In the Security Council debates some states (the UK, France, Canada, and China) supported the right of Lebanon to request and the USA to send troops, but on the facts this cannot be interpreted as amounting to an endorsement of the actual use of force in the exercise of collective self-defence. It can be seen as simply an endorsement of the right of the USA to send in its troops to help the government of Lebanon. Certain states such as the UAR, the USSR, and Sweden, denied the existence of an armed attack and said that because of this the USA had no right to use force against the UAR.[48] Lebanon, in later defending its position against the criticisms that had been made by other states in the Security Council, expressly justified its invitation to the USA on the basis that there had been an armed attack. It affirmed a conception of armed attack that did not include the mere supply of arms, but only armed attack by regular army and irregular troops.[49]

---

[46] *Nicaragua* case para 230. The Court was criticized by some for its reluctance to attribute these actions to Nicaragua, but its position on this point is consistent with its position on the *contras*. Just as the Court did not make the USA responsible for all the acts of the *contras* and did not accept that the *contras* were mere agents of the USA, so it did not attribute to Nicaragua all action helping the opposition in El Salvador; see Gill, 'The Law of Armed Attack in the Context of the *Nicaragua* case', 1 Hague Yearbook of International Law (1988) 30.

Judge Schwebel disagreed with the conclusion of the Court on these facts (Dissenting Opinion para 166). On the question of fact, Judge Jennings (Dissenting Opinion 544) said:

As to the case before the Court, I remain somewhat doubtful whether the Nicaraguan involvement with Salvadorian rebels had not involved some forms of 'other support' besides the possible provision, whether officially or unofficially, of weapons. There seems to have been perhaps overmuch concentration on the question of the supply, or transit, of arms; as if that were of itself crucial, which it is not. Yet one is bound to observe that here, where questions of fact may be every bit as important as the law, the United States can hardly complain at the inevitable consequences of its failure to plead during the substantive phase of the case.

[47] SC 827th meeting (1958).
[48] SC 827th–831st meetings (1958).
[49] SC 833rd meeting (1958).

The US justification of its intervention in Vietnam also at first seemed to be based on a wide view of armed attack. In its 1966 Department of State *Memorandum on The Legality of US Participation in the Defense of Vietnam* it said in the first paragraph that it was assisting South Vietnam to defend itself against armed attack from the North and that 'this armed attack took the form of externally supported subversion, the clandestine supply of arms and the infiltration of armed personnel'.[50] But the USA subsequently focused on the movement of troops across the border between North and South Vietnam; in its reports to the Security Council the USA, in claiming to act in collective self-defence, generally spoke only of the use of force by regular and irregular troops.[51] The lesson that emerges from this practice is that the supply of arms alone does not constitute an armed attack. This position was acceptable to Judges Schwebel and Jennings, but some commentators have apparently taken a more extreme position.[52]

FRONTIER INCIDENTS

Also controversial was the distinction made by the International Court of Justice in the *Nicaragua* case between armed attack and frontier incident. The distinction requires detailed discussion because of the prevalence of frontier incidents in state practice; this is the most common form of force between states, and the least discussed. The Court first drew this distinction in the context of its discussion of the applicable law. It said that as regards certain aspects of the principle prohibiting the use of force, it would be necessary to distinguish the most grave forms of the use of force (those involving an armed attack) from less grave forms. Accordingly, in its examination of the exceptions to the prohibition on the use of force, and specifically in its consideration of the right of individual and collective self-defence, the Court discussed the nature of an armed attack and referred expressly to frontier incidents. It said that just as individual self-defence is subject to the state concerned having been the victim of an armed attack, reliance on collective self-defence does not remove the need for this: 'The Court sees no reason to deny that, in customary law, the prohibition of armed attacks may apply to the sending by a state of armed

---

[50] 60 AJIL (1966) 565.

[51] Thus on the extension of the war into Cambodia, see 1972 UNYB 153; Stevenson, 'US Military Actions in Cambodia: Questions of International Law', in Falk (ed.), *The Vietnam War and International Law*, Vol 3 (1972), 23 at 31.

[52] Norton Moore, 'The *Nicaragua* case and the Deterioration of World Order', 81 AJIL (1987) 151 at 154; Norton Moore, 'The Secret War in Central America and the Future of World Order', 80 AJIL (1986) 43; Reisman, 'Allocating Competences to Use Coercion in the Post-Cold War World', in Damrosch and Scheffer (eds), *Law and Force in the New International Order* (1991), 26.

bands to the territory of another state, if such an operation, because of its scale and effects, would have been classified as an armed attack *rather than as a mere frontier incident* had it been carried out by regular armed forces.'[53]

When the Court came to apply customary international law to the facts of the case, it asked whether the US actions using force against Nicaragua were justified as collective self-defence.[54] Did Nicaragua engage in an armed attack against El Salvador, Costa Rica, and Honduras? The Court said that the limited provision of arms from Nicaragua to the opposition in El Salvador did not amount to an armed attack.[55] Therefore the concept of frontier incident did not play a decisive role in this part of the judgment. In contrast, the Court held that there had been certain transborder incursions from Nicaragua into Costa Rica and Honduras imputable to the government of Nicaragua.[56] Here, it seems that the distinction between frontier incident and armed attack was important to the Court. If these trans-border incursions amounted to armed attacks, then it would be possible that the USA might have a claim to collective self-defence of Costa Rica and El Salvador. However, the Court was rather non-committal (and it did not expressly mention frontier incidents or elaborate on the distinction between armed attack and frontier incident at this point in its judgment). It said only that it had very little information as to the circumstances or possible motivations of the incursions and this rendered it difficult to decide whether they could be treated for legal purposes as amounting either singly or collectively to an armed attack by Nicaragua on either or both of these states.

The distinction between armed attack and frontier incident in the *nicaragua* case

The Court did not elaborate in any detail on the distinction between frontier incidents and armed attack. The first distinguishing features it mentioned were the 'scale and effects' of the attack;[57] this formula is comparable to the exclusion of 'acts and consequences not of sufficient gravity' from the *Definition of Aggression* and would seem to cover scale in place and time and also the scale of the impact of the attack. It is clear from the context of the Court's pronouncement that the difference envisaged is one of degree rather than of kind; that is, both frontier incidents and

---

[53] *Nicaragua* case para 195.
[54] *Nicaragua* case, paras 226, 229.
[55] Ibid., para 230.
[56] Ibid., para 231.
[57] *Nicaragua* case para 195.

armed attacks were attributable to the state. The Court's concept of frontier incident was not limited to acts of non-state organs.

The second set of distinguishing features mentioned by the Court are more obscure; they are the 'circumstances and motivations' of the attack.[58] This phrase is very general; the implication seems to be that the Court would include within 'frontier incident' episodes where there was no intent to carry out an armed attack, including accidental incursions and incidents where officials disobeyed orders. The question of motivation is a controversial one. Can a state's motive be anything more than an inference from the action in question? Is the intent of individual soldiers to be attributed to the state? Factors of motive and intent were much discussed during the drafting of the *Definition of Aggression*; there was fundamental disagreement as to whether an act could constitute an act of aggression simply because the use of force was intentional or whether there should be some further intention on the part of the state to commit aggression (*animus aggressionis*).[59] The Court in *Nicaragua* left these questions of intent and motive with regard to frontier incidents unresolved.[60]

Criticism of the distinction between armed attack and frontier incident

At first sight it might seem that the distinction drawn in a sketchy way in the *Nicaragua* case between armed attacks and lesser incursions such as frontier incidents was illogical and unnecessary. Given that all self-defence, whether individual or collective, must be necessary and proportionate, a minor frontier incursion would justify only a very limited response. Thus there would seem to be no need to distinguish between armed attacks allowing self-defence and mere frontier incidents. The necessity and proportionality requirements would provide adequate safeguard against excessive use of force.[61]

Many harsh criticisms were made of the Court for its narrow view of armed attack, and its consequent limitation of the US right to act in collective self-defence. As part of this, writers condemned the Court's distinction between frontier incidents and armed attacks. In the context of the law on self-defence Dinstein is critical of the Court in *Nicaragua*. He says that 'In reality there is no cause to remove small scale armed attacks from the

---

[58] Ibid., para 231.

[59] Schwebel, 'Aggression, Intervention and Self-Defense in Modern International Law', 136 RCADI (1972–II) 463; Ferencz, 'Defining Aggression: Where it stands and where it's going', 66 AJIL (1972) 491.

[60] For discussion of intent and armed attack in the *Oil Platforms* case, see Chapter 4 above.

[61] For example, this is the view of Higgins, *Problems and Process* (1994), 251.

spectrum of armed attacks' and he describes the question of frontier incidents as 'particularly bothersome'.[62] Many others writing on the *Nicaragua* case also throw doubt on the distinction.[63] For example, Hargrove says Article 51 in no way limits itself to especially large, direct or important attacks.[64] Reisman accuses the Court of developing a theory that is tolerant of different forms of protracted and low-intensity conflict; he argues that this will lead to an increase in violence in international politics.[65] This argument echoes that of Fitzmaurice, writing in 1933, who argued that it was important not to treat frontier incidents as a justified resort to force; this would encourage frontier incidents and place innocent states in a difficult position.[66]

The writers critical of the reasoning in the *Nicaragua* case follow the same line as earlier commentators on the UN Charter who said that any attack, even small border incidents, allowed self-defence.[67] Thus Brownlie had expressed doubts about the concept of frontier incidents. He writes of the concept as 'vague', and says that from the point of view of assessing responsibility the distinction between frontier incident and armed attack is only relevant in so far as the minor nature of the attack is *prima facie* evidence of absence of intention to attack, of honest mistake, or simply the limited objectives of an attack. For him, the question as to whether the particular use of force is permissible self-defence is merely one of proportionality.[68]

Arguments for the distinction between armed attack and frontier incident

But it is clear, despite the criticisms of the *Nicaragua* case, that there were nevertheless serious reasons for the Court's distinction between

[62] Dinstein, *War, Aggression and Self-Defence* (4th edn, 2005), 195. But Dinstein accepts the distinction between frontier incidents and other more significant uses of force in the context of determining whether a state of war exists.

[63] For example, Schacter, 'In Defense of International Rules on the Use of Force', 53 University of Chicago Law Review (1986) 113; Macdonald, 'The *Nicaragua* case: New Answers to Old Questions', 1986 Canadian Yearbook of International Law 127 at 151.

[64] Hargrove, 'The *Nicaragua* Judgment and the Future of the Law of Force and Self-defense', 81 AJIL (1987) 135 at 139.

[65] Reisman, 'Allocating Competences to use Coercion in the post Cold-War World, Practises, Conditions, and Prospects', in Damrosch and Scheffer (eds), *Law and Force in the New International Order* (1991), 26 at 39–40.

[66] Fitzmaurice in Ferencz (ed.) *Defining International Aggression: The Search for World Peace* (1975), Vol 2 at 152.

[67] For example, Kunz, 'Individual and Collective Self-Defense in Article 51 of the Charter of the United Nations', 41 AJIL (1947) 872 at 878; Badr, 'The Exculpatory Effect of Self-defense in State Responsibility', 10 Georgia Journal of International and Comparative Law (1980) 1.

[68] Brownlie, *The Use of Force by States* (1963) at 366. He referred to intent, mistake, and limited objective as distinguishing features of frontier incidents.

armed attacks and mere frontier incidents. Its concern was with *collective* self-defence; it wanted to limit *third state* involvement. Its insistence on a high threshold for armed attack would serve to limit third party involvement. If there was no armed attack, there could be no collective self-defence. The use of necessity and proportionality alone would not exclude third party involvement, merely limit the scope of their permissible response.[69]

Judge Jennings, in his Dissenting Opinion in the *Nicaragua* case, expressed some limited sympathy with the Court's approach to collective self-defence. He said that, 'It is of course a fact that collective self-defence is a concept that lends itself to abuse. One must therefore sympathize with the anxiety of the court to define it in terms of some strictness. There is a question, however, whether the court has perhaps gone too far in this direction.'[70] Jennings did not, however, specifically criticize the concept of frontier incident.

Interestingly, Judge Schwebel, in his otherwise sweeping rejection of the majority judgment in the *Nicaragua* case, did not uncompromisingly reject the Court's position on this question of the scope of armed attack. He said:

While I disagree with its legal *conclusions*—particularly as they turn on the holding that there has been no action by Nicaragua tantamount to an armed attack upon El Salvador to which the United States may respond in collective self-defence—I recognize that there is room for the Court's *construction of the legal meaning of an armed attack*, as well as for some of its other conclusions of law. The Court could have produced a plausible judgment—unsound in its ultimate conclusions, in my view, but not implausible—which would have recognized not only the facts of United States intervention in Nicaragua but the facts of Nicaragua's prior and continuing intervention in El Salvador; which would have treated Nicaragua's intervention as unlawful (as it undeniably is); but which would also have held that it nevertheless was not tantamount to an armed attack upon El Salvador or that, even if it were, the response of the United States was unnecessary, ill-timed or disproportionate.[71]

More recently, the Legal Adviser to the US State Department in his reaction to the Court's decision in the *Oil Platforms* case, actually accepted the distinction between armed attack and frontier incident.[72]

---

[69] For some support for this view, see Farer, 'Drawing the Right Line', 81 AJIL (1987) 112; Diaz Barrado, *El Consentimento Causa de Exclusion de la Ilicitud del Uso de la Fuerza en Derecho Internacional* (1989).

[70] Jennings, Dissenting Opinion 528 at 543.

[71] Schwebel, Dissenting Opinion 272, para 15 (italics added).

[72] Taft, 'Self-Defense and the *Oil Platforms* Decision', 29 Yale Journal of International Law (2004) 295 at 302.

The distinction and the *Definition of Aggression*

The distinction between mere frontier incidents and other more significant uses of force is not one that was invented by the Court. Although
the concept of frontier incident had not before *Nicaragua* attained the status of a term of art, it was already familiar from earlier practice and had
been specifically discussed during the protracted attempts of states to
define aggression, particularly during the drafting of the 1974 *Definition of
Aggression*. The proposal to include a *de minimis* clause (to exclude minor
incidents, including frontier incidents, from the category of aggression)
was first made by Finland in 1972 in order to give the Security Council the
opportunity not to condemn when the acts or the consequences are not
grave.[73] Eventually Article 2 of the *Definition of Aggression* was adopted:

> The first use of armed force by a state in contravention of the Charter shall con-
> stitute prima facie evidence of aggression although the Security Council may, in
> conformity with the Charter, conclude that a determination that an act of aggres-
> sion has been committed would not be justified in the light of other relevant cir-
> cumstances, *including the fact that the acts concerned or their consequences are not of
> sufficient gravity.*

Although this does not expressly refer to frontier incidents, it reflects the
general support for a distinction between frontier incidents and aggression and followed extensive discussion of frontier incidents.[74]

Of course, the flexibility of Article 39 of the UN Charter means that the
distinction between aggression and frontier incident is not likely to be crucial for the decision-making of the Security Council under Chapter VII; its
powers are the same whether it finds an act of aggression, a breach of the
peace or a threat to the peace. Moreover, the Security Council in practice
has been reluctant to identify and denounce acts of aggression.[75] The less
dramatic choice, but more important in this context, will be whether the
frontier incident amounts to a breach of the peace or a threat to the peace.[76]

Furthermore, there are questions about the interrelationship of aggression, frontier incident, and armed attack. As part of the debate about the

---

[73] See Ferencz, *Defining International Aggression: The Search for World Peace* (2 vols, 1975)
at 367.

[74] Ibid., at 248; Schwebel, 'Aggression, Intervention and Self-Defense in Modern International
Law', 136 RCADI (1972–II) 463 at 467–8; Fitzmaurice, 'The Definition of Aggression', 1 ICLQ
(1952) 137 at 139.

[75] Cot and Pellet (eds), *La Charte des Nations Unies* (1991) 661.

[76] Higgins, *The Development of International Law through the Political Organs of the United
Nations* (1963), 181; as Higgins pointed out, it is important to remember that just because an
act is too minor to count as aggression does not mean that it is legal; it could still be a breach
of the peace, open to condemnation by the UN. In the early days of the UN the Security
Council condemned even minor uses of force, but this does not seem to be true today.

role that a definition of aggression might play, and of the usefulness of such a definition, the lack of any express correlation between the terms used in Articles 2(4) ('the use of force'), 51 ('armed attack') and 39 ('act of aggression') of the UN Charter gave rise to considerable controversy.[77] During the early discussions of the *Definition of Aggression* the Netherlands representative suggested that it might be more useful to define armed attack rather than aggression. In this context he said that insignificant incidents did not amount to armed attack allowing self-defence.[78] However, his proposal to define armed attack was not accepted. But, just because the concept of frontier incident was being discussed in the context of work on a definition of aggression, this does not mean that these discussions have no relevance for the scope of the right of self-defence. Some commentators apparently assumed that any act of aggression would necessarily allow self-defence. Thus Broms said that the *de minimis* clause limits the likelihood of a state arguing that a very minor incident amounts to an act of aggression leading to self-defence.[79] If this is a complete identification of aggression and armed attack it goes too far. But in *Nicaragua* the Court itself used the *Definition of Aggression* to help it to determine the scope of an armed attack; it was in this context that it drew the distinction with frontier incident. Some later writers supported this and said that Article 51 required serious acts, and that small border incidents did not count.[80] The legality of the third state use of force was controversial in all the cases where collective self-defence was invoked by states. But, although the existence of an armed attack was problematic in most of the above episodes, in none of them has the distinction between armed attack and frontier incident been a relevant consideration.[81]

---

[77] Bowett, *Self-Defence in International Law* (1958) at 250–6; Roling, 'The Ban on the Use of Force and the UN Charter', in Cassese (ed.), *The Current Legal Regulation of the Use of Force* (1986); Mullerson, 'The Principle of the Non-Threat and Non-Use of Force in the Modern World', in Butler (ed.), *The Non-Use of Force in International Law* (1989), 29.

[78] Ferencz, *Defining International Aggression: The Search for World Peace* (1975) at 238; see also Fitzmaurice, 'Definition of Aggression', 1 ICLQ (1952) 137 at 142.

[79] Broms, *The Definition of Aggression in the UN* (1968), 151; 'The Definition of Aggression', 154 RCADI (1977–I) 299 at 346; see also Hargrove, 'The Nicaragua Judgment and the Future of the Law of Force and Self-defense', 81 AJIL (1987) 135 at 139.

[80] Mullerson, 'Self-Defense in the Contemporary World', in Damrosch and Scheffer (eds), *Law and Force in the New International Order* (1991), 13; Lamberti Zanardi, 'Indirect Military Aggression', in Cassese (ed.), *The Current Legal Regulation of the Use of Force* (1986), 111; see also Rifaat, *International Aggression* (1979), Chapter 11.

[81] In the case of Tajikistan questions arose as to whether cross-border incursions from Afghanistan constituted armed attacks allowing collective self defence. However, the central issue was the responsibility of Afghanistan rather than the characterization of the incursions.

OTHER LIMITS ON THE RIGHT OF COLLECTIVE SELF-DEFENCE

As mentioned above, the Court's findings in the *Nicaragua* case on the nature of the incursions from Nicaragua into Costa Rica and Honduras were somewhat inconclusive as regards the question whether these were frontier incidents not amounting to an armed attack. After the Court had looked at these incursions and at the supply of arms to the opposition in El Salvador it continued, 'There are however *other* considerations which justify the court in finding that neither these incursions nor the alleged supply of arms to the opposition in El Salvador may be relied on as justifying the exercise of the right of collective self-defence.'[82] The Court went on to apply the conditions that it had identified as limiting the right to collective self-defence in its earlier discussion of customary international law. It found that there had been no timely declaration by El Salvador that it was the victim of an attack and no declaration at all by Honduras and Costa Rica. Also none of the three had made any request for help to the USA before its forcible intervention. These factors together all showed that the USA was not acting in self-defence of the three states.[83]

The only authority the Court mentioned for its requirement of a request by the victim state was the *Rio Treaty*, Article 3(2), which says that measures of collective self-defence are decided 'on the request of the state or states directly attacked'. As regards its requirement of a declaration by the victim state that it had been the victim of an armed attack, the Court offered no authority. That is, it offered almost no justification for the conditions it apparently imposed on collective self-defence. One obvious inference is that the Court was influenced by the fact that the parties were actually bound by a treaty commitment that the victim state request assistance.[84] Moreover, the approach adopted by the Court seems correct in principle, as any other approach would allow the third state to pronounce on the existence of an armed attack and to decide that it was going to use force even against the wishes of the victim state.[85]

Judges Jennings and Schwebel, however, attacked the Court's reasoning and conclusion on these points. Their arguments seem to be based on policy considerations. Both were critical of the court's 'formalistic' model of collective self-defence. Schwebel's concern was with covert action; he asked, 'Where is it written that a victim state may not

---

[82] *Nicaragua* case para 231.
[83] Ibid., paras 232–4.
[84] *Inter-American Treaty of Reciprocal Assistance* (1947) 21 UNTS 77.
[85] See *contra* Macdonald, 'The *Nicaragua* case: New Answers to Old Questions', 1986 Canadian Yearbook of International Law 127 at 143.

informally and quietly seek foreign assistance?'[86] Jennings showed some sympathy with the Court's desire to limit the scope of collective self-defence:

Obviously the notion of collective self-defence is open to abuse and it is necessary to ensure that it is not employable as a mere cover for aggression disguised as protection, and the Court is therefore right to define it somewhat strictly. Even so, it may be doubted whether it is helpful to suggest that the attacked state must in some more or less formal way have 'declared' itself the victim of an attack and then have as an additional 'requirement' made a formal request to a particular third state for assistance.

Jennings' argument is apparently based on policy. He goes on, 'It may readily be agreed that the victim state must both be in real need of assistance and must want it and that the fulfilment of both these conditions must be shown. But to ask that these requirements take the form of some sort of formal declaration and request might sometimes be unrealistic.'[87]

Writers similarly have been critical of the Court's reasoning on the grounds of its formalism.[88] Simma's commentary on the UN Charter states categorically, but without any attempt at justification beyond references to secondary sources, that the Court was wrong to require an express request by the victim state.[89] Macdonald agrees that the requirement of a request for help was a 'wholly new and unconsidered limitation on the right to collective self-defence'.[90] These pronouncements by writers are not only misguided as a matter of principle and in the light of state practice; they also rest on a misreading of the Court's judgment.

The Court's judgment could be interpreted in a much less formalistic way than that adopted by the writers critical of the Court. When it came to apply the rule that it had earlier in its discussion of the applicable law stated in apparently rather categorical terms the Court took a more relaxed approach to the requirement of a declaration and a request. It said that it is evident that it is the victim state, being most directly aware of that fact, which is *most likely* to draw general attention to its plight. It is also evident

---

[86] Schwebel, Dissenting Opinion paras 191, 221–7. He argued particularly that these requirements were not appropriate in cases of covert action. But this seems to mistake the nature of the right and the role of the Security Council.

[87] Jennings, Dissenting Opinion 544–5.

[88] Norton Moore, 'The Nicaragua case and the Deterioration of World Order', 81 AJIL (1987) 151; Morrison, 'Legal Issues in the Nicaragua Opinion', 81 AJIL (1987) 160.

[89] Simma (ed.), *The Charter of the United Nations: A Commentary* (2nd edn 2002) 803 at para 38.

[90] See Macdonald, 'The *Nicaragua* case: New Answers to Old Questions', 1986 Canadian Yearbook of International Law, 127 at 150.

that if a victim state wants help it will *normally* make an express request.[91] This is clearly something less than a strict formal rule:

Thus in the present instance the Court is entitled to take account, in judging the asserted justification of the exercise of collective self-defence by the United States, of the actual conduct of El Salvador, Honduras and Costa Rica at the relevant time, as indicative of a belief by the State in question that it was the victim of an armed attack by Nicaragua, and of the making of a request by the victim State to the United States for help in the exercise of collective self-defence.[92]

In fact it is clear that the Court did not *require* a declaration and a request.

Nor did it intend the declaration and request to be *decisive* as to legality. After its examination of whether there had been a declaration and a request, the Court concluded that 'the condition *sine qua non* required for the exercise of the right of collective self-defence by the United States is not fulfilled in this case'. The reference to 'the condition *sine qua non*' apparently refers to an armed attack.[93] The Court thus apparently took the absence of a declaration, request for assistance (and of a report to the Security Council) simply as *confirmation* that there had been no armed attack.[94] However, in the *Oil Platforms* case the Court seemed to take a more categorical position. It said, 'Despite having referred to attacks on vessels and aircraft of other nationalities, the United States has not claimed to have been exercising collective self-defence on behalf of neutral states engaged in shipping in the Persian Gulf; this would have required the existence of a request made to the United States by the State which regards itself as the victim of an armed attack.'[95] That is, although it was not actually called on to pronounce on collective self-defence, the Court treated the Court's position in the Nicaragua case as authoritative, and it now made clear that it regarded the existence of a request by the victim state as a necessary element of self-defence.

State practice also supports the Court's position that normally a request and a declaration would be made. Some collective self-defence treaties, like the *Rio Treaty*, expressly require a request by the victim state.[96] In every case where a third state has invoked collective self-defence it has based its claim on the request of the victim state even where there was no express

---

[91] *Nicaragua* case para 232.
[92] Ibid., paras 233, 234.
[93] Ibid., paras 236–7.
[94] Greig, 'Self-Defence and the Security Council: What does Article 51 require?', 40 ICLQ (1991) 366 at 375, supports this view.
[95] ICJ Reports (2003) 161 para 51.
[96] The Arab League *Treaty of Joint Defence*, Article IV(3), 55 AJIL Supplement 51, and the France/Djibouti Protocol (1982), 1430 UNTS 103 also require a request. Other treaties require 'consultation' (UK/Mauritius *Agreement on Mutual Defence and Assistance* (1968) 648 UNTS 3; UK/Malta *Agreement on Mutual Defence* (1964) 588 UNTS 55) or 'agreement' on the response to an armed attack (USA/Liberia *Agreement on Cooperation* (1959) 357 UNTS 94).

treaty provision requiring this.[97] Also the state claiming to be the victim has generally asserted that it has been the victim of an armed attack. But in almost all the cases of collective self-defence listed above there has been controversy over the existence or the genuineness of the request. With regard to the interventions in Lebanon and Jordan in 1958, the USSR argued that the USA put pressure on Lebanon to issue an invitation,[98] and that the UK intervention was planned before the request from Jordan and that the request was not free. The true motive of the USA and the UK was to repress the rise of Arab nationalism.[99] With regard to Vietnam, those who challenged the legality of the US intervention said that South Vietnam was not a separate state and had no right to seek outside assistance.[100] In the Soviet invasions of Czechoslovakia and Afghanistan the invitations came from governments installed by the invading state.[101] In Chad there was an ongoing civil war and the legitimacy of the government and its right to request outside help was not always clear. But Libya relied on a request in 1980 and said that it had left when so requested.[102] France also said that a request was necessary and it responded to a request.[103]

Third state interest?

After his criticism of the Court's requirement of a declaration and a request by the victim state, Judge Jennings went on to say that the reasoning was also objectionable in that the Court was giving the impression that the third state need not itself have an interest for it to exercise collective self-defence.[104] Many others follow the Jennings approach.[105] Some have even argued that

[97] USSR/Hungary (1956), 1956 UNYB 67; USA/Lebanon (1958) SC 827th meeting (1958), 1958 UNYB 36 at 38; UK/Jordan (1958) 1958 UNYB 41; USA/Vietnam (1965) UN doc S/6174 (1965), 60 AJIL (1966) 565; USSR/Czechoslovakia (1968) SC 1441st meeting (1968), 1968 UNYB 298; USSR/Afghanistan (1979), 1980 UNYB 296; Libya/Chad (1980) 1981 UNYB 222; France/Chad (1983, 1986) 1983 UNYB 180, 1986 UNYB 168, 1987 UNYB 176, UN docs S/17837, 18 February 1986, S/18554, 2 November 1987; Angola/Cuba (from 1975) SC 2440th, 2481st meetings (1983), 1983 UNYB 173; USA/Honduras (1988) SC 2802nd meeting (1988), UN doc S/19643, 17 March 1988, 1988 UNYB 170; USA and UK/Kuwait (1990) UN Publications, *The UN and the Iraq/Kuwait Conflict 1990–1996* at 16; Russia/Tajikistan (1993) UN doc S/26241, 5 August 1993, 1993 UNYB 514; Angola, Namibia and Zimbabwe/DRC 1998 UNYB 82–6. On *Operation Enduring Freedom* in Afghanistan, see Chapter 6 below.

[98] 1958 UNYB 36.

[99] 1958 UNYB 41.

[100] Wright, 'Legal Aspects of the Viet-Nam Situation', 60 AJIL (1966) 750.

[101] Doswald-Beck, 'The Legal Validity of Military Intervention by Invitation of the Government', 56 BYIL (1985) 189.

[102] 1981 UNYB 223.

[103] France 1983 UNYB 180, 1984 UNYB 185, 1986 UNYB 168, 1987 UNYB 176, UN docs S/17837, 18 February 1986, S/18554, 2 January 1987, SC 2721st meeting (1986); *Repertoire of the Practice of the Security Council (1981–84)* 261; see Alibert, 'L'Affaire du Tchad', 90 RGDIP (1986) 368.

[104] Jennings, Dissenting Opinion 545.

[105] Dinstein, *War, Aggression and Self-Defence* (4th edn, 2005), Chapter 9; Bowett, *Self-Defence in International Law* (1958) at 216; Macdonald, 'The *Nicaragua* case: New answers to

the right to collective self-defence is essentially the right of the party giving aid to the victim, and that the International Court of Justice itself should not be taken to have rejected this position.[106] But this insistence on a third party interest all seems rather far-fetched in the light of state practice since 1945. States themselves have not used this argument; criticisms by states of the legality of actions taken in the name of collective self-defence have not mentioned the absence of a third state interest or of a treaty commitment as a ground of illegality. In many of the episodes the intervening state did in fact have a pre-existing treaty relationship with the 'victim' state,[107] but in the other cases where there was no such treaty this was not mentioned as a ground of illegality even by those otherwise critical of the use of force.[108]

The duty to report to the Security Council under Article 51

Also the failure of the USA to report on its use of force to the Security Council under Article 51 was taken by the Court as an indication that the USA was not exercising the right of collective self-defence.[109] Judge Schwebel criticized this, but the Court's position is an accurate reflection of earlier practice on collective self-defence. The USA itself, with regard to its intervention in Vietnam, pointed out that it was not bound under Article 51 to report because neither North nor South Vietnam were members of the UN. Nevertheless, it said it would report because Article 51 was an appropriate guide.[110] The other states claiming to use collective

old questions', 1986 Canadian Yearbook of International Law at 151; Delivanis, *La légitime défense en droit international public moderne* (1971).

[106] Macdonald 'The *Nicaragua* case: New Answers to Old Questions', 1986 Canadian Yearbook of International Law 127 argued that 'if there is an armed attack, what the victim believes to have occurred is otiose because the aid-giving state is also subject to the armed attack'.

[107] There were pre-existing treaties between Hungary, Czechoslovakia, Ethiopia, Afghanistan, and the USSR; the UK and the South Arabian Federation; El Salvador, Costa Rica and Honduras and the USA; Chad and France (France invoked a 1976 Cooperation Agreement, but had to stretch its terms; see Alibert, 'L'Affaire du Tchad', 90 RGDIP (1986) 343). To justify its collective self-defence of Tajikistan Russia invoked a bilateral Treaty of Friendship (UN doc S/26110, 19 July 1993) and an agreement between five members of the CIS (UN doc S/26892, 18 December 1993, 1993 UNYB 514). In some of these cases the treaty was concluded not long before the use of force, so it seems that even though it is not a legal requirement it may be seen as adding legitimacy. NATO invoked Article 5 of its constituent treaty for the first time in response to 9/11: see Chapter 6.

[108] Thus the absence of a treaty in the cases of USA/Lebanon (1958), UK/Jordan (1958), Cuba/Angola (from 1975), USA and UK/Kuwait (1990), and Angola, Namibia and Zimbabwe/ DRC (1998) was not singled out as a ground for criticism.

[109] *Nicaragua* case para 235; see Greig, 'Self-Defence and the Security Council: What does Article 51 require?', 40 ICLQ (1991) 366.

[110] As discussed in the previous chapter, the USA did not just report to the Security Council once at the start of the conflict, but made several separate reports of individual actions or series of actions; 1965 UNYB 185, 1966 UNYB 153, 1970 UNYB 215.

self-defence in other episodes also reported under Article 51. Indeed, there is a contrast here with individual self-defence, with regard to which states' reporting was much more erratic and which has improved only since the *Nicaragua* case. In collective self-defence all the states expressly invoking collective self-defence reported.[111] And after the decision on the merits of the *Nicaragua* case the Central American states and the USA referred their subsequent claims to collective self-defence to the Security Council.[112] Moreover, several collective self-defence treaties specifically require parties to report to the Security Council.[113] It may not be mandatory to report in the sense that failure to report will not in itself mean that the action cannot be self-defence, but failure will be *evidence* that the action was not in fact self-defence. As with the UK's controversial intervention to protect the South Arabian Federation (before it was a member of the UN), the USSR and the USA both said that the UK should have gone to the Security Council earlier if its action had been justified as self-defence.[114] The UK itself repeated this argument against the USSR and its failure to turn earlier to the Security Council over Afghanistan.[115]

CONCLUSION

Writers on collective self-defence are clearly split into two camps, and their reactions to the *Nicaragua* case reflect these different viewpoints. First, some view collective self-defence as a valuable means to help protect weak victim states from oppression.[116] They therefore attack the Court's limitations on collective self-defence. For them the Court's view of armed attack is too narrow, and the alleged requirements of a declaration and

---

[111] USA/Lebanon, SC 827th meeting (1958), 1958 UNYB 38; Jordan/UK, UN docs S/4053, 17 July 1958, S/4071, 1958 UNYB 40; USA/Vietnam, 1965 UNYB 185, 1966 UNYB 146, 1970 UNYB 215, 1972 UNYB 153, S/1063, 9 May 1982; USSR/Czechoslovakia, SC 1441st meeting (1968), 1968 UNYB 298; Libya/Chad, 1981 UNYB 223; France/Chad, SC 2721st meeting (1986), UN docs S/17837, 18 February 1986, S/18554, 2 January 1987, S/19136, 15 September 1987, 1983 UNYB 180, 1984 UNYB 185, 1986 UNYB 168, 1987 UNYB 176; USSR/Afghanistan, 1980 UNYB 296 at 299,300; Cuba/Angola, SC 2440th, 2481st meetings (1983), 1983 UNYB 173; USA/Honduras, 1988 UNYB 170; USA and the UK/Kuwait, 1990 UNYB 195; Russia/Tajikistan, UN docs S/26110, 19 July 1993, S/26241, 5 August 1993, 1993 UNYB 514; DRC/Angola, Namibia and Zimbabwe, UN doc S/1998/891, 1998 UNYB 85–6; USA/Afghanistan, UN docs S/2001/946, S/2001/947.
[112] For example, 1988 UNYB 170; SC 2800th, 2802nd meetings (1988), UN doc A/42/931, 17 March 1988.
[113] Australia/New Zealand/USA 131 UNTS 83; USA/Japan 373 UNTS 179; S E Asia 209 UNTS 28; Arab League 70 UNTS 237.
[114] 1964 UNYB 181 at 184.
[115] 1980 UNYB 300.
[116] For example, Macdonald, 'The *Nicaragua* case: New Answers to Old Questions', 1986 Canadian Yearbook of International Law 127 at 151.

request by the victim state are unduly formalistic and restrictive. They argue that the Court's approach will encourage aggression of a low-key kind.[117] This sort of enthusiasm for collective self-defence was also apparent in earlier writers on the Charter; they were clearly writing under the influence of the Second World War and saw the provision for collective self-defence in Article 51 as a useful means to protect small states. For example, McDougal and Feliciano said that defence must be collective if it is not to be an exercise in individual suicide.[118]

The opposing camp comprises those writers who have taken a much more suspicious approach to collective self-defence. They see it rather as a threat to world peace. Thus they argue that there is a need for a high threshold of armed attack and distinction between armed attack and lesser use of force in order to reduce the involvement of superpowers. Otherwise there would be a risk of the internationalization of civil conflicts and the expansion of inter-state conflicts.[119] They also said that there is a danger that Article 51 on collective self-defence would help remote, undemocratic states.

In this regard it is interesting that the Court itself in *Nicaragua*, although concerned to limit the right of collective self-defence, expressly ruled out any consideration of the *motives* of states engaged in collective self-defence. Thus it declined to undertake an examination of any additional motive beyond the protection of El Salvador, Costa Rica, and Honduras that the USA might have in using force against Nicaragua.[120] The USA asserted that it had responded to requests for assistance from El Salvador, Honduras, and Costa Rica in their self-defence against aggression by Nicaragua. Nicaragua claimed that the references made by the USA to the justification of self-defence were merely pretexts for its activities. The true motive was to impose its will on Nicaragua and force it to comply with US demands. However, the Court said that if the USA could establish that Nicaragua had supported the opposition in El Salvador and that this support amounted to an armed attack and the other appropriate conditions for collective self-defence were met, then it could legally invoke collective self-defence. The possibility of an additional motive, even one perhaps

---

[117] Reisman, 'Allocating Competences to use Coercion in the post Cold-War World, Practises, Conditions, and Prospects' in Damrosch and Scheffer (eds), *Law and Force in the New International Order* (1991, 26).

[118] McDougal and Feliciano, *Law and Minimum World Public Order* (1961) at 246; Delbruck, 'Collective Self-Defence', *Encyclopaedia of Public International Law,* Bernhardt (ed. 1982), Vol 13, 114.

[119] Farer, 'Drawing the Right Line', 81 AJIL (1987) 112; Higgins, 'The Attitude of Western States towards Legal Aspects of the Use of Force', in Cassese (ed.), *Current Legal Regulation of the Use of Force* (1986); also Delivanis, *La légitime défense en droit international public moderne* (1971), Part II, Chapter 2.

[120] *Nicaragua* case para 127.

more decisive for the USA, could not deprive the USA of its right to resort to collective self-defence. The only significance of the alleged additional motive was that special caution was called for in considering the allegations of the USA concerning conduct by Nicaragua which might provide a sufficient basis for self-defence. This provides a marked contrast to the policy-oriented approach of McDougal and Feliciano. In their discussion of collective self-defence they say, 'A first step in the determination of reasonableness (that is lawfulness) is thus an inquiry into the substantiality of the collective "self " alleged for security and defence, and *into whether a purported grouping for common protection is in reality a facade for other unlawfully expansive purposes.'*[121]

Does state practice reflect the ideal picture of collective self-defence as a protection for small states rather than as a pretext for furthering Cold War or neo-colonial interests? The more cynical view appears to be the more accurate as regards the actual use of force. All the state practice on collective self-defence since the Second World War has been controversial. The USSR has subsequently disavowed its invasion of Hungary and Czechoslovakia and acknowledged that the Brezhnev doctrine of limited sovereignty was not compatible with international law.[122] Some of the other episodes may be seen as showing a fundamental clash of perceptions; the situation could be seen either as one of a civil war with outside interference to further the political aims of the third state or as collective self-defence against an outside attack. The US intervention in Vietnam is just the most dramatic instance of this. The episodes where the USA or the UK intervened in Arab states may also be seen in this way: were they propping up unpopular rulers against regional pressure for change or were they saving the victims of outside aggression? And the same question arose of the French intervention in Chad. In Tajikistan the key question was how far Afghanistan was responsible for the operations across its border into Tajikistan. The legality of *Operation Enduring Freedom* in Afghanistan and its impact on the law of collective self-defence will be discussed in the next chapter.

On the positive side, it is possible to argue that during the Cold War the simple existence of collective self-defence treaties—not only NATO[123] and the now defunct Warsaw Pact, but also the treaties between the USA, the USSR and former colonial powers and smaller states—may have acted as a deterrent to attack and thus protected small states. But this conclusion is

---

[121] McDougal and Feliciano, *Law and Minimum World Public Order* (1961) at 248, 252.

[122] McWhinney, 'New Thinking in Soviet International Law', 1990 Canadian Yearbook of International Law 309 at 332; Gray, 'Self-determination and the Break-up of the Soviet Union', 12 Yearbook of European Law (1992) 465.

[123] Since the end of the Cold War, and in particular since 9/11, NATO has been seeking a new role: see 213 below.

necessarily speculative. The same state practice would be equally open to an alternative construction that these treaties in fact served to legitimate intervention by states parties.

The USA walked out of the Court hearings in the *Nicaragua* case after it lost its attempt to challenge the admissibility and jurisdiction.[124] In view of its conformity with state practice and the failure of the dissenting judges and critical commentators to demonstrate that the decision was wrong in law rather than on the facts, the ICJ's judgment on the merits of the *Nicaragua* case remains an authoritative statement of the law in this area, and was reaffirmed recently in the *Oil Platforms* case.[125]

---

[124] 24 ILM (1985) 246.
[125] ICJ Reports (2003) 161 para 51.

6

The use of force against terrorism: a new war for a new century?

The massive terrorist attacks on the World Trade Center and the Pentagon on September 11, 2001 (hereafter 9/11) led to a fundamental reappraisal of the law on self-defence.[1] The US response was to announce 'a different kind of war against a different kind of enemy', a global war on terrorism. But it is open to question how far any change in the law on the use of force has resulted from the terrorist attacks and their aftermath.

Responsibility for 9/11 was quickly attributed to the Al Qaida terrorist organization led by Osama bin Laden which had been responsible for several earlier terrorist attacks on US targets dating back to 1993.[2] The immediate international reaction was one of impressive unity among governments. The UN Security Council and General Assembly passed unanimous resolutions condemning the terrorist attacks;[3] Security Council Resolution 1368 (2001) implicitly affirmed the right of self-defence in response to terrorist attacks for the first time. NATO invoked Article 5 of its treaty for the first time in its history and declared that the attack on the USA was an attack on all member states and that they were prepared to act in collective self-defence.[4] The OAS also invoked collective self-defence;[5] Russia, China and Japan all gave support to military action.[6] Only Iraq directly challenged the legality of the military action.[7]

---

[1] For an account of the events, see Murphy, 'Contemporary Practice of the United States relating to International Law', 96 AJIL (2002) 237 and Keesings (2001) 44333, 44391.

[2] Murphy, 'Contemporary Practice of the United States relating to International Law', 96 AJIL (2002) 237 at 239; O'Connell, 'Evidence of Terror', 7 Journal of Conflict and Security Law (2002) 19.

[3] SC Res 1368 (2001) and 1373 (2001); GA Res/56/1 (2001).

[4] 40 ILM (2001) 1267, 1268. Article 5 provides: The Parties agree that an armed attack against one of more of them in Europe or North America shall be considered an attack against them all and consequently they agree that, if such an armed attack occurs, each of them, in exercise of the right of individual or collective self-defence recognized by Article 51 of the Charter of the UN, will assist the Party or Parties so attacked by taking forthwith, individually and in concert with the other Parties, such action as it deems necessary, including the use of armed force, to restore and maintain the security of the North Atlantic area.

[5] 40 ILM (2001) 1270, 1273. See also Ratner, 'Ius ad bellum and ius in bello after September 11', 96 AJIL (2002) 905 at 909.

[6] Murphy, 'Contemporary Practice of the United States relating to International Law', 96 AJIL (2002) 237 at 248.

[7] Keesings (2001) 4435–6, 44393; The Guardian, 8 October 2001.

The USA demanded that the Taliban regime in Afghanistan close Al Qaida terrorist training camps in Afghanistan, surrender Osama bin Laden and other members of Al Qaida, and open Afghanistan to US inspections. But the Taliban refused.[8] The USA with the military assistance of the UK, and pledges of military support from France, Germany, Australia, Canada and others, began *Operation Enduring Freedom* in Afghanistan on 7 October 2001;[9] this operation still continues over six years later. At the start of their military action both the USA and the UK wrote to the Security Council under Article 51, asserting that they were acting in individual and collective self-defence.[10] Although NATO had indicated its willingness to act in collective self-defence, the USA preferred not to act through NATO. Nevertheless many member states had forces directly involved in *Operation Enduring Freedom* at some stage.[11] The EU declared its 'whole-hearted support for the action that is being taken in self-defence in conformity with the UN Charter and the UN SC Resolution 1368'.[12]

It is not yet clear whether these events have brought about a radical and lasting transformation of the law of self-defence or whether their significance should be narrowly construed in that *Operation Enduring Freedom* was essentially a one-off, a response to a particular incident based on Security Council affirmation and (almost) universal acceptance by states. Even in the immediate aftermath of 9/11 there was a certain lack of clarity as to the exact scope of the right to use force in self-defence against terrorism and as to whether such a right could be invoked unilaterally. Radically opposing versions of the significance of 9/11 and *Operation Enduring Freedom* are possible. The temporary agreement between those few states which argued that the legal right to use force against terrorist attacks was already established and those far more numerous states who after 9/11 were apparently for the first time willing to accept it as a new development in the interpretation of Article 51 later dissipated in the disagreement as to whether to use military force against Iraq. Apart from the obvious question of the impact on the law of self-defence, *Operation Enduring Freedom*'s significance for the controversial doctrines of regime change and intervention should also be considered.

---

[8] Murphy, 'Contemporary Practice of the United States relating to International Law', 96 AJIL (2002) 237 at 243; Keesings (2001) 44337.

[9] Keesings (2001) 44391, 44448; Murphy, 'Contemporary Practice of the United States relating to International Law', 96 AJIL (2002) 237 at 246; Katselli and Shah, 'September 11 and the UK Response', 52 ICLQ (2003) 245; Byers, 'Terrorism, the Use of Force and International Law after 11 September 2001', 51 ICLQ (2002) 401.

[10] UN docs S/2001/946, S/2001/947; 40 ILM (2001)1280.

[11] See NATO website; <www.nato.int/terrorism/index.htm>.

[12] Press Release, Brussels, 7 October 2001.

The invocation of self-defence to justify the use of force in response to terrorist attacks had been made by only a few states before 9/11. The USA and Israel had invoked Article 51 to justify the use of force in response to terrorist attacks on nationals abroad, but many regarded their use of force as going far beyond the bounds of this provision. Force was used in response to past terrorist attacks by Israel in 1968 against Beirut and in 1985 against Tunis and by the USA against Libya in 1986, Iraq in 1993 and Sudan and Afghanistan in 1998. In all these episodes force was used against the state allegedly harbouring the terrorist organisation responsible. Israel and the USA used language that combined claims to be acting in response to past attacks and to deter future attacks.[13]

The first instance was the attack by the Israeli air force on Beirut airport in December 1968; Israel attempted to justify this action as a response to the earlier terrorist attack on an Israeli plane in Athens airport. It said that Lebanon had permitted Arab terrorist organisations to set up their headquarters in Beirut and to maintain training bases in Lebanon, thus officially encouraging warfare by terror against Israel. The Lebanese government had assumed responsibility for the activities of terror organizations. The attack on the Israeli civil aircraft at Athens airport had violated the ceasefire between Israel and Lebanon, and Israel was entitled to exercise its right of self-defence. The Security Council unanimously condemned the Israeli action in Resolution 262 (1968). It is striking that although the USA joined in the condemnation it made a point of explaining that it did so only because Lebanon had not in fact been responsible for the terrorist attack on Athens airport and the Israeli action was not proportionate; it accepted the principle on which the Israeli action was based. A state subject to continuing terrorist attacks could respond by appropriate use of force to defend itself against further attacks; this was an aspect of the inherent right of self-defence recognized in the UN Charter.[14]

This was not the view of the other states in the Security Council in 1968, but it has been repeated by the USA and Israel in later episodes. Israel in its 1985 attack on Tunis claimed that it was acting against the PLO headquarters in response to terrorist attacks on Israelis abroad by Palestinians.

---

[13] Alexandrov, Self-Defense against the Use of Force in *International Law* (1996) at 182; Arend and Beck, *International Law and the Use of Force: Beyond the UN Charter Paradigm* (1993) at 138; O'Brien, 'Reprisals, Deterrence and Self-Defense in Counterterror Operations', 30 Virginia Journal of International Law (1990) 421.

[14] 1968 UNYB 228. See Falk, 'The Beirut Raid and the International Law of Retaliation', 63 AJIL (1969) 415; Blum, 'The Beirut Raid and the International Double Standard', 64 AJIL (1970) 73.

It also claimed that Tunisia had a duty to prevent such attacks being carried out from its territory. Israel said that it was acting in self-defence and the USA in the Security Council debate accepted this argument. But the other member states did not agree and the action was vigorously condemned as an act of armed aggression against Tunisia's territory in flagrant violation of the UN Charter by 14–0–1 in Resolution 573 (1985). For the other member states the Israeli conception of self-defence was very far from that in international law.[15]

The USA itself undertook this type of action in 1986 against Libya. In response to terrorist attacks against US citizens abroad for which it said Libya was responsible, US aircraft, flying from bases in the UK with the support of the UK government, attacked targets in Tripoli. The USA reported the action to the Security Council as self-defence under Article 51; its action was a response to past terrorist attacks on nationals and also taken to deter such attacks in the future. Most states rejected this claim saying that self-defence should be narrowly interpreted and could not be pre-emptive. However, the UK and France joined the USA in vetoing the resolution condemning its action.[16] The UK accepted that 'the right of self-defence is not an entirely passive right'; it was within the inherent right of self-defence to try to turn the tide of terrorism and to discourage further attacks.[17]

The USA used the same wide doctrine of self-defence to justify its action in its response to the alleged assassination attempt on ex-President Bush by Iraqi agents in Kuwait in April 1993. The USA responded in June 1993 by firing missiles at the Iraqi Intelligence Headquarters in Baghdad. It again invoked Article 51 in its letter to the Security Council. The response of the Security Council showed considerable sympathy with the USA and some commentators have tried to argue that this marked the emergence of a new rule of international law allowing such actions in response to terrorism. But in the Security Council it was only Russia and the UK which offered express support for the US legal argument. The UK took a fairly cautious line; it said that force may be used in self-defence against threats to one's nationals if the target continues to be used in support of terrorist

---

[15] 1985 UNYB 285; SC 2610th, 2615th meetings (1985).

[16] 1986 UNYB 247; the USA reported to the Security Council in UN doc S/17990, 14 April 1986; SC 2677th, 2679th, 2680th meetings (1986); see 'Contemporary Practice of the US', 80 AJIL (1986) 632; on UK position see 'UK Materials on International Law', 57 BYIL (1986) 641; Greenwood, 'International Law and the United States Air Operation Against Libya', 89 West Virginia Law Review (1987) 933.

[17] The USA denied that there was any parallel between the South African attacks on Zambia, Zimbabwe and Botswana and its own acts against Libya; the UK apparently accepted this, 'UK Materials on International Law', 57 BYIL (1986) 621, but other states said there was such a parallel between the actions of the USA and of South Africa, SC 2684th, 2686th meetings (1986).

acts against one's nationals and there is no other way to respond.[18] Several states expressed concern, although only China actually condemned the US action. Other states generally said that they understood the US action.[19]

Similarly, when the USA responded to terrorist attacks on its embassies in Kenya and Tanzania in August 1998 by missile attacks on a terrorist training camp in Afghanistan and a pharmaceutical plant in Sudan, the response of the rest of the world was generally muted. The USA said that the camp had been used by the Al Qaida organization to support terrorism and that the pharmaceutical plant also produced chemical weapons for terrorist activities. It reported its actions to the Security Council under Article 51; it wished to report that the USA had exercised its right of self-defence in responding to a series of armed attacks against US embassies and nationals. It said that it was acting in response to those terrorist attacks and to prevent and deter their continuation. Its attacks were carried out after repeated efforts to convince Sudan and the Taliban regime in Afghanistan to shut down the terrorist facilities. The targets struck and the timing and method of attack used were designed to comply with rules of international law, including the rules of necessity and proportionality.[20] Sudan requested a meeting of the Security Council but the issue was not put on the agenda and there was only a very brief meeting with no action taken. There were condemnations of the use of force by the USA by Arab states, the Non-Aligned Movement, Pakistan and Russia. As before, those who refrained from condemnation or expressed support were careful not to adopt the US doctrine of self-defence.[21]

All these episodes were justified by the states using force as self-defence, but on the basis of the explanations given by Israel and the USA themselves the actions look more like reprisals, because they were punitive rather than defensive. Even if the actions were aimed at those actually responsible for the terrorist attacks, and even if the response could be accepted as proportionate, it is difficult to see how the use of force was

---

[18] 'UK Materials on International Law', 64 BYIL (1993) 732.

[19] 1993 UNYB 431; US letter to the Security Council UN doc S/26003, 26 June 1993; Kritsiotis, 'The legality of the 1993 US Missile Strike on Iraq and the right of self-defence in international law', 45 ICLQ (1996) 162; Gray, 'After the Cease fire: Iraq, the Security Council and the Use of Force', 65 BYIL (1994) 135; Reisman, 'The raid on Baghdad: some reflections on its lawfulness and implications', 5 EJIL (1994) 120; Condorelli, A propos de l'attaque américaine contre l'Iraq du 26 Juin 1993', 5 EJIL (1994) 134.

[20] UN doc S/1998/780; 1998 UNYB 1218.

[21] 'Contemporary Practice of the United States relating to International Law', 93 AJIL (1999) 161. There was considerable doubt as to whether the plant in Sudan was really a chemical weapons factory linked to international terrorism, Keesings (1999) 42766. The UK position showed some uncertainty; the PM defended the legality of the US action but the Foreign Secretary took a much more cautious line. It is noteworthy that the UK Materials on International Law for BYIL (1998), prepared with the help of the UK FCO, do not include any materials on the UK reaction.

necessary, given that the attacks on the nationals had already taken place. The USA and Israel aimed to retaliate and deter and said that their actions were pre-emptive because there was a danger of future terrorist attacks. The problem for the USA and Israel is that all states agree that in principle forcible reprisals are unlawful.[22] The General Assembly made this clear in the *Declaration on Friendly Relations* and the *Resolution on the Inadmissibility of Intervention*. The Security Council also passed Resolution 188 in 1964, in response to a British attack on Yemen, but declaring in absolute terms that it condemned reprisals as incompatible with the purposes and principles of the UN. This universal agreement that reprisals are not lawful led Israel and the USA to try to stretch the meaning of Article 51, but although other states were not prepared formally to condemn the USA for its attacks on Baghdad, Afghanistan and Sudan, they did not accept the legal argument. Only Russia and the UK were prepared openly to support the legality of the US action in 1993. Russia has since abandoned its brief moment of enthusiasm and returned to a critical approach; even the UK, as so often the main supporter of the USA, took an ambivalent position in 1998. Failure to condemn the USA should be taken to indicate sympathy and understanding rather than acceptance of a legal doctrine which destroys the distinction between reprisals and self-defence and which the USA would never contemplate being used against itself.

THE IMPACT OF 9/11

Therefore, before 9/11 it was clear that the right to use force in self-defence against terrorist attacks was controversial. But the almost universal support of states for a US right of self-defence in response to 9/11 may be seen as raising the question whether there has been a significant change in the law. For some this is just a continuation of the existing wide right of self-defence; for others it is a new right based on a re-interpretation of Article 51 of the UN Charter, justified by the fiction of instant custom or, more realistically, by universal acceptance by states of a new legal rule; for others the acceptance was merely political and did not serve to create a wider right of self-defence. After 9/11 it seemed that the members of the Security Council

---

[22] Once again writers have gone further than states in claiming that it is unrealistic to outlaw reprisals. Some have tried to argue that certain reprisals may be legitimate, although technically illegal. Bowett was the first to make this claim with regard to Israel. He said that failure to condemn by the Security Council was an indication that the action was permissible, Bowett, 'Reprisals involving recourse to armed force', 66 AJIL (1972) 31. O'Brien followed this line and updated it, O'Brien, 'Reprisals, Deterrence and Self-Defense in Counterterror Operations', 30 Virginia Journal of International Law (1990) 421. But this argument was forcefully and successfully refuted by Barsotti, 'Armed Reprisals', in Cassese (ed.) *Current Legal Regulation of the Use of Force* (1986) 79.

were willing to accept the legality of action in self-defence in response to the terrorist attacks on the World Trade Center and the Pentagon as they unanimously passed Resolution 1368 on 12 September and Resolution 1373 on 28 September 2001. These both assert in the preamble that the Security Council is 'determined to combat by all means threats to international peace and security caused by terrorist acts' and that it recognizes 'the inherent right of individual or collective self-defence in accordance with the Charter'.

Although some have expressed doubt as to whether these resolutions actually support self-defence against terrorist actions, because the reference to this is found in the preamble rather than the operative part of the resolutions and the language is that of 'threat to international peace and security' rather than 'armed attack' under Article 51,[23] it seems clear that the members of the Security Council were in fact willing to accept the use of force in self-defence by the USA in response to the terrorist attacks. The reference to self-defence in the preamble is of greater significance than might appear taken in isolation, because the Security Council does not commonly make any express reference to the right of self defence in its resolutions. That is, it seems from the international response to 9/11 that there could, under certain conditions, be a right of self-defence against non-state actors for terrorist attacks. But there are difficulties in establishing the exact scope of this right.

The concept of armed attack after 9/11

One of the most difficult questions arising out of 9/11 is whether the concept of 'armed attack' in Article 51 has undergone a revolutionary change so that it now extends to attacks by non-state actors even if there is very little or no state complicity. It is true that Article 51 does not specify that an armed attack must be by a state. But even if there could hypothetically be an armed attack in the absence of state complicity in that attack, the question of the permissible response is much more problematic. For many states and commentators the concept of self-defence against non-state actors was unacceptable before 9/11. Few were willing openly to support a right to use force against a state where the terrorists operated or were present in the absence of the complicity of that state in the terrorist acts.[24] The test generally accepted by states was that in the *Definition of Aggression*,

[23] For example, Cassese, 'Terrorism is also disrupting some crucial legal categories of international law,' 12 EJIL (2001) 993; Myjer and White, 'The Twin Towers Attack: an Unlimited Right to Self-defence', 7 Journal of Conflict and Security (2002) 5.
[24] In the cases discussed above the states against whom action was taken in response to prior terrorist acts were all accused of involvement in the terrorism, with the exception of Tunisia. Israel's attack on Tunis in 1985 was condemned by the Security Council (see note 15 above).

taken by the International Court of Justice in the *Nicaragua* case as applicable to the concept of armed attack: that the use of force by individuals constituted an armed attack only when there had been a *'sending by or on behalf of a state* of armed bands, groups, irregulars or mercenaries, which carry out acts of armed force against another State of such gravity as to amount to acts of aggression'.[25]

After 9/11 President Bush announced that the USA would make no distinction between terrorists and those who 'harboured' them, and that it would treat any nation that harboured terrorists as a hostile regime.[26] Also the Joint Resolution of Congress authorizing force did so against states which 'planned, authorized, committed or aided the terrorist attacks... or harboured such organizations'.[27] This has been seen by some as a widening of the right of self-defence. But the USA did not use this language in its letter to the Security Council under Article 51; here it said that it had 'obtained clear and compelling information that the Al-Qaida organization, which is supported by the Taliban regime in Afghanistan, had a central role in the attacks.... The attacks on September 11, 2001 and the ongoing threat to the United States and its nationals posed by the Al-Qaida organization have been made possible by the decision of the Taliban regime to allow the parts of Afghanistan that it controls to be used by this organization as a base of operation'. Despite efforts by the international community the Taliban regime had refused to change its policy. From the territory of Afghanistan Al Qaida continued to train and support terrorists who target US nationals and interests in the USA and abroad.[28]

The UK argued that Al Qaida was something between a traditional terrorist organization and a state. Osama bin Laden and Al Qaida had been able to commit the atrocities because of their close alliance with the Taliban regime which allowed them to operate with impunity in pursuing their terrorist activity.[29] In its letter to the Security Council the UK said that the military action was directed against Osama bin Laden's Al Qaida terrorist organization and the Taliban regime that was supporting it.[30] However, after the event the UK did retrospectively claim that their use of force against Al Qaida and the Taliban in Afghanistan had been undertaken on the basis of a right of self-defence against those who planned and perpetrated large-scale terrorist acts and those who 'harboured' terrorists.[31]

---

[25] *Nicaragua* case. ICJ Reports (1986) 14 at para 195; see 130 above.
[26] Murphy, 'Contemporary Practice of the United States relating to International Law', 96 AJIL (2002) 237.
[27] 40 ILM (2001)1282.
[28] UN doc S/2001/946; 40 ILM (2001)1280.
[29] FCO Paper, *Responsibility for the terrorist atrocities* (2001).
[30] UN doc S/2001/947.
[31] Attorney-General Speech in the House of Lords, HL Debates 21 April 2004 Vol 660 c369–372; UK Materials in International Law, 75 BYIL (2004) 822–3.

Both states thus left uncertain what degree of involvement, if any, by Afghanistan was necessary to justify the use of force against its territory. Commentators disagree on their interpretation of the facts and of the significance of the language of the USA and the UK. Some have argued that there has been a change in the law to widen it to allow self-defence against states harbouring terrorists;[32] others say that such an attempt to widen the law would be impermissible;[33] others that on the facts the relationship between Al Qaida and the Taliban regime was sufficiently close to come within the traditional requirements as set out in the *Definition of Aggression*, even though the USA had used the language of harbouring.[34] In this particular case the Security Council had passed repeated resolutions strongly condemning the continuing use of Afghan territory for the sheltering and training of terrorists and planning of terrorist acts, deploring the fact that the Taliban continued to provide a safe haven to Osama bin Laden and demanding that the Taliban regime stop providing sanctuary and training for international terrorists and their organizations.[35] Considerable uncertainty thus remains on this long-standing controversy as to the definition of armed attack. Those who argue that the law has changed or should be changed—that the requirements of the *Definition of Aggression* as applied by the International Court of Justice in the *Nicaragua* case should be modified in such a way that self-defence may be invoked against non-state actors operating from a state which has tolerated their activities or is unable to control them— have not been able to adduce state practice in support of their argument other than that of *Operation Enduring Freedom*.[36] In so far as their arguments are based on policy considerations they bear the heavy burden of establishing that widening the permissible use of force would be effective in the 'war on terror'.

---

[32] Ratner, '*Ius ad Bellum* and *Ius in Bello* after September 11', 96 AJIL (2002) 906. The 2005 AU *Non-Aggression and Common Defence Pact* (not yet in force) in Article 1(c) includes 'harbouring' in its definition of aggression. But the drafting here is not clear.

[33] Paust, 'Use of armed force against terrorists in Afghanistan, Iraq and beyond', 35 Cornell ILJ (2002) 532; Corten and Dubuisson, 'Operation Liberté Immuable: une extension abusive du concept de légitime défense', 106 RGDIP (2002) 51; Myjer and White, 'The Twin Towers Attack: an Unlimited Right to Self-defence', 7 Journal of Conflict and Security (2002) 5.

[34] Byers, 'Terrorism, the Use of Force and International Law after 11 September', 51 ICLQ (2002) 401.

[35] SC Res 1193 (1998),1214 (1998), 1267 (1999), 1333 (2000).

[36] See discussion by Becker, *Terrorism and the State* (2006); Jinks, 'State responsibility for the acts of private armed groups', 4 Chicago JIL (2003) 83; Kammerhofer, 'The Armed Activities case and non-state actors in self-defence law', 20 Leiden JIL (2007) 89; Murphy, 'Terrorism and the concept of armed attack in Article 51 of the UN Charter', 43 Harvard JIL (2002) 41; Ruys and Verhoeven, 'Attacks by private actors and the right of self-defence', 10 Journal of Conflict and Security law (2005) 289; Tams, 'Note Analytique: Swimming with the tide or seeking to stem it', 18 Revue québécoise de droit int (2005) 275; Travalio and Altenburg, 'Terrorism, State responsibility and the use of military force', 4 Chicago JIL (2003) 97.

As was shown in Chapter 4, the International Court of Justice in the *Wall Opinion* did not make a clear pronouncement on these questions as to whether there can be an armed attack by a non-state actor and as to what would be the permissible response to such an attack in self-defence.[37] Many interpret its brief paragraph on Article 51 as expressly ruling out self-defence against non-state actors. Whether or not the Court took such a categorical position, it clearly adopted a restrictive interpretation of Security Council Resolutions 1368 (2001) and 1373 (2001) in holding that these did not support a claim to self-defence by Israel in this case: 'The Court also notes that Israel exercises control in the Occupied Palestinian Territory and that, as Israel itself states, the threat which it regards as justifying the construction of the wall originates within, and not outside, that territory. The situation is thus different from that contemplated by Security Council Resolutions 1368 (2001) and 1373 (2001), and therefore Israel could not in any event invoke those resolutions in support of its claim to be exercising a right of self-defence. Consequently, the Court concludes that Article 51 has no relevance in this case.' Thus the Court treated the applicable law as that of occupation. There could be no right under Article 51 against terrorist attacks originating in the Palestinian territory occupied by Israel.[38] In *Armed Activities on the Territory of the Congo (DRC v Uganda)*—not a case on terrorists, but on opposition groups conducting cross-border attacks— the Court deliberately and explicitly avoided the controversial issue of self-defence against non-state actors in the absence of state involvement in an armed attack.[39]

Another issue that arises about the scope of 'armed attack' after 9/11 is whether it extends beyond attacks on territory to attacks on nationals abroad. Before 9/11 states were divided on this issue.[40] The terrorist attacks of 9/11 were on US territory rather than against nationals abroad as they had been in the earlier terrorist episodes discussed above. And the attacks were clearly of a sufficient gravity according to the *Definition of Aggression* to constitute an 'armed attack' under Article 51. Questions must remain as to how far the majority of states would be willing to accept smaller scale terrorist attacks on nationals abroad as giving rise to a right of self-defence against non-state actors in a non-complicit state.

---

[37] ICJ Reports (2004) 136 para 139.

[38] Israel repeatedly claims a right to self-defence against terrorist actions originating in the occupied territories in its communications to the Security Council. It invokes Article 51, but in accordance with its usual practice, the SC has not expressly pronounced on the validity of these claims.

[39] ICJ Reports (2005) 168 at para 147. See Okowa, 'Congo's War', 77 BYIL (2006) 203.

[40] See 156 above.

Necessity and proportionality

Another problem arising out of any new right of self-defence against past terrorist actions is the application of the requirement that self-defence be necessary and proportionate. If force is used in response to *past* attacks, it is not necessary self-defence as the harm has already been done. In so far as self-defence against terrorism is designed to deter and prevent *future* terrorist acts it is difficult, if not impossible, to employ these central criteria of self-defence in the absence of detailed evidence about a specific threatened attack. The USA and the UK, which both support a wide right of self-defence against imminent attacks, claim that they may take measures proportionate to the *threat* of a future attack, rather than merely to a specific armed attack which has already taken place.[41] This was also the approach adopted by Israel in the 2006 conflict in Lebanon.[42] It raises the questions how it would be possible to determine what would be necessary and proportionate to deter a possible, but indeterminate, future attack? If these criteria of necessity and proportionality are not applicable then there are no limits on self-defence. There are more fundamental questions as to how far the use of force is an effective response to terrorism. It is not clear that the forcible response to 9/11 will in fact deter future terrorist attacks: if it is not an effective response, then it could be argued that it cannot be a necessary response.

Operation Enduring Freedom

At the time of writing, *Operation Enduring Freedom* continues in Afghanistan six years after its inception. Some commentators have expressed doubts as to how far *Operation Enduring Freedom* is necessary and proportionate, because it started as an aerial bombardment rather than as a more selective ground campaign and because it involved actions not just against Al Qaida but also against the Taliban regime.[43] Further questions now arise because the operation has continued for such a long time. It began in October 2001 with an air campaign against fixed targets such as air defence, communication centres and command and control centres, air bases and training camps. It then went on to target the positions of Taliban and Al Qaida forces. At first, the US military campaign operated in cooperation with the Northern

---

[41] UK Attorney-General's Speech in the House of Lords, HL Debates 21 April 2004 Vol 660 c369–372; UK Materials in International Law, 75 BYIL (2004) 822–3; US State Department Legal Adviser, Taft, 'Self-Defense and the Oil Platforms decision', 29 Yale Journal of International Law (2004) 295.

[42] See 237 below.

[43] See, for example, Cassese, 'Terrorism is also disrupting some crucial legal categories of international law,' 12 EJIL (2001) 993; Corten and Dubuisson, 'Operation Liberté Immuable: une extension abusive du concept de légitime défense', 106 RGDIP (2002) 51.

Alliance, Afghan opposition forces which had been fighting the Taliban regime in Afghanistan for many years. Together they forced the Taliban to evacuate Kabul in November 2001 and drove them from power. The defeat of the Taliban weakened Al Qaida's support base in Afghanistan.[44]

But the political settlement in the *Bonn Agreement* in December 2001 and the establishment of a UN-authorized force, ISAF,[45] in January 2002, to assist the government of Afghanistan in the maintenance of security, did not bring peace or stability to Afghanistan. Military operations by *Operation Enduring Freedom* continued in pursuit of Al Qaida and Taliban forces; a significant operation in the south was initiated on the same day as action against Iraq began in March 2003.[46] The pronouncement by US Defense Secretary Rumsfeld in May 2003 that major combat operations were over has proved distinctly premature.[47] ISAF was initially restricted to the area of Kabul until its sphere of operation was extended by Resolution 1510 in October 2003.[48] Despite pleas from UN officials and from the President of Afghanistan, the USA was reluctant to accept its expansion beyond Kabul before that date, in case ISAF's operations interfered with those of *Operation Enduring Freedom*.[49] ISAF's size and sphere of operation were incrementally increased until it finally extended its area of responsibility to the whole of Afghanistan in October 2006.[50] But *Operation Enduring Freedom* also continues to operate.[51]

The situation is still unstable, despite the agreement on a new constitution in January 2004, the holding of presidential and parliamentary elections, and the replacement of the transitional *Bonn Agreement* with the *Afghanistan Compact* in January 2006.[52] The Taliban is resurgent. Insurgent forces increasingly engage in conventional conflicts with Afghan government and international security forces.[53] There has also been a growing

---

[44] UK Foreign Affairs Committee Report HC 196 para 76; Report HC 384, para 87.
[45] ISAF was authorized by the *Bonn Agreement* of December 2001 and endorsed by UN SC Res 1386 under Chapter VII, 42 ILM (2002) 1032. It was initially 5,000 strong and was gradually expanded until it reached 35,000 in 2007, Keesings (2007) 47756.
[46] Keesings (2003) 45289.
[47] Keesings (2003) 45403.
[48] UN Press Release SC/7894, 13 October 2003. NATO assumed command of ISAF on 11 August 2003, Keesings (2003) 45552.
[49] UN Press Release SC/7751, 6 May 2003; UN News Centre report 13 August 2003; *The Observer*, 8 June 2003.
[50] Report of the SC Mission to Afghanistan, S/2006/935 para 13.
[51] In February 2007 it numbered 8,000 troops, Report of the Secretary-General, The situation in Afghanistan and its implications for international peace and security, S/2007/152 para 33.
[52] Report of the SC Mission to Afghanistan, S/2006/935. Some have expressed doubts as to the compatibility of the two operations; see, for example, the statements of the Italian Foreign Minister, *International Herald Tribune*, 25 July 2007.
[53] Report of the SC Mission to Afghanistan, S/2006/935 para 8–10; Keesings (2003) 45241, 45345, (2004) 45789, (2005) 46821, (2006) 47099, 47150, (2007) 47756, 47989, 48138, 48193. The

number of suicide attacks; according to the UN Secretary-General, these represent the most visible link between the insurgency and international terrorism.[54] The Security Council has expressed its concern at the increasing violence and terrorist activities in a series of resolutions starting in 2005.[55]

Much of the country outside Kabul remains lawless, and there have been reports that drug production has increased to record levels.[56] In 2002 and 2003 there was factional fighting between various militias and ethnic groups,[57] and outside states were reported to maintain support for the different ethnic groups involved in ongoing conflict.[58] This factional fighting has now declined but ethnic divisions still affect the country.[59] At the end of 2002 Afghanistan concluded a non-aggression pact with its neighbours, China, Pakistan, Iran, Turkmenistan, Uzbekistan and Tajikistan. This was intended to end foreign interference in Afghanistan, something which had contributed to the continuation of 20 years of conflict; the pact was welcomed by the Security Council in Resolution 1453 (2002).[60] However, the USA has repeatedly expressed concern that Al Qaida terrorists have fled into Pakistan and are operating from there and it has put pressure on Pakistan's government to act more strongly against them.[61] The USA has also made accusations of Iranian involvement in the insurgency in Afghanistan.[62]

UN Secretary-General reported in March 2007 that: 'Popular alienation remains a key factor behind the revitalized insurgency, and stems from inappropriate Government appointments, tribal nepotism and monopolization of power, the marginalization of those outside the dominant social and political groups' (Report of the Secretary-General, The situation in Afghanistan and its implications for international peace and security, S/2007/152 para 5).

[54] Report of the Secretary-General, The situation in Afghanistan and its implications for international peace and security, S/2007/152 para 7. In September 2007 he reported further that 'An intensifying Taliban-led insurgency that increasingly relies on suicide bombing and other terrorist tactics is undermining confidence in the future.', S/2007/755 para 2.

[55] SC Res 1589 (2005), 1662 (2006), 1707 (2006) 1746 (2007).

[56] Keesings (2004) 45846, 46120, 46312, (2006) 47413, (2007) 47809, 47990; UN Office on Drugs and Crime Report, *Afghanistan Opium Survey*, August 2007.

[57] Report of the SC Mission to Afghanistan, S/2003/1074 para 24; UN Press Release SC/7753, 6 May 2003; Keesings (2002) 45041, 44981, (2003) 45345; *The Observer* 12 February 2003; *The Guardian*, 8 December 2003, 22, 29 March 2004, 9 April 2004, 18 August 2004.

[58] The Pashtun, from whom the Taliban were mostly derived, offered resistance to the government, *The Guardian*, 6 March 2002. Tajiks and Uzbeks dominate in the Northern Alliance, allegedly with Russian sponsorship, *The Guardian*, 23 October 2001. There have been many reports of Iranian assistance to Tajik militias, *The Guardian*, 24 January, 4 February 2002, Keesings (2002) 44553. See also *The Guardian*, 23 December 2002, 29 January 2003.

[59] Report of the SC Mission to Afghanistan, S/2006/935.

[60] Keesings (2002) 45142.

[61] See, for example, Keesings (2002) 44724, (2006) 47520, (2006) 47467, (2007) 47694, 47695, 47755. The governments of Afghanistan and Pakistan also accuse each other of failing to act against Taliban and Al Qaida forces on their territory: Keesings (2006) 47150, 47149, 47208, 47464, 47641.

[62] Keesings (2007) 47867, 47989; see 113 above.

The USA has involved other states—initially Australia, Poland and the UK—directly in *Operation Enduring Freedom* in what may be seen as a quest for political legitimacy, even though it has not been willing to accept the constraints of acting through NATO or the UN. Many other states have participated in *Operation Enduring Freedom* in a support capacity.[63] The USA can thus argue that its action is not unilateral but that of a 'Coalition against Terror'. This search for legitimacy through wider international participation became increasingly important as *Operation Enduring Freedom* continued, with no express UN basis beyond the initial reference to self-defence in Security Council Resolutions 1368 (2001) and 1373 (2001). The longer *Operation Enduring Freedom* continues, the further it is detached from its initial basis in self-defence. It may be that awareness of this led to express reference to *Operation Enduring Freedom* in Security Council resolutions; the first reference was in Resolution 1510 (2003) which called upon ISAF to continue to work in close consultation with the *Operation Enduring Freedom* coalition in the implementation of its mandate.[64] Resolution 1659 (2006) went further and called for 'closer operational synergy' between the two forces, and Resolution 1707 (2006) welcomed the increased coordination between them. Also, in Resolution 1589 (2005) the Security Council called on the Government of Afghanistan, with the assistance of the international community, including the *Operation Enduring Freedom* coalition and ISAF, 'to continue to address the threat to the security and stability of Afghanistan posed by Al Qaida operatives, the Taliban and other extremist groups, factional violence among militia forces and criminal activities, in particular violence involving the drug trade'.[65] These resolutions may be seen as implicit acceptance of the legality of *Operation Enduring Freedom* by the Security Council, but they contain nothing express on its legal basis, and there was no discussion of this in the Security Council.

In September 2007 the legal basis of the maritime operations conducted by eight states as part of *Operation Enduring Freedom* did attract some attention in the Security Council. The question apparently arose because there were indications that Japan for domestic political reasons would not agree to continue its navy's participation in these maritime operations unless there was express Security Council authorization.[66] Accordingly,

---

[63] Murphy, 'Contemporary Practice of the United States relating to International Law', 97 AJIL (2003) 419 at 428; Keesings (2003) 45315. For current information on those taking part, see 'Coalition Fighting Terror' on the US Department of Defense website; <www.defenselink.mil/>.

[64] SC Res 1563 (2004) and 1623 (2005) also called for cooperation between ISAF and *Operation Enduring Freedom*.

[65] See also Res 1662 (2006), 1746 (2007).

[66] Keesings (2007) 48197. However, Japan did later decide to resume its involvement in *Operation Enduring Freedom*, and this was welcomed by the Secretary-General, UN Press Release SG/SM/11370, 14 January 2008.

the Security Council in resolution 1776 (2007) extending the authority of ISAF, for the first time made express reference to the maritime operations of *Operation Enduring Freedom*: 'expressing its appreciation for the leadership provided by the North Atlantic Treaty Organization (NATO), and for the contribution of many nations to ISAF and to the OEF coalition, including its maritime interdiction component'. Russia abstained on this resolution, because there had been no clarity with regard to the new wording. It said that the activities of the *Operation Enduring Freedom* coalition were carried out outside the context of the UN, and the Security Council had not been informed in detail about them.[67] This indicates an unwillingness to accept the legality of all aspects of the activities of *Operation Enduring Freedom*.

Initially, perhaps this military campaign in Afghanistan could be seen as a new war against an unprecedented act of terrorism. The USA today maintains that the conflict, like that in Iraq, is the front line in the war on terror.[68] But there are many who argue that the conflict in Afghanistan demonstrates that the 'war on terror' is self-perpetuating and cannot be won by military means.[69] In its prolonged support for an Afghan government unable to retain power on its own against fundamentalist Islamist and ethnic opposition forces, *Operation Enduring Freedom* seems somewhat reminiscent of the Soviet occupation of Afghanistan from 1979–89. The legal basis of the continuing operations is today left unclear: there is room for doubt as to whether it should still be seen as self-defence against terrorism or whether the authority for the operation now comes from the consent of the new regime in Afghanistan and the fight has become one to secure the stability of the government. The new government established under the auspices of the UN still does not control large areas of its territory and, the longer *Operation Enduring Freedom* continues, the more questions arise with regard to Afghanistan. The US and UK press releases on the conduct of the campaign give no clear indication on this matter, nor is it discussed in the UN.

---

[67] SC 5744th meeting (2007). Russia said that it believed 'that the maritime component is necessary solely to combat terrorism in Afghanistan and should not be used for other purposes'. Russia and China regretted the manner in which the resolution was adopted (under the coordination of Italy) without adequate consultation.

[68] See, for example, 2006 US *National Security Strategy* 12 (available on White House website; <www.whitehouse.gov/>). Afghanistan also maintained that insecurity arises from the international terrorist network, not from ethnic divisions within the country; the threat comes from the remnants of the Taliban and Al Qaida, UN Press Release GA/10215, 5 December 2003.

[69] Military occupation, and the deaths of civilians caused by US air attacks aimed at Al Qaida and insurgent forces inevitably lead to new recruits for those opposed to the US presence. If the 'war on terror' is to continue until the threat of terrorism is defeated then it is difficult to see an end. Indeed President Bush has spoken of the 'war on terror' as an intergenerational war in his 2007 State of the Union Address, Keesings (2007) 47683.

Pre-emptive self-defence

Another difficult question arising out of 9/11 and its aftermath is whether self-defence against terrorist attacks is permissible only when there has been an actual past attack or whether a purely pre-emptive action is lawful, and if so, how such a purely pre-emptive action could be necessary and proportionate. Moreover, would pre-emptive action be legal only against terrorism or also against other dangers?

The US letter to the Security Council under Article 51 of the UN Charter said that, 'In response to these attacks and in accordance with the inherent right of individual and collective self-defence, United States armed forces have initiated actions designed to prevent and deter further attacks on the United States.'[70] The UK letter said, 'These forces have been employed in exercise of the inherent right of individual and collective self-defence, recognized in Article 51, following the terrorist outrage of 11 September, to avert the continuing threat of attacks from the same source.'[71] These are claims to preventive and deterrent action which before 9/11 would have been regarded by many as unlawful reprisals rather than lawful self-defence, but even these wide claims were limited by the fact that there had been an actual attack. The apparent attempt by the USA subsequently to extend the right of self-defence to cover purely pre-emptive action has proved extremely controversial.[72]

How far has *Operation Enduring Freedom* been a turning point in the law on the use of force?

The operation against Afghanistan can be interpreted in radically opposing ways, as a wide or a narrow precedent in the development of the law on the use of force. On the narrowest view, self-defence would be limited to the situation where there had been an actual massive terrorist attack on a state's territory, where there was a continuing threat of global terrorism from those responsible and where the response was directed against the organization directly responsible in a state which had allowed it to operate and which then refused to expel it; and then only after the Security Council had determined the existence of a threat to international peace

---

[70] UN doc S/2001/946; 40 ILM (2001) 1280.

[71] UN doc S/2001/947; 'UK Materials on International Law', 72 BYIL (2001) at 682.

[72] See, for example, Bothe, Terrorism and the Legality of Pre-emptive Force', 14 EJIL (2003) 227; Glennon, 'The Fog of Law: Self-defense, inherence and incoherence in Article 51 of the UN Charter', 25 Harvard Journal of Law and Public Policy (2002) 539; O'Connell, 'The Myth of Pre-emptive self-defense', American Society of International Law Task Force on Terrorism (2002); <www.asil.org/taskforce/oconnell,pdf>; and Sofaer, 'On the need of pre-emption', 14 EJIL (2003) 209.

and security; and where the Security Council had asserted a right of self-defence, even if not in the operative part of the resolutions. In the case of Afghanistan, Security Council Resolutions 1368 (2001) and 1373 (2001) could be cited as crucial by states explaining their willingness not to condemn the US action.[73]

In contrast a wide view of the precedential significance of *Operation Enduring Freedom* might be asserted whereby states are now free to act in self-defence against the threat of any sort of terrorist attack on their nationals or their territory, even in the absence of any Security Council resolution, and even where the state against whose territory the action is taken had no involvement in any sort of support for the terrorists.

THE BUSH DOCTRINE OF PRE-EMPTIVE SELF-DEFENCE

The USA in its letter to the Security Council under Article 51 at the start of *Operation Enduring Freedom*, having asserted its right to act in self-defence in response to 9/11, went on to say 'There is much we do not know. Our inquiry is still in its early stages. We may find that our self-defense requires further actions with respect to *other organizations* and *other States.*'[74] It is not entirely clear whether the USA envisaged action only against those directly involved in the attacks of 9/11 or whether it was already widening the right of self-defence in the war against terrorism. The USA has subsequently gone further, apparently indicating that force may be used even where there has been no actual attack, purely in order to pre-empt future, even non-imminent, attacks. This controversial doctrine is regarded with considerable suspicion by most other states. In 2002 it was initially open to question how far the aim of the USA was really to introduce a radical change in the law or whether the doctrine was designed mainly to stir up fear in certain states, to put pressure on them to modify their behaviour, or to justify targeted killings.[75]

---

[73] *Combating Terrorism*, A Policy Report of the UN Association of the USA, (2002) at 23.

[74] UN doc S/2001/946.

[75] The USA apparently envisaged a series of measures, ranging from invasion to targeted killings. Thus in Yemen in November 2002 the USA, with the apparent consent of the government, assassinated six alleged Al Qaida members, using an unmanned drone (Keesings (2002) 45118; *The Guardian*, 5 and 6 November 2002). A similar operation was carried out in Pakistan in 2006 with the apparent acquiescence of the government at the time (Keesings (2006) 40738). The President later protested about the infringement of its sovereignty (*The Guardian*, 28 April 2006). More recently, the USA undertook targeted killings in Somalia (see 249 below). The UK reaction to targeted killings has not been enthusiastic. When asked by the Foreign Affairs Committee what was its attitude to this policy of targeted killings, the Government replied cautiously, 'The scale and unpredictable nature of the terrorist threat posed by Al Qaida and related groups requires a preparedness to take rigorous action in self-defence. We cannot prejudge the action that may be required. But, in protecting the

In his *State of the Union Address* in January 2002 President Bush said that the 'war against terrorism' was just beginning. Although *Operation Enduring Freedom* in Afghanistan was far from over, he shifted the focus of the war towards the 'Axis of Evil' consisting of Iraq, Iran and North Korea. His concern was that these states were developing weapons of mass destruction which they might use themselves or supply to terrorist organizations hostile to the USA. It was with regard to these states that the question of pre-emptive self-defence came to the fore. The USA in September 2002 produced a *National Security Strategy* in response to the new terrorist threat.[76] This was a dramatic document which combined triumph at the victory of the West in the Cold War with alarmism at the threat of terrorism. As President Bush said in his covering letter, 'Defending our Nation against its enemies is the first and fundamental commitment of the Federal Government. Today, that task has changed dramatically. Enemies in the past needed great armies and great industrial capabilities to endanger America. Now, shadowy networks of individuals can bring great chaos and suffering to our shores for less than it costs to purchase a single tank. Terrorists are organized to penetrate open societies and to turn the power of modern technologies against us.' The 2002 *National Security Strategy* warned, 'While the US will constantly strive to enlist the support of the international community, we will not hesitate to act alone if necessary, to exercise our right of self-defense by acting pre-emptively against such terrorists, to prevent them from doing harm against our people and our country.'

The third US goal in the 2002 *National Security Strategy* was *to strengthen alliances to defeat global terrorism and to work to prevent attacks against us and our friends*. The aim was to disrupt and destroy terrorist organisations, to identify and destroy the threat before it reached their borders. This third goal was linked to the fifth, *to prevent our enemies from threatening us, our allies and our friends with weapons of mass destruction*. This link between states developing weapons of mass destruction—the US singled out Iraq and North Korea in this regard—and terrorists was used further to extend the right of self-defence. The USA was now putting forward a new 'Bush doctrine', extending the right of self-defence far beyond its traditional scope. The USA must be prepared to stop rogue states and their terrorist

UK and its citizens, we would act in accordance with international and domestic law.' (Response of the Secretary of State for Foreign and Commonwealth Affairs to the Second Report of the Foreign Affairs Committee, Session 2002–3, Cm 5793 at p.5). The UK government later said expressly that targeted killings are unlawful (UK Materials on International Law, 76 BYIL (2005) 903.) See also the Israeli Supreme Court decision in *The Public Committee against Torture in Israel v the Government of Israel*, 45 ILM (2007) 375 for a discussion of the legality of this practice.

[76] Available on the US Department of State website; <www.state.gov/>.

clients before they are able to threaten to use weapons of mass destruction. 'Given the goals of rogue states and terrorists, the US can no longer rely on a reactive posture as we have in the past. The inability to deter a potential attacker does not permit that option. We cannot let our enemies strike first…We must be prepared to stop rogue states and their terrorist clients before they are able to threaten or use weapons of mass destruction against the US. The doctrine of self-defence needs to be revised in the light of modern conditions. In particular the requirement that a threat be imminent needs to be revisited.' The USA asserts that pre-emptive self-defence has been recognized for centuries, a controversial claim in the light of the divisions between states on this subject.[77] But even this is not enough: the USA now argues that circumstances have changed and that the requirement of imminent attack should be adapted to the capabilities and objectives of today's adversaries.

This argument was repeated by President Bush in his 2003 *State of the Union Address*, with express reference to Iraq, when he said, 'Some have said that we must not act until the threat is imminent. Since when have terrorists and tyrants announced their intentions, politely putting us on notice before they strike? If this threat is permitted to fully and suddenly emerge, all actions, all words, and all recriminations would come to late. Trusting in the sanity and restraint of Saddam Hussein is not a strategy and not an option.'[78]

This apparent attempt to extend the war against terrorism to cover purely pre-emptive action in the absence of an imminent threat provoked much controversy.[79] President Bush seemed to be taking advantage of the rhetoric of the 'war against terrorism' and the legitimacy conferred by that war to stretch the boundaries of self-defence.[80] There is some uncertainty as to the exact scope of the US claims. The terms anticipatory, preventive and pre-emptive are not technical terms of art with clear meanings

---

[77] See 160 above.

[78] Keesings (2003) 45178 at 45181.

[79] See, for example, Bothe, Terrorism and the Legality of Pre-emptive Force', 14 EJIL (2003) 227; Glennon, 'The Fog of Law: Self-defense, inherence and incoherence in Article 51 of the UN Charter', 25 Harvard Journal of Law and Public Policy (2002) 539; O'Connell, 'The Myth of Pre-emptive self-defense', American Society of International Law Task Force on Terrorism (2002); <www.asil.org/taskforce/oconnell,pdf>; Sofaer, 'On the need of pre-emption', 14 EJIL (2003) 209; Farer, 'Beyond the Charter Frame: Unilateralism or Condominium?', 96 AJIL (2002) 359; 'Agora: Future Implications of the Iraq Conflict', 97 AJIL (2003) 553.

[80] Though some commentators argue that the USA had adopted this wide position much earlier. See, for example, Reisman and Armstrong, 'The past and future of claims of pre-emptive self-defense', 100 AJIL (2006) 525, and discussion by Murphy, 'The doctrine of pre-emptive self-defense', 50 Villanova LR (2005) 699. The US State Department Legal Adviser in a 2002 roundtable discussion argued that the concept of pre-emptive self-defence was not a novel concept. He maintained support for the requirement that there be an imminent threat, but took a very wide view of 'imminence.' Taft, The Legal Basis for Preemption, 18 November 2002; <www.cfr.org/publication.html?id=5250>.

and they are used in different ways by different authors. But the crucial question of substance is whether the USA is claiming a right to use force against non-imminent threats. This was certainly the impression given by President Bush in the speech quoted above. And this was the UK Attorney-General's understanding of the US position. In his advice on the legality of the use of force against Iraq, he said, 'I am aware that the USA has been arguing for recognition of a broad doctrine of a right to use force to pre-empt danger in the future. If this means more than a right to respond proportionately to an imminent attack (and I understand that the doctrine is intended to carry that connotation) this is not a doctrine which, in my opinion exists or is recognized in international law.'[81]

Whereas states did not challenge the legality of *Operation Enduring Freedom*, there is little sign of any willingness by states to abandon the requirement that for self-defence to be permissible a terrorist attack should already have occurred, be underway, or at the most extensive, be imminent. The opposition by many states to *Operation Iraqi Freedom* (which started in March 2003) made it clear that they were not willing to accept pre-emptive self-defence as a legal basis for that particular action.[82]

The High-level Panel Report and the Secretary-General's Report *In Larger Freedom* both expressly rejected the doctrine of pre-emptive self-defence which they understood as action against non-imminent threats. These reports addressed the issue whether the right of self-defence should be expanded to meet the new threats facing the world. Although both reports controversially accepted anticipatory self-defence against an imminent attack, they were not prepared to go any further. Where the threat is not imminent—for example, the acquisition of nuclear weapons-making capacity—a state cannot act pre-emptively against a non-imminent or non-proximate threat. In such a situation it was for the UN Security Council to authorize action. Unilateral pre-emptive action posed too great a threat to global order.[83] Nor was there any widespread support by states for the US doctrine.[84]

Nevertheless the USA strongly rejected the position of the High-level Panel Report: 'Given today's threats we should not be putting new constraints on self-defence. But that is what would happen if the proposal

---

[81] 54 ICLQ (2005) 767 para 3. In contrast the Dutch government interpreted the 2002 *US National Security Strategy* as allowing force only against imminent threats; it also itself rejected the use of force in pre-emptive action against non-imminent threats: Government letter to the House of Representatives, 29 October 2004, 29800 V, No. 56.

[82] See, for example, the express rejection of the doctrine by Malaysia, Yemen, Vietnam, Iran and Lebanon in SC 4726th meeting (2003). See further Chapter 8 below at 354.

[83] High-level Panel Report, UN doc A/59/565, para 189–92. *In Larger Freedom*, UN doc A/59/2005, 21 March 2005, para 125, said, 'where the threat is not imminent but merely latent the Charter gives full authority to the Security Council to use military force'.

[84] See 213 below.

that only the Security Council could authorize the prevention of the use of force were adopted. Even in cases where terrorists have a nuclear weapon, the report says that a state should go to the Security Council first for authorization to take preventative military action…Such constraints will never be acceptable to the United States.'[85] And in 2006 the USA issued a new *National Security Strategy*. In this it repeated its commitment to pre-emptive self-defence.[86] It said, 'The place of pre-emption in our national security strategy remains the same' and it reaffirmed all the relevant sections of the 2002 Strategy on the use of force. But its identification of the nature of the threat in the war on terror had shifted since 2002: the main danger was now said to come not from shadowy networks of individuals but from 'Islamic extremists',[87] and it was now Iran and Syria (rather than Iraq and North Korea) which posed the greatest threat as 'sponsors of terror'.[88]

The 2006 Strategy, like its predecessor, leaves many questions about pre-emption unanswered. It does not make clear what will trigger the right of pre-emptive action and what is the proper scope of such action. It repeats the words of the 2002 Strategy that 'under long-standing principles of self-defence we do not rule out the use of force before attacks occur, even if uncertainty remains as to the time and place of the enemy's attack',[89] and adds only that, 'The reasons for our actions will be clear, the force measured, and the cause just.' There is no further discussion of the imminence requirement. Indeed there is no mention of international law in the 2006 Strategy and almost no mention of the role of the UN in the maintenance of international peace and security.

There is very little international support for this doctrine of pre-emptive self-defence.[90] The General Assembly debates on *In Larger Freedom* showed that most states were not willing to accept anticipatory, let alone pre-emptive self-defence.[91] The 118 member Non-Aligned Movement has repeatedly rejected the doctrine of pre-emptive self-defence.[92] NATO, which had been given only very limited mention in the 2002 and the 2006 *US National Security Strategy*, has not openly adopted the Bush doctrine of effectively unlimited self-defence. It is in the process of trying to re-define its role after

---

[85] Assistant Secretary of State Kim Holmes, speech of December 2004, 99 AJIL (2005) 494.
[86] Available on the White House website.
[87] 2006 USNSS 9.
[88] Ibid., 9, 20.
[89] Ibid., 23.
[90] Reisman and Armstrong make the opposing argument, based on a creative interpretation of general statements: 'The past and future of claims of preemptive self-defence', 100 AJIL (2006) 525.
[91] UN doc GA/10377, 10388, 10399, 6–8 April 2005.
[92] For example, in the 2006 Havana Declaration, UN doc S/2006/780, 29 September 2006, para 20, 22.5.

the end of the Cold War, and in the light of 9/11.[93] At its Prague Summit in November 2002 it considered the future of NATO in adapting to the threat of terrorism. Its original basis of protecting western Europe from the USSR during the Cold War was obsolete. Since the end of the Cold War its membership has been expanded to twenty-six to include many of the former eastern bloc states.

The NATO states agreed that the threat to its members now comes from international terrorism and weapons of mass destruction; they decided to meet threats to collective security wherever they arise. As part of its *New Capabilities Initiative* NATO announced the formation of a new rapid reaction force, the 20,000 strong NATO Response Force to strike terrorist bases anywhere in the world.[94] At the Prague Summit NATO leaders also agreed a *New Military Concept for Defence against Terrorism* making clear their readiness to act against terrorist attacks or the threat of such attacks, to assist national authorities in dealing with the consequences of terrorist attacks and to deploy forces as and where required to carry out such missions.[95] In 2006 it adopted a *Comprehensive Political Guidance*, setting out the political direction for NATO's continuing transformation: 'Collective defence will remain the core purpose of the Alliance. The character of potential Article 5 challenges is continuing to evolve. Large scale conventional aggression against the Alliance will continue to be highly unlikely; however, as shown by the terrorist attacks on the US in 2001 following which NATO invoked Article 5 for the first time, future attacks may originate from outside the Euro-Atlantic area and involve unconventional forms of armed assault. Future attacks could also entail an increased risk of the use of asymmetric means, and could involve the use of weapons of mass destruction. Defence against terrorism and the ability to respond to challenges from wherever they may come have assumed and will retain an increased importance.' But NATO has not expressly adopted a doctrine of pre-emptive self-defence.

Similarly the CIS has agreed to create a rapid reaction force to respond to regional threats including terrorism and Islamic extremism, but no details are yet available as to the scope of the right claimed.[96] The EU in its 2003 *Security Strategy* identifies five key threats: terrorism, the proliferation of weapons of mass destruction, regional conflicts, state failure and

---

[93] On its role in crisis management in Bosnia and Herzegovina, Kosovo and elsewhere, see 40 above.

[94] Prague Summit Declaration, 21 November 2002, 42 ILM (2003) 244; <www.nato.int/ims/docu/terrorism.htm>; see also, NATO Briefing, *NATO and the fight against terrorism*, March 2006, available on NATO website. There is an ongoing debate as to whether the NATO Treaty should be amended to allow the transformation of NATO into a global organization open to states such as Australia, New Zealand and Japan, *The Guardian*, 25 November 2006.

[95] <www.nato.int/ims/docu/terrorism.htm>.

[96] Keesings (2001) 44173, (2002) 45050.

organized crime.[97] It goes on to say that with the new threats the first line of defence will often be abroad. This implies that it must be ready to act before a crisis occurs. But the EU still does not expressly adopt the doctrine of pre-emptive self-defence, in marked contrast to the US *National Security Strategy*.

Even the UK government, recently the USA's strongest supporter, has not openly accepted a wide doctrine of pre-emption.[98] After 9/11 the Parliamentary Foreign Affairs Committee invited the government 'to reconsider the notion of imminence in the light of new threats to international peace and security' but the government initially resisted this request.[99] In 2004 the Attorney-General said 'It is therefore the Government's view that international law permits the use of force in self-defence against an imminent attack but does not authorise the use of force to mount a pre-emptive strike against a threat that is more remote.' This apparently remains the official position. However, the UK seems now to have adopted a wide view of imminence: 'The concept of what constitutes an imminent attack will develop to meet new circumstances and new threats. For example, the resolutions passed by the Security Council in the wake of 11 September 2001 recognised both that large-scale terrorist action could constitute an armed attack that will give rise to the right of self-defence and that force might, in certain circumstances, be used in self-defence against those who plan and perpetrate such acts and against those harbouring them, if that is necessary to avert further such terrorist attacks. It was on that basis that UK forces participated in military action against Al Qaeda and the Taliban in Afghanistan. It must be right that states are able to act in self-defence in circumstances where there is evidence of further imminent attacks by terrorist groups, even if there is no specific evidence of where such an attack will take place or of the precise nature of the attack.'[100] Such a wide view deprives the requirement of 'imminence' of any content.

---

[97] <ue.eu.int/uedocs/cmsUpload/78367.pdf>.

[98] The Foreign Secretary clearly disavowed such a doctrine, Foreign Affairs Committee, Second Report, *Foreign Policy Aspects of the War against Terrorism*, Session 2002–2003, HC 196 at para 150. See also The Attorney-General's advice on the legality of the invasion of Iraq, 54 ICLQ (2005) 767 para 3.

[99] Response of the Secretary of State for Foreign and Commonwealth Affairs to the Second Report of the Foreign Affairs Committee, *Foreign Policy Aspects of the War against Terrorism*, Session 2002–2003, Cm 5793, at 8. The Foreign Affairs Committee later questioned the government's long-held position that there is a right of anticipatory action; in response the UK government reasserted its traditional view (Foreign Affairs Committee Seventh Report, *Foreign Policy Aspects of the War against Terrorism*, Session 2003–2004, HC 441-I, para 415–429).

[100] Attorney-General Speech in the House of Lords, HL Debates 21 April 2004 Vol 660 c369–372; UK Materials on International Law, 75 BYIL (2004) 822–3.

Australia has been the most outspoken supporter of the US doctrine; in the aftermath of the bomb attack on the Bali night club in December 2002 it asserted a right of pre-emptive self-defence against terrorists in neighbouring states.[101] Early indignation by Indonesia, Malaysia, Philippines and Thailand, was increased by later suspicion that Australia was really trying to justify future action against Iraq.[102] The Australian Prime Minister later repeated his commitment to pre-emptive military force, but this doctrine is not included in the Australian 2005 Defence Update.[103]

As was described in Chapter 4, the International Court of Justice has avoided any pronouncement on anticipatory self-defence. But in *Armed Activities on the Territory of the Congo (DRC v Uganda)* Uganda in invoking its right to self-defence against an armed attack had argued that its use of force was necessary 'to secure its legitimate security interests'. The Court said that the specified security interests were essentially preventative—to ensure that the political vacuum in the border area did not adversely affect Uganda, to prevent attacks from genocidal elements, to be in a position to safeguard Uganda from irresponsible threats of invasion, to deny the Sudan the opportunity to use the territory of the DRC to destabilize Uganda.[104] Later in the judgment the Court said 'Article 51 of the Charter may justify the use of force in self-defence only within the strict confines there laid down. It does not allow the use of force by a State to protect perceived security interests beyond these parameters. Other means are available to a concerned State, including, in particular, recourse to the Security Council.'[105] The Court therefore implicitly indicated that it would not accept pre-emptive action as self-defence.

IRAQ AND PRE-EMPTIVE SELF-DEFENCE

After President George W Bush's *State of the Union Address* in January 2002,[106] with its destabilizing—and self-fulfilling—rhetoric about the threat from Iran, Iraq and North Korea, the states in the 'Axis of Evil', most discussion of the precedential significance of the action against Afghanistan focused on the question how far the further use of force against Iraq could

---

[101] *The Guardian*, 2 and 4 December 2002.
[102] Keesings (2002) 45147; *The Guardian*, 2 and 4 December 2002. In fact Australia did not use this justification for its participation in *Operation Iraqi Freedom* in 2003, see below at note 152.
[103] <www.defence.gov.au/update2005>.
[104] ICJ Reports (2005) 168 para 143.
[105] Ibid., para 148.
[106] Keesings (2002) 44545.

be justified as part of the war against terrorism, or whether some other justification would be used.[107]

Allegations of links between Al Qaida and Saddam Hussein

In their apparent determination to embark on the use of force against Iraq in response to its repeated violations of the ceasefire regime established in Security Council Resolution 687 (1991) and its non-cooperation with UN weapons inspectors, some members of the US administration made claims of links between Al Qaida and President Saddam Hussein of Iraq.[108] Even where there was no claim of any direct involvement of Saddam Hussein in the terrorist attacks of 9/11, the assertions of ongoing links were clearly designed to bring any attack on Iraq within the scope of the war against terrorism, thus giving the doctrine of self-defence based on the precedent of Afghanistan a very wide interpretation. Such attempts to link Al Qaida and Saddam Hussein increased following the identification of a threat from the Axis of Evil when President Bush singled out Iran, Iraq and North Korea in his 2002 *State of the Union Address*. He spoke of a grave and growing danger to the USA and of the need to prevent terrorists and regimes who seek weapons of mass destruction from threatening the USA and the world.[109]

Rhetorical flourishes like that of President Bush in his 2003 *State of the Union Address* stopped short of the assertion of an actual direct link between Saddam Hussein and Al Qaida: 'Before September the 11th, many in the world believed that Saddam Hussein could be contained. But chemical agents, lethal viruses and shadowy terrorist networks are not easily contained. Imagine those 19 hijackers with other weapons and other plans—this time armed by Saddam Hussein. It would take one vial, one canister, one crate slipped into this country to bring a day of horror like none we have ever known.'[110] Jack Straw, the UK Foreign Secretary, less dramatically, and also without drawing any direct link, spoke of Saddam Hussein and Al Qaida as 'part of the same picture'.[111] But

---

[107] See McGoldrick, *From 9/11 to Iraq* (2004).
[108] Keesings (2002) 45009, 45029, (2003) 45265, 45546, 45588.
[109] Keesings (2002) 44545.
[110] Keesings (2003) 45181.
[111] *The Guardian*, 6 January 2003. The UK government set out its position in February 2003 in response to the Select Committee conclusion that, although the possibility that Saddam Hussein might employ terrorist methods must be taken seriously, there is no compelling evidence linking the Iraqi regime to Al Qaida. Neither the British nor the US Government had thus far provided any evidence that Iraq had any involvement in the attacks of 11 September 2001. Until such evidence was provided, any military action against the Iraqi regime must be justified on grounds other than its past or current involvement with the Al Qaida network. The UK government in reply said that 'We must also guard against

intelligence agencies in the USA and the UK were unwilling to assert any significant link between Al Qaida and Saddam Hussein. They acknowledged that Saddam Hussein had no involvement in the Al Qaida attacks on the WTC and Pentagon.[112] Nevertheless the US administration made renewed claims of a link immediately before the use of force against Iraq.[113] President Bush and Vice-President Cheney continue to make such connections even today, even after official investigations have discredited these claims.[114]

Pre-emptive self-defence against the threat of Iraq's weapons of mass destruction

In the period between 9/11 and the eventual attack on Iraq in March 2003 there were deep divisions between states on whether to use force against Iraq and whether there was any legal justification for *Operation Iraqi Freedom*.[115] Many states warned against any extension of the right of self-defence against terrorism beyond *Operation Enduring Freedom* in Afghanistan, saying that an invasion of Iraq would be a dangerous distraction from the 'war on terror'. They expressed serious doubts about the Axis of Evil rhetoric of the USA, and the attempt to extend the war against terrorism against certain states developing weapons of mass destruction.[116] NATO states were bitterly divided; they produced only a cautious declaration on Iraq in the November 2002 *Prague Summit Statement* with no commitment to the use of force, let alone to the doctrine of pre-emption.[117] This was apparently the result of the split between the states

the terrifying prospect of Saddam Hussein passing weapons of mass destruction to terrorists such as Al Qaida. Saddam Hussein is developing them. Al Qaida is seeking them and would use them. Saddam Hussein and Al Qaida have a common disregard for others. Both are prepared to use terror to achieve their objectives. We have no evidence that Iraq was involved in the September 11 attacks. But there are links between Iraq and Al Qaida.' Response of the Secretary of State for Foreign and Commonwealth Affairs to the Second Report of the Foreign Affairs Committee, Session 2002–2003, Cm 5793 at 6; Foreign Affairs Committee, Second Report 2002–2003, HC 196 at para 79–86.

[112] UK Foreign Affairs Committee, Seventh Report of Session 2001–02, *Foreign Policy Aspects of the War Against Terrorism*, HC 384, para 215; *The Guardian*, 9 October 2002, 10 June 2003, 6 October 2004, 16 February 2007.

[113] See, for example, Keesings (2003) 45009; *The Guardian*, 27 September 2002, 29 January 2003.

[114] On the reports, see Keesings (2003) 45588, (2004) 46049, 46108, (2006) 47451. On the continued claims of a link between Iraq and the 9/11 attacks, see Keesings (2005) 46674, (2006) 47451, 47855, (2007) 48030.

[115] See 354 below on the justification of UN authorization as the basis for the use of force against Iraq.

[116] Keesings (2002) 45005, 45067, (2003) 45216, 45313. Russia, China and many EU states did not accept the case for the use of force against Iraq. For a statement of the Russian position, see 52 ICLQ (2003) 1059.

[117] 42 ILM (2003) 244; NATO Press Release (2002) 133–21 November 2002.

who opposed the use of force against Iraq, identified by US Defense Secretary Rumsfeld as 'Old Europe', led by France and Germany, and 'New Europe', ready to contemplate the use of force, which included the UK, Spain and most of the East European states.[118]

For those states supporting action against Iraq, the crucial question became whether it was possible to extend the war against terrorism to cover action against Iraq—that is, whether such an action could be a use of self-defence against terrorism. Or, alternatively, should action against Iraq be justified on the basis of non-compliance with the ceasefire regime binding on Iraq under Resolution 687 (1991) and subsequent resolutions? Or, as is characteristic of legal argument, it might be that a combination of these weak arguments would be used. It is interesting that the Resolution of the US Houses of Congress in October 2002 used *both* implied authorization and self-defence. This 'Authorization for the Use of Military Force against Iraq' authorized the President 'to use the armed forces of the United States as he determines to be necessary and appropriate in order to (1) defend the national security of the United States against the continuing threat posed by Iraq; and (2) enforce all relevant United Nations Security Council Resolutions regarding Iraq'.[119] Similarly John Negroponte, the US representative to the UN Security Council, speaking after the unanimous adoption of Security Council Resolution 1441 on Iraq in November 2002, said that 'If the Security Council fails to act decisively in the event of further Iraqi violations this resolution does not constrain any member state from acting to defend itself against the threat posed by Iraq or to enforce relevant United Nations resolutions and protect world peace and security.'[120] Clearly the USA was deliberately keeping both options open. President Bush's Address to the Nation on 19 March 2003 as military operations against Iraq began and the US letter to the Security Council on 20 March 2003 also used this combination of arguments.[121]

But the UK and Australia, the only other states to contribute forces to *Operation Iraqi Freedom*, did not use pre-emptive self-defence as any part of their legal case for the invasion of Iraq; they preferred to rely on authorization by the Security Council, an indication of the doubt over the doctrine of pre-emptive action.[122] Nor did the other states offering military or political support expressly put forward a justification based on

---

[118] Keesings (2003) 45216; *The Guardian*, 24 January, 11 February 2003.
[119] 41 (2002) ILM 1440.
[120] UN Press Release SC/7564, 8 November 2002.
[121] <www.whitehouse.gov/news/releases/2003/03/20030319-17.html>; UN doc S/2003/351.
[122] UN docs S/2003/350; S/2003/352. Australia expressly said that there was no need to consider self-defence: *Memorandum of Advice on the Use of Force against Iraq provided by the Attorney-General's department and the Department of Foreign Affairs and Trade*, 18 March 2003.

pre-emption.[123] Several states which opposed the use of force against Iraq expressly rejected the legality of pre-emptive use of force.[124]

Any case for pre-emption rested on the existence of a threat of attack on the USA and others arising from Iraq's possession or development of weapons of mass destruction. But the problems with this doctrine were apparent when the US and UK case for forcible action against Iraq was challenged by other states. Germany, France, Russia and China all preferred to continue the UN weapons inspections established under the ceasefire regime in Resolution 687 (1991) and reintroduced in November 2002 under Resolution 1441 to secure the disarmament of Iraq; they did not accept the existence of an imminent threat.[125] And even within the USA and the UK there were reports that the intelligence services did not accept that Iraq posed an imminent threat to their states.[126] In the absence of any imminent threat, force could be used in self-defence only under a very wide 'Bush doctrine'. Although the USA referred to the need to defend the USA as a possible basis for *Operation Iraqi Freedom*, it did not go into detail as to the scope of this doctrine; the UK and Australia placed no reliance on pre-emptive self-defence.

After *Operation Iraqi Freedom* drove Saddam Hussein from power in Iraq in April 2003, the US and UK occupying forces did not find weapons of mass destruction. Hans Blix, the head of the UN weapons inspectors in Iraq, criticized as unfounded the US and UK claims about Iraq's weapons programme.[127] In both the USA and the UK there was debate over the intelligence data on the basis of which the case for the use of force against Iraq was made; in both the USA and the UK (and in Australia) there were serious political concerns as to whether the governments had deliberately misled their people as to the nature of the threat posed by Iraq and as to the case for the use of force.[128] The Iraq Survey Group, formed in May 2003 to hunt for WMD in Iraq, stated in its final report that after 1,500 inspectors had spent sixteen months in searching Iraq they had not

---

[123] The USA claimed that more states were involved in the 'coalition' in favour of military action than had been involved in the 1991 operation authorized by the UN. Forty-five states were involved in *Operation Iraqi Freedom*, Keesings (2003) 45315; *The Guardian*, 5 and 19 March 2003; Murphy, 'Contemporary Practice of the United States relating to International Law', 97 AJIL (2003) 419 at 428.

[124] See, for example, Yemen and Iran, SC 4625th meeting (2002); Malaysia, Yemen, Vietnam, Iran and Lebanon, SC 4726th meeting (2003).

[125] Keesings (2003) 45216, 45264; *The Guardian*, 28 January 2003; 6, 7, 10, 18 February 2003. The UN Secretary-General also expressed doubts over a resort to force rather than the continuation of the work of the weapons inspectors, Keesings (2003) 45217; *The Guardian*, 1 January 2003.

[126] *The Guardian*, 9 and 10 October 2002.

[127] *The Guardian*, 6 and 7 June 2003.

[128] Keesings (2003), 45453, 45508, 45520, 45588; *The Guardian*, 3 June, 7 July 2003.

unearthed any WMD or any programmes to manufacture them.[129] It is generally agreed that Al Qaida did not operate in Iraq before *Operation Iraqi Freedom*, but the USA now argues that Al Qaida-linked terrorists are operating there.[130] The USA started to characterize Iraq as the front line in the war on terror from September 2003.[131]

Thus pre-emptive self-defence remains extremely problematic. The doctrine as set out by the USA in its 2002 and 2006 *National Security Strategies* is not clear; it contains a central uncertainty as to what will trigger pre-emptive action, what form pre-emptive action will take and as to the role envisaged for the UN, if any.[132] The apparent unity of states on the scope of self-defence after 9/11 has broken down; a clear split emerged between those who had supported the attack on Afghanistan as to whether to go further and act against Iraq. Although about forty-five states were willing to offer military or political support to the USA in its use of force against Iraq, it seems that none did so on the basis of the doctrine of pre-emptive self-defence. The move away from response to past terrorist attacks to possible armed action against states in alleged possession of weapons of mass destruction who might give them to terrorists, the stress on military rather than peaceful mechanisms and on unilateral rather than multilateral decisions on the existence and seriousness of a threat were not acceptable to many states and commentators.[133] Many argue that concern over the spread of nuclear weapons should be addressed through existing multilateral treaties. The UN Deputy Secretary-General acknowledged the fear of how much more damage terrorists could do if they were to acquire weapons of mass destruction, but stressed the importance of a multilateral approach through the Non-Proliferation Treaty:

If the competition of nuclear-armed superpowers was terrifying, so—in a different way—is the thought of such weapons in the hands of terrorists...Here too we have a number of international instruments which have undoubtedly played an important part in restraining the spread of such weapons. Particularly important is the

---

[129] Keesings (2004) 46280. The report did suggest that Saddam Hussein intended to restart WMD production when possible, but it did not give any evidence for this.

[130] See *Country Reports on Terrorism* (2004, 2005, 2006) available on US Department of State website. Very soon after *Operation Iraqi Freedom* many foreign fighters moved in to Iraq, Keesings (2003) 45571, 45587, 45623, 45671. The White House website, in *Myth/Fact: Iraq Fact Check: Responding to Key Myths*, asserts that Al Qaida in Iraq is the same organization which attacked the USA on 9/11, an organization founded and led by foreign terrorists loyal to Osama bin Laden and not a homegrown groups of Iraqi Sunnis; <www.whitehouse.gov/news/releases/2007/09>.

[131] Keesings (2003) 45587, 45623.

[132] For an attempt to draw up a framework governing pre-emptive action, see Buchanan and Keohane, 'The pre-emptive use of force: a cosmopolitan institutional perspective', 2004 Ethics and International Affairs 1.

[133] 'Agora: Future Implications of the Iraq Conflict', 97 AJIL (2003) 553; 'Unilateralism in International Law: A US-European Symposium', 11 EJIL (2000) 1 at 349.

Nuclear Non-Proliferation Treaty...The vast majority of States appear to value the treaty, and to respect its provisions. But this acceptance is gradually being undermined as non-nuclear-weapon states hear nuclear-weapon states propounding doctrines of first use; as they see new nuclear weapons being used; and as reduction of existing weapons stocks proceeds more slowly than had been hoped.[134]

The next steps: North Korea and Iran

At first it seemed that the rhetoric of pre-emption was employed by the USA primarily in order to put pressure not only on Iraq, but also on Iran and North Korea—states which the USA saw as a potential threat because of their possible development of weapons of mass destruction and because of the alleged risk that they might provide such weapons to terrorists hostile to the USA. The USA's unfriendly language towards these states since President Bush's 'Axis of Evil' speech in January 2002 gave rise to speculation that the USA was planning to use pre-emptive force to prevent their development of nuclear weapons.[135] The 2002 *US National Security Strategy* focused on the threat posed by Iraq, Iran and North Korea. The UN Secretary-General warned that the development of a policy calling for pre-emptive and, if necessary, unilateral action against the threat of weapons of mass destruction was a challenge to the existing multilateral treaty regimes on disarmament and arms limitation.[136] In particular the nuclear non-proliferation regime faced a major crisis of confidence. India, Israel and Pakistan had never joined the *Treaty on the Non-Proliferation of Nuclear Weapons* (NPT) and had all developed nuclear weapons, North Korea had withdrawn from the treaty, and there were concerns about Iran's nuclear programme. States had been unable to strengthen the NPT at a 2005 Review Conference and at the World Summit because they could not agree whether non-proliferation or disarmament should come first.[137]

North Korea

The USA initially adopted extremely hostile rhetoric towards North Korea when President Bush took power, denouncing it as a member of the 'Axis

---

[134] UN Press Release DSG/SM/196, 12 May 2003. See also UN Press Release GA/DIS/3247, 3 October 2003, for further expression of concern about challenges to existing disarmament and arms limitation regimes.

[135] The USA had designated Iran, Iraq and North Korea as 'state sponsors of terrorism'. It also included Cuba, Libya, Sudan and Syria in this category. In December 2003 Libya announced that it would abandon voluntarily its programmes for developing weapons of mass destruction and would fulfil its obligations under the relevant treaties on non-proliferation (UN Press Releases SC/7967, SG/SM/9091).

[136] UN Press Release GA/DIS/3247, 3 October 2003.

[137] Ibid. See also Secretary-General's Press Release, SG/SM/10527, 21 June 2006. For a discussion of pre-emption and deterrence, see Verdirame, 'The sinews of peace', 77 BYIL (2006) 83.

of Evil', and expressing concern about its possible acquisition of nuclear weapons.[138] This decline in relations brought to an end the 1994 US/North Korea *Agreed Framework*,[139] concluded after North Korea had threatened to withdraw from the NPT in 1993.[140] Under this agreement North Korea had agreed to freeze its nuclear weapons programme in exchange for US aid for the production of peaceful nuclear energy and oil supplies. The decline in relations also undermined the improvement in relations between North and South Korea and led to concern among the states of the region.[141] In response North Korea proclaimed the existence of its nuclear weapons programme in October 2002, stepped up its nuclear programme, and in January 2003 announced its withdrawal from the NPT.[142] The USA on several occasions threatened pre-emptive action (or refused to rule it out) to stop North Korea from developing nuclear weapons.[143] North Korea said that it was therefore entitled to take a pre-emptive strike against the USA because of US threats and that it had withdrawn from the NPT as a measure of legitimate self-defence in face of US threats.[144] Japan in turn asserted that it would take pre-emptive action against North Korea if it feared imminent attack.[145] North Korea demanded a non-aggression pact with the USA in return for easing security tensions.[146]

Attempts to negotiate a settlement proved fruitless.[147] In its 2006 *National Security Strategy* the USA stated that the tyrannical regime in North Korea was defying the international community in its illicit nuclear programme.[148] In 2006 North Korea test fired long-range ballistic missiles. In response the Security Council unanimously passed Resolution 1695 (2006), its first resolution on North Korea since 1993. This deplored North Korea's announcement of withdrawal from the NPT and its stated pursuit of nuclear weapons. It condemned the launch of the ballistic

---

[138] Keesings (2001) 44545.
[139] Keesings (1994) 40140, 40227. On the decline in relations between the USA and North Korea, see Keesings (2001) 44006, 44055, 44214, (2002) 44619, 44676, 44939, 45088, 45138.
[140] SC Res 825 (1993) called on North Korea to reconsider its announcement, to reaffirm its commitment to the NPT and to honour its non-proliferation obligations.
[141] Keesings (2001) 44104, 44402, (2002) 44619, 44788, (2003) 45407; *The Guardian*, 6 February 2003.
[142] Keesings (2002) 45039, 45138; (2003) 45187.
[143] Keesings (2002) 44619, 44676, 45287.
[144] Keesings (2003) 45238; UN doc S/2003/91, 27 January 2003.
[145] Keesings (2003) 45239.
[146] Keesings (2003) 45187.
[147] A breakthrough was reached in 2005 when North Korea agreed to end its nuclear weapons programme in return for US security guarantees and economic aid. The UN Secretary-General welcomed the consensus, UN Press Release SG/SM/10111, 20 September 2005. However, the imposition of new sanctions by the USA on North Korean banks and businesses in Macau derailed the agreement, Keesings (2005) 46827, 46828; *The Guardian*, 20 September, 10, 14 October 2005.
[148] 2006 US *National Security Strategy* 3, 19, 21.

missiles, 'given the potential of such systems to be used as a means to deliver nuclear, chemical or biological payloads'. North Korea said in reply that the launches were part of routine military exercises to increase its military capacity for self-defence.[149] Japan again raised the possibility of pre-emptive action against missile bases in North Korea.[150]

North Korea then took the dramatic step of carrying out a nuclear weapons test in October 2006. It said, 'The US extreme threat of a nuclear war and sanctions and pressure compel the DPRK to conduct a nuclear test, an essential process for bolstering nuclear deterrent, as a self-defence measure in response.'[151] The Security Council in Resolution 1718 (2006) condemned the test, demanded that North Korea return to the NPT, and decided that it must abandon its nuclear weapons and its ballistic missiles programmes; in order to secure compliance with these demands it imposed sanctions on North Korea.[152] North Korea rejected the resolution: 'It is gangster-like of the Security Council to have adopted today a coercive resolution while neglecting the nuclear threat and moves for sanctions and pressure of the United States against the DPRK.' North Korea accused the Security Council of double standards, saying that it was disappointed that the Council was incapable of offering a single word of concern when the United States threatened to launch pre-emptive nuclear attacks, reinforced its armed forces and conducted large-scale military exercises near the Korean peninsula. It had felt compelled to prove its possession of nuclear weapons to protect itself from the danger of war from the United States.[153]

In 2007 a settlement was finally reached in a deal similar to that of 1994 *Agreed Framework*. North Korea undertook to shut down its nuclear reactor and readmit international inspectors in return for oil supplies.[154] In July 2007 North Korea shut down its nuclear reactor.[155] Some interpret this episode as a demonstration of the counter-productive impact of threats of pre-emption: they, coupled with calls for regime change, provide a perverse incentive to acquire weapons of mass destruction.

Iran

The USA also repeatedly expressed concern that Iran was developing a nuclear weapons programmes.[156] In the 2006 *US National Security Strategy*

---

[149] SC 5490th meeting (2006).
[150] Keesings (2006) 47368; *The Washington Post* 11 July 2006; *The New York Times* 12 July 2006; *The Guardian*, 14 July 2006.
[151] Keesings (2006) 47515; *The Guardian*, 4 October 2006.
[152] This resolution was carefully drafted so as to exclude any claim that it could be interpreted as authorizing the use of force against North Korea. See Chapter 8 below.
[153] SC 5551st meeting (2006).
[154] Keesings (2007) 47759; *The Guardian* 14 February 2007.
[155] Keesings (2007) 48042, 48141, 48252.
[156] See, for example, Keesings (2003) 45267, 45320, 45432, 45492.

it said that Iran harboured terrorists at home and sponsored terrorist activity abroad. The USA was concerned about Iran, not only because of its attempts to develop nuclear weapons, but also because of broader concerns: 'The Iranian regime sponsors terrorism, threatens Israel, seeks to thwart Middle East peace, disrupts democracy in Iraq; and denies the aspirations of its people for freedom.'[157] In his 2007 *State of the Union Address* President Bush devoted a section to the 'war on terror', saying that America was still a nation at war. He again accused Iran of funding and arming terrorists like Hezbollah.[158] As with Iraq under Saddam Hussein, there were no established links between Iran and Al Qaida; rather the USA accused (Shia) Iran of support for Hezbollah and Hamas, in Lebanon, the West Bank and Gaza. President Bush said that (Sunni) Al Qaida was just one camp in the Islamist radical movement: 'In recent times it had become clear that the USA faced an escalating danger from Shia extremists who are just as hostile to America and are also determined to dominate the Middle East...The Shia and Sunni extremists are different faces of the same totalitarian threat.'[159] As earlier with regard to Iraq, the USA now expressed concern about the danger posed by Iran because of the link between its alleged development of WMD and support for terrorists. The USA has called for regime change in Iran and has supplied funds for the 'promotion of democracy'.[160]

Iran maintained that it was merely working to develop peaceful nuclear energy as it was entitled to under the NPT to which it was a party.[161] It claimed a legal right to develop a uranium enrichment programme for civil nuclear purposes under the oversight of the International Atomic Energy Agency (IAEA). The 118-member Non-Aligned Movement supported this legal right.[162] The USA and other western states opposed any Iranian uranium enrichment programme as this would allow Iran to produce weapons-grade uranium. Prolonged negotiations failed to resolve this dispute. The reluctance of European and other states to offer any pretext to the USA for the use of force against Iran made it difficult for the IAEA to adopt a resolution on Iran's compliance with the IAEA regime; states were very cautious about allowing any language that might allow the USA to claim implied authority to use force, as it had done in the case of Iraq.[163]

---

[157] 2006 *US National Security Strategy* 20.
[158] Keesings (2007) 47682–3.
[159] Ibid. See also, speech of President Bush on 28 August 2007, *The Guardian*, 29 August 2007.
[160] Keesings (2005) 46453, 46600, *The Guardian* 31 January, 29 August 2007.
[161] Unlike Israel, India and Pakistan which have all developed nuclear weapons outside the NPT regime.
[162] Final Document, Havana Conference 2006, UN doc S/2006/780, Annex IV; see also, UN doc S/2006/1018.
[163] See 368 below.

In September 2005 the IAEA found Iran in non-compliance with its NPT obligations, and in February 2006 it referred the matter to the Security Council.[164] In April 2006 Iran claimed it had successfully enriched uranium.[165] The Security Council demanded in Resolution 1696 (2006) that Iran suspend enrichment-related activities, to be verified by the IAEA. If Iran did not comply by 31 August 2006 the Security Council intended to adopt appropriate measures under Article 41. When the IAEA reported that Iran had not taken the steps required by the IAEA the Security Council imposed sanctions in Resolutions 1737 (2006) and 1747 (2007). The language of these resolutions was deliberately very cautious; there is nothing to authorize unilateral use of force.[166] But there have been many reports that there are those in the US administration who are determined to pursue pre-emptive military action against Iran to prevent its acquisition of nuclear weapons capacity. President Bush refused to rule out the use of force against Iran.[167] He maintained his hostile rhetoric towards Iran even after a joint intelligence report was issued in 2007; this judged with high confidence that in autumn 2003 Iran had halted its nuclear weapons programme.[168] President Bush nevertheless continued to assert that Iran remained a dangerous threat.[169] There has been a large build up of US forces in the region[170] and a regional arms race is under way.[171]

The doctrine of pre-emptive self-defence thus apparently allows the USA to make plausible threats against what it regards as rogue states, while maintaining lip service to international law. But the problems are obvious: these threats go far beyond the traditional conception of self-defence and beyond the force used in *Operation Enduring Freedom*. The

---

[164] Keesings (2005) 46854, (2006) 47122.

[165] Keesings (2006) 47230.

[166] In the Security Council debates leading up to these resolutions Russia pointed out that the language of the resolutions excluded the use of force, SC 5500th, 5612th (2006), 5647th meetings (2007).

[167] Keesings (2005) 46494, (2006) 47230, (2007) 47679, 47723, 47780, 48015, 48102, 48163; *The Guardian*, 10 August 2004, 18 January, 7 February 2005, 31 January, 12, 26 February, 15 May, 16, 23 July, 18 September 2007. France also refused to rule out the use of force against Iran; the UN chief weapons inspector warned against such rhetoric and reminded states of the lessons of Iraq, *The Guardian*, 17, 18 September 2007. Russia also spoke out against the use of force, *The Guardian*, 17 October 2007. Iran has warned Israel against taking pre-emptive measures against it like those it took against the Iraqi nuclear reactor in 1981, Keesings (2006) 47607. It has complained to the Security Council about 'the daily threats of resort to force against Iran, even the threat of using nuclear weapons, uttered at the highest levels by the US, UK and the lawless Israeli regime in violation of Article 2(4) of the Charter', UN doc S/2006/603.

[168] National Intelligence Estimate, *Iran: Nuclear Intentions and Capabilities*, November 2007; *The Guardian*, 4, 8 December 2007.

[169] *The Guardian*, 5 December 2007. Israel took the same position, *The Guardian*, 8 December 2007.

[170] Keesings (2007) 47723; *The Guardian*, 16, 31 January, 21, 23 February 2007.

[171] *The New York Times*, 4 March 2007; *The Guardian*, 1 August 2007.

responses of North Korea and of Japan make clear the dangers of escalation inherent in the doctrine of pre-emptive action. France in particular had earlier warned of the dangers of the doctrine of pre-emptive self-defence: 'As soon as one nation claims the right to take preventive action, other countries will naturally do the same. And what would you say, in the entirely hypothetical event that China wanted to take preventive action against Taiwan, saying that Taiwan was a threat to it? How would the Americans, the Europeans and others react? Or what if India decided to take preventive action against Pakistan, or vice versa?'[172]

TERRORIST ATTACKS AFTER 9/11 AND THE INTERNATIONAL RESPONSE

Since 9/11 there have been many further terrorist attacks, some of which have been attributed to Al Qaida.[173] But the international response to the terrorist threat has not to date involved the use of force. The Security Council in response to certain of these attacks has again, as in Security Council Resolutions 1368 (2001) and 1373 (2001), asserted that acts of terrorism are threats to international peace and security, but it has not made express reference to Chapter VII in so doing. Nor has it expressly asserted any right of self-defence with regard to these further terrorist episodes. Its focus in the 'war against terrorism' has been on peaceful means. Thus in Resolution 1438 (2002) the Security Council condemned the attack on the Bali night club and repeated that it regards such acts, like any act of international terrorism, as a threat to international peace and security. But no reference was made to self-defence, only to a 'reinforced determination to combat all forms of terrorism, in accordance with its responsibilities under the Charter of the UN'. Resolution 1440 (2002) condemning the heinous act of taking hostages in Moscow, Resolution 1465 (2003) on a bomb attack in Colombia, Resolution 1516 (2003) on the bomb attacks in Istanbul, Turkey, Resolution 1530 (2004) on the Madrid bombing and Resolution 1611(2005) on the London bombs followed the same pattern. Resolution 1450 (2004)

---

[172] *New York Times*, 9 September 2002.
[173] For example, Bali, nightclub in Indonesia, Keesings (2002) 45034; Yemen, Keesings (2002) 45070; Moscow, Keesings (2002) 45047; Kenya, Keesings (2002) 45076; Istanbul, Turkey (UN Press Release SC/7929); Madrid, Keesings (2004) 45910; Uzbekistan, Keesings (2004) 46119; Beslan school in Russia, Keesings (2004) 46212; London, Keesings (2005) 46747, 46837; Bali Keesings (2005) 46883; Amman, Jordan, Keesings (2005) 46959; Lebanon, Keesings, (2005) 46714, 46798; Egypt, Keesings (2005) 46758; Mumbai, India, Keesings (2006) 47362; Egypt, Keesings (2006) 47234. There is much debate as to the nature of Al Qaida; many agree that it is a global network of groups unbound by any organizational structure but held together by overlapping goals. This question is clearly of crucial importance to the Al Qaida and Taliban sanctions committee, established pursuant to SC Res 1267 (1999).

was adopted in response to the acts of terror in Kenya; this expressly deplored the claims of responsibility by Al Qaida for the acts. But even in this case no reference was made to self-defence.[174]

The Security Council's general declaration on the issue of combatting terrorism in Resolution 1456 (2003) also limited itself to peaceful means with no mention of self-defence. The same is true of the Global Counter-terrorism Strategy unanimously adopted by the UN General Assembly in 2006.[175] The failure to refer to self-defence in this context, or to take the opportunity to reaffirm the right to use force in self-defence mentioned in earlier resolutions, seems significant. It may be taken as an indication that the right to use force in self-defence against past terrorist acts should remain exceptional, perhaps available only in cases of attacks on territory rather than on nationals abroad. Certainly the Security Council has not demonstrated any willingness to assert a wide right of preemptive self-defence.

INTERVENTION AFTER *OPERATION ENDURING FREEDOM*

Difficult questions also arise as to how far the war against terrorism in Afghanistan has affected the law on intervention. The traditional rule was that states should not intervene to assist opposition forces to overthrow a government. And although it was permissible to respond to a request for help by a government, states should not intervene in a conflict which had escalated to a civil war unless there had been outside intervention against the government.[176] If states claim that the opposition are terrorists then this might be used not only to justify non-military, repressive actions by the government, but also to justify a shift in legal argument on forcible intervention.

The UN Secretary-General has expressed concern that states are increasingly using the 'T word'—terrorism—to demonize political opponents and to de-legitimize legitimate political grievances. 'States fighting various forms of unrest or insurgency are finding it tempting to abandon the sometimes slow process of political negotiation for the deceptively easy option of military action.'[177] Thus Israel tried to draw a parallel between its position and that of the USA in order to avoid criticism for the escalation

---

[174] The many SC presidential statements passed in response to terrorist acts take the same approach.
[175] UN docs A/60/825, 27 April 2006, GA/10488, 8 September 2006, GA/10502, 19 September 2006. Similarly, the OAS *Convention on Terrorism* (2003) included only peaceful means: 42 ILM (2003) 19.
[176] See 92 above.
[177] UN News Centre; <www.un.org/apps/news/printnews.asp?nid=5923>.

of its massive retaliation against Palestinian attacks and obstruction of the peace process.[178] China also drew a parallel between its position and that of the USA and rounded up Muslims in Xinjiang on the basis of an alleged link with Al Qaida.[179] There is a danger that states are using the threat of terrorism as an excuse to abandon the domestic protection of human rights, and also to modify international law doctrine on forcible intervention by third states.

The USA has turned to the new language of the war against terrorism to justify the establishment of new bases round the world, and also to support military intervention on behalf of insecure governments. For example, the US military has been present in Colombia for many years; its justifications for involvement have shifted over time. First, it was involved in the 'fight against communism', then in helping the government in its so-called war on drugs. But the USA always took pains to claim that it was not intervening in a civil war; it maintained that its contribution was limited to the maintenance of law and order, or the provision of training. Since 9/11 the USA now says that is helping the government in its unified war on narcotics and terrorism—even though there are no reported links of the opposition forces with Al Qaida or Islamic groups—and the USA continues to provide vast amounts of aid.[180]

In the Philippines large numbers of US troops have been deployed, initially 'in support of counter-terrorism exercises'. In February 2002 the USA undertook their first major military operation outside Afghanistan, lasting about six months against an Islamic group, the Abu Sayyaf Group, accused of involvement in terrorism and of having links with Al Qaida.[181] In February 2003 an increase in the number of US troops was planned, but there was some controversy over the description of the US participation, whether the role of the US troops was just 'training' or whether the US forces were to have a combat role. The Philippines Constitution does not allow foreign troops to engage in combat on its territory, but US Defense Secretary Rumsfeld argued that there was no substantive difference between the two states over the actual US role but only about its

---

[178] UN Press Release SC/7242, 14 December 2001; Keesings (2001) 44371.

[179] SC4413th meeting (2001); *The Guardian*, 22 October 2001, 22 February 2002.

[180] Keesings (2002) 44931, (2003) 45234; *The Guardian*, 25 February, 21 March 2002, 4 and 24 February 2003. There have also been reports of UK special forces involvement to assist the government, *The Guardian* 2 September 2003. See also, Feickert, *US Military Operations in the Global War on Terrorism*, at 16, 26 August 2005, Congressional Research Service, Order Code RL 32758.

[181] Keesings (2002) 44622, 44662, 44901, (2003) 45197, (2004) 46306, (2005) 46617, 46772, (2006) 47304; *The Guardian*, 1 February 2002. See also, Feickert, *US Military Operations in the Global War on Terrorism*, at 14, 26 August 2005, Congressional Research Service, Order Code RL 32758.

description.[182] There have been further 'joint military exercises'.[183] US troops remain in the Philippines to provide anti-terrorism training to Philippine forces.[184] The Philippine government began a major offensive against the Abu Sayyaf Group in August 2006, with the backing of the USA, and the conflict continues.[185]

In marked contrast, the USA was reluctant to accept any right of Russia to use force in self-defence against terrorism with regard to the situation in Georgia where Chechen forces operate in the Pankrisi Gorge area.[186] Russia bombarded Chechen positions in Georgia several times in response to terrorist attacks by Chechens in Russia. In a letter to the Security Council on the first anniversary of 9/11 it used the language of self-defence:

The Chechen Republic, where international terrorist organizations, including the not unknown Al Qaida, have expanded their activities on a full-scale basis, has for a long time remained a source of extremism and terrorism in our country's territory. The continued existence in separate parts of the world of territorial enclaves outside the control of national governments, which, owing to the most diverse circumstances, are unable or unwilling to counteract the terrorist threat is one of the reasons that complicate efforts to combat terrorism effectively. The Pankisi Gorge is one such place. From 1999 Russia has attempted to arrange cooperation with Georgia on issues relating to combatting terrorism. If the Georgian leadership is unable to establish a security zone in the area of the border, continues to ignore Security Council Resolution 1373 and does not put an end to the bandit sorties and attacks on adjoining areas of Russia, we reserve the right to act in accordance with Article 51 of the UN Charter.[187]

The USA in response stressed the rights of Georgia. It seemed not to accept the Russian claims; it deplored the violations of Georgian sovereignty

---

[182] Keesings (2003) 45247; *The Guardian*, 22 February 2003; <www.defenselink.mil/news/Feb2003/t02282003>.

[183] Keesings (2004) 45852.

[184] Feickert, *US Military Operations in the Global War on Terrorism*, 14, 26 August 2005, Congressional Research Service, Order Code RL 32758; Lum, *US Foreign Aid to East and South East Asia*, Congressional Research Service, Order Code RL 31362, 21, 22 August 2007.

[185] Keesings (2005) 46472, (2006) 47417, (2007) 47701, 48044, 48085, 48143; The *International Herald Tribune*, 25 August 2007. There are reports that Australia has made a security pact with the Philippines to train and equip the government in its fight against Islamic insurgents, Keesings (2007) 47934.

[186] Keesings (2002) 44630, 44662, 44686, 44747, 44810, 44951, 44998, 45050; *The Guardian*, 6 January 2004. In contrast, the USA has been more sympathetic to Russian attempts to secure a settlement within Chechnya since 9/11: *The Guardian*, 15 May 2003.

[187] UN doc S/2002/1012. For Georgia's reply see UN doc S/2002/1033. Georgia accused Russia of violations of its sovereignty by bombers and military helicopters and spoke of the 'unaptness' of the reference by Russia which allows an attacked state to render armed resistance in order to defend its territorial integrity and sovereignty. Russia has not been subjected to armed aggression by Georgia. Repeated attempts are being made to blame Georgia for its inability to provide security for Russia on the Chechen segment of the Georgian-Russian state border, where the current situation has been deliberately created by the Russian Federation itself.

and spoke of bombings by Russian aircraft *'under the guise of* antiterrorist operations', even though it acknowledged that Georgia had not been able to establish effective control over the eastern part of the country and accepted a link between the Chechen forces and Al Qaida.[188] The USA itself provided training and other assistance to help the Georgian authorities to implement tighter anti-terrorism controls and so did the UK.[189] This reluctance by the USA to acknowledge the right of another state to invoke self-defence against terrorism, even in a neighbouring state, and even where it may legitimately claim to have a strong case, seems to make it more difficult to claim that the events of 9/11 and the response have established a new customary rule. Here, as elsewhere, we see the USA claiming rights for itself that it is unwilling to see exercised by others.[190]

REGIME CHANGE

The question of the impact of 9/11 on the development of international law on the use of force also arises with regard to the related issue of regime change. This question has divided even the USA and the UK: the former seems to have abandoned any lip service to the idea that it is illegal forcibly to intervene to overthrow a government in the absence of Security Council authorization, whereas the latter is not willing openly to espouse this position. However, the reasoning of the Court in the *Nicaragua* case suggests that this difference may be one of limited legal significance.

When it began *Operation Enduring Freedom* in Afghanistan, the USA claimed to be acting in self-defence, but it subsequently went on to say that it wanted to overthrow the Taliban regime and install a new government. The UK was not quite so overt; in its campaign objectives it stated that its aims were to bring Osama bin Laden and other leaders to justice, to prevent them from posing a continuing terrorist threat and to ensure that Afghanistan ceased to harbour and sustain international terrorism. The UK required sufficient change in the leadership to ensure that Afghanistan's links to international terrorism were broken. It would take all means, political and military, to isolate the Taliban regime unless the Taliban regime complied with the US ultimatum, taking action against Osama bin Laden, the Al Qaida network and where necessary taking action to fragment the present Taliban regime.[191] There were no real

---

[188] *The Guardian*, 24, 26 August 2002.
[189] Keesings (2002) 44630, 44686, 44749, 44951; *The Guardian*, 22 and 28 February, 20 March, 23 October, 21 November 2002.
[190] Similarly, the USA was initially reluctant to accept the right of Turkey to take cross-border action against PKK terrorist forces in northern Iraq: see 140 above.
[191] <www.operations.mod.uk/veritas/faq/objectives.htm>.

objections by other states with regard to the overthrow of the Taliban—
the regime had been isolated in the international community, it had not
been recognized by the UN as the legitimate government of Afghanistan
and had been subjected to sanctions by the UN—but this question of
regime change has proved much more problematic with regard to Iraq.

Very soon after 9/11 the USA said that it wanted regime change in Iraq.
Following President Bush's identification of Iraq as part of the Axis of Evil
in the 2002 *State of the Union Address* there were press reports of members
of the administration openly setting out a US policy of regime change.[192]
The administration began to implement the 1998 *Iraq Liberation Act* signed
into law by President Clinton at a time of political weakness, but never
implemented by him. This provides that 'It should be the policy of the
United States to support efforts to remove the regime headed by Saddam
Hussein from power in Iraq and to promote the emergence of a democratic
government to replace that regime.' The USA was to supply massive aid,
including military equipment to designated Iraqi 'democratic opposition
organizations'. Under President Bush a much more enthusiastic approach
was adopted with many expressions of desire for regime change despite
the problems with identifying a viable Iraqi opposition and the divisions
between the different groups.[193] In December 2002 the USA promised $92
million to train Iraqi militia to form a new army.[194] Those states opposed to
the use of force against Iraq, such as France, Germany, Russia and China,
all accused the USA of using force without legal justification in order to
secure an illegal regime change.[195]

The legal position of the UK after 9/11 was that it would welcome
a regime change in Iraq if that was a *consequence* of its actions, but that
this would not be the *aim* of any use of force. Whereas the US policy was
regime change, it was not that of the UK; the UK's purpose was disarmament.[196] The Attorney-General in his advice on the legality of the war in
Iraq expressly ruled out forcible regime change as the basis for the use of
force; he said, 'regime change cannot be the objective of military action'.[197]
But the difference between the positions of the two states seems very

---

[192] Foreign Affairs Committee Seventh Report of Session 2001–02, *Foreign Policy Aspects
of the War Against Terrorism*, HC 384, para 204; Second Report of Session 2002–03, HC 196,
para 111. See Reisman, 'Why regime change is (almost always) a bad idea', 98 AJIL (2004) 516.

[193] *The Observer*, 16 February 2003, *The Guardian*, 21 February 2003. Accusations of corruption had led to threats to cut off aid to opposition groups (Keesings (2002) 44585; *The
Guardian*, 9 January, 22 February 2002). And there were reports of internal divisions within
the US administration on this issue (*The Guardian*, 22 February, 11 December 2002).

[194] *The Guardian*, 11 December 2002.

[195] UN Press Releases SC/7705, 26 March 2003, SC/7707, 27 March 2003; *Le Monde*,
30 September 2002; *The Guardian*, 1 October 2002.

[196] UK Materials on International Law, 73 BYIL (2002) 877 at 16/43; *The Guardian*, 3,
8 October 2002.

[197] Attorney-General's Advice on the Iraq War, 54 ICLQ (2005) 767 at para 36.

small in the government's reply to the Foreign Affairs Committee's recommendation that it clarify whether its policy was to bring about regime
change in Iraq. The reply was 'The government's policy is to secure full
implementation of the Security Council resolutions elating to Iraq. It is
also the Government's view that Iraq would be a better place without
Saddam Hussein. As the Prime Minister has made clear we are determined to deal with the threat posed by Iraq's possession of Weapons of
Mass Destruction.'[198] And immediately before the intervention the government increased its emphasis on the desirability of the overthrow of
Saddam Hussein for humanitarian reasons, apparently in order to increase
the popular support for military action. Prime Minister Blair, in response
to the mass protest in London in February 2003, argued that he wanted an
end to the regime of Saddam Hussein, although 'this is not our aim', the
aim was disarmament.[199]

However, the *Nicaragua* case suggests that in international law what is
decisive is not the intent of the intervening state, whether proclaimed or
otherwise. The test as to whether an act of intervention is unlawful is an
objective one. The Court said in response to Nicaragua's claim that it was
the aim of the USA to overthrow the government that it did not consider it
necessary to seek to establish whether the intention of the United States to
secure a change of governmental policies in Nicaragua went so far as to be
equated with an endeavour to overthrow the Nicaraguan government. The
Court said that in international law, if one state, with a view to the coercion of another state, supports and assists armed bands in that state whose
purpose is to overthrow the government of that state, that amounts to an
intervention by the one state in the internal affairs of the other, whether
or not the political objective of the state giving such support and assistance is equally far-reaching. It did not therefore examine the intentions of
the United States in this context.[200] The Court confirmed this approach in
Armed Activities in the Territory of the Congo (DRC v Uganda).[201] Thus, if the
UK actions in fact had the effect of overthrowing Saddam Hussein then
it would be no defence that this had not been their aim. Nevertheless, it
is significant that even if the UK line of argument on regime change is

---

[198] Response of the Secretary of State for Foreign and Commonwealth Affairs to the
Seventh Report of the Foreign Affairs Committee on Foreign Policy Aspects of Terrorism,
Cm 5589, p.13.

[199] *The Observer*, 16 February 2003; *The Guardian*, 17, 18 February 2003. The Prime Minister
of Australia, in authorizing defence forces to take part in operations against Iraq, said, 'The
government's principal objective is the disarmament of Iraq; however, should military
action be required to achieve this, it is axiomatic that such action will result in the removal
of Saddam Hussein's regime.'; <www.pm.gov.au/news/speeches/2003/speech2201.htm>.

[200] *Case concerning Military and Paramilitary Activities in and against Nicaragua*, ICJ Reports
(1986) 14 at para 241.

[201] ICJ Reports (2005) 168. See Chapter 3.

not sufficient to save it from responsibility, the UK unlike the USA still goes out of its way to pay lip service to the traditional doctrine of non-intervention. UK Prime Minister Blair subsequently adopted new language: he argued that since 9/11 the USA 'has embarked on a policy of intervention in order to protect its own and our future security. Hence Afghanistan. Hence Iraq. Hence the broader Middle East initiative in support of moves towards democracy in the Arab world. The point about these interventions, military and otherwise, is that they are not just about changing regimes but changing the values systems governing the nations concerned. The banner was not actually 'regime change', it was 'values change'.[202]

THE 'WAR ON TERROR' EXTENDS

Israel, Syria and Lebanon 2001–2006

The scope of the right to use force against terrorism after 9/11 has predictably proved especially controversial in the Middle East. Israel repeatedly said that it was acting in self-defence against terrorism in its use of force against Lebanon since 9/11, including its regular incursions into Lebanon's airspace by warplanes and helicopters. It argued that Hezbollah was a terrorist organization, operating from Lebanon, and responsible for a series of attacks on Israeli nationals and armed forces. Israel claimed that Hezbollah has the full support and blessing of Lebanon, Syria and Iran which had persistently refused to meet their obligations to prevent terrorism under Security Council Resolution 1373 (2001). Israel had ended its (almost) twenty year occupation of south Lebanon in June 2000, but Lebanon had not reasserted its governmental authority in the area, as required by Security Council Resolutions 1310 (2000) and 1337 (2001), to prevent cross-border terrorist attacks and ensure effective peace and security. It permitted Hezbollah complete freedom of movement. Syria provided financial, logistical and political support to Hezbollah; it offered a safe harbour in Syrian controlled territory and was therefore responsible for Hezbollah's actions. Israel said that it would adopt the necessary measures to protect its citizens in accordance with the right of self-defence.[203]

After 9/11 Israel adopted language similar to that of the USA on the war against terrorism; it employed the key concepts of 'global terrorism' and 'harbouring'. Israel claimed that Hezbollah was an organization

---

[202] Speech to the World Affairs Council in Los Angeles, 1 August 2006; <www.number10. gov.uk/output/Page 9948>.
[203] UN docs S/2003/806, S/2003/758, S/2003/96, S/2002/373, S/2002/986; 2001 UNYB 448. 2002 UNYB 473, 2003 UNYB 516, 2004 UNYB 505.

with extensive terrorist networks around the globe and a lengthy history of global terrorism.[204] It also accused Syria and Lebanon of 'harbouring' Hezbollah. But Israel also argued that Syria and Lebanon actively supported Hezbollah and it was that active involvement which meant that they were responsible for its actions and that Israel was entitled to use force in self-defence against Lebanon and Syrian targets within Lebanon. Israel stressed that Lebanon and Syria were colluding with Hezbollah; that is, it did not expressly claim a right to act against non-state actors in the absence of territorial state involvement. Israel also argued after 9/11 that there were links between Al Qaida and Hezbollah; it said that there was an Al Qaida presence in Lebanon.[205]

Lebanon's position was complex. It was on the strongest ground in objecting to the series of Israeli incursions into Lebanon's airspace and in claiming the right to respond in self-defence. It said that these Israeli acts were acts of aggression and provocation and entitled Lebanon to exercise its right of self-defence, including anti-aircraft fire against Israeli aircraft.[206] More controversially, it also argued that Israel remained in illegal occupation of certain Lebanese territory—in the Shab'a farms area—after the withdrawal of its forces in June 2000.[207] Therefore the acts of legitimate resistance against the Israeli occupation were not being carried out on Israeli territory, but in occupied territory and against Israeli military positions in that territory. Lebanon refused to condemn Hezbollah as it was acting in response to Israel's continued illegal occupation of Lebanese territory, in the disputed Shab'a farms area: there was a dividing line between legitimate resistance to occupation in self-defence and terrorism. The actions were not terrorism under Security Council Resolution 1373, but were covered by General Assembly Resolution 46/51 (1991) which distinguished between terrorism and the rights of people to struggle against foreign occupation. If Israeli military aircraft intruded into Lebanon and Hezbollah fired in self-defence, this was part of a legitimate struggle to liberate territory.[208] Syria also maintained this position which is essentially a continuation of the support for Hezbollah in its earlier efforts to end the Israeli occupation of southern Lebanon.[209]

The UN Secretary-General reported that the commitment of Hezbollah to the launching of hostile attacks across the Blue Line established

---

[204] UN doc S/2003/96.
[205] Keesings (2002) 45010; S/2002/743. For Lebanon's denial, see UN docs S/2002/687, S/2002/829. The USA has also asserted that there are links between Hezbollah and Al Qaida (Keesings (2002) 44918).
[206] UN docs S/2002/135, S/2002/1038, S/2003/148.
[207] 2001 UNYB 448, UN Press Releases SC/7352, 3 April 2002, SC/7358, 8 April 2002. See 104 above.
[208] UN docs S/2002/135, S/2002/1038, S/2003/148.
[209] UN docs S/2001/438, S/2003/178.

between the two states when Israel withdrew its forces from Lebanon, and the Lebanese government's unwillingness to fulfil its commitment to ensure full respect for the Blue Line, contravened Security Council decisions. That line was drawn by the United Nations and recognized by the Security Council as confirming the withdrawal of Israeli forces from southern Lebanon under Resolution 425 (1978).[210] The Shab'a farms area lies in an area occupied by Israel in 1967 and is therefore subject to a negotiated settlement.[211]

When Israel extended its 'war on terrorism' beyond Lebanon and Syrian targets within Lebanon,[212] and into Syria itself, on the basis that Syria was harbouring terrorists, there was a strong international rejection of the legality of its use of force. In October 2003, after a Palestinian suicide bomb in a restaurant in Haifa, Israel responded by its deepest raid into Syria since the 1973 war. Israel said that it was acting against a Palestinian terrorist training camp for Islamic Jihad; it warned terrorists not to hide in neighbouring states.[213] The UN Secretary-General strongly deplored the Israeli air-strike on Syrian territory as well as condemning the preceding terrorist attack.[214] The Security Council met at Syria's request, and Syria accused Israel of aggression and a breach of the 1974 *Disengagement Agreement* between the two states. Israel claimed that it was acting in self-defence against a state which supported terrorism.[215]

In the Security Council the majority of states condemned the Israeli action as a violation of international law. Arab states argued that this was a disproportionate armed reprisal and proceeded from a political desire to destroy the peace process and destabilize the region. For Spain, France, and China it was a patent violation of international law. Pakistan accused

---

[210] The Security Council had repeatedly expressed its recognition of the Blue Line as valid for the purpose of confirming Israel's withdrawal; it had expressed concern at the persistence of tension and violence along the Blue Line and condemned all such acts of violence, including both Hezbollah's firing of rockets and Israel's air incursions: SC Res 1583 (2005), 1614 (2005), 1655 (2006).

[211] Report of the Secretary-General on UNIFIL, S/2002/746.

[212] Israel attacked Syrian positions in Lebanon in April and July 2001. It said that Syria was the main power broker in Lebanon with 30,000 troops there, that it supported Hezbollah and allowed it to maintain terrorist training facilities in the Syrian-controlled Bekaa valley. Israel was acting in self-defence against Hezbollah attacks on Israeli forces on the Israeli side of Blue Line (2000 UNYB 472, 2001 UNYB 448). The EU condemned this as a disproportionate and excessive response to Hezbollah attacks. That is, it did not enter into question of the legality of the use of force against terrorism.

[213] There was considerable speculation at the time that this action was taken because the Israeli government wanted to be seen to act against ongoing terrorist attacks by Palestinians, but was under US pressure not to implement its Security Cabinet decision to 'remove' (that is, to exile or assassinate) the Palestinian leader, Yasser Arafat (UN Press Releases SC/7875, 16 September 2003, GA/10152, 19 September 2003; Keesings (2003) 45673; *The Guardian* 6, 7, 8, 10 October 2003).

[214] UN Press Release SG/SM/8918, 6 October 2003.

[215] SC 4836th meeting (2003), UN Press Release SC/7887, 5 October 2003.

Israel of exploitation of the campaign against terrorism for other purposes: 'the answer to individual acts of terrorism is not state terrorism, nor is it wanton attacks against other countries'. Germany said that Israel's action was 'unacceptable' and a violation of the sovereignty of a neighbouring state; the UK said only that the action was unacceptable and did not expressly enter into the question of legality; Russia was also cautious. The USA called for restraint, but it said that Syria was 'on the wrong side in the war on terrorism'; it was still considered a state sponsor of terrorism and a host to Islamic militant groups. Certain states such as Mexico and Jordan said that the action was clearly a reprisal not self-defence; in the case of self-defence the right to use force was subject to the commission of an advance military aggression against that state. That is, no general support was expressed for a wide right to use force against terrorist camps in a third state. In contrast, when Israel carried out a mysterious air raid on an unknown target in Syria in September 2007 there was little international condemnation, even though Israel did not offer any legal justification for its use of force. There was speculation that the target was nuclear technology from North Korea, although Syria denied these accusations and they were not substantiated. There was also speculation that Israel had carried out the raid as a warning to Iran, in order to deter it from developing nuclear weapons. Syria protested to the Security Council, but the UN took no action.[216]

Israel/Lebanon 2006

The issues raised by the 2002 and 2006 US *National Security Strategies* concerning the scope of the right to use force—the legality of pre-emptive force, the question of what will trigger pre-emptive action, the scope of self-defence against non-state actors such as terrorists and against their rogue state sponsors, the role of the UN—have all arisen with regard to the recent conflict between Israel and Hezbollah. The conflict in Lebanon and the international response to it demonstrate a deep doctrinal divide on the scope of self-defence, in particular with regard to proportionality. The central question is whether the 'war on terror' gives Israel a wide right to use force, even a pre-emptive right.

It is commonly said that the conflict began on 12 July 2006 when Hezbollah launched a cross-border attack on Israeli forces in northern Israel, killed eight Israeli soldiers and abducted two.[217] The UN Secretary-General

---

[216] Keesings (2007) 48164, 48224; *The Guardian* 18 September, 15 October 2007; *The Observer* 16 September 2007; Syria's letter to the UN, UN doc S/2007/537.
[217] See Secretary-General's Reports on UNIFIL, S/2006/560, S/2007/392 para 2, for an account of the outbreak of the conflict.

condemned the Hezbollah attacks and called for the release of the Israeli captives.[218] The same day Israel wrote to the UN Security Council saying that the attack was a 'clear declaration of war' and reserving the right to act in self-defence.[219] There was a heavy exchange of fire and Israel mounted increasingly extensive attacks on Lebanon. Its use of force by land, sea and air continued for a month and involved massive destruction. The UN reported that Israel destroyed roads, airports, bridges, ports, power stations, as well as thousands of houses. The Israeli attacks caused about one thousand civilian Lebanese deaths, injured over 3,500 and displaced almost a million people.[220] The air, sea and land blockade of Lebanon continued after the ceasefire. During the conflict Hezbollah fired hundreds of rockets into Israel, causing fifty civilian casualties and an estimated 114 military deaths, and disrupting the lives of hundreds of thousands of civilians.[221]

The question arose whether Israel had the right of self-defence against such attacks, and how far its response was proportionate. Israel's letter of 12 July 2006 to the Security Council was brief. It reserved the right 'to act in accordance with Article 51 of the UN Charter and exercise its right of self-defence when an armed attack is launched against a Member of the UN'.[222] This is a cautious formulation, based on the universally agreed principle that there is a right of self-defence in response to an actual armed attack. As it turned out, Israel's use of force went rather beyond this narrow right.

States were divided in their response to the conflict. This may be seen clearly in the Security Council debates.[223] Initially, at the first meeting held after the outbreak of the conflict, most members of the Security Council seemed sympathetic to Israel's claim to self-defence. Only China and Qatar (and, to a lesser extent, Ghana) openly condemned the Israeli actions at this stage. All the European members of the Security Council apart from Russia asserted that Israel had a right to self-defence. Interestingly the USA made no mention of self-defence at this meeting. Japan, Peru, Argentina and Tanzania also said that Israel had a right of self-defence. The states supporting this right did so in rather general terms which left the scope of the doctrine unclear.[224]

Many states accepted that the incidents of 12 July 2006 were the start of the conflict. The UN Secretary-General said that 'Hezbollah's provocative

[218] UN doc SG/SM/10563, 12 July 2006.
[219] UN doc S/2006/515, 12 July 2006.
[220] UN Press Releases, Humanitarian Fact sheets on Lebanon, IHA/1215, 11 August 2006; IHA/1216, 14 August 2006.
[221] UN Press Release, SC/8808, 11 August 2006.
[222] UN doc S/2006/515.
[223] SC 5489th meeting (2006); SC 5493rd meeting (2006).
[224] SC 5489th meeting (2006); UN Press Release SC/8776, 14 July 2006.

attack on 12 July was the trigger of this crisis'.[225] But other contested this; they said there was no right of self-defence. These incidents were not of sufficient gravity to amount to an armed attack. It was important not to take the minor incident of 12 July out of context; this was one in a series of cross border incidents, and should be seen in the context of the history of the region and Israel's continued occupation of the Palestinian territories and the Golan Heights.[226] The UN Secretary-General's Report on the UN Interim Force in Lebanon (UNIFIL) of 21 July 2006 listed a long sequence of such cross-border incidents pre-dating 12 July.[227] Thus, for example, in February 2006 there had been a series of cross-border incidents following the alleged shooting by Israeli troops of a Lebanese shepherd. In May 2006 there was a rocket attack from Lebanon on an Israeli Defence Force base in north Israel; in response, the Israeli air force attacked Palestinian bases inside Lebanon. It was also reported that Israeli forces were responsible for the targeted assassination of an Islamic jihad leader in Sidon. Such cross-border incidents were commonplace in the years following the Israeli withdrawal from Lebanon in 2000. Over the years Hezbollah had fired many rockets from Lebanon over the border into Israel; Israel had conducted what the Secretary-General's Report called 'persistent and provocative air incursions' over Lebanon. But previous incidents had not led to such a massive response by Israel since 1982.[228]

Non-state actors

This conflict raises the question of the degree of state complicity, if any, necessary to justify a forcible response against a state from which non-state actors are operating. Although many states accepted Israel's right to self-defence, it is not clear from their statements in the Security Council debates whether they accepted that Israel was entitled to use force against Hezbollah in the absence of complicity of Lebanon. Israel itself was careful to attribute responsibility to Lebanon; in its letter to the Security Council on 12 July it said, 'Responsibility for this belligerent act of war lies with the government of Lebanon from whose territory these acts have been launched into Israel. Responsibility also lies with the governments of Iran and Syria, which embrace and support those who carried out this attack.'[229]

---

[225] UN Press Release SC/8781, 20 July 2006.
[226] This was the position of Qatar, SC 5489th meeting, 14 July, and of many Arab states at the 20 July meeting, SC 5493rd meeting.
[227] Report of the Secretary-General S/2006/560.
[228] In many regards the 2006 conflict mirrors that of 1982 when a terrorist attack on the Israeli ambassador in London triggered a massive invasion, the siege of Beirut and the occupation of southern Lebanon for nearly twenty years. In that case there was limited international support for Israel; its invasion and prolonged occupation were seen as clearly disproportionate (1982 UNYB 428–497).
[229] UN doc S/2006/515.

Lebanon said that it was not responsible for the actions of Hezbollah and accused Israel of an act of aggression.[230] At the first Security Council debate on the conflict Lebanon regretted that Israel had held Lebanon responsible for Hezbollah's acts, even though the Lebanese government had issued a statement on 12 July, declaring that it was not aware of the incident, that it did not take responsibility for it, and did not endorse what had happened.[231] Since the departure of the Syrian forces from Lebanon in 2005 following Security Council Resolution 1559 (2004), Lebanon had worked to regain independence with a full commitment to the Council resolutions.[232] Israel's aggression had hampered the efforts exerted towards fostering democracy, since it undermined Lebanon's sovereignty and attempts to exercise its authority over its entire territory.[233]

The role of the UN

The UN Security Council played a very limited role in the conflict; it was effectively side-lined (as in the 2006 US *National Security Strategy*) in what the USA, the UK and Israel portrayed as part of the 'war on terror.' The USA and the UK indicated that they would not accept a call for an immediate ceasefire by the G8 or by the Security Council, even though Lebanon had called for a ceasefire from the start of the conflict, and even though the UN Secretary-General had subsequently supported this call, saying that the authority and standing of the Security Council were at stake if it did not play a role in securing an end to the conflict.[234] The Non-Aligned Movement and ASEAN also called for a ceasefire.[235] However, the USA and the UK said that it was necessary to secure a 'durable and sustainable ceasefire': the violence would end only when Hezbollah had been disarmed or removed from the border. The UK and the USA were not willing to allow the Security Council to call for an immediate end to the fighting. This was taken as a green light by Israel to continue its military campaign.[236] In its first resolution after the outbreak of the conflict the

---

[230] UN doc S/2006/529, 17 July 2006.
[231] UN doc S/2006/518, 13 July 2006, UN Press Release SC 8776, 14 July 2006.
[232] Syrian forces had been present in Lebanon at the invitation of the government since the civil war of 1975–1976. From 2004 the USA and France exerted strong pressure on Syria to secure its withdrawal; they secured the adoption of SC Resolution 1559 (2004) calling for the withdrawal of all foreign forces and the disbanding of all militias. Elections held in 2005 produced a coalition government of national unity, including two members of Hezbollah: Keesings (2005) 46759. See Chapter 3.
[233] SC 5489th meeting (2006), UN Press Release SC/8776, 14 July 2006.
[234] Lebanon called for an immediate ceasefire in UN Press Release SC/8776, 14 July 2006, UN doc S/2006/500, 19 July 2006. The Secretary-General also called for a ceasefire in UN Press Releases SC/8781, 20 July 2006, SC/8790, 30 July 2006.
[235] UN docs S/2006/548, S/2006/569.
[236] *The Guardian*, 14, 19, 27 July 2006; 2, 10 August 2006; US and UK speeches in SC 5493rd meeting (2006); Speech by Tony Blair, 18 July 2006; <www.number10.gov.uk/output/Page 9870.asp>.

Security Council merely expressed deepest concern at the escalation of hostilities since 12 July 2006.[237] It was not until 11 August that it called for a 'full cessation of hostilities' in Resolution 1701 (2006). The Secretary-General indicated his regret that the Security Council had not called for the immediate cessation of hostilities earlier.[238]

Proportionality

Israel's massive use of force was clearly not proportionate if seen as a response to the events of 12 July 2006 or to past attacks by Hezbollah, even if those attacks could be taken cumulatively. Israel claimed that its acts were aimed at Hezbollah, not at Lebanon; they were targeted at Hezbollah strongholds and infrastructure, not at civilian targets.[239] Lebanon strongly rejected this argument; it said 'from the start it had been clear that it was not Hezbollah that was the target, but Lebanon. Its infrastructure was the target and hundreds of civilians had been killed before Israel had even taken up any campaign against Hezbollah and its positions'.[240] The Secretary-General also seemed sceptical about Israel's claim.[241]

Most states condemned Israel's use of force as disproportionate.[242] A few members of the Security Council were not willing to do this; they merely called on Israel to ensure that its acts were not disproportionate.[243] But many others such as France and Argentina, which had initially asserted that Israel had a right to self-defence, subsequently condemned its actions. India, Brazil, Chile, Djibouti, Switzerland and New Zealand, as well as many Arab states, all condemned the excessive use of force. China did not repeat its earlier strong denunciation of the armed aggression of Israel against Lebanon, but simply condemned attacks targeting civilians and civilian infrastructure in general terms. It urged all parties concerned to exercise maximum restraint.[244]

But Israel, the USA and the UK demonstrated a different understanding of proportionality in this case. Israel said in its letter to the Security Council, 'These acts pose a grave threat not just to Israel's northern border, but also to the region and the entire world.' It argued that the conflict should be seen as part of the 'war on terror'.[245] 'In this vacuum [of southern Lebanon] festers the Axis of Terror: Hezbollah and the terrorist states of Iran and Syria, which have today opened another chapter in their war of

---

[237] SC Res 1697 (2006).
[238] SC 5511th meeting (2006).
[239] SC 5493rd meeting (2006).
[240] UN Press Release SC/8789, 30 July 2006; see also SC/8808, 11 August 2006.
[241] UN Press Release SC/8781, 20 July 2006.
[242] Ibid.
[243] This was the position of the UK, Denmark and Greece.
[244] SC 5493rd meeting (2006).
[245] UN doc S/2006/515.

International Law and the Use of Force

terror.'[246] Israel argued that the aim of Hezbollah, supported by Iran, was to destroy Israel and that therefore Israel's use of force was proportionate to the threat posed by Hezbollah. The conflict was portrayed as part of a wider 'war on terror.'[247]

The Secretary-General's Special Adviser reported to the Security Council that the Prime Minister of Israel had 'made clear that Israel had decided that military operations would continue until Hezbollah was seriously weakened; this was not, as in the past, a response to a particular incident but was a definitive response to an unacceptable strategic threat posed by Hezbollah and a message to Iran and Syria that threats by proxies would no longer be tolerated'.[248] The actions of Israel were pre-emptive in so far as they were designed to stop future attacks by Hezbollah. Hezbollah was portrayed as a threat to the existence of Israel. But, however intolerable its rocket attacks on the civilians of Israel, this is not a convincing picture, given the vast disparity of resources. As Ghana said, 'The reality of Israel's absolute military dominance in the region belies the oft-repeated claim that this powerful country must take extreme measures to protect itself, even if that means laying waste to another sovereign state that is obviously very weak.'[249]

The USA and the UK accepted the Israeli position, and refused to condemn Israel's actions as disproportionate, or to allow a call for an immediate ceasefire by the Security Council. They used the ongoing 'war on terror' as justification for their support for Israel's campaign to wipe out Hezbollah.[250] As US Representative John Bolton put it in the Security Council, 'All of us in this Chamber face a common and shared enemy...That enemy is terrorism.'[251] After the Security Council's adoption of the ceasefire resolution, President Bush said that responsibility for the suffering lies with Hezbollah. 'It was an unprovoked attack by Hezbollah on Israel that started this conflict. Responsibility for the suffering of the Lebanese people also rests with Hezbollah's states sponsors, Iran and Syria. The regime in Iran provides Hezbollah with financial support, weapons and training. Iran has made clear that it seeks the destruction of Israel. We can only imagine how much more dangerous this conflict would be if Iran had the nuclear weapon it seeks. Syria is another state sponsor of Hezbollah. Syria allows Iranian weapons to pass through its territory into Lebanon. Syria permits Hezbollah's leaders to operate out of Damascus and gives political support to Hezbollah's cause. Syria supports Hezbollah because it wants

---

[246] SC 5511th meeting (2006), UN Press Release SC/8808, 11 August 2006.
[247] UN Press Release SC/8808, 11 August 2006.
[248] SC 5493rd meeting (2006) at 4–5.
[249] SC 5493rd meeting (2006) at 8.
[250] *The Guardian*, 19, 29 and 31 July 2006.
[251] SC 5493rd meeting (2006) at 16.

to undermine Lebanon's democratic government and regain its position of dominance in the country.'[252] This view was not convincing to a majority of states; the 118-member Non-Aligned Movement condemned the Israeli use of force against Lebanon as aggression.[253]

A ceasefire was finally agreed under Resolution 1701(2006), passed unanimously, but the resolution perpetuated the dispute about the scope of self-defence. The resolution seemed weighted in favour of Israel in that it called for 'a full cessation of hostilities based upon, in particular, the immediate cessation by Hezbollah of all attacks and the immediate cessation by Israel of all offensive military operations'. This left open the prospect that Israel would take a wide view of defensive action, to include further pre-emptive actions against Hezbollah.[254] Some states expressed reservations about this language during the negotiations and at the time of adoption.[255] And it turned out that their concerns were justified: on 19 August there was an Israeli air incursion into Lebanon in pursuit of Hezbollah fighters, and to block the supply of arms to Hezbollah from Syria. The Secretary-General expressed deep concern about this breach of the ceasefire.[256] Israel said that it was acting defensively and also that it had the right to use force to implement Resolution 1701.[257]

Although the government of Lebanon, working with the UN force UNIFIL, has now extended its control over almost the whole of southern Lebanon,[258] the situation in Lebanon remains unstable.[259] Israel maintains that Hezbollah has rebuilt its military presence and capacity, but it has not provided UNIFIL with specific intelligence.[260] There are allegations

---

[252] <www.whitehouse.gov/news/releases/2006/08/200608143.html>.

[253] 2006 Havana Conference, Final Declaration, UN doc S/2006/780, 29 September 2006, at para 142–143; SC 5629th meeting (2007). The Organization of the Islamic Conference also expressed strong condemnation of Israeli aggression, UN doc S/2006/959, 11 December 2006.

[254] Israel said that 'Thus a clear distinction is made between the two parties to the military hostilities, and Israel is given permission by the Security Council to continue defensive actions against a terrorist organization.' (Israeli Ministry of Foreign Affairs, 'Behind the Headlines: UN Security Council Resolution 1701', 12 August 2006.)

[255] The Arab League expressed concern during negotiations, UN Press Release SC/8804, 8 August 2006; Lebanon also expressed dissatisfaction with Resolution 1701, UN Press Release SC/8808, 11 August 2006. See also the letter from Qatar to the Security Council, UN doc S/2006/655, 15 August 2006.

[256] UN Press Release SG/SM/10602, 19 August 2006; *The Guardian*, 21 August 2006.

[257] Israel Ministry of Foreign Affairs, 'MFA: IDF Bekaa operation in response to violation of the ceasefire', 20 August 2006. There were further serious Israeli violations of resolution 1701 in February 2007, Report of the Secretary-General S/2007/147 para 3–8.

[258] Israel has withdrawn its troops from Lebanon apart from the northern part of the village of Ghajar, where it remains in violation of Resolution 1701 (2006), Report of the Secretary-General S/2007/641 para 71.

[259] See Reports of the Secretary-General S/2006/670, S/2006/780, S/2006/933, S/2006/730, S/2007/147, S/2007/641.

[260] Report of the Secretary-General S/2007/641 para 20, 33.

of violations along the Syrian/Lebanese border of the arms embargo imposed in Resolution 1701 (2006). The Security Council has expressed concern at any allegation of the re-arming of Lebanese and non-Lebanese armed groups and militias; it also expressed concern about the statement by Hezbollah that it retains the capacity to strike all parts of Israel.[261] The Secretary-General said that Hezbollah's maintenance of an infrastructure of arms that remains separate from the State has had an adverse effect on the efforts of the government to assert its exclusive control over the entire territory of Lebanon in accordance with Resolution 1701 (2006). He also reported that there have been almost daily violations by Israel of Lebanese airspace. These not only constitute violations of Scrutiny Council Resolutions, but also undermine the credibility of the UN as well as the Lebanese Armed Forces in the eyes of the local population and damage efforts to reduce tension, build confidence and stabilize the situation in southern Lebanon.[262] The two Israeli soldiers whose seizure precipitated the conflict had not been returned at the end of 2007.

Ethiopia/Somalia 2006

The 2006 conflict in Somalia also raises interesting questions about self-defence, but the failure of the states involved adequately to explain their actions in legal terms and the reluctance of other states to enter into legal debate in the Security Council or elsewhere makes assessment difficult. One possible explanation for the lack of international response to the significant Ethiopian intervention in Somalia is the impact of the end of the Cold War; there is no longer any almost automatic challenge by one bloc to the legality of the use of force by the other bloc. In this instance states were apparently not willing to risk offence to the USA, the main supporter of Ethiopia, by condemning what looked like an excessive use of force or by even by querying its legal basis, especially when that use of force was linked to the 'war on terror'. Also the fact that the UN Security Council had repeatedly asserted the legitimacy of the Transitional Federal Government of Somalia helps to explain the reluctance of states to condemn Ethiopian intervention in support of that government. The public silence of China, Russia and the NAM was striking.

Ever since the overthrow of President Siad Barre and the outbreak of civil war in 1991 Somalia has been without an effective government. The UN intervention from 1993–1995 did not reestablish peace and security; the US-led force UNITAF failed to carry out its mandate of disarming the

---

[261] S/PRST/2007/29. For Hezbollah's claims, see S/2007/147 para 15.
[262] S/2007/641 para 72, 75.

warlords.[263] The Secretary-General told the Security Council that the UN's ability to provide security had been reduced by troop withdrawals, budget restrictions and military actions by the Somali factions. Wider problems included the lack of commitment to peace by the factions and insufficient political will by member states.[264] The UN force withdrew in March 1995. The arms embargo imposed by resolution 733 (1992) remained in force. Ever since there have been repeated attempts to establish a government. The Secretary-General reported that during the years without a functioning government the country suffered tremendous destruction and neglect. In addition to the physical damage, the foundations and institutions of the society have been almost completely destroyed.[265]

In 2004 agreement was reached between the competing groups on the establishment of a Transitional Federal Government (TFG) under President Yusuf, backed by Ethiopia.[266] This government was given express AU and Security Council support.[267] Most explicitly, in July 2006 the Security Council said that it supported the TFG and its parliament as 'the internationally recognized authorities to restore peace, stability and governance to Somalia' and that it was ready to consider a limited modification of the arms embargo to enable the TFG to develop Somalia's security sector and national institutions. The Security Council called on all parties inside and outside Somalia to refrain from action that could provoke or perpetuate violence.[268] However, the TFG did not exercise control over the territory; its hopes for an AU peacekeeping force to secure the transitional government were not met before the conflict broke out.[269] The TFG faced a serious challenge from the Union of Islamic Courts (UIC) which had been established in Somalia in 1999. Ethiopia and the USA accused the UIC of being a terrorist organization with strong links to Al Qaida and with plans to create a greater Somalia incorporating parts of Ethiopia and Kenya. Others regarded it as a more disparate coalition of moderates and extremists.[270]

The continuing instability was fuelled by increasing arms flows into Somalia in violation of the arms embargo. These were repeatedly

---

[263] See 286 below.
[264] 1994 UNYB 317, <www.un.org/Depts/dpko/dpko/co_mission/unosom2backgrl.html>.
[265] Report of the Secretary-General on the situation in Somalia, S/2007/381, para 34.
[266] 2004 UNYB 256.
[267] Ibid at 261; SC Res 1587 (2005), 1676 (2006).
[268] S/PRST/2006/31.
[269] Keesings (2006) 47444.
[270] *The Guardian*, 6 June, 27 December 2006, *The Observer*, 10, 31 December 2006; Keesings (2006) 47444. In the SC debate on 6 December 2006 John Bolton, the US representative, said that the UIC had sought to destabilize the Horn of Africa region through irredentist claims on the Somali-populated regions of neighbouring states and support for insurgent groups in Ethiopia, SC 5579th meeting.

condemned by the Security Council.[271] A series of UN reports set out the details of foreign intervention: the main assistance to the TFG came from Ethiopia and to the UIC from Eritrea.[272] Both states rejected these accusations,[273] but the UN reports expressed concern that the regional rivalry between the two states manifested in the 1998–2000 conflict between them was being played out in Somalia.

In June 2006 the UIC seized the capital, Mogadishu. It defeated an alliance of warlords, reported to have been supported by the USA in an attempt to combat the danger it perceived of Islamic extremism in Somalia.[274] The UIC brought about an overall improvement in security and reopened the international airport and the main seaport which had been out of operation for more than a decade.[275] A ceasefire was then agreed—the Khartoum declaration—but the two sides subsequently accused each other of violating its provisions. The UIC accused Ethiopia of sending troops into Somalia to assist the TFG.[276] In November 2006 a UN report alleged that both sides were actively supported inside Somalia by the presence of combat troops, military trainers and advisers from certain states: the UIC was supported by 2,000 Eritrean troops and the TFG by 8,000 Ethiopian and Ugandan troops. The report also made accusations that other states—Djibouti, Egypt, Iran, Libya, Saudi Arabia, and Syria—supported the UIC:[277] 'The military build-up facilitated by aggressive state support not only perpetuates widespread instability and rising tensions, but also helps to sustain a clearly discernible momentum towards the possibility of a major military conflict involving most of Somalia.'[278]

And so it turned out. Clashes between the UIC and the TFG escalated from July 2006. The UIC made significant advances.[279] It accused Ethiopia

---

[271] SC Res 1630 (2005), 1676 (2006), 1724 (2006).

[272] Reports of Monitoring Group on Somalia, S/2005/153, S/2005/625, S/2006/229; Reports of the Secretary-General on the situation in Somalia, S/2005/392, S/2006/838; Report of the Security Council Committee under Resolution 751 (1992), S/2006/913. The last of these reports claims that 720 members of the UIC fought alongside Hezbollah in the 2006 conflict with Israel (para 95–101); this was challenged by commentators: *The Guardian*, 16 November 2006.

[273] Report of Monitoring Group on Somalia, S/2006/229, Annex III; Report of the Security Council Committee under Resolution 751 (1992), S/2006/913, Annex V, VI, X. Ethiopia said it was distressing that the current context in Somalia had been overlooked. It said 'The Horn of Africa region is currently the target of active destabilization by dangerous international terrorist groups.' See also SC 5614th meeting (2006), Report of the Secretary-General's Special Representative.

[274] *The Guardian*, 3 March, 23 May, 27 December 2006; Keesings (2006) 47134, 47240, 47296.

[275] Report of the Secretary-General on the situation in Somalia, S/2006/838, para 2, 28.

[276] Ibid., para 4–5; *The Guardian*, 21 July 2006; Keesings (2006) 47296.

[277] Report of the Security Council Committee under Resolution 751 (1992), S/2006/913 at para 56–86; 15–55; 129–131, 204.

[278] Ibid., at para 215.

[279] Keesings (2006) 47353, 47444.

of intervention to help the TFG; Ethiopia denied any significant presence in Somalia.[280] Ethiopia and the UIC accused each other of moving troops to the Somali/Ethiopian border.[281] On 30 November the Ethiopian Parliament authorized military action to counter any attacks or incursions on or into Ethiopia.[282]

On 6 December the Security Council called for the resumption of peace talks. Resolution 1725 (2006), passed unanimously under Chapter VII of the UN Charter, clearly supported the TFG against the UIC. In the preamble it called upon the UIC to cease any further military expansion and to reject those with an extremist agenda or links to international terrorism. It also called upon all parties inside Somalia and all other states to refrain from action that could provoke or perpetuate violence, contribute to unnecessary tension and mistrust and endanger the ceasefire. In the operative part of the resolution the Security Council reiterated that the TFG offered the only route to achieving peace and stability in Somalia and emphasized the need for dialogue. It stated its intention to consider taking measures against those that seek to prevent a peaceful dialogue process, overthrow the TFG or take action that further threatens regional stability. It authorized the establishment of a regional protection and training mission in Somalia, modified the arms embargo accordingly, and specified that those states that border Somalia should not deploy troops.[283]

But the Security Council's call for dialogue proved ineffective. The TFG welcomed the resolution, but the UIC rejected it, saying that the deployment of foreign troops in Somalia would be tantamount to an invasion.[284] The UIC called for the withdrawal of Ethiopian troops; when they did not leave it launched a major offensive. It called for jihad against Ethiopian troops and appealed to foreign fighters for support.[285] Both sides accused each other of receiving support from foreign forces: there were consistent reports of the involvement of Ethiopian troops in the conflict and also of Eritrean assistance to the UIC.[286] At first Ethiopia denied that it had sent troops; then on 24 December it admitted that it had done so and claimed that it had acted in self-defence. It sent tanks and helicopters to assist the TFG and its ground troops penetrated deep into Somalia. It also carried out air attacks on the main airports to prevent the UIC from bringing in military supplies.[287]

---

[280] Keesings (2006) 47398, 47503.
[281] Keesings (2006) 47503, 47562; *The Guardian*, 27 November 2006.
[282] Keesings (2006) 47562.
[283] SC 5579th meeting (2006).
[284] Report of the Secretary-General on the situation in Somalia, S/2007/115 para 4.
[285] SC 5614th meeting (2006); Report of the Secretary-General on the situation in Somalia, S/2007/115; Keesings (2006) 47620.
[286] SC 5614th meeting (2006); Report of the Secretary-General on the situation in Somalia, S/2007/115.
[287] Ibid. See also *The Guardian*, 23, 27, December 2006; Keesings (2006) 47620.

It is interesting that Ethiopia did not report this action to the Security Council under Article 51 of the UN Charter, especially as it had so reported in its earlier conflict with Eritrea.[288] However, the Special Representative of the Secretary-General reported that the Prime Minister of Ethiopia had said in an official statement that it had 'taken self-defensive measures and started counter-attacking the aggressive extremist forces of the Islamic Courts and foreign terrorist groups'.[289] In a letter to a British newspaper the Ethiopian Ambassador said that Ethiopia went into Somalia for reasons of self-defence. The UIC had declared a jihad against Ethiopia; twenty terrorist actions had been taken against Ethiopia by the leaders of the UIC.[290]

On 2 January 2007 the Prime Minister of Ethiopia in a speech to parliament set out the justification for the use of force at greater length. He referred to the 'rightful and historic' resolution of the Ethiopian parliament asking the government to take the necessary legal measures to protect the country from any attack. Attempts to negotiate a peaceful settlement had failed; the extremist leadership of the UIC had completed its preparation to launch an all out war against the TFG. It had reached a stage where it could assemble around the Ethiopian border anti-peace forces in its relentless effort to facilitate infiltration of these forces into Ethiopia. Ethiopia accordingly had prepared a plan for a counter-offensive to protect the country from attack and had implemented the plan in coordination with the TFG. It identified as enemies the extremist leadership of the UIC, extremist terrorists assembled from different countries and soldiers of the Eritrean government. The Prime Minister claimed the unequivocal and public support of the African Union.[291] He said that only one state in the Security Council had challenged the self-defence measure of Ethiopia. 'Therefore the UN Security Council did not put into question the measures we took in self-defense. Similarly various governments in different parts of the world have supported our right to self-defense and have refrained from putting out any kinds of declarations which might have put into question our inherent right of self-defense.' He said that the only party which took a different position on the issue was the creator of the problem, the government of Eritrea. Although the main aim of Ethiopia was to protect itself from attacks, it also supported the efforts of the people of Somalia to disengage themselves from the Taliban-like rule

---

[288] See 122 above.
[289] SC 5614th meeting (2006).
[290] *The Guardian*, 9 January 2007.
[291] There had been a statement by the AU Deputy-Commissioner that Ethiopia was acting in self-defence, but it is not clear that this was an official statement reflecting the views of member states, *The Guardian*, 27 December 2006.

of extremists. Upon completion of the final phase of the mission Ethiopia would withdraw its forces as soon as possible.[292]

Both the USA and Ethiopia portrayed the conflict as part of the 'war on terror'. They claimed that the UIC was controlled by Al Qaida members.[293] The USA tacitly supported the Ethiopian action. There were newspaper reports that the USA had provided practical help and that it was conducting a counter-terrorism operation against Al Qaida by proxy through Ethiopia.[294] The USA also intervened directly after the main conflict was over. In January 2007 it carried out an air attack on Hayo village, against suspected terrorists linked with Al Qaida. This was apparently aimed at those allegedly involved in the 1998 terrorist attacks on the US embassies in Kenya and Tanzania.[295] There were also reports of a second strike against suspected Al Qaida operatives in southern Somalia.[296] But the USA offered no legal explanation in the UN or elsewhere. It remains unclear whether its justification was self-defence as part of the war on terror, or that it was operating with the consent of the government, as in its earlier targeted killings in Yemen in 2002.[297] Some concern was expressed about this US intervention but its legality was not discussed in the Security Council.[298]

By early January 2007 the Ethiopian army and the TFG had driven UIC forces out of Mogadishu and the regions they controlled. The Ethiopian troops pursued some UIC forces to the southern border. The UIC abandoned the battle.[299] The AU Peace and Security Council issued an optimistic communiqué on 19 January 2006 proclaiming that there was 'Today a unique and unprecedented opportunity to restore structures of government in Somalia and to bring about lasting peace and reconciliation.' It authorized deployment of a regional peacekeeping force, AMISOM.[300]

---

[292] <www.mfa.gov.et/Press_Section/publication.php?Main_Page_Number= 3311>.
[293] *The Guardian*, 10 January 2007; Keesings (2006) 47296.
[294] *The Guardian*, 28 December 2006, 13 January 2007, *The Observer*, 31 December 2006; Keesings (2007) 47735. The USA had provided military aid to Ethiopia since 2002; the two states shared intelligence and the USA provided arms, aid and training.
[295] Report of the Secretary-General on the situation in Somalia, S/2007/115, para 6, 10; Keesings (2007) 47672, 47735; *The Guardian*, 10, 12 January 2007.
[296] *The Guardian*, 25 January, 24 February 2007.
[297] See Chapter 6 note 75.
[298] The UN Secretary-General expressed concern over the American air strikes, particularly their humanitarian aspect, UN News Service, 9 January 2007. An EU spokesman also expressed concern, *The Guardian*, 10 January 2007. The UK did not comment on the legality of the US action; but the Foreign Secretary did say that action had to be taken to stop terrorist activity and that there could not be a safe haven for international terrorists (House of Commons Hansard Debates for 16 January 2007).
[299] Report of the Secretary-General on the situation in Somalia, S/2007/115; Keesings (2007) 47672; *The Guardian* 29, 30 December 2006, 2, 6 January 2007, *The Observer*, 31 December 2006.
[300] UN doc S/2007/34, 24 January 2007. On AMISOM, see 378 below.

A small part of this force was eventually deployed in March 2007 under Security Council Resolution 1744 (2007).[301] However, the UN Secretary-General reported at the end of February that the 'semblance of law and order that the UIC had created in Mogadishu' had begun to deteriorate. Insecurity had increased. The TFG was not able to establish effective authority. There were repeated attacks on Ethiopian forces. Public resentment of the continued presence of Ethiopian troops in Somalia had created a volatile situation.[302] Later reports do not indicate any great improvement in the situation.[303] The 'deputy leader' of Al Qaida had called for resistance to Ethiopian troops in Somalia, and foreign fighters had responded to this call.[304] Ethiopian troops remained in Somalia despite repeated promises to leave.[305] The USA blamed Eritrea for the violence and said that the insurgency was part of a global jihadist network.[306] It could be argued that here, as in Iraq, the use of force as a means to fight the 'war on terror' has not improved the situation and may actually have made it worse.

There is some uncertainty as to the precise legal basis for the Ethiopian action.[307] Ethiopia generally denied the presence of its forces in Somalia until December 2006. It then claimed self-defence. This was clearly not self-defence against an armed attack by government forces, but apparently self-defence as part of the 'war on terror' against the threat posed by the UIC, and against its past terrorist attacks. There was no report to the Security Council under Article 51. Ethiopia did not offer any reasoned legal case in defence of its use of force in the UN. Its major military operations extending far beyond the border area look more like action to protect the TFG government against the UIC than self-defence of Ethiopia.[308] A stronger legal basis for intervention might have been intervention at the invitation of the legitimate (though ineffective) government supported by the UN, in response to prior foreign intervention as set out in the UN

---

[301] Report of the Secretary-General on the situation in Somalia, S/2007/204, para 32.

[302] Report of the Secretary-General on the situation in Somalia, S/2007/115, para 7–13.

[303] Reports of the Secretary-General on the situation in Somalia, S/2007/204, S/2007/381. The latter (para 12–17, 48) describes the operations of the TFG, supported by Ethiopian troops, to disarm insurgents in Mogadishu; these operations involved heavy fighting from 21 March until 27 April 2007 and led to the displacement of 400,000 people from the capital. See also Keesings (2007) 47792, 47852, 48232. In a later report the Secretary-General said that the situation had not improved, S/2007/658 para 15.

[304] Keesings (2007) 47672; Reports of the Secretary-General on the situation in Somalia, S/2007/204, para 25–26, S/2007/381.

[305] Keesings (2007) 47672; *The Guardian*, 30 December 2006, 3, 24 January, 16 July 2007.

[306] Keesings (2007) 47852, 48121; *The Guardian*, 9 April 2007.

[307] For an account broadly sympathetic to Ethiopia, see Yihdego, 'Ethiopia's Military Action against the Union of Islamic Courts and others in Somalia', 56 ICLQ (2007) 666; see also, Corten, 'La licéité douteuse de l'action militaire de l'Ethiopie en Somalia', 111 RGDIP (2007) 513.

[308] Cf. *Armed Activities on the Territory of the Congo, (DRC v Uganda)*, ICJ Reports (2005) 168 para 147.

reports. The Prime Minister of the TFG after the event spoke of 'Ethiopia's intervention on behalf of the UN-backed TFG'.[309] There were indications in the speech of the Prime Minister to the Ethiopian parliament on 2 January 2007 that this was an additional basis for its use of force, but it was not entirely clear how far this was being put forward as a legal argument.[310]

There was very little international discussion of the legality of the conflict. At the start of the conflict the Security Council issued a Presidential Statement expressing deep concern and calling on all parties to draw back from conflict.[311] The Secretary-General subsequently urged a cessation of hostilities.[312] The Security Council met to discuss the conflict on 26–27 December 2006, but there is no record of any discussion. On 10 January and 28 June 2007 it met in closed session. On 20 February it unanimously passed Resolution 1744 (2007) authorizing AU member states to set up a regional force, AMISOM, in Somalia. Again there was no discussion of the legality of the use of force. In its preamble Resolution 1744 welcomed the decision of Ethiopia to withdraw its troops from Somalia, and took note that it had already started the withdrawal. It underlined that the deployment of AMISOM would help avoid a security vacuum and create the conditions for a full withdrawal.[313] Thus there has been no public Security Council debate on the Ethiopian use of force, there was no call by the Security Council for an end to the fighting, and no determination of the legality of the Ethiopian action.[314]

The AU seemed sympathetic to Ethiopia. The first public statement came from a Deputy-Commissioner in support of the right of Ethiopia to self-defence.[315] However, on 27 December the Chair of the AU Commission took a more cautious approach and called for a ceasefire and for the withdrawal of Ethiopian and other foreign forces.[316] Later the AU Assembly—held in Ethiopia in January 2007—issued a decision in which it 'noted with satisfaction the recent positive developments in Somalia which have resulted from Ethiopia's intervention upon the invitation of the legitimate

---

[309] Press Conference by Prime Minster, 28 June 2007; <www.un.org/News/briefings/docs/2007/070628_Somalia.doc.htm>

[310] See note 292 above. For a discussion of the justification of intervention by invitation in this case: Corten, 'La licéité douteuse de l'action militaire de l'Ethiopie en Somalia', 111 RGDIP (2007) 513.

[311] S/PRST/2006/59.

[312] SC 5614th meeting (2006).

[313] SC 5633rd meeting (2007).

[314] Similarly the Security Council did not call for an end to the fighting in the 2006 conflict in Lebanon. In this case and that of Somalia – both seen by some as part of a 'war on terror' – the USA and the UK were unwilling to allow the Security Council to make any such call (*The Guardian*, 28 December 2006; US and UK speeches in SC 5493rd meeting (2006)).

[315] *The Guardian*, 27 December 2006.

[316] Joint Communiqué—AU, League of Arab States and IGAD on the current situation in Somalia, 27 December 2007.

TFG of Somalia, and which has created unprecedented opportunity for lasting peace in the country'. It welcomed the decision of Ethiopia to withdraw its troops from Somalia.[317] At present the troops remain; the regional force has not reached its authorized strength, and the situation in Somalia is, as it has been since 1991, far from stable.[318]

CONCLUSION

The question as to whether the events of 9/11 and the experience in Afghanistan should be seen as a turning point in the development of the law on the use of force may be seen as part of the wider—and sometimes rather apocalyptic—debate as to whether USA now feels itself free from any constraint of international law and the implications of this for the UN and for other states. Before *Operation Iraqi Freedom* the UN Secretary-General stressed the unique legitimacy available only through the UN,[319] and suggested that 'If the US and others were to go outside the Council and take military action, it would not be in conformity with the Charter.'[320] The USA nevertheless went ahead with the use of force against Iraq. But even so it went out of its way to claim that it was not acting unilaterally and that more nations were involved in the coalition against terror than participated in the 1991 Persian Gulf War.[321] And although it did not abandon its claim to act in self-defence its main justification was clearly that it had the authority of the UN Security Council to use force. Although it has adopted the rhetoric of the war against terrorism, and in so doing has abandoned the traditional doctrine of regime change, the extent to which it has also moved to a wide 'Bush doctrine' of pre-emptive self-defence is not yet clear. What is clear is that other states have so far proved reluctant to accept any such doctrine. Many are doubtful as to whether the use of the doctrine to put pressure on North Korea and Iran has been effective. And there has not been general support for any modification of the traditional rules on regime change.

The rhetoric of the 'war on terror' has been invoked with regard to the recent conflicts in Somalia and in Lebanon to justify the extensive use of force. In both it was open to question whether there had been an armed attack justifying the use of force in self-defence; in both there was little

---

[317] Assembly/AU/Dec.142(VIII), Decisions and Declarations, 29–30 January 2007.
[318] Reports of the Secretary-General on the situation in Somalia, S/2007/381, para 29, 99, S/2007/658 para 15, 33.
[319] For example; <www.un.org/News/Press/docs/2002/SGSM8378.doc.htm>.
[320] <www.un.org/apps.sg/offthe cuff.asp?nid=394>.
[321] <www.defenselink.mil/news/Feb2003/n02282003_200302286.html>; *The Guardian*, 5, 19 March 2003.

if any international discussion of this issue. With regard to the Ethiopian intervention in Somalia there was almost no international response; states were reluctant openly to challenge the legality of this use of force. The reasons for this must be speculative, but it seems likely that now the Cold War is over states will refrain from criticism of the USA and its allies unless they are directly involved or they feel very strongly. The contrast between the intense international criticism of *Operation Iraqi Freedom* and the much more muted response to the conflict in Somalia is striking. With regard to the Israeli invasion of Lebanon, unlike the Ethiopian intervention in Somalia, there was public debate in the UN. The main focus of debate was on the issue of proportionality and a fundamental division emerged; the majority of states were not willing to accept the very wide doctrine proposed by Israel, the USA and the UK.

7
The UN and the use of force

The Security Council has been more active in its use and authorization of the use of force in recent years than at any time in the history of the UN, but its activities bear little relation to the original scheme of the Charter. Since 1988 it has initiated more peacekeeping operations than in the previous forty years, ranging from minor operations such as UNMOT on the border of Tajikistan and Afghanistan to major operations such as those in Cambodia, Angola, Liberia and the DRC, Kosovo and East Timor. In recent years there has been a massive surge in peacekeeping.[1] All these operations have been conducted without any express provision for peacekeeping in the Charter. The Security Council has also authorized member states to use force against Iraq and in Yugoslavia, Somalia, and several other states.[2] These operations too are rather different from the original plan of those who established the UN.

The aim of the drafters of the UN Charter was not only to prohibit the unilateral use of force by states in Article 2(4) but also to centralize control of the use of force in the Security Council under Chapter VII.[3] The initial plan was that the Security Council would have its own standing army to use in response to threats to the peace, breaches of the peace and acts of aggression. But the standing army never materialized; states did not make the agreements to provide troops to the UN as set out in Article 43. It is notorious that during the Cold War the Security Council was not able to carry out its 'primary responsibility for the maintenance of international peace and security' under Article 24 and its power to take decisions binding on member states under Article 25 was little used because of the veto power of the five permanent members of the Security Council under Article 27 of the UN Charter. The formal scheme of Chapter VII under which the Security Council could take provisional measures (Article 40) or determine that there was a threat to the peace or breach of the peace or act of aggression (under Article 39) and take economic measures (Article 41) or (should the Security Council consider that measures under Article 41 would be inadequate or had proved inadequate) action by air, sea

---

[1] UN Press Release DSG/SM/334, 4 September 2007.
[2] See Chapter 8 below.
[3] On Chapter VII of the UN Charter, see Simma (ed.), *The Charter of the United Nations: A Commentary* (2nd edn, 2002), 701; Cot and Pellet (eds), *La Charte des Nations Unies* (1991). Article 2(7) of the UN Charter provides that the application of enforcement measures under Chapter VII shall not be prejudiced by the principle that the UN should not intervene in matters which are essentially within the domestic jurisdiction of states.

or land forces (Article 42) did not stand up to the pressure of the Cold War. I will give only a brief account of the Security Council's actions during the Cold War in order to determine how far the early actions set the pattern for more recent action. This chapter will show how the Charter scheme has been transformed in practice, how the UN Security Council has used its powers to respond to threats to the peace, breaches of the peace, and acts of aggression. The focus will be on the practice of the UN, and certain operations will be considered in detail in order to illuminate the application in practice of Chapter VII of the Charter and the development through practice of the institution of peacekeeping.

THE UN IN THE COLD WAR

Chapter VII action

The veto of the five permanent members of the Security Council under Article 27(3) was used 279 times between 1945 and 1985; from 1946 until 1970 it was almost exclusively the USSR, facing a western majority in the General Assembly, that prevented the adoption of resolutions by the Security Council. In 1970 the USA made its first veto, and from then on came to replace the USSR as overwhelmingly the main user of the veto.[4] But of course it was not only the actual use of the veto that prevented action by the Security Council; threats to use the veto also prevented the adoption of resolutions or secured their revision to something more acceptable to the permanent member concerned.

During the Cold War the Security Council occasionally threatened to use Chapter VII; often it called for action without taking any binding decisions. Very rarely did it succeed in taking binding decisions under Chapter VII in response to threats to the peace, breach of the peace, and acts of aggression.[5] When it did act under Chapter VII its approach was generally flexible rather than formalistic; it did not usually specify the exact article of the Charter under which it was acting.[6] Security Council

---

[4] Article 27(3) of the UN Charter provides that decisions of the Security Council on non-procedural matters shall be made by an affirmative vote of nine members, including the concurring votes of the permanent members. See Patil, *The UN Veto in World Affairs* (1992); Sonnenfeld, *Resolutions of the United Nations Security Council* (1988), 43–52; Bailey and Daws, *The Procedure of the UN Security Council* (3rd edn, 1998) at 226.

[5] For a list of resolutions passed under Chapter VII, see Bailey and Daws, *The Procedure of the UN Security Council* (3rd edn, 1998) at 272–3.

[6] See Sarooshi, *The United Nations and the Development of Collective Security* (1999) for a detailed discussion of the possible bases of Security Council action in the UN Charter. However, the justification of implied or revived Security Council authorization for *Operation Iraqi Freedom* in 2003 prompted Security Council members to specify the Charter articles under which they were acting in recent resolutions on Iran and North Korea: see 367.

Resolution 598 (1987), belatedly demanding a mandatory ceasefire in the 1980–88 Iran–Iraq conflict, was unusual in that it expressly stated that the Security Council was acting under Articles 39 and 40. This reluctance by the Security Council to identify the precise legal basis, if any, for its resolutions has led to protracted and not always fruitful speculation by some commentators as to the legal basis of Security Council operations. It seems clear from the practice of the Council that no formal pronouncement with an express reference to Article 39 is required for action under Chapter VII; the use of the language of Article 39 is apparently sufficient.[7]

The Security Council has been extremely reluctant to find that there has been an act of aggression; it has done so only with regard to Israel, South Africa, and Rhodesia.[8] It is also generally reluctant to condemn states by name. It has been only slightly readier to find a breach of the peace; it has done so with regard to Korea, Iraq/Kuwait, Argentina's invasion of the Falklands, and the 1980–88 Iran–Iraq conflict. These are all inter-state conflicts. However, the Security Council has passed many resolutions determining the existence of a threat to the peace.[9]

The first time the Security Council took economic measures under Article 41 was against Rhodesia (now Zimbabwe) after the Smith regime illegally declared independence of the UK in 1965 in order to establish white minority rule. In 1966 the Security Council imposed an embargo on raw materials, oil, and arms in Resolution 232; this expressly stated that it was acting under Articles 39 and 41. In 1968 it expanded this to a more comprehensive embargo in Resolution 253, which stated that the Security Council was acting under Chapter VII. It made no reference to Article 41 until paragraph 9, which requested 'all member states to take all possible action under Article 41 to deal with the situation in Southern Rhodesia, not excluding any of the measures provided in that article'. The later resolutions designed to strengthen sanctions against Southern Rhodesia also made express reference to Article 41. In contrast, when the Security Council subsequently took economic measures with regard to other states

---

[7] See Freudenschuss, 'Article 39 of the UN Charter Revisited: Threats to the Peace and Recent Practice of the UN Security Council', 46 Austrian Journal of Public and International Law (1993) 1; Bailey and Daws, *The Procedure of the UN Security Council* (3rd edn, 1998) at 271.

[8] SC Res 573 (1985), 611 (1988), 387(1976), 567 (1985), 568 (1985), 571 (1985), 574 (1985), 577 (1985), 455 (1979). The General Assembly has been ready to denounce acts of aggression; such resolutions were usually discounted by permanent members as not authoritative findings under Chapter VII.

[9] On practice under Article 39, see Kirgis, 'The Security Council's First Fifty Years', 89 AJIL (1995) 506; Simma, (ed.), *The Charter of the United Nations: A Commentary* (2nd edn, 2002) 717; Wellens, 'The UN Security Council and New Threats to the Peace: Back to the Future', 8 Journal of Conflict and Security Law (2003) 15; Matheson, *Council Unbound: the Growth of UN decision-making on conflict and post-conflict issues after the Cold War* (2006) Chapter 2.

it did so without express reference to Article 41. In other ways these first sanctions set the pattern for subsequent measures.

First, the Security Council has consistently taken a wide view of the phrase 'threat to international peace and security' under Article 39. In these first resolutions on Southern Rhodesia it said that the situation resulting from the proclamation of independence by the illegal authorities in Southern Rhodesia was extremely grave and its continuance constituted a threat to international peace and security. This readiness to look at the wider consequences of a civil conflict or illegal overthrow of a government and to treat it as a threat to international peace and security has been apparent in much of the later practice of the Security Council. Second, the resolutions imposing sanctions were directed against a non-state entity and addressed to non-member states as well as members. Resolutions 232 (1966) and 253 (1968) specifically urged non-member states to act in accordance with the provisions of the present resolution. Resolution 314 (1972) was addressed to 'all states'. The legal basis for this was spelled out in Resolutions 314 (1972) and 409 (1977) as residing in Article 2(6) of the UN Charter.[10] Subsequent resolutions followed this pattern of reference to 'all states'.

Third, in Resolution 221 (1966), passed to secure the effectiveness of the voluntary embargo called for in Resolution 217 (1965), the Security Council authorized the UK to use force to intercept ships on the high seas. This resolution did not include any reference to Chapter VII or to any specific article, although it did determine that the possibility of a breach of the oil embargo by tankers discharging oil intended for Southern Rhodesia in Mozambique amounted to a threat to the peace. It called upon the UK to prevent, by the use of force if necessary, the arrival in Mozambique of oil destined for Southern Rhodesia. Clearly such authorization does not fit within Article 41 which expressly excludes 'measures involving the use of armed force'. But Resolution 221(1966) has been the model for many subsequent resolutions; it is sometimes said to be based on Article 42 and sometimes Chapter VII in general. This lack of concern with the specification of a precise legal basis for its actions has proved typical of the Security Council. Many commentators are content to base such resolutions authorizing force to secure the implementation of economic measures on 'Article 41 and a half'.[11]

Again in Resolution 418 (1977) imposing an arms embargo on South Africa, the first mandatory sanctions against a member state, the Security Council did not refer to Article 41 specifically; it made only a general

---

[10] Article 2(6) of the UN Charter says, 'The Organization shall ensure that states which are not Members of the United Nations act in accordance with these Principles so far as may be necessary for the maintenance of international peace and security.'

[11] See Sarooshi, *The United Nations and the Development of Collective Security* (1999), 194.

reference to Chapter VII. This approach was followed in almost all sub-sequent resolutions authorising economic measures or the use of force.[12] The resolution held that the military build-up by South Africa and its persistent acts of aggression against neighbouring states seriously disturbed the security of those states; South Africa was at the threshold of producing nuclear weapons. Therefore, having regard to the policies and acts of the South African government, the acquisition of arms by South Africa constituted a threat to the maintenance of international peace and security. The Security Council decided that all states should observe a mandatory arms embargo.

The action against Korea in 1950 was the only use of force authorized by the Security Council during the Cold War in response to a breach of the peace by a state.[13] It was not quite what was envisaged in Chapter VII of the Charter and there is still controversy about its legality. The Security Council determined in Resolution 82 (1950) that North Korea had made an armed attack against South Korea and this constituted a breach of the peace. Neither was a member state and some states saw this conflict as a struggle within one divided state for decolonization rather than an invasion of one pro-western state by a socialist state. The absence of the USSR (in protest at the representation of China in the United Nations by the Taiwan government) enabled the Security Council to act.[14] It passed Resolution 83 (1950) recommending member states to 'furnish such assistance to South Korea as may be necessary to repel the armed attack and to restore international peace and security in the area'. But this action was far from what was provided in the Charter. The Council (in the absence of any standing army under Article 43 agreements) recommended action by states; it did not take any binding decision. And it did not itself establish a UN force. In Resolution 84 (1950) it recommended all member states providing military force and other assistance to make such forces available to a unified command under the USA; it requested the USA to designate a commander, but authorized the force to use the UN flag. Sixteen states contributed forces, but the USA played the dominant role. It was requested to provide the Security Council with reports as appropriate on the course of the action taken.[15]

---

[12] However, the Security Council did expressly refer to Article 41 in SC Res 1718, 1737 (2006), 1747 (2007) on Iran and North Korea, in order to make it quite clear that the resolutions could not be interpreted as an implied authorization to use force: see 367.

[13] 1950 UNYB 220; Sarooshi, *The United Nations and the Development of Collective Security* (1999), at 169.

[14] On the controversy about the interpretation of Article 27(3) on voting in the Security Council see Simma (ed.), *The Charter of the United Nations: A Commentary* (2nd edn, 2002) at 493; Bailey and Daws, *The Procedure of the UN Security Council* (3rd edn, 1998) at 257.

[15] On the return of the USSR, the Security Council was again unable to act; the General Assembly stepped in: 1950 UNYB 220; Franck, *Nation against Nation* (1985), 33–5.

The exact legal basis for the action against North Korea was not specified in the resolution recommending states to send troops and this has led to speculation ever since. Some argue that the action could not have been under Article 42 because that provision is not autonomous but depends on member states having made agreements under Article 43. Others reject this because Article 42 makes no reference to Article 43 and there is no indication elsewhere in the Charter that Article 42 must remain inoperative in the absence of Article 43 agreements. Moreover, given that Article 42 allows Security Council decisions to use force, this must be taken to include the lesser power to make recommendations to member states. Other writers argue that the Korean action was taken under Article 39 or under Chapter VII generally, or that it was collective self-defence.[16] There is little in the resolutions or in the Security Council debates to resolve this controversy and it is not clear that it had any practical significance.

The division of powers between the Security Council and the General Assembly

The inaction of the Security Council during the Cold War led the General Assembly to assume a role greater than originally envisaged. The Charter provides for a division of functions between the two organs. Article 11(2) says that the General Assembly may discuss questions relating to the maintenance of international peace and security and make recommendations (except as provided in Article 12); but any such question on which action is necessary shall be referred to the Security Council. Article 12 is designed to prevent clashes between the two bodies; it provides that, while the Security Council is exercising its functions with regard to a particular dispute or situation, the General Assembly shall not make any recommendation unless the Security Council so requests. But these two provisions have been flexibly interpreted in such a way that there is no strict division of functions.[17]

The General Assembly, concerned at the inaction of the Security Council and its failure to play the role provided in the Charter, passed the *Uniting for Peace Resolution* in 1950. This allowed it to call emergency meetings in the event of Security Council failure because of lack of unanimity of the permanent members to exercise its primary responsibility for the maintenance of peace and security in any case where there appears to be a

---

[16] See Simma (ed.), *The Charter of the United Nations: A Commentary* (2nd edn, 2002) 750 at 757. The *Certain Expenses* case, ICJ Reports (1962) 151 at 167, rejected the argument that Article 42 is inoperative in the absence of agreements under Article 43. The Court said that 'It cannot be said that the Charter has left the Security Council impotent in the face of an emergency situation when agreements under Article 43 have not been concluded.'

[17] On the drafting history, see Franck, *Recourse to Force* (2002) at 31.

threat to the peace, breach of the peace or act of aggression. The General Assembly may then recommend collective measures, including the use of armed force if necessary.[18] Using this procedure it recommended the establishment of peacekeeping forces in the Middle East. The legality of this was upheld by the International Court of Justice in the *Certain Expenses* case; it explained away the provision of Article 11(2) that 'any such question on which action is necessary shall be referred to the Security Council by the General Assembly' on the basis that the Security Council has a primary but not an exclusive responsibility for the maintenance of international peace and security. The Court also relied on the less convincing argument that it is only enforcement action and not peacekeeping action that must be referred to the Security Council.[19]

Article 12 has also been gradually eroded. The General Assembly has made recommendations even when the Security Council was dealing actively with an issue. If the Security Council was not actually exercising its functions at that moment, or if a resolution was blocked by a veto, the General Assembly has assumed it is free to make recommendations, provided that these did not directly contradict a Security Council resolution.[20] The General Assembly has accordingly passed series of resolutions condemning certain behaviour when the Security Council could not agree on a resolution or could not take measures against a wrongdoing state. Some western states were unhappy at this; they said that the repetition of resolutions condemning states was a pointless rhetorical exercise. This was the response when the General Assembly called for the imposition of sanctions on South Africa after the USA and the UK had blocked this in the Security Council. More recently the General Assembly regarded itself as free to call on the Security Council to lift the arms embargo on Bosnia-Herzegovina when the Security Council had been divided as to whether to do so. Technically it may be possible to make out a case on the basis of the practice of the two bodies that this did not contravene Article 12, but it seems to be precisely the type of situation that Article 12 was designed to prevent.[21]

Another blurring of the divide between the General Assembly and the Security Council during the Cold War occurred because many states not members of the Security Council chose to address the Security Council

---

[18] GA Res 377(V).

[19] *Certain Expenses* case, ICJ Reports (1962) 151. Since UNEF it has been the Security Council rather than the General Assembly which has established peacekeeping forces.

[20] Simma (ed.), *The Charter of the United Nations: A Commentary* (2nd edn, 2002) at 288; Blum, *Eroding the United Nations Charter* (1993) 103. See also, the ICJ Advisory Opinion *Legal Consequences of the Construction of a Wall in the Palestinian Occupied Territory*, ICJ Reports (2004) 136 para 25.

[21] Gray, 'Bosnia and Herzegovina: Civil War or Inter-State Conflict: Characterisation and Consequences', 67 BYIL (1996) 155.

to set out their positions.[22] States such as France, Australia and the UK repeatedly complained that this was inappropriate; they accused these states of turning the Security Council into a mini-General Assembly. Thus France said that there was a growing tendency to transform the debates of the Security Council, which should be action-oriented, into a substitute for General Assembly debate and a forum for confrontation. The UK said that it would prefer speeches to be given only by member states and those specially affected.[23] In recent years this use of the Security Council by non-members has become much less common. In contrast, developing states have taken to accusing the Security Council of encroaching on matters properly within the sphere of the General Assembly since the end of the Cold War.[24] The Security Council has addressed issues of terrorism,[25] proliferation of weapons of mass destruction[26] and climate change.[27]

Peacekeeping during the Cold War

In response to the inability of the Security Council to take enforcement action under Chapter VII the institution of peacekeeping evolved during the Cold War.[28] There was no express basis for this in the Charter, but the institution has evolved through the practice of the United Nations and its legality is no longer challenged by any state. Commentators have speculated that a legal basis may be found in the power of the General Assembly to establish subsidiary organs, or under Chapter VI on peaceful

[22] On participation of non-member states, see UN Charter Articles 32, 34, 35; Bailey and Daws, *The Procedure of the UN Security Council* (3rd edn, 1998) 154.
[23] For example, Australia SC 2619th meeting (1985); France SC 2608th meeting (1985); UK SC 2713th meeting (1986).
[24] See, for example, the position of the Non-Aligned Movement in UN doc S/2007/31, comments by Iran in GA/L/3322, 17 October 2007, Egypt in SC 5632nd meeting (2007). On the role of the Security Council, see Matheson, *Council Unbound: the Growth of UN decision-making on conflict and post-conflict issues after the Cold War* (2006); Talmon, 'The Security Council as world legislature', 99 AJIL (2005) 175.
[25] SC Res 1373 (2001). See Happold, 'Security Council Resolution 1373 and the Constitution of the UN', (16) Leiden Journal of International Law (2003) 593.
[26] SC Res 1540 (2004), 1673 (2006). See Joyner, 'Non-proliferation law and the UN system', (20) Leiden Journal of International Law (2007) 489; Sur, 'La resolution 1540 du conseil de securité', 108 RGDIP (2004) 855.
[27] When the Security Council held a debate on climate change in 2007 at the request of the UK (in UN doc S/2007/186) many states expressed concern that it was not the proper forum to discuss the issue: see SC 5663rd meeting (2007), UN Press Release SC/5663, 17 April 2007.
[28] UN Publications, *The Blue Helmets: A Review of United Nations Peacekeeping* (3rd edn, 1996); Higgins, *United Nations Peacekeeping 1946–1967* (4 vols); Morphet, 'UN Peacekeeping and Election-Monitoring', in Roberts and Kingsbury (eds), *United Nations, Divided World* (2nd edn 1993), 183; Hill and Malik, *Peacekeeping and the United Nations* (1996); White, *Keeping the Peace* (1993).

settlement, or under Article 40 on provisional measures.[29] All of these may be theoretical possibilities, but in practice there has been no express reference to any of these in the resolutions establishing peacekeeping forces and the debate seems to be without practical significance. The UN Blue Books on Peacekeeping and the UN Peacekeeping website do not concern themselves with this problem.

Between 1948 and 1988 thirteen peacekeeping forces were established. It is common to divide the practice of peacekeeping in the Cold War into four periods; the nascent, (1948–56), the assertive (1956–67), the dormant (1967–73) and the resurgent (1974–87).[30] Different writers have drawn up different lists of these forces over the years, but the UN's own list can probably be treated as authoritative.[31] There was a wide variety of types of operation which came to share the name of peacekeeping. Most of the Cold War peacekeeping operations were interposed between states; few were established to play a role in ending civil conflict.

The earliest were limited observation forces; the first major forces were UNEF, established by the General Assembly in the Middle East from 1956 to 1967, and ONUC, established by the Secretary-General with Security Council authorization in the Congo[32] from 1960 to 1964. The former operation led to agreement on the basic principles underlying what later came to be known as peacekeeping operations; the latter revealed the difficulties that arise when these principles are compromised.

After UNEF was terminated the UN Secretary-General produced a report examining the 'new and unique experiment' and setting out guidance for future operations.[33] The mandate of UNEF under General Assembly Resolutions 998 (1956) and 1000 (1956) had been 'to secure and supervise' the ceasefire and withdrawal of foreign forces from Egypt, and later to maintain peaceful conditions in the area by its deployment along the armistice line between Egypt and Israel. It had been agreed that the force should not include troops from the permanent members of the Security Council or of any other country which for geographical or other reasons might have a special interest in the conflict. It operated with the consent of the host state and was withdrawn when Egypt terminated its consent in 1967. In determining the composition of the force serious consideration was to be given to the views of the host state. UNEF

---

[29] Simma (ed.), *The Charter of the United Nations: A Commentary* (2nd edn, 2002) at 648.

[30] Hill and Malik, *Peacekeeping and the United Nations* (1996) Chapter 2.

[31] UNDPKO website; <http://www.un.org/Depts/dpko>; UN Publications, *The Blue Helmets: A Review of United Nations Peacekeeping* (3rd edn, 1996).

[32] Subsequently Zaire, and now the Democratic Republic of the Congo.

[33] Report of the Secretary-General, *Summary study of the experience derived from the establishment and operation of the Force*, A/3943, 9 October 1958.

had been interposed between regular, national military forces which were subject to a ceasefire. It had a clear-cut mandate and was neutral in relation to international political issues. It operated under a Status of Forces Agreement (SOFA), with the host state establishing the rights and privileges of the UN forces.

Interestingly, the Secretary-General said that the nature of peace-keeping precluded the employment of UN forces in situations of an essentially internal nature. Nor should such a force enforce any specific political solution; it would require specific authority for offensive action. It should use force only in self-defence. A wide interpretation of this right was not acceptable because it would blur the distinction between these operations and those under Chapter VII.

Most of the UN operations which later became known as peacekeeping operations followed these principles. But ONUC departed from them and showed the dangers of so doing. It was originally created to assist the government of Congo in the chaotic aftermath of independence in 1960. Its mandate was to give the government military and technical assistance after the collapse of essential services until national security forces were able fully to meet their tasks, but it became embroiled in the conflict when its original mandate was expanded. Resolution 161 (1961), although not formally passed under Chapter VII, used the language of Article 39 in its concern that the danger of civil war constituted a threat to international peace and security. It authorized ONUC to use force going beyond self-defence in order to prevent civil war; the resolution urged ONUC 'to take all appropriate measures to prevent the occurrence of civil war in the Congo...including the use of force, if necessary, in the last resort'. Later Resolution 169 (1961) went further and not only affirmed the territorial integrity of Congo but authorized the Secretary-General to use force to end the attempted secession of the province of Katanga and to expel foreign mercenaries. This led ONUC to assume responsibilities that went beyond normal peacekeeping. Its numbers were increased to 20,000 to respond to the expansion of its mandate and it was involved in fighting against those seeking secession.[34] The type of controversy that arose over the extension of peacekeeping in the Congo has recurred with regard to the operations in Yugoslavia and Somalia.

Of the fifteen forces established in the Cold War five still exist: three in the Middle East, UNMOGIP in Kashmir, and UNFICYP in Cyprus. This highlights a problematic characteristic of peacekeeping: that it may help to freeze the situation, or even protect an aggressor's territorial gains.[35]

---

[34] See Higgins, *United Nations Peacekeeping 1946–1967*, Vol III, 5; Abi-Saab, *The United Nations Operations in the Congo 1960–1964* (1978); Virally, 'Les Nations Unies et L'affaire du Congo', 1960 AFDI 557.
[35] This has led to argument about payment with regard to UNIFIL in Lebanon and UNFICYP in Cyprus; some states have argued that payment should be by Israel and Turkey

A NEW LEGAL ORDER? CHAPTER VII AFTER THE COLD WAR

The end of the Cold War brought with it a steep decline in the use of the veto and a massive increase in the activity of the Security Council. In 1990 the only vetos were two by the USA, one on a resolution about its 1989 intervention in Panama and one on a resolution to establish a Commission on Israel's activities in the occupied territories. There were then no vetos until 1993; the first was by Russia on the funding of the peacekeeping force in Cyprus. The USA did not use its veto for five years from 1990; when it did revert to this, it was again to protect Israel from condemnation of its breaches of international humanitarian law in the occupied territories. This was its thirtieth veto in protection of Israel since 1972.[36] It has continued to use its veto for this purpose.[37] China has used its veto to prevent the renewal of a UN mission in Guatemala, to block the extension of the preventive peacekeeping force in Macedonia, and with Russia to prevent the condemnation of Myanmar (Burma) for human rights violations.[38]

The UN response to the Iraqi invasion of Kuwait gave rise to hopes of a new era for the UN and of a New World Order.[39] This was only the second time that the Security Council had authorized armed action against an aggressor state. The Security Council met the day after the invasion and passed Resolution 660 (1990), declaring that there had been a breach of international peace and security; expressly acting under Articles 39 and 40 it condemned the invasion and demanded the withdrawal of Iraqi forces from Kuwait. It called on Iraq to withdraw and imposed economic sanctions in Resolution 661 (1990). When this proved ineffective to secure Iraq's withdrawal from Kuwait, Resolution 678 (1990) authorized member states cooperating with the government of Kuwait to use 'all necessary means' to uphold and implement Resolution 660 (1990), calling on Iraq to withdraw from Kuwait and to restore international peace and security in the area.[40] It is clear from the Security Council debates that this formula was

respectively. See Martinez, 'Le financement des opérations de maintien de la paix de l'Organisation des Nations Unies', 81 RGDIP (1987) 102.

[36] In 2003 the USA vetoed a resolution declaring illegal the construction by Israel of a wall in the occupied territories (UN Press Release SC/7896, 14 October 2003) and a resolution demanding Israel desist from any act of deportation or assassination of the elected President of the Palestinian Authority (UN Press Release SC/7875, 16 September 2003).

[37] UN Press Releases SC/7896, 14 October 2003, SC/7875, 16 September 2003, SC/8207, 5 October 2004, SC/8039, 25 March 2004, SC/8867, 11 November 2006, SC/8775, 13 July 2006.

[38] UN Press Releases SC/6311, 10 June 1997, SC/6648, 25 February 1999, SC/8939, 12 January 2007. Russia also used its veto with regards to Cyprus, UN Press Release SC/8066, 21 April 2004.

[39] UN Blue Book Series, Vol IX, *The UN and the Iraq/Kuwait Conflict 1990–1996*.

[40] The resolution was passed by 12–2 (Cuba, Yemen) – 1 (China), 1990 UNYB 189 at 204. On abstentions in the Security Council, see Bailey and Daws, *The Procedure of the UN Security Council* (3rd edn 1998) at 250.

understood to mean the use of force. The same (or similar) euphemistic formula has been used in almost all the subsequent resolutions authorising the use of force by states. In the case of Iraq no further resolution was passed until the ceasefire three months later and there was considerable controversy over lack of UN control over the operation conducted by the coalition forces. No time limit was set to the member state action; Security Council involvement was secured only by the duty on the member states to keep it informed.[41]

As with the Korean action, there was debate as to the legal foundation of the coalition action in *Operation Desert Storm* against Iraq. Unlike the resolutions on Korea, Resolution 678 (1990) does refer to Chapter VII, but it does not refer to any specific article. Also in contrast to the Korean action, the coalition forces in Iraq did not operate under UN flag or UN command; they were simply authorized to act against Iraq by the Security Council. Some claim this as an Article 42 action, others regard it as justified by Chapter VII generally; yet others say that it was collective self-defence authorized by the Security Council.[42] The Secretary-General, in his *Agenda for Peace*, did not treat it as Article 42 action, but said simply that the Security Council had authorized member states to use force.[43] The question is only of practical significance if the legal basis affects the scope of the permissible action that could be taken by states. Because the coalition forces did not in fact continue to use force to secure the overthrow of the government of Saddam Hussein, the disagreement as to the legal basis of the operation does not seem to have had practical consequences at the time.[44] It is doubtful whether this would have counted as necessary and proportionate action if the force had been based on collective self-defence, but it could conceivably have been justified under Chapter VII as action necessary to restore international peace and security. Despite the uncertainty as to its legal basis, this operation marked the start of a new era for the UN and Resolution 678 (1990) provided a model for later authorization of the use of force by member states. However, the optimism prevalent at the time of Resolution 678 (1990) has since dissipated.

---

[41] The Security Council met in private during the operation: 1991 UNYB 168. On the concern over lack of Security Council control see, for example, Sarooshi, *The United Nations and the Development of Collective Security* (1999) at 174 and works cited there.

[42] Sarooshi, ibid; Greenwood, 'New World Order or Old? The Invasion of Kuwait and the Rule of Law', 55 MLR (1992) 153.

[43] 31 ILM (1992) 953.

[44] It later became of great practical significance in the context of the argument as to whether the authorization to use force in SC Res 678 (1990) had later been revived to justify the use of force against Iraq in 1993, 1998, and, most importantly, in *Operation Iraqi Freedom* in 2003: see Chapter 8 below.

ARTICLE 41: TRANSFORMATION

The Security Council has made vastly increased use of Article 41 in recent years.[45] It has imposed sanctions to reverse aggression, to respond to serious violations of human rights and humanitarian law, to restore a democratically elected government, to counter terrorism and to prevent nuclear proliferation.[46] It is only if such measures under Article 41 would be inadequate or have already proved to be inadequate that the Security Council may turn to measures involving armed force under Article 42. As in the case of the measures against South Africa, it has imposed measures without express mention of Article 41; for many years the Security Council simply referred to Chapter VII in general. However, in taking measures against Iran and North Korea it was careful to specify that it was acting under Article 41 in order to ensure that no claim could be made that the Security Council was implicitly authorizing the use of force.[47] Starting with the comprehensive sanctions against Iraq after its invasion of Kuwait, the Security Council has taken measures with regard to Yugoslavia, Somalia, Libya, Liberia, Haiti, Angola, Rwanda, Sudan, Sierra Leone, Kosovo, Afghanistan, Ethiopia and Eritrea, the DRC, Côte d'Ivoire, Iran and North Korea. It has authorized force to secure the effective implementation of measures in a few of these cases (those of Iraq, Yugoslavia, Somalia, Haiti, and Sierra Leone).[48] For example, Resolution 787 (1992) on sanctions against Yugoslavia (Serbia and Montenegro) 'calls upon states acting nationally or through regional agencies or arrangements to use such measures commensurate with the specific circumstances as may be necessary under the authority of the Security Council to halt all inward and outward maritime shipping in order to inspect and verify their cargoes and destinations and to ensure strict implementation of the provisions of resolutions 713 (1991) and 757 (1992)'. As in the earlier authorization of the UK to use force to enforce the embargo on Rhodesia, the precise legal basis for this was not specified and remains unclear. More recently, the Security Council has authorized UN peacekeeping forces to assist in monitoring arms embargoes in Liberia, Côte d'Ivoire, the DRC and Lebanon.[49]

---

[45] For an overview, see Simma (ed.) *The Charter of the United Nations: A Commentary* (2nd edn, 2002) at 736; <www.un.org/Docs/sc/committees/INTRO.htm>. See also, Matheson, *Council Unbound: the Growth of UN decision-making on conflict and post-conflict issues after the Cold War* (2006).

[46] UN Press Release SC/9010, 30 April 2007; High-level Panel Report, A/59/565 para 77.

[47] See 270, 367 below.

[48] Iraq: SC Res 665 (1990), 670 (1990); Yugoslavia: SC Res 757 (1992), 787 (1992); Somalia: SC Res 794 (1992); Haiti: SC Res 875 (1993); Sierra Leone: SC Res 1132 (1997).

[49] Liberia, SC Res 1343 (2001), 1408 (2002); DRC, SC Res 1533 , 1565 (2004), Côte d'Ivoire, SC Res 1609 (2005), Lebanon, SC Res 1701 (2006).

The above list of Article 41 measures includes several cases of sanctions against non-state actors, as in the first measures against Rhodesia; Article 41 does not specify any limitation on those against whom sanctions may be taken. Thus the Security Council condemned the failure of the Khmer Rouge in Cambodia to carry out their obligations under the 1991 *Paris Peace Agreements* and called for the implementation of an embargo imposed in the peace agreements on the supply of petroleum products to areas occupied by any party not complying with the agreements.[50] Second, binding and more extensive measures were taken against UNITA in Angola when it refused to comply with the peace agreement and with Security Council resolutions.[51] Third, in September 1994 sanctions were imposed against the Bosnian Serbs for their refusal to accept the peace settlement for the former Yugoslavia.[52] Fourth, sanctions were imposed on the unrecognized Taliban regime in Afghanistan after their failure to surrender the terrorist leader, Usama Bin Laden, to a country where he would be brought to justice; these sanctions were subsequently extended to Al Qaida.[53] Sanctions have also been imposed on named individuals responsible for behaviour in violation of Security Council demands or which threatens international peace and security.[54]

The Secretary-General's view is that Article 41 measures are designed not to punish but to secure compliance with international obligations.[55] Some of the measures are clearly not directed against any wrongdoer. Thus, certain of the arms embargoes were imposed not because a state had broken international law, but to try to ensure that a conflict did not escalate. The arms embargoes on Yugoslavia, Somalia, Liberia, under Resolution 788 (1992), Rwanda, Ethiopia and Eritrea, and the DRC were of this type, and the embargoes on Yugoslavia and Somalia were imposed with the consent of the governments. More recently, arms embargoes that were initially imposed as blanket prohibitions on the export of arms to a state have been modified to allow the provision of arms to the legitimate

---

[50] SC Res 792 (1992).
[51] SC Res 864 (1993), 1127, 1173, 1176, 1295 (1997). These sanctions were suspended and then terminated in December 2002 after the death of the leader of UNITA and its acceptance of the peace process: SC Res 1412, 1432, 1439, 1448 (2002).
[52] SC Res 942 (1994). These measures were suspended in SC Res 1022 (1995) and terminated in SC Res 1074 (1996).
[53] SC Res 1267 (1999), 1333 (2000).
[54] These have been provided for (although not always imposed) in SC Res 1267 (1999), 1333 (2000), 1343 (2001), 1532 (2004), 1572 (2004),1591 (2005), 1596 (2005), 1649 (2005), 1672 (2006), 1718 (2006), 1737 (2006). This has given rise to serious questions as to the compatibility of Security Council decision-making with international human rights: Bulterman, 'Fundamental Rights and the UN financial sanctions regime', 19 Leiden Journal of International Law (2006) 753. See also, O'Donnell, 'Naming and Shaming: the sorry tale of SC Res 1530', 17 EJIL (2006) 945.
[55] See, for example, UN Press Release SC/9010, 30 April 2007.

government or international forces but to prohibit their supply to illegitimate forces. This was done with regard to Rwanda, Sierra Leone, the DRC, Liberia and Somalia.[56] Some of these measures have been described as a symbolic substitute for any real action by the international community, faced with the need to be seen to take some action in response to serious conflict.

Other arms embargoes were imposed in response to a breach of international law, such as those against the illegal regimes in Rhodesia and South Africa, and subsequently those against Libya for its sponsorship of terrorism; those against the FRY in 1998 for its behaviour in Kosovo;[57] and those against Liberia for its unlawful intervention in Sierra Leone.[58] Arms embargoes were also imposed against those who seized power illegally in Haiti[59] and Sierra Leone,[60] and an arms embargo was imposed on Côte d'Ivoire after the government had resorted to force in violation of a ceasefire.[61] In some of these cases the state affected by the arms embargo challenged its legality or sought its removal on the ground that the embargo violated its right to self-defence. This was argued unsuccessfully by Bosnia-Herzegovina in an attempt to secure exemption from the arms embargo imposed on the whole of Yugoslavia, by Liberia to try to escape the measures imposed for its intervention in Sierra Leone, and with more success by Rwanda where the embargo was lifted as far as arms destined for the government were concerned, but otherwise remained in place.[62]

Generally, the resolutions passed under Article 41, in response to a violation of a Security Council requirement, specify the justification for the imposition of the measures and the action needed to secure their termination. For example, Resolution 757 (1992) imposing sanctions on Yugoslavia (Serbia and Montenegro) specified that this was in response to non-compliance with Resolution 752 (1992) demanding an end to intervention in Bosnia; it said that all states should adopt the comprehensive measures listed until the Security Council decided that Yugoslavia (Serbia and Montenegro) had complied with Resolution 752 (1992). Resolutions designed to stop the prolongation of a conflict may also specify the

---

[56] Rwanda, SC Res 918 (1994), 1011 (1995); Sierra Leone, SC Res 1132 (1997), 1171 (1998), 1299 (2000); DRC, SC Res 1493 (2003); Liberia SC Res 1521 (2003), 1683 (2006); Somalia SC Res 1744 (2007).

[57] SC Res 1160 (1998). Even in this case Russia insisted that the aim of the arms embargo was not to punish Yugoslavia, SC 3868th meeting (1998). The measures were terminated in SC Res 1367 (2001).

[58] SC Res 1343 (2001), 1478 (2003). These measures were modified in 2003 after the departure of President Taylor and the installation of a Transitional Government: SC Res 1521 (2003). They were terminated in SC Res 1731 (2006), 1753 (2007).

[59] SC Res 841, 861, 873, 875 (1993); these measures were terminated in SC Res 944 (1994).

[60] SC Res 1132 (1997), 1171 (1998).

[61] SC Res 1572 (2004).

[62] See 126 above.

measures to be taken, or the conditions to be met, to secure the end of an embargo. Resolution 1521 (2003) extending the arms embargo and imposing an import ban on rough diamonds and timber from Liberia spells out in considerable detail the conditions that would have to be met for the termination of these measures. The measures taken against Côte d'Ivoire in Resolution 1572 (2004) were subject to review in the light of progress in the peace and national reconciliation process; the Security Council expressed its readiness to consider the modification or termination of the measures if the peace agreements had been fully implemented.

But sometimes it is unclear or controversial exactly what action would be required by the state subject to the Article 41 measures. The question of terminating the comprehensive sanctions against Iraq, in place since Resolution 661 (1990), led to divisions between members of the Security Council. The ceasefire Resolution 687 (1991) required the destruction of Iraq's chemical, biological, and nuclear weapons and long-range ballistic missiles and an undertaking by Iraq not to develop any such weapons in the future; when this was achieved the Security Council would lift the sanctions imposed in Resolution 661 (1990). There were many conflicts over the implementation of this provision. Iraq repeatedly claimed to have complied with its disarmament obligations and was repeatedly found by the UN inspection team to have been concealing its weapons. Nevertheless, there were reports that certain members of the Security Council were ready to consider lifting the sanctions. As the Secretary-General said, the humanitarian situation in Iraq posed a serious moral dilemma for the UN. The UN had always been on the side of the weak and the vulnerable, yet here it was accused of causing suffering to an entire population. The UN was in danger of losing the propaganda war about who was responsible for the situation in Iraq, President Saddam Hussein or the UN.[63] Eventually the USA and others turned to force in *Operation Iraqi Freedom*, rather than continue to rely on sanctions as a means of securing disarmament.[64]

There was also some concern over the sanctions against Libya, imposed in Resolution 748 (1992), adopted by 10–0–5; this said that the sanctions were imposed because of Libya's refusal to provide a full and effective response to US, UK and French requests for the surrender of Libyan nationals, allegedly responsible for terrorist attacks. The sanctions would be lifted after Libya demonstrated by concrete actions its renunciation of terrorism. Libya challenged the validity of this resolution in the *Lockerbie* case before the ICJ. It argued either that the resolution did not in fact

---

[63] UN Press Release SC/6834, 24 March 2000.
[64] See Chapter 6 above. The sanctions were ended by SC Res 1483 (2003), and the weapons inspection was finally terminated by SC Res 1762 (2007).

require the surrender of the alleged terrorists or, if it did, it was *ultra vires* and invalid.[65] Support for the sanctions from African and Arab states showed signs of crumbling from 1997 onwards. After the two alleged terrorists were surrendered for trial in a Scottish court in the Netherlands the sanctions were suspended in 1999 and finally terminated in 2003.[66] Similar resolutions more explicitly seeking the surrender of alleged terrorists from Sudan and Afghanistan were also passed and followed by the imposition of sanctions.[67]

Sanctions were imposed on North Korea and Iran in 2006 because of concerns over the proliferation of nuclear weapons. When North Korea carried out a nuclear weapons test in October 2006, Resolution 1718 (2006), passed unanimously, condemned the nuclear test; demanded that North Korea not conduct any further nuclear tests or launch of ballistic missile, retract its announcement of its withdrawal from the Non-Proliferation Treaty; and decided that it should suspend all activities related to its ballistic missile programme and should abandon its nuclear weapons programme in a verifiable and irreversible manner. Resolution 1718 (2006) also prohibited the provision of large-scale arms, nuclear technology and related training to North Korea, and imposed an asset freeze and travel ban on persons related to the nuclear-weapon programme. The conditions to be met for the lifting of the sanctions were that North Korea was to comply with the provisions of the resolution.

When Iran refused to abandon its nuclear enrichment programme, as required by Security Council Resolution 1696 (2006), the Security Council unanimously passed Resolution 1737 (2006). This subjected Iran to an import and export embargo on sensitive nuclear material and equipment as well as to a freeze on the assets of those involved in proliferation-sensitive nuclear activities. The IAEA was to report on Iran's suspension of its uranium enrichment-related activities; the Security Council would terminate its measures when Iran had complied with the obligations imposed on it by the IAEA and the Security Council.

The increased use of sanctions after the end of the Cold War intensified concern over effectiveness, humanitarian considerations of the impact of the measures on the population of the target state and the economic

---

[65] *Cases Concerning Questions of Interpretation and Application of the 1971 Montreal Convention arising from the Aerial Incident at Lockerbie (Jurisdiction and Admissibility)*, ICJ Reports (1998); 37 ILM (1998) 587.

[66] The measures were suspended by SC Res 1192 (1998). They were finally terminated in September 2003 by SC Res 1506 (13–0–2, USA and France) after Libya wrote to the Security Council accepting responsibility for the acts of its officials, renounced terrorism and arranged for payment of appropriate compensation for the families of the victims, UN doc S/2003/818. For the US and UK response, see UN doc S/2003/819.

[67] SC Res 1044, 1054, 1070 (1996) on Sudan; these measures were lifted in SC Res 1372 (2001). SC Res 1267 (1999) on Afghanistan.

impact on neighbouring states.[68] The Secretary-General, in his *Supplement to the Agenda for Peace*, wrote of the difficulties of determining the objectives of Article 41 measures, of monitoring and of avoiding unintended effects. He described sanctions as a blunt instrument that may harm vulnerable groups, interfere with the work of humanitarian agencies, and conflict with the development objectives of a state. Also they may be counter-productive in that they may provoke a patriotic response as opposed to a rejection of those whose behaviour led to the imposition of sanctions.[69] The measures imposed on Iraq in 1990, the most comprehensive and long-lasting in the history of the UN, prompted a reappraisal of Security Council sanctions. The Council shifted away from comprehensive sanctions to 'smart' or 'targeted' measures aimed at decision-making elites, that directly affect those responsible for the transgression without unduly harming the general population.[70] Thus in many cases the measures were designed to restrict the freedom to travel of those who had illegally violated peace agreements or Security Council resolutions and also to freeze foreign bank accounts of those responsible for the unlawful action.[71] The Security Council has also attempted to restrict the trade in 'conflict diamonds' and other natural resources which have been used by the warring parties to fund the conflict in states such as Angola, Sierra Leone, Liberia, the DRC and Côte d'Ivoire.[72]

There have been several attempts to draw up guidelines for an effective and humane system.[73] It is now regular practice to appoint not only

[68] Leigh, 'The Political Consequences of Economic Embargoes', 89 AJIL (1999) 74; Forum on 'Sanctions and the Operation of Humanitarian Exceptions', 13 EJIL(2002) 43; see also, for example, the SC debate on sanctions against Iraq, SC 4120th meeting(1999). Under Article 50 of the UN Charter states have the right to consult the Security Council on special economic problems resulting from sanctions imposed on other states.

[69] *Supplement to Agenda for Peace* S/1995/1.

[70] The UN GA called for the use of such smart sanctions in GA Res 51/242 (1997). It is significant that since this shift in practice there have been no communications by member states to sanctions committees in the last five years to report special economic problems resulting from sanctions against others: General Assembly L/3113, 7 February 2007.

[71] An early example is the case of UNITA, where the measures implemented by SC Res 1173 and 1176 (1998) were directed against the leaders of UNITA and the areas of Angola controlled by it. The prohibition on the sale of diamonds from these areas was reinforced by the creation of a panel of experts in SC Res 1237 (1999) to make the sanctions effective. Targeted measures were also taken against those responsible for the coup in Haiti, SC Res 917 (1994), and against the Taliban regime in Afghanistan, SC Res 1267 (1999), 1333 (2002). More recently asset freezes and travel bans have been in imposed on individuals in the DRC, SC Res 1596 (2005); Liberia, SC Res 1521 (2003) 1532 (2004); Côte d'Ivoire, SC Res 1572 (2004); Sudan, SC Res 1591 (2005); North Korea, SC Res 1718 (2006); and Iran, SC Res 1737 (2006).

[72] See, for example SC Res 1521 (2003) and SC Res 1607 (2005) on Liberia; the embargo on timber was terminated by SC Res 1731 (2006) and that on diamonds by SC Res 1753 (2007). On conflict diamonds, see <www.un.org/peace/africa/Diamond.html>.

[73] There is now a *Sanctions Assessment Handbook* (2004) and a complementary set of Field Guidelines: UN Press Release IHA/964, 19 November 2004. Guidelines are also contained

sanctions committees, but also independent expert groups to monitor the implementation of sanctions. An informal working group on General Issues of Sanctions was established in 2000 and issued its report in 2006.[74] This made recommendations on the working methods of sanctions committees, the design of sanctions resolutions, the unintended impact of sanctions and other issues; it was welcomed by the Security Council in Resolution 1732 (2006). The Security Council is currently still working on the improvement of the sanctions system.[75]

PEACEKEEPING AFTER THE COLD WAR

The Security Council vastly increased its peacekeeping activities after the Cold War. The numbers give a clear picture of the scope of the change. In total there have been 63 operations. In the forty years from 1948 to 1988 there were thirteen operations; in the ten years from 1988 to 1998 over thirty new peacekeeping forces were established; and seventeen more in the last ten years.[76] The majority of these new forces were deployed within states involved in civil wars rather than between states. In his 1995 *Supplement to An Agenda for Peace* the Secretary-General noted this transformation in the nature of peacekeeping. He wrote of peacekeeping as being in a time of transition and discussed the difficulties that had arisen. Because most peacekeeping after the Cold War had been within states, challenges had arisen that had not been encountered since the Congo operation in the 1960s. UN forces were faced by irregular forces rather than regular armies, civilians were the main victims of the conflicts, civil conflict brought humanitarian emergencies and refugees, state institutions collapsed. All these factors meant that international intervention had to go beyond military and humanitarian operations to bringing about national reconciliation and re-establishing effective government. Peacekeeping in such contexts was more complex and more expensive than more limited operations such as monitoring a ceasefire or controlling a buffer zone. This was to be a second generation of peacekeeping.[77] According to the

in the 2005 *World Summit Outcome Document*, A/60/L.70 para 106, (following the recommendations of the Secretary-General in *In Larger Freedom* A/59/2005 para 109) and in GA Res 51/242 and SC Res 1730 and 1732 (2006).

[74] UN doc S/2006/997.

[75] The Special Committee on the UN Charter discussed this issue in its 2007 session: 251st meeting, General Assembly L/3113, 7 February 2007. See also UN Press Release GA/L/3322, 17 October 2007, and UN doc A/C.6/62/L.6.

[76] See list of peacekeeping forces on UN website; <www.un.org/Depts/dpko>.

[77] UN doc S/1995/1; 1995 UNYB 175. See Ratner, *The New UN Peacekeeping* (1995).

Secretary-General, the concept of peacekeeping is not static; there are as many types of peacekeeping operations as there are types of conflict.[78] The forces established in 1999 in Kosovo and East Timor marked a further development:

[T]hey are qualitatively different from almost any other the Organisation has ever undertaken. In each place the United Nations is the administration, responsible for fulfilling all the functions of a State—from fiscal management and judicial affairs to everyday municipal services, such as cleaning the streets and conducting customs formalities at the borders. This is a new order of magnitude for an organization that more customarily provides States with technical assistance in such areas, rather than assuming complete responsibility for them. And it is a new order of magnitude for peacekeeping operations as well, making them extraordinarily complex and almost as dependent on civilian experts as on military personnel.[79]

Accordingly UNMIK and UNTAET could be seen as the third generation of peacekeeping.[80]

Most recently the UN has created new types of operation in Darfur and in Chad and the CAR. UNAMID and MINURCAT are hybrid operations involving cooperation between the UN and the AU and the EU; these mark a new era of cooperation with regional organizations.

Other significant developments include the greater emphasis on peace-building,[81] conflict prevention and the establishment of preventive peacekeeping forces, and cooperation between UN and regional peacekeeping forces.[82] At the start of the 21st century the UN Secretary-General set up the *Brahimi Panel* to make recommendations on conflict prevention, peacekeeping doctrine, peace-building strategy and administrative reform of the UN Department of Peacekeeping. The *Brahimi Report* was a central feature of the Millennium Summit of the UN Security Council in September 2000 and many of its recommendations have subsequently been implemented.[83]

The subsequent surge in peacekeeping has brought new challenges. The *Brahimi Report* had been based on the assumption that the DPKO would launch only one large new mission a year, but this has turned out to be an underestimate. The 140,000 peacekeepers authorized for deployment in

[78] 1993 UNYB 3.
[79] Address of Deputy-Secretary-General, Press Release DSG/SM/91, 3 April 2000.
[80] See, for example, Ruffert, 'The Administration of Kosovo and East Timor by the International Community', 50 ICLQ (2001) 613; Wilde, 'From Danzig to East Timor and Beyond: The Role of International Territorial Adminstration', 95 AJIL (2001) 583; Chesterman, *You, The People: Transitional Administration, State-Building and the UN* (2004).
[81] See 323 below.
[82] See Chapter 9 below.
[83] Gray, 'Peacekeeping after the Brahimi Report: is there a crisis of credibility for the UN?', 6 Journal of Conflict and Security Law (2001) 267. See 307 below.

twenty missions at the end of 2007 is the highest number in the history of the UN. This has placed a strain on systems and personnel in the field and on Headquarters staff. The Under-Secretary-General for Peacekeeping has spoken of the enormity of the current challenge; he argued that the situation requires a more systematic structural response. Therefore an ambitious reform project by the name of Peace Operations 2010 was initiated in 2006 with the aim of improving the professionalism, management and efficiency of UN peacekeeping.[84] As part of this project, the new Secretary-General, shortly after taking office at the start of 2007, divided the DPKO into two, a Department of Peace Operations and a Department of Field Support.[85] The Under-Secretary-General insisted that the priority of doctrine must stay uppermost in the restructuring process: 'A doctrine of UN peacekeeping should ensure that, in the face of diverse operational environments, personnel and mandates, field activities should be guided by a coherent body of principles and procedures to enhance security and effectiveness.' At the end of 2007 the DPKO was working to produce a Capstone Document to set out core doctrine on peacekeeping.

The end of Cold War conflicts

UN peacekeeping forces played a major role in the settlement of long-standing conflicts that had been fuelled by the Cold War. In 1988 the USSR announced its intention of withdrawing its troops from Afghanistan; this was followed by the 1988 *Geneva Accords*, a set of four agreements involving Afghanistan, Pakistan, the USA and the USSR. As part of this settlement the Security Council established UNGOMAP with the relatively limited mandate to investigate and report on possible violations of the *Geneva Accords*. Although it was set up as part of the UN Secretary-General's Good Offices Mission, its use of military personnel meant that it was classified as a peacekeeping operation. It monitored the withdrawal of Soviet forces and also operated on the border between Afghanistan and Pakistan, investigating reports of violations of the non-interference and non-intervention obligations in the peace accords. It was terminated in 1990.[86]

The interconnected peace settlements in Namibia, Angola, and Mozambique also involved the creation of new UN peacekeeping operations. The United Nations had been concerned with Namibia since 1948,

---

[84] Special Committee on Peacekeeping Operations, 195th and 196th meetings, UN Press Release GA/PK/192, 26 February 2007.

[85] UN doc A/61/858; UN Press Release GA/10579, 15 March 2007.

[86] UN Publications, *The Blue Helmets: A Review of United Nations Peacekeeping* (3rd edn, 1996) at 661.

when South Africa first purported to incorporate the mandated territory. In 1966 the UN General Assembly terminated the South African mandate over Namibia and placed it under the responsibility of the UN, but South Africa continued illegally to occupy Namibia. In 1978 the Security Council agreed on a plan for Namibian independence in Resolution 435; western states sought a negotiated solution and the USA and the UK opposed further Chapter VII action against South Africa other than the arms embargo in Resolution 918 (1994). South Africa subsequently linked the question of the independence of Namibia and its compliance with Resolution 435 (1978) with the withdrawal of Cuban forces from Angola. The General Assembly and the Security Council rejected this linkage, but it nevertheless formed the basis of the agreement eventually reached in 1988 between Angola, Cuba, and South Africa. In 1989 the Security Council finally began to implement the Resolution 435 Settlement and, as part of this, agreed on the establishment of UNTAG. This was at the time an unusual operation, with functions going beyond traditional peacekeeping; it was the first of the 'second generation of peacekeeping'. At its maximum it comprised 8,000 personnel. Its mandate was to ensure free and fair elections and to create the conditions that would make such elections possible. UNTAG included military, civilian, and police components. The military section was responsible for monitoring the ceasefire, the withdrawal of South African troops and some border monitoring. In March 1990 Namibia finally reached independence and UNTAG was terminated.[87]

The fate of Angola was tied to that of Namibia; it had been subjected to civil war ever since its independence from Portugal in 1975, with Cuba and the USSR supporting the government, and South Africa and the USA supporting the opposing UNITA forces.[88] Also SWAPO operated from Angola in its operations to liberate Namibia from South African occupation. As part of the wider regional settlement in 1988, Angola, South Africa and Cuba agreed on the withdrawal of Cuban troops from Angola; Angola and Cuba asked for the establishment of a UN military observer force to verify compliance with their bilateral agreement on troop withdrawal. A small force, UNAVEM, was created and successfully completed this limited mission. Negotiations on the settlement of the internal conflict in Angola between the government and UNITA led to the 1991 *Peace Accords* for Angola and the creation of UNAVEM II. This was now given a much more extensive mandate; it was to verify implementation of the Peace Accords. This involved monitoring the ceasefire, the collection of the armed forces of the two parties into assembly areas and the demobilization of those forces, the formation of joint armed forces, the police, and

[87] Ibid., 201.
[88] Ibid., 231.

supervising the elections. But serious problems arose; after the elections in October 1992 UNITA resorted to fighting and the situation deteriorated in early 1993. UNAVEM II operated as a channel for communications between the parties but its mandate came to seem unrealistic in the absence of an effective ceasefire. The Security Council reacted to UNITA's non-cooperation with the peace process by imposing an arms and oil embargo on it. Negotiations eventually led to the *Lusaka Protocol* in October 1994 and a new attempt at securing a cease-fire. In 1995 UNAVEM III took over from UNAVEM II; it was assigned political, military, police, humanitarian and electoral functions. But the authorized number of troops were not provided and like its predecessor, it ran into difficulties because of delays and non-cooperation, mainly by UNITA. Its mandate was terminated in July 1997 and it was replaced by an observer mission (MONUA). But the security situation worsened and MONUA was not able to carry out its mandate; it was terminated in February 1999. Angola was once again in a state of war. The United Nations held UNITA and its leader, Jonas Savimbi, responsible for this crisis and imposed a series of sanctions on UNITA.[89] After Savimbi's death in February 2002 an effective ceasefire was agreed and approved by the UN and a peace-building force was created.[90] Angola began to enjoy peace for the first time since its independence.

The UN experience in Mozambique was happier. Like Angola, Mozambique had been involved in civil war almost since the date of its independence from Portugal in 1975; again South Africa and western states denied the legitimacy of its government and supported forces aiming to overthrow it. The SWAPO liberation movement operated from Mozambique against South African occupation of Namibia. In 1992 a *General Peace Agreement* was signed between the parties and the UN was asked to oversee the implementation of this Agreement. The Security Council created UNOMOZ and over two years it verified the ceasefire and secured the assembly and demobilization of the opposing armed forces; it assisted in the creation of a new joint army; its police component monitored the national police; it coordinated humanitarian activities; assisted the massive repatriation programme; and secured the implementation of free and fair elections in October 1994.[91]

In Cambodia the 1991 *Paris Agreements* were intended to end many years of conflict. After the 1978 intervention in Cambodia by Vietnam to overthrow the Khmer Rouge regime of Pol Pot, states' support for the competing parties divided partly on Cold War lines. The Vietnamese

---

[89] S/PRST/1999/3; Report of the Secretary-General S/1999/49.
[90] SC Res 1433 (2002), Keesings (2002) 44969.
[91] UN Publications, *The Blue Helmets: A Review of United Nations Peacekeeping* (3rd edn, 1996) at 319; UN Blue Book Series, Vol V, *The United Nations and Mozambique 1992–1995*.

announced the withdrawal of their troops in 1989 and the permanent members of the Security Council worked together to achieve a negotiated solution. Under the Peace Agreement the UN was to organize free elections, coordinate the repatriation of refugees, coordinate economic rehabilitation and reconstruction, supervise and verify the withdrawal of foreign forces, the ceasefire and demobilization; coordinate the release of prisoners of war and foster an environment of peace and stability. The UN sent in an advance mission, UNAMIC; then UNTAC, one of the largest and most ambitious peacekeeping forces in the history of the UN, was deployed in 1992. UNTAC was made up of seven distinct components: human rights, electoral, military, civil administration, police, repatriation, and rehabilitation. At its largest it comprised 20,000 personnel. It was terminated in 1993.[92]

Finally, in Central America the long-lasting conflicts involving significant outside intervention by Eastern and Western blocs were terminated by the 1986 *Esquipulas II Agreement* between the five states of the region. As part of this agreement Costa Rica, El Salvador, Guatemala, Honduras, and Nicaragua agreed on the deployment of the first substantial UN peacekeeping operation in Latin America. Initially ONUCA was established to verify the commitments by the states parties to stop aid to opposition forces in other states and not to allow the use of their territory for attacks on other states. Mobile teams of military observers were created. The mandate was subsequently expanded to include verification of the cessation of hostilities and demobilization of irregular forces; and subsequently to monitor the separation of forces and the ceasefire in Nicaragua. ONUCA completed its mandate in 1992.[93]

In El Salvador it was replaced by ONUSAL in 1991; negotiations between the government and the opposition FMLN led to a series of agreements, culminating in the 1992 *Chapultepec Agreement*. Under these preliminary agreements ONUSAL was to monitor agreements between the government and FMLN; its initial mandate was to verify compliance with the *Human Rights Agreement*. The *Chapultepec Agreement* further expanded the role of ONUSAL to cover verification of the ceasefire and the separation of forces, prevention of the movement of forces, and the supervision of the destruction of its weapons by FMLN. ONUSAL was to have three, later four, divisions: Human Rights, Military, Police, and Electoral to supervise the different aspects of the peace agreement. It completed its functions in 1995.[94]

---

[92] *The Blue Helmets* at 447; UN Blue Book Series, Vol II, *The United Nations and Cambodia 1991–1995*.
[93] Ibid., 413.
[94] Ibid., 423; UN Blue Book Series, Vol IV, *The United Nations and El Salvador 1990–1995*.

This brief survey of UN peacekeeping operations in those conflicts where the end of the Cold War facilitated settlement shows that the forces played an extensive role involving a very wide range of activities. Only UNGOMAP in Afghanistan was a limited force of a traditional kind; the others were large and complex operations with functions including disarmament, election monitoring, human rights, and the re-establishment of civil society. They involved significant civilian participation as well as more traditional military functions such as monitoring ceasefires. In the terms of the *Agenda for Peace* these were peace-building as well as peace-keeping operations.

The start of new conflicts

But the end of the Cold War also contributed to the outbreak of new conflicts. The break-up of Yugoslavia and the competing claims of Croats, Bosnians, and Serbs, led to conflict; the UN undertook several operations in the former Yugoslavia. The break-up of the USSR into its fifteen constituent republics also brought with it pressures for further subdivision on ethnic lines and the first UN peacekeeping force in the former USSR was established in Georgia in 1993. Conflict had broken out because of the determination of the Abkhazians to pursue independence, although at the time that Georgia became independent the Abkhazians were only a 20 per cent minority within Abkhazia. After a ceasefire was agreed between Georgian government and Abkhaz secessionist forces in July 1993 the Security Council created UNOMIG, an observer force of up to eighty-eight members with a traditional mandate to verify compliance with the ceasefire and investigate reports of violations. However, as soon as deployment began the ceasefire broke down; Abkhaz forces occupied the whole of the territory and displaced the Georgian inhabitants. Resolution 881 in November 1993 authorized the continued presence of UNOMIG, with an interim mandate to suit the changed circumstances. It was simply to maintain contacts with both sides and monitor the situation. After another ceasefire was agreed CIS peacekeeping forces were deployed; accordingly the mandate of UNOMIG was amended. Its strength was increased to 136 observers and it was given new tasks: the verification of the new ceasefire, the observation of the CIS peacekeeping forces, verification that the parties and their heavy military equipment were withdrawn from certain security zones, and monitoring the withdrawal of volunteer forces from outside Abkhazia.[95] Political stalemate continued because of the fundamental disagreements between the government and the Abkhaz

---

[95] SC Res 937 (1994).

separatists on the recognition of the territorial integrity of Georgia and the repatriation of refugees.[96] The Security Council repeatedly expressed regret that the Abkhaz side refused to engage in substantive political discussions.[97] The situation deteriorated in 2006 and the Security Council also urged the Georgian side 'to address seriously legitimate Abkhaz security concerns, to avoid steps which could be seen as threatening and to refrain from militant rhetoric'.[98] But Georgia expressed its dissatisfaction with the settlement process and Georgian special forces conducted an operation in Abkhazia on 25 July 2006.[99] The situation has been complicated by the deterioration in relations between Russia and Georgia following the 2003 'Rose Revolution' in Georgia which brought to power a president committed to closer relations with the west and NATO. Georgia has accused Russia of support for the Abkhaz separatists and of unlawful intervention in its territory.[100] In September 2007 the most serious clashes between Georgian and Abkhaz forces for many years led the Secretary-General to call for an expansion of the size and mandate of UNOMIG.[101] He expressed concern over the suspension of meetings between the two sides. There was no prospect of a political settlement at the end of 2007.

After the former USSR republic Tajikistan became an independent state, previous political and economic structures broke down and civil war broke out; initially many of the opposition forces retreated to Afghanistan and conducted cross-border attacks. The UN became involved in seeking a peaceful settlement and the *Tehran Agreement* was reached between the opposing Tajik forces in September 1994. In this the parties agreed to halt hostile acts on the Tajik/Afghan border and within Tajikistan and to establish a Joint Commission to oversee the implementation of the agreement. The Security Council created UNMOT, a small operation initially of fifty-five mixed military and civilian personnel, to investigate ceasefire allegations on its own initiative or at the request of the Joint Commission. The situation worsened in 1996, but talks continued. In November 1997 the situation was calmer and UNMOT's mandate was expanded to include monitoring disarmament and demobilization. Its civilian component was to take on new functions in monitoring human rights, police, and elections. After the successful holding of the first multi-party elections UNMOT was terminated in May 2000.[102]

---

[96] *The Blue Helmets* at 569; 2000 UNYB 386.
[97] For example, SC Res 1582 (2005) 1615 (2005).
[98] SC Res 1666 (2006).
[99] The SC acknowledged with concern in Res 1716 (2006) that a new and tense situation had emerged. See Keesings (2006) 47377.
[100] Keesings (2006) 47054, 47116, 47271, 47377, 47484, 47532, 47603, (2007) 47831, 48093. See also UN Press Releases SC/8997, 13 April 2007, SC/9142, 15 October 2007.
[101] Report of the Secretary-General on the situation in Abkhazia, S/2007/588.
[102] 2000 UNYB 589.

Also, when the USSR and the USA and other powers withdrew support from governments which they had helped to keep in power during the Cold War, those governments were weakened and in many cases civil war resulted. UN peacekeeping operations played a role in some of these conflicts. Thus, for example, the UN became involved in peacekeeping operations in Somalia when civil war broke out after the overthrow of the Siad Barre regime, which had long been supported by western states. In Liberia, when the government of the western-backed President Doe was overthrown, the UN sent a peacekeeping force to supplement the work of a regional force.[103] In the Central African Republic the reluctance of France to continue to prop up the government contributed to instability; a UN force was successfully deployed.[104]

In other African states it was internal as much as Cold War factors which contributed to the outbreak of conflict or prevented its resolution.[105] The DRC plunged into conflict after the overthrow of President Mobutu who had been supported in power by France during the Cold War; conflicts in neighbouring Rwanda, Uganda, Burundi and Angola spread into the DRC. The Security Council provided for the establishment of a UN force in the DRC, but its deployment was delayed. Here and in Sierra Leone the parties struggled for power and control of the rich resources of the state; internal conflicts spilled over into regional instability involving other states in the region. In Sierra Leone a UN peacekeeping force was established in 1999 but ran into difficulty; UN forces were also established in response to civil conflict in the neighbouring states of Côte d'Ivoire and Liberia. New operations have been set up to help to resolve the long-lasting ethnic conflicts in Burundi and Sudan.

Ethiopia and Eritrea embarked on what the UN Secretary-General called a 'senseless' territorial war in 1998;[106] a traditional UN peacekeeping force was established to monitor the cease-fire and the Temporary Security Sone (TSZ) created in Eritrean territory in support of the cease-fire.[107] The parties then concluded a Peace Agreement providing for the establishment of a Boundary Commission to make a final and binding delimitation and demarcation of the contested boundary.[108] However, the 4,200-strong force

---

[103] See 392 below.

[104] See 303 below.

[105] See Report of the Secretary-General, *The causes of conflict and the promotion of durable peace and sustainable development in Africa*, S/1998/318, 37 ILM (1998) 913.

[106] The Eritrea/Ethiopia Claims Commission attributed responsibility for the outbreak of the conflict to Eritrea in a controversial decision, Ethiopia's *Ius ad Bellum* Claims 1–8, 45 ILM (2006) 430. See Gray, 'The Eritrea/Ethiopia Claims Commission oversteps its boundaries', 17 EJIL (2006) 699.

[107] UNMEE was established by SC Res 1320 (2000).

[108] See 40 ILM (2001) 259. SC Res 1430 (2002) then expanded the mandate of UNMEE to assist the Boundary Commission in the implementation of its delimitation decision.

(UNMEE) ran into difficulties. Ethiopia refused to implement the binding award made by the Boundary Commission in 2002; in retaliation Eritrea limited its cooperation with UNMEE and obstructed its deployment and operations.[109] At the end of 2004 Ethiopia moved its troops closer to the TSZ.[110] The Security Council repeatedly called on Ethiopia to implement the delimitation decision and on Eritrea to cooperate with UNMEE.[111] The situation worsened and in 2006 the Secretary-General warned of disastrous consequences if the situation was allowed to fester.[112] The Security Council in Resolution 1710 (2006) announced that it would transform or reconfigure UNMEE if no progress was made. This may be seen as an indication of the Security Council's desire not to allow the existence of a peacekeeping force to freeze the situation. But Eritrea sent its troops into the TSZ and Ethiopia moved more forces towards the zone.[113] The Security Council responded by reducing the strength of UNMEE; it called on Eritrea to withdraw its troops and on Ethiopia to reduce the number of its forces next to the zone.[114] The problems with peacekeeping in Africa were a major concern of the *Brahimi Report*.[115]

PEACEKEEPING AND ENFORCEMENT ACTION IN YUGOSLAVIA AND
SOMALIA: THE BLURRING OF TRADITIONAL DISTINCTIONS

The extension of peacekeeping

Optimism about the role that peacekeeping forces would be able to play after the end of the Cold War was one of the factors that led to an expansion of their mandates. They not only took on wider roles in the re-creation of civil society as described above, there was also a blurring of the differences between peacekeeping and enforcement action. The Secretary-General, in his 1992 *Agenda for Peace*, had envisaged a more ambitious role for peacekeeping forces. He wrote of a new concept of 'peacemaking'; this would involve UN forces operating under Article 40 of the UN

---

[109] Report of the Secretary-General S/2005/553; UN Press Releases SC/7972, 7 January 2004; SC/8085, 4 May 2004; SC/8519, 4 October 2005; SC/ 8561, 23 November 2005; SC/8584, 14 December 2005; SC/8736, 31 May 2006.
[110] UN Press Release SC/8334, 14 March 2005.
[111] SC Res 1560 (2004), 1622 (2005), 1640 (2005), 1681 (2006).
[112] Report of the Secretary-General S/2006/749; UN Press Release SC/8842, 29 September 2006. See also, Report of the Secretary-General S/2007/33.
[113] Reports of Secretary-General S/2006/992, S/2007/33; UN Press Release SC/9086, 30 July 2007. For a statement of Eritrea's position, see UN docs S/2006/840, 23 October 2006, S/2007/4, 4 January 2007.
[114] SC Res 1681 (2006), SC Res 1741 (2007), 1767 (2007).
[115] See 307 below.

Charter to enforce rather than merely monitor ceasefires.[116] The expansion of the traditional model of peacekeeping and blurring of the distinction between peacekeeping and enforcement was most marked in Yugoslavia and Somalia; UN experience in these conflicts led to a rethinking of the relationship and a much more cautious attitude, by both the Secretary-General in his 1995 *Supplement to An Agenda for Peace* and the Security Council. Thus in Yugoslavia and Somalia the traditional distinctions between the two types of operation seemed to break down. As described above, the generally agreed principles that had evolved through state practice required that peacekeeping forces should be impartial, not take sides, lightly armed, not use force except in self-defence, operate with the consent of the host state and should not usually include forces from permanent members of the Security Council or states with a political interest in the host state. They had no express basis in the UN Charter and did not operate under Chapter VII of the Charter.

Yugoslavia

In Yugoslavia and Somalia peacekeeping and enforcement action blurred together when peacekeeping forces were given functions that went beyond traditional peacekeeping. In Yugoslavia UNPROFOR was set up in 1991 as a traditional peacekeeping force, The first sixteen resolutions on UNPROFOR were all passed without any reference to Chapter VII. But it was sent in to Croatia and then Bosnia in the absence of a firm cease-fire and without the cooperation of the parties. Divisions in the Security Council and lack of agreement as to strategy led to a long series of over thirty resolutions on UNPROFOR and the gradual expansion of its mandate. Its initial mandate under Resolution 743 in February 1992 was 'to create the conditions of peace and security required for the negotiation of an overall settlement of the Yugoslav crisis'. This was expanded to authorize the protection and operation of Sarajevo airport in Bosnia, the monitoring of UN protected areas in Croatia, and the delivery of humanitarian aid.

The first major expansion of its mandate was in Resolution 776 (1992) (12–0–3) which authorized UNPROFOR to use force to secure the delivery of humanitarian aid. China abstained on this vote because the resolution impliedly referred to Chapter VII through its reference back to Resolution 770 (1992), which had been passed under Chapter VII. China said that this changed the nature of the peacekeeping force; UNPROFOR should, as a UN peacekeeping operation, follow the generally recognized guidelines established in past UN peacekeeping operations in implementing its mandate. This resolution contained disturbing elements which departed from these guidelines. On the one hand, it recognized that UNPROFOR

---

[116] *Agenda for Peace* para 44, 31 ILM (1992) 953.

should observe the normal rules of engagement of UN peacekeeping forces in implementing its new mandate, namely to use force in self-defence. On the other hand, it approved the use of force in self-defence when troops were blocked by armed forces. China was concerned that UNPROFOR would run the risk of plunging into armed conflict.[117] This fear was borne out by events; it proved difficult for UNPROFOR to secure the delivery of aid by force and each party saw the delivery of aid to the other parties as a threat to it and so they were not willing to cooperate.

From February 1993 the Security Council began to use Chapter VII in its resolutions on UNPROFOR. The first time it did this was apparently on the initiative of France which said that, given the problems encountered by UNPROFOR, it was unthinkable to continue the present mandate in its current form. France said that the reference to Chapter VII was not intended to change the nature of the force from peacekeeping to peacemaking; it was motivated by the need to guarantee the safety of UNPROFOR. China challenged this, saying that the resolution establishing UNPROFOR had not invoked Chapter VII and that the safety of UNPROFOR personnel could be dealt with by their right of self-defence without invoking Chapter VII. Resolution 807 (1993) expressed concern at the lack of cooperation of the parties and at the ceasefire violations; it determined that the situation constituted a threat to peace and security in the region and then went on: 'determined to ensure the security of UNPROFOR, and to this end acting under Chapter VII' they demanded that the parties comply fully with the UN peacekeeping plan in Croatia, observe Security Council resolutions, and respect fully UNPROFOR's unimpeded freedom of movement.[118] Almost all the subsequent resolutions on UNPROFOR also invoked Chapter VII; as France acknowledged, not to have resorted to Chapter VII in later resolutions would have been the worst of signals for the parties. France said that the reference to Chapter VII did not imply any automatic authority to resort to force other than in self-defence, but gave UNPROFOR the authority it needed to surmount the obstacles in the way of the execution of its mandate.[119]

UNPROFOR was later also authorized to use force in protection of the safe havens. The Security Council, faced with calls to act in response to ethnic cleansing, especially that by the Bosnian Serbs, proclaimed several 'safe areas' in 1993. It followed this by extending the mandate of UNPROFOR in Resolution 836 (1993) to enable it not only to monitor the ceasefire and to participate in the delivery of humanitarian relief in the safe areas, but also 'acting in self-defence to take the necessary measures

---

[117] SC 3114th meeting (1992) at 11–12.
[118] SC 3174th meeting (1993).
[119] SC 3344th meeting (1994); 3527th meeting (1995).

including the use of force' in reply to bombardments and armed incursions into the safe areas. But member states were not willing to provide the 30,000 troops estimated by the UN Secretary-General to be necessary for the performance of this mandate. The 7,000 troops actually provided were militarily incapable of protecting the safe areas against attack by the Bosnian Serbs and the protection for one ethnic group was seen as undermining the impartiality of UNPROFOR.[120]

Despite the invocation of Chapter VII in these resolutions, UNPROFOR was still obstructed in the performance of its mandate by all the parties; the Security Council responded with the creation of the Rapid Reaction Force (RRF) in June 1995. This was a mobile, well-armed force, to operate under the existing mandate of UNPROFOR. But states were divided as to whether this was really a continuation of UNPROFOR or a new enforcement force. China argued that the RRF would constitute a *de facto* change in the peacekeeping status of UNPROFOR; it was being established for enforcement action and would thus become a party to the conflict. Russia agreed that the resolution gave the impression that the RRF was intended to operate against one party to the conflict, the Bosnian Serbs. But the UK and France insisted that no change in the nature of UNPROFOR was intended. Both Croatia and Bosnia put obstacles in the way of the operation of the RRF on the ground.[121]

In Macedonia the Security Council established the first preventive peacekeeping force, UNPREDEP, in 1995 to stop the conflict in Bosnia from spreading to Macedonia.[122] The Secretary-General, in his *Agenda for Peace*, had stressed the desirability of acting to prevent conflicts. He has since repeatedly argued that the international community needs to move from a culture of reaction to a culture of prevention and this has become a more prominent concern for the Security Council.[123] UNPREDEP was subsequently retained in response to the danger that the conflict in Kosovo in 1998 might spill over into neighbouring states with significant Albanian population. But it was terminated in February 1999, against the wishes of the government of Macedonia, when a veto by China prevented the renewal of the force. China took the position that peacekeeping forces should not be open-ended and that the situation was stable.[124] When this view proved over-optimistic and ethnic conflict did break out

---

[120] Akashi, 'The Use of Force in a UN Peacekeeping Operation: Lessons Learnt from the Safe Areas Mandate', 19 Fordham ILJ (1995) 312; 1994 UNYB 522; Report of the Secretary-General pursuant to GA Resolution 53/35 (1998), *Srebrenica Report*.

[121] Gray, 'Host-State Consent and UN Peacekeeping in Yugoslavia', 7 Duke Journal of Comparative and International Law (1996) 241.

[122] 1995 UNYB 596.

[123] UN Secretary-General's Reports on Conflict Prevention: S/2001/574; S/2003/888; SC Res 1366 (2001); GA Res 57/337 (2003); UN Press Release GA/10145, 3 July 2003.

[124] 1999 UNYB 370.

in Macedonia, UNPREDEP was replaced, first by a NATO force in 2001, and then by the first EU peacekeeping force in 2003, both at the invitation of the government of Macedonia.[125]

When in 1995 Croatia demanded the withdrawal of UNPROFOR from its territory, it was replaced by UNCRO. The Security Council affirmed its determination to ensure the security and freedom of movement of personnel of the new peacekeeping operation and to that end acted under Chapter VII in Resolution 981 (1995) establishing UNCRO. The force was nevertheless still regarded as a peacekeeping force, dependent on Croatia's consent for its deployment in its territory. It was given a mandate more acceptable to Croatia because the name of the force (UN Confidence Restoration Operation in Croatia) was designed to acknowledge Croatia's sovereignty over the whole of its territory. Its mandate was essentially to create the conditions that would facilitate a negotiated settlement consistent with the territorial integrity of Croatia and which guaranteed the security and rights of all communities living in a particular area of Croatia. Despite Croatia's success in renegotiating the mandate of the force it did not cooperate with UNCRO. It overran the areas where UNCRO operated in 1995 and its mandate became unworkable.[126]

After the 1995 Peace Agreement the UN created new peacekeeping operations. In Bosnia UNMIBH replaced UNPROFOR; in Croatia UNCRO was replaced by UNTAES and UNMOP.[127] The last was to monitor the demilitarization of the Prevlaka peninsula and was established without any reference to Chapter VII. But the Security Council again blurred the distinction between peacekeeping and enforcement operations in its creation of UNTAES; this alone of the three operations was created under Chapter VII, even though with the consent of Croatia. The Security Council in Resolution 1037 (1996) determined that the situation in Croatia continued to constitute a threat to international peace and security. 'Acting under Chapter VII', it decided to establish a UN peacekeeping operation for an initial period of twelve months. The reference to Chapter VII seems to have been inspired by concern over the need to ensure the security and freedom of movement of the personnel of the UN peacekeeping operation in Croatia. The mandate of the military component of UNTAES was to supervise the demilitarization agreed in the Basic Agreement on the Region of Eastern Slavonia, Baranja and Western Sirmium between the government of Croatia and the local Serbian community, to monitor the safe return of refugees, to contribute by its presence to the maintenance

---

[125] Keesings (2001) 44232,44305; (2003) 45214, 45312.
[126] UN Publications, *The Blue Helmets: A Review of United Nations Peacekeeping* (3rd edn, 1996) at 543.
[127] UNMIBH and UNMOP terminated in December 2002.

of peace and security in the region, and otherwise to assist in implementation of the Basic Agreement. The UN Secretary-General had expressed some concern over the creation of this force; he argued that it should have proper enforcement powers if it was to be able to carry out its functions. There was a danger that it would run into the same sort of problems as UNPROFOR had earlier. But despite the reference to Chapter VII, the new force was not given enforcement powers. It was member states who were authorized to take all necessary measures in defence of UNTAES.[128] The force was terminated in January 1998 although a major part of its mandate, the repatriation of displaced Serbs, was left undone.

Thus the use of Chapter VII in the resolutions on UNPROFOR, UNCRO, and UNTAES increased expectations as to what they might achieve, but did not in itself give these forces enforcement powers in the absence of further express provision. The lack of realistic mandates and of adequate resources meant that the forces were not able to fulfil the expectations raised. In contrast UNMIBH and UNMOP were regarded as successes: 'with the right mandate, the cooperation of the parties and strong support of the Security Council and member states, UN peacekeeping could make an important difference'.[129] The termination of UNMIBH and UNMOP in December 2002 brought an end to an era of UN involvement in the former Yugoslavia.[130]

Somalia

The UN commitments in the former Yugoslavia led to reluctance to get involved in Somalia even though the scale of the loss of life there was much greater than that in the former Yugoslavia.[131] This led to accusations of double standards; the Security Council was said to care less about conflict in Africa than in Europe. The Security Council first responded to the civil war in Somalia by issuing a statement in January 1991, but it was not until a year later in January 1992 that the Security Council passed Resolution 733, expressing grave alarm at the rapid deterioration of the situation and the heavy loss of life and widespread material damage. It determined that the situation was a threat to peace and security and imposed an arms embargo. In April 1992 it established a peacekeeping force; Resolution 751 said that the Security Council was deeply disturbed by the magnitude of

---

[128] SC Res 1037 (1996), 1120 (1997).
[129] UN Press Release SC/7632, 14 January 2003.
[130] On the continued UN involvement in Kosovo, see 295.
[131] UN Publications, *The Blue Helmets: A Review of United Nations Peacekeeping* (3rd edn, 1996) at 285; UN Department of Peacekeeping, Lessons Learned Unit, *The Comprehensive Report on Lessons learned from UN Operations in Somalia, April 1992–March 1995*; Clarke and Herbst (eds), *Learning from Somalia: The Lessons of Armed Humanitarian Intervention* (1997); UN Blue Book Series, Vol VIII, *The United Nations and Somalia 1992–1996*.

the human suffering caused by the conflict and concerned that the continuation of the situation constituted a threat to international peace and security.

As in Bosnia, there was no real ceasefire in place and the peacekeeping force was sent in even though there was no peace to keep. Its mandate led it into conflict with the warring parties. Its initial mandate was not only to monitor the ceasefire in the capital, Mogadishu, but also to provide security for those delivering humanitarian aid. This was the first time in the history of the UN that a force was established with the primary purpose of making possible the delivery of emergency assistance to a civilian population. Its purpose was to deter attacks on humanitarian relief operations and it was to use force only in self-defence. But UNOSOM I proved unable to operate beyond Mogadishu or to carry out its mandate in the absence of cooperation of the warring parties.

The Security Council responded to this by sending a different type of force. In December 1992 it authorized the deployment of member states in a multinational non-UN force, UNITAF, to 'use all necessary means to establish a secure environment' for humanitarian relief operations. Operational command was assumed by the USA and it contributed more than two thirds of the troops. The authorization of this operation was another new departure for the UN.[132] It was the first time that Chapter VII was used, not to authorize force against a wrongdoing state such as Iraq, but for humanitarian aims in a civil war. More than twenty states contributed forces and at the maximum UNITAF reached 37,000 troops, of which the vast majority were US citizens. It was created as a temporary operation, and when the USA decided to terminate its participation the force could not go on. It achieved limited success in securing the delivery of humanitarian relief, but it was not able to operate throughout Somalia and it did not secure the disarmament of the warring factions. It handed over to another UN force in March 1993 without having established a secure environment for humanitarian operations.

The Security Council in Resolution 814 (1993) (adopted unanimously) replaced both UNOSOM I and UNITAF by UNOSOM II, the first peace-enforcement operation under the command of the UN, created under Chapter VII, with functions that went beyond traditional peacekeeping.[133]

---

[132] On authorization to member states to use force, see 289 below and Chapter 8.

[133] For the first time the USA contributed troops to serve under UN command; this led to serious problems in securing unity of command. The USA tended to operate outside the UN command structure. The Secretary-General, in the *Supplement to an Agenda for Peace* (S/1995/1 at para 41), said that the experience in Somalia underlined again the necessity for a peacekeeping force to act as an integrated whole. That necessity is all the more imperative when the mission is operating in dangerous conditions. There must be no attempt by troop contributing governments to provide guidance, let alone give orders, to their contingents on operational matters. To do so creates divisions within the force. It can also create the

UNOSOM II was mandated in Resolution 814 (1993) to operate throughout Somalia: to monitor the cessation of hostilities and compliance with the ceasefire agreements; to prevent any resumption of violence and, if necessary, to take appropriate action against any faction violating the ceasefire; to secure disarmament of the organized factions; to maintain security at ports, airports and lines of communication needed for deliveries of humanitarian assistance; to protect the UN civilian staff; to clear mines; and to assist refugees to return home. This innovative combination of peacekeeping and Chapter VII proved only partially successful. UNOSOM II was drawn into conflict with one of the warring factions and was not able to carry out its mandate in the absence of an effective ceasefire. Resolution 837 (1993) was passed in response to the murder of UN peacekeepers by one of the factions led by General Aidid; it extended UNOSOM II's mandate and drew it into conflict with the faction. This resolution authorized the UN forces to arrest and try those responsible for the killings. Under this mandate US troops suffered losses when their operation in pursuit of General Aidid went wrong. After this the USA was no longer willing to continue the operation and announced a complete withdrawal of its forces by March 1994.

Accordingly UNOSOM II's mandate was redefined in a more limited way in February 1994 in Resolution 897; this determined that there was still a threat to international peace and security and was again passed under Chapter VII, but nevertheless marked a return to traditional peacekeeping. UNOSOM II was no longer to use force to secure disarmament or in response to cease-fire violations. It would use force only in self-defence. In the continued absence of cooperation from the warring parties and the reluctance of contributing states to maintain their troops in Somalia the operation was terminated in March 1995. According to the Secretary-General, this was the first UN operation to be withdrawn by the Security Council before completing its mission.[134] The UN continued to pursue attempts at a political settlement in combination with regional organizations. But these proved unsuccessful and Somalia never achieved an effective central government with control over the whole territory.[135] In 2006 Ethiopia invaded in support of the weak Transitional Federal Government supported by the UN and the AU but its intervention did

---

impression that the operation is serving the policy objectives of the contributing governments rather than the collective will of the UN as formulated by the Security Council. Such impressions inevitably undermine an operation's legitimacy and effectiveness.

[134] Report of the Secretary-General, *The causes of conflict and the promotion of durable peace and sustainable development in Africa*, S/1998/318, 37 ILM (1998) 913 para 31.

[135] Within Somalia Somaliland (which declared independence in 1991) in the north did achieve effective autonomy and stability; Puntland (which proclaims autonomy) in the north-east was also relatively stable. However, conflict between these two entities broke out in 2007: Report of the Secretary-General S/2007/658 para 14.

not bring peace and stability.[136] The situation at the end of 2007 was too violent and unstable for the establishment of a UN peacekeeping force. The Security Council had authorized an 8,000 strong AU force to establish a mission to support dialogue and reconciliation in Somalia, but this force never reached its full strength; it was too small and too weak to cope with the very difficult security situation.[137] The AU called on the UN to send a UN force, but the UN Secretary-General reported that the deployment of a UN peacekeeping operation could not be considered a realistic and viable option. It had not even been possible to send an assessment mission to Somalia. A UN operation could only succeed if it was deployed in support of a political process, not as a substitute for one. Given the 'complex security situation' in Somalia he reported that it might be advisable to consider the deployment of a robust multinational force or coalition of the willing.[138]

Contemporaneous peacekeeping and enforcement operations

The second way in which the Security Council blurred the traditional distinctions between peacekeeping and enforcement action in Yugoslavia and Somalia was through the establishment of both peacekeeping and enforcement forces to operate at the same time. In these conflicts the Security Council first established a peacekeeping force and later authorized states to take enforcement action. This happened first in Yugoslavia, where UNPROFOR was operating on the ground as a peacekeeping force; the Security Council subsequently authorized NATO member states to use force under Chapter VII. The first resolution to do this was Resolution 770 in August 1992; it called upon states acting nationally or through regional arrangements or agencies to take all measures necessary to facilitate, in coordination with the UN, the delivery by relevant UN humanitarian organizations and others of humanitarian assistance to Sarajevo and other parts of Bosnia. That is, it authorized the use of force to ensure the safety of humanitarian convoys, if necessary by clearing a path through hostile forces. It was followed by Resolution 816 (1993) authorizing states 'under the authority of the Security Council and subject to close coordination with the Secretary-General and UNPROFOR' to take all necessary measures in the airspace of Bosnia to ensure compliance with the ban on flights over Bosnia that the Security Council had imposed earlier in an attempt to secure the safety of humanitarian operations. Under this resolution NATO

---

[136] See 244 above.
[137] SC Res 1744 (2007), 1772 (2007).
[138] For the AU request, see UN doc S/2007/499. See also the UN Secretary-General Reports S/2007/115, S/2007/204, S/2007/381, S/2007/ 658.

set up *Operation Deny Flight*. The scope of the right to use force was limited to responding to violations of the no-fly ban, it did not allow pre-emptive action against surface-to-air weapons systems on the ground. Resolution 836 (1993) on the protection of safe havens proved more important. The Security Council had declared that six towns were safe havens, but had failed either to demilitarize them (except Srebrenica and Zepa) or to provide adequate numbers of peacekeeping forces to protect them. Therefore it turned to NATO to protect the safe havens. Resolution 836 (1993) decided that member states could take all necessary measures, through the use of air power, in and around the safe areas in Bosnia to support UNPROFOR in the performance of its mandate to deter attacks and reply to bombardments and armed incursions on the safe areas.[139]

The first use of force by NATO under these resolutions was in February 1994 against aircraft violating the no-fly zone. It followed this by at first minor and then more serious uses of force to protect the safe areas in 1994 and 1995. It became clear that NATO air attacks could not deter action on the ground by the Bosnian Serbs against the safe areas; also UN peacekeeping forces on the ground were vulnerable to attack and were endangered by member state operations against Bosnian Serbs. This was made very clear when the Bosnian Serbs responded to a NATO air attack in April 1995 by taking UNPROFOR troops hostage. UNPROFOR forces were unable to defend the safe areas of Srebrenica and Zepa; the Security Council subsequently withdrew its forces from areas it could not defend and thus made it possible for the NATO air forces to act. Finally NATO used force in *Operation Deliberate Force*, a major operation to defend Sarajevo under Resolution 836 (1993). This brought an end to the conflict in Bosnia and led to the conclusion of the December 1995 Peace Agreement.[140]

All these resolutions authorizing states to use force, to secure the delivery of humanitarian aid, to enforce the no-fly zone, and to protect safe havens asserted the obligation on member states to act in close coordination with the Secretary-General. In practice this was interpreted to require not merely that NATO inform the Secretary-General of its use of force, but that the Secretary-General's consent was needed before NATO could act. This was to secure coordination with UNPROFOR operations and to avoid actions that would endanger UNPROFOR forces on the ground. This restriction on NATO's freedom to use force led to divisions in the Security Council; the USA, without troops on the ground, was more enthusiastic about air strikes against Bosnian Serbs than

---

[139] SC Res 908 and 958 (1994) later supplemented this provision to deal with actions against safe areas originating in Croatia.

[140] See UN Publications, *The Blue Helmets: A Review of United Nations Peacekeeping* (3rd edn, 1996), 485; 1994 UNYB 522 at 523, 525; *Srebrenica Report* para 117–23, 452; *General Framework Agreement* 38 ILM (1999) 75.

troop-contributing states France and the UK, and called for greater freedom for NATO to act. Again this shows the difficulties of combining the two types of operations.

After the end of the conflict the combination of the two types of force was more successful. Following the Peace Agreement the Security Council combined in Bosnia a UN Mission (UNMIBH) and IFOR. The latter was a multinational force of NATO and non-NATO member states under unified command established under Chapter VII. In Resolution 1031 (1995) the Security Council determined that the situation in Bosnia was still a threat to international peace and security. It authorized member states to establish IFOR; this 50,000 strong force was to 'use all necessary means to effect the implementation of and to ensure compliance' with the Peace Agreement. At the end of 1996 IFOR was replaced by a smaller multinational stabilization force, SFOR;[141] in 2004 this was in turn replaced by an EU force.[142]

Again in Somalia the Security Council's attempts to combine peacekeeping and enforcement forces proved not wholly successful. As described above, it first established a peacekeeping force, UNOSOM I, then in Resolution 794 (1992) authorized states to conduct a joint operation (UNITAF) to 'use all necessary means to establish as soon as possible a secure environment for humanitarian relief operation'. There was meant to be a clear division of functions between the two forces, but UNITAF failed to deliver the secure environment for humanitarian assistance that it was mandated to provide. It was unwilling to undertake the disarmament functions that the UN had expected it to carry out and which would have given the peacekeeping force the security to carry out its mandate.[143]

Thus the combination of two different types of operations at the same time during on-going armed conflict led to serious problems in Yugoslavia and in Somalia. It emerged that peacekeeping and enforcement actions were not necessarily compatible during armed conflict. Peacekeeping operations were endangered by forcible intervention and the states authorized to use force were hampered by the presence on the ground of vulnerable peacekeeping forces. There were fundamental problems as to who could authorize operations and of coordination between the two

---

[141] SC Res 1088 (1996).

[142] SC Res 1551 (2004) and 1575 (2004).

[143] See UN Department of Peacekeeping, Lessons Learned Unit, *The Comprehensive Report on Lessons Learned from UN Operations in Somalia, April 1992–March 1995*. Subsequently, when UNITAF and UNOSOM I were replaced by UNOSOM II, the USA at the same time maintained its own forces in support of UNOSOM II but outside the UN command; UN Publications, *The Blue Helmets: A Review of United Nations Peacekeeping* (3rd edn, 1996) at 301.

forces. The combination of the two types of operation has proved more successful after the conclusion of conflict.[144]

The UN's experience of peacekeeping in Rwanda produced lessons which contrasted and even conflicted with those of Yugoslavia and Somalia. The Security Council's role in Rwanda reflected a marked caution.[145] Member states were not willing to commit resources to Rwanda at the same time that they were heavily involved in the former Yugoslavia and Somalia. The Security Council's first involvement was in response to incursions by Tutsi rebels (the RPF) against the government of Rwanda from Uganda. In July 1993 the Security Council established a border monitoring force, UNOMUR, on the Uganda side of the border with Rwanda.[146] When a comprehensive peace agreement was made between government and opposition forces in Rwanda, the UN agreed to assist in the implementation of the agreement. In October 1993 the Security Council established UNAMIR at the joint request of the government and the RPF opposition with the mandate of 'contributing to the establishment and maintenance of a climate conducive to the secure installation and subsequent operation of the transitional government'. It was to monitor the ceasefire and oversee demilitarization and demobilization and assist with mine clearance. It comprised 2,500 lightly armed and equipped military personnel.[147]

However, the parties were not all committed to the implementation of the peace agreement and in April 1994, after the Presidents of Rwanda and Burundi died together in a plane crash, the country sank into conflict. There were terrible massacres of Tutsis and moderate Hutus by supporters of the Rwandan government; between 500,000 and a million people were killed in three months. UNAMIR's mandate to implement the peace agreement became irrelevant; and it did not have the resources to prevent the genocide. The Belgian contingent was unilaterally withdrawn from

---

[144] This may also be seen in Kosovo and East Timor; see 295 below. In Côte d'Ivoire a small UN peacekeeping force, MINUCI, was created in 2003 under SC Res 1479 at the same time that UN-authorized ECOWAS and French forces were present to protect the elected government; in the DRC first an ECOWAS member state force, and then two EU forces, operated at the same time as the MONUC UN peacekeeping force in order to make up for the weakness of that force. There was no conflict between the mandates of these forces.

[145] UN Publications, *The Blue Helmets: A Review of United Nations Peacekeeping* (3rd edn, 1996) at 339; UN Department of Peacekeeping, *Comprehensive Report on Lessons Learned from UNAMIR*; UN Blue Book Series, Vol X, *The United Nations and Rwanda 1993–1996.*

[146] UNOMUR ended in 1994 when RPF became the new government of Rwanda.

[147] 1993 UNYB 282.

UNAMIR and its strength was reduced to 1,500.[148] Senior military officials said that 'the force level was too small for military action to protect the victims of the slaughter and the force's capabilities had not been put together with a conflict situation in mind. With an extremely weak logistics base, UNAMIR was also rapidly running out of food and medical supplies... It had no ambulances and mainly soft-skin vehicles for the transportation of troops'.[149]

During the massacres in April 1994 the Secretary-General accordingly gave the Security Council a choice between three options: a large Chapter VII force with the power to avert massacres, a small group of around two hundred and seventy military personnel to act as intermediary between the two parties, or complete withdrawal. The Security Council chose the second option. Resolution 912 (1994) altered UNAMIR's mandate; it was to act as an intermediary in an attempt to secure a ceasefire, assist in humanitarian operations, and monitor developments. The situation deteriorated and there were mass movements out of the state. It was not until May 1994 that the Security Council attempted to authorize more effective action. In Resolution 918 (1994) it imposed an arms embargo on Rwanda and expanded UNAMIR's mandate to authorize it to contribute to the security of refugees and civilians through the establishment of secure humanitarian areas and the provision of security for humanitarian operations; it was to take action in self-defence against persons or groups who threaten protected sites and populations. But the Secretary-General ran into serious difficulty in trying to obtain more troops; states did not want to become involved in another civil war. After the massacres UNAMIR had only 500 troops on the ground.

The RPF forces gained control over almost the whole of the country and declared a ceasefire in July 1994. Many of the defeated government forces took refuge in the DRC from where they continued to operate against Rwanda.[150] After the civil war ended UNAMIR finally reached its full strength of 5,500 troops in October 1994; states were still reluctant to contribute civilian police to assist in the rebuilding of society.[151] In early 1995 former government forces were rearming and the situation was tense. The new government of Rwanda informed the UN that UNAMIR no longer had a role to play; it had been established at a time of genocide and civil war in order to contribute to the security of displaced persons. This was

---

[148] The participation of Belgian forces was an example of a departure from the convention that states with historic interests in an area should not participate in peacekeeping forces there.

[149] UN Department of Peacekeeping, *Comprehensive Report on Lessons Learned from UNAMIR*, Part 2, para 10; 1994 UNYB 281.

[150] See 68 above.

[151] 1994 UNYB 281.

now the responsibility of the new government, as was national security and the protection of humanitarian convoys. Accordingly UNAMIR's mandate was redefined in a more limited way in June 1995 and its size was reduced until it was eventually withdrawn by March 1996.[152]

It is clear that states' reluctance to play a major role in Rwanda was strongly influenced by the experience of Yugoslavia and Somalia. The failure to prevent the genocide in Rwanda has, according to the Secretary-General, 'had especially profound consequences in Africa. Throughout the continent, the perception of near indifference on the part of the international community has left a poisonous legacy that continues to undermine confidence in the Organization.'[153] It was this experience that contributed to the development of the concept of the 'responsibility to protect'.[154] But recent experience in Darfur and Somalia demonstrates that Security Council members may still be reluctant to undertake military intervention to prevent humanitarian catastrophe in Africa.

THE RELATION OF UN PEACEKEEPING AND CHAPTER VII

In the light of the experience of Yugoslavia and Somalia the Secretary-General, in his 1995 *Supplement to An Agenda for Peace*, abandoned the expansive optimism of the earlier *Agenda for Peace* and retreated to the more traditional concept of peacekeeping. He stressed the basic principles of consent of the parties, impartiality, and the non-use of force except in self-defence. He said that three aspects of recent mandates had led peacekeeping operations to undermine these basic principles: the tasks of protecting humanitarian operations during continuing warfare, protecting civilian populations in safe areas, and pressing the parties to achieve national reconciliation at a pace faster than they were ready to accept. It has repeatedly been asserted that peacekeeping forces must never again be deployed into an environment in which there is no cease-fire or peace agreement, and that UN peacekeeping is not a substitute for a political process. The Security Council in a Statement welcomed the Secretary-General's analysis in the *Supplement to the Agenda for Peace* and also reiterated the practical requirements of successful peacekeeping: the need for a clear mandate, a fixed time frame, an effective command structure, and secure financing.[155]

---

[152] 1995 UNYB 370, 1996 UNYB 59.

[153] Report of the Secretary-General, *The causes of conflict and the promotion of durable peace and sustainable development in Africa*, S/1998/318, 37 ILM (1998) 913 para 11.

[154] See 51 above.

[155] S/PRST/1995/9; see also Special Peacekeeping Committee Press Release GA/PK/163, 26 April 1999.

For a significant period after the operations in Yugoslavia, Somalia and Rwanda the Security Council did not set up peace-enforcement operations during armed conflict; it did not base its establishment of new peacekeeping operations on Chapter VII. Thus the forces in Georgia, Liberia,[156] Tajikistan, Central African Republic, Sierra Leone, Ethiopia and Eritrea, Côte d'Ivoire and the DRC were not established under Chapter VII. However, Chapter VII is still used for some peacekeeping operations. A distinction has emerged between limited observer and monitoring missions, where there is normally no reference to Chapter VII, and more ambitious operations where the Security Council has continued to use Chapter VII, either for the establishment of an operation, or else within the body of a resolution on a peacekeeping operation. This basic distinction is clear, but there is no clear pattern in the Security Council's use of Chapter VII or in its authorization of force by peace operations. There seem to be various possible explanations for the choice to create an operation under Chapter VII: to indicate that it has a mandate going beyond mere observation or monitoring, to allow the force to regulate matters that would normally be within the domestic jurisdiction of the state concerned, or to make it clear that the operation does not depend on the consent of that state, and that there is a duty on all parties to cooperate with the UN force. Of course the mere reference to Chapter VII does not in itself authorize the use of force. When Chapter VII is used within the body of a resolution this is usually, but not always, done in order to authorize the use of force.[157]

In 1999 both UNMIK in Kosovo and UNTAET in East Timor were created under Chapter VII. After the end of the 1999 NATO operation against Yugoslavia to bring an end to the humanitarian catastrophe in Kosovo, Yugoslavia accepted a political solution to the Kosovo crisis. This included the withdrawal of its military, police, and paramilitary forces from Kosovo. The Security Council re-engaged in the search for peace in Kosovo. Under Resolution 1244 (1999) it both authorized member states in KFOR to use force and also authorized the Secretary-General to establish an international civilian administration, UNMIK. This was to promote the establishment of substantial autonomy and self-government in Kosovo, perform basic civilian administration functions, organize the development of provisional institutions for democratic and autonomous self-government, facilitate a political process designed to determine Kosovo's future status, support the reconstruction of key infrastructure,

---

[156] The first UN force in Liberia, UNOMIL (1993–97) under SC Res 866 (1993) was not established under Chapter VII, but a later force, UNMIL, created in 2003 under SC Res 1497 and 1509 (2003), was set up under Chapter VII.

[157] On the use of force by peace operations, see 302 below. One of Sudan's professed concerns about the establishment of a UN peacekeeping force in Darfur was that it would be created under Chapter VII (see UN Press Release SC/8750, 15 June 2006).

support humanitarian aid, and maintain civil law and order, including establishing local police forces. Never before had the United Nations assumed such broad, far-reaching, and important executive tasks.[158] The invocation of Chapter VII was thus necessary not to give UNMIK any wide right to use force, but, first, to authorize force by member states and, second, to legitimize the very wide powers of UNMIK to restore a semblance of normal life to the province and to make clear that its operations do not depend on the consent of Yugoslavia. At the end of 2007 the future of Kosovo is uncertain.[159]

In East Timor UNTAET, initially referred to in Resolution 1264 (1999) as a peacekeeping force, was also established under Chapter VII. In 1999 Indonesia had finally agreed to the holding of a consultation process, organized by the UN through UNAMET, to determine the wishes of the inhabitants of East Timor, the Portuguese territory it had invaded and occupied in 1975. After the inhabitants had indicated in the consultation process that they sought independence, widespread and serious disorder broke out as pro-Indonesia militias spread terror by their attacks on the people of East Timor; nearly half of the population fled their homes. The UN Security Council in Resolution 1264 (1999) first authorized a multi-national force (INTERFET) to restore peace and security; it also agreed that this force would be replaced as soon as possible by a peacekeeping force. Accordingly in Resolution 1272 (1999) it acted under Chapter VII in establishing UNTAET, to be endowed with overall responsibility for the administration of East Timor and empowered to exercise all legislative and executive authority.[160] It was to have a military component of up to 8,950 troops and was also authorized 'to take all necessary measures' to fulfil its mandate. The resolution (in contrast to Resolution 1264) did not refer to any consent by Indonesia to the establishment of UNTAET, beyond a reference to the importance of cooperation between Indonesia, Portugal, and UNTAET in the implementation of the resolution. Here the reference to Chapter VII was necessary because UNTAET was to take over the enforcement powers of the multinational force as soon as possible; also UNTAET itself was 'given a robust mandate' and empowered to use force by the reference to all necessary measures.[161] Several later resolutions referred back to this and called on UNTAET to use the robust powers it

---

[158] 1999 UNYB 332 at 353; for a discussion of the extensive role of UNIMK and UNTAET see, for example, Ruffert, 'The Administration of Kosovo and East Timor by the International Community', 50 ICLQ (2001) 613; Wilde, 'From Danzig to East Timor and Beyond: The Role of International Territorial Adminstration', 95 AJIL (2001) 583; Chesterman, *You, The People: Transitional Administration, State-Building and the UN* (2004).

[159] Report of the Secretary-General, S/2007/582, 28.

[160] 1999 UNYB 279 at 292.

[161] Report of the Secretary-General on the Situation in East Timor, S/1999/1024.

had been given in Resolution 1272 (1999).[162] In February 2000 the multi-national force INTERFET transferred military command of the territory to UNTAET,[163] which in turn handed over to UNMISET, a new peacekeeping force with a more limited military role, in May 2002 when East Timor finally gained independence.[164] UNMISET terminated in 2005 and was generally seen as a success. But violence broke out again in 2006.[165] The former colonial power, Portugal, and regional states, Australia, New Zealand and Malaysia provided a (non-UN) peacekeeping force at the request of the government,[166] and in 2006 the UN established UNMIT, a mainly police mission, to assist the government in the restoration of security.[167] In 2007 the situation remained 'fragile and volatile'.[168]

Another multidimensional UN peacekeeping force (with an initially authorized strength of 15,000) was established in Liberia under Chapter VII in 2003, the first such multidimensional force in Africa.[169] It replaced a member state force authorized by the Security Council.[170] But although UNMIL was created under Chapter VII there was no express authorization to use force within the resolution creating the force. Similarly MINUSTAH, the peacekeeping force created in Haiti in 2004, ten years after the first UN mission was established there, was set up under Chapter VII but without any express reference to the use of force.[171] In contrast, the multidimensional peacekeeping operation created in Côte d'Ivoire and the smaller force established in Burundi in 2004 were both set up by resolutions passed under Chapter VII which also contained authorization to use force.[172] When the size and mandate of UNIFIL in Lebanon were expanded after the Israeli invasion of 2006, Resolution 1701 (2006) made no

---

[162] SC Res 1319 (2000), 1338 (2001). These both underlined 'that UNTAET should respond robustly to the militia threat in East Timor, consistent with its resolution 1272(1999)'.
[163] 2000 UNYB 278.
[164] UNMISET (which includes a 5,000 strong military component) was established by SC Res 1410 (2002); it was not created under Chapter VII, but within Res 1410 para. 6 gave it certain Chapter VII powers: to take the necessary actions, for the duration of its mandate, to fulfil its mandate. This mandate was spelled out in the Secretary-General's Report, S/2002/432. On East Timor's independence and admission to the UN, see Keesings (2002) 44781, 44987.
[165] SC 5457th meeting (2006), 5469th meeting (2006).
[166] SC Res 1690 (2006); Keesings (2006) 47372, *The Guardian*, 25–26 May 2006.
[167] SC Res 1704 (2006). This made no reference to Chapter VII.
[168] SC Res 1745 (2007); Report of Secretary-General S/2007/513.
[169] SC Res 1509 (2003) set up UNMIL, with political, military, civilian police, criminal justice, civil affairs, human rights, gender, child protection, disarmament, demobilization, reintegration, public information, and support components (Secretary-General's Report S/2003/875 para 53). The military component was to create a secure and stable environment throughout Liberia after the recent civil war and the prolonged instability. See further 320 below.
[170] SC Res 1497 (2003). See 338 below.
[171] SC Res 1542 (2004).
[172] See 305 below.

express reference to Chapter VII, but did determine in the preamble that the situation was a threat to international peace and security. However, the Commander of the force later made it clear that the enhanced UNIFIL was a Chapter VI mission. The role of UNIFIL was to assist the parties and work with each of them to make sure they fully implemented Resolution 1701 and respected the cessation of hostilities.[173]

Consent to peacekeeping

Traditionally peacekeeping forces have operated with the consent of the host state.[174] This ostensibly simple principle masks considerable complexity. The difficulties that can arise in practice, and the complexity of the notion of consent, were particularly apparent in the case of Yugoslavia, where UNPROFOR was originally established at the request of the government of Yugoslavia.[175] The parties were clearly reluctant to go beyond formal consent to the establishment and deployment of UNPROFOR to real cooperation with those forces. Lack of cooperation was the main factor that made it impossible for UNPROFOR to fulfil its mandate. The parties sought a military solution and saw UNPROFOR as an obstruction to this; they interfered with its freedom of movement, undertook offensives across its positions, and even attacked its forces and took them hostage. It was partly in response to these problems that the Security Council turned to Chapter VII in its resolutions on UNPROFOR. The lack of cooperation by the governments of Croatia and Bosnia with UNPROFOR and their reluctance to respect its freedom of movement were further manifested in the difficulties experienced by the UN in securing the conclusion of *Status of Forces Agreements* (SOFAs) on the rights, duties, privileges, and immunities of the UN forces. Such agreements had been concluded between host states and the UN since UNEF.[176]

---

[173] Press Conference by Lebanon Force Commander, 5 September 2007; <www.un.org. News/briefings/docs/2007/070905_UNIFIL.doc.htm>. Qatar also stressed that this was a Chapter VI resolution in the debate on the adoption of SC Res 1701, SC 5511th meeting (2006).

[174] *Certain Expenses* case, ICJ Reports (1962) 151; White, *Keeping the Peace* (1993), 202; Higgins, *United Nations Peacekeeping* (4 vols, 1972).

[175] On host-state consent, see Gray, 'Host-State Consent and UN Peacekeeping in Yugoslavia', 7 Duke Journal of Comparative and International Law (1996) 241; Wippman, 'Treaty-Based Intervention: Who Can Say No?', 62 University of Chicago Law Review (1995) 607, and 'Military Intervention, Regional Organization and Host-State Consent', 7 Duke Journal of International and Comparative Law (1996) 209.

[176] Morphet, 'UN peacekeeping and Election Monitoring', in Roberts and Kingsbury (eds) *United Nations, Divided World* (2nd edn, 1993) at 187–8; Higgins, *United Nations Peacekeeping 1946–1967*, Vol 1 at 372. In 1990 the UN produced a model SOFA: UN Document A/45/594. But in Yugoslavia no SOFA was concluded with Bosnia until May 1993 and no agreement with Croatia was made on UNPROFOR though Croatia did conclude an agreement on the

The traditional requirement that UN peacekeeping operations have the consent of the host state was established in the case of the first major UN peacekeeping operation, UNEF. When Egypt withdrew its consent to the stationing of UNEF on its territory the UN Secretary-General regarded this as final and the UN forces were precipitately withdrawn.[177] In Yugoslavia Croatia's withdrawal of consent to the continuation of UNPROFOR on its territory led to the withdrawal of this force and its replacement by UNCRO. Rwanda's notification of the end of its consent to UNAMIR terminated that operation, to the regret of the UN Secretary-General; at roughly the same time Burundi refused to consent to the establishment of a UN peacekeeping force on its territory.[178] Recently Chad refused to accept a UN peacekeeping force, preferring an EU military force in combination with UN police.[179] And Sudan resisted the deployment of a hybrid AU/UN force in Darfur until 2007.[180] Although it had accepted a major UN force under the North/South *Comprehensive Peace Agreement* of 2005, it was reluctant to accept a UN force in Darfur. It accused the Security Council of having taken a 'path characterized by imbalance' with regard to Darfur because it had made no mention of ceasefire violations by opposition groups, but had threatened sanctions against the government.[181]

In cases where UN peacekeeping forces have been established in states involved in civil conflict the UN has increasingly sought the consent not only of the government but also of the warring parties. It seems that this has been done not out of legal obligation, but as a matter of securing the effectiveness of the operation. Thus in Yugoslavia the UN Secretary-General sought the consent of all the concerned parties to the initial deployment of UNPROFOR in Croatia and its subsequent deployment in Bosnia. This followed the earlier practice in Angola, Namibia, Cambodia, and Mozambique, but was formalized in that the early Security Council

successor to UNPROFOR, UNCRO. Similar difficulties in other conflicts have also reflected the problems that UN peacekeeping forces face in the absence of cooperation. The Security Council has repeatedly stressed the importance of the conclusion of these agreements, in SC Res 854 (1993), 858 (1993), 937 (1994) on Georgia, SC Res 872 (1993) and 1029 (1995) on Rwanda, SC Res 976 (1994) on Angola, SC Res 1369 (2001) on Eritrea, SC Res 1410 (2002) on East Timor.

[177] Report of the Secretary-General on UNEF, UN doc A/3943.

[178] On the withdrawal of consent by Croatia, see Gray, 'Host-State Consent and UN Peacekeeping in Yugoslavia', 7 Duke Journal of Comparative and International Law (1996) 241 at 265; on Burundi, see UN Publications, *The Blue Helmets: A Review of United Nations Peacekeeping* (3rd edn, 1996) at 366; on Rwanda, UN doc S/1995/1018, UN Blue Book Series, Vol X, *The United Nations and Rwanda 1993–1996* at 600.

[179] Report of the Secretary-General, S/2007/288 para 21–28.

[180] SC 5706th meeting (2007). Earlier plans for a UN force had failed in the absence of Sudan's consent. In 2006 plans were made for a transition from the AU force in Sudan since 2004 to a UN force (SC 5634th, 5392nd, 5434th, 5439th meetings, SC Res 1679, 1706 (2006)). But the government of Sudan did not consent to the establishment of a UN force, SC 5462nd, 5520th, 5528th, 5571st meetings (2006).

[181] SC 5520th, 5528th meetings (2006).

resolutions on UNPROFOR expressly referred to the consent of the concerned parties.[182] The Secretary-General has continued to consult all parties where possible before the establishment of recent peacekeeping operations in Liberia, Burundi, Côte d'Ivoire and Sudan, but no express reference to this has been made in Security Council resolutions.[183]

The caution learned from the experience in Yugoslavia and Somalia may, however, conflict with the determination by many states, especially African states, to avoid a repetition of the terrible events in Rwanda. The need for urgent action to stop massacres or serious fighting may conflict with the requirement of a ceasefire and commitment to cooperation with a UN force. This tension can be seen in regard to Sierra Leone and the DRC. In the DRC there were delays in the deployment of the peacekeeping force (MONUC) authorized by the Security Council. Resolution 1291 (2000) establishing the peacekeeping force had stipulated that the deployment of MONUC personnel would be carried out only after the Secretary-General had received credible assurances from the parties to the *Lusaka Ceasefire Agreement* regarding adequate security to allow UN personnel to carry out their functions. Certain states expressed unhappiness at this situation and complained of double standards despite the efforts of the Security Council to address the special problems of peacekeeping in Africa.[184] Uganda, Tanzania, and Zimbabwe all called for swift action; China called on the Security Council to act in Africa as readily as it had in Kosovo and East Timor.[185] But several later resolutions altering the

---

[182] See Gray, 'Host-State Consent and UN Peacekeeping in Yugoslavia', 7 Duke Journal of Comparative and International Law (1996) 241.

[183] Secretary-General Reports, S/2004/210, S/2004/5, S/2003/875, S/2005/57.

[184] The Secretary-General produced at the request of the Security Council a report on *The causes of conflict and the promotion of durable peace and sustainable development in Africa*, S/1998/318, 37 ILM (1998) 913; this said that the UN had deployed more of its peacekeeping operations in Africa than in any other single region. The deployment in 1989 of operations in Angola and Namibia began a new era of complex, post-Cold-War peacekeeping. Of the thirty-two operations launched by the UN during the succeeding nine years, thirteen were deployed in Africa. However, he acknowledged that the setback suffered in Somalia and the bitter experience in the former Yugoslavia had made the international community reluctant to assume the political and financial exposure associated with deploying peacekeeping operations. This reluctance appeared to go well beyond the lessons that Somalia offered and has had a particularly harsh impact upon Africa (para 29). See also the Report of the Secretary-General on *Enhancement of African Peacekeeping Capacity*, A/54/63 (1999). The Security Council set up an Ad hoc Working Group on Conflict Prevention and Resolution in Africa in 2002 (UN Press Release SC/7632, 14 January 2003). Each year special debates are held on Conflict Prevention and Resolution in Africa, and many SC meetings are devoted to Africa, but there are still delays in securing troops for peacekeeping operations in Africa and there was no third generation force like UNTAET or UNMIK in Africa until the creation of a multidimensional force in Liberia in 2003.

[185] See, for example, Fifth Committee Debate (Press Release GA/AB/3363, 29 March 2000) and Fourth Committee Debate on peacekeeping (Press Release GA/SPD/165, 19 October 1999).

mandate of MONUC reaffirmed the need for cooperation and continued to lay down conditions for the implementation of later phases of MONUC.[186] In the case of Yugoslavia there was consultation not only on the establishment of the force but also on its initial mandate and composition. The latter had in the early days of peacekeeping been the subject of some debate between host states and the UN as to who should have the final say in determining the nationality of the troops in the peacekeeping force. Through practice it became established that the final word was with the UN, but in fact behind-the-scenes discussions take place between the host state, the members of the Security Council, and troop-contributing states. Recently, when Eritrea rejected the participation of troops from certain states in UNMEE, it was condemned by the Security Council for this action.[187] Even more controversially, this question of consent to the composition and mandate of the force was an issue with regard to the deployment of UNAMID, the hybrid AU/UN force in Darfur. Sudan made its acceptance of a hybrid AU/UN force conditional on its African character, having earlier rejected a UN force as a means of re-colonization. The Security Council accepted this condition and Resolution 1769 (2007) recalled the agreement 'that the hybrid operation should have a predominantly African character and the troops should, as far as possible, be sourced from African countries'. However, it has proved difficult to obtain troops with adequate capabilities. The government of Sudan was unwilling to accept troops from Thailand, Nepal and Nordic states. Prolonged negotiations about the composition of the force and its freedom of action continued at the end of 2007.[188]

In the first peacekeeping operations troops were not accepted from permanent members of the Security Council or from states with interests in the host state. But this practice was abandoned in Cyprus and Lebanon (where the UK and France respectively contributed troops) and was not followed in Yugoslavia. Faced with the difficulty of obtaining troops and the need for well-trained and equipped forces to meet the more ambitious mandates the former restrictions on troop contribution were abandoned. The end of the Cold War meant that the reasons behind the restrictions on participation in peacekeeping forces have partly disappeared in that the fear that contribution of troops by the USA or the USSR would threaten the impartiality of the force and draw the UN into the Cold War

---

[186] SC Res 1355 (2001); SC Res 1376 (2001) set out in considerable detail the actions required by the parties before the next phase of the deployment could begin.

[187] UN Press Releases SC/8572, 7 December 2005; SC/8584, 14 December 2005.

[188] UN Press Release SC/9178, 27 November 2007; Report of the Secretary-General S/2007/759. On the problems caused by the combination of different peace agreements in Sudan, see Nouwen, Sudan's divided and divisive peace agreements', 19 Hague Yearbook of International Law (2006) 113.

is no longer applicable. However, the experience with US participation in UNOSOM II showed that there were difficulties with the participation of the one remaining superpower. The Secretary-General, in speaking of the dangers of a divided command in Somalia, showed that US unwillingness to submit to UN command led to the perception that the operation was serving the policy objectives of the contributing governments rather than the collective will of the UN as formulated by the Security Council.[189] Such impressions inevitably undermined an operation's legitimacy and effectiveness. This problem is clear also in the 1994 US Presidential Decision Directive, which made express the US reluctance to accept UN command: 'The greater the US military role, the less likely it will be that the US will agree to have a UN commander exercise operational control over US forces. Any large scale participation of US forces in a major peace enforcement mission that is likely to involve combat should ordinarily be conducted under US command and operational control or through competent regional organisations such as NATO or *ad hoc* coalitions.'[190] The USA now provides only a tiny number of peacekeeping troops, but it has the responsibility to contribute over a quarter of peacekeeping budget. And developed states collectively are not major troop contributors to UN peacekeeping force, with the exception of their significant contributions to UNIFIL when it was expanded in 2006. It is developing states which are the largest contributors of troops to UN peacekeeping.[191]

The use of force by peacekeeping operations

Traditionally peacekeeping forces were limited to the use of force in self-defence. This was not expressly spelled out in the resolutions establishing their mandates, but was affirmed in the reports of the Secretary-General that usually set out the details of the operations. Thus in the case of UNEF the Secretary-General affirmed the right of self-defence and warned that this should be used only under strictly defined conditions, because if there was a wide interpretation of self-defence this might blur the distinction between peacekeeping and Chapter VII action.[192] Nevertheless, it was understood that this right to self-defence included the right to resist attempts by forceful means to prevent the force from discharging its duties under its mandate. This was also generally set out in the UN Secretary-General's reports rather than made express in Security

---

[189] See note 133 above.
[190] 33 ILM (1994) 795.
[191] See 307 below.
[192] Report of the Secretary-General on UNEF, A/3943 (1958) para 179.

Council resolutions.[193] UNIFIL was exceptional in that Resolution 467 (1980) expressly quoted the Secretary-General's report on the operation and provided that 'The Force shall not use force except in self-defence.' Also 'Self-defence would include resistance to attempts by forceful means to prevent it from discharging its duties under the mandate of the Security Council.'

When UNPROFOR ran into problems in Bosnia and Croatia the Security Council made express its right to self-defence in Resolutions 776 (1992), 836 (1993), and 871 (1993). In the first of these UNPROFOR was authorized, in accordance with the Secretary-General's report, to use force to protect humanitarian convoys; this authorized it to act in self-defence, including situations in which armed persons attempted by force to prevent them from carrying out their mandate. Resolution 836 (1993) on the protection of safe areas was unusual in that it expressly authorized UNPROFOR to use force in self-defence. This approach was followed in Resolution 871 (1993), which authorized UNPROFOR in carrying out its mandate in Croatia, acting in self-defence, to take the necessary measures, including the use of force, to ensure its security and freedom of movement. Some concern arose that express provision in some resolutions for self-defence might give rise to the false inference that if a resolution did not expressly authorize the right of self-defence a peacekeeping force could not legally use force in self-defence.

Perhaps in response to this concern, in later resolutions on Rwanda and Angola a different approach was adopted. Instead of *authorizing* the use of force the resolutions *recognized* the right of peacekeeping operations to use force in self-defence. Resolution 918 (1994) on UNAMIR thus 'recognizes that UNAMIR may be required to take action in self-defence against persons or groups who threaten protected sites and populations, United Nations and other humanitarian personnel or the means of delivery and distribution of humanitarian relief'. Subsequently even this more cautious approach has been abandoned and a different formulation was adopted with regard to MINURCA, the first new peacekeeping force created in Africa since 1993. This was established in response to a crisis in the Central African Republic beginning in 1996; it was to replace a member state force, MISAB, set up after the *Bangui Peace Agreements* of January 1997. Resolution 1159 (1998) 'affirms that MINURCA may take action to ensure its security and freedom of movement'. This mission was successfully completed in February 2000; the Secretary-General said that MINURCA had done much to restore peace and security in the CAR and to create conditions conducive to the successful conduct of national

---

[193] For example, UN Publications, *The Blue Helmets: A Review of United Nations Peacekeeping* (3rd edn, 1996) at 60, 84.

elections, the restructuring of the security forces, the training of the
national police, and the launching of major economic and social reforms.
The Secretary-General said that it showed how much could be achieved
by peacekeeping operations in Africa with the cooperation and political
will of the parties, their commitment to peace and national reconciliation,
a clear mandate, appropriate resources, and the strong and consistent
support of the international community. It had also broken new ground
through its close cooperation with international financial institutions to
promote political and financial stability.[194] However, the situation deteriorated; there was a series of attempted coups and in 2003 there was a successful coup.[195] The situation remained unstable, and the conflict in Darfur
spilled over into the CAR and Chad. In 2007 a new UN/EU operation was
established in the CAR and Chad to supplement the new AU/UN force
in Darfur.[196] These operations would be deployed almost to the centre of
Africa over extended supply lines in inhospitable terrain. Without a viable
ceasefire and political process there was a real risk that hostilities might
continue.[197]

Thus it seems that where there is no express reference to the use of force
in a resolution then a peacekeeping force will have the right to use force
in self-defence and possibly also in the implementation of its mission. For
example, UNMEE between Ethiopia and Eritrea and MINUCI within
Côte D'Ivoire were traditional peacekeeping operations. They were established under resolutions not passed under Chapter VII and which did not
authorize force under Chapter VII or even make any reference to self-
defence or other use of force. UNMEE was a force of 4,200 troops set up to
monitor the cessation of hostilities and the redeployment of troops after
an *Agreement on the Cessation of Hostilities* had brought to an end the conflict which had broken out again between the parties in 2000.[198] In Côte
d'Ivoire MINUCI was a limited military liaison force with a mandate to
facilitate the implementation by the Ivoirian parties of the *Linas-Marcoussis
Agreement* (2003), which had ended an attempt by rebels to overthrow the
government.[199]

In more complex operations the Security Council has employed a
range of different formulae in its resolutions without any discussion of
the choice of formula in a particular case. There is no obvious reason for

[194] UN Press Release GA/SPD/164, 18 October 1999.
[195] Keesings (2001) 44142, 44494, (2002) 44715, 44926, (2003) 45276).
[196] See 340 below.
[197] Speech of Under-Secretary-General to Fourth Committee, GA/SPD/382, 31 October
2007.
[198] SC Res 1312 (2000), 1320 (2000), 1430 (2002), 1466 (2003), 1507 (2003).
[199] It was set up under SC Res 1479 (2003) in accordance with the Secretary-General's recommendations in his Report, S/2003/374. Initially classified as a peacekeeping force, it was
later re-labelled as a political mission.

the diversity, and there have been calls for more clarity in this regard. In marked contrast to UNMEE and MINUCI, the peacekeeping forces created for Sierra Leone and the DRC were established in much less promising circumstances and ran into serious difficulties. They were expressly given wide responsibilities under Chapter VII and authorized 'to take the necessary action' to ensure the security and freedom of movement of their personnel, and also within their capabilities and areas of deployment to offer protection to civilians under imminent threat of physical violence.[200] Later the mandate of the force in the DRC, MONUC, was expanded; in Resolution 1493 (2003), passed under Chapter VII, the Security Council authorized MONUC 'to take the necessary measures' also to contribute to the improvement of the security conditions in which humanitarian assistance is provided and 'to use all necessary means to fulfil its mandate' in certain regions of the DRC. This mandate was adjusted in Resolutions 1565 (2004) and 1756 (2007), also passed under Chapter VII, which authorized MONUC to 'use all necessary means' to carry out certain of the tasks listed in its mandate. In 2004 the resolutions establishing UNOCI in Côte d'Ivoire and ONUB in Burundi were both passed under Chapter VII and each resolution authorized the peacekeeping force to 'use all necessary means to carry out its mandate'.[201]

Resolution 1590 (2005) creating a peacekeeping force in Sudan, after a comprehensive peace agreement had finally been concluded between the north and the south to end their long civil war, was not passed under Chapter VII. But the preamble did refer to the situation in Sudan as constituting a threat to international peace and security. And within the resolution the Security Council acted under Chapter VII to authorize UNMIS to 'take the necessary action' to protect UN personnel, ensure their security and freedom of movement and that of humanitarian workers, and to protect civilians under imminent threat of physical violence. The Resolution creating a hybrid AU/UN force in Darfur followed the same pattern. In contrast UNMIL, the 'UN stabilization force' set up in Liberia in 2003 to support implementation of a ceasefire agreement, was created under Chapter VII to create a secure and stable environment throughout Liberia.[202] Although it was given a wide mandate including the duty to protect UN personnel, to ensure the security and freedom of movement of its personnel and to protect civilians under imminent threat of physical violence, there was no reference to 'necessary means' or 'necessary action'. Again, when the mandate of UNIFIL in Lebanon was expanded after the

---

[200] SC Res 1270 (1999), SC Res 1291 (2000). See 312 below.
[201] SC Res 1528 (2004), SC Res 1545 (2004).
[202] SC Res 1497 (2003), 1509 (2003); Secretary-General's Reports S/2003/875 para 53; S/2003/1175.

Israeli invasion of 2006, Resolution 1701 (2006) made no express reference to Chapter VII, but did determine in the preamble that the situation was a threat to international peace and security. It authorized UNIFIL 'to take necessary action' to ensure that its area of operations was not utilized for hostile activities of any kind, to resist attempts by forceful means to prevent it from discharging its duties, and to protect UN personnel and civilians. The resolution makes clear that the authorization is 'in support of a request from the Government of Lebanon'. Despite the absence of express Chapter VII authorization, the enhanced force was nevertheless given robust rules of engagement.[203]

There is thus considerable diversity in the language of the Security Council for the authorization of force going beyond self-defence.[204] The ongoing Peace Operations 2010 reform project is in the process of trying to establish general doctrine on the use of force by peacekeeping operations, but this is proving a controversial enterprise.[205]

REFORM OF UN PEACEKEEPING

The UN has clearly experienced problems in its attempts to provide effective peacekeeping in hostile environments; there is an unresolved, and perhaps unresolvable, controversy about the proper role of peacekeeping forces in civil conflicts, a tension between impartiality and effectiveness. The UN Secretary-General set up the *Brahimi Panel* to examine UN peacekeeping because the 'UN simply could not continue to conduct business as usual when it came to peacekeeping operations. Too many times, in too many places, over the past decade, inadequate mandates and insufficient means and Headquarters support had led to calamities for the weak and vulnerable people the Organization sought to serve, for the brave and committed peacekeepers in the field, and for the Organization itself.'[206] In fact many of the Report's recommendations were not new; the Panel followed earlier calls for change by the Lessons Learned Units, the

---

[203] Report of the Secretary-General, S/2006/670 para 26.

[204] In the 2007 session of the Special Committee on Peacekeeping Operations Australia commented that 'the language of Security Council resolutions on the use of force in peacekeeping operations often led to differing interpretations and inconsistencies in the rules of engagement for peacekeepers and policing elements. It was necessary to examine that issue in order to promote a more systematic approach'. (UN Press Release GA/PK/192, 26 February 2007. On the problems posed by national states' own rules of engagement for UN peacekeeping troops, see Stephens, 'The lawful use of force by peacekeeping forces: the tactical imperative', 12 International Peacekeeping (2005) 157.

[205] See 323 below.

[206] UN Press Release, GA/AB/3414, 30 November 2000.

Special Committee on Peacekeeping and the Secretary-General's own reports.

The *Brahimi Report* and its implementation

The *Brahimi Report* was produced for the 2000 Millennium Summit of the UN Security Council; it provided a far-reaching examination of peacekeeping, and an ambitious set of proposals for reform. The Security Council made a *Declaration on Ensuring an Effective Role for the Security Council in the Maintenance of International Peace and Security, particularly in Africa* in Resolution 1318 (2000) unanimously welcoming the work of the Panel. The Report has had a great influence on the practical and administrative reform of UN peacekeeping.[207] There was a clear political willingness to implement the Brahimi proposals and to avoid what the Secretary-General warned would be a 'crisis of credibility' for the UN if changes were not made. Many of the practical proposals for institutional change have been implemented and have had a major impact in the transformation of the Department of Peacekeeping. Progress has also been made in speeding up the deployment of peacekeeping forces. The original plan for a standing UN army able to take enforcement action under Article 43 agreements has not been revived, but the UN has established a standby arrangements system of peacekeeping forces; over eighty states have made standby arrangements.[208] This has helped the UN to come nearer to meeting the goal set by the *Brahimi Report* of securing rapid deployment of peacekeeping forces: 30 days for simple operations and 90 days for more complex operations.[209]

The *Brahimi Report* pointed out the difficulties faced by the UN in securing troops for peacekeeping. As the Security Council became more active in peacekeeping and involved in more complex, dangerous, and expensive operations, it became difficult for it to find enough troops and personnel. A Security Council resolution mandating an operation was no longer a guarantee that the operation would be carried out as authorized. This was notoriously the experience in Yugoslavia and Rwanda, and subsequently also in Sierra Leone and the DRC. In contrast to the long tradition of developed states providing the bulk of troops for UN peacekeeping operations during the UN's first fifty years, in recent years a

---

[207] On the implementation of the *Brahimi Report*, see the Reports of the Special Committee on Peacekeeping Operations, A/56/863 (2002); A/57/767 (2003) and the Reports of the Secretary-General, A/55/502 (2000); A/57/711 (2003); GA Res 56/225 (2002); GA Res 57/129 (2002); GA Res 57/336 (2003); SC Res 1318 (2000), 1327 (2000), 1353 (2001).

[208] <www.un.org/Depts/dpko/milad/fgs2/unsas_files/sba.htm>.

[209] Special Committee on Peacekeeping Operations Report, A/57/767, para 80, (2003); UN Press Release GA/PK/178, 4 March 2003; Report of Secretary-General, A/57/711 (2003).

majority of troops have been contributed by developing countries.[210] The Secretary-General had also expressed concern that peacekeeping duties were not shared equally by member states, and that not all missions mandated by the Security Council received equal or even adequate support. Many delegations had deplored the 'commitment gap', the gap between the commitments undertaken in Security Council Resolutions and the actual contributions of states in practice; the lack of political will to contribute to peacekeeping operations in Africa was striking.[211]

In his first report on the implementation of the *Brahimi Report* the Secretary-General said that peacekeeping was the responsibility of all member states, first and foremost the members of the Security Council. The performance of the UN in this area would not improve until member states, and particularly those possessing the greatest capacity and means to do so, were ready to participate.[212] But Security Council Resolution 1327 (2000), passed in response to the *Brahimi Report,* reflects the lack of unanimity among states as to the need for greater permanent member participation in UN peacekeeping; while it recognized that the problem of the commitment gap required the assumption by all states of the shared responsibility to support UN peacekeeping, not surprisingly given the composition of the Security Council, the resolution stopped short of expressly calling on permanent members in particular or developed states in general to provide more troops. The resolution seems to accept that the shared responsibility could take the form of logistical support or provision of equipment. Developed states apparently advocate a division of labour: in complex and dangerous operations, especially those in Africa, developing states will provide troops and developed states will provide financial and logistical support.[213] Many states still call on developed states to provide more troops for peacekeeping operations, but they have preferred to take part in UN-authorized Chapter VII operations as 'coalitions of the willing' and to offer direct assistance to governments or regional organizations.[214]

---

[210] The *Brahimi Report,* paras 103–104, 60–61.

[211] UN Press Release GA/AB/3414, 30 November 2000. See also the comments of the Secretary-General in *In Larger Freedom,* UN doc A/59/2005 para 111.

[212] Report of Secretary-General S/2000/1081.

[213] India has complained of this situation. In a debate on peacekeeping it said that the UN should do more for Africa instead of seeking to disengage by sub-contracting peacekeeping to regional arrangements. Developed states should participate in peacekeeping operations in Africa. Other states also called on developed states to contribute troops. (UN Press Release GA/PK/177). These calls have been repeated many times: see, for example, Fourth Committee debates, GA/SPD/353, 20 October 2006, GA/SPD/383, 1 November 2007, GA/SPD/384, 2 November 2007, GA/SPD/385, 5 November 2007.

[214] See Gray, 'Peacekeeping and enforcement action in Africa: the role of Europe and the obligations of multilateralism', 31 Review of International Studies (2005) 207.

The *Brahimi Report* also called for a new three-way relationship between the Security Council, the Secretariat and troop-contributing countries (TCCs) on the basis that this would help to address such problems as commitment gaps in the contribution of troops or shortcomings in the operations. The need for greater consultation with TCCs had already been discussed by the Security Council in the past; the increased risks involved in peacekeeping in the former Yugoslavia and Somalia led TCCs to call for a greater input into decision-making.[215] The *Brahimi Report* suggested improvements in the consultation process. Security Council Resolution 1327 (2000) accordingly underlined the importance of an improved system of consultation between TCCs, the Secretary-General and the Security Council in order to foster a common understanding of the situation on the ground, of the mission's mandate and of its implementation. The Council agreed to strengthen the existing system of consultations, in particular during the implementation phase of an operation, or when considering a change in, or renewal of, or completion of, a peacekeeping operation, or when a rapid deterioration on the ground threatens the peace and safety of UN peacekeepers. The seven-page Resolution 1353 (2001) accordingly set out a new system for closer collaboration and involvement with TCCs. Despite the significant progress made, it was clear in Security Council debates that there are fundamental splits as to how much say TCCs should have in peacekeeping operations. Is the right of TCCs merely to communication and consultation or is there a more substantive right to participation? The permanent members stressed that the powers of the Security Council should not be undermined. But if developing states' troops are to die because developed states are not willing to send their troops to UN peacekeeping operations in Africa, there may be a political price to pay. As Jordan said, the distribution of the burden in dangerous operations was uneven; as a major troop contributor it was not prepared to be the servant of others, blindly obeying, unquestioning.[216] But finding the right balance is problematic; there is a danger that TCCs might use the process cynically or hold up decision-making. The TCCs are still calling for a greater role in decision-making.[217]

The second main priority for reform which emerged from the *Brahimi Report* was the need for well-conceived and clearly defined peacekeeping mandates. This clearly raises fundamental questions about

---

[215] UN doc S/2001/21; S/PRST/1994/62; S/PRST/1996/13; SC 4527th meeting (2002).
[216] SC 4257th meeting (2001).
[217] See, for example, Fourth Committee debates, GA/SPD/353, 20 October 2006, GA/SPD/383, 1 November 2007, GA/SPD/384, 2 November 2007, GA/SPD/385, 5 November 2007; Special Committee on Peacekeeping Operations 2007 session, GA/PK/193, 27 February 2007.

the nature of peacekeeping. The *Brahimi Report* itself made a case for 'robust peacekeeping', but it has subsequently become clear that this was not acceptable to those who support a more limited concept of peacekeeping, based on the traditional principles of impartiality, consent and self-defence. The call for bigger forces, better equipped and more costly, able to pose a credible deterrent, contrasts with the traditional non-threatening presence that characterized traditional peacekeeping.[218] This question about the principles governing the use of force by peacekeeping operations later proved controversial in discussion of the Capstone Document to be adopted as part of the Peace Operations 2010 reform project.[219]

The *Brahimi Report* recommended that the Security Council adopt only clear, credible and achievable mandates for peacekeeping forces. This has been a concern for many years and the apparent simplicity of this aim masks the fact that it is inextricably linked to fundamental questions about the proper role and legal powers of peacekeeping forces. The experience of the UN in the former Yugoslavia, Somalia and Rwanda led the *Brahimi Report* to recommend reform. UNPROFOR's mandate had changed many times, Chapter VII of the Charter was used to give powers to UNPROFOR, peacekeeping and enforcement action were combined. These frequent changes of mandate reflected the lack of agreement in the Security Council on the strategy to be adopted. Some of the problems of UNPROFOR in Yugoslavia may be seen as an instance of failures occurring 'because the Security Council and the member states crafted and supported ambiguous, inconsistent and under-funded mandates and then stood back and watched as they failed'.[220] After the tragedies of Somalia and Rwanda the UN Lessons Learned Unit again identified the failure to provide a clear and workable mandate as a serious problem for the UN peacekeeping forces. First, the experience of Somalia between 1992–95 led to the conclusion that the operation's mandate was vague, changed frequently during the process and open to myriad interpretations. The mandate changed from protecting the delivery of humanitarian assistance, to encouraging and assisting in political reconciliation, to establishing and maintaining a secure environment, to capturing a leader of one of the factions and later to encouraging negotiations with that same leader. The Unit said that these mandates were in many respects contradictory, and most often the changes were decided on with little explanation to member states, TCCs, humanitarian agencies or the Somali people.[221] Second,

---

[218] *Brahimi Report* paras 48–51.
[219] See 323 below.
[220] *Brahimi Report* para 266.
[221] The Comprehensive Report on Lessons Learned from UNOSOM; <www.un.org/Depts/dpko/lessons/somalia.htm>.

with regard to Rwanda, the Lessons Learned Unit reported that a lightly equipped and armed peacekeeping force of only 400 troops had been left without a clear mandate or the means or the necessary support to stop the massacres of 1994. From inception to withdrawal UNAMIR was always one step behind the realities of the situation. On the basis of this and other experience,[222] the *Brahimi Report* made four specific recommendations: (i) that, before the Security Council agrees to implement a ceasefire or peace agreement with a UN-led peacekeeping operation, the Council assures itself that the agreement meets conditions, such as consistency with international human rights standards and practicability of the specified tasks and time lines; (ii) the Security Council should leave in a draft form resolutions authorizing missions with sizable troop levels until such time as the Secretary-General has firm commitments of troops and other critical mission support elements from member states; (iii) Security Council resolutions should meet the requirements of peacekeeping operations when they deploy into potentially dangerous situations, especially the need for a clear chain of command and unity of effort; (iv) the Secretariat must tell the Security Council what it needs to know, not what it wants to hear, when formulating or changing mission mandates.[223]

Following the *Brahimi Report*, the Security Council in Resolution 1327 (2000) resolved 'to give peacekeeping operations clear, credible and achievable mandates'. It undertook to ensure that the mandated tasks of peacekeeping operations were appropriate to the situation on the ground, taking account of such factors as the prospects of success, the potential need to protect civilians and the possibility that some parties may seek to undermine peace through violence; it also emphasized that the rules of engagement of UN peacekeeping forces should be fully consistent with the legal basis of the operation and with any relevant Security Council resolutions, and clearly set out the circumstances in which force may be used to protect all mission components and personnel. This resolution has been described as creating a new doctrine of peacekeeping, but subsequent experience leaves it open to doubt how far it can have any significant practical impact.

Some claim that reform of the Security Council is a precondition for the implementation of the *Brahimi Report*. Although the developing world dominated the Security Council's agenda, developing countries had little say in its decisions.[224] Others urged member states not to hold the implementation of the Panel's recommendations hostage to the resolution

---

[222] See Gray, 'Peacekeeping after the *Brahimi Report*: Is there a Crisis of Credibility for the UN?', 6 Journal of Conflict and Security Law (2001) 267.

[223] *Brahimi Report*, para 64.

[224] UN Press Release GA/SPD/200, 9 November 2000.

of this issue.[225] The intractable issue of the expansion of the Security Council to make it a more representative body has been the subject of serious debate for the last fifteen years. But the High-level Panel set up by the Secretary-General was unable to agree on proposals on this issue,[226] and the World Summit Outcome Document did not address this issue.[227] It may be true that the Security Council as currently constituted is guilty of the charges of double standards levelled at it over its treatment of Africa, and that a changed membership would alter the focus of its concerns, but unless a reformed Security Council can secure resources from developed states it will not be any more able to take effective action in Africa than it is now.[228] The problems with the implementation of these apparently reasonable recommendations in practice were very apparent with regard to the UN operations in Sierra Leone and the DRC.

Sierra Leone and the DRC

In Sierra Leone a military coup in May 1997 led to disorder; a small UN force, UNOMSIL, was sent in to supplement an existing ECOMOG regional force.[229] The democratically elected President Kabbah was restored in May 1998, but the opposition RUF, led by Sankoh, did not fully accept the election result and disorder continued. After the *Lomé Peace Agreement* of July 1999 UNOMSIL was replaced by UNAMSIL, a larger force of up to 6,000 military personnel, to cooperate with the government in the implementation of the agreement and to assist in the implementation of the disarmament, demobilization and reintegration plan.[230] The Secretary-General had recommended that the new force should be large and capable and should operate on the basis of robust rules of engagement.[231] Resolution 1270 (1999), adopted unanimously, was not itself passed under Chapter VII, but in paragraph 14 the Security Council decided under Chapter VII that in the discharge of its mandate UNAMSIL may take the necessary action to ensure the security and freedom

---

[225] UN Press Release GA/SPD/200, Report of Secretary-General S/2000/1081.

[226] They proposed two different models for reform: High-level Panel Report, A/59/565. The divisive issues are the size of the expanded Council, which states should become new members, whether they should be permanent members and, if so, whether they should have the veto. See also the recent General Assembly debates on SC reform: UN Press Releases GA/10656 – 8, 12–14 November 2007; Schrijver, Reforming the UN SC in pursuance of collective security', 12 Journal of Conflict and Security Law (2007) 127.

[227] UN doc A/59/2005.

[228] See note 307 above.

[229] See 411 below; 1997 UNYB 129; <www.un.org/Depts/DPKO/Missions/unosil>.

[230] 1999 UNYB 152 at 164.

[231] Reports of the Secretary-General on UNOMSIL, S/1999/836, S/1999/1003; Report of the Secretary-General on UNAMSIL, S/1999/1223; UN Press Release SC/6742, 22 October 1999.

of movement of its personnel. It also went further, apparently in response to the Rwanda experience; it also authorized UNAMSIL 'within its capabilities and areas of deployment, to afford protection to civilians under imminent threat of physical violence'. In the debate on this resolution Argentina commented on the use of Chapter VII; it said that it was appropriate that the draft resolution strengthened UNAMSIL's rules of engagement with the additional authority of Chapter VII of the Charter. The protection of civilians under Chapter VII was a pertinent development. It introduced a new legal and moral dimension. It indicated that the Council had learned from its own experiences and would not be unresponsive when innocent civilians were attacked.[232]

Later the Security Council expanded the role and size of UNAMSIL in order to enable it to take over ECOMOG's role. Resolution 1289 (2000) again invoked Chapter VII in the body of the resolution (paragraph 10) in order to revise UNAMSIL's mandate to authorize it to provide security at key locations, important intersections, and major airports; facilitate the free flow of people, goods and humanitarian assistance; and provide security in the disarmament process. The government of Sierra Leone welcomed the fact that the revised mandate and additional responsibilities of UNAMSIL were fully backed by Chapter VII of the Charter. His government regarded as one of the most significant provisions of the resolution the Council's decision to authorize UNAMSIL to afford protection to civilians under imminent threat of physical violence.[233] The UK stressed that UNAMSIL was not a Chapter VII peace enforcement operation but said that it was necessary to adopt a robust and serious stance against possible threats.[234] The Secretary-General said that the force would function with the cooperation of the parties, but, through its military presence, capabilities, and posture, would be able to deter attempts to derail the peace process. However, in practice UNAMSIL was not able to fulfil this wide mandate when the RUF opposition forces resorted to violence again in 2000.[235] Hundreds of UN forces were taken hostage by the RUF in May 2000. The Secretary-General said that UNAMSIL had been designed as a peacekeeping force and was not equipped for an enforcement operation. It was attacked by one of the parties that had pledged cooperation before it was properly deployed.[236]

The emergency Security Council debate revealed a division between states. Some, including several West African states, called for the revision of the mandate of UNAMSIL to make it into a Chapter VII force

[232] SC 4054th meeting (1999); UN Press Release SC/6742, 22 October 1999.
[233] SC 4099th meeting (2000); UN Press Release SC/6801, 7 February 2000.
[234] Ibid.
[235] 2000 UNYB 195; SC 4139th meeting (2000); UN Press Release SC/6857, 11 May 2000.
[236] Ibid. For further discussion of the lessons from UNAMSIL's experience, see UN Press Releases SC/7456, 18 July 2002, GA/PK/178, 4 March 2003.

with greater powers; others argued that the existing mandate with its already wide powers under Chapter VII was adequate, and that the immediate problem was to ensure that the mission had the capacity to carry out the tasks this mandate imposed.[237] The Security Council sub-sequently strengthened UNAMSIL's mandate in the face of continued non-cooperation by the RUF, but its later resolutions were still not passed under Chapter VII and no further reference to Chapter VII was made in the body of its resolutions. Resolution 1313 (passed unanimously in August 2000 and without further public debate in the Security Council) acknowledged the difficulties UNAMSIL had faced. With unprecedented openness the Security Council said in the resolution that 'the RUF offensive had revealed serious inherent weaknesses in the mission's structure, command and control and resources'.

Resolution 1313 (2000) therefore strengthened the mandate of UNAMSIL: it was to maintain the security of certain crucial regions; to deter and, where necessary, decisively counter the threat of RUF attack by responding robustly to any hostile actions or threat of imminent and direct use of force; to assist the government to extend state authority, restore law and order, and, within its capabilities and areas of deployment, to afford protection to civilians under threat of imminent physical violence; to patrol main access routes to the capital in order to dominate ground, ensure freedom of movement and facilitate the provision of humanitarian assistance; to assist in the promotion of the political process. Despite these ambitious functions, the Security Council made no further reference to Chapter VII, beyond that in its earlier resolutions on UNAMSIL.[238] It was only when UNAMSIL was given a new role to facilitate the smooth holding of elections in Resolution 1389 (2002) that the Security Council once more referred expressly to Chapter VII in reiterating its authorization in Resolutions 1270 (1999) and 1289 (2000) to take the necessary action for fulfil its new tasks.

---

[237] 2000 UNYB 189; UN Press Release SC/6857, 11 May 2000. In 2000 the UN force was supplemented by UK troops, present at the invitation of the government of Sierra Leone to allow for the safe evacuation of British nationals. The UK made it clear that UK forces would not be deployed in a combat role as part of UNAMSIL, but their presence on the ground helped to stabilize the situation; they also provided 'technical military advice' to the UN and to the government (Statement by the Secretary of State for Defence in the House of Commons, 15 May 2000; Keesings (2000) 43552, 43613). The UK then kept a substantial force in Sierra Leone to train the national army (Secretary-General's Reports S/2000/751 para 20, S/2000/832 para 12, S/2000/1055 para 18, 47, S/2000/1199 para 30; S/2001/228 para 18; S/2001/627 para 24; the UK force was withdrawn in July 2002 (Keesings (2002) 44888.

[238] Again, Resolution 1346 (2001) which further increased the authorized size of the military component of UNAMSIL to 17,500, and further revised UNAMSIL's concept of operations (in accordance with the Secretary-General's Report, S/2001/228) made no further reference to Chapter VII.

But the Security Council's resolutions and the Secretary-General's Reports reflect the problems in securing adequate troops for UNAMSIL.[239] Resolution 1313 (2000) paragraph 6 stressed that the successful achievement of the objectives of the mission would depend on the provision to UNAMSIL of fully equipped, complete units, with the required capabilities, effective command and control structure and capacity, a single chain of command, adequate resources and the commitment to implement the mandate of the mission in full. Member states were still not immediately willing to contribute the authorized number of troops. Resolution 1334 (2002) again strongly urged all states in a position to do so seriously to consider contributing peacekeeping forces for Sierra Leone.[240]

The peace process based on the November 2000 *Abuja Peace Agreement*[241] made good progress in 2002 and the government continued gradually to extend its authority throughout its territory; elections were successfully held in May 2002.[242] The Security Council accordingly planned to reduce the military component of UNAMSIL and to end the operation by December 2004.[243] There was a brief interruption in this process because of fears for the stability of the region, caused by events in Liberia (under sanction by the Security Council for its intervention in support of the RUF opposition forces in Sierra Leone) and Côte d'Ivoire. But the reduction in UNAMSIL then resumed and the operation terminated successfully at the end of 2005.[244]

---

[239] The Secretary-General appealed to states, in particular to those with large and well-equipped armed forces, to participate in UNAMSIL with troops and equipment (Report of the Secretary-General S/2000/1055; UN Press Release SC 6946, 3 November 2000). As the *Brahimi Report* pointed out at para 104–6 no developed state currently contributed troops to the most difficult UN-led peacekeeping operations from a security perspective, UNAMSIL and MONUC. A mission such as UNAMSIL would probably not have faced the difficulties it did in Spring 2000 had it been provided with forces as strong as those then keeping the peace as part of KFOR in Kosovo. Yet the likelihood of a KFOR-type operation being deployed in Africa in the near future seemed remote.

[240] The Security Council did not increase UNASMIL's mandate until it secured commitments of more troops. The Secretary-General in several reports called for an expansion of the mandate of UNAMSIL to make it more effective, but he made it clear that more troops would be needed for this. In the absence of commitments of more troops the Security Council simply recorded its intent to increase the mandate. It did not actually do so until Resolution 1346 (2001) when it revised the concept of operations and authorized a force of 17,500 troops.

[241] Keesings (2000) 43840.

[242] The UK sent 300 troops to Sierra Leone to assist the government in February 2003, because of its concern at possible destabilisation from Liberia (Keesings (2003) 45231).

[243] SC Res 1436 (2002), SC Res 1492 (2003), Secretary-General's Report S/2002/987.

[244] The Security Council commended the valuable contribution made by UNAMSIL to Sierra Leone's recovery from conflict over the last six years and to its progress towards peace, democracy and prosperity. Sierra Leone said that the Mission was a testimony to the triangular partnership—regional organizations, troop contributors and the UN, UN Press Release SC/8592, 20 December 2006. However, the country was still fragile and the new

Similar references to Chapter VII were made in the Security Council resolutions providing for a peacekeeping force in the DRC. Chapter 3 of this book described the outbreak of conflict in the DRC, the overthrow of President Mobutu, and the intervention of Uganda, Rwanda, Namibia, Angola, and Zimbabwe in the fighting in 1998. The Security Council expressed concern, but took no further action until the conclusion of the Lusaka Ceasefire Agreement in July 1999. This agreement proposed the establishment of an appropriate force to be constituted, facilitated, and deployed by the UN in collaboration with the OAU.[245] The Secretary-General pointed out that in order to be effective any UN peacekeeping mission in the DRC would have to be large and expensive. It would require the deployment of thousands of international troops. It would face tremendous difficulties and be beset by risks. Deployment would be slow. The huge size of the country, the degradation of its infrastructure, the intensity of its climate, the intractable nature of some aspects of its conflict, the number of parties, the high levels of mutual suspicion, the large population displacements, the ready availability of small arms, the general climate of impunity and the substitute of armed force for the rule of law in much of the territory combine to make the DRC a highly complex environment for peacekeeping.[246]

The preliminary deployment of a small number of UN liaison officers deepened the Secretary-General's appreciation of the difficulties. The Security Council went on to establish an observer mission, MONUC, but the peace agreement remained fragile and the situation deteriorated.[247] Six months after the peace agreement the Security Council passed Resolution 1291 in February 2000, providing for the expansion of the mandate of MONUC and of the size of the force up to 5,537 military personnel. It was to monitor the implementation of the ceasefire agreement, to investigate violations of the ceasefire; and to develop an action plan for the overall implementation of the ceasefire agreement with particular emphasis on disengagement, disarmament, demobilization and resettlement. In paragraph 8 the Security Council acted under Chapter VII in deciding that MONUC might 'take the necessary action in the areas of deployment of its infantry battalions and, as it deems within its capabilities', to protect UN personnel, facilities, installations, and equipment; ensure the security and freedom of movement of its personnel; and protect civilians under imminent threat of physical violence. Many states expressed concern about this

Peacebuilding Commission took on the task of working to ensure that it did not relapse into conflict.

[245] Lusaka Ceasefire Agreement, S/1999/790.
[246] Report of the Secretary-General on the UN Preliminary Deployment in the DRC, S/1999/790.
[247] <http://www.un.org/Depts/dpko/monuc/monucM>.

resolution; it had been adopted as a compromise. It fell far short of matching the mission's mandate with the resources needed for it to succeed. The deployment of a MONUC peacekeeping operation might create inflated and unrealistic expectations.[248]

In fact fighting prevented full deployment; the prolonged fighting was funded by the rich resources of the DRC, plundered by all outside states and all groups involved in the conflict.[249] There were repeated delays and MONUC's mandate was adjusted many times in the light of developments in the DRC.[250] MONUC faced serious problems in securing its full complement of 5,537 troops, and the Security Council called for more troops to be provided.[251] Significant progress in the implementation of the *Lusaka Ceasefire Agreement* was finally made in 2002 when Rwanda and Uganda concluded separate agreements with the DRC agreeing once more to withdraw their troops.[252] But conflicts continued between armed groups in many different areas of the huge country. Nevertheless the various DRC parties eventually concluded transition agreements on power-sharing and the creation of a new constitution; they endorsed these in April 2003.[253]

In the light of these favourable developments and of encouraging developments on the ground, including the withdrawal of 20,000 Rwandan troops and also of troops from those states which had supported the government of the DRC,[254] the Security Council passed Resolution 1445 (2002). This expanded MONUC to 8,700 and further revised its mandate to create two robust task forces to help with disarmament, demobilization and repatriation; it was also to continue to monitor the withdrawal of foreign troops from the DRC. But there were still serious problems; armed groups continued to plunder the natural resources, and fighting in the gold-rich Ituri province escalated in 2003. The 700-strong section of MONUC stationed in the city of Bunia in the Ituri province was not able to provide protection to the civilians who had suffered during months of terrible fighting between the armed groups. The Security Council eventually sent in a member state force (IEMF) as a temporary measure at the request of the Secretary-General.[255]

---

[248] SC 4104th meeting (2001); UN Press Release SC/6809, 24 February 2001.
[249] See reports of the Panel of Experts on the illegal exploitation of the natural resources of the DRC: S/2001/357; S/2001/1072; S/2002/1146.
[250] SC Res 1341 (2001), 1355 (2001), 1376 (2001), 1399 (2002).
[251] SC Res 1417 (2002). The DRC itself proposed the increase of MONUC to 20,000 (UN Press Release SC/7105, 24 July 2001).
[252] *Pretoria Agreement* with Rwanda, 30 July 2002, UN Press Release SC/7483, 15 August 2002, 41 ILM (2002) 1053; *Luanda Agreement* with Uganda, 6 September 2002 (UN Press Release SC/7498, 6 September 2002).
[253] UN Press Releases, SC/7611, 18 December 2002; SC/7699, 20 March 2003; SG/SM/8654, 2 April 2003.
[254] Report of Secretary-General, S/2002/1180.
[255] See 336 below.

In July 2003 in Resolution 1493 it for the first time put MONUC in the context of Chapter VII and authorized it to use 'all necessary means' to fulfil its mandate in the eastern part of the country where armed conflict continued.[256] The overall strength of MONUC was to be increased to 10,800. The new Ituri Brigade of MONUC took over from the IEMF on 1 September 2003.[257] A government of national unity was installed in July 2003 and it looked as if the prolonged conflict which had left 4.7 million dead was finally drawing to an end.[258] However, the violence and instability continued. The Secretary-General was outspoken about his serious concerns about the mandate given to MONUC in Resolution 1493 (2003). He said that the interpretation of this resolution had been a major challenge for MONUC. The establishment of the peacekeeping mandate under Chapter VII had raised expectations that the Mission would enforce the peace throughout the country. However, there was a wide gap between such expectations and the Mission's capacity to fulfil them. This gap had put UN personnel at risk. Moreover, the lack of specificity as to its tasks under the resolution did not lend itself to the most effective use of the resources provided to the Mission. He therefore made proposals for the expansion of MONUC and the major revision of its mandate.[259] The Security Council accordingly passed Resolution 1565 (2004) under Chapter VII; this revised the mandate and also significantly increased the size of MONUC by 5,900, but this increase still fell far below the figure recommended by the Secretary-General.[260] The first democratic elections in more than forty years were successfully held in 2006; an EU force assisted a further expanded MONUC in keeping the peace.[261] MONUC was subsequently given a revised mandate to assist the government in the establishment of a stable security environment.[262] But hopes that MONUC could be wound up in 2007 were frustrated, first, by the resort to violence of supporters of the defeated Presidential

---

[256] UN Press Release SC/7828, 28 July 2003. It also repeated its Chapter VII authorization in Resolution 1291, para. 8, and added new authorization to protect humanitarian workers and to contribute to the improvement of security conditions in which humanitarian assistance was provided.
[257] UN Press Release SG/SM/8842, 2 September 2003.
[258] UN Press Release SG/SM/8785, 17 July 2003.
[259] Report of the Secretary-General on MONUC, S/2004/650.
[260] Ibid. Again in 2005 the Security Council authorized a further increase of 300 rather than the 2,580 requested by the Secretary-General in response to the attacks on MONUC and the increased hostilities by armed groups and militias in the east, UN Press Release SC/8491, 6 September 2005, Special Report of the Secretary-General on elections in the DRC, S/2005/320, 26 May 2005.
[261] See Chapter 8 below.
[262] SC Res 1756 (2007).

candidate in the capital, Kinshasa, and, more seriously, by the growing crisis in the east.[263]

This practice shows that agreement on clear, credible and achievable mandates is not a simple matter. The *Brahimi Report* stressed both the need for a robust force in the face of non-cooperation and the need for the Security Council to secure guarantees of adequate resources before establishing a peacekeeping force. A force must be large and strong enough to cope with resistance on the ground; no force should be deployed until it has adequate resources for the performance of its mandate. The impact of these two factors in combination may well be inaction, although this was clearly not the intent of the *Brahimi Report*. The other requirements for a clear mandate which have been identified also appear to run the danger of inherent contradiction: the competing requirements of clarity and flexibility, the need for robust missions on the one hand but to avoid mission creep on the other, indicate that clear, credible and achievable mandates will be difficult in practice. The apparently simple and reasonable recommendations of Brahimi are actually far from straightforward. The experiences in Africa show the serious problems facing UN peacekeeping.

Recent peacekeeping operations

It has proved easier to stipulate conditions for successful peacekeeping than to live up to them in practice. The relation of peacekeeping and Chapter VII is still problematic. The use of Chapter VII in resolutions on peacekeeping has raised expectations, but the repeated failure by member states to establish realistic mandates and to provide the necessary resources has led peacekeeping forces into difficulty. Criticism has been directed at the UN and its forces, criticism that should often more appropriately be directed at member states. More recent peacekeeping operations—again those in Africa—have encountered some of the same problems that MONUC and UNAMSIL experienced. Thus, ONUB, established in 2004 in Burundi after a long internal conflict between a largely Tutsi army and a Hutu rebel group, was created as a robust force with an extensive mandate, including the authorization under Chapter VII to use all necessary means to carry out its mandate. It was given robust rules of engagement in view of the security situation on the ground where one group remained outside the peace process and intermittent fighting continued.[264] But the Secretary-General complained that deployment was delayed because of problems with securing enough troops to implement

---

[263] Report of the Secretary-General, S/2007/671.
[264] Report of the Secretary-General, S/2004/210.

the mandate.[265] However, these were not serious delays and the operation proved successful. With its assistance Burundi conducted its first democratic elections for twelve years, the installation of a national government, the disarmament and demobilization of combatants and the creation of integrated defence and police forces. The operation terminated at the end of 2005.[266]

The operation in Liberia also ran into some difficulties. UNMIL was established after a protracted conflict which had led to the displacement of nearly one third of the population. This 15,000-strong force was set up under Chapter VII, but with no express reference to the use of force within the resolution. It was to establish a secure and stable environment. The Secretary-General reminded states of the lessons of the past: 'in planning the structure and deployment of the UN force, emphasis has been placed on incorporating the lessons of past deployment when insufficient and inadequately equipped troops were deployed for peacekeeping duties with disastrous consequences'.[267] But 'the process of generating troops for UNMIL has not proved completely satisfactory'.[268] In particular the Secretary-General found it difficult to secure enough specialist units and helicopters. However, these delays lasted only around six months and the operation then made good progress.[269] But the security situation remained fragile and Liberia was heavily dependent on UNMIL for providing security. The unpredictable situation in neighbouring Côte d'Ivoire also contributed to the insecurity. Accordingly a reduced force was maintained in Liberia.[270]

UNOCI in Côte d'Ivoire experienced more serious problems. This 6,240 multidimensional force was set up under Chapter VII in 2004 after the *Linas-Marcoussis Peace Agreement* was concluded to end the situation in which the country was effectively divided into two, with rebels controlling the north and the government holding the south.[271] Here, as in the DRC and Sierra Leone, there were problems in securing adequate troops at the start of the operation, and in particular the UN found it very difficult to secure the helicopters it required.[272] There were also more serious problems when the Security Council did not accept the repeated pleas of the Secretary-General for an increase in the size of the force to enable

---

[265] Reports of the Secretary-General, S/2004/682, S/2004/902.
[266] Report of the Secretary-General S/2005/728.
[267] Report of the Secretary-General S/2003/875.
[268] Report of the Secretary-General, S/2003/1175.
[269] Reports of the Secretary-General on UNMIL, S/2004/229, S/2004/430.
[270] SC Res 1694 (2006), 1750, 1777 (2007).
[271] 2004 UNYB 170.
[272] The Secretary-General again stressed the crucial issue of resources: Report of the Secretary-General, S/2004/443, para 88. See also, Reports of the Secretary-General, S/2004/697, S/2004/962, S/2005/186, paras 25, 85.

it to carry out its mandate in deteriorating conditions.[273] The Secretary-General argued that an increase was indispensable to enable UNOCI to discharge effectively the multiple responsibilities assigned to it by the Security Council.[274] When the Security Council did authorize increases it never allowed the full number requested by the Secretary-General.[275]

There were also difficulties in establishing a clear, credible and achievable mandate. The situation on the ground deteriorated at the end of 2004 when government forces attacked the French forces and UNOCI in violation of the ceasefire. The Security Council repeatedly modified UNOCI's mandate in an attempt to address the changing situation.[276] As Algeria said in a Security Council debate on the role of UNOCI, it had been created to help implement a peace agreement, but the changing conditions meant that it was led to take up tasks for which it was not prepared.[277] There were delays in the disarmament process and repeated attacks on the UN force and interference with its freedom of movement. Leaders of the various parties repeatedly rejected the peace process and the elections provided for in the *Linas-Marcoussis Peace Agreement* were twice postponed. The situation finally improved in 2006, and UNOCI troops were able to move beyond the separation of the two sides to increasing their presence and mobility throughout the country.[278] In March 2007 the parties concluded the *Ouagadougou Agreement*. This was hailed as a unique turning point: it was the first time that the parties had undertaken dialogue on their own initiative.[279] UNOCI's mandate was accordingly adjusted in Resolution 1765 (2007) to adapt its role to the new phase of relations.

In contrast, UNMIS in Sudan, established in 2005 to support the implementation of the January 2005 *Comprehensive Peace Agreement* which ended the twenty-one year north/south civil war was given a much more limited mandate under Resolution 1590 (2005).[280] It did experience difficulties in obtaining the authorized number of troops;[281] and there were delays in

---

[273] Report of the Secretary-General, S/2004/962 para 64.

[274] Report of the Secretary-General, S/2005/186, paras 25, 85.

[275] Reports of the Secretary-General, S/2005/398, S/2006/2, S/2006/939. There were some divisions between member states on this issue: UN Press Releases SC/8345, 28 March 2005, SC/8522, 13 October 2005.

[276] Reports of the Secretary-General, S/2004/962, S/2005/186, S/2005/398, S/2005/604, S/2006/2, S/2006/821, S/2006/939; UN Press Release SC/8367, 24 April 2005; SC Res 1603, 1609 (2005), SC Res 1633 (2005), 1682 (2006), 1721 (2006), 1739, 1765 (2007).

[277] UN Press Release SC/8345, 28 March 2005.

[278] Report of the Secretary-General, S/2006/939.

[279] Report of the Secretary-General, S/2007/275.

[280] The Secretary-General proposed that it should be a Chapter VI multidimensional force: Report of the Secretary-General S/2005/57. However, the Security Council in Res 1590 (2005) expressly gave it a Chapter VII authorization within the resolution to take the necessary action to protect UN personnel, humanitarian workers and civilians.

[281] Reports of the Secretary-General S/2005/579, S/2005/821.

securing a SOFA with the government of Sudan.[282] However, its initial mandate has survived the challenges posed by the slow progress of the peace process to date.

The hybrid AU/UN force in Darfur also faced difficulties in securing adequate troops. The insistence of the government of Sudan that the force should have a predominantly African character, and the need for specialized forces able to meet the extremely challenging mandate, together posed serious problems for the formation of the force. The Under-Secretary-General for peacekeeping warned that UNAMID still lacked twenty-four helicopters and specialized forces. The overall security situation in Darfur continued to deteriorate and the mission would be at risk if the full force could not be deployed. The security situation on the Chad-Sudan border has also worsened. The UN was experiencing difficulties in negotiating the SOFA with the government. If discussions failed to clear the way to deployment of an effective force the international community would be confronted by hard choices: should the UN move ahead with the deployment of a force that would not make a difference or be able to defend itself?[283]

The difficulties in securing troops and the delayed deployment experienced by most African peacekeeping forces contrast with the enhancement of UNIFIL in 2006. Resolution 1701 (2006), passed unanimously after the Israeli invasion of Lebanon, gave the 2,000-strong force an expanded mandate, better equipment and increased its authorized size to 7,000; the enhanced force was deployed with unprecedented speed. The Secretary-General hailed this as an important milestone for UN peacekeeping: it marked European re-engagement with UN peacekeeping and the organization's first major naval force. Italy, Spain, France and Germany all made major contributions.[284] But the developed states were still reluctant to submit their troops to UN control; they set up a 'strategic military cell' within the DPKO staffed by officers from the TCCs under the nominal supervision of the Under-Secretary-General for Peacekeeping.[285] There was some controversy about this novel arrangement,[286] and the

---

[282] Reports of the Secretary-General S/2005/579, S/2006/160 para 81.

[283] UN Press Release SC/9178, 27 November 2007. See also Reports of the Secretary-General, S/2007/653, S/2007/759; Abass, 'The UN, the AU and the Darfur crisis', 54 Netherlands International Law Review (2007) 416.

[284] *Report of the Secretary-General on the Work of the Organization*, UN doc A/61/1 at para 53; see also GA/SPD/353, 20 October 2006.

[285] UN doc S/2006/9333, 1 December 2006, Report of the Secretary-General, S/2007/641, para 62.

[286] The Special Committee on Peacekeeping stressed the need for equitable treatment of all peacekeeping operations with respect to their needs for adequate military capacity: UN Press Release GA/10605, 24 July 2007. Pakistan argued that the principle of unified command and control under the UN must apply to all missions. Any discrimination and unequal treatment between missions in terms of structure and resource allocations would

Secretary-General was asked by the General Assembly to provide an evaluation of the Strategic Military Cell.[287]

Peace Operations 2010

The surge in peacekeeping since 2003 has brought further reappraisal of UN peacekeeping. The Under-Secretary-General for Peacekeeping has said that the DPKO should focus on two strategic priorities. The first was to run the machinery of peacekeeping effectively. The second was to run itself out of business.[288] With regard to the second priority, the prevention of conflict has attracted increasing attention in recent years. Article 1(1) of the UN Charter commits member states to take effective collective measures for the prevention and removal of threats to the peace. Prevention of armed conflict by peaceful means is the cheapest and most effective way to promote international peace and security.[289] The UN Secretary-General published a major report on this in 2001, and in 2006 he issued a progress report.[290] As he said, 'Over the last five years we have spent $18 billion on UN peacekeeping that was necessary partly because of inadequate preventive measures. A fraction of that investment on preventive action would surely have saved both lives and money.' However, the main problem remained that the utility of any given prevention strategy was very difficult to prove.[291]

Another major concern is the need to prevent a state relapsing into conflict after a UN peacekeeping operation has ended. The experience of Haiti, Liberia and East Timor, in all of which conflict broke out again after the termination of a UN peacekeeping operation, has strengthened the call for post-conflict peacebuilding. The World Summit Outcome Document, on the basis of the recommendations of the High-Level Panel[292] and the Secretary-General,[293] called for the establishment of a Peacebuilding Commission to ensure the transition from conflict to peace, development

seriously undermine efforts to strengthen UN peacekeeping: GA/SPD/383, 1 November 2007.

[287] Report of the Secretary-General, S/2007/641 para 62. He provided an interim review in April 2007 (UN doc A/61/883, 26 April 2007). This stressed that the Strategic Military Cell was established to deal with the particular military, security and operation conditions in which UNIFIL was strengthened in the immediate aftermath of the recent conflict in Lebanon. It was a temporary means of augmenting overstretched capacities and a means of engaging TCCs' experience and resources in support of UN peacekeeping.

[288] Remarks to the Fourth Committee of the General Assembly, 19 October 2006, summarized in UN Press Release GA/SPD/352, 19 October 2006.

[289] UN Press Release DSG/SM/251, 12 April 2005.

[290] UN doc A/60/891 (2006).

[291] UN Press Release GA/10487, 7 September 2006.

[292] A/59/565 para 261.

[293] UN doc A/59/2005 para 114.

and reconstruction.[294] The Security Council, acting concurrently with the General Assembly, accordingly passed Resolution 1645 (2005) to establish a Peacebuilding Commission as an inter-governmental advisory body.[295] The Commission began its work in 2006 by focusing on Burundi and Sierra Leone.[296]

In order to cope with the surge in demand for peacekeeping forces in recent years the Security Council has increased its cooperation with regional organizations.[297] It has also adopted a regional approach to conflict in Africa, in recognition that conflict in one state may have a serious impact on the security of its neighbours. It has increasingly held meetings seeking regional solutions to conflicts. It has held meetings on West Africa, Central Africa, and on the Great Lakes region. It has also provided for inter-mission cooperation and for the exchange of troops between UN peacekeeping missions in a particular region where this would increase the efficiency of an operation. For example, Resolution 1609 (2005) provides for cooperation between UNMIL, UNAMSIL and UNOCI. In 2007 the Security Council created complementary forces in Darfur on the one hand and in Chad and the CAR on the other in response to the interconnected conflicts in the three states. These are new types of force, the former a hybrid AU/UN force and the latter a combination of EU military troops and UN police.[298]

As regards the first strategic priority, the Under-Secretary-General for Peacekeeping Operations initiated *Peace Operations 2010*, a reform project to increase the professionalism, management and efficiency of UN peacekeeping. As part of this project the DPKO is working on a Capstone Document.[299] Chapter Four of the latest draft suggests 'Guiding principles of UN Peacekeeping Operations'. It reaffirms the need for consent and impartiality, but proposes an alteration in the basic principle that peacekeeping forces should not use force except in self-defence. Instead it calls for 'restraint in use of force'. It elaborates on this as follows: that UN peacekeeping operations should use force as a last resort. The ultimate aim is to influence and deter those working against the peace

---

[294] World Summit Outcome Document A/60/L.70 para 97.

[295] UN Press Releases SC/8593, GA/10439, 20 December 2005, GA/10444, 27 December 2005, PBC/1, 23 June 2006.

[296] It issued its first annual report in 2007, UN doc A/62/137 (2007). See also the General Assembly debate, UN Press Release GA/10635, 10 October 2007, and the Security Council debate, UN Press Release SC/9144, 17 October 2007. At the end of 2007 the PBC added Guniea-Bissau to its agenda: UN Press Release PBC/26, 19 December 2007.

[297] See Chapter 9 below.

[298] Speech of Under-Secretary-General to Fourth Committee, GA/SPD/382, 31 October 2007.

[299] See the Best Practices Unit on the UN Peacekeeping website; <www.un.org/Depts/dpko/dpko/>.

process or seeking to harm civilians. The mission may have to use force pre-emptively to implement its mandate and to protect civilians. The draft also suggests the addition of three new principles, credibility (taken as requiring rapid deployment, proper resources and a unified command), legitimacy (taken as requiring that the operation should be seen as representative of the will of the international community and proper conduct by the mission) and promotion of national and local ownership. The last three are relatively uncontroversial, but the recommendations on 'restraint in use of force' have provoked a hostile response from many developing states. Many involved in the follow-up to the *Brahimi Report* appeared doubtful about any shift away from traditional peacekeeping to a more robust approach. The Special Committee and the Secretary-General have both taken a cautious approach.[300] The Non-Aligned Movement and many developing states have expressed their unhappiness with the DPKO's draft Capstone Document and their support for the traditional principles of peacekeeping.[301] There is concern by many states at suggestions that the traditional principle on the use of force should be replaced.[302]

The Special Committee on Peacekeeping Operations reaffirmed at its 2007 session that it is the only UN forum mandated to review comprehensively the whole questions of peacekeeping operations in all their aspects, including measures aimed at enhancing the capacity of the Organization to conduct UN peacekeeping operations. In its report it repeated the traditional position: The Special Committee believes that respect for the basic principles of peacekeeping, such as the consent of the parties, impartiality and the non-use of force except in self-defence and in the defence of a mandate authorized by the Security Council, is essential to its success.[303] It recognized that peacekeeping operations had become more complex and that a common understanding of terminology was required in order to promote clarity, common approaches and cooperation.[304] At the end of 2007 it remains to be seen whether there will be any modification of the traditional doctrine by the UN. The call for increased clarity about the significance of reference to Chapter VII in Security Council resolutions on peacekeeping and for consistent terminology within the resolution seems appealing, but may prove impracticable as other apparently sensible suggestions for reform have in the past.

---

[300] A/54/839; A/55/502 at para 7(e); A/57/767 at para 45.
[301] GA/PK 193, 27 February 2007; GA/SPD/383, 1 November 2007, GA/SPD/384, 2 November 2007, GA/SPD/385, 5 November 2007, GA/SPD/353, 20 October 2006.
[302] Fourth Committee debates, UN Press Releases GA/SPD/382, 31 October 2007. GA/SPD/384, 2 November 2007.
[303] UN doc A/61/19 (Part II) (2007).
[304] Ibid at para 116–118.

CONCLUSION

The period since the end of the Cold War has seen a vast expansion in Security Council activity. There has also been a marked decline in the number of armed conflicts in that period and some have attributed the decline to the activities of the UN.[305] An overview of the Security Council's activity in this area makes it clear that it has departed radically from what was originally planned by the founders. The Security Council has shown itself to be flexible and non-formalistic in its exercise of its powers; it has not been concerned with establishing the formal basis for its actions; and it has not generally referred to the particular articles of the Charter, if any, under which it is acting.

The UN has authorized force under Chapter VII in ways very different from those originally planned. The absence of a UN standing army under Article 43 has not inhibited it. It has authorized force to implement economic measures; it has authorized member states to use force under UN command (Korea); it has authorized member states to act together against wrongdoing states (Iraq). It has also used Chapter VII to authorize peacekeeping forces to use force going beyond self-defence (as in Yugoslavia and Somalia) and as the basis for the establishment of peacekeeping or peace enforcement forces. Thus the distinction between peacekeeping and enforcement action has been blurred in some operations.

Peacekeeping, an institution that emerged without clear, formal legal basis in the Charter, in response to the inability of the Security Council to implement Chapter VII of the UN Charter in the Cold War, and which has developed through practice to enable the Security Council to carry out its primary responsibility for the maintenance of international peace and security under the Charter, has evolved over the years. The majority of peacekeeping operations since the end of the Cold War have been established within rather than between states and they have ranged from simple, small operations to complex rebuilding of societies torn apart by civil war. The term 'peacekeeping' covers a very wide range of operations and it is clear that peacekeeping is a flexible institution which adapts to meet new needs. But the blurring of peacekeeping and enforcement as in Yugoslavia and Somalia and the use of Chapter VII in peacekeeping operations led to problems; it seems that abandoning the defining principles of peacekeeping, endangered the success of operations. However, robust operations are still necessary. The UN is now trying to devise a coherent legal framework which will govern the use of Chapter VII and provide a consistent terminology, while maintaining the flexibility necessary for the wide range of peacekeeping operations.

[305] Human Security Report, *War and Peace in the 21st Century* (2005).

8

Security Council authorization for member states to use force

Because the use of peacekeeping forces for enforcement purposes proved unworkable, and because the UN itself is not capable of extensive enforcement action, the Security Council has continued to authorize states to use force under Chapter VII, following the models of the operation against Iraq in *Operation Desert Storm* (1990) and the use of NATO member states in Yugoslavia in 1994–5 and UNITAF in Somalia (1992).[1] *Operation Desert Storm* against Iraq may be seen as a revolutionary development, made possible by unprecedented agreement among states, and which proved to be the catalyst for fundamental change in the international regulation of the use of force. Thus in Rwanda (1994), Haiti (1994 and 2004), Albania (1997), the Central African Republic (1997), and East Timor (1999) the Security Council acted under Chapter VII in authorizing member states to use force.[2] In 2003 it authorized three more such forces in Africa: in Liberia, the DRC and Côte d'Ivoire; and in 2006 it authorized another force in the DRC. It has also authorized longer-term operations in Bosnia and Herzegovina,[3] Kosovo and Afghanistan, and a new multinational force in Iraq. Most recently it has provided for an EU force in Chad and the Central African Republic. It is clear that these are not the type of operations originally envisaged by Chapter VII.[4]

At first it seemed that the action taken against Iraq in *Operation Desert Storm* was unique, the product of a never to be repeated set of circumstances. The UN Secretary-General stressed this unique character:

The Iraqi invasion and occupation of Kuwait was the first instance since the founding of the Organization in which one Member State sought to completely overpower and annex another. The unique demands presented by this situation

---

[1] See Chapter 7 above.

[2] In 1996 it also authorized states in SC Res 1078, SC Res 1080 (1996) to go into Zaire on a fixed-term, humanitarian mission because of its concern with the situation in the Great Lakes region of Africa (though with the consent of Zaire, UN doc S/1996/920), but the operation turned out to be unnecessary.

[3] See 291 above.

[4] For a full discussion of the legal basis of these actions, see Sarooshi, *The United Nations and the Development of Collective Security* (1999); Quigley, 'The Privatization of Security Council Enforcement Actions: A Threat to Multilateralism', 17 Michigan JIL (1995–6) 249.; Franck, *Recourse to Force* (2002) 24.

have summoned forth innovative measures which have given practical expression to the Charter's concepts of how international peace and security might be maintained.

Certainly the inter-state use of force in the years since 1991 has not produced anything like the international response triggered by the Iraqi invasion of Kuwait. The conflicts which broke out between Ethiopia and Eritrea, Armenia and Azerbaijan, Cameroon and Nigeria, Israel and Lebanon, and Ethiopia and Somalia did not provoke the UN to identify an aggressor and to authorize action against it. The reaction of the Security Council to the outbreak of inter-state conflict since the end of the Cold War, just as during the Cold War, has generally been to avoid condemnation and the attribution of responsibility and rather to call for a ceasefire and the restoration of peace. It is in internal conflicts rather then inter-state conflicts that the experience of Iraq seems to have had a more significant impact.

With regard to Iraq, Resolution 678 (1990) authorized member states to use 'all necessary means' to ensure Iraq immediately and unconditionally withdrew all its forces from Kuwait and to restore international peace and security in the area.[5] There now seems to be general agreement that the original scheme of Chapter VII of the UN Charter, even after the end of the Cold War, is not workable, and that it should not be for the UN itself to conduct enforcement operations. Instead there is consensus that it is for the Security Council to authorize member states to take enforcement action, even if the precise legal basis for this in the Charter is not clear.

The Security Council has not again authorized member states to use force against an aggressor state in the same way as it did against Iraq. In most cases the host state has consented to the UN-authorized operation, or even requested it. The situations nearest to that of Iraq are those where the Security Council authorized the use of force against a group involved in an internal conflict when that group did not comply with its obligations under a UN-brokered or approved ceasefire. This was the situation in Bosnia-Herzegovina where member states were authorized to enforce the no-fly zones over Bosnia and to protect the 'safe havens'; these measures were in fact directed against the Bosnian Serbs.[6]

The 1994 operation in Haiti can be seen as an action against a state, or rather against a military junta that had illegally seized power. This may be seen as a new development in UN action: the authorization to

---

[5] Subsequent resolutions use either the phrase 'all necessary means' or 'all necessary measures'. There is no obvious significance in the distinction.

[6] See 289 above.

use force to restore a democratically elected government. In response to a military coup in 1991 overthrowing the first democratically elected government in the history of Haiti, the Security Council condemned the coup and demanded the replacement of the constitutionally elected President, Jean-Bertrand Aristide. After the Security Council agreed on the imposition of an oil and arms embargo in 1993, the junta and the ousted President concluded the *Governors Island Agreement*, requiring the return of the lawful President and the restoration of democracy. The agreement included provision for a peacekeeping force, UNMIH. However, when an advance party of UNMIH tried to land in Haiti they were rebuffed.

The Security Council decided that in the absence of the implementation of the *Governors Island Agreement*, UNMIH could not be deployed. Accordingly in Resolution 940 (1994), (12–0–2, China, Brazil), acting under Chapter VII, it authorized member states to create a multinational force to 'use all necessary means' to facilitate the departure from Haiti of the military leadership and the prompt return of the legitimately elected President, the restoration of the legitimate authorities of the government of Haiti, and to establish and maintain a secure and stable environment that would permit implementation of the *Governors Island Agreement* on the restoration of democratic government. It also authorized the revision and expansion of the mandate of UNMIH, which was to take over from the multinational force when it had established a secure and stable environment necessary to restore and maintain democracy in Haiti. As it turned out, the US-led multinational force was able to land and carry out its mandate peacefully; it was duly replaced by UNMIH in March 1995. However, the situation in Haiti remained precarious and the re-established democracy was not secure.[7]

From its first resolutions on Haiti the Security Council stressed that this was a unique and exceptional case. Certainly the willingness of the Security Council to find that the situation in Haiti created by the failure of the military authorities to fulfil their obligations under the *Governors Island Agreement* and to comply with relevant Security Council resolutions calling for the restoration of the democratically elected government constituted a threat to peace and security in the region went further in its discretion under Article 39 than any other such finding.[8]

---

[7] UN Publications, *The Blue Helmets: A Review of United Nations Peacekeeping* (3rd edn, 1996) at 613; UN Blue Book Series, Vol XI, *Les Nations Unies et Haiti 1990–1996*; 1993 UNYB 334, 1994 UNYB 412, 1995 UNYB 440, 2000 UNYB 628.
[8] In the Security Council debate Mexico and Brazil expressed doubts as to whether the situation came within Article 39 and justified the authorization of force, SC 3413rd meeting (1994).

Ten years later in 2004 the Security Council again voted to establish a multinational force to intervene in Haiti. This time it no longer stressed the unique and exceptional nature of the case, and this time it is difficult to portray the intervention as pro-democratic. The USA was no longer willing to support President Aristide whose left wing political views were not attractive to the Bush administration. After controversial legislative elections in 2000 returned Aristide to power, the main bilateral donors cut international assistance to the government of Haiti, the poorest state in the western hemisphere, and withdrew their support from President Aristide.[9] The situation in Haiti deteriorated and violent disorder spread. In 2004 armed insurrection broke out; opposition forces seized control of half the territory.[10] The regional organizations CARICOM and the OAS made proposals to seek a political solution by the creation of a new government. President Aristide agreed, but the opposition did not. The Security Council initially condemned the opposition for this rejection.[11] CARICOM and the OAS accordingly went to the Security Council in February 2004, asking for the establishment of a peacekeeping force in Haiti. There was considerable support for this proposal.[12]

But three days later the Security Council chose to follow a different route.[13] France, the former colonial power, and the USA put pressure on President Aristide to step down.[14] He left the country and subsequently accused the USA of forcing him into exile. The USA denied this.[15] In Resolution 1529 (2004) the Security Council unanimously (without public debate) determined that the situation in Haiti constituted a 'threat to international peace and security and to stability in the Caribbean, especially through the potential outflow of people to other States in the subregion'. Acting under Chapter VII it authorized the immediate deployment of a Multinational Interim Force for a period of not more than three months, to contribute to a secure and stable environment and facilitate the provision of humanitarian need. It authorized member states participating in the force to take 'all necessary measures to fulfil its mandate'. The USA, France, Canada and Chile provided the 3,400 strong US-led force.[16] CARICOM subsequently expressed criticism of the path taken by the Security Council; it regretted that it had not chosen to establish a

---

[9] 2000 UNYB 249; Keesings (2000) 43566, 43852, 43668, (2001) 43996, (2004) 45841; *The Guardian*, 4 March 2004. In 2002 the OAS urged the resumption of aid and loans to avert humanitarian disaster in Haiti, Keesings (2002) 44976.
[10] 2004 UNYB 288; *The Guardian*, 23 February 2004.
[11] 2004 UNYB 288–90; SC Press Release 8009, 25 February 2004; Keesings (2004) 45784.
[12] UN doc S/2004/148, SC 4917th meeting (2004).
[13] SC 4919th meeting (2004).
[14] UN doc S/2004/145; *The Guardian*, 18, 26, 28, February 2004.
[15] Keesings (2004) 45895; *The Guardian*, 3 March, 1 June 2004, *The Observer*, 7 March 2004.
[16] 2004 UNYB 290–92; *The Guardian*, 1, 2, 11 March 2004.

peacekeeping force.[17] After three months the MIF was replaced by a UN stabilization force, MINUSTAH, which remains today.[18] The situation in Haiti at the end of 2007 has improved, but is still not secure.[19]

In Rwanda and Albania the Security Council used Chapter VII to authorize force to further humanitarian ends, as it had earlier in Yugoslavia and Somalia.[20] Thus in Rwanda the Security Council responded to the request from France for authorization under Chapter VII to establish a safe humanitarian zone; in Resolution 929 (1994), passed by 10–0–5, the Security Council stressed the strictly humanitarian character of the operation which was to be conducted in an impartial and neutral fashion; determined that the magnitude of the humanitarian crisis in Rwanda constituted a threat to peace and security in the region; and acting under Chapter VII authorized member states to conduct a temporary operation under national command aimed at contributing in an impartial way to the security and protection of displaced persons at risk in Rwanda and to use 'all necessary means' to achieve its humanitarian objectives.[21] In Albania the Security Council expressly affirmed the sovereignty, independence, and territorial integrity of Albania, and determined that the breakdown of law and order in Albania and the collapse of effective government constituted a threat to peace and security in the region. It therefore welcomed the offer by certain member states to establish a temporary and limited multinational protection force to facilitate the safe and prompt delivery of humanitarian assistance, and to help create a secure environment for the missions of international organizations in Albania. It authorized member states participating in the multinational protection force to conduct the operation in a neutral and impartial way. In contrast to the other operations, it did not use the phrase 'use all necessary means' (or 'all necessary measures'); rather, it used Chapter VII only to authorize member states to ensure the security and freedom of movement of the personnel of the multinational force.[22] The Security Council also used this formula in the case of the Central African Republic; in Resolution 1125 (1997) it welcomed the establishment of MISAB, the Inter-African Mission to Monitor the Implementation of the *Bangui Agreements*, set up in January 1997 at the

---

[17] 2004 UNYB 292; Keesings (2004) 45896.
[18] SC Res 1542 (2004); 2004 UNYB 294.
[19] SC 5631st, 5758th meetings (2007).
[20] See Chapter 7 above.
[21] Here again there was some concern about the combination of peacekeeping and Chapter VII action at the same time. New Zealand expressed concern that the combination of two separate operations with different command arrangements did not work; there was clear evidence that the initiative was having a negative impact on UNAMIR (1994 UNYB 291).
[22] Kritsiotis, 'Security Council Resolution 1101 (1997) and the Multinational Protection Force of Operation Alba in Albania', 12 Leiden Journal of International Law (1999) 511.

request of the Central African Republic and, acting under Chapter VII, authorized those states to ensure the security and freedom of movement of their personnel. In April 1998 this force was replaced by a UN force, MINURCA, when France withdrew its logistical and financial support from MISAB and it was unable to continue on its own.[23] The situation remained unstable and after the termination of MINURCA in 2000 another regional force was established; this remained in the Central African Republic at the end of 2007. The stability of the Central African Republic was further threatened by the crisis in Darfur and in 2007 the Security Council agreed to establish a new EU military force in the Central African Republic and Chad. This was authorized to use all necessary measures to fulfil its mandate 'to contribute to the protection of civilians in danger, to facilitate the delivery of humanitarian aid, to contribute to the protection of UN personnel'.[24]

In East Timor the authorization of force was more far-reaching. The breakdown of law and order and widespread killing after the consultation process led the Security Council to authorize a multinational force (INTERFET) led by Australia to intervene. Under Resolution 1264 (1999), passed under Chapter VII, the Security Council authorized the establishment of a multinational force under a unified command structure, pursuant to the request of the government of Indonesia, to restore peace and security in East Timor, to protect and support the UN mission in carrying out its tasks and, within force capabilities, to facilitate humanitarian assistance operations; it authorized the states participating in the multinational force to take 'all necessary measures' to fulfil this mandate. This multinational force was to be deployed until replaced as soon as possible by a UN peacekeeping operation and six months later it handed over to UNTAET.[25]

The Secretary-General has recognized that this delegation of UN functions to member states is necessary, given the limited resources at the disposal of the UN and its inability to mount an enforcement action. In the *Supplement to the Agenda for Peace* he acknowledged that the Security Council did not then have the capacity to deploy, command, and control an enforcement action. Although it was desirable that in the long term the UN should be able to conduct such operations, it would be folly to

[23] 1998 UN Yearbook 127; <www.un.org/Depts/DPKO/Missions/minurcaB.htm>; UN Press Release SC/6476, 5 February 1998; see McFarlane and Malan, 'Crisis and Response in the Central African Republic: A new trend in African peacekeeping?', 7 African Security Review (1998) 1.
[24] See 382 below.
[25] 1999 UNYB 278; 2000 UNYB 277. UNTAET in turn handed over to UNMISET after East Timor attained independence in May 2002. But serious disorder broke out again in 2006 and a multinational peacekeeping force was deployed with the consent of the government (see 387 below).

undertake them at a time when the UN was hard pressed even to carry out its peacekeeping commitments. However, he spoke of the dangers to the UN if it seemed to be sidelined; its stature and credibility might be adversely affected. *Operation Desert Storm* had given rise to concern among states about the need to limit the discretion of member states authorized to use force and to a determination not to repeat what came to be seen as flaws in the mandate of the operations. Thus, at the time of the operation there was concern about the lack of UN control over the decision as to when to start the operation and over the conduct of the campaign, about the wide and unclear mandate and about the lack of a time limit on the coalition action.[26] Yemen and Cuba voted against Resolution 678 (1990), partly on these grounds. Yemen said that the resolution was vague and not related to any specific article of Chapter VII. The Security Council would not have any control over the forces and command was not with the UN. Cuba argued that the text of Resolution 678 (1990) violated the Charter in that it authorized member states to use military force in total disregard of Charter procedures. China abstained because it sought a peaceful solution and had difficulty with accepting the resolution because the phrase 'all necessary means' permitted the use of military action.[27] When the Security Council subsequently authorized member state operations it increasingly took care to ensure a greater degree of Security Council control. States which abstained on, or opposed, Security Council resolutions authorizing new member state forces did so, not because of doubt about the constitutionality of such operations, but because they had concerns about the particular operation. China most often expressed such concerns.[28]

After the operation against Iraq, only UNITAF in Somalia and the 1994–95 NATO operations during the conflict in the former Yugoslavia (and KFOR in Kosovo) were not time-limited, but even these UNITAF and NATO member state forces were subject to greater limits than *Operation Desert Storm* had been. Member states were required to act in close coordination with the Secretary-General; in the former Yugoslavia this was interpreted to require the consent of the Secretary-General to any use of force by NATO in order to guarantee coordination and to avoid danger to

---

[26] Weston, 'Security Council Resolution 678 and Persian Gulf Decision-Making: Precarious Legitimacy', 85 AJIL (1991) 516; Lobel and Ratner, 'Bypassing the Security Council: Ambiguous Authorization to Use Force, Ceasefires and the Iraqi Inspection Regime', 93 AJIL (1999) 124; Sarooshi, *The United Nations and the Development of Collective Security* (1999) at 174.
[27] SC 2963rd meeting (1990).
[28] As, for example, in China's abstentions on the resolutions on Rwanda, Albania and Haiti. However, the resolutions authorizing force in the CAR, Côte d'Ivoire and the DRC were passed unanimously, as were those on all other member state forces except KFOR when China abstained on SC Res 1244 (1999).

the UN peacekeeping forces on the ground. The member state operations in Rwanda, Haiti and Albania, and all subsequent operations except for KFOR,[29] were subject to fixed time limits and all had to be renewed by the Security Council. Also in all these operations the states concerned were required to report to the Council on a regular basis on the implementation of the resolution.

There is also a danger that interested states operating under UN authorization would gain legitimacy to further their own interests. The early tradition of not using the forces of permanent members of the Security Council or of those states with geographical or historical interests in the state concerned has been further circumvented through this type of operation. Thus it was the USA that led the 1994 and 2004 operations in Haiti, France in Rwanda and the Central African Republic (1997), Italy in Albania, and Australia in East Timor. There was some suspicion of the motives of these states. In Rwanda *Operation Turquoise* was criticized for providing a safe haven for the perpetrators of genocide. These were, however, all temporary, limited forces operating with the consent of the host states even where this was not expressly indicated in the relevant resolutions. It is not clear that the use of the EU to lead an operation instead of a single member state will necessarily meet this concern as to ulterior motives. There were newspaper reports that the use of the EU in the DRC was interpreted by some as evidence of foreign state support for the incumbent President in the elections.[30] And Chad seems to have regarded an EU force led by its former colonial power and current supporter, France, as more acceptable than a UN force.[31]

Member state operations in Africa (2003–2007)

The three operations authorized in 2003 were also all limited, temporary operations. The first was in the Côte d'Ivoire, and was designed to help in the implementation of a political agreement between the different factions.[32] A coup attempt in September 2002 led to fears for the stability not only of Côte d'Ivoire, but of the region. There were deep divisions between the government-controlled south and the rebel-controlled north of Côte d'Ivoire. ECOWAS forces were quickly sent and the French troops already in Côte d'Ivoire by agreement with the government were increased.[33] Agreement between the different parties in Côte d'Ivoire was

---

[29] See 341 below.
[30] See 338 below.
[31] See 340 below.
[32] For an overview, see Report of the Secretary-General on the UN Mission in Côte d'Ivoire, S/2004/3.
[33] Keesings (2002) 45131, (2003) 45175, 45230; Secretary-General Report S/2003/374 para 15. Some accused France of pursuing its own interests, of putting pressure on the government (*The Guardian*, 2 October 2002). After the conclusion of a constitutional settlement

reached in January 2003 in the *Linas-Marcoussis Agreement*, but there was still considerable unrest and the states in the region called for Security Council authority to be given to the ECOWAS and French forces.[34] Accordingly Resolution 1464 (2003), passed unanimously, welcomed the deployment of ECOWAS and the French forces with a view to contributing to a peaceful solution to the crisis and the implementation of the peace agreement. Under Chapter VII it authorized member states participating in the ECOWAS forces, together with the French forces supporting them, to take 'the necessary steps to guarantee the security and freedom of movement of their personnel' and to ensure the protection of civilians immediately threatened with physical violence within their zones of operation.[35] This went further than the authority given to the member state forces in Albania and the CAR, but, like them, the member state force in Côte d'Ivoire was not actually established under Chapter VII.

This authorization continued until the establishment of a UN force, UNOCI, under Chapter VII in April 2004.[36] The 4,000 French troops remaining in Côte d'Ivoire were then authorized by Resolution 1528 (2004) to use 'all necessary means' to support UNOCI in the performance of its mandate. This authorization was given for an initial period of 12 months and has been renewed many times up to the present. France was requested to report 'periodically' to the Security Council. France was not willing to put its troops under UN command and it stipulated the functions they were and were not (disarmament, demobilization and reintegration) to carry out.[37] It would continue to oversee compliance with the ceasefire between government and rebel forces and to act as a rapid reaction force.

There was some anti-French feeling in Côte d'Ivoire and suspicion that the French force was not truly neutral, but that France was putting pressure on the government for its own ends. Anti-French riots broke out in 2003 and 2004.[38] However, the Security Council clearly supported the French intervention. The Secretary-General had made it clear in his report on the establishment of a UN force that without French assistance a much larger UN force would have been needed.[39] When government forces attacked opposition forces in November 2004, and in the process

there were anti-French riots by those angry that the settlement was too favourable to the rebels (Keesings (2003) 45175).

[34] 2003 UNYB 165–184; UN Press Release SC/7758, 13 May 2003.

[35] Secretary-General's Reports S/2003/374, S/2003/801 para 59. The initial six-month authorization was renewed in Resolution 1498 (2003).

[36] For further discussion of UNOCI see 320 above.

[37] Report of the Secretary-General on the UN Mission in Côte d'Ivoire, S/2004/3 para 52–3, 61–70.

[38] Keesings (2003) 45175, 45731; Secretary-General's Reports S/2004/3 para 13, S/2004/697 para 3–4, S/2004/962 para 7, 18–19, 30.

[39] Report of the Secretary-General on the UN Mission in Côte d'Ivoire, S/2004/3 para 64 –67.

harmed the French forces, in violation of the ceasefire, France responded by destroying the small Côte d'Ivoire air force.[40] In Resolution 1572 (2004), passed unanimously, the Security Council condemned the attack by the government of Côte d'Ivoire; it confirmed that the French forces and UNOCI were authorized to use all necessary means to carry out their mandate under Resolution 1528 (2004) and expressed full support for the action taken by the French forces. It imposed an arms embargo on Côte d'Ivoire. Interestingly, the Security Council expressly referred not only to UNOCI, but also to the French forces, as 'impartial forces' in the preamble to Resolution 1721 (2006) and in some, but not all, subsequent resolutions; this phrase was apparently taken from the Secretary-General's reports.[41] UNOCI and the French forces remained in Côte d'Ivoire at the end of 2007.

The second member state force authorized in 2003 was the Interim Emergency Multinational Force (IEMF) in the DRC.[42] This had a crucial military role in ending factional fighting, but only in one small area of the DRC. The IEMF's role was to end the factional fighting in Bunia when MONUC, the UN peacekeeping force, had not been able to do so. Fighting had been going on in the resource-rich DRC since 1998 and many neighbouring states were involved in the conflict. After the *Lusaka Peace Agreement* in 1999 the Security Council had created a UN peacekeeping force, MONUC, but it faced serious difficulties in securing enough troops and delays in deployment because of the insecure situation.[43] A further peace agreement in May 2003 did not end the fighting in the gold-rich Ituri province in the north-east of the country. The small and lightly armed UN peacekeeping force stationed in Bunia, the main town in the Ituri province, proved unable to cope with the extreme violence which broke out between opposing militias.[44] In May the UN Secretary-General asked the Security Council to act; he expressed deep concern about the rapidly deteriorating situation in the region and requested the Security Council urgently to consider his proposal for the rapid deployment of a highly trained and well-equipped multinational force under the lead of

---

[40] 2004 UNYB 185–6. Secretary-General's Third Progress Report on UNOCI, S/2004/962 para 14–23.

[41] The same formula was used in SC Res 1726 (2006) and 1763(2007) but not in Res 1739 (2007) or 1765 (2007). After the 2004 clashes the Secretary-General reported that the key assumptions underlying the original concept of UNOCI's operations had now changed. UNOCI's structure was predicated on the ability of the Licorne force to provide quick reaction capacity when needed. However, the recent events had illustrated the complexities of the balance between the two forces, and how difficult it could be to reconcile the emergency requirements of each when both are severely stretched (Secretary-General's Third Progress Report on UNOCI, S/2004/962 para 64–65).

[42] On the background to this conflict, see 68 above, and 2003 UNYB 113–137.

[43] See 316 above.

[44] Secretary-General's Report S/2003/566; 2003 UNYB 113 at 124–7.

a member state.[45] The President of the DRC, the parties in Ituri and the governments of Rwanda and Uganda supported the Secretary-General's request, and the Security Council in Resolution 1484 (2003) unanimously authorized under Chapter VII the deployment of a 1,500 strong Interim Force, authorized to take 'all necessary measures' to fulfil its mandate. The IEMF was led by the EU in its first military operation outside Europe, *Operation Artemis*. In contrast to those in Albania, Central African Republic and Côte d'Ivoire, the IEMF was established under Chapter VII, as befitted its more military role. It was to act in close coordination with MONUC, to contribute to the stabilization of the security conditions and the improvement of the humanitarian situation in Bunia, to ensure the protection of the airport, the internally displaced persons in the camps in Bunia and, if the situation required it, to contribute to the safety of the civilian population, UN personnel and the humanitarian presence in the town. It was expressly said to be deployed on a 'strictly temporary' basis to allow the Secretary-General to reinforce MONUC's presence in Bunia. It was replaced by a 2,500 strong MONUC brigade with a robust mandate on 1st September 2003.[46] Over the subsequent years MONUC was incrementally expanded to meet the challenging conditions until it was the largest, most expensive peacekeeping operation in the world.[47]

When presidential and parliamentary elections were finally held in 2006 the Security Council once again turned to the EU to provide military assistance to MONUC. In Resolution 1671 (2006), passed under Chapter VII, it established EUFOR-RDC on a strictly temporary basis, with a fixed-term mandate, authorizing it to take 'all necessary measures' to support MONUC during the elections in case the mission faced serious difficulties in fulfilling its mandate. The government of the DRC supported the temporary deployment of an EU force. EUFOR-RDC was also to contribute to the protection of civilians under imminent threat of physical violence, to ensure the security and free movement of its own personnel and to execute limited operations to extract individuals in danger. These tasks were to be taken upon a request by the Secretary-General, or in emergency cases, in close consultation with MONUC. The EU was to report regularly not only to the Security Council, but also to the government of the DRC on the implementation of this mandate. The EU reported that the deterrent effect of EUFOR-RDC was a significant factor in limiting the number of incidents. The 2,400 strong EU force was decisive in containing the potential spread of violence at a sensitive moment in the election process.[48]

---

[45] UN doc S/2003/574.
[46] UN Press Releases SC/7862, 3 September 2003, SG/SM/8842, 2 September 2003; 2003 UNYB 113 at 130–133.
[47] SC 5616th meeting (2007), UN Press Release SC/8936, 9 January 2007.
[48] Ibid.

The EU claimed that EUFOR-RDC had confirmed its position of neutrality in the eyes of the Congolese population and had reinforced its credibility.[49] However, there were newspaper reports that the European presence confirmed that foreign governments were backing President Kabila, just as they had propped up President Mobutu in order to secure access to the mineral resources of the DRC.[50] As in the case of Côte d'Ivoire, EU members were not willing to participate in the UN force, but preferred to operate under a separate Chapter VII authorization. The UK representative to the Security Council said, 'Whereas the EU member states were less active in UN peacekeeping, they hoped to be able to build the capacity to rapidly deploy when necessary, thereby contributing strongly to international efforts when needed.'[51]

Third, the Security Council established a force in Liberia, also on the initiative of the Secretary-General; it again turned to ECOWAS.[52] Here Security Council action was delayed, apparently for political reasons. The USA was unwilling to intervene in its former creation. Ever since President Charles Taylor was elected in 1997 after a prolonged civil war, other states had accused him of intervention in neighbouring states. Sanctions were imposed on Liberia by Resolution 1343 (2001) for its interference in the civil war in Sierra Leone. In June 2003 President Taylor was also indicted by the Sierra Leone Special Court for war crimes committed during the ten-year civil war.[53] Armed opposition to him in Liberia had been increasing since 2002, and in 2003 opposition forces gained control of much of the country and advanced on the capital, Monrovia. On 4 June 2003 President Taylor agreed to stand down and this was welcomed by the Security Council.[54] A ceasefire was then agreed between the warring parties, but soon broke down. The UN Secretary-General wrote to the Security Council, expressing deep concern at the flagrant violations of the ceasefire.[55] The intense fighting around Monrovia had made it evident that international action was urgently needed to reverse Liberia's drift towards total disintegration. The consequences of allowing the situation to spiral out of control were too terrible to contemplate, not only for Liberia but also for the states of the sub-region, particularly Sierra Leone and Côte d'Ivoire. He therefore requested the Security Council to take urgent action to authorize the deployment of a highly trained and well-equipped multinational force under the lead of a member state, to prevent a major humanitarian

---

[49] Javier Solana, EU High Representative at the SC 5616th meeting (2007).
[50] *The Guardian*, 15 November 2006.
[51] SC 5616th (2007), UN Press Release SC/8936, 9 January 2007.
[52] Secretary-General Report S/2003/875.
[53] Keesings (2003) 45451.
[54] 2003 UNYB 188, UN Press Release SC/7787, 11 June 2003.
[55] 2003 UNYB 189, UN doc S/2003/678.

tragedy and to stabilize the situation in Liberia. He regretted that this was the second such initiative he had had to propose in recent months, but he was again compelled to do so by a grave humanitarian and security situation with massive potential for exacerbating regional instability. He later requested the USA, the former quasi-colonial power, to consider spearheading the deployment of the force.[56]

Despite this plea the Security Council delayed in order to obtain further reports on the situation; it did not send in a force to restore law and order until it was confident that President Taylor would actually depart.[57] ECOWAS informed the Security Council that it was willing to deploy 1,500 troops to Liberia by mid-August to serve as the vanguard for the multinational force proposed by the Secretary-General. In July 2003 the Secretary-General repeated his deep concern at the dramatic deterioration of the situation on the ground and said it was absolutely essential to accelerate the deployment of the ECOWAS vanguard force, ECOMIL, followed by a full multinational force and then a UN peacekeeping operation.[58] The Security Council at the start of August in Resolution 1497 (2003) finally authorized member states under Chapter VII to establish a Multinational Force to support the implementation of the ceasefire agreement, including establishing conditions for initial stages of disarmament, demobilization and reintegration, to help establish security in the period after the departure of the current President, to secure the environment for the delivery of humanitarian assistance and to prepare for the introduction of a longer term, 15,000 strong, UN stabilization force to replace the Multinational Force.[59] It authorized member states in the Multinational Force to take 'all necessary measures' to carry out its mandate. The USA did not directly take part, but it provided a task force of over 2,000 marines off the coast of Liberia.[60] Like the IEMF in the DRC, this force was actually established under Chapter VII because of the significant military role assigned to it. The deployment of the substantial French-led force was followed by a comprehensive peace agreement in August 2003 and the situation in Liberia improved.[61]

---

[56] UN doc S/2003/875 para 10.
[57] UN Press Release SC/7824, 24 July 2003, 2003 UNYB 184.
[58] 2003 UNYB 190, UN doc S/2003/769.
[59] This resolution was passed by 12–0–3. Mexico, Germany and France abstained because the resolution provided (at the insistence of the USA) that personnel from a contributing state which was not a party to the Rome Statute of the International Criminal Court should be exempted from its jurisdiction. See Secretary-General's Report S/2003/875. The UN peacekeeping force was subsequently set up by SC Res 1509.
[60] Secretary-General Report S/2003/875 para 12. The Secretary-General expressed gratitude to the USA for its support to the deployment and operation of ECOMIL, and for positioning significant US military capabilities off the coast of Liberia, para 104.
[61] Secretary-General's Report S/2003/875 para 15. On the UN force, see 320 above.

Europe in Africa

These forces authorized under Chapter VII by the Security Council reveal the pattern of European involvement in African conflict. As was shown in the previous chapter, developed states have generally been reluctant to contribute troops to UN peacekeeping, especially in Africa. They prefer to contribute to limited Chapter VII action when authorized by the UN. They may also provide direct assistance to the governments of their former colonies or to regional organizations. The EU has recently taken a much more active role in undertaking Chapter VII action in Africa.[62] These operations have been created after a UN force has proved unable to act effectively because of limited resources, as in the DRC in 2003, and Côte d'Ivoire in 2006; or to prepare for a UN operation, as with the French-led multinational force in Liberia, and with the ECOWAS and French forces in Côte d'Ivoire in 2003. The Security Council has also turned to the member states of the AU to take action in Sudan and Somalia.[63]

Chad and the Central African Republic (CAR)

In 2007 the Security Council authorized a new EU military force in Chad and the CAR to help to bring an end to the long-lasting regional instability. The governments in Chad and the CAR were both under threat from armed opposition forces, and since 2003 the conflict in neighbouring Darfur had further destabilized the region. The significant cross-border movement of rebels and refugees had a serious impact on security. Chadian rebels operate from Sudan, and Sudan in turn accuses the government of Chad of supporting the opposition forces in Darfur. The UN Panel of Experts reported in 2006 that, 'The Sudan/Chadian border is no more than a line in the desert, the concept of a border being often ignored by nationals of both countries. Insurgents from the Sudan and Chad regularly cross the border unhindered. Since December 2005 there has been an increase in attacks on both Sudanese and Chadian villages along the common border... The ongoing crisis stems from tribal conflicts in the two countries and a power struggle in Chad... The territory of Sudan has been used as a staging ground to topple at least two Chadian presidents.'[64] The Security Council expressed deep concern at the deteriorating relations between Chad and Sudan.[65] It was also concerned that the deterioration of relations between Chad and Sudan might negatively affect the

---

[62] See White, 'The ties that bind: the EU, the UN and international law', 37 Netherlands Yearbook of International Law (2006) 57; 11International Peacekeeping (2004) 395, special issue on the EU's military operations.
[63] See 378, 380 below.
[64] Report of Panel of Experts, S/2006/250. See also UN doc S/2006/256.
[65] S/PRST/2006/19, 25.

security and stability of the CAR. It called for the adoption of a sub-regional approach to stabilize the borders.[66] The situation in the CAR was worsening, especially along the borders with Chad and Sudan. The government of the CAR accused Sudan of supporting the rebellion against it.[67]

The UN Secretary-General initially suggested the creation of a multi-dimensional UN force along the borders of Chad and the CAR with Sudan, but this was not acceptable to Chad.[68] Chad later agreed to accept an EU military force; the UN would provide only civilian staff.[69] Accordingly Resolution 1778 (2007), passed under Chapter VII, authorized the EU to deploy for one year and 'to take all necessary measures' in eastern Chad and north-eastern CAR to contribute to the protection of civilians in danger, to facilitate the delivery of humanitarian aid, to contribute to the protection of UN personnel. The EU was to liaise with the UN and with the governments of Chad and the CAR, and to report twice during the year to the Security Council.

Thus the 3,000-strong EU force was to have a more robust mandate than that of the AU peacekeeping force then operating under great pressure in Darfur until it could be replaced by a hybrid UN/AU force by the end of 2007.[70] France was to lead the EU force; it already maintained a substantial military presence in its former colony, Chad (now a significant oil producer) in support of the government of President Déby. This may help to explain why the EU force, under French leadership, was more acceptable to the government of Chad than a UN force. France also maintains some forces in the CAR, another former colony, where it assisted the government to maintain power against rebel attacks in 2006–7.[71]

Kosovo

The UN-authorized operations in Kosovo and Afghanistan were longer-term and more complex. In the former, the NATO operation against Yugoslavia in 1999 was followed by an agreement on the principles of a political settlement. Yugoslavia agreed to end the violence in Kosovo and to complete a rapid withdrawal of all its military, police, and paramilitary forces. These were to be replaced by international civil and security presences.[72] The Security Council reasserted its involvement in Kosovo

---

[66] UN Press Releases SC/8771, 7 July 2006, SC/8876, 22 November 2006, S/PRST/2006/47.
[67] Report of the Secretary-General on the situation in the CAR, S/2006/1034.
[68] Report of the Secretary-General on Chad and the CAR, S/2007/97, Report of the Secretary-General on the situation in the CAR, S/2007/376.
[69] Report of the Secretary-General on Chad and the CAR, S/2007/488.
[70] See 380 below.
[71] Keesings (2006) 47563; *The Independent*, 18 July 2007. And see also 89 above.
[72] 1999 UNYB 333.

after the NATO operation; in Resolution 1244 (1999) (14–0–1) it acted under Chapter VII in authorizing member states and relevant international organizations to establish the 50,000 strong international security presence (KFOR) in Kosovo. This followed the model of SFOR in Bosnia.[73] KFOR was to include substantial NATO participation, to be deployed under unified command and control and authorized to establish a safe environment for all people in Kosovo and to facilitate the safe return to their homes of all displaced persons and refugees.[74] A large UN mission, UNMIK, was to be responsible for the administration of Kosovo.

The resolution spelled out in detail the responsibilities of KFOR; it did not expressly authorize force and it did not say that member states could use or take all necessary means to carry out its mandate. The formula adopted in paragraph 7 of Resolution 1244 (1999) was that the Security Council authorized member states and relevant international organizations to establish the international security presence in Kosovo as set out in Annex 2 *'with all necessary means to fulfil its responsibilities under the resolution'*. This was apparently a compromise formula, seen by the West as wide enough to cover enforcement action, but by China and Russia as not an express authorization to use force. Russia said that the presence in Kosovo of the international civil and military contingents would be carried out under the Council's thorough control; the resolution's reference to Chapter VII contained no hint of the possibility of any type of force except that set out in the peace agreement.[75] China abstained, to show its unhappiness with the failure to condemn the NATO bombing; it was also unhappy that the resolution failed to impose necessary restrictions on invoking Chapter VII. However, in view of the fact (among other considerations) that Yugoslavia had already accepted the peace plan, China would abstain.[76] The *Military Technical Agreement* between KFOR and the federal and state governments of Yugoslavia was more specific.[77] This recorded the agreement of the government that KFOR would deploy with the authority to take all necessary action to establish and maintain a secure environment for all citizens of Kosovo and otherwise to carry out its mission. Unusually no time limit was set, and there have been no subsequent resolutions on KFOR. Although there was agreement by Yugoslavia to the deployment and mandate of KFOR, the language and tone of the resolution were less conciliatory than other resolutions authorizing member states to use force, apart from that regarding Haiti. It *demanded* that Yugoslavia put an immediate end to violence and repression in Kosovo

---

[73] See 291 above.
[74] 1999 UNYB 332.
[75] UN Press Release SC/6686, 10 June 1999.
[76] Ibid.
[77] 38 ILM (1999) 1217.

and begin complete and verifiable withdrawal of all forces according to a rapid timetable. It also demanded the full cooperation of Yugoslavia in the implementation of the political settlement. The aim was to establish a stable, peaceful, multiethnic Kosovo.

But the presence of KFOR did not prevent the displacement and mistreatment of the minority Serb population.[78] The security situation finally improved in 2006.[79] But there was continuing deadlock between the ethnic Albanians and the ethnic Serbs on the question of the final status of Kosovo, with the former seeking independence and the latter resisting this. The Security Council has been unable to agree on a new resolution to replace Resolution 1244 (1999) and to bring an end to KFOR and UNMIK.[80]

Afghanistan

In Afghanistan *Operation Enduring Freedom*, taken in response to 9/11, brought about the overthrow of the Taliban regime and the installation of a new government. The UN authorized the creation of a 5,000 strong International Security Assistance Force (ISAF) to assist the interim Afghan government in the maintenance of security in Kabul and its surrounding areas, so that the government and the personnel of the UN involved in peace-building operations could operate in a secure environment. Resolution 1386 (2001) (passed unanimously) authorized it to 'take all necessary measures' to fulfil its mandate and required it to report periodically to the Security Council.[81] Regarding the relationship between ISAF and *Operation Enduring Freedom*, the USA was initially to have final authority over both operations so that the activities of the two bodies did not conflict with each other and to ensure that there was no interference with the successful completion of *Operation Enduring Freedom*.[82] Questions have recently been raised about the compatibility of the two operations: ISAF is to work for the stabilization of Afghanistan whereas *Operation Enduring Freedom* is still pursuing the 'war on terror'.[83] In September 2007 the Secretary-General reported that 'the inherent dangers of two forces

---

[78] Keesings (1999) 43174, 43218, 43286 (2004) 45924; 2000 UNYB 358, 2001 UNYB 345, 2002 UNYB 367, 2003 UNYB 412, 2004 UNYB 404.

[79] UN Secretary-General Report on UNMIK, S/2006/906. The size of KFOR has been gradually reduced to 16,000, NATO website; <www.nato.int/issues/kfor/evolution.html>.

[80] UN Secretary-General Report on UNMIK, S/2007/582 para 3; *The Guardian*, 9 July 2007; Keesings (2007) 48006, 48501.

[81] This was later changed to a requirement of quarterly reports in SC Res 1563 (2004).

[82] UN Press Release SC/7248, 20 December 2001; UN doc S/2001/1217.

[83] See 204 above.

operating in the same battle space with different mandates requires more proactive coordination to ensure the success of the ISAF mission'.[84]

Despite the presence of the two forces much of the country remained lawless; the Secretary-General's Special Representative accordingly proposed the expansion of ISAF.[85] But the USA and others at first opposed any wider deployment of ISAF beyond the environs of Kabul in order to allow *Operation Enduring Freedom* to take action in pursuit of Taliban and Al Qaida forces anywhere in Afghanistan without impediment.[86] However, as conflict continued in many areas of Afghanistan the USA indicated a willingness to expand the role of ISAF beyond Kabul,[87] and the Security Council authorized this in October 2003. Resolution 1510 (2003) authorized the expansion of ISAF to allow it to support the Afghan Transitional Authority and its successors in the maintenance of security in areas outside Kabul, so that the Afghani authorities and UN personnel and other international personnel engaged in reconstruction and humanitarian efforts could operate in a secure environment. NATO took over the command of ISAF in its first military operation outside Europe. Subsequently ISAF incrementally expanded its area of operation until in Resolution 1746 (2007) the Security Council welcomed the completion of its expansion throughout Afghanistan.[88] However, ISAF has struggled to address the challenges facing it; the future of NATO has been put in some doubt by the reluctance of member states to contribute sufficient troops to this operation.[89] The Security Council has repeatedly stressed the need to strengthen the force,[90] and at the end of 2007 ISAF reached the size of 40,000 troops from thirty-seven states. However, the Security Council in Resolution 1707 (2006) and Resolution 1746 (2007) expressed concern about the security situation in Afghanistan, in particular the increased violent and terrorist activity by the Taliban, Al Qaida, illegally armed groups and those involved in the narcotics trade. And recent UN reports on the situation in Afghanistan have made it clear that Afghanistan's security situation continues to be dragged down by an ever-expanding opium economy, endemic corruption and mounting violence from an emboldened insurgency.[91] There is no prospect of an end to ISAF's mission.

---

[84] Report of the Secretary-General on the Situation in Afghanistan, S/2007/555 para 34.
[85] UN Press Release SC/7458, 19 July 2002.
[86] Ibid. Turkey, France, the UK and Russia also opposed wider deployment of ISAF.
[87] 2003 UNYB 290, 308; *The Guardian*, 8, 19 September 2003.
[88] NATO website; <www.nato.int/issues/isaf/evolution.html>.
[89] Keesings (2007) 48193.
[90] SC Res 1563 (2004), 1623 (2005), 1707 (2006), 1776 (2007).
[91] SC 5641st meeting (2007), UN Press Release SC/8972, 2007); Report of the Secretary-General on the Situation in Afghanistan, S/2007/555, 21 September 2007.

The multinational force in Iraq (2003)

In contrast to the arrangements in Afghanistan, after *Operation Iraqi Freedom* the USA was at first not willing to accept UN or UN-authorized forces in Iraq at the same time as its 'coalition' forces were working to occupy the territory, to reorganize the economy and to establish a new government. But ongoing violence and the increasing costs of occupation eventually persuaded the USA to seek military and financial assistance through the UN in September 2003.[92] The capture of Saddam Hussein did not bring an end to the attacks on the US troops.[93] Negotiations on a Security Council resolution were difficult; those states which had opposed the war were not willing to include any provision which would indicate acceptance of the legality of *Operation Iraqi Freedom*. They sought a much greater role for the UN and a swift end to the occupation and return of sovereignty to the Iraqi people.[94] In an attempt to secure assistance from other states, the USA tried to depict the ongoing attacks on occupying forces, the UN headquarters in Iraq[95] and on humanitarian organizations not as resistance to occupation but as terrorist attacks: President Bush said that Iraq was now the 'central front in the war against terrorism'.[96]

Eventually Resolution 1511 was passed unanimously in October 2003. Acting under Chapter VII, the Security Council authorized a multinational force (MNF) under unified command to 'take all necessary measures to contribute to the maintenance of security and stability in Iraq'. The force was to be under US command, and the USA was to report to the Security Council on its efforts and progress. The Security Council was to review the requirements and mission of the force not later than one year from the date of the resolution, and the mandate of the force was to expire 'upon the completion of the political process' described in the resolution. As in Afghanistan, this MNF faced an enormously difficult task. At the end of 2003 the Secretary-General reported that the dangers posed by insurgents were growing; the mounting insecurity problem could not be solved through military means alone. A political solution was required through an inclusive and transparent transition process, designed to make clearer that the foreign occupation of Iraq was to be short-lived. The role to be played by the UN in terms of assistance to the political transition was still undefined.[97] The MNF was

---

[92] *The Guardian*, 9 September 2003.
[93] UN Press Release SC/7955, 16 December 2003.
[94] Keesings (2003) 45623; *The Guardian*, 4, 5, 6, 9, 10, 24, 25 September 2003.
[95] SC 4811th meeting (2003).
[96] Keesings (2003) 45587.
[97] UN Press Release SC/7955, 16 December 2003.

involved in a wide spectrum of military activities, from offensive combat operations to reconstruction.[98]

In both Afghanistan and Iraq the UN-authorized member state force established under Chapter VII complemented a US-led invasion force. In the former ISAF was present under the *Bonn Agreement* between the various groups in Afghanistan; its mandate was to assist the provisional Afghan government and its legitimacy was little challenged.[99] In Iraq the situation was more complex, given the divisions as to the legality of *Operation Iraqi Freedom* and the disagreement as to the role to be played by the UN in the reorganization of Iraq. The USA made the choice to establish a force through the UN because this increased the likelihood that states would be willing to contribute troops. However, as in earlier cases, there was a clear danger for the UN in that it may seem to be allowing the USA to further its own interests through the multinational force authorized by Resolution 1511 (2003). Some concern was expressed during the debate on Resolution 1511 (2003).[100] Pakistan had advocated that the multinational force in Iraq should have a distinct identity from the coalition forces and should be deployed on the invitation of the Iraqi people. Because these considerations had not been reflected in the resolution it would not contribute troops. France, Germany and Russia issued a joint statement on the adoption of Resolution 1511 (2003), regretting the lack of a timetable for the political transition and the insufficient role of the UN in the political process. In that context the resolution had not created conditions for military commitments or further financial contributions.

The situation changed when the Security Council passed Resolution 1546 (2004) unanimously; this accepted that the occupation had ended on 30 June 2004 and endorsed the formation of an interim Iraqi government.[101] The 140,000 strong MNF was now said to be present with the consent of the sovereign government. It was authorized to take 'all necessary measures to contribute to the maintenance of security and stability in Iraq' in accordance with letters from the Iraqi Prime Minister and the US Secretary of State annexed to the resolution. Iraq and the MNF were to agree policy on sensitive offensive operations.[102] The MNF mandate was for twelve months; it could be reviewed at the request of the Iraqi government and would terminate on the completion of the political process, or earlier if the Iraqi government so requested. The USA was to report to

---

[98] UN Press Release SC/8060, 16 April 2004.
[99] See 204 above.
[100] UN Press Release SC/7898, 16 October 2003.
[101] 2004 UNYB 346.
[102] France expressed concern that the resolution did not spell out what would happen in the event of disagreement between the Iraqi government and the force, SC 4987th meeting (2004).

the Security Council on behalf of the MNF.[103] Although many states have contributed to the MNF since 2004, the vast majority of the force are US troops.

Resolution 1546 (2004) also announced that there would be a leading role for the UN assistance mission (UNAMI) to assist in the establishment of an elected government, the production of a new constitution and the development of civil and social services. China hailed this resolution as a new page in the relationship between Iraq and the UN and said that it would further strengthen the authority and rule of the Security Council.[104] But some had wanted a larger role for UN: Spain would have preferred the UN to have assumed military leadership in the transition phase.[105] And in practice UNAMI could play only a very limited role because of the lack of security in Iraq.[106]

The Secretary-General's reports under this resolution and those of his Special Representative described the evolving situation in Iraq. Despite progress in the establishment of a constitutional government, and in the training of Iraqi armed forces to take over responsibility for the security of Iraq, the MNF was not able to bring an end to the violence. Figures on civilian casualties in Iraq since March 2003 vary between 50,000 and one million.[107] There has also been a massive flow of people—about 2.2 million—out of the country. In September 2006 it was reported that Iraq had become one of the most violent conflict areas in the world. The Secretary-General warned that if current patterns of discord and violence prevailed there was a grave danger of a breakdown of the Iraqi state and of civil war.[108] By December 2006 the prospects of an all-out civil war and even a regional conflict had increased. The efforts by the Iraqi Government and the MNF could not prevent the continuous deterioration of the security situation.[109] Some members of the Security Council argued that a timetable should be set for the withdrawal of the MNF. France said that this could contribute to stabilizing the situation; it welcomed Resolution 1723

---

[103] This mandate was renewed in 1637 (2005) and 1723 (2006).

[104] SC 4987th meeting (2004).

[105] Ibid.

[106] UNAMI was initially created by SC Res 1500 (2003). After the attack on UN HQ in Baghdad in August 2003 it effectively stopped operating in Iraq for a year (SC 5247th meeting, UN Press Release SC/8473, 11 August 2005). On the problems that it faced, see SC 5583rd meeting (2006). After the completion of the process of establishing a constitutional government, Resolution 1770 (2007) set out plans to expand the role of the UN and to bolster regional dialogue; the MNF was to have an important role in supporting UNAMI (see UNAMI website; <uniraq.org>).

[107] SC 5583rd meeting (2006). UNAMI has expressed regret that the government of Iraq does not publish figures of casualties (Human Rights Report 1 April—30 June 2007; <uniraq.org>), *The Guardian*, 19 March 2008.

[108] SC 5523rd meeting (2006).

[109] SC 5583rd meeting (2006).

(2006) which for the first time integrated prospects for a withdrawal in its preamble; China said that it was necessary for the MNF to signal that it would not be a permanent presence in Iraq.[110] Russia said that it was necessary to identify when the MNF, 'a serious irritant for many', would leave the country.[111] But the USA chose instead to increase the numbers of the MNF and in January 2007 announced a surge of about 20,000 in its strength in order to secure Baghdad.[112] By the end of 2007 there were some signs of improvement, but the situation is still far from secure.[113] In December 2007 the MNF's mandate was renewed by the Security Council for what the Iraqi Representative said would be the last time.[114] Iraq still faced 'an exceptionally complex series of overlapping sectarian, political and ethnic conflicts'.[115]

IMPLIED (OR REVIVED) AUTHORIZATION
TO USE FORCE

Iraq 1991–2002

Where they were not able to secure express authority to use force, certain states have recently sought to justify their use of force as impliedly authorized by the Security Council. The first indications of this controversial argument emerged with regard to US and UK action against Iraq.[116] After Iraq was driven out of Kuwait by the coalition forces the government of Iraq turned on the Kurds and Shiites who had been incited to rise against the government during the conflict. The Security Council displayed some initial reluctance to involve themselves in what they at first saw as an internal matter for Iraq, but then passed Resolution 688 (1991)(10–3–2) condemning the repression of the Kurds and Shiites, demanding that Iraq stop the repression and calling on Iraq to allow access to international humanitarian organizations. This resolution was not passed under Chapter VII and did not authorize force to protect the Kurds and Shiites. Nevertheless,

---

[110] SC 5583rd meeting (2006).
[111] SC 5693rd meeting (2007).
[112] Keesings (2007) 47721.
[113] Report of the Secretary-General, S/2007/608; SC 5763rd meeting (2007), SC 5823rd meeting (2008).
[114] SC 58058th meeting (2007); SC Res 1790 (2007), Annex I, objective 5.
[115] SC 5693rd meeting (2007).
[116] See Kritsiotis, 'The Legality of the 1993 US Missile Strike on Iraq and the Right of Self-defence in International Law', 45 ICLQ (1996) 162; Wedgwood, 'The Enforcement of SC Resolution 687', 92 AJIL (1998) 724; Lobel and Ratner, 'Bypassing the Security Council: ambiguous authorisations to use force, ceasefires and the Iraqi inspection regime', 93 AJIL (1999) 124; Sicilianos, 'L'autorisation par le conseil de sécurité de recourir à la force: une tentative d'evaluation', 106 RGDIP (2002) 5.

the USA, the UK, and France referred to this resolution in explanation of their action in intervening in Iraq to establish safe havens. They did not offer a full legal argument in justification of this action and the later establishment of no-fly zones over Iraq, first in the north, then in the south.

In the course of a series of clashes between the USA and the UK and Iraq over the no-fly zones the doctrine of implied authorization did not take any clearer form; the UK and the USA spoke of Resolution 688 (1991) allowing a response to Iraqi action and said that action to ensure the safety of aircraft in the no-fly zone was 'consistent with', in implementation of', 'in support of', and 'pursuant to' the resolution.[117] The UK also belatedly invoked a justification of humanitarian intervention. Russia and China objected strongly to the US and UK interventions. US and UK action in the no-fly zones escalated dramatically from December 1998; they widened the rules of engagement of their air forces, allowing pre-emptive attacks on ground defences and command centres.[118] All this was done without extensive legal justification. In the face of continued criticism from Russia and China and a call from the Arab League to halt all acts not authorized by the Security Council, the UK simply said that its operations were purely reactive and not aggressive. The no-fly zones were necessary both to limit Iraq's capacity to oppress its own people and to monitor its compliance with obligations. The USA repeated that it was acting in support of Resolution 688 (1991).[119]

The question of the legal basis for action taken to enforce the no-fly zones arose again in February 2001 when the USA and the UK undertook another major operation in response to increased Iraqi activity in the no-fly zones and improvements in Iraq's air defence systems. The UN Secretary-General, responding to calls from Iraq to condemn the US and UK air attacks emphasized that only the Security Council could determine the legality of actions in the no-fly zones; only the Security Council was competent to determine whether its resolutions were of such a nature and effect as to provide a lawful basis for the no-fly zones and for the actions that have been taken in their enforcement.[120] This statement implicitly rejects any claims by the USA and the UK to justify their action unilaterally on the basis of Resolution 688 (1991). The UK has accepted this. Although still invoking Resolution 688 (1991) as supporting the legitimacy of its actions, it openly acknowledges that, 'The legal justification for the patrolling of the no-fly zones does not rest on Security Council Resolution 688 (1991). That has not been the government's position. In terms of

---

[117] See, for example, 64 BYIL (1993) 728, 65 BYIL (1994) 683.
[118] Keesings (1999) 42754, 42811, 42866.
[119] UN Press Release SC/6683, 21 May 1999.
[120] 2001 UNYB 295.

humanitarian justification, we are entitled to patrol the no-fly zones to prevent a grave humanitarian crisis. That is the legal justification in international law. It does not rest on Resolution 688 (1991), although that resolution supports the position that we have adopted.'[121] The international response to the US and UK operation in February 2001 showed that they were isolated. Very few states expressed any support for the US and UK action; Russia, China and France all regarded it as illegal.[122] The enforcement of the unilaterally proclaimed no-fly zones has thus come to be seen as illegal, despite UK protestations of humanitarian necessity.

The doctrine of implied (or revived) authorization was used more clearly to justify the use of force against Iraq to secure its cooperation with the ceasefire regime established by Resolution 687 (1991) after Iraq had been driven out of Kuwait. This regime obliged Iraq to destroy its weapons of mass destruction and created UNSCOM and IAEA teams to monitor and verify Iraq's compliance; despite Iraq's formal acceptance of Resolution 687 (1991), there was great trouble over the implementation of this regime. Iraq's obstruction of the weapons inspectors led to military intervention by the USA and the UK. The first major confrontation came in January 1993 when, in response to Iraq's withdrawal of cooperation, the USA, the UK and France launched large-scale missile and air attacks on facilities connected with Iraq's nuclear weapons programme.[123] The UN Secretary-General said, 'The raid yesterday, and the forces that carried out the raid, have received a mandate from the Security Council, according to Resolution 678 (1990), and the cause of the raid was the violation by Iraq of Resolution 687 (1991) concerning the ceasefire. So, as Secretary-General of the United Nations, I can say that this action was taken and conforms to the resolutions of the Security Council and conforms to the Charter of the United Nations.'[124] This is apparently the first, brief, appearance of an argument that was subsequently to prove very divisive. The UK based its legal justification on this argument.[125]

The difficulties in securing Iraqi compliance with the ceasefire regime escalated from 1996 and in response the Security Council passed two resolutions under Chapter VII. The first, Resolution 1154 (1998), stressed that compliance by Iraq with its obligations to accord immediate and unrestricted

---

[121] 'UK Materials on International Law', 72 BYIL (2001) 693. The UK had expressed this position earlier, see Gray, 'After the Ceasefire: Iraq, the Security Council and the Use of Force', 65 BYIL (1994) 135 at 165.

[122] Keesings (2001) 44026; for divisions on earlier operations in the no-fly zones, see 'Contemporary Practice of the United States', 93 AJIL (1999) 471; 94 AJIL (2000) 102.

[123] Keesings (1993) 39291.

[124] 'UK Materials on International Law', 64 BYIL (1993) 736. See also the references back to the Secretary-General's statement by the USA in its letter to the Security Council at the start of *Operation Iraqi Freedom*, S/2003/351, and by the UK, (52) ICLQ (2003) 812.

[125] 'UK Materials on International Law', 64 BYIL (1993) 736–40.

access to UNSCOM and the IAEA was necessary for the implementation of Resolution 687 (1991) and that any violation would have severest consequences for Iraq. When Iraq again limited its cooperation with the weapons inspectors, the Security Council passed Resolution 1205 (1998), expressing alarm and condemning the decision of Iraq to cease cooperation with UNSCOM and demanding that Iraq rescind its decision. When the UN weapons inspectors reported that Iraq was still obstructing their work the USA and the UK began *Operation Desert Fox* in December 1998, a series of air strikes that continued for four days and nights; it used more Cruise missiles than had been used in the whole 1991 campaign to drive Iraq out of Kuwait. The aim was to degrade Iraq's capability to build and use weapons of mass destruction and to diminish the military threat Iraq poses to its neighbours.

At the Security Council debate the USA and the UK put forward an argument of implied or revived authorization. The UK said that there was a clear legal basis for military action in the resolutions adopted by the Security Council. By Resolution 1205 (1998) the Security Council had implicitly revived the authority to use force given in Resolution 678 (1990).[126] The USA similarly said that its forces were acting under the authority provided by Security Council resolutions. Iraq had flagrantly committed material breaches of the ceasefire regime in Resolution 687 (1991). Several member states supported the action without any discussion of its legality, but a majority of the states speaking in the debate did not accept the legality of the action. According to Russia, the action violated international law; the USA and the UK had no right to act independently on behalf of the UN or to assume the function of world policemen. The ceasefire regime in Resolution 687 (1991) did not allow unilateral use of force without further Security Council resolutions.[127] These divisions as to whether Resolution 678 (1990) could be invoked unilaterally to justify the use of force against Iraq in the event of further material breaches of the ceasefire regime were to arise again in 2003.

The 1999 Kosovo operation

The USA, the UK and other NATO states relied on implied authorization as part of the justification for the NATO operation against Yugoslavia in

---

[126] It is interesting that the UK Attorney-General in his advice on the invasion of Iraq published in 2005 said that the revival doctrine used in 1993 and 1998 was controversial and not widely accepted among academic commentators; it was not more than reasonably arguable 54 ICLQ (2005) 767 para 7–11, 30.

[127] UN Press Release SC/6611, 16 December 1998; 'Contemporary Practice of the United States relation to International Law', 93 AJIL (1999) 470; Lobel and Ratner, 'Bypassing the Security Council: ambiguous authorisations to use force, ceasefires and the Iraqi inspection regime', 93 AJIL (1999) 124.

1999. This aroused even more controversy than the actions against Iraq; strong arguments were made that such action was incompatible with the Charter and undermined the role of the Security Council.

The Security Council passed three resolutions in 1998 in response to events in Kosovo. It is clear that these did not *expressly* authorize the use of force. Nor did the words of Resolutions 1160 (1998), 1199 (1998) and 1203 (1998) amount to an *implied* authorization of force. This interpretation is confirmed by the fierce opposition of China and Russia in 1998 to any UN authorization of the use of force against Yugoslavia. Thus Russia, in the debate leading up to the adoption of Resolution 1199 (1998), warned that 'the use of unilateral measures of force in order to settle this conflict is fraught with the risk of destabilizing the Balkan region and all of Europe and would have long-term adverse consequences for the international system which relies on the central role of the United Nations'.[128] In the debate leading to Resolution 1203 (1998) it said that 'Enforcement elements have been excluded from the draft resolution, and there are no provisions in it that would directly or indirectly sanction the automatic use of force, which would be to the detriment of the prerogatives of the Security Council under the Charter.'[129] Costa Rica also warned against any attempt to claim implied authorization under Resolution 1203 (1998); it said that any action which implies the use of force requires clear authorization by the Security Council for each specific case.

The resolutions were all passed under Chapter VII of the UN Charter; they all condemned the use of excessive force by Serbian forces against civilians and also acts of terrorism by the Kosovo Liberation Army. In March 1998 Resolution 1160, passed by 14–0–1 (China), imposed an arms embargo on Yugoslavia and called for a political solution to the issue of Kosovo. It concluded by emphasizing that failure to make constructive progress towards the peaceful resolution of the situation in Kosovo would lead to the consideration of additional measures.[130] Resolution 1199, passed by 14–0–1 (China) in September 1998, expressed grave concern at the excessive and indiscriminate use of force by Serbian security forces and the Yugoslav army which had resulted in numerous civilian casualties and the displacement of over 230,000 persons from their homes. It now determined that the deterioration of the situation in Kosovo constituted a threat to peace and security in the region and demanded an end to hostilities. It demanded that the authorities of Yugoslavia and the

---

[128] SC 3930th meeting (1998).
[129] SC 3937th meeting (1998).
[130] This resolution was adopted without express reference to a determination by the Security Council that there exists a threat to international peace and security as required by Article 39, because of Russian and Chinese opposition to such a statement (SC 3868th meeting, UN Press Release 6496, 31 March 1998).

Kosovo Albanian leadership should take immediate steps to improve the humanitarian situation and to avert the impending humanitarian catastrophe. In particular it spelled out certain concrete measures to be taken by Yugoslavia, including the cessation of all action by the security forces and the withdrawal of security units used for civilian repression. It also called for the full implementation of the commitments made by President Milosevic of Yugoslavia in June 1998 to resolve problems by peaceful means and not to use repression against the peaceful population. It concluded by deciding that, should the concrete measures demanded in this resolution and Resolution 1160 (1998) not be taken, it would consider further action and additional measures to maintain or restore peace and stability in the region. Resolution 1203 was passed by 13–0–2 (China, Russia) in October 1998 to welcome the agreements between Yugoslavia and the OSCE and NATO concerning the verification of compliance by Yugoslavia with the requirements of Resolution 1199 (1998). It affirmed that the unresolved situation in Kosovo constituted a continuing threat to peace and security in the region; this characterization of the situation was not acceptable to China and Russia. The Security Council demanded full implementation of the agreements. These three resolutions may justify a claim that NATO was acting in pursuance of the aims of the international community, but they cannot support any claim of implied authorization of force against Yugoslavia by NATO.[131]

In the Security Council debates after the NATO campaign started some states stressed the earlier Security Council resolutions passed under Chapter VII calling on Yugoslavia to stop its actions.[132] Although these resolutions did not expressly authorize the use of force by NATO, several states seemed to argue that they nevertheless justified the NATO action. Thus France, the Netherlands, and Slovenia all emphasized that the Security Council had adopted resolutions under Chapter VII, affirming that the situation posed a threat to regional peace and security, and had imposed certain requirements on Yugoslavia; because Yugoslavia flagrantly violated these requirements, NATO had been entitled to act.

Yugoslavia challenged the legality of the NATO action by bringing cases against ten NATO member states before the ICJ. At the provisional

---

[131] On implied authorization, see Lobel and Ratner, 'Bypassing the Security Council: ambiguous authorisations to use force, ceasefires and the Iraqi inspection regime', 93 AJIL (1999) 124; Sicilianos, 'L'autorisation par le conseil de securité de recourir à la force: une tentative d'evaluation', 106 RGDIP (2002) 5. For a rejection of the legality of the NATO claim, see Simma, 'NATO, The UN and the use of force: Legal Aspects', 10 EJIL (1999) 1. Rosalyn Higgins, in response to the claim that Resolution 1199 was enough to justify military action, said 'One must necessarily ask whether this is not to stretch too far legal flexibility in the cause of good': Higgins, 'International Law in a Changing International System', 58 Cambridge Law Journal (1999) 78.
[132] SC 3989th meeting (1999).

measures stage of the case most of the defendant states did not set out their justification for the use of force. But Belgium did go into the law on the use of force; it argued that the armed intervention was in fact 'based on' Security Council resolutions; this is another instance of the argument of implied Security Council authorization. However, Belgium said that it was necessary to go further and to set out also the doctrine of humanitarian intervention.[133]

Thus there was some uncertainty as to the legal basis for the NATO air campaign; some states focused on implied authorization by the Security Council, others on humanitarian intervention. It was clear, despite the failure by the Security Council to condemn the NATO bombing, that a majority of states were not willing to accept a doctrine of implied authorization. Ever since the end of the NATO action many states have gone out of their way to register their rejection of the unilateral action by NATO and to stress the primary role of the Security Council and the need for express authorization. The Non-Aligned Movement, at a Ministerial Meeting in September 1999, rejected the legality of the NATO operation.[134] Russia and China remain adamant in their opposition. The UN Secretary-General, in his 1999 *Report on the Work of the Organization*, said that '[T]he moral rights and wrongs of this complex and contentious issue will be the subject of debate for years to come, but what is clear is that enforcement actions without Security Council authorization threaten the very core of the international security system founded on the Charter of the United Nations. Only the Charter provides a universally accepted legal basis for the use of force.'[135]

Operation Iraqi Freedom (2003)

The most recent, the most extensive, and the most controversial, instance of reliance on the doctrine of implied or revived authorization was against Iraq in March 2003.[136] *Operation Iraqi Freedom* was undertaken by the USA, the UK and Australia to secure the disarmament of Iraq of weapons of mass destruction.[137] States were bitterly divided as to the legality of any

---

[133] *The Legality of Use of Force* Yugoslavia v Belgium, Canada, France, Germany, Italy, Netherlands, Portugal, Spain, United Kingdom, United States of America: Provisional Measures, Belgium oral pleadings.

[134] UN Press Release GA/SPD/164, 18 October 1999.

[135] UN doc A/54/1 (1999) para 66.

[136] For a wide range of views on the legality and wider significance of this operation, see 'Agora: Future Implications of the Iraq Conflict', 97 AJIL (2003) 553. See also Corten, 'Opération Iraqi Freedom: peut-on admettre l'argument de l'autorisation implicite du conseil de sécurité?', 2003 Revue Belge de Droit International 205; Murphy, 'Assessing the legality of invading Iraq', 92 Georgetown Law Journal (2004) 173.

[137] Murphy (ed.), 'Contemporary Practice of the United States relating to International Law', 97 AJIL (2003) 419.

use of force against Iraq; not only did Russia and China reject the US and UK case for force, but also other NATO and EU states argued that force should not be used without express Security Council authorization. Ever since 9/11 the US administration had seemed determined to expand the 'war against terrorism' to cover Iraq. President Bush in his first *State of the Union* Address in January 2002 employed dramatic rhetoric about the dangers posed by the 'Axis of Evil', Iraq, Iran and North Korea.[138] In particular he expressed concern that Iraq was developing weapons of mass destruction in violation of the ceasefire regime imposed under Resolution 687 (1991).

The divisions that obstructed Security Council decision-making on Iraq led states and commentators to question the role of the United Nations; the apparent determination of the USA to use force against Iraq led to questions how far, if at all, the USA was constrained by international law. But the USA did offer a legal justification for its use of force, that of authorization by the Security Council under a combination of Security Council resolutions. And although *Operation Iraqi Freedom* was not a UN force or even a NATO force, the USA in its search for legitimacy proclaimed that it was acting with the support of 'a coalition' of at least forty states, including Spain, Italy, Denmark, many East European states, and Japan, even though few states were directly involved in the military action.[139]

The UN weapons inspectors empowered under Resolution 687(1991) to monitor the disarmament of Iraq of its weapons of mass destruction had been withdrawn from Iraq in December 1998. This was done at the request of the USA, in response to Iraqi non-cooperation with the inspections, to allow it to resort to unilateral military action in *Operation Desert Fox* to try to enforce cooperation.[140] Iraq subsequently refused to allow the weapons inspectors to return. The USA and the UK expressed suspicion that in their absence Iraq was developing weapons of mass destruction and might be planning to supply those weapons to terrorists. After many years of debate, in a final attempt to secure a peaceful solution and to allow the UN weapons inspectors to resume their work, the Security Council passed Resolution 1441 unanimously in November 2002 and Iraq accepted the resolution.[141]

---

[138] For further discussion of the build-up to the use of force against Iraq and of the doctrine of pre-emptive self-defence, see Chapter 6.

[139] Keesings (2003) 45315; *The Guardian*, 5, 19 March 2003.

[140] See 351 above.

[141] On the negotiations leading to the adoption of resolution 1441, see Murphy (ed), 'Contemporary Practice of the United States relating to International Law', 96 AJIL (2002) 956. Iraq's acceptance of SC Res 1441 was communicated to the Security Council in S/2002/1034 (16 September 2002) and S/2002/1242 (13 November 2002).

Security Council Resolution 1441 (2002)

Resolution 1441 (2002) recalled all the Security Council's previous relevant resolutions, including Resolution 678 (1990) which had authorized 'Member States cooperating with the Government of Kuwait... to use all necessary means' to drive Iraq out of Kuwait and to restore international peace and security in the area, and Resolution 687 (1991), the ceasefire resolution. Acting under Chapter VII of the UN Charter, the Security Council decided that Iraq 'has been and remains in material breach of its obligations under relevant resolutions, including resolution 687'. It went on to decide to afford Iraq 'a final opportunity to comply' with its disarmament obligations, and accordingly it set up an enhanced inspection regime. Iraq was to provide the weapons inspectors and the Security Council with a complete declaration of all aspects of its weapons programmes. Any false statements or omissions would constitute a further material breach of Iraq's obligations and should be reported to the Council for assessment (paragraph 4). The resolution set out detailed rules on the enhanced inspection regime. The weapons inspectors were to report immediately to the Security Council any interference or failure to comply by Iraq (paragraph 11). The Security Council was to convene immediately upon receipt of a report under paragraphs 4 or 11, 'in order to consider the situation and the need for full compliance with all of the relevant Security Council resolutions in order to secure international peace and security' (paragraph 12). The resolution concluded by recalling that the Council had repeatedly warned Iraq that it would face serious consequences as a result of its continued violations of its obligations (paragraph 13).

This resolution does not expressly authorize force against Iraq; it is apparent from the debate leading up to the resolution that several permanent members were not willing to give such authority. The Security Council was still divided between, on the one hand, the USA and the UK who wanted a single resolution which authorized force and, on the other, Russia, China, Germany and France who were not ready to accept this and who wanted a two stage process, leading to another resolution expressly authorizing force in the event of continued Iraqi non-compliance and further material breach. Debate initially focused on whether Resolution 1441 (2002) alone was enough to authorize force by the USA and the UK or a 'coalition' of states without a second resolution, but the Security Council records made it clear that this was not the understanding of member states at the time. China, Russia and France would not have agreed to the resolution if it had contained any immediate authorization of military action.[142] Even the USA and the UK were in agreement that there was no

[142] 2003 UNYB 315–336; SC 4625th 4644th meetings (2002); Murphy 'Contemporary Practice of the United States relating to International Law', 97 AJIL (2003) 419.

'automaticity' in the resolution and the 'coalition' did not in fact rely on Resolution 1441 (2002) alone as the basis for military action.[143]

The UN weapons inspectors returned to Iraq to set up the new inspection regime under Resolution 1441 (2002) and Iraq produced a massive 12,000 page declaration on the state of its weapons programme.[144] The weapons inspectors at first reported some delays in cooperation and that Iraq did not initially take the pro-active approach demanded by the new enhanced inspection regime. The inspectors did not find any weapons of mass destruction, but many banned weapons remained unaccounted for and could only be resolved by Iraq's immediate, unconditional and active cooperation. Iraq's cooperation improved in February 2003.[145] The USA and the UK argued that Iraq was in material breach, but there was no new formal determination by the Security Council itself other than that in Resolution 1441 (2002).[146]

The states which resorted to force thus did not rely on Resolution 1441 (2002) alone as the basis for military action. However, they maintained that no second resolution was necessary. They argued that the crucial fact was that Resolution 1441 (2002) did not expressly stipulate that another resolution was necessary; it did not say that there had to be a second Security Council resolution to authorize military action. Therefore Resolution 1441(2002) did not require a further Security Council *decision*; paragraph 12 required only that the Security Council meet to '*consider* the situation'.[147] States were thus free unilaterally to resort to force against Iraq in the event of further material breaches of the ceasefire regime.[148]

Nevertheless the USA and the UK made persistent attempts to secure another resolution. The UK repeatedly stressed its strong preference for a second resolution.[149] But for France, Germany and Russia the preferred

---

[143] This was expressly accepted by the UK in the FCO *Legal Basis for the Use of Force* (17 March 2003) para 11, 52 ICLQ (2003) 812; 'UK Materials on International Law', 73 BYIL (2002) 787, 879–90.

[144] 2002 UNYB 289.

[145] For UNMOVIC's and the IAEA's reports to the Security Council and subsequent debates, see 2002 UNYB 285–296; 2003 UNYB 316–333.

[146] See, for example, 2003 UNYB 330–332; SC 4701st meeting, UN Press Release SC/7658, 5 February 2003; SC 4721st meeting, UN Press Release 7696, 19 March 2003; FCO Press Statement, 28 January 2003.

[147] See FCO *Legal Basis for the Use of Force* (17 March 2003) para 11, ICLQ (2003); Australian Attorney-General's *Memorandum of Advice on the Use of Force against Iraq* (18 March 2003), 24 Australian Yearbook of International Law (2003) 415.

[148] The UK Attorney-General in his legal advice published after the invasion considered this crucial argument at some length, 54 ICLQ (2005) 767 at para 22–31. He concluded that the language of the resolution left the position unclear and the statements made on adoption of the resolution suggest that there were differences of view within the SC as to the legal effect of the resolution.

[149] Speech by the Foreign Secretary, 25 November 2002, Hansard, House of Commons Debates Vol 395, Columns 49–50; *The Guardian* 8 November 2002, 1 February 2003.

solution was to continue with weapons inspections and to strengthen the inspection regime.[150] On 24 February 2003 a draft resolution authorizing force was put forward by the USA, the UK and Spain, but was later withdrawn when it became clear that it would not attract sufficient support in the Security Council and would be vetoed by France and Russia.[151]

The 'coalition' case for action

The 'coalition' of the USA, the UK and Australia, with the political and other support of about forty states, therefore went ahead with *Operation Iraqi Freedom* without a second resolution. They did so on the basis of the revival of the authority to use force in Resolution 678 (1990).

The UK and Australian Attorney-Generals set out the legal case for military action against Iraq. Both did so in response to domestic pressure and demands for legal justification; they took very similar approaches.[152] The UK position was as follows:

The UK Attorney-General was of the opinion that the 'safest legal course would be to secure the adoption of a further resolution to authorise the use of force.' (54 ICLQ (2005) 767 at para 27).

[150] For their joint memoranda, see S/2003/214, 24 February 2003; S/2003/253, 3 March 2003; *The Guardian* 10, 11, 24 February 2003.

[151] Keesings (2003) 45313–15; UN Press Release SC/7682 at 12, 7 March 2003; *The Independent*, 27 February 2003; *The Guardian*, 12 March 2003. There was some debate as to whether one or all of these vetos could be discounted as long as there was a majority in the Security Council in favour of the use of force. President Chirac was reported as having announced on 10 March 2003 that France would use its veto to block any resolution containing an ultimatum to Iraq 'whatever the circumstances'. The UK Prime Minister responded that this would be an unreasonable veto and could be discounted. 'I define an unreasonable veto as follows. In resolution 1441, we said that it was Saddam's final opportunity and that he had to comply. That was agreed by all members of the Security Council. What is surely unreasonable is for a country to come forward now, at the very point when we might reach agreement and when we are saying that he must comply with the UN, after all these months without full compliance, on the basis of the six tests or action will follow. For that country to say that it will veto such a resolution in all circumstances is what I would call unreasonable.' (House of Commons Hansard, 18 March 2003, Col764–767). But legally this argument that if the Security Council were prevented from acting by an unreasonable veto then the USA and the UK could go ahead to implement the will of international community as expressed in SC Res 1441 is difficult to sustain. As critics pointed out, the UK itself had used the veto over thirty times in a way that might be seen by others as unreasonable; the veto was an integral part of the UN system and could not be ignored when it was inconvenient. The UK did not pursue this line of argument after the draft resolution allowing the use of force failed to secure a majority in the Security Council. The UK Attorney-General in his advice on the legality of the invasion rejected any doctrine of an unreasonable veto: 'I do not believe there is any basis in law for arguing that there is an implied condition of reasonableness which can be read into the power of veto conferred on the permanent members of the Security Council by the UN Charter...In any event, if the majority of world opinion remains opposed to military action it is likely to be difficult on the facts to categorise a French veto as unreasonable.' (54 ICLQ (2005) 767 at para 31).

[152] For UK case, see 52 ICLQ (2003) 811; for a fuller version, see 54 ICLQ (2005) 767. For Australia's case, see Attorney-General's *Memorandum of Advice on the Use of Force against Iraq* (18 March 2003), 24 Australian Yearbook of International Law (2003) 415.

Authority to use force against Iraq exists from the combined effects of resolutions 678, 687 and 1441. All of these resolutions were adopted under Chapter VII of the UN Charter which allows the use of force for the express purpose of restoring international peace and security:

1. In resolution 678 the Security Council authorized force against Iraq, to eject it from Kuwait and to restore peace and security in the area.

2. In resolution 687, which set out the ceasefire conditions after Operation Desert Storm, the Security Council imposed continuing obligations on Iraq to eliminate its weapons of mass destruction in order to restore international peace and security in the area. Resolution 687 suspended but did not terminate the authority to use force under resolution 678.

3. A material breach of resolution 687 revives the authority to use force under resolution 678.

4. In resolution 1441 the Security Council determined that Iraq has been and remains in material breach of resolution 687, because it has not fully complied with its obligations to disarm under that resolution.

5. The Security Council in resolution 1441 gave Iraq 'a final opportunity to comply with its disarmament obligations' and warned Iraq of the 'serious consequences' if it did not.

6. The Security Council also decided in resolution 1441 that, if Iraq failed at any time to comply with and cooperate fully in the implementation of resolution 1441, that constitutes a further material breach.

7. It is plain that Iraq has failed so to comply and therefore Iraq was at the time of resolution 1441 and continues to be in material breach.

8. Thus, the authority to use force under resolution 678 has revived and so continues today.

9. Resolution 1441 would in terms have provided that a further decision of the Security Council to sanction force was required if that had been intended. Thus, all that resolution 1441 requires is reporting to and discussion by the Security Council of Iraq's failures, but not an express further decision to authorize force.

This is an impressively concise and cleverly argued case, even if it ultimately failed to convince the vast majority of other states.[153] The fuller legal advice given by the UK Attorney-General was not made public at the time; this provided a much more cautious approach and a detailed consideration of the competing arguments. He said, 'To sum up, the language of resolution 1441 leaves the position unclear and the statements made on the adoption of the resolution suggest that there were differences of view within the Council as to the legal effect of the resolution. Arguments can

---

[153] A slightly longer version was provided by the Foreign and Commonwealth Office, *Legal Basis for the Use of Force* (17 March 2003), 52 ICLQ (2003) 812.

be made on both sides.'[154] The USA did not publish a comparable formal legal case, but did set out its position in speeches and communications to the Security Council.[155] The pressure on the USA to offer a plausible legal case came not so much from any strong domestic opposition to war, but rather from other states whose help the USA was asking, to provide rights of overflight and other support. States such as Turkey, Saudi Arabia, Italy and Japan needed to be able to justify their support role in *Operation Iraqi Freedom* to their own domestic constituencies and to reconcile their participation with the relevant constitutional limits on the use of force.

In March 2003 the USA, the UK and Australia each sent a letter to the Security Council at the start of *Operation Iraqi Freedom*. The USA reported that coalition forces had commenced military operations in Iraq. These were necessary in view of Iraq's continued material breaches of its disarmament obligations under relevant Security Council resolutions, including Resolution 1441 (2002). The actions being taken were authorized under Resolutions 678 (1990) and 687 (1991). The USA said that this had been the basis for 'coalition' use of force in the past; it expressly referred back to its use of force in 1993.[156] The UN Secretary-General had then accepted the doctrine of the revival of Resolution 678 (1990) following Iraq's material breach of Resolution 687 (1991). The Security Council had decided that Iraq had been and remained in material breach and that it would face serious consequences. Iraq had decided not to avail itself of the 'final opportunity' to comply and had committed additional breaches. In view of this the basis for the ceasefire had been removed and the use of force was authorized under Resolution 678 (1990). The USA would use force 'to defend the United States and the international community from the threat posed by Iraq and to restore international peace and security in the area'.[157]

The UK and Australia followed a similar line, although it is interesting to note that whereas the USA mentioned self-defence in its letter, the UK and Australia relied only on Security Council authority.[158] They wrote that in Resolution 1441(2002) the Council had reiterated that Iraq's possession of weapons of mass destruction constituted a threat to international peace

---

[154] 54 ICLQ (2005) 767 at para 26.

[155] The Legal Adviser and Assistant Legal Adviser to the US State Department did provide an account of the US position after the operation: Taft and Buchwald, 'Pre-emption, Iraq and International Law', 97 AJIL (2003) 553. This followed broadly the same approach as that of the UK and Australia.

[156] See 350 above.

[157] UN doc S/2003/351.

[158] UN docs S/2003/350, S/2003/352. On pre-emptive self-defence as a possible justification for action against Iraq, see Chapter 6 above. The UK Foreign Affairs Select Committee had earlier expressed a qualified preference that any military action against Iraq should not be taken on the basis of self-defence, unless new evidence emerged that Iraq posed an imminent threat to the security of the UK, (Second Report from the Foreign Affairs Committee, *Foreign Policy Aspects of the War against Terrorism, Session 2002–2003*, HC 196 at 7).

and security; that Iraq had failed to disarm and that in consequence Iraq was in material breach of the conditions for the ceasefire in Resolution 687 (1991). Military action was undertaken only when it became apparent that there was no other way of achieving compliance by Iraq.

Thus the coalition was not able to secure any new express Security Council authority to use force, but the USA, the UK and Australia claimed that the sequence of Resolutions 678, 687 and 1441 in combination was enough to give Security Council authority under Chapter VII. This assumes that the authority to use 'all necessary means' in Resolution 678 (1990) continued and that it could be invoked unilaterally despite the ceasefire in Resolution 687 (1991). The main questions provoked by this line of argument are, first, how could Resolution 678 (1990) provide authority to use force twelve years after it was originally passed and in very different circumstances? Resolution 678 (1990) was passed in response to the invasion of Kuwait by Iraq; it authorized member states 'acting in cooperation with government of Kuwait' to use all necessary means to drive Iraq out of Kuwait and to restore international peace and security in the area. The context was very different in 2003, but the coalition argued that the need to restore international peace and security in the area remained. Iraq's behaviour continued to pose a threat to international peace and security, and force could now be used to disarm Iraq of its weapons of mass destruction.

Australia directly addressed this problem of the revival of Resolution 678 (1990) many years after it was passed in the Attorney-General's *Memorandum of Advice on the Use of Force against Iraq*; it argued that there had been no time limit in the operative part of Resolution 678 (1990). Nor was its purpose confined to restoration of the sovereignty and independence of Kuwait; the authority to use force was also to restore international peace and security in the region. 'There is no finite time under the Charter in which the authority given in a Security Council resolution expires. Nor is there any indication in resolutions subsequent to SCR 678 that the authority for the use of force contained in that resolution has expired.'[159] Iraq continued to be a threat to international peace and security and so action could be taken against it. The UK took a similar line: the authorization to use force in Resolution 678(1990) was suspended but not terminated by Resolution 687 (1991); it was revived by Resolution 1441 (2002).[160] The UK referred to the controversial precedents of 1993 and 1998 as examples where 'the coalition' had taken military action under the

---

[159] Attorney-General's *Memorandum of Advice on the Use of Force against Iraq* (18 March 2003) para 15, 24 Australian Yearbook of International Law (2003) 415.
[160] FCO *Legal Basis for the Use of Force* (17 March 2003) 52 ICLQ (2003) 812; 54 ICLQ (2005) 767 at para 7–11.

revived authority of Resolution 678 (1990) to deal with the threat to international peace and security posed by Iraqi violations of the ceasefire.[161]
In his fuller legal advice published after the invasion the UK Attorney-
General acknowledged that the revival argument was controversial and
not widely accepted among academic commentators. However, he argued
that Resolution 1441 (2002) strengthened the revival argument, given that
it expressly recalled the authorization to use force in Resolution 678 (1990),
that it provided that Iraq had been and remained in material breach of its
obligations, and that it had been warned of serious consequences from
continued violations. He asserted that the previous practice of the Council
and the statements made during the negotiation of Resolution 1441 (2002)
demonstrated that the phrase 'material breach' signified a finding by the
Council of a sufficiently serious breach of the ceasefire conditions to revive
the authorization in Resolution 678 (1990) and that 'serious consequences'
was accepted as indicating the use of force.[162] However, he accepted that
the language of Resolution 1441 (2002) left the position unclear.

The second main problem with the 'coalition' case is its essentially unilateral nature. There was significant uncertainty as to two of the central
questions arising out of Resolution 1441 (2002): what is a material breach
and who is to make that determination?[163] Resolution 1441 (paragraph 4)
specified that Iraq was already in material breach but now had a final
opportunity to comply. False statements or omissions in the declaration
and failure at any time to comply with and cooperate fully with the implementation of the resolution would constitute further material breaches.

The US position was that a material breach was a matter of objective fact
which did not require a Security Council determination. The USA was
therefore free to resort to force under the revived authority in Resolution
678 (1990) on the basis of its own finding of material breach.[164] The UK
Attorney-General acknowledged that this was an issue of critical importance when considering the effect of Resolution 1441 (2002).[165] He said that
the UK government position was that it was for the Security Council to
determine the existence of a material breach 'such that the basis of the
ceasefire is destroyed'. It could be argued that the Security Council had
already pre-determined the issue in Resolution 1441 (2002). However, he
acknowledged that this was a narrow textual argument at odds with public statements.[166] He also accepted that the Security Council did not intend

---

[161] See 350 above.
[162] 54 ICLQ (2005) 767 para 10.
[163] Ibid, for a detailed discussion of the opposing arguments.
[164] Ibid., para 9, 22. The UK Attorney-General said, 'I am not aware of any other state
which supports this view.'
[165] Ibid., para 9.
[166] Ibid., paras 9, 15, 17 and 26.

that the authorization in Resolution 678 (1990) should revive *immediately* following the adoption of Resolution 1441 (2002) since it offered Iraq a final opportunity to comply with its disarmament obligations. In the event of a report of further material breach there was to be a meeting of the Security Council to consider the situation. The Council would thus have the opportunity to take a further decision expressly authorizing force, or to decide that other enforcement means should be used. But the Council might fail to act. In that case the UK argued that it was open to member states to resort to force in the absence of any further Security Council resolution.[167] However, the Attorney-General said the argument that Resolution 1441 (2002) had revived the authorization to use force in Resolution 678 (1990) would only be sustainable if there were strong factual grounds for concluding that Iraq had failed to take the final opportunity offered to it. There had to be hard evidence of non-compliance and non-cooperation.[168] As it turned out, there was no such hard evidence.[169]

Thus it seems that both the USA and the UK asserted a right to determine for themselves whether there was a further material breach by Iraq and also a right to decide whether to resort to force. Other states were not willing to accept this interpretation of the relevant resolutions; the decisions on material breach and on the use of force were for the Security Council. How could the USA and the UK argue that a material breach—even a non-forcible breach—by Iraq of the ceasefire regime in Resolution 687 (1991) ended the ceasefire and revived the authority to use force under Resolution 678 in the absence of a determination by the Security Council that the ceasefire was over? There was no express Security Council authority to use force in 2003 and no formal determination by the Security Council of a further material breach by Iraq apart from those in Resolution 1441 (2002).

The USA stressed that *Operation Iraqi Freedom* was not unilateral but undertaken by a 'coalition', bigger than that for the UN-authorized action in 1991.[170] The USA had used this term to cover action by itself and the UK in the no-fly zones and in *Operation Desert Fox* (1998). Nevertheless the determination of a material breach after Resolution 1441 was unilateral in the sense that it was made by the USA, the UK and Australia rather than by the Security Council. The crucial question of the existence of a material breach allowing force was not to be left in the hands of the Security Council, but was one for the 'coalition'. In Resolution 1441 (2002) the Security Council had found that Iraq 'has been and remains in material

---

[167] Ibid., para 21, 22–25. The Attorney-General made it clear that he took a more cautious (and not entirely clear) view on this point than the USA.
[168] Ibid., para 29.
[169] See 220 above.
[170] Keesings (2003) 45315; *The Guardian*, 5, 19 March 2003.

breach' of its obligations under the relevant Security Council resolutions, but it did not authorize force because of the opposition of France, Russia and China. For the coalition this was enough to end a Security Council imposed ceasefire and to allow military action, even in the absence of any express authorization, and in the face of the opposition of a majority of the Security Council.

Operation Iraqi Freedom started on 20 March 2003, and by 9 April the government of Iraq had been defeated.[171] Many states continued to argue that the use of force was not legal. Very unusually the UN Secretary-General spoke out in public to say that the invasion of Iraq was illegal.[172] The Non-Aligned Movement (then 116 states), the League of Arab States and several other states wrote to the Security Council to put on record their view that the 'coalition' was guilty of aggression in violation of the UN Charter.[173] Russia said that 'Nothing can justify this military action—neither accusations that Iraq is supporting international terrorism (we have never had, and still do not have, information of this kind), nor the desire to change the political regime in that country, which is in direct contradiction with international law. Finally, there was no need to launch military action in order to answer the key question that was posed directly by the international community, namely, does Iraq have or does it not have, weapons of mass destruction, and if it does, what should be done, and within what time frame, in order to liquidate them?' In Security Council debates during the conflict France, Germany, Russia and China all said that US and UK allegations about Iraq's weapons of mass destruction and support for terrorism had not been substantiated; they were using force to secure regime change in a sovereign state contrary to the UN Charter.[174] The Non-Aligned Movement and the Arab League did not accept the coalition case that the operation was legal because it had been authorized by the Security Council.[175]

Nor did the end of the conflict bring acquiescence by the states which had denied the legality of *Operation Iraqi Freedom*, even though most welcomed the overthrow of President Saddam Hussein.[176] The USA announced on 1 May 2003 that major combat operations had ended, but coalition forces would remain in Iraq as long as necessary to help the

---

[171] Murphy (ed), 'Contemporary Practice of the United States relating to International Law', 97 AJIL (2003) 419. Despite the name of the operation, the USA and the UK did not use the doctrine of humanitarian intervention as a legal justification for the operation; see Chapter 2 above.

[172] 'Iraq war illegal says Annan', BBC News, 16 September 2004, available on BBC website; *The Guardian*, 17 September 2007.

[173] UN docs S/2003/365, S/2003/357.

[174] SC 4726th meeting (2003).

[175] Ibid.

[176] Keesings (2003) 45370.

Iraqi people to build their own political institutions and reconstruct their country. Civil disorder and attacks on occupying forces continued. Debates in the Security Council about the future of Iraq made it clear that states opposed to the military action were determined not to legitimize it retrospectively.[177] Some repeated their accusations of illegality; others called for members to look to the future and not to rake up the embers of old quarrels. Given the failure of the occupying forces to find evidence of weapons of mass destruction, there was also considerable scepticism as to the basis on which the coalition had gone to war: the fear that Iraq was developing weapons of mass destruction in violation of Resolution 687 (1991) and that it posed a real threat to other states. Security Council Resolutions on Iraq passed after the start of *Operation Iraqi Freedom* took the pragmatic approach of simply accepting the status quo without any express or implied observation on the legality of the military operation.[178] The rules governing belligerent occupation were accepted as applicable to their forces in Iraq by the USA and the UK; in a letter to the President of the Security Council they acknowledged their obligations as occupying powers under the unified command of 'the Authority'.[179] These rules apply regardless of the legality or otherwise of the initial military action. Resolution 1483 (2003) accordingly recognized the US-led occupation force as a provisional authority in Iraq, but made no pronouncement on the legality of *Operation Iraqi Freedom*.

States were divided as to the future administration of Iraq. Those who had opposed the use of force now insisted that the UN should play the central role in reconstruction. But the USA initially was willing to accept only a more limited role for the UN. Resolution 1483 (2003) was a compromise; it provided that the UN should play 'a vital role' in humanitarian relief, the reconstruction of Iraq, and the restoration and establishment of national and local institutions for representative governance. But bitter divisions persisted. Many states called for a much stronger UN role and refused to offer assistance to the occupying forces unless the UN was given this role.[180] In October 2003 Resolution 1511 was passed unanimously after protracted negotiations; like the previous resolutions it did not indicate acquiescence in the legality of *Operation Iraqi Freedom*. It outlined the roles of the UN, the US-led 'Authority' and the Iraqi Governing Council set up by the 'Authority'. It emphasized the temporary nature of the coalition 'Authority', called on it to return governing authority to the people of that country as soon as practicable, and invited the Iraqi Governing Council

---

[177] SC 4761st, 4791st meetings (2003).
[178] SC Res 1472, 1483, 1500 (2003).
[179] UN doc S/2003/538.
[180] SC 4761st, 4791st, 4812th meetings (2003).

to provide a timetable for drafting a new constitution and holding democratic elections. But France, Germany and Russia, although they voted for the resolution, were still not satisfied that it gave a large enough role to the UN in the reorganization of Iraq.[181]

CONCLUSION

It is clear that *Operation Desert Storm* served as a crucial precedent, a catalyst for a shift in the UN system. The *Brahimi Report* operated on the premise that 'while the UN has acquired considerable expertise in planning, mounting and executing traditional peacekeeping operations, it has yet to acquire the capacity needed to deploy more complex operations rapidly and to sustain them effectively'.[182] The Panel went so far as to say that 'the UN does not wage war. Where enforcement action is required it has consistently been entrusted to coalitions of willing states with the authorization of the Security Council, acting under Chapter VII of the Charter.'[183] Thus it has become the new orthodoxy that it is for member states to undertake enforcement action. Developed states have generally preferred to undertake this type of operation rather than submit their forces to UN command.

But the doctrine of implied authorization is much more controversial. The use of the doctrine of implied authorization by the Security Council to justify the military action by the USA and the UK in Iraq in 1993 and 1998, by NATO in Kosovo and most recently by the USA, the UK and Australia in *Operation Iraqi Freedom* shows lip service to the authority of the UN, but an unwillingness actually to accept the decisions of the Security Council. Some have welcomed the fact that the USA has turned to this doctrine; they see it as preferable to a complete abandonment of any attempt at a legal justification. For others the doctrine of implied authorization is a dangerous one which risks undermining the authority of the United Nations. There is also a serious risk that the Security Council will become unwilling to pass resolutions under Chapter VII condemning state action if there is a possibility that such resolutions might be claimed as implied justification for regional or unilateral use of force despite their drafting history. The impact of the justifications used for the invasion of Iraq on subsequent Security Council decision-making may be seen very clearly with regard to the DPRK and Iran. When the Security Council wished to express its concern that these states were in violation of their

---

[181] SC 4844th meeting (2003). See 346 for subsequent developments.
[182] *Brahimi Report*, A/55/305 (2000) para 6(h).
[183] Ibid., para 53.

non-proliferation obligations the language it used in its resolutions was extremely careful and was designed deliberately to exclude any possible invocation of implied Security Council authorization by the USA or any other state wishing to take forcible action against the DPRK and Iran.[184]

In response to the DPRK's withdrawal from the *Treaty on the Non-Proliferation of Nuclear Weapons* (NPT) and its test firing of long range ballistic missiles in 2006 the Security Council unanimously passed Resolution 1695 (2006); this expressed grave concern at the launch of the missiles and deplored the announced withdrawal from the NPT, but it was not expressly passed under Chapter VII of the Charter. Instead there was in the preamble a statement that the Security Council was 'acting under its special responsibility for the maintenance of international peace and security'. There was no express reference to Chapter VII, and no formal determination that there was a threat to international peace and security. It was clear from the debate that the resolution was a compromise.[185] When the DPRK later carried out a nuclear weapons test on 9 October 2006, the Security Council resolution again was clearly designed to exclude any authorization of military action. Unusually the Security Council in Resolution 1718 (2006) (passed unanimously) expressly referred to the Article of the Charter under which it was taking action. This resolution condemning the test, and demanding that the DPRK retract the announcement of its withdrawal from the NPT and that it suspend its ballistic missile programme and abandon its nuclear weapons programme was expressly passed under Chapter VII, and specified that it was taking measures under Article 41 in imposing sanctions on the DPRK. The resolution ended by expressly underlining 'that further decisions will be required should additional measures be necessary'. This was clearly designed to avoid the type of argument made by the USA and the UK in the case of Iraq; they had claimed that because Resolution 1441 (2002) did not expressly require a further Security Council *decision*, but said only that the Security Council should *consider* the situation if Iraq committed further material breaches of its obligations, therefore it was open to them to resort to force even without a further Security Council resolution.[186] In the debate on Resolution 1718 (2006) Russia said that this resolution was the result of tense negotiations; China stipulated that it was firmly opposed to the use of force.[187]

---

[184] See 367 above. On the interpretation of SC resolutions, see Wood, 'The interpretation of Security Council resolutions', 1998 (2) Max Planck Yearbook of UN Law 73; Papastavridis, 'Interpretation of Security Council Resolutions under Chapter VII in the aftermath of the Iraqi Crisis', 56 ICLQ (2007) 83.
[185] SC 5490th meeting (2006).
[186] See 359 above.
[187] SC 5551st meeting (2006).

The same caution in the drafting of Security Council resolutions was apparent with regard to Iran. Iran's official policy was to pursue the development of nuclear energy, but the IAEA had expressed concern that Iran had not cooperated with its efforts to establish that Iran's nuclear programme was exclusively for peaceful purposes. The Security Council in Resolution 1696 (2006) expressly said that it was acting under Article 40, the power to take provisional measures.[188] It called on Iran to take the steps required by the IAEA and to suspend all enrichment-related and reprocessing activities to be verified by the IAEA. In the ante-penultimate paragraph it expressed its intention in the event that Iran had not complied with this resolution by 31 August 2006 then to adopt appropriate measures under Article 41 to persuade Iran to comply; it 'underlines that further decisions will be required should such additional measures be necessary'. There is clearly nothing here that could be seized on by states wishing to use force.[189] In the debate on Resolution 1696 (2006) Russia said that it was 'crucial to note that it followed from the resolution that any additional measures that could be required to implement the resolution ruled out the use of military force'.[190] The next two resolutions, passed unanimously, impose sanctions on Iran under Article 41. They express concern at the proliferation risks presented by the Iranian nuclear programme and by Iran's continuing failure to meet the IAEA requirements. Both call for further reports on Iran's compliance with the measures required by the IAEA and affirm that if these reports show that Iran has not complied with the resolution then the Security Council 'shall adopt further measures under Article 41', again underlining that further decisions shall be required should such additional measures be necessary.[191] Russia again stressed that the text of the two resolutions—the product of long and difficult consultations—did not permit the use of force.[192] It is evident from the text of all these resolutions that members of the Security Council have learned lessons from the use made of Resolution 1441 (2002) to justify the 2003 invasion of Iraq.

Clear divisions have emerged between those states claiming to act on behalf of the international community and those who reject such claims in the absence of express Security Council authorization of force. The former offer a justification for the use of force based on implied authorization by

---

[188] Passed by 14–0–1 (Qatar); Qatar called for further time to be given to be Iran.

[189] On the legality of possible use of force against Iran, see O'Connell, 'The Ban on the Bomb and Bombing', 57 Syracuse LR (2007) 497; Maggs, 'How the United States might justify a preemptive strike on a rogue nation's nuclear weapon development under the UN Charter', 57 Syracuse LR (2006/7) 465.

[190] SC 5500th meeting (2006).

[191] SC Res 1737 (2006) and 1747 (2007).

[192] SC 5612th meeting (2006); SC 5647th meeting (2007).

the Security Council in response to material breach of a Security Council resolution. The USA and the UK have based their case for force on the words of particular resolutions and have discounted the drafting history which showed an unwillingness by other states to accept that the resolutions in question could be interpreted to authorize force. It is no longer simply a case of interpreting euphemisms such as 'all necessary means' to allow the use of force when it is clear from the preceding debate that force is envisaged, as was the case with Resolution 678 in 1990. The USA, the UK and others have gone far beyond this in order to claim to be acting on behalf of the international community. The latter group of states who oppose the use of force on this basis proclaim adherence to the existing UN system, accepting the risk of inaction by the Security Council as the price to pay for the maintenance of that system and as preferable to accepting claims by states acting unilaterally that they do so to fulfil the true wishes of the international community.

The USA in its justification of *Operation Iraqi Freedom* referred to the acceptance by a former UN Secretary-General of the doctrine of implied authority under Resolution 678 in 1993.[193] But in September 2002 the then Secretary-General said 'Any state, if attacked, retains the inherent right of self-defence under Article 51 of the Charter. But beyond that, when states decide to use force to deal with broader threats to international peace and security, there is no substitute for the unique legitimacy provided by the UN.'[194] In March 2003 he warned more directly, 'If the US and others were to go outside the Council and take military action, it would not be in conformity with the Charter.'[195] For a majority of states this remains the legal position.

---

[193] UN doc S/2003/351.
[194] UN Press Release GA/10045, 12 September 2002.
[195] Keesings (2003) 45313; <www.un.org/apps/sg/offthecuff.asp?nid=394>, 10 March 2003; *The Guardian*, 24 September 2003, 17 September 2004.

9
Regional peacekeeping and enforcement action

INTRODUCTION

The end of the Cold War brought a transformation in regional action to match that in UN action. Not only has there been a significant increase in regional activity, especially in the last ten years, but this has also given rise to fundamental questions as to the relationship between the UN and regional organizations and the interpretation of the Charter. Regional action is governed by three articles in Chapter VIII of the UN Charter. Article 52 provides that regional arrangements or agencies may deal with such matters relating to the maintenance of international peace and security as are appropriate for regional action, provided that such arrangements or agencies and their activities are consistent with the purposes and principles of the UN. Article 53 allows the Security Council to utilize regional arrangements or agencies for enforcement action; they are not permitted to take enforcement action without the authorization of the Security Council. Article 54 requires regional arrangements and agencies to keep the Security Council fully informed of their activities for the maintenance of international peace and security.[1]

The increase in UN activity after the end of the Cold War overstretched the UN financially; it also ran into difficulty in securing an adequate number of troops from member states to carry out the peacekeeping operations the Security Council mandated. It was therefore proposed by many that the UN should turn to regional organizations to share the burden. The UN Secretary-General, in his 1991 *Agenda for Peace*, was optimistic as to the role to be played by regional organizations now that the Cold War was over. He wrote that the Cold War had impaired the proper use of Chapter VIII and indeed that regional arrangements had on occasion worked against resolving disputes in the manner foreseen in the Charter. This verdict seems justified in so far as it was based on action by the OAS with regard to Cuba (1962) and the Dominican Republic (1965), Arab League action in Lebanon (1976–83), OAU action in Chad (1981), and Organization of Eastern Caribbean States (OECS) in Grenada (1983).

[1] On Chapter VIII of the UN Charter, see Simma (ed.), *The Charter of the United Nations: A Commentary* (2nd edn, 2002), 807; Cot and Pellet (eds), *La Charte des Nations Unies* (1991).

There was controversy as to the legality of all these operations.[2] They have been discussed in detail by many writers, so in its discussion of this early practice this chapter will focus on the general lessons to be learned from an overview; it will examine the common themes that emerged, the limitations on what may be expected from regional peacekeeping, and the uncertainties about the applicable law that remained at the end of the Cold War. During the Cold War there was not much regional peacekeeping activity, and what there was was controversial. Partly because of the divisions between states, little in the way of clear rules emerged from Security Council debates and resolutions. Recent practice shows a significant increase in regional activity and a new awareness of the possibilities offered by regional organizations. The surge in UN peacekeeping since 2003 has led to increasing calls for partnership with regional organizations to share the burden;[3] the creation of the AU as the successor to the OAU has led to greater regional activity in Africa; NATO has operated alongside UN missions in Afghanistan and Kosovo; the EU has taken on a new role in cooperation with the UN.[4] However, some legal uncertainties remain and the practical problems with regional operations have become even more apparent outside the Cold War context.

The Secretary-General, in his *Agenda for Peace*, did not set forth any formal pattern of relations between the UN and regional organizations or call for any specific division of labour. But he argued that regional organizations possessed a potential that should be utilized for preventive diplomacy, peacekeeping, peacemaking, and post-conflict peace building. The Security Council would keep its primary role in the maintenance of international peace and security, but 'regional action, as a matter of decentralisation, delegation and cooperation with UN efforts could not only lighten the burden of the Council, but also contribute to a deeper sense

---

[2] See Pellet (ed.), *Les forces régionales du maintien de la paix* (1982); Akehurst, 'Enforcement Action by Regional Agencies, with special reference to the Organization of American States', 42 BYIL (1967) 175; Alibert, 'L'Affaire du Tchad', 90 RGDIP (1986) 368; Miller, 'Regional Organization and the Regulation of Internal Conflict', 19 World Politics (1967) 582; Naldi, 'Peacekeeping Attempts by the OAU', 34 ICLQ (1985) 593; Pogany, 'The Arab League and Regional Peacekeeping', 34 Netherlands ILR (1987) 54; Cot, 'The Role of the Inter-African Peacekeeping Force in Chad', in Cassese (ed.), *The Current Legal Regulation of the Use of Force* (1986), 167; Issele, 'The Arab Deterrent Force in Lebanon 1976–83', ibid.179; Pirrone, 'The Use of Force in the Framework of the OAS', ibid. 223; Weiler, 'Armed Intervention in a Dichotomized World: the case of Grenada', ibid. 241.

[3] The Special Committee on Peacekeeping Operations in its Report, UN doc A/61/19 (2007), highlighted the importance of partnerships with regional arrangements. The Committee recommended that the DPKO establish a framework for practical cooperation and replace *ad hoc* arrangements with effective coordination techniques (para 182–187).

[4] See EU statement in SC 5776th meeting (2007) on EU cooperation with the UN and regional organizations; White, 'The ties that bind: the EU, the UN and international law', 37 Netherlands Yearbook of International Law (2006) 57; 11 International Peacekeeping (2004) 395, special issue on the EU.

of participation, consensus and democratization in international affairs'. The Secretary-General explained how this might be achieved. First, consultations between the UN and regional arrangements or agencies could help to build international consensus on the nature of the problem and the measures required to address it. Second, complementary efforts by regional organizations and the UN in joint undertakings would encourage states outside the region to act supportively. Third, if the Security Council were to choose to authorize a regional arrangement or organization to take the lead in addressing a crisis within its region it could lend the weight of the UN to the validity of the regional effort.[5]

COOPERATION BETWEEN THE UN AND
REGIONAL ORGANIZATIONS

The years since the *Agenda for Peace* have partly fulfilled the Secretary-General's hopes. There has been a significant increase in consultation and cooperation between the Security Council and regional organizations.[6] The resolutions of the Security Council reflect the transformation of the Cold War situation as regards regional action. These resolutions show an increased awareness of regional organizations and of their growing role in international peace and security. A 1988 study of Security Council resolutions found that references to regional organizations were rare; it cited only two such references in the entire history of the UN.[7] In 1989 there were no references and in 1990 only one, but since 1991 this picture has been transformed. Many resolutions referred to regional organizations in the context of the former Yugoslavia, Western Sahara, Rwanda, Mozambique, Angola, Somalia, Burundi, Liberia, Sierra Leone, Eritrea and Ethiopia, Haiti, and the former USSR. Such resolutions sometimes expressly recalled Chapter VIII of the UN Charter, or expressed appreciation of regional efforts aimed at settlement of a conflict, or supported cooperation between the UN and regional organizations, or endorsed regional efforts. Most of these references concerned attempts at the peaceful settlement of a dispute. Some showed the Security Council urging the regional organization to take the leading role; others authorised

---

[5] 31 ILM (1992) 953.

[6] On cooperation between UN and regional organizations from the first meeting between the UN Secretary-General and heads of regional organizations, see 1994 UNYB 88; 1995 UNYB 1439; 1996 UNYB 1352; 1997 UNYB 63, 1491; 1998 UNYB 61, 556, 1339; 1999 UNYB 74, 1354; 2000 UNYB 230, 1378; 2001 UNYB 107, 1368; 2002 UNYB 234, 1437; 2003 UNYB 12, 271, 2004 UNYB 13, 282, 306, 1452. See also UN Department of Peacekeeping, Lessons Learned, *Cooperation between the United Nations and Regional Organizations/Arrangements in a Peacekeeping Environment: Suggested Principles and Mechanisms* (March 1999).

[7] Sonnenfeld, *Resolutions of the UN Security Council* (1988), 103.

joint operations; yet others authorised the use of force by a regional organization.[8]

The High-level Panel,[9] the Secretary-General in his report *In Larger Freedom*,[10] and the 2005 World Summit all called for a stronger relationship between the UN and regional and subregional organizations, pursuant to Chapter VIII of the Charter. The World Summit Outcome Document resolved to expand consultation and cooperation through formalized agreements between the respective secretariats, and to ensure that regional organizations that have a capacity for the prevention of armed conflict or peacekeeping consider placing such capacity in the framework of the UN Standby Arrangements System.[11]

In response to the World Summit Outcome Document, the Security Council passed Resolution 1631 (2005), its first resolution on cooperation with regional and subregional organizations. This emphasized that the growing contribution by regional organizations could usefully complement the work of the UN in maintaining peace and security, and stressed that such contribution must be made in accordance with Chapter VIII of the UN Charter. The Security Council expressed its determination to take steps towards further cooperation, and invited regional and subregional organizations to place their capacities in the framework of the UN standby arrangements system. It urged all states to contribute to strengthening the capacity of regional and subregional organizations, in particular in Africa, including through the provision of human, technical and financial assistance. It stressed that it was important to develop the ability of regional organizations to deploy peacekeeping forces rapidly in support of UN peacekeeping operations or other Security Council mandated operations. The Security Council called for better communication between the UN and regional and sub-regional organizations; it recalled the obligation for regional organization to keep the Security Council fully informed under Article 54 of the UN Charter.[12] It also requested the Secretary-General to report on the opportunities and challenges involved and to explore the possibility of framework agreements on cooperation.

In 2006 the Secretary-General published his Report, *A regional-global security partnership: challenges and opportunities*.[13] This said that it had long been recognized that the UN was not equipped to handle every crisis in

---

[8] Gray, 'Regional Arrangements and the United Nations', in Fox (ed.), *The Changing Constitution of the United Nations* (1998), 91.
[9] UN doc A/59/565 (2004) para 270–273.
[10] UN doc A/59/2005 (2005) para 213–215.
[11] UN doc A/60/L.1 (2005) para 170.
[12] The Solomon Islands said recently that 'one of the glaring gaps in cooperation' was the lack of observation of Article 54: SC 5776th meeting (2007).
[13] UN doc A/61/204 (2006).

the world on its own: a partnership between the UN and regional and other intergovernmental organizations should be developed if peace and security were to be maintained. The report described the history of cooperation between the UN and regional organizations and current operational cooperation.[14] It then made proposals for the establishment of a more effective partnership, based on a clear division of labour that reflects the comparative advantage of each organization in conflict prevention, peacemaking, peacekeeping and peacebuilding. Also important was the development of a programme of action for capacity building, especially in Africa. The UN was exploring cooperation on standby arrangements and rapid deployment.

The Report noted that the Secretary-General holds annual meetings with the heads of regional organizations; he makes regular reports on cooperation between the UN and regional organizations.[15] The Security Council also holds annual meetings with representatives of regional organizations to consider various aspects of cooperation.[16] It has issued a series of statements which call for increased cooperation based on complementarity and the comparative advantages of the different organizations.[17] In the Security Council debates states have shown general enthusiasm for cooperation. Many argue that regional organizations have not only the advantage of proximity to threats, but also a greater understanding of them, and that a regional organization is in a better position to detect early symptoms of conflict and to act promptly. It may be able to provide a rapid response when the UN is not able to act; NATO, the EU and the AU have developed, or are developing, rapid response capabilities. But there is also recognition that the capacity of regional organizations for sustained operations may be limited, and that it may be necessary for the UN to step in when the threat goes beyond regional capabilities. Some warn that there can be no enforcement action without Security Council authorization.

In practice the aspirations of the Secretary-General as set out in the *Agenda for Peace* have been met in some respects. Regional organizations have taken the leading role in some conflicts. The Security Council has left it to the CSCE (now the OSCE) to take the leading role in the conflict between Armenia and Azerbaijan over the Armenian-populated enclave of Nagorno-Karabakh in Azerbaijan. After the escalation of the conflict in 1993 the Security Council saw its role as essentially one of support for the

---

[14] See also, *Report on the Implementation of the recommendations of the Special Committee on Peacekeeping operations*, A/58/694 (2004) para 83–92.

[15] See, for example, *Cooperation between the UN and regional and other organizations*, A/61/256 (2006).

[16] SC 5007th meeting (2004), 5282nd meeting (2005), 5529th meeting (2006), 5649th meeting, 5776th meeting (2007).

[17] S/PRST/2004/27, S/PRST/2006/39, S/PRST/2007/7, S/PRST/2007/42.

efforts of the CSCE. The CSCE agreed in principle on the establishment of peacekeeping forces, but these were never deployed.[18] The Security Council has also relied on the CSCE to deal with ethnic conflict in other former USSR republics, in Moldova, in South Ossetia in Georgia, and in Chechenya in Russia. In the Federal Republic of Yugoslavia in 1998 the OSCE agreed on the deployment of 2,000 unarmed observers in Kosovo in response to the conflict between the federal government and the ethnic Albanian population of Kosovo.[19]

It is in Africa that regional and subregional organizations have played the most significant role in recent years. ECOWAS, a sub-regional organization, established peacekeeping operations in Liberia (1990–97, 2003), Sierra Leone, Guinea-Bissau and Côte d'Ivoire. The Security Council turned to the OAU to take the leading role in Burundi.[20] After the abortive coup of October 1993 the OAU announced that it was sending a team of military observers. Burundi had originally asked the UN for 1,000 troops but the UN, apparently made cautious by its experience in Somalia, refused this request. The Security Council limited its involvement to welcoming the OAU military observers.[21] After the coup in July 1996 the Security Council again limited itself to a resolution welcoming OAU efforts and mentioning the possibility of sanctions.[22] Subsequently South Africa took a leading role in pursuing a peace settlement, and following the 2000 *Arusha Peace Agreement* it sent in a peacekeeping force in October 2001 with the consent of the government.[23] Subsequently, an AU observer mission, AMIB, made up of troops from Mozambique, Ethiopia and South Africa, was established.[24] This was the first ever AU peacekeeping mission. However, AMIB ran into funding problems, and the AU requested UN assistance.[25] This is a recurring problem for the AU and one which has weakened its peacekeeping capacity. In Resolution 1545 (2004) the Security Council welcomed the efforts of AMIB; it noted the statement of

---

[18] 1994 *Annual Register* 433.

[19] 38 ILM (1999) 24. The force was withdrawn in March 1999.

[20] 1994 UNYB 276.

[21] S/PRST/1994/60 and 82. When the UN Secretary-General proposed a Chapter VII force in January 1996 no member state was willing to take the lead and Burundi was hostile to the deployment of a UN force: 1996 UNYB 73–89.

[22] SC Res 1072 (1996), 1996 UNYB 673.

[23] 2000 UNYB 143; 2001 UNYB 145; Keesings (2001) 44380; UN Press Release SC/7189, 29 October 2001; Report of the Secretary-General S/2001/1013; SC Res 1375 (2001).

[24] 2003 UNYB 145; African Union Communiqués: Central Organ/MEC/AMB/2(LXXVIII); Central Organ/MEC/AMB/Comm.(LXXXVIII); Central Organ/MEC/AHG/Comm.(VII); Central Organ/MEC/AMB/COMM.(XCIII); Keesings (2003) 45331. The UK provided significant financial aid to the Mozambican government to help equip their contingent (UK FCO Press Release, 19 October 2003) and also to the AU (UK FCO Press Release, 10 December 2003).

[25] 2004 UNYB 141 at 145, UN doc S/2004/270, 17 March 2004; UN Press Releases SC/7944, 4 December 2003, SC/9001, 17 February 2004.

the President of Burundi in favour of transforming the AU force into a UN peacekeeping operation and accordingly provided for the establishment of ONUB to take over from AMIB.[26] The AU also later took the lead in creating operations in Darfur and Somalia.

The UN and the AU

In the 1990s the UN sought to induce the OAU (now the AU) to take a more active role in the resolution of conflicts in Africa. Following an OAU/ UN cooperation agreement in 1990, the OAU established a *Mechanism for Conflict Prevention, Management and Resolution* in 1993. These provisions were adopted despite the traditional opposition of the OAU to intervention.[27] In 1997 the Security Council welcomed the important contributions of the OAU through its Mechanism to preventing and resolving conflicts in Africa and looked forward to a stronger partnership in conformity with Chapter VIII.[28] The Security Council went on to support enhancement of the capacity of African states to contribute to peacekeeping operations and asked the UN Secretary-General to submit a report with concrete recommendations on the sources of conflict in Africa and ways to prevent and address these conflicts. Accordingly in 1998 the Secretary-General issued a *Report on the causes of conflict and the promotion of durable peace and sustainable development in Africa*.[29] The overall approach is very cautious. The Secretary-General discussed three possibilities for UN support of regional and subregional activity. First, the authorization of the use of force by member states. But he said that this raised the problem of the ability properly to monitor such action. Second, the co-deployment of UN and regional forces. This might be modelled on the UNOMIL collaboration with ECOMOG in Liberia,[30] but it could not be concluded that it would always be possible to delegate to regional organizations. The impartiality of member states could be open to question. Third, the strengthening of African capacity for peacekeeping. On the last possibility, assistance in the form of training, joint peacekeeping exercises, and partnerships between African states and donor states all had a role.[31]

---

[26] 2004 UNYB 141.

[27] 1993 *Annual Register* 425; 1993 UNYB 304.

[28] S/PRST/1997/46.

[29] 37 ILM (1998) 913; also Secretary-General's *Report on the Enhancement of African Peacekeeping Capacity*, S/1999/171; and SC Res 1625 (2005) Declaration on strengthening the effectiveness of the SC's role in conflict prevention, particularly in Africa.

[30] See below at 405.

[31] The Secretary-General said that the recommendations of the previous Secretary-General in S/1995/1911 remained valid on these points.

The OAU's successor organization, the AU, has taken a more active approach to peacekeeping; its *Constitutive Act* is more positive about AU intervention in member states than the earlier OAU Charter. Under Article 4 it allows not only the right of the AU to intervene in respect of war crimes, genocide and crimes against humanity, but also the right of member states to request intervention from the AU in order to restore peace and security.[32] The AU has made formal provision for peace support operations in the 2002 *Protocol relating to the establishment of the Peace and Security Council of the AU.*[33] This set up a fifteen-member Peace and Security Council as a standing decision-making organ for the prevention, management and resolution of conflicts: 'The Peace and Security Council shall be a collective security and early-warning arrangement to facilitate timely and efficient response to conflict and crisis situations in Africa.' The Protocol also provides for the creation of an African Standby Force.[34] The Security Council welcomed the Protocol and called on the international community to support AU efforts through provision of training, expertise and resources. It also underlined the importance of the Security Council being kept fully informed of regional activities under Article 54.[35]

The UN has been active in encouraging the enhancement of African peacekeeping capacity and in encouraging financial, technical and training assistance.[36] The World Summit Outcome Document called for a ten-year capacity-building programme for the AU,[37] and the UN Secretary-General is working to implement this.[38] The 2006 *Declaration on Enhancing UN–AU Cooperation* adopted a framework for the programme.[39] The General Assembly has expressed its support, and has called on the UN system to intensify its assistance to the AU in strengthening the institutional and operational capacity of its Peace and Security Council.[40] As part of this ten-year capacity-building programme, the EU has established the Peace Facility for Africa with the purpose of financing costs incurred

---

[32] The Constitutive Act of the AU entered into force 26 May 2001; <www.africa-union.org/About_AU/Constitutive_Act.htm>; 12 African Journal of International and Comparative Law (2000) 629; see Packer and Rukare, 'The New African Union and its Constitutive Act', 96 AJIL (2002) 365; Magliveras and Naldi, 'The African Union – A New Dawn for Africa?', 51 ICLQ (2002) 415; Rechner, 'From the OAU to the AU', (39) Vanderbilt J.I.L (2006) 543.

[33] Text available on AU website; <www.africa-union.org>; see Levitt, 'The Peace and Security Council of the AU and the UN Security Council', in Blokker and Schrijver (eds), *The Security Council and the Use of Force* (2005) at 213.

[34] Article 13.

[35] S/PRST/2004/44.

[36] See UN doc A/59/591 (2004).

[37] UN doc A/60/L.1 (2005) para 93.

[38] *A regional-global security partnership*, S/2006/590 (2006) para 64–70.

[39] UN doc A/61/630, annex (2006).

[40] GA Res 61/296 (2007).

by peacekeeping forces.[41] There have been increasing calls for the UN to finance AU peacekeeping operations, especially where the Security Council has authorized the creation of the force under Chapter VII.[42]

In March 2007 the Security Council held an open debate on the relationship between the UN and regional organizations, in particular the AU, in the maintenance of international peace and security. The peace and security challenges being addressed by the AU in Darfur and Somalia had raised new questions. The Assistant Secretary-General for Peacekeeping said that the partnership between the UN and the AU was the most intense of all regional partnerships, encompassing all phases of conflict management throughout the whole continent. The creation of the AU, with its commitment to develop peacekeeping capabilities, had opened up new avenues and challenges for cooperation. Over 75 per cent of UN peacekeepers were deployed in Africa, and Africa provided up to 40 per cent of peacekeepers to the UN.[43]

The Security Council recognized that in some cases the AU may be authorized by the Security Council to deal with collective security challenges on the African continent. It stressed the importance of supporting and maintaining in a sustained way the resource base and capacity of the AU. It requested the Secretary-General to provide a report on specific proposals on how the UN could better support arrangements for further cooperation and coordination with regional organizations, in particular the AU.[44]

The AU in Somalia: AMISOM

The recent experience in Somalia and Darfur has demonstrated the problems facing AU peacekeeping. As described in Chapter 8 above, the situation in Somalia had remained unstable since the withdrawal of the UN force in 1995. Attempts to establish an effective government repeatedly failed; the Transitional Federal Government (TFG) recognized by the UN and the AU could not exercise control over the territory of Somalia and was challenged by the Union of Islamic Courts (UIC). IGAD and the AU were playing the leading role in seeking a negotiated settlement, and there were proposals for the establishment of an IGAD or AU force in support of the TFG.[45] The UIC stated its intention violently to oppose any such

---

[41] *A regional-global security partnership*, S/2006/590 (2006) para 65.
[42] See, for example, the speech of AU Commissioner for Peace and Security, SC 5649th meeting (2007).
[43] SC 5649th meeting (2007).
[44] S/PRST/2007/7.
[45] The TFG President requested the AU to provide a substantial force, AU document PSC/PR/2 (XXII). It was initially agreed that an IGAD force should be deployed, AU document PSC/PR/Comm. (XXIX), to be followed by an AU force, S/PRST/2006/11. IGAD and the

force.[46] Nevertheless the Security Council welcomed the involvement of IGAD and the AU, and in Resolution 1725 (2006), under Chapter VII, it authorized IGAD and the member states of the AU to establish a protection and training mission in Somalia. This was to monitor progress by the transitional government and the UIC in implementing agreements.[47] However, the large-scale invasion of Somalia by Ethiopia in support of the TFG in December 2006 meant that this force was never deployed.[48] There were also some concerns that an IGAD force could not be impartial, given that the membership of IGAD included states with an interest in the situation in Somalia.[49]

After the Ethiopian invasion the Security Council unanimously passed Resolution 1744 (2007). Under Chapter VII it authorized the member states of the AU to establish AMISOM, an 8,000-strong stabilization force; AMISOM was authorized to take all necessary measures to carry out its mandate. It was to evolve into a UN operation that would support the long-term stabilization and post-conflict restoration of Somalia.[50] The AU Peace and Security Council stated its conviction that, 'following the recent developments (ie the Ethiopian invasion) that have enabled the TFG to take over Mogadishu and take control of the country, there exists today a unique and unprecedented opportunity to restore structures of government in Somalia and bring about lasting peace and reconciliation'.[51] The Secretary-General also said that 'the current situation may represent the best opportunity that Somalia has had in years to find a long-term solution to its protracted conflicts by putting in place a functioning and effective state'.[52] This was to prove wildly over-optimistic: the TFG was not able to assert effective control over the territory; the security situation in Mogadishu deteriorated after the defeat of the UIC; there was public resentment at the continued presence of the Ethiopian troops and serious clan-related fighting was resurgent.

The AU had serious difficulties in securing the troops for AMISOM: only Uganda contributed forces in 2007 and AMISOM fell far below the authorized numbers. It was subject to repeated attacks and was not able to carry

AU proposed the deployment of this joint peace support mission, Report of the Secretary-General, S/2006/838, at para 16–18, 68. The Secretary-General said that ideally, the deployment of such a force should be in support of a peace agreement or political process and should enjoy the consent of all major parties.

[46] UN Press Release SC/8880, 29 November 2006.
[47] UN Press Release SC/8887, 6 December 2006.
[48] See Report of the Secretary-General, S/2007/115 para 23.
[49] Report of the Secretary-General, S/2006/838 para 18.
[50] AMISOM was to be exempt from the SC Res 733 (1992) arms embargo on Somalia.
[51] UN doc S/2007/34.
[52] Report of the Secretary-General, S/2007/115 para 62.

out its mandate effectively.[53] The Secretary-General commended the AU for its strong determination to contribute to the stability of Somalia. The deployment of the AU mission in such a challenging and volatile security environment was a daunting task that required and deserved the full support of the international community.[54] The Security Council urged member states to provide resources to AMISOM.[55] The AU told the Security Council that AMISOM was suffering from serious financial and logistical constraints, the task was far beyond the capabilities of the AU, and there was a need for a UN force to take over.[56] But the Secretary-General reported that under the prevailing political and security situation the deployment of a UN peace-keeping operation could not be considered a realistic and viable option.[57]

The AU in Darfur: AMIS

When conflict broke out in Darfur in 2003 it was again the AU which took the lead in seeking a solution.[58] It helped the government and rebel groups to conclude the *N'Djamena Humanitarian Ceasefire Agreement* in April 2004, and initially agreed to send a small monitoring force.[59] It then incrementally expanded the force (AMIS) from a monitoring force to a peacekeeping force with a final authorized strength of 6,171 military personnel: its mandate was to monitor and ensure compliance with the *N'Djamena Agreement*, to assist in confidence building and to contribute to a secure environment for the delivery of humanitarian relief and the return of displaced persons. Within this framework AMIS was also to protect civilians from imminent threat, although this was limited to those it encountered and it was understood that the protection of the civilian population was the responsibility of the government.[60] The government of Sudan and various rebel groups consented to the deployment of AMIS.[61] Canada, the EU and the USA pledged financial support and the

---

[53] Reports of the Secretary-General, S/2007/204, S/2007/381, S/2007/658; S/PRST/2007/19.

[54] Report of the Secretary-General, S/2007/204 para 31–34.

[55] S/PRST 2007/13; SC Res 1772 (2007). The USA and the EU offered financial and strategic support, Report of the Secretary-General, UN doc S/2007/115.

[56] Report of the Secretary-General, S/2007/204 para 33–34; UN doc S/2007/499.

[57] Report of the Secretary-General, S/2007/658 para 33.

[58] See Abass, 'The UN, the AU and the Darfur crisis', 54 Netherlands International Law Review (2007) 416.

[59] AU Press Release 51/2004, 28 May 2004, Communiqué of the 12th Meeting of the AUPSC, PSC/MIN/Comm.(XII).

[60] UN doc S/2004/603; Communiqué of the 17th Meeting of the AUPSC, PSC/PR/Comm.(XVII), Communiqué of the 28th Meeting of the AUPSC, PSC/PR/Comm.(XXVIII), Communiqué of the 34th Meeting of the AUPSC, PSC/MIN/Comm.(XXXIV).

[61] Abuja Protocol between the Government of Sudan, the Sudan Liberation Movement and the Justice and Equality Movement on the Improvement of the Humanitarian Situation in Darfur, 9 November 2004; AU Press Release, 21 December 2004; SC Res 1564 (2004).

EU, NATO and the USA participated in the airlift of the African troops.[62] The UN Security Council endorsed the initial deployment of AMIS and its later expansion and urged the international community to continue to support it.[63]

But there were repeated violations of the ceasefire by all parties.[64] The government of Sudan did not carry out the obligations imposed on it by the Security Council to secure the disarmament of the 'janjaweed' militias, and the Security Council threatened to impose sanctions on it.[65] The government of Sudan accused the Security Council of bias and was reluctant to accept a UN force to replace AMIS when the Security Council called for this at the start of 2006.[66] AMIS had been repeatedly commended by the Secretary-General for its proactive and positive role, carried out with limited resources, but it was subject to repeated attacks and was too small and inadequately equipped to provide security throughout the vast area of Darfur.[67] As the AU envoy for Darfur put it in a briefing to the Security Council, AMIS, as presently constituted, was not optimally equipped to fulfil its mandate.[68] A *Comprehensive Peace Agreement* for Darfur was finally concluded in May 2006, and this made a further expansion of AMIS necessary until it could be replaced by a much larger and more mobile UN operation, better equipped and with a stronger mandate.[69] The Security Council therefore unanimously passed Resolution 1679 (2006) under Chapter VII calling on the AU to agree with the UN on requirements to strengthen the capacity of AMIS to enforce the security arrangements of the *Comprehensive Peace Agreement* with a

[62] AU Press Release 27/2005, 30 May 2005; AU Darfur Integrated Taskforce, Information Update No 1, 20 July 2005; UN Press Release SG/SM/9925, 10 June 2005; <www.nato.int/issues/darfur/index.html>.

[63] SC Res 1556, 1564 (2004), SC Res 1590 (2005).

[64] Report of the Secretary-General, S/2004/703, UN Press Releases SC/8180, 2 September 2004, SC/8346, 29 March 2005, SC/8668, 21 March 2006.

[65] SC Res 1556 (2004), passed by 13–0–2 (China, Pakistan). SC Res 1564 (2004), passed by 11–0–4 (Algeria, China, Pakistan, Russia); SC Res 1591 (2005). The government said that the Security Council was attempting to hijack the issue of Darfur from the AU, UN Press Release SC/8160, 30 July 2004.

[66] UN Press Release SC/8628, 3 February 2006; SC Res 1663 (2006). The AUPSC sent a communique on 12 January 2006 expressing support for the transition. The UN Secretary-General said in Report S/2005/148 that it would be erroneous to characterize any transition to the UN as a substitution of an African force by an international force, pointing out that the current AMIS was already an international force, operating under an AU mandate, with the endorsement of the Security Council and the participation of troops and personnel from more than 29 countries. See also SC Res 1679 (2006).

[67] UN Press Releases SC/8262, 7 December 2004, SC/8383, 12 May 2005, SC/8521, 13 October 2005; Reports of the Secretary-General S/2006/591 at para 41, S/2007/104 at para 13

[68] UN Press Release SC/8694, 18 April 2006.

[69] UN Press Release SC/8713, 9 May 2006. Not all the parties to the conflict signed the Peace Agreement.

view to a follow-on UN operation.[70] It then attempted to expand the mandate of the UN Mission in Sudan (already present under the 2005 North/South Peace Agreement) to Darfur, but this proved unacceptable to the government of Sudan.[71] So negotiations began on the deployment of a hybrid UN/AU force.[72] It was not until June 2007 that the government of Sudan finally agreed to the deployment of a hybrid UN/AU force to replace AMIS.[73]

Joint operations

As envisaged in the *Agenda for Peace*, the Security Council has now undertaken joint operations: UN and regional peacekeeping forces have cooperated in Liberia, Georgia, Tajikistan, Sierra Leone and Côte d'Ivoire; the UN has cooperated with EU-led forces in the DRC. The Security Council has also for the first time acted under Chapter VII of the UN Charter to authorize the use of force by a regional arrangement or agency in the former Yugoslavia, Haiti, Sierra Leone, Côte d'Ivoire, Liberia (2003), the DRC (2003 and 2006) and Somalia. In 2007 the Security Council created two new operations. In Darfur after many years of serious violence the UN authorized a 20,000 strong hybrid UN/AU force (UNAMID); this new form of operation was chosen because of the government's prolonged resistance to the deployment of a purely UN force in Darfur.[74] UNAMID took over from the earlier AU force at the end of 2007. And the UN also established a combined UN/regional force (MINURCAT) in Chad and the CAR: the EU was to provide the military component of the operation and the UN, the civilian component. This arrangement was adopted because Chad was reluctant to accept UN peacekeepers.[75]

---

[70] UN Press Release SC/8721, 16 May 2006. Russia and China expressed reservations about the reference to Chapter VII; their position was that the deployment of a UN peacekeeping mission in Darfur required the agreement of the government of Sudan. The government of Sudan was also concerned about the adoption of SC Res 1679 under Chapter VII. Other states such as the UK and Tanzania argued that the reference to Chapter VII was necessary to allow the protection of civilians and of the mission's own forces, UN Press Release SC/8750, 15 June 2006.

[71] SC Res 1706 (2006), passed by 12–0–3 (China, Qatar, Russia); UN Press Releases SC/8821, 31 August 2006, SC/8823, 11 September 2006, SC/8833, 18 September 2006.

[72] UN Press Releases SC/8875, 22 November 2006, SG/SM/10772, 30 November 2006. A three-phased UN support package for AMIS was planned, Report of the Secretary-General S/2007/104 para 32–44. This package was accepted by the government of Sudan in April 2007: UN Press Release SC/8999, 17 April 2007.

[73] UN Press Release SC/9061, 26 June 2007.

[74] SC Res 1769 (2007).

[75] See 299 above.

'REGIONAL ARRANGEMENTS AND AGENCIES'

All these recent resolutions and actions by the Security Council reflect a flexible approach to the once problematic question as to what counts as a 'regional arrangement or agency' under Chapter VIII. In the early days of the UN there was some controversy over this issue, reflected in the absence of any definition of regional arrangement in the UN Charter.[76] The UN Secretary-General, in his 1995 report to the General Assembly on cooperation with regional organizations,[77] put a positive gloss on the absence of a definition; he said that the Charter had anticipated the need for flexibility by not giving any precise definition of regional arrangement or organization, thus enabling diverse organizations to contribute to the maintenance of peace and security.[78] More recently there have been some calls for more precision in this regard, for an express distinction between regional and subregional organizations and other inter-governmental organizations outside Chapter VIII.[79]

There was even in the early days of the UN some disagreement as to whether there should be any cooperation between the UN and regional bodies. Formal cooperation between the UN and regional organizations began in 1948 with the OAS, established in the same year. This organization is expressly proclaimed in Article 1 of the OAS Charter to be a regional organization.[80] The General Assembly, in Resolution 253, invited the Secretary-General of the OAS to assist as an observer at General Assembly sessions. When Argentina initiated this proposal the Eastern bloc states were hostile, arguing that there was no provision in the Charter for such an arrangement. It seemed that they feared that it would reinforce western domination of the UN. But the resolution was passed and the OAS was accepted by the UN as a regional organization under Chapter VIII. This was followed by an invitation to the Arab League in 1950. There was further controversy over the Arab League; this does not expressly claim to be a regional organization under Chapter VIII in its constituent treaty, but it had passed resolutions claiming this status.[81] Israel's challenge to

---

[76] Cot and Pellet (eds), *La Charte des Nations Unies* (1991) at 801, 810; Simma (ed.), *The Charter of the United Nations: A Commentary* (2nd edn, 2002) at 820, 828.

[77] It is striking that UN organs often use the terms organization, arrangement and agency interchangeably.

[78] 1995 UNYB 116.

[79] Report of the Secretary-General, *A regional-global security partnership: challenges and opportunities*, S/2006/590 (2006) para 72–84. Greece supported this call for greater clarity in the identification of regional and subregional agencies and of the criteria by which they could be distinguished from other organizations for the purpose of applying Chapter VIII: SC 5529th meeting (2006); UN doc S/2006/719.

[80] 119 UNTS 48; 33 ILM (1994) 981.

[81] Established in 1945, 70 UNTS 248.

the extension of an invitation to the Arab League and the subsequent debate led to some clarification of issues deliberately left unresolved in Chapter VIII, such as the question of what constitutes a regional agency or arrangement.[82] The subsequent acceptance of the Arab League as an observer amounted to an implicit rejection of Israel's arguments on this issue and made it clear that the concept of region was flexible, that to qualify as a regional organization the Organization did not have to be open to all the states in the region and that no express reference to Chapter VIII or even to the UN Charter in the constituent instrument of the regional organization was necessary. The OAU[83] and the Islamic Conference[84] were granted observer status as regional organizations in 1965 and 1975 respectively.

These invitations to regional organizations to be observers at the General Assembly were followed by General Assembly requests to report annually on what was being done to promote cooperation with these organizations. Even such an apparently innocuous request was the subject of some controversy in the cases of the Islamic Conference and the Arab League. On the former, some states expressed doubts because it served to promote one religion only; on the latter, Israel challenged the initial General Assembly requesting the Secretary-General to report, and twenty-three states abstained. From 1983 onwards Israel and the USA, with some support from the EC and Canada, resisted that part of the General Assembly's resolution on cooperation with the Arab League which requested the UN Secretary-General to intensify efforts towards the implementation of UN resolutions on Palestine and the Middle East.[85]

Since the end of the Cold War the CSCE and CIS have also been given observer status by the General Assembly. These organizations were not originally seen by their member states as Chapter VIII organizations.[86] The General Assembly resolution on observer status for the CSCE included express reference to Chapter VIII; that on the CIS did not.[87] The CSCE had declared at the Helsinki summit of July 1992 that it was a regional organization in the sense of Chapter VIII;[88] it reaffirmed this in its 2000 *Charter for European Security* and declared its intention of reinforcing its

---

[82] Cot and Pellet (eds), *La Charte des Nations Unies* (1991) at 795.

[83] Established in 1963, 479 UNTS 70.

[84] Established in 1972, 914 UNTS 111.

[85] Gray, 'Regional Arrangements and the United Nations', in Fox (ed.), *The Changing Constitution of the United Nations* (1998), 91 at 94.

[86] The CSCE was established in 1975: 14 ILM (1975) 1292. The CIS was established in 1991: 31 ILM (1992) 138.

[87] On the CSCE, see 1993 UNYB 219, 1994 UNYB 610; on the CIS, see 1994 UNYB 255; 1994 (2) UN Chronicle 36.

[88] 31 ILM (1992) 1385; Bothe, Ronzitti and Rosas (eds), *The OSCE in the Maintenance of Peace and Security* (1997).

peacekeeping role.[89] The CIS referred to itself in this way with regard to its action in Tajikistan in 1993; in 1996 it formally declared itself a Chapter VIII organization in its provision for peacekeeping.[90] The Security Council has apparently taken a flexible approach in its resolutions; it has expressly referred to the EC and CSCE in resolutions referring to Chapter VIII.[91] The Security Council has also implicitly referred to NATO and the WEU as regional organizations in its resolutions on the former Yugoslavia and the Secretary-General included them in his meeting with regional organizations in 1994.[92] None of these had initially been set up as regional organizations under Chapter VIII, but the Security Council did not trouble itself with this question.

Since 2003 the EU has taken on a more active role under its European Security and Defence Policy. It undertook its first peacekeeping operation in Macedonia, in succession to NATO, on the basis of the consent of the government of Macedonia.[93] Next the Security Council authorized an EU-led force to use force in the DRC when MONUC was not able to cope with the outbreak of fighting in Bunia; Security Council Resolution 1484 (2003) was passed under Chapter VII, without express reference to Chapter VIII or to the EU.[94] This was the EU's first military operation outside Europe. Similarly, when the EU conducted another operation in the DRC in support of MONUC during the 2006 elections, it was authorized to do so under Chapter VII with no reference to Chapter VIII.[95] However, this resolution did make express reference to the EU and called on it to report regularly to the Security Council. The EU also took over from the NATO-led SFOR in Bosnia-Herzegovina and deployed EUFOR at the end of 2004.[96] Most recently the EU has been authorized to establish a peacekeeping operation in Chad and the CAR by Resolution 1778 (2007). Again this made no reference to Chapter VIII; this lack of reference to Chapter VIII with regard to the EU operations is not surprising in that these were clearly not the type of regional operations originally

---

[89] 39 ILM (2000) 255. However, this has not been important in practice.

[90] 1993 UNYB 516; 35 ILM (1996) 783. In 2002 six members of the CIS made an agreement to establish the CSTO as the military core of the CIS; see UN doc A/59/195 (2004). See also Nikitkin, 'The end of the Post-Soviet space', Chatham House Briefing paper, REP BP 07/01. In 2004 the CSTO was granted observer status at the UN, 2004 UNYB 1459.

[91] See 423 below.

[92] 1994 UNYB 88. The Secretary-General invited the CIS, the Commonwealth, CSCE, EU, NATO, Arab League, OAU, OAS, Islamic Conference, WEU, and ECOWAS. On the status of NATO, see Simma (ed.), *The Charter of the United Nations: A Commentary* (2nd edn, 2002) at 819.

[93] SC Res 1371 (2001); Keesings (2003) 45312; see Chapter 7 above.

[94] See 336 above.

[95] SC Res 1671(2006).

[96] SC Res 1551, 1571 (2004). It is planned that the EU will also take over from KFOR in Kosovo if agreement can be reached on the future status of the province.

envisaged under Chapter VIII; they were not carried out *within* EU member states. Nevertheless, the Secretary-General in his report on the work of the organization includes cooperation between the UN and the EU in the section on 'The UN and regional organizations'. The UN and the EU have since 2003 increased their cooperation on conflict prevention and post-conflict reconstruction; in September 2004 they made a Joint Declaration on UN–EU Cooperation in Crisis Management.[97]

However, it has become clear that the question whether an organization was expressly established under Chapter VIII, or was understood by its founder states to be a Chapter VIII organization, is of limited importance. The crucial factor is not the nature of the organization but the type of action that is undertaken and the attitude of the Security Council. Various peacekeeping operations have been undertaken by *ad hoc* groups of states and the legality of their actions has not been challenged on the ground that they were not regional organizations under Chapter VIII.[98] Among these was the operation undertaken by MISAB, the Inter-African Mission to Monitor the Implementation of the Bangui Agreement, in the Central African Republic in 1997. It was established at the request of the Central African Republic and its legitimacy was assumed by the Security Council in its resolutions approving the conduct by member states of MISAB of operations in an impartial and neutral way to facilitate the return to peace and security; under Chapter VII it authorised the states participating in MISAB to ensure the security and freedom of movement of the force.[99] South Africa sent peacekeeping forces to Burundi,[100] and Australian-led forces were sent into Bougainville in 1998[101] and the Solomon Islands in

---

[97] 2004 UNYB 13.

[98] Wiseman, 'The UN and International Peacekeeping: A Comparative Analysis', in UNITAR, *The UN and the Maintenance of International Peace and Security* (1987), 263 at 315; Brouillet, 'La Force Multinationale d'interposition à Beyrouth', 1982 AFDI 293.

[99] On MISAB, see 1997 UNYB 91;1998 UNYB 127. It was later replaced by a UN force, MINURCA, which was terminated in February 2000, see also 1999 UNYB 118, 2000 UNYB 161; <http://www.un.org/Depts/DPKO/Missions/car.htm>. MINURCA was succeeded by BONUCA, a UN peace-building mission: 1999 UNYB 128, 2000 UNYB 161. When the situation deteriorated after an attempted coup in May 2001 a peacekeeping force of CEN-SAD, the Community of Sahel-Saharan states, was established: 2001 UNYB 152, 158. The CEN-SAD force was in turn replaced by FOMUC, a CEMAC/ECCAS force in December 2002 (S/2003/5, 3 January 2003; Keesings (2003) 45276), at the request of the government. FOMUC remained, supplemented by Chadian troops, after a successful coup in March 2003, at the request of the new government (S/2003/661, 20 June 2003, 2003 UNYB 155). It received substantial financial and logistical support from France (UN Press Release SC/7626). On FOMUC, see further at note 110 below. See also Zwanenburg, 'Regional Organisations and the Maintenance of International Peace and Security', (11) Journal of Armed Conflict and Security Law (2006) 483.

[100] 2000 UNYB 143; 2001 UNYB 145; Keesings (2002) 44380; UN Press Release SC/7189, 29 October 2001; Secretary-General's Report S/2001/1013.

[101] Keesings (1998) 42205.

2003 at the request of the government.[102] Another Australian-led multi-national force was invited by the government of East Timor to assist it to restore and maintain security after a serious breakdown in law and order in 2006 (after UNMISET had withdrawn); this was welcomed by the Security Council in a series of resolutions.[103]

THE CONSTITUTIONAL BASES FOR REGIONAL PEACEKEEPING

Similarly the question whether an organization has, under its own constitution, the power to take action involving the use of force has not in practice proved controversial in the majority of cases. It is striking that when most of the regional and subregional organizations were set up their constituent instruments did not make any express provision for peacekeeping activity or for enforcement action.[104] The OAU (now the AU),[105] Arab League, OECS, ECOWAS, SADC, CEMAC/ECCAS, IGAD, CSCE (now the OSCE), EU and CIS did not at their creation include in their constituent treaties the express power to take peacekeeping action. But recently, as awareness of the possibilities of regional action has increased, some of these organizations have made new agreements expressly providing for peacekeeping powers. Thus the CSCE in 1992 at its Helsinki summit decided to provide itself with the capability to undertake peacekeeping operations. The member states declared their understanding that the CSCE is a regional arrangement in the sense of Chapter VIII. In the Declaration they laid down detailed rules on CSCE peacekeeping; such operations would be conducted within the framework of Chapter VIII.[106] The CSCE Declaration to a large extent codifies the UN rules on peacekeeping

---

[102] Keesings (2003) 45474, 45520, (2004) 45960, 46066, (2006) 47374, (2007) 48145. See Ponzio, 'The Solomon Islands; the UN and intervention by coalitions of the willing', 12 International Peacekeeping (2005) 173.

[103] SC 5457th meeting, 13 June 2006; Keesings (2006) 47257; SC Res 1690 (2006), 1704, 1745 (2007). Australia reported its intervention to the SC in UN doc S/2006/321.

[104] Only the *Rio Treaty* of the OAS, 21 UNTS 78, 43 AJIL Supplement (1949) 53, contains a provision that could possibly be interpreted to cover such action. Article 6 of the *Rio Treaty* provides:

If the inviolability or the integrity of the territory or the sovereignty or political independence of any American State should be affected by an aggression which is not an armed attack or by an extra-continental or intra-continental conflict, or by any other fact or situation that might endanger the peace of America, the Organ of Consultation shall meet immediately in order to agree on measures which must be taken in case of aggression to assist the victim of the aggression or, in any case, the measures which should be taken for the common defence and for the maintenance of the peace and security of the Continent.

[105] The AU made express provision for peacekeeping in its 2002 Peace and Security Protocol: see note 33 above.

[106] 31 ILM (1992) 1385 at 1399.

that have emerged through practice. It also clearly reflects the lessons learned from UN experience in Yugoslavia and Somalia.

The CSCE Declaration recognizes the wide variety of peacekeeping operations: 'a CSCE peacekeeping operation, according to its mandate, will involve civilian and/or military personnel, may range from small-scale to large-scale, and may assume a variety of forms including observer and monitor missions and larger deployment of forces. Peacekeeping activities could be used inter alia to supervise and help maintain cease-fires, to monitor troop withdrawals, to support the maintenance of law and order, to provide humanitarian and medical aid and to assist refugees'. The Declaration provides that the peacekeeping operations shall not entail enforcement action, and that they require the consent of the parties directly concerned. This formalizes the practice of the Security Council in recent years in seeking the consent not just of the government but of all parties involved in a conflict. This cautious approach is developed further in the requirement that certain conditions must be fulfilled before the decision to dispatch a mission is taken; an effective and durable cease-fire must be established, and the necessary memoranda of understanding must have been agreed with the parties concerned. As with UN peace-keeping, operations should be conducted impartially, and there must be a clear and precise mandate. Detailed rules are laid down on political control and the chain of command. Finally, the Declaration provides for cooperation with the EC, NATO, and the WEU; the CSCE will depend on them for troops and expertise. To date the CSCE has not conducted any peacekeeping operations apart from its dispatch of unarmed observers into Kosovo in 1998.

The CIS in 1996 agreed on the *Concept for Prevention and Settlement of Conflicts in the territory of states members of the Commonwealth of Independent States*.[107] They said that the CIS should, in its capacity as a regional organization, take the steps required to settle conflicts in the territory of member states in accordance with Chapter VIII of the Charter; this would include peacekeeping operations. They set out the essential conditions for the conduct of peacekeeping operations: like the CSCE Declaration, these follow the general principles of UN peacekeeping and also build on recent UN experience. Accordingly six of the member states adopted a Statute on Collective Peace-keeping force in the Commonwealth of Independent States.[108] The CSTO, established in 2002 as the functional military core of the CIS, is in the process of concluding institutional and practical arrangements for peacekeeping.[109]

---

[107] 35 ILM (1996) 783.
[108] 35 ILM (1996) 783.
[109] See note 90 above on the establishment of the CTSO as the functional core of the CIS.

Certain subregional organizations have also accepted or provided for the possibility of peacekeeping action.[110] ECOWAS has taken on a major role in peacekeeping in West Africa; it was established in 1975 as a subregional organization of fifteen member states, concerned with economic matters.[111] Its constituent treaty made no provision for the establishment of peacekeeping forces, but two subsequent treaties expanded ECOWAS's concerns beyond the economic. These are the 1978 *Protocol on Non-Aggression* and the 1981 *Protocol on Mutual Assistance on Defence*.[112] The latter includes provision for the establishment of allied forces of the community to be used if there is a conflict between two member states or 'in the case where an internal armed conflict in a member state of the Community is actively maintained and sustained from outside likely to endanger the security and peace in the entire community'. Express provision for peacekeeping was finally made when ECOWAS concluded the 1999 *Protocol Relating to the Mechanism for Conflict Prevention, Management, Resolution, Peacekeeping and Security*.[113] This provides detailed rules on institutions

[110] The SADDC was originally created in 1980 to further development of the frontline states in the face of apartheid South Africa; in 1992 it became the SADC and changed its aim to the establishment of a common market. It has since concluded a *Protocol on Politics, Defence and Security* enabling it to intervene in internal conflict at the request of a member state (11 African Journal of International and Comparative Law (1999) 197; see Chigara, 'The SAD community—a litmus test for the UN's resolve to banish oppression', 11 African Journal of International and Comparative Law (1999) 522, and 'Operation of the SADC Protocol on Politics, Defence and Security in the DRC', 12 African Journal of International and Comparative Law (2000) 58; <www.africa-union.org/root/au/RECs/sadc.htm>.
IGAD (initially IGADD) was set up in 1986 to deal with drought and development; it subsequently broadened its concerns to include resolution of inter and intra-state conflict; <www.africa-union.org/root/au/RECs/igad.htm>. SADC and IGAD have involved themselves with seeking diplomatic settlements to the conflicts in Sudan, Somalia, Lesotho, Angola, and the DRC (see, for example, Keesings (1998) 42115, 42426, 42538, 42539; (1999) 42929, 43050, 43093; (2000) 43348, 43393; UN Press Releases SC/7466, SC/7530; SG/SM/8960, 24 October 2003).
CEMAC was initially set up as an economic and monetary community. It had overlapping membership with ECCAS, also initially an economic community (founded in 1983), with which it merged in 2003 under pressure from the EU. This joint organization has adopted a 1996 Non-Aggression Pact and it has also made provision for peacekeeping in its *Pact for Mutual Assistance* of February 2000: UN Press Release DC/2894, 22 October 2003; <www.ceeac-eccas>. CEMAC/ECCAS set up FOMUC, a peacekeeping force in the CAR (see note 99 above), when its forces replaced those of CEN-SAD; <www.africa-union.org/root/au/RECs/cen_sad.htm>. This force remains in the CAR at the end of 2007.
[111] 35 ILM (1996) 660.
[112] Weller (ed.), *Regional Peacekeeping and International Enforcement: The Liberian Crisis* (1994) at 18 and 19 respectively.
[113] 12 African Journal of International and Comparative Law (1999) 629; Abass, 'The new collective security mechanism of ECOWAS', 5 Journal of Conflict and Security Law (2000) 211. The Protocol needs nine ratifications to enter into force, but it was treated as already operative before this: *Report of the ECOAWS Workshop*, Accra, 10–11 February 2005, at note 10. ECOWAS was given observer status at the UN in 2004: 2004 UNYB 1459.

and decision-making procedures. It has undertaken operations in Liberia, Sierra Leone, Guinea-Bissau,[114] and Côte d'Ivoire.[115]

But the fundamental question whether an organization has the power under its own constitution to engage in peacekeeping activities has been treated as unimportant in practice. When regional organizations have engaged in the use of force the legality of such action has been assessed by the rest of the world not in terms of the organization's own constitution but rather in terms of the UN Charter and general international law. Only in the case of Grenada was there any significant debate in the Security Council on this issue of the organization's own constitution.[116] Following a coup in 1983 in which a government sympathetic to Cuba and to the USSR seized power, the USA led a forcible intervention to 'restore government and order, and to facilitate the departure of those United States citizens and other foreign nationals who wish to be evacuated'. In a letter to the Security Council the USA claimed that its action was taken pursuant to an invitation by the OECS. It later elaborated on this in the Security Council debate on the intervention; the USA position was that the OECS had sought its assistance to undertake collective regional action because of the vacuum of authority in Grenada. The consent to regional action had come from the Governor-General.[117] The representative of Grenada itself raised the point as to whether the action by the USA and OECS member states was legitimate under the OECS constitution; it argued persuasively that the OECS Treaty made no provision for peacekeeping action and that the US action went beyond what was allowed in the Treaty. The USA relied on Article 8 of the OECS treaty as one of the justifications for its actions, but actually this clearly provides for collective self-defence against external aggression, not for intervention by a non-member state

---

[114] The ECOMOG operation in Guinea-Bissau was established under the *Abuja Agreement* between the government and the junta that had opposed it: 38 ILM (1999) 28; ECOWAS communiqué, UN doc S/1998/638. This provided for the withdrawal from Guinea-Bissau of all foreign troops and the simultaneous deployment of ECOMOG interposition forces. The ECOMOG forces were to keep the warring parties apart, to guarantee security along the border with Senegal, and to guarantee free access to humanitarian organizations. That is, the regional force was to help a government without the military resources itself to maintain order and stability. The Security Council welcomed the deployment of ECOMOG to implement this peacekeeping mandate in SC Res 1233 (1999). However, a May 1999 coup ended the truce (Keesings (1999) 42924) and led to the withdrawal of ECOMOG: *Report of the Secretary-General Pursuant to Security Council Resolution 1233 (1999) relative to the Situation in Guinea-Bissau* (S/1999/741).

[115] See 419 below.

[116] 1983 UNYB 211; UN SC 2487th–2491st Meetings (1983). On Grenada, see Gilmore, *The Grenada Intervention* (1984).

[117] The USA set out its position in UN doc S/16076 (1983); SC 2487th meeting para 52, 187; 2491st meeting para 51.

in the internal affairs of Grenada.[118] Many other states disagreed with the US interpretation of Article 8.[119] However, the Security Council resolution calling for the withdrawal of foreign troops from Grenada was vetoed by the USA. It is striking that the actual member states of the OECS did not themselves adopt the same argument on Article 8 as the USA; they preferred to invoke the equally doubtful argument of 'pre-emptive defensive strike' under the OECS provisions for collective self-defence. However, most of the debate did not focus exclusively on the OECS Treaty; rather, states concerned themselves with the legality of the operation under the UN Charter.

Again in the Security Council debates on the OAS measures against Cuba in 1962 and the Dominican Republic in 1965 there was some discussion about whether the OAS Charter outlawed forcible intervention of the types undertaken.[120] However, there was no real discussion of the scope and application of Article 6 of the Rio Treaty or of the constitutionality of the action in terms of Article 6. The debate focused on whether the forcible interventions were compatible with the UN Charter and general international law. The Arab League intervention in Lebanon from 1976–83 was not discussed in the Security Council[121] and the OAU action in Chad in 1981 led to a split as to whether it was Chapter VIII regional peacekeeping or simply a domestic matter for Chad.[122] Thus neither episode was discussed by the Security Council in terms of its legality under the Arab League or OAU Charter. Therefore, by default, it seems to have been accepted by states during the Cold War that regional organizations

---

[118] Article 8 provides for the composition and functions of the Defence and Security Committee. Paragraph 4 provides that :

The Defence and Security Committee shall have responsibility for coordinating the efforts of Member States for collective self-defence and the preservation of peace and security against external aggression and for the development of close ties among the Member States of the Organization in matters of external defence and security, including measures to combat the activities of mercenaries, operating with or without the support of internal or national elements, in the exercise of the inherent right of individual or collective self-defence recognised by Article 51 of the Charter of the United Nations.

[119] Grenada, SC 2487th meeting (1983) para 88. See also Mexico, Nicaragua, Cuba, Democratic Yemen, 2487th meeting. Also Poland and Ethiopia, 2489th meeting (1983); Afghanistan, 2491st meeting (1983).

[120] For a full discussion of these episodes, see Akehurst, 'Enforcement Action by Regional Agencies, with special reference to the Organization of American States', 42 BYIL (1967) 175.

[121] See Pogany, 'The Arab League and Regional Peacekeeping', 34 Netherlands ILR (1987) 54; Issele, 'The Arab Deterrent Force in Lebanon 1976–83', in Cassese (ed.), *The Current Legal Regulation of the Use of Force* (1986) at 179.

[122] SC 2358th meeting (1982). On Chad, see Naldi, 'Peacekeeping Attempts by the OAU', 34 ICLQ (1985) 593; Cot, 'The Role of the Inter-African Peacekeeping Force in Chad', in Cassese (ed.), *The Current Legal Regulation of the Use of Force* (1986), 167.

have implied powers to establish peacekeeping forces, and also that they need not follow the formal procedures for decision-making laid down in the respective treaties, even if the peacekeeping action is taken in the name of the organization. Apparently the basis for this was that states can do together, even in the name of the organization, what they could do separately. That is, because individual states may undertake peacekeeping activities, groups of states acting through a regional organization may do the same; whether or not an entity qualified as a regional arrangement or agency under Article 52 did not affect its power to undertake peacekeeping activities.[123] It seems to follow that only a member state of an organization may challenge the constitutionality of its peacekeeping action on grounds of non-compliance with the organization's constituent treaty. Otherwise, provided that the organization limits itself to peacekeeping and does not embark on enforcement action needing Security Council authorization, this would not be a ground for legal challenge by a non-member state.

ECOWAS action in Liberia

This lack of concern over the constitutional basis for regional action may be seen also in the response to regional action. With regard to ECOWAS action in Liberia, other states did not go into questions of the ECOWAS constitution or the procedures followed.[124] This conflict and that in Sierra Leone will be discussed in detail in order to demonstrate clearly the application of Chapter VIII and the legal issues that have arisen in post-Cold War regional action. In December 1989 there was an uprising against President Doe who had been in power since 1980. The uprising was led by Charles Taylor, a former member of the Doe government, who came from the Côte d'Ivoire with a small force (the NPFL). The rebels grew in number and were successful, though the opposition movement split in February 1990 when Prince Johnson broke away. By summer 1990 the rebels controlled about 90 per cent of Liberia and were advancing on the capital, Monrovia.

The government had sought UN intervention in June 1990, but the Security Council did not become involved until January 1991. Nor did the USA intervene, despite its major role in Liberia since its creation as a

---

[123] Akehurst, 'Enforcement Action by Regional Agencies, with special reference to the Organization of American States', 42 BYIL (1967) 175.

[124] The following account of events in Liberia is taken from Gray, 'Regional Arrangements and the United Nations', in Fox (ed.), *The Changing Constitution of the United Nations* (1998), 91; see also Nolte, 'Restoring Peace by Regional Action: International Legal Aspects of the Liberian Conflict', 53 Zeitschrift für ausländisches öffentliches Recht und Völkerrecht (1993) 603; Weller (ed.), *Regional Peacekeeping and International Enforcement: The Liberian Crisis* (1994); Mindua, 'Intervention armée de la CEDAO au Liberia', 7 African Journal of International and Comparative Law (1995) 257.

state in 1847. The USA had maintained and even increased its links with Liberia after Doe seized power in 1980. But when civil war broke out in December 1989 the USA ruled out direct intervention. In the absence of UN or US intervention ECOWAS stepped in. It established a Mediation Committee and in August 1990 the Committee called for a ceasefire and established ECOMOG with troops from Nigeria, Ghana, Gambia, Guinea, and Sierra Leone. About 3,000 troops went to Liberia and secured Monrovia against the NPFL. Various attempts were made to reach a peaceful settlement and at one of these conferences it was agreed to establish an interim government under President Sawyer. He was installed in Monrovia in December 1990 and a ceasefire held from then until August 1992. During this time attempts to produce a peaceful settlement continued and in October 1991 the *Yamoussoukro IV Agreement* was accepted by the Doe forces, the NPFL, and Prince Johnson. This provided for a ceasefire, the disarmament of the warring parties, and the encampment of all forces under the supervision of ECOMOG.

But in 1992 fighting broke out again; the NPFL forces attacked Monrovia and ECOMOG not only drove them off, it went onto the offensive and took territory formerly occupied by the NPFL in an action that appeared to go beyond peacekeeping. In July 1993 a peace agreement was concluded at Cotonou, Benin, but this was not observed and it was followed by a whole sequence of supplementary peace agreements. It was not until August 1996 that a final peace agreement was made; a year later elections were held and Charles Taylor was elected President by a large majority.

The constitutional question of the legal basis for the ECOMOG operation was not much discussed by those involved or by the UN. Little attention was paid to the legality of the action under ECOMOG's own mandate and under its constitution. ECOMOG's mandate from the ECOWAS Mediation Committee was that 'ECOMOG shall assist the Committee in supervising the implementation, and ensuring strict compliance, of the cease-fire by all the parties to the conflict'. In its report to the Security Council on the establishment of ECOMOG Nigeria said that 'ECOMOG is going to Liberia first and foremost to stop the senseless killing of innocent civilian nationals and foreigners and to help the Liberian people to restore their democratic institutions. The ECOWAS intervention is in no way designed to save one part or to punish another.'[125]

Did ECOWAS have the power under its own constitution to establish peacekeeping forces? The 1981 *Protocol on Mutual Defence* offered a possible legal basis for the establishment of ECOWAS forces, given the apparent existence of outside involvement by Burkina Faso and Libya in supporting Charles Taylor and the NPFL. This was referred to in passing by the

---

[125] UN doc S/21485 (1990).

ECOWAS Mediation Committee when it first took action in August 1990, but was not subsequently mentioned by ECOWAS.[126] But, as with earlier regional operations, there was little international concern or express discussion about the legality of the ECOMOG operation in terms of ECOMOG's constitution. In ECOWAS's communications to the Security Council after the establishment of ECOMOG there was no mention of the legal basis for the establishment and deployment of ECOMOG.[127] Nor was this referred to in the Security Council statements[128] or resolutions[129] on Liberia, or in the first Security Council debate on the situation in Liberia in January 1991.[130] During this debate Liberia itself said nothing about the constitutional basis for ECOWAS peacekeeping. Nigeria said only that 'ECOWAS should be commended for promoting the principles of the UN Charter by stepping in to prevent the situation in Liberia from degenerating into a situation likely to constitute a real threat to international peace and security.'

In the second Security Council debate on Liberia in November 1992 there was again little interest in the legal basis of the ECOWAS action in terms of its own constitution and treaties.[131] The Côte d'Ivoire was alone in its express reference to the 1981 *Protocol on Mutual Assistance and Defence.* Sierra Leone referred to ECOWAS acting under the UN Charter and the Treaty of ECOWAS in sending a peacekeeping force. The USA said simply that the dispatch of peacekeeping forces had been a decision by ECOWAS governments on their own initiative. In his later report to the Security Council on events in Liberia the Secretary-General stated without elaboration that ECOWAS was acting under both the 1981 Protocol and the 1978 *Protocol on Non-Aggression* in establishing ECOMOG.[132]

Given the non-invocation of the latter Protocol as well as the fact that it provides for response to external attacks, it seems unlikely that the Secretary-General was correct in referring to the *Protocol on Non-Aggression* as a basis for ECOMOG. As for the 1981 Protocol, it is clear that the normal decision-making processes of ECOWAS were not followed. The decision to set up ECOMOG was not made unanimously by all ECOWAS member states. As in earlier peacekeeping operations, an extremely relaxed attitude, or indifference, on the part of those concerned is very noticeable with regard to this issue of the constitutional propriety of the creation of peacekeeping forces.

---

[126] Weller (ed.), *Regional Peacekeeping and International Enforcement: The Liberian Crisis* (1994) at 67.

[127] UN docs S/21485, S/22025 (1990).

[128] UN docs S/22133 (1991), S/23886 (1992).

[129] SC Res 788 (1992), 813 (1993), 856, 866 (1993).

[130] SC 2974th meeting (1991).

[131] SC 3138th meeting (1992).

[132] Weller (ed.), *Regional Peacekeeping and International Enforcement: The Liberian Crisis* (1994) at 283; S/25402 (1993) para 15.

ECOWAS action in Sierra Leone

Even more striking was the lack of inquiry into constitutionality of the action in Sierra Leone in 1997. In May 1997 there was a coup overthrowing the government that had been democratically elected as part of the peace process ending the six-year civil conflict in Sierra Leone. There were already ECOMOG forces (Nigerian and Guinean troops) in Sierra Leone at the time of the coup, apparently there at the request of the government because of the overspill of the Liberian conflict into Sierra Leone.[133] Nigerian forces were also present under a bilateral agreement with the government of Sierra Leone. After the coup, Nigeria and Guinea sent more troops and, claiming to act under the aegis of ECOWAS, became involved in the conflict. The normal ECOWAS decision-making procedures do not seem to have been followed at this stage; Nigeria and Guinea simply assumed the right to use force to resist the coup and to try to restore the legitimate government at the request of the deposed President. It was not until June 1997 that ECOWAS met and issued a formal statement. This said that ECOWAS's objectives were to reinstate the legitimate government, restore peace and security, and resolve the refugee problem. They called for non-recognition of the junta that had seized power and said that they would reinstate the democratically elected government by dialogue, sanctions, and the use of force. ECOWAS did not specify the legal basis for its operations.[134] But other states did not speak out against the Nigerian and Guinean military action on the ground that it was not really constitutional ECOWAS action. The use of force by Nigeria, itself ruled by a military junta that had seized power from a democratically elected government, to restore democracy in Sierra Leone met with a very muted response. There was not even much discussion of the legitimacy of the action in the light of UN and general international law rules on peacekeeping.[135]

A similar lack of concern over constitutional basis was apparent in the ECOWAS intervention in Côte d'Ivoire. After an attempted coup in September 2002 Nigeria and Ghana sent planes and troops at the request of the democratically elected President; Nigeria said that these were ECOWAS forces, even though the formal ECOWAS meeting was not held until later;[136] plans for an ECOWAS peacekeeping force were formally agreed at a summit meeting on 23 October 2002.[137]

The constitutionality of CIS action in Tajikistan and Georgia also passed without discussion. The former seems to have been unproblematic; five of

---

[133] Keesings (1991) 38136; (1992) 38900; (1995) 40491.
[134] UN doc S/1997/499.
[135] See 411 below.
[136] Keesings (2002) 44968.
[137] UN Press Release SC/7588, 6 December 2002.

the CIS member states established coalition forces in Tajikistan in August 1993; they expressly stated that they viewed this as a regional arrangement, concluded in accordance with the principles and purposes of Chapter VIII of the UN Charter.[138] There was apparently no discussion of constitutionality of this operation in the UN. Similarly there were no inquiries into constitutional propriety with regard to the more controversial CIS operation established in 1994 in Abkhazia, Georgia—more controversial because of Georgian suspicion of the motives of Russia.[139] Russian troops had remained in Georgia after the break-up of the USSR; they stayed there with the reluctant consent of the President of Georgia when it became clear that Georgian forces alone were not able to prevent the forcible secession of the Abkhaz people and their expulsion of the Georgian population from Abkhazia. These Russian forces were nominally transformed into CIS peacekeeping forces after a May 1994 ceasefire agreement between the Georgian and Abkhaz authorities; this provided that CIS forces would ensure respect for the ceasefire and for a weapons exclusion zone. Even though it is not clear that any formal decision-making process had taken place in the CIS, the UN Security Council accepted the Russian troops as a CIS force and there was no discussion of constitutional propriety.[140] Again there was no apparent concern about the continuation of the CIS operation despite the expiration of the mandate of the CIS peacekeeping force on 30 June 1998; the UN Secretary-General, after reporting a continuing good working relationship with the CIS forces, simply said that the expiry of the mandate had not affected its presence and that it continued to operate.[141] It seems that no issues about the constitutionality of regional action arose with regard to AU peacekeeping operations.

THE LEGALITY OF REGIONAL ACTION IN TERMS OF THE UN
CHARTER AND GENERAL INTERNATIONAL LAW

In practice, debate on the legality of regional action has centred on the compatibility of the use of force with the UN Charter and with general international law. During the Cold War the Security Council debates

---

[138] UN doc S/26610 (1993). See Iji, 'Cooperation, coordination and complementarity in international peacekeeping: the Tajikistan experience', 12 International Peacekeeping (2005) 189.
[139] 33 ILM (1994) 577; 1994 UNYB 577; see also Greco, 'Third Party Peacekeeping and the Interaction between Russia in the OSCE in the CIS area', in Bothe, Ronzitti and Rosas (eds), *The OSCE in the Maintenance of Peace and Security* (1997), 267.
[140] For the later report by Russia of a CIS decision to establish a peacekeeping operation, see 1994 UNYB 583, UN doc S/1994/732.
[141] UN doc S/1999/60. The Secretary-General has not raised the question of the constitutionality of the CIS force in subsequent reports.

centred on fundamental issues such as what was meant by enforcement action under Article 53 of the UN Charter, whether the particular regional action was legitimate peacekeeping or enforcement action that needed Security Council authorization under Article 53. Did the requirement in Article 53 of Security Council authorization for enforcement action apply to the imposition of economic measures by the regional organization? Did failure to condemn amount to authorization? These questions were crucial in the cases of Cuba and the Dominican Republic. In the former, the OAS responded to the 1959 socialist revolution which brought President Castro to power by suspending Cuba from the organization and imposing economic sanctions because Cuba's 'aims and principles were incompatible with the aims and principles of the inter-American system'; it subsequently authorized member states to take all measures including the use of armed force to ensure that Cuba did not receive from the USSR missiles that endangered the peace and safety of the continent. In the Dominican Republic the USA again responded to a socialist revolution by intervention; it initially sent in US forces, but later sought to transform its forces into an OAS force. The USA took a narrow view of enforcement action under Article 53 and claimed that the OAS was undertaking peacekeeping activities. It also took a wide view of authorization and relied on Security Council acquiescence as authorization under Article 53. These issues concerning the scope of peacekeeping and the need for Security Council authorization could not be authoritatively resolved by the Security Council during the Cold War.[142]

Other issues that emerged in practice during the Cold War with regard to the legitimacy of regional action related to the complex question of impartiality. Concern that one state would be able to manipulate a regional organization and use it to further its own ends arose in several cases during the Cold War. The role of the USA in the OAS action over Cuba and the Dominican Republic, of the USA (a non-member) in the OECS action in Grenada, and of Syria in the Arab League intervention in Lebanon all gave rise to serious criticism. Factors such as the composition, control, and financing of peacekeeping forces may be significant in the assessment of impartiality.

---

[142] See Pellet (ed.), *Les forces régionales du maintien de la paix* (1982); Akehurst, 'Enforcement Action by Regional Agencies, with special reference to the Organization of American States', 42 BYIL (1967) 175. The question of priority of jurisdiction as between the OAS and the UN was divisive during the Cold War, but has not been a problem in recent years, see Simma (ed.), *The Charter of the United Nations: A Commentary* (2nd edn, 2002) at 838. However, the AU in its 2002 *Protocol on Peace and Security* claims in Article 16 that it has the *primary* responsibility for promoting peace and security in Africa: see Levitt, 'The Peace and Security Council of the AU and the UN Security Council', in Blokker and Schrijver (eds), *The Security Council and the Use of Force* (2005) Chapter 11 at 228.

Impartiality, now seen as a necessary characteristic of peacekeeping activity, involves the duty not to take sides in a particular dispute. But questions have arisen as to how far a regional force may use force to keep a particular government in power in the absence of Security Council authority. The starting point of any examination of this issue is the mandate given to the force by the regional organization. In some cases there has been ambiguity. With regard to Chad there was some uncertainty over the exact mandate. The relevant OAU resolution said that the task of the peacekeeping force was to 'ensure the defence and security of the country while awaiting the integration of government forces'. But the Chairman of the OAU said that the force's role was to enable the people of Chad to decide on a national government through free and fair elections supervised by the OAU with the help of the African peacekeeping force, and the OAU standing committee on Chad said that the force was to help the government maintain peace and security, and to help form a united national army. There were also agreements between the government of Chad and the OAU on the presence of the OAU forces providing that the forces should contain and moderate hostilities, safeguard the security of the states, and assist the government in the formation of a united national army. There was thus some ambiguity as to whether the role of the force was simply to act as a buffer between opposing forces or whether it was to help the government that issued the invitation to defeat the opposition.

The OAU forces had been invited in by President Goukouni in 1981, but when the civil war started to go against him they remained strictly impartial. President Goukouni became hostile to the OAU forces because they would not support him and they withdrew. The OAU forces had chosen not to impose a military solution. There are radically opposing views of the success of this operation among the writers who discussed it: for Cot it was a success in that it permitted the orderly transfer of power and it reduced foreign intervention, but for Naldi it was an 'abject failure' in that it did not stop the civil war.[143]

The OAU also ran into difficulties over the financing of the peacekeeping force.[144] It appealed to the UN for financial help, the first such

---

[143] Naldi, 'Peacekeeping Attempts by the OAU', 34 ICLQ (1985) 593; Cot, 'The Role of the Inter-African Peacekeeping Force in Chad', in Cassese (ed.), *The Current Legal Regulation of the Use of Force* (1986), 167.

[144] On the OAU action in Chad, see Alibert, 'L'Affaire du Tchad', 90 RGDIP (1986) 368; Naldi, 'Peacekeeping Attempts by the OAU', 34 ICLQ (1985) 593; Cot, 'The Role of the Inter-African Peacekeeping Force in Chad', in Cassese (ed.), *The Current Legal Regulation of the Use of Force* (1986), 167; Wiseman, 'The UN and International Peacekeeping: A Comparative Analysis' in UNITAR, *The UN and the Maintenance of International Peace and Security* (1987), 263 at 309.

request from a regional organization. In April 1982 the Security Council responded by Resolution 504, calling on the Secretary-General to establish a fund to which UN member states could contribute in order to provide financial assistance to the OAU force.[145] Only a limited number of states contributed troops to the OAU operation: Nigeria, Senegal, and Zaire. It is interesting that Senegal's troops were supported financially by France and those of Nigeria and Zaire received contributions from the USA. Such financial support inevitably raised questions about the independence of the regional decision-making and led to doubts as to how far regional peacekeeping could really contribute to a greater democratization in international affairs, as hoped by the UN Secretary-General in his *Agenda for Peace*. Other organizations have also subsequently turned to developed states for assistance.[146] The UN implicitly legitimized the OAU intervention in Security Council Resolution 504 (1982), calling on members to support the Fund to assist the operation, but there was no express reference in this resolution to Chapter VIII. The USSR argued that it was purely an internal matter for Chad. But the *Repertoire of the Practice of the Security Council* did include an account of the action under its section on Chapter VIII.[147]

In Lebanon similar questions arose over the scope of the mandate and the impartiality of the Arab forces. The initial limited Arab Security Force was mandated by the Arab League in 1976 to 'maintain security and stability' after the civil war; it was replaced by a much larger Arab Deterrent Force with a more ambitious mandate to ensure the observance of the ceasefire, separate the parties, implement the *Cairo Agreement* and collect heavy weapons. The force was a very large one, and was overwhelmingly Syrian. When the Syrian forces exceeded their peacekeeping mandate and went beyond self-defence, taking action against Christian forces, other states withdrew their contingents and suspended their financial contributions. The force was now even more clearly Syrian-dominated, and doubts about its legality were strengthened when it remained in Lebanon even after the ADF mandate expired in July 1982. In theory the forces were under the control of the President of Lebanon, but in reality it was Syria that was in charge.[148] The Syrian troops remained until 2005.[149]

---

[145] 1982 UNYB 318. In the event, the fund was not set up because the OAU intervention in Chad ended in June 1982.

[146] See 421–22 below.

[147] *Repertoire of the Practice of the Security Council 1981–84*, 348.

[148] On the Arab League action in Lebanon, see Pogany, 'The Arab League and Regional Peacekeeping', 34 Netherlands ILR (1987) 54; Issele, 'The Arab Deterrent Force in Lebanon 1976–83' in Cassese (ed.), *The Current Legal Regulation of the Use of Force* (1986) at 179.

[149] See 100 above.

ECOWAS action in Liberia (1990–97)

After the end of the Cold War questions of impartiality and of the distinction between peacekeeping and enforcement action arose again. The ECOWAS operation in Liberia provokes fundamental questions about the role of regional organizations, but (as in the cases of Chad and Lebanon) it is striking that not much attention was paid in the Security Council to the question of the legality of this operation under the UN Charter.

The legality of the operation under the UN Charter

The ECOWAS communications to the Security Council made no express reference to Chapter VIII of the UN Charter, but Nigeria spoke of ECOMOG as holding the fort for the UN in accordance with Chapter VIII.[150] States in the Security Council debates simply assumed that ECOWAS had legally established peacekeeping forces. The USA and China spoke of the 'peacekeeping forces' set up by ECOWAS and appeared to assume their legality.[151] But the first Security Council resolution on Liberia, Resolution 788 (passed in November 1992) imposing an arms embargo, was cautious in its language; it recalled Chapter VIII and commended ECOWAS for its attempts to secure a peaceful settlement, but did not mention ECOMOG by name.

In contrast, those resolutions passed *after* the *Cotonou Peace Agreement* in 1993 do refer to ECOMOG expressly and clearly assume its legality as a peacekeeping force. Resolution 866 (1993) establishing the UN observer force refers to ECOMOG as 'a peacekeeping mission already set up by another organization'. Later resolutions not only repeatedly commend the positive role of ECOWAS in its continuing efforts to restore peace, security, and stability in Liberia, but also call for states to contribute troops to ECOMOG, and then commend those that did this. They demand that all factions in Liberia strictly respect the status of ECOMOG personnel and urge member states to provide support for the peace process in Liberia through a UN Trust Fund for Liberia, in order to enable ECOMOG to fulfil its mandate.[152] These resolutions clearly indicate acceptance of the legality of ECOMOG's deployment under the *Cotonou Agreement* and later peace agreements.[153] The existence of the peace agreement was clearly crucial in establishing the legality of the force.

---

[150] SC 3138th meeting (1992); The Head of State of Nigeria also made a speech outside the UN referring to Chapter VIII, see Weller, *Regional Peacekeeping and International Enforcement: The Liberian Crisis* (1994) at 105.

[151] SC 3138th meeting (1992).

[152] SC Res 866 (1993), 950 (1994), 1014, 1020 (1995), 1041 (1996).

[153] Similarly with regard to Guinea-Bissau, the Security Council, after the *Abuja Peace Agreement*, was prepared in SC Res 1233 (1999) to mention ECOMOG by name and to assume the legality of its deployment.

Consent of the host state

One central issue in establishing the legality of peacekeeping action is the need for the consent of the host state for the establishment and deployment of peacekeeping forces. This was problematic in the case of Liberia. In contrast to the stress on this need for consent in General Assembly Resolution 49/57, *The Declaration on the Enhancement of Cooperation between the UN and Regional Arrangements or Agencies in the Maintenance of International Peace and Security,*[154] on regional action, this was passed over in almost complete silence by states and in the Security Council's statements and resolutions with regard to the initial deployment of ECOMOG in Liberia. It was not mentioned in the first ECOWAS communication to the Security Council in August 1990.[155] In its second communication in December 1990 ECOWAS said that an agreement between itself and Liberia was necessary on the status and operations of ECOMOG.[156] The ECOWAS Authority mandated such an agreement to be made with the interim government under President Sawyer set up under the auspices of ECOWAS in December 1990.[157] Generally the UN treated the Sawyer government as the body with power to represent Liberia; the issue of the credentials of the Liberian representative to the UN was not raised. And the Secretary-General's reports spoke of the UN and the OAU as recognizing the Sawyer government until it was replaced by the Transitional Government under the *Cotonou Agreement.*[158]

At the time that ECOMOG was established and entered Liberia, there were newspaper reports that President Doe and Prince Johnson consented to its presence. But Charles Taylor whose troops controlled 90 per cent of Liberia did not consent and opposed the deployment. And in the Security Council debates on Liberia in January 1991 and November 1992 Liberia itself implied that consent was not necessary, at any rate for UN intervention. Liberia regretted that the UN had not involved itself earlier and called for a review and reinterpretation of the Charter, particularly of the provisions on non-intervention. It said that a strict application of this principle had hampered the effectiveness of the Security Council and its principal objective of maintaining international peace and security. In the second debate it said that opinion was divided between those supporting humanitarian intervention and those favouring classical conceptions of sovereignty, however anachronistic. It said that ECOWAS had taken a bold and courageous decision to deploy ECOMOG.

---

[154] 1994 UNYB 124.
[155] UN doc S/21485 (1990), Weller, *Regional Peacekeeping and International Enforcement: The Liberian Crisis* (1994) at 75.
[156] UN doc S/22025 (1990), Weller, ibid., at 121.
[157] UN doc S/25402 (1993); Weller, ibid., at 280.
[158] UN doc S/25402 (1993) para 17, Weller, ibid., at 280.

So there was considerable uncertainty on the consent issue as far as the initial deployment of ECOMOG was concerned. The readiness of the international community to acquiesce in the ECOMOG peacekeeping even in the absence of clear consent from the government and even though the government was no longer effective finds precedents in the flexible approach to the consent requirement in the cases of peacekeeping forces in Chad, Lebanon, and Somalia.[159] Subsequently it seems that the Security Council regarded the 1993 *Cotonou Peace Agreement* and its successors as providing legitimacy for the continued deployment of ECOMOG. Resolution 866 (1993) and later resolutions refer to ECOMOG expressly and note that the Peace Agreements assign to ECOMOG the primary responsibility of supervising the military provisions of the agreement.

The impartiality of ECOMOG

Legal and practical problems have also continued since the end of the Cold War over the financing, control, and impartiality of regional forces. Thus in Liberia the question arose whether ECOMOG was really an impartial force. Was it a neutral force solely concerned to implement a ceasefire as Nigeria maintained, or was it a Nigerian-dominated force designed to stop Charles Taylor becoming President? Because Charles Taylor opposed its intervention, ECOMOG became involved in action against the NPFL and undertook action that seemed to go beyond peacekeeping and throw doubt on its impartiality. First, in October 1990 ECOMOG ousted the NPFL from Monrovia and established a security zone around the city. Much more far-reaching was its action in October 1992. After the NPFL attacked Monrovia, ECOMOG went on the offensive, using Nigerian planes to bomb NPFL positions outside Monrovia and driving them back to allow the Sawyer government to gain control of more territory.[160] The UN Secretary-General, in his March 1993 Report, said that the NPFL attack had obliged ECOMOG to adopt a peace enforcement model to defend and protect the capital.[161]

The ECOMOG force was initially made up of troops from Nigeria, Ghana, Gambia, Guinea, and Sierra Leone, with the largest contingent coming from Nigeria. The original Ghanaian commander was removed and replaced by a Nigerian. At first the francophone members of ECOWAS

---

[159] Nolte, 'Restoring Peace by Regional Action: International Legal Aspects of the Liberian Conflict', 53 Zeitschrift für ausländisches öffentliches Recht und Völkerrecht (1993) 603; Wippman, 'Treaty-Based Intervention: Who Can Say No?', 62 University of Chicago Law Review (1995) 607, and 'Military Intervention, Regional Organization and Host-State Consent,' 7 Duke Journal of Comparative and International Law (1996) 71.

[160] Weller, *Regional Peacekeeping and International Enforcement: The Liberian Crisis* (1994) at 99, 100.

[161] UN doc S/25402 (1993) para 17, Weller, ibid., at 280.

were suspicious, seeing ECOMOG as designed to further Nigerian policy and to stop Charles Taylor from becoming President. Burkina Faso and the Côte d'Ivoire at first supported Charles Taylor. But there were newspaper reports that both were put under pressure by the USA to support ECOMOG and by November 1992 they had ended their opposition. Also Senegal was induced to contribute 3,000 troops to ECOMOG when the USA supplied funds for this purpose.[162] ECOWAS had difficulties in securing adequate funding for ECOMOG and its ability to carry out its responsibilities was hampered by the limited financing available.[163] The UN Secretary General set up a trust fund to help support ECOMOG;[164] this again highlights the practical problem of turning to regional organizations in the absence of adequate resources.

Charles Taylor, not surprisingly, was hostile to ECOMOG and said that its intervention was an attempt by Nigeria to save the Doe government. He accused Nigeria of using Liberia to prove that it was an African superpower, criticized the composition of ECOMOG, and called for the UN to replace it. When a ceasefire was agreed at Cotonou in July 1993 the parties agreed to expand the participation of states in ECOMOG and to give the UN a role in establishing peace. As the Secretary-General commented in his March 1993 report, these measures were necessary because of the NPFL mistrust of ECOMOG and insistence on UN participation. A similar concern to secure UN participation and thus apparently to secure greater legitimacy for an operation may be seen also in later operations.[165]

Enforcement action

The disagreement that emerged in the Cold War over the meaning of 'enforcement action' and whether it included economic measures, and over the need for authorization under Article 53 did not give rise to discussion in the Security Council in the case of Liberia, even though the actions of ECOWAS could have given rise to controversy on these subjects. First, when ECOWAS imposed economic sanctions on those factions that did not accept the *Yamoussoukro IV Peace Agreement* in October 1992, it asked the Security Council to make these sanctions mandatory for the entire international community. That is, it did not request Security Council authorization but simply assistance. The implication is that ECOWAS did not regard economic sanctions as enforcement action under Article 53, an issue raised earlier with regard to the OAS action against Cuba. The view that economic sanctions by a regional organization do not need Security Council

---

[162] Weller, ibid., at 174.
[163] 1994 UNYB 379.
[164] UN doc S/26422 (1993), Weller, ibid., at 374.
[165] See below at 408, 420.

authorization was controversial when the OAS took measures against Cuba,[166] but has been implicitly confirmed by the many sanctions imposed subsequently without recourse to the UN. This view is confirmed by the action with regard to Haiti. The OAS imposed sanctions in 1991. The UN General Assembly supported this, but the Security Council did not act until June 1993 when it passed Resolution 841 unanimously imposing an oil and arms embargo on Haiti. Thus without discussion it was assumed that OAS economic sanctions did not require Security Council authorization.

With regard to Liberia, the Security Council did not go so far as to make the ECOWAS sanctions mandatory for all states, although it did impose an arms embargo. It unanimously passed Resolution 788 (1992); this recalled Chapter VIII, commended ECOWAS for its efforts to restore peace in Liberia, reaffirmed the *Yamoussoukro IV Peace Agreement*, and condemned the continuing armed attacks against the peacekeeping forces of ECOWAS by one of the parties to the conflict. It requested all states to respect the measures established by ECOWAS to bring about a peaceful solution to the conflict in Liberia.

Second, ECOWAS did not seek UN Security Council authorization for the deployment of the ECOMOG force. It seems, therefore, that ECOWAS did not regard ECOMOG action as enforcement action for which Article 53 authorization was necessary. Nor did any state in the Security Council claim that ECOMOG needed its authorization. But ECOWAS did inform the UN of its actions, even if its initial report came some months after the deployment of ECOMOG. Approval was given by the Secretary-General and by the Security Council in statements and resolutions commending ECOWAS for its actions. The Security Council did not demonstrate concern that ECOMOG had gone beyond legitimate peacekeeping even after its 1992 offensive. Later resolutions such as Resolution 911 recognized that the *Cotonou Peace Agreement* assigned ECOMOG to assist in the implementation of the Agreement. Later peace agreements gave ECOMOG and the Transitional Government 'peace enforcement powers' and the Security Council welcomed the action of ECOMOG in helping to defeat a coup attempt in September 1994.[167]

In Resolution 866 (1993), following the *Cotonou Peace Agreement*, the Security Council established UNOMIL, a UN peacekeeping force to complement ECOMOG. The resolution actually spelled out that this was the first time the UN had undertaken a peacekeeping mission in cooperation with a force set up by another organization. A clear understanding about the roles

---

[166] Akehurst, 'Enforcement Action by Regional Agencies, with special reference to the Organization of American States', 42 BYIL (1967) 175; Simma *The Charter of the United Nations: A Commentary* (2nd edn 2002) 860.
[167] 1994 UNYB 380.

of the two forces was crucial.[168] Under the Peace Agreement[169] ECOMOG, which was initially to be 4,000 strong, had the primary responsibility for supervising the implementation of the military provisions of the agreement. It was to be stationed at entry points, ports, and airports to ensure compliance with the Resolution 788 (1992) arms embargo; and also to be deployed throughout the country to supervise the disarmament and demobilization of the combatants. African states from outside the region were to contribute forces.[170] Like the establishment of a UN force, this provision for other states to contribute was designed to overcome the mistrust of those who saw ECOMOG as not truly impartial. Tanzania, Uganda, and Zimbabwe agreed to provide troops. The Agreement provided that ECOMOG was to be a neutral peacekeeping force. It included a heading 'peace enforcement powers', but in fact this made no express provision for the use of force except in self-defence. ECOMOG was to ensure the safety of UNOMIL observers.

Under Resolution 866 (1993) UNOMIL, a force of 300 military observers, was to monitor compliance with the ceasefire and the Peace Agreement and, *'without participation in enforcement operations,* to coordinate with ECOMOG in the discharge of ECOMOG's separate responsibilities both formally and informally'. This express exclusion of a peace enforcement role for UNOMIL seems to refer to the Peace Agreement and to imply that ECOMOG could undertake peace enforcement. But it does not amount to an express authorization of enforcement action by ECOMOG under Article 53 of the UN Charter and so the implication seems to be that ECOMOG was not involved in enforcement action under Article 53 in this case. The Security Council seemed to assume that some legal basis existed for peace enforcement operations by ECOMOG, that peace enforcement was not incompatible with peacekeeping.[171] The *Cotonou Peace Agreement* described ECOMOG as a peacekeeping force.

ECOWAS cooperation with a UN force

UNOMIL was to monitor the various implementation procedures in order to verify their impartial application. The UN involvement contributed

---

[168] The Secretary-General made a report defining the respective roles of UNOMIL and ECOMOG: S/26422, Weller, *Regional Peacekeeping and International Enforcement: The Liberian Crisis* (1994) at 374; an agreement was subsequently concluded: S/26868, Weller, ibid. at 440.
[169] *The Cotonou Agreement*, UN doc S/26272 (1993), Weller, ibid., at 343.
[170] UN doc S/26868 (1993), Weller, ibid., at 440; S/1994/168, Weller, ibid., at 455. A Trust Fund was established to help pay for the ECOMOG forces. The USA, the UK, and Denmark contributed.
[171] This type of uncertainty may be traced to the UN Secretary-General's categorization of peacekeeping in his *Agenda for Peace*. He has later, in his Lessons Learned Report on *Cooperation between the United Nations and Regional Organizations/Arrangements in a Peacekeeping Environment* (1999) para 36, stressed the need for a uniform terminology, common to the UN and to regional organizations.

significantly to the eventual implementation of the Peace Agreement and served to underline the international community's commitment to conflict resolution in Liberia. In all its subsequent resolutions on Liberia the Security Council stated that UNOMIL's ability to carry out its mandate depended on the capacity of ECOMOG to discharge its responsibilities.

But the peace process ran into repeated difficulties; there were delays in the establishment of an effective Transitional Government and hostilities prevented ECOMOG and UNOMIL from carrying out their respective mandates. UNOMIL was reduced in size at the end of 1994 and the peace process was at a standstill.[172] Its mandate was subsequently adjusted to reflect the breakdown of the *Cotonou Peace Agreement* and the succession of subsequent peace agreements, but in essentials UNOMIL's functions remained the same.[173] Later resolutions stressed the need for close contacts and enhanced coordination between ECOMOG and UNOMIL. They also called for ECOMOG to intensify the necessary action to provide security for UNOMIL.[174] It was not until August 1996, after another outburst of fighting, that the final *Abuja II Peace Agreement* was concluded and ECOMOG and UNOMIL were able to discharge their responsibilities. After elections were held and President Taylor came to power UNOMIL was terminated in September 1997. A small contingent of ECOMOG remained to help the Liberian government not only to provide security throughout Liberia, but also to restructure the Liberian army and police. It finally left in 1999.[175]

Conclusion

The ECOWAS intervention in Liberia between 1990 and 1997 may be seen as a success in that it helped to secure a ceasefire and a political settlement. Alternatively, it may be seen as a Nigerian-inspired operation that merely prolonged the conflict and postponed the coming to power of Charles Taylor. It highlights the problems over consent and impartiality; there was considerable uncertainty about the Liberian consent to the ECOMOG intervention and also controversy over ECOMOG's role in the civil war. A regional organization may run into the danger of seeming to take sides and of being dominated by one powerful member state. A condition of the Peace Agreement was the inclusion of states from outside ECOWAS in ECOMOG; UN involvement also proved necessary to secure the commitment of all the parties to the peace process. There were also financial problems which throw doubt on the ability of regional or

---

[172] Report of the Secretary-General S/1995/158; 1994 UNYB 371, 1995 UNYB 350.
[173] SC Res 1020 (1995).
[174] SC Res 1014, 1020 (1995), 1041, 1059, 1071, 1083 (1996).
[175] Final Report of the Secretary-General on UNOMIL, S/1997/712 para 5; Report of the Secretary-General S/2003/875 para 3.

subregional organizations to carry out extensive peacekeeping operations. The UN had to establish a special fund, and bilateral aid was also provided.[176] Nevertheless, there was much talk of the ECOWAS operation being an important precedent for future regional action and for UN/regional cooperation.[177]

The question also arises whether the operation has a fundamental legal significance in indicating that humanitarian intervention or pro-democratic or other enforcement action by a regional organization may now be legal even without express Security Council authorization under Article 53. The approval by the Security Council of the ECOWAS action led some commentators to infer from this and other episodes an important change in the interpretation of the Charter provisions governing regional organizations, giving them a legal right to greater autonomy, even in enforcement action.[178]

The former USSR

This precedent of cooperation between a regional and a UN force was followed in the cooperation between the CIS and the UN in the former USSR, in Tajikistan, and Georgia. In both operations a small UN force of military observers was supplemented by a larger regional force which was to maintain security. This division of labour reflects that adopted in Liberia. It seems that the cooperation in Tajikistan was regarded as relatively unproblematic, whereas at the inception of the operation in Georgia there were some questions about the impartiality of the CIS forces, and since 2003 Georgia has increasingly expressed concern about the presence and mandate of the CIS forces.

Tajikistan

After the outbreak of civil war in Tajikistan in May 1992 Russia wrote to the Secretary-General in April 1993 proposing the deployment of a military contingent of forces from Kirgizstan, Kazakhstan, Russia, Tajikistan, and Uzbekistan.[179] The five states made a formal Declaration after a summit meeting in August 1993; they said that the CIS would undertake

---

[176] See note 152 above. Many of the African sub-regional organizations are not financially independent, but depend on support from developed states.
[177] SC 3138th meeting (1992); UN doc S/24815 (1992).
[178] Deen-Racsmány, 'A Redistribution of authority between the UN and regional organizations in the field of maintenance of peace and security', 13 Leiden Journal of International Law (2000) 297; Franck, *Recourse to Force* (2002) at 155. For a more cautious approach, see Simma (ed.), *The Charter of the United Nations: A Commentary* (2nd edn, 2002) at 863. See further 417 below.
[179] UN doc S/25720 (1993).

regional peacekeeping under Chapter VIII. They agreed that the conflict was essentially an internal one, but that there was cross-border infiltration from Afghanistan.[180] There were already CIS border forces in Tajikistan deployed to act in collective self-defence of that state. The Security Council welcomed these efforts by the regional states.[181] The five states then made the *Moscow Accord* in September 1993 to establish a coalition force in Tajikistan; again they spoke of this as a regional arrangement concluded in accordance with the principles and purposes of Chapter VIII of the UN Charter.[182] Tajikistan was a party to the agreement and hence clearly consented to the deployment of this force and welcomed it as an important step in de-escalation of the conflict. But nevertheless it asked the Security Council to consider giving the CIS forces the status of UN peacekeeping forces. The Security Council did not accede to this request although it was repeated many times during the conflict and may indicate not only a desire for relief from the financial burden to the CIS, but also the higher status and perhaps also the clearer impartiality of UN forces.[183] Throughout 1993 and for most of 1994 there was fighting within Tajikistan and across the border. In September 1994 the parties concluded the *Tehran Agreement*; this provided for a temporary ceasefire and for the cessation of hostile acts across the border.[184]

After the *Tehran Agreement* the UN established a new UNMOT, to replace earlier temporary missions; this was to be a small team of observers with the mandate under Resolution 968 (1994) to monitor the ceasefire, investigate reports of ceasefire violations and to provide its good offices. It was to liaise closely with CIS peacekeeping forces and with the border forces. In this resolution the Security Council made no reference to Chapter VIII. As regards the role of the CIS forces, it showed less enthusiasm than it had with regard to ECOWAS in Liberia and later in Sierra Leone; the Security Council merely acknowledged positively the readiness of the collective peace-keeping forces of the CIS in Tajikistan to work together with UN observers to assist in maintaining the ceasefire and underlined the importance of close liaison between UNMOT and the CIS collective peacekeeping forces and the border forces.

In later resolutions it went on to express satisfaction over the close liaison between UNMOT and the CIS forces; it underlined the need to pursue this and develop it further. Later it expressed its satisfaction at the regular contacts between UNMOT and the CIS forces and the border

---

[180] UN doc S/26290 (1993).
[181] UN doc S/26341 (1993), 1993 UNYB 514.
[182] UN docs S/26357, S/26610 (1993).
[183] 1994 UNYB 591.
[184] Ibid.

forces.[185] But it was not until after the conclusion of the *General Agreement on the Establishment of Peace* in 1997 that the Security Council expressed any gratitude to the CIS forces, and then it was only for their readiness to assist in providing security for UN personnel at the request of UNMOT.[186] By 1998 they had become more appreciative; in Resolution 1167 (1998) they welcomed the cooperative liaison between UNMOT and the CIS forces and encouraged them to continue discussion of options for improving security cooperation. Resolution 1206 (1998) welcomed the continued contribution by the CIS peacekeeping in assisting parties in the implementation of the General Agreement, and in a statement the Security Council welcomed the readiness of the CIS force to arrange for the guarding of UN premises in Dushanbe.[187]

Abkhazia, Georgia

With regard to Abkhazia, Georgia, the UN was at first even more cautious in expressly regulating the relations between the UN force and the regional force; here again there was some apparent suspicion of the regional force. In this conflict the UN observer mission pre-dated the official establishment of the CIS force (although Russian forces that later made up the CIS force were already in Georgia). Abkhaz claims for secession grew while Georgia was riven by civil discord; in August 1992 armed conflict broke out. Georgia accused Russian forces of siding with the Abkhazians.[188] In July 1993 the UN Security Council began to plan the deployment of military observers once a ceasefire was implemented. Resolution 849 (1993) welcomed the participation of Russia as a facilitator in the UN Secretary-General's attempts to launch a peace process. In August 1993 the Security Council in Resolution 858 (1993) established UNOMIG to verify compliance with the July 1993 ceasefire and to investigate reports of violations. However, the ceasefire broke down and the Abkhaz offensive led to their occupation of almost the whole of Abkhazia and the displacement of the Georgian population. Accordingly UNOMIG could not carry out its original mandate; the Security Council produced a revised interim mandate for UNOMIG in Resolution 881(1993): it was to maintain contacts with both sides and also with the Russian military contingents. In December

---

[185] SC Res 1030, 1061, 1089 (1996).
[186] SC Res 1128, 1138 (1997).
[187] S/PRST/1998/4. The mandate of UNMOT was expanded after the 1997 Peace Agreement and it was given a security unit to protect its personnel. But progress in establishing peace was slow and the situation remained precarious. The first multi-party elections were held in March 2000: UN Press Release SC/6827, 21 March 2000. UNMOT was terminated in May 2000.
[188] UN doc S/26031 (1993), 1993 UNYB 506.

1993 Resolution 892 welcomed the readiness of Russia to help ensure the security of UNOMIG.

In May 1994 a more lasting ceasefire was agreed. This gave formal authority not to the Russian troops but to the 'CIS peacekeeping force'. This marked the transformation of the Russian forces into CIS forces, with the mandate to ensure respect for the ceasefire and the weapons exclusion zone.[189] Russia wrote to the Secretary-General, reporting that the CIS had decided under Chapter VIII to send a collective peacekeeping force to Abkhazia. The advance contingent of Russian troops already in Abkhazia would be deployed immediately.[190] The Security Council was willing to take this at face value and did not inquire into constitutional propriety; in Resolution 934 (1994) it noted with satisfaction the beginning of CIS assistance in zones of conflict, in response to the request of the parties on the basis of the May Agreement in continued coordination with UNOMIG. However, the Security Council made no reference to Chapter VIII. Further coordinating arrangements with UNOMIG were to be agreed and the Secretary-General was to report on these arrangements. Resolution 937 (1994) welcomed the May Agreement; it expressly recognized that the deployment of the CIS peacekeeping force was predicated upon the request and consent of the parties to the conflict. It noted with satisfaction the readiness of Russia to continue to inform the members of the Security Council on the activities of the CIS peacekeeping force. The Security Council now expanded UNOMIG and gave it the mandate of monitoring and verifying the implementation by the parties of the May ceasefire; to verify respect for the security zones and to monitor the withdrawal of troops and patrol and investigate violations of the Agreement.

UNOMIG was also 'to observe the operation of the CIS peacekeeping force'; this apparently reflected a perception that it was necessary to secure the impartiality of the CIS operations because of suspicion about the role of Russia. This provision for observation of the operation of the CIS force went far beyond any provision on the relation between UNOMIL and ECOWAS or UNMOT and the CIS forces. But many subsequent resolutions reported satisfaction at the cooperation and coordination between the two forces.[191] Resolution 1150 (1998) welcomed the contribution that the CIS force had made to stabilizing the situation in the zone of conflict and noted that the cooperation between UNOMIG and the CIS was good and had continued to develop. Resolution 1225 (1999) went further and noted that the working relationship between UNOMIG and the CIS peacekeeping force had been good at all levels; later resolutions spoke of

---

[189]   UN doc S/1994/583.
[190]   1994 UNYB 582, UN docs S/1994/476, S/1994/732.
[191]   From SC Res 971, 993 (1995).

an 'excellent relationship'.[192] However, the dispute in Abkhazia remained unresolved and the conflict zone remained volatile.

Relations between Georgia and Russia deteriorated when the pro-western President Saakashvili took power in Georgia in 2003.[193] Georgia repeatedly accused Russia of intervention, and the Georgian parliament called on its government to request the withdrawal of the CIS force.[194] The situation in Abkhazia worsened in 2006;[195] and in September 2007 the most serious clash for many years between Georgian and Abkhazian forces took place outside the area of operation of UNOMIG and the CIS forces. There were also several incidents in which Georgian forces challenged the CIS forces.[196] Georgia has increasingly expressed its dissatisfaction with the UN peace process.[197] But the Security Council has continued to support the CIS forces; most recently, in Resolution 1781(2007) it stressed 'the importance of close and effective cooperation between UNOMIG and the CIS peacekeeping force as they currently play an important stabilizing role in the conflict zone' and recalled that a lasting a comprehensive settlement of the conflict would require appropriate security guarantees.

ECOWAS action in Sierra Leone

Some of the questions about constitutionality, impartiality, and the interpretation of Article 53 which arose with regard to the ECOWAS action in Liberia arose again with regard to Sierra Leone. Here also a UN force was established to work with the regional force after the restoration of the democratically elected government. In contrast to Liberia, there was clear consent to the presence of the Nigerian and Guinean troops in Sierra Leone from the democratically elected President, both before the coup in May 1997 and after he was overthrown. But there are doubts as to whether the action taken in the name of ECOWAS did in fact constitute regional peacekeeping. ECOWAS, in June 1997, called for the restoration of the democratically elected government. It said that there were three means of achieving this: dialogue, sanctions, and, if necessary, the use of force. But the actual use of force seemed to go beyond impartial peacekeeping action; ECOWAS used force to remove the junta and restore democratic government. In contrast to the Security Council's express authority to use force in Haiti to restore democratic government, it did not expressly

---

[192] SC Res 1311 (2000), 1339 (2001); 2000 UNYB 386 at 390, 393; 2001 UNYB 374.
[193] See, for example, Keesings (2006) 47054, 47271, 47377, 47484, 47532, (2007) 47831, 48093.
[194] Press Conference by Georgia, UN, 31 October 2007; <www.un.org/News/briefings/docs/2007/071031_Georgia.doc.htm>; UN Press Release SC/8940, 12 January 2007, page 31.
[195] UN Press Release SC/8851, 13 October 2006, SC Res 1716 (2006).
[196] Report of the Secretary-General, S/2007/588, para 16–23.
[197] Ibid., para 6, 45.

authorize a comparable use of force by ECOWAS. There is, therefore, controversy as to the legal significance of this ECOWAS action and whether it supports a new right of pro-democratic or humanitarian intervention or the reinterpretation of Article 53.[198]

The first Security Council reaction to the coup was prompt but limited. It issued a statement on 27 May 1997 expressing concern. Especially given that the UN had assisted the attempts at reconciliation in Sierra Leone, the Security Council deplored the attempt to overthrow the democratically elected government and called for the immediate restoration of constitutional order.[199] The first ECOWAS communiqué was issued when ECOWAS met in June 1997, some time after the first involvement of the Nigerian and Guinean forces in the fighting in Sierra Leone.[200] This said that the ECOWAS objectives were to reinstate the legitimate government, restore peace and security, and resolve the serious refugee problem. It called for non-recognition of the junta and said that it would reinstate the previous government by force if necessary. Nigeria then requested a meeting of the Security Council; it said that the countries of the subregion had once again risen to the challenge of serving the cause of peace and security in the neighbouring country of Sierra Leone. It referred to the ECOWAS communiqué of June 1997; it acknowledged that some delegations had expressed concern about the use of force, but argued that negotiation and sanctions could not be achieved without the use of some military force. The meeting of the Security Council in July 1997 was held in closed session.[201] The product was a statement, expressing concern at the atrocities committed by the supporters of the junta against civilians, foreigners, and members of the ECOWAS monitoring group.[202] It welcomed the mediation efforts initiated by ECOWAS and said that it would monitor the progress of efforts aimed at the peaceful resolution of the crisis; it was ready to consider appropriate measures if constitutional order was not restored. It is clear that the Security Council's language endorsing ECOWAS attempts at peaceful settlement was very cautious and stopped far short of an authorization of the use of force.

This pattern was repeated in the subsequent Security Council statements and resolutions. It was not until Resolution 1132 (1997), imposing sanctions on Sierra Leone in October 1997, that the Security Council gave

---

[198] See Franck, *Recourse to Force* (2002), at 155; Deen-Racsmány, 'A Redistribution of Authority between the UN and Regional Organizations in the Field of the Maintenance of Peace and Security', 13 Leiden Journal of International Law (2000) 297; de Wet, *The Chapter VII powers of the UN Security Council* (2003), at 290.

[199] S/PRST/1997/29.

[200] UN doc S/1997/499.

[201] S/1997/531; SC 3797th meeting (1997).

[202] S/PRST/1997/36.

any express authorization of the use of force by ECOWAS. From the time of the coup ECOMOG forces had imposed a *de facto* embargo on Sierra Leone through interception of ships and aircraft. This was formalized in the June 1997 meeting of ECOWAS. In October 1997 ECOWAS sought Security Council support for its efforts. Nigeria reported that the junta was intransigent and the situation was a threat to international peace and security. The subregion was anxious to avoid a costly and long engagement like that in Liberia and sought UN support and endorsement for the ECOWAS sanctions and for enforcement of those sanctions.[203] The Security Council passed Resolution 1132 unanimously under Chapter VII; this expressed strong support for the efforts of the ECOWAS Committee to resolve the crisis and imposed sanctions against the members of the junta designed to restrict their freedom of movement. It also imposed an oil and arms embargo on Sierra Leone.[204] Resolution 1132 invoked Chapter VIII, as well as Chapter VII, specifically authorizing ECOWAS to ensure the strict implementation of this resolution by halting inward shipping. Member states could provide technical and logistical support to ECOWAS to carry out these responsibilities. This follows the precedents of the authorization to 'member states acting nationally or through regional organizations' to use force to secure compliance with arms embargos on Yugoslavia and Haiti. But, unlike these earlier resolutions, it referred to the relevant regional organization by name. The authorization was not to UN member states acting nationally or through regional agencies or arrangements but only to ECOWAS itself, not to individual members of ECOWAS. The matter was not discussed in the Security Council debate leading up to the resolution, but it seems that the intention was to ensure that ECOWAS acted collectively.[205]

The language of Resolution 1132 (1997) was cautious and did not amount to an authorization for enforcement action apart from that needed to implement the sanctions. However, the reference to ECOWAS could be taken as an endorsement of Nigeria's claim to be acting through the regional organization rather than unilaterally. The debate leading up to the resolution also shows some caution.[206] Several states spoke of their support for

---

[203] SC 3822nd meeting (1997).

[204] An express exception was made allowing the import of oil by the previous government and ECOWAS forces, but (apparently through an oversight) at first no comparable exception was made for the supply of arms to the previous government or ECOWAS. The sanctions regime was later modified to allow the supply of arms to ECOMOG and the legitimate government in SC Res 1156 and 1171(1998); later SC Res 1299 (2000) extended this exception to UNAMSIL. On the breaking of the blanket arms embargo by the UK see the UK government publication, *Report of the Sierra Leone Arms Investigation* (1998).

[205] Express reference was also made to ECOWAS in SC Res 1464 (2003) on Côte d'Ivoire: see below at 419.

[206] SC 3822nd meeting (1997).

International Law and the Use of Force

ECOWAS attempts to bring about the return of the government *through negotiations*. Russia in particular spoke of the need to strengthen coordination between the Security Council and ECOWAS; it said that its main premise was that the Charter required that enforcement action could not be undertaken by regional organizations without the authority of the Security Council.

After the imposition of sanctions the parties concluded the *Conakry Peace Agreement* in October 1997, on the basis of a peace plan produced by the ECOWAS Committee. This provided for ECOMOG to monitor and verify the cessation of hostilities, disarmament, and demobilization.[207] This peace plan was welcomed by the Security Council, but there was no immediate ceasefire.[208] ECOMOG continued to be involved in the conflict; it used force extensively, but in its reports to the Security Council under Resolution 1132 (1997) it was careful to claim only to be acting in self-defence or in enforcing the arms and oil embargo.[209] Nigeria also reported to the Security Council saying that ECOMOG forces had been the target of attacks by the junta. They claimed that the final engagement which led to the overthrow of the junta was the direct result of unprovoked attacks on ECOMOG.[210] On 12 February 1998 ECOMOG forces ousted the junta. The democratically elected government was returned and the peace agreement was implemented.[211]

The Security Council, in Resolution 1162 (1998), commended ECOMOG on its important role in the ongoing restoration of peace and security. For the first time in a resolution it expressly referred to the ECOMOG forces. As in the case of Liberia, this express reference to ECOMOG and the apparent acceptance of the legality of its operations followed the conclusion of a peace treaty between the parties. The Secretary-General, in his reports on the situation in Sierra Leone, avoided any pronouncement on the legality of the ECOMOG action; his report on the action leading to the restoration of the President in March 1998 does not challenge the legality of the final ECOMOG action even if it did not expressly accept at face value the ECOWAS claims to be acting in self-defence. He said that 'responding to an attack by the junta forces, ECOMOG launched a military attack on the junta which culminated approximately one week later in the collapse of the junta and its expulsion by force from Freetown after heavy fighting'. ECOMOG subsequently took control of almost every major town.

---

[207] UN doc S/1997/824.
[208] S/PRST/1997/52.
[209] UN docs S/1997/895, S/1998/14, S/1998/107, S/1998/170; see also address by President Kabbah of Sierra Leone, UN doc S/1999/186, saying that ECOMOG forces were acting in self-defence; 1998 UNYB 163 at 167.
[210] UN docs S/1998/123, S/1998/170.
[211] UN doc S/1998/215; SC Res 1156; 1998 UNYB 163.

The Secretary-General commended the contribution by ECOMOG officers and men to the removal of the military junta.[212]

The ECOMOG forces were then supplemented by UNOMSIL, a small UN force of seventy military observers established in June 1998 by Resolution 1181 to monitor the military and security situation and the disarmament and demobilization process, including the role of ECOMOG in the provision of security and in the collection and destruction of arms.[213] This express injunction to monitor the regional peacekeeping force mirrors the precedent of the mandate of UNOMIG in Georgia and may reflect a suspicion of Nigeria comparable to that of Russia; at least it reflects the primacy of the United Nations and the need to secure the propriety of ECOMOG's actions. The combination of a small UN force and a larger, pre-existing regional force follows the precedents of Liberia, Tajikistan, and Georgia.

The rebels returned to the attack and occupied the capital, Freetown, in January 1999. ECOMOG played a major role in driving them back from the capital and in launching a counter attack.[214] ECOMOG's role was to defend the legitimate government that it had helped to restore; it seems rather far-fetched to claim that this action could constitute self-defence of ECOMOG.[215] But no concern was expressed about the ECOMOG action. The UN Secretary-General said that ECOMOG was to be congratulated on its success in repelling the rebels from Freetown and restoring a measure of order to the city. Donor governments, the Netherlands, Canada, the UK and the USA, were also thanked for their logistical support.[216] The Security Council, in Resolution 1231 (1999), also commended the efforts of ECOMOG towards the restoration of peace, security, and stability, and called on all member states to provide ECOMOG with financial and logistical support. Thus there was clear support for ECOWAS and apparent acceptance of the legality of its actions, but without any discussion of their legal basis.

In July 1999 the warring parties concluded the *Lomé Peace Agreement*.[217] This stipulated the adoption of a new mandate for ECOMOG; it was to

---

[212] Fourth Report of the Secretary-General on the Situation in Sierra Leone, S/1998/249.
[213] 1998 UNYB 172.
[214] Fifth Report of the Secretary-General on UNOMSIL, S/1999/237; 1999 UNYB 152.
[215] Also, it may be that some states were willing to accept the legality of this operation because of the fact that there had been foreign support for the rebels from Liberia (S/PRST/1991/1). On the accusation by Sierra Leone against Liberia, see UN doc S/1999/73, 1999 UNYB 154. This argument was used by the UK to justify its substantial aid to the democratically elected government and to ECOMOG (Private notice question answered by the Foreign Secretary, House of Commons, 19 January 1999). Liberia denied intervention and attributed the actions to mercenaries (UN docs S/1999/17, S/1999/193); 1999 UNYB 154.
[216] Fifth Report of the Secretary-General on UNOMSIL, S/1999/237.
[217] UN doc S/1999/1073; 1999 UNYB 159.

cover four areas: peacekeeping; security of the State of Sierra Leone; protection of UNOMSIL; and protection of disarmament, demobilization and reintegration personnel. Also a timetable was to be drawn up for the phased withdrawal of ECOMOG; it was to be replaced by a neutral peacekeeping force comprising UNOMSIL and ECOMOG.[218] In August 1999 ECOWAS accordingly adopted a revised mandate for ECOMOG.[219]

The Security Council approved this revised ECOMOG mandate in Resolution 1270 (1999), but it did not refer to Chapter VII or Chapter VIII. The implication is that it did not regard ECOMOG as an enforcement force needing authorization under Article 53 and that it saw it as deriving its legal basis from the *Lomé Peace Agreement*. In contrast, Security Council did invoke Chapter VII with regard to UNAMSIL. This new 6,000 strong UN force was to replace UNOMSIL. It was to cooperate with the government and the other parties to the peace agreement in the implementation of the agreement. Its main purpose was to assist the government in the disarmament and demobilization and the creation of conditions of confidence and stability. The force was not mandated to ensure the security of Freetown and the international airport or to provide protection for the government. These tasks and 'operations against rogue elements' would remain the responsibility of ECOMOG.[220] Under Chapter VII UNAMSIL was authorized to take the necessary action to ensure the security and freedom of movement of its personnel and, within its capabilities and areas of deployment, to afford protection to civilians under imminent threat of physical violence.

The division of functions between the two forces was agreed. The initial mandate of UNAMSIL under Resolution 1270 (1999) rested on the assumption that ECOMOG would continue. But Nigeria decided in December 1999 to withdraw its forces.[221] Accordingly the Security Council, in Resolution 1289 in February 2000, expanded the numbers of UNAMSIL to 11,000 and redrew its mandate to allow it to take over the functions of ECOMOG. It was given increased powers under Chapter VII, but the Secretary-General underscored that these tasks would not fundamentally change the nature of the mandate, which was based on the requirement in the *Lomé Peace Agreement* for a neutral peacekeeping force.[222] ECOMOG forces were subsequently incorporated (re-hatted) into UNAMSIL.[223]

---

[218] Seventh Report of the Secretary-General on UNOMSIL, S/1999/836; 1999 UNYB 160.
[219] Eighth Report of the Secretary-General on UNOMSIL, S/1999/1003.
[220] SC 4054th meeting (1999); see also Press Release SC/6742, 22 October 1999; 1999 UNYB 164.
[221] First Report of the Secretary-General on UNAMSIL, S/1999/1223; 1999 UNYB 167.
[222] Second Report of the Secretary-General on UNAMSIL, S/2000/13; Press Release SC/6800, 7 February 2000; 2000 UNYB 190.
[223] Third Report of the Secretary-General on UNAMSIL, S/2000/186; UN Press Release SC/6821, 13 March 2000.

Thus in Sierra Leone a regional force operated with Security Council initial acquiescence and later express approval to restore a democratically elected government and to maintain it in power when the national army was not able to do so on its own. It was clear, through its repeated commendations of ECOMOG's role in the restoration and maintenance of peace and security, that the Security Council approved the regional action, but did not make clear the legal basis for this. In the absence of express provision or illuminating debate the most plausible solution seems to be that this was created as a regional peacekeeping force, operating with the consent of the democratically elected President. It was authorized to use force to implement the Security Council embargo, but apart from this the Security Council made no further reference to Chapter VII or VIII with regard to ECOWAS. ECOWAS itself based its use of force on Resolution 1132 (1997) and on self-defence. Subsequently it could base its legal authority on the more far-reaching provisions of the peace agreements. But it needed outside help to carry out its operations; the USA provided significant assistance to ECOWAS.[224]

A REINTERPRETATION OF ARTICLE 53 OF THE UN CHARTER?

Some commentators have argued on the basis of the ECOWAS operations in Liberia and Sierra Leone (and, even more controversially, on the basis of the NATO operation in Kosovo) that not only has there been in practice a redistribution of powers between the UN and regional organizations, but also that Article 53 should be reinterpreted to allow certain humanitarian or pro-democratic enforcement action without prior Security Council authorization; that regional organizations now have an increasing range of rights and responsibilities in the field of enforcement action.[225] They argue not only that *ex post facto* approval by the Security Council may make up for the lack of prior authorization under Article 53, but also that such approval may amount to implicit authorization or even indicate that no authorization is needed in certain cases.

Franck suggests that 'such *ex post facto* approval effectively reinterprets the text of Article 53'.[226] But it is not clear that the practice supports any radical conclusions. In the absence of clear language by the Security Council, it seems unjustified to claim as a matter of law that 'regional organizations enjoy a considerably larger degree of freedom even in the field of

---

[224] 1998 UNYB 171; <http://usembassy.state.gov/nigeria/wwwhawfc.html>.
[225] Deen-Racsmány, 'A Redistribution of Authority between the UN and Regional Organizations in the Field of the Maintenance of Peace and Security', 13 Leiden Journal of International Law (2000) 297; Franck, *Recourse to Force* (2002) at 155.
[226] Franck, *Recourse to Force* (2002) at 162.

enforcement measures involving the use of armed force than they did'[227] if this is taken to mean that express prior authority is no longer legally required, rather than simply that the Security Council may in exceptional circumstances acquiesce in the use of force by regional organizations which has arguably crossed the line between peacekeeping and enforcement action. Such an argument seems to threaten the Charter scheme on the relationship between the Council and regional organizations, and to be reading too much into general statements by the Council; it ignores the absence of wide claims by ECOWAS itself and the clear caution of the approach of the Security Council. It is difficult in cases such as that of Liberia and Sierra Leone to deduce the exact scope of any implicit *ex post facto* authority when the Security Council's approval is expressed in general terms and ECOWAS did not itself claim a wide right to use force. The more recent practice of the Security Council in authorizing force by ECOWAS in Côte d'Ivoire and Liberia (2003) and by the AU in Somalia may indicate a deliberate reassertion of direct Security Council control of enforcement action.[228]

A regional right to use force to restore democratic government?

Some have claimed that the ECOWAS intervention in Sierra Leone shows acceptance of a regional right to use force to restore democracy, comparable to the Security Council- authorized operation in the case of Haiti, and perhaps even supporting a unilateral right to use force to further democracy, but this also seems open to doubt. In the absence of express or even implied Security Council authorization under Chapter VII to allow the restoration of democracy, and in the absence of any discussion of this question in Security Council debates, this is another example of reinterpretation of state practice, looking at what states did and not at what they said. The 'restoration of democracy' was an aim of ECOWAS, but not the express legal basis for their action. ECOWAS did not itself claim a legal right of pro-democratic intervention; its use of force was based on the implementation of Resolution 1132 (1997), self-defence, and the various peace agreements. In the absence of any express claim by a regional organization, and given that the Security Council has not acknowledged any autonomous right of regional organizations to use force to restore democracy, it is difficult to accept the emergence of a radical new right

---

[227] Deen-Racsmány, 'A Redistribution of Authority between the UN and Regional Organizations in the Field of the Maintenance of Peace and Security', 13 Leiden Journal of International Law (2000) 297.

[228] The SC also authorized the use of force by the EU in the DRC and in Chad and the CAR.

involving a fundamental change to the role of regional organizations under the Charter. This question came up again, in less dramatic form, in the 2003 ECOWAS operations in Côte d'Ivoire and Liberia and in the FOMUC operation in the CAR.

Côte d'Ivoire

In Côte d'Ivoire plans were made for an ECOWAS peacekeeping force (ECOMICI) to assist the government after an attempted coup in 2002.[229] The Security Council commended ECOWAS for its efforts to promote a peaceful settlement of the conflict and called on the international community to help with the deployment of ECOMOG. In the meanwhile the Security Council expressed its appreciation to France, the former colonial power, for using its troops to prevent further fighting at the request of the legitimate authorities pending the deployment of ECOMOG.[230] In December 2002 the Security Council expressed concern at the situation, support for the legitimate government, support for the deployment of a six member state ECOMOG force under Senegal's command and appreciation of the efforts of France, at the request of the government, to prevent further fighting.[231]

In January 2003 the *Linas-Marcoussis Agreement* was concluded between the opposing parties in Côte d'Ivoire and was approved by the Security Council.[232] Resolution 1464 (2003), passed unanimously, endorsed the agreement and welcomed the deployment of ECOWAS and French troops with a view to contributing to a peaceful solution to the crisis. Under Chapter VII it authorized 'member states participating in the ECOWAS force in accordance with Chapter VIII together with the French forces supporting them to take the necessary steps to guarantee the security and freedom of movement of their personnel and to ensure…the protection of civilians immediately threatened with physical violence within their zones of operation, using the means available to them, for a period of six months'.[233] ECOWAS determined that it needed a force of 3,200 to implement the Peace Agreement. However, owing to severe lack of financial resources the force was not able to reach that level.[234] In February 2003 the

---

[229] UN Press Release SC/7588, 6 December 2002.
[230] Ibid. Some suspicion was expressed of French motives and there was considerable local hostility to France's involvement. There was concern as to whether France was actually helping the government or whether it was really taking advantage of the situation to impose conditions on that government. Anti-French riots broke out at the terms of the peace settlement, *The Guardian*, 27 September 2002, 2 October 2002, Keesings (2003) 45230.
[231] UN Press Release SC/7619, 20 December 2002.
[232] UN Press Release SC/7646, 28 January 2003, 2003 UNYB 165.
[233] This follows the pattern of the authorization to the UN force, UNOMSIL, in SC Res 1270 (1999) in Sierra Leone.
[234] Report of the Secretary-General S/2004/3 para 48–51.

Security Council called on member states to provide appropriate financial and logistical support; the Netherlands responded with substantial
aid for ECOWAS.[235] Given the situation facing the ECOMICI force, all
Ivorian parties called for the deployment of a UN peacekeeping force that
would include the ECOWAS forces. The Chair of ECOWAS stressed that
the resources of ECOWAS were overstretched and that ECOMICI could
no longer be sustained. They stressed the unique legitimacy, impartiality
and capabilities that the UN could bring to bear.[236] The heads of state of
concerned African countries had also called for a UN role and expressed
the wish that the Security Council would endorse the peacekeeping operation launched by ECOWAS and France in order to confer greater legitimacy on it.[237]

A government of national reconciliation was set up in April 2003.[238]
And in May 2003 the Security Council/established MINUCI, a small UN
mission to complement existing ECOWAS and French forces, to facilitate
the implementation of the *Linas-Marcoussis Agreement*.[239] In July 2003 the
Security Council welcomed the progress made, but voiced concern at the
continued existence of regional factors of instability: the use of mercenaries and child soldiers, the spread of small arms and light weapons. It was
encouraged that efforts had been made to resolve the conflict in Liberia
which had been the primary source of instability in the subregion.[240] The
presence of ECOWAS forces was indispensable if the stability was to be
sustained. But the Security Council was concerned about the financial
difficulties ECOWAS continued to face; lack of adequate funding could
jeopardize operations.[241] In November 2003 ECOWAS requested that the
Security Council establish a UN force, and accordingly in Resolution
1528 (2004), passed unanimously under Chapter VII, the Security Council
created a 6,240 strong multidimensional force, UNOCI, to take over
from ECOMICI and MINUCI.[242] ECOMICI could be seen as a regional

---

[235] ECOWAS Press Release: <sec.ecowas.int.presse.en/presseshow.php?nb=19/2003>;
ECOWAS Press Release: <sec.ecowas.int.presse.en/presseshow.php?nb=30/2003>; *The
Guardian*, 25 April 2003. Assistance was also provided by France, the USA and the UK:
UN Press Release SC/7724, 11 April 2003. The Secretary-General repeatedly reported that
ECOWAS needed more financial assistance: see, for example, S/2003/801 para 59.
[236] Report of the Secretary-General S/2004/3 para 48–51.
[237] UN Press Release SC/7758, SC 4754th meeting (2003).
[238] UN Press Release SC/7732, 15 April 2003.
[239] Under SC Res 1479 (2003), passed unanimously. This was originally categorized by
the UN as a peacekeeping force, but was re-labelled as a special political mission in October
2003.
[240] UN Press Release SC/7758, 13 May 2003 para 62. The Secretary-General welcomed
the unique opportunity which had arisen for a regional solution to the problems of Côte
d'Ivoire, Liberia and Sierra Leone: UN doc S/2003/1069 para 52.
[241] Secretary-General's Reports S/2003/801 para 59, S/2003/1069 para 33.
[242] 2004 UNYB 170.

peacekeeping operation to preserve democracy in Côte d'Ivoire. But issues of the legality of enforcement action to restore democratic government without Security Council authority did not arise on the facts.

Liberia (2003) and the Central African Republic

Neither does the 2003 ECOWAS operation in Liberia provide support for any suggested new right of regional organizations to use force to restore democratic government without express Security Council authority. In this instance the Security Council authorized the deployment of ECOMIL as the vanguard for a multinational force, to be followed by a UN force.[243] The elected President of Liberia, Charles Taylor, was under considerable international pressure.[244] Sanctions had been imposed on Liberia for its support for the opposition in Sierra Leone, and the President had been indicted by the Sierra Leone Special Court for his involvement in the conflict in Sierra Leone. Opposition forces had gained control of much of the country and were advancing on the capital, Monrovia. ECOWAS offered to send in peacekeeping forces, but it was not until President Taylor undertook to stand down that the Security Council was willing to take up ECOWAS's offer. In Resolution 1497 (2003) the Security Council authorized member states under Chapter VII to establish a multinational force in Liberia to support the implementation of a ceasefire agreement, and to prepare for the introduction of a longer-term UN stabilization force. ECOWAS deployed 3,500 forces on 4 August;[245] President Taylor handed over power and left for Nigeria on 11 August 2003; a *Comprehensive Peace Agreement* was agreed on 18 August.[246] This was clearly not an operation in support of the maintenance or restoration of a democratically elected government; the intervention was delayed until after the commitment of President Taylor to stand down, despite the desperate conditions in Liberia and the pleas of the UN Secretary-General.[247] ECOMIL was replaced by a UN force in October 2003.[248]

The CEMAC peacekeeping operation in the Central African Republic (CAR) also gives a mixed message as far as support for a doctrine of

---

[243] SC Res 1497 (2003); Report of the Secretary-General, S/2003/875.

[244] Report of the Secretary-General S/2003/875.

[245] Report of the Secretary-General S/2003/875. The USA promised US$10 million to Nigeria for financial and logistical support to ECOWAS; <http://allafrica.com/stories/printable/200307290624.html>, and further support to ECOWAS: UN Press Release GA/SPD/267 (2003). Germany also provided a large amount of assistance to ECOWAS: ECOWAS Press Release 66/2003, 1 July 2003.

[246] Secretary-General Report S/2003/875.

[247] Some limited support for democratic principles may be found in SC Res 1497 (2003), paras. 12 and 13. Para 13 urges the LURD and MODEL opposition forces to refrain from any attempt to seize power by force, bearing in mind the position of the African Union on unconstitutional changes of government.

[248] SC Res 1509 (2003), Report of the Secretary-General S/2003/1175.

forcible regional restoration of democracy is concerned. A peacekeeping force (FOMUC) was set up in response to a series of attempted coups against the democratically elected government.[249] When there was a successful coup in March 2003 FOMUC did not act against the new regime to restore the previous government, as it had in Sierra Leone. Rather the new government asked FOMUC to remain in order to help to restore stability.[250] The Security Council subsequently expressed support for FOMUC.[251] Presidential and legislative elections were successfully held in 2005 and the Security Council commended FOMUC for providing decisive support to the defence and security forces of the CAR. It appreciated the vital role played by FOMUC and expressed its support for continuing efforts by FOMUC to back the consolidation of the constitutional order.[252] The security situation deteriorated in 2006; the government was not able to repel armed groups in the north and north-east. Also the conflict in Darfur spilled over into the CAR. 'The CAR is a victim of the tension between Chad and Sudan, which accuse each other of supporting rebels hostile to their respective regimes, even though the provision of such support is prohibited under the Tripoli Agreement signed by the two leaders on 8 February 2006.'[253] The Security Council called on FOMUC to continue supporting the CAR armed forces.[254] In 2007 the Security Council in Resolution 1778 authorized the establishment of MINURCAT, a joint EU and UN force in the CAR and Chad. FOMUC was also to remain in the CAR;[255] the Security Council while expressing concern about the ongoing insecurity in the CAR which had led to a severe humanitarian crisis, welcomed the extension of its mandate.[256]

It is, therefore, difficult to argue on the basis of the practice in Sierra Leone, Liberia, Côte d'Ivoire and the CAR that there is any new right of regional organizations to act without Security Council authority to use force to restore democracy or for humanitarian purposes. The Security Council's acquiescence in the actions of ECOMOG in Sierra Leone does not seem to be enough to justify such a doctrine. Recent discussions on

---

[249] See note 99 above. See also, Zwanenburg, 'Regional Organizations and the Maintenance of International Peace and Security', 11 Journal of Armed Conflict and Security Law (2006) 483.

[250] France provided major logistical and financial support for this operation (UN Press Releases SC/7593, 10 December 2002, SC/7626, 8 January 2003).

[251] S/PRST/2004/39.

[252] S/PRST/2005/35.

[253] Report of the Secretary-General, S/2006/441; UN Press Release GA/SPD/383, 1 November 2007.

[254] S/PRST/2006/47.

[255] A joint mission of the EU, Council of Europe and the AU visited the CAR to discuss the further extension and strengthening of the mandate of the regional force, Report of the Secretary-General, S/2007/697.

[256] UN Press Release SC/9196, 12 December 2007.

the future of cooperation between the UN and regional organizations revealed states such as Russia continuing to insist strongly on the need for Security Council authorization for any enforcement action by regional organizations.[257]

SECURITY COUNCIL AUTHORIZATION OF USE OF FORCE BY REGIONAL ORGANIZATIONS

In Yugoslavia the Security Council for the first time used its powers to authorize enforcement action by what it apparently regarded as a regional organization. Its flexible approach to the question what counts as a regional arrangement or agency under Chapter VIII was apparent: the Security Council apparently viewed the EC, CSCE, and possibly also the WEU and NATO as regional bodies in that it referred to Chapter VIII to commend their activities or to authorize force by them.[258] The Security Council's initial response to the situation in Croatia and later in Bosnia was to impose an arms embargo on the whole of the former Yugoslavia. It subsequently in May 1992 imposed a complete trade embargo on Serbia and Montenegro; in November 1992 it reinforced these measures in Resolution 787: 'Acting under Chapter VII and Chapter VIII, the Security Council calls upon States acting nationally or through regional agencies or arrangements, to use such measures commensurate with the specific circumstances as may be necessary under the authority of the Security Council to halt all inward and outward maritime shipping in order to inspect and verify their cargoes and destinations and to ensure strict implementation of the provisions of resolutions 713 and 757.' Under this authorization NATO and the WEU intercepted ships in the Adriatic and on the Danube.

The Security Council also authorized the use of force to secure the implementation of an Article 41 embargo in Haiti and Sierra Leone.[259]

---

[257] See, for example, UN Press Releases SC/7724, 11 April 2003, SC/8526, 17 October 2005 at 9, GA/PK/192, 26 February 2007, at 8, 9, GA/PK 193, 27 February 2007, at 9, 10.

[258] As regards the EC and the CSCE, typically resolutions said: 'Recalling also the provisions of Chapter VIII of the Charter of the United Nations, commending the efforts undertaken by the European Community and its Member States, with the support of the States participating in the CSCE, to restore peace and dialogue in Yugoslavia.' The implication was that the EC and the CSCE are regional organizations. Similarly, some of the resolutions authorizing member states to use force refer to Chapter VIII; although there was no express reference to NATO, it was understood by the member states that it would be NATO that implemented the resolution.

[259] In response to the 1993 coup in Haiti the Security Council imposed an oil and arms embargo; in Resolution 875: 'Acting under Chapters VII and VIII of the Charter of the United Nations, Calls upon Member States, acting nationally or through regional agencies or arrangements, cooperating with the legitimate Government of Haiti, to use such measures commensurate with the specific circumstances as may be necessary under the authority

The resolutions on Yugoslavia and Haiti do not in their operative paragraphs refer to any regional organization by name. They could nevertheless be seen as the first use by the Security Council of Article 53 of the UN Charter in that they call on member states of regional agencies or arrangements to take enforcement action. But no express reference is made to Article 53 and it is typical of the Security Council not to concern itself with the exact article under which it is acting if this makes no difference to its powers. The Security Council action with regard to Sierra Leone seems more obviously to fall within Article 53 in that Resolution 1132 (1997) 'authorizes' rather than 'calls on' states to take action and it expressly refers to the regional organization, ECOWAS, by name. But even this resolution makes no express reference to Article 53.[260]

The Security Council has gone further than authorizing force to implement a trade embargo. With regard to the former Yugoslavia it acted under Chapter VII, and sometimes also Chapter VIII, to call on states to use force for humanitarian purposes and also to enforce the no-fly zone and to protect safe havens. In Resolution 770 (1992), acting under Chapter VII, it called upon states acting nationally or through regional agencies or arrangements to take all measures necessary to facilitate the delivery by relevant UN humanitarian organizations and others of humanitarian assistance. In Resolution 816 (1993) it authorized member states 'acting nationally or through regional organizations' to take measures to ensure compliance with the ban on flights in Bosnia's airspace. In this resolution the Security Council said that it was acting under Chapter VII, but it also recalled Chapter VIII. The authorization to member states to use force made it clear that they were under the authority of the Security Council and subject to close coordination with the Secretary-General and UNPROFOR. Also member states were required to coordinate their activities, including their rules of engagement, with the Secretary-General and UNPROFOR and to inform the Secretary-General of any measure taken. Resolution 836 (1993) on the use of force to protect the safe areas established by the Security Council is slightly different in that it did not make any express reference to Chapter VIII.[261] It expanded UNPROFOR's mandate by authorizing it to use force in reply to attacks on the six designated

---

of the Security Council to ensure strict implementation of the provisions of resolutions 841 (1993) and 873 (1993)…and in particular to halt inward maritime shipping as necessary to inspect and verify their cargoes and destinations.' In Resolution 917 it extended this to outward shipping.

[260] SC Res 1132 (1997), 'Acting also under Chapter VIII of the Charter of the United Nations, authorizes ECOWAS, cooperating with the democratically elected Government of Sierra Leone, to ensure strict implementation' of the oil and arms embargo.

[261] Later SC Res 908 (1994), 1037 (1996), 1120 (1997) on Croatia also refer only to Chapter VII, not to Chapter VIII, in authorizing force by member states acting nationally or through regional agencies to protect UNPROFOR and its successors in Croatia.

safe areas, and also 'decided that' member states acting nationally or through regional organizations or arrangements may take 'all necessary measures' through the use of air power to support UNPROFOR under the authority of the Security Council. Again the Security Council called for close coordination between member states, the Secretary-General, and UNPROFOR. Under these resolutions NATO deployed planes to monitor the no-fly zones and safe areas in Bosnia. Early in 1994 NATO took its first action. For NATO, these resolutions and subsequent military actions were a new departure; they constituted its first out-of-area action and its first use of force.[262]

The Security Council in 2003 'authorized' force by regional organizations in Côte d'Ivoire and Liberia. It also authorized force by the AU in Somalia and by the EU in the DRC,[263] and in Chad and the CAR.[264] No reference was made to Article 53 in any of these cases. As regards Côte d'Ivoire, the Security Council invoked Chapters VII and VIII; in Resolution 1464 it authorized member states participating in the ECOWAS forces in accordance with Chapter VIII to take the necessary steps to protect their own personnel and also civilians immediately threatened with physical violence in their zones of operation. This is clearly a limited mandate, unlikely to be based on Article 53. With regard to Liberia, the Security Council went further. Security Council Resolution 1497 in its preamble referred to Chapter VIII in commending the role of ECOWAS. Then, 'acting under Chapter VII', it authorized member states to establish a multinational force (IEMF) to support the implementation of the Peace Agreement; it specifically mentioned ECOWAS as forward element of IEMF.[265] Member states were authorized to take all necessary measures to fulfil the mandate of the IEMF. It was to operate until a longer-term UN stabilization force could take over.[266] The express authorization of force in these two contrasting cases created no problem over the legality of enforcement action by regional organizations—unlike the earlier operations in Liberia and Sierra Leone. The issue of the distinction between peacekeeping and enforcement action and the possible emergence of a wide new right of regional bodies to use force did not arise. The Security Council played the lead role, even though its action was delayed, and

---

[262] UN Publications, *The Blue Helmets: A Review of United Nations Peacekeeping* (3rd edn, 1996) at 531; Gazzini, 'NATO Coercive Military Activities in the Yugoslav Crisis', 12 EJIL (2001) 391.

[263] SC Res 1484 (2003), passed under Chapter VII, established a member state force in the DRC, to be led by the EU, but made no reference to Chapter VIII or the EU. SC Res 1671 (2006), also passed under Chapter VII, did expressly refer to the EU.

[264] SC Res 1778 (2007) referred expressly to the EU and, within the body of the resolution, authorized it to use force under Chapter VII.

[265] In accordance with Secretary-General's Report, S/2003/769.

[266] See 421 above.

Chapter VII authority was given from the start of the ECOWAS intervention in Liberia (2003).

It seems that the question whether the Security Council has in these instances—Yugoslavia, Sierra Leone, Côte d'Ivoire, Liberia (2003), Somalia and Chad and the CAR—authorized states to use force under Article 53 of Chapter VIII or simply under Chapter VII is not of any great legal significance, though it may be of symbolic importance for the role of regional organizations. The express use of Article 53 would represent an acknowledgement of the importance of their special role. Similarly, when Security Council resolutions refer to member states of a regional agency or arrangement rather than to the organization itself, this may reflect a lack of concern with any question of constitutionality; in contrast, the reference to the organization by name with regard to Sierra Leone, Côte d'Ivoire and Liberia (2003), to ECOWAS rather than (or as well as) its member states, may be taken as showing greater concern that the member states should act collectively and as an acceptance of the special role of regional organizations. But this may be reading too much into the difference of terminology.

CONCLUSION

The wide variety of recent developments with regard to regional action—the cooperation between the UN and regional organizations in seeking peaceful settlement of disputes, as reflected in the large number of Security Council resolutions referring to regional action; the joint operations in Liberia, Sierra Leone, Georgia, Tajikistan, Côte d'Ivoire and the DRC; the new forms of cooperation in Darfur and Char/CAR; the use of regional organizations for enforcement action, possibly under Article 53—suggests that regional arrangements will continue to play a larger role in international peacekeeping and enforcement in the future. Although it is now clear that regional organizations may contribute to a deeper sense of participation, consensus, and democratisation, as the UN Secretary-General had envisaged in his *Agenda for Peace*, there is still a need for caution.

In all the recent discussions about the role of regional organizations, and about their relationship with the UN, there has been a consistent commitment to the existing legal framework of Chapter VIII. The radical claims made by some commentators, that there has been a reinterpretation of Article 53 based on the practice in Liberia and Sierra Leone, allowing regional enforcement action or pro-democratic intervention in the absence of Security Council authorization, have not been supported by recent practice. Nor has there been any support for these claims in the High-level Panel report or that of the Secretary-General or in the World

Summit Outcome Document. Russia repeatedly stresses the need for Security Council authorization for enforcement action; many states have reaffirmed in more general terms the need to work within the Chapter VIII framework.[267] In all the calls for stronger cooperation between regional organizations and the UN there have been repeated demands for proper reports by regional bodies under Article 54, intended to reinforce the primary role of the Security Council. Thus Resolution 1631 (2005) stresses the need for regional organizations to keep the Security Council fully informed of their activities for the maintenance of international peace and security.

There are some slight indications of a return to a more formalistic approach, echoing the concerns of the 1940s. The question as to what constitutes a regional organization under Chapter VIII has resurfaced. Thus the calls for greater clarity on the interpretation of Article 52 may lead to a less flexible approach to this issue than that apparent in earlier Security Council resolutions. But it is not yet clear what difference, if any, this would make in practice. There is also support for formalized agreements between regional organizations and the UN, and perhaps also between regional and subregional organizations. The question as to what may be 'appropriate for regional action' under Article 52 arises out of the calls for a clear division of labour between the UN and regional organizations.

Some states members of regional organizations will continue to prefer UN to regional intervention where they are concerned that one powerful state dominates a regional or subregional organization. As with the authorization to UN member states to use force, so the authorization to the member states of a regional organization raises issues of UN supervision and control. The express requirement that a UN force should monitor the regional force, as in Georgia and Sierra Leone, indicates the greater faith in the impartiality of the UN. In contrast Sudan and Chad recently displayed suspicion of the UN, and were not willing to accept a traditional UN force.

It is also clear that some problems handled initially at the regional level cannot be resolved at that level, but will require the greater authority and resources of the UN. It is clear from the practice of ECOWAS and of the AU that regional organizations depend on developed states not only for financial support but also for logistical support. Thus regional organizations may be able to provide a rapid response, but may not be equipped for long-term operations in difficult circumstances. Regional organizations

---

[267] See, for example, the NAM statement in the Fourth Committee that the role of regional organizations should be in accordance with Chapter VII, UN Press Release GA/SPD/353, 20 October 2006. See also the Report of the Special Committee on Peacekeeping Operations, A/61/19 (2007) para 182.

were the first to become involved in Liberia, Sierra Leone, Tajikistan, Georgia, Burundi and Côte d'Ivoire but were later supplemented (or replaced) by the UN, partly to guarantee their impartiality and to remove fears of sphere of influence peacekeeping.[268] The AU took action in Darfur and Somalia when the UN was not willing to do so, but the AU experienced serious difficulties, and turned to the UN to take over in both cases. The African sub-regional organizations, especially ECOWAS, have played a major role, but they have depended on outside financial assistance to carry out their operations. The USA, France and other European states have all made substantial contributions. A major concern in recent reports and debates is therefore with the practical question of capacity building, especially of the AU. There is currently a debate as to how far the UN itself should fund regional action in cases where the Security Council has authorized the creation of the regional force, and as to whether regional standby forces should be placed at the disposal of UN.

This must cast some doubt on whether the use of regional organizations actually indicates 'a greater sense of participation, consensus and democratization', as the Secretary-General had hoped in his *Agenda for Peace*, or whether it provides a convenient opportunity for developed states to subcontract operations in Africa, as some fear. Developed states have shown themselves more willing to provide training and resources for regional peacekeeping in Africa than to participate in UN peacekeeping operations themselves. There is suspicion in some quarters that developed states are simply seeking to reduce the direct engagement of non-African countries in peacekeeping in Africa.[269] The UN Secretary-General has stressed that UN partnerships with regional organizations must provide the means to meet, rather than to avoid, responsibilities under the Charter to provide an effective response to violent conflict, wherever it occurs.[270]

---

[268] Report of the Secretary-General on the Work of the Organizations, A/54/1 (1999) para 112.

[269] 1998 UNYB 61; 1999 UNYB 74, 2000 UNYB 107, 230; 2001 UNYB 9; UN Press Releases GA/PK/177 and 178, 3–4 March 2003, GA/SPD/265, 15 October 2003. See also Berman and Sams, *Peacekeeping in Africa: Capabilities and Culpabilities* (2000), Gray, 'Peacekeeping and enforcement action in Africa: the role of Europe and the obligations of multilateralism', (31) Review of International Studies (2005) 207. In the more recent debates on cooperation between the UN and regional organizations, states such as Jamaica and India have stressed that the UN should not use regional action to avoid its responsibilities: UN Press Release GA/PK/184, 1 February 2005, GA/SPD/326, 24 October 2005.

[270] SC 5282nd meeting (2005).

Index

Abkhazia (Georgia)
Chapter VIII of UN Charter 410
Commonwealth of Independent State's
operation 396, 409–10
mandates 410
peacekeeping operations 410–12
regional arrangements and enforcement
action 409–11
Russia 396, 409–11
SC resolutions 278–9, 409–11
Security Council 409–11
UNOMIG 278–9, 409–11
Afghanistan *see also Operation Enduring
Freedom* in Afghanistan
Al Qaida 193, 194, 197, 200–1
armed attacks, self-defence and 140, 174, 175
authorization for use of force by Security
Council 343–4
civil wars, intervention in 110, 112
Geneva Accords 274
Pakistan 110, 112
September 11, 2001 terrorist attacks on
United States 194, 252
Tajikistan 140, 175, 279, 408
Taliban 112, 194, 200–1
terrorist attacks, self-defence against 197
training camps 194
UNGOMAP 274, 278
USSR intervention 92–4, 110, 112, 174
'war on terror' 1–2, 194, 252
Africa *see also* African Union (AC);
Organization of African Unity
(OAU); particular countries (eg Côte
d'Ivoire)
2003–2007, member state operations
during 334–9
authorization for use of force by Security
Council 334–41
Brahimi Report 310–12
consent to peacekeeping 299–301
Peace Operations 2010 324
peacekeeping 5–6
Portugal, colonial territories of 21, 136–8,
139
African Union (AU)
AMIB 375–6
AMIS 380–2
AMISOM 378–80
authorization of use of force 376, 378
Burundi 375–6

Chad, MINURCAT in 382
Chapter VII of UN Charter 382
Darfur, Sudan 54–5, 322, 380–2
*Declaration on Enhancing UN–AU
Cooperation* 377
Ethiopia/Somalia 2006 245, 248–52
European Union 377–8, 382
joint operations, list of 382
Peace and Security Council 377–8
peacekeeping 273, 376–8, 382
request intervention, right to 377
responsibility to protect principle 53
Security Council 377–8
Somalia 245, 248–52, 288–9, 378–80
Standby Force 377
World Summit Outcome Department 377
aggression
armed attacks, self-defence and 130–1
Chapter VII of UN Charter 256, 258
civil wars, intervention in 110, 112
frontier incidents 178–9, 182–3
General Assembly 18–19, 22
Operation Iraqi Freedom 364
SC resolutions 18–19, 22–3
self-defence 130–1, 178–9, 182–3
South Africa 18–19
Al Qaida
Afghanistan 193, 197, 200–1
anticipatory self-defence 217–18
Chapter VII of UN Charter 267
Ethiopia/Somalia 2006 249, 250
Iraq, alleged links with 217–18
Operation Enduring Freedom in
Afghanistan 203–6, 344
Pakistan 205
sanctions 267
self-defence 197
'war on terror' 193–4, 228
Albania 32, 331
AMIB 375–6
AMIS 54, 380–2
AMISOM 249–51, 378–80
Angola
armed attacks, self-defence and 138–40
ceasefires 275–6
civil wars, intervention in 107–9, 111, 113
collective self-defence 168–9
Cuba 108, 111, 168–9, 275
end of conflict 111
MONUA 276

Angola (*cont.*)
  Namibia 275–6
  peacekeeping operations 303
  SC resolutions 138, 140, 303
  South Africa 107–9, 111, 138–9, 169
  UNAVEM 275
  UNAVEM II 275–6
  UNAVEM III 276
  United States 75–8, 80–1, 108–9, 111, 113
  war on terror 113
anticipatory or pre-emptive self-defence *see
    also* anticipatory or pre-emptive self-
    defence, 'war on terror' and
  academic debate 117–18
  armed attacks 160–1, 165
  Article 51 of UN Charter 160, 165, 208
  Bush doctrine 114, 209–16, 252
  Chapter VIII of UN Charter on regional
    peacekeeping 161–2
  Cuban missile crisis 161–2
  customary international law 165
  Democratic Republic of Congo, Uganda
    and 164
  GA resolutions 160
  Grenada, United States action in 391
  *High-level Panel on Threats, Challenges and
    Changes* (Security Council) 165
  imminence of attacks 165
  International Court of Justice 165
  Iran 162, 224–7
  Iraq 162–3, 216–27
  Israel 161, 163–4
  justification 161, 164
  legality 163–4
  necessity and proportionality 150, 154,
    165, 208
  North Korea 222–5
  Operation Enduring Freedom in
    Afghanistan 209
  regional arrangements and enforcement
    action 391
  Security Council 121, 163
  state practice 163–5
  Uganda 164
  United States 216–27, 391
  'war on terror' 2, 208–27, 252
anticipatory or pre-emptive self-defence, 'war
    on terror' and
  alliances, strengthening 210
  Article 51 of UN Charter 216
  Australia 216
  'Axis of Evil' 210
  Bush strategy 210–11
  Commonwealth of Independent States 214
  Democratic Republic of Congo, Uganda
    and 216
  European Union 214–15

*High-level Panel on Threats, Challenges and
    Changes* (Security Council) 212–13
  imminence, concept of 211–12
  International Court of Justice 216
  National Security Strategy 210, 213, 215
  NATO 213–14
  non-imminent threats 211–12
  nuclear weapons, acquisition of 212
  Operation Enduring Freedom in
    Afghanistan 209–10
  SC resolutions 215
  Uganda 216
  United Kingdom 215
  weapons of mass destruction 210–14
Arab League 383–4, 391, 399
armed attacks, self-defence and 115–19,
    128–48
  Afghanistan 140, 174–5
  aggression 130–1
  Angola 138–40
  anticipatory self-defence 160–1, 165
  armed bands, actions of 173–5
  arms, provision of 131–2, 172, 175–6, 178
  Article 51 of UN Charter 141–4
  assistance to rebels 130–1, 172
  circumstances and motives 179
  collective self-defence 130, 177–83
  colonialism 136–8, 139
  cross-border action by irregular
    forces 132–40
  cumulative minor attacks 129
  customary international law 172, 177–8
  cyber-attacks 129
  declarations by victim state 184–6
  Definition of Aggression resolutions 130–4,
    173–4, 199–200
  degree of state involvement 132
  Democratic Republic of Congo, Uganda
    and 132–4
  Ethiopia/Eritrea 148
  existence of 115–19, 128–9
  frontier attacks 177–83
  gravity, degree of 129–30, 143–4, 146–8,
    177, 178, 202
  hot pursuit, doctrine of 137
  intent 129, 146
  International Court of Justice 129–36,
    143–7, 173–83
  Iran–Iraq conflict 143–7
  Iranian Oil Platforms case 143–7
  Iraq 140–7
  irregulars, attacks by 130, 132–40, 173–5,
    177
  Israel 135–40
  Kurds in Iraq 141–5
  Lebanon 139, 174, 176
  meaning 169, 171–7

mines 145–7
missiles 128–9, 145–7
national liberation movements 130–1,
  136–7, 172
naval mines 128–9
necessity and proportionality 147
neighbouring states, irregular forces
  operating from 140
Nicaragua case 129–32, 138, 147–8, 171–2,
  175–6, 178–83, 200
non-state actors 199–202
Operation Enduring Freedom in
  Afghanistan 169
Operation Iraqi Freedom 142
Palestinian Wall, construction of 135–6
Portugal, colonial territories in Africa
  of 136–8, 139
proportionality 139
regular armies, attacks by 130, 138, 172,
  177
reports to Security Council 174
Russia 175
SC resolutions 136, 138–40
Security Council 131–2, 136–42, 174, 176
self-defence 199–202
self-determination 138
September 11, 2001 terrorist attacks on
  United States 135
South Africa 137–9
state practice 131–2, 173, 176
Tajikistan 140, 175
terrorism 142
third state assistance 174, 181
Turkey, cross-border attacks on Kurds in
  Iraq by 140–5
Uganda 132–4
UN Charter Chapter VII 131
United States 143–7, 174–7
USSR 174
Vietnam 174–5, 177
weapons, supply of 131–2, 172
arms *see also* **arms embargoes; weapons of
  mass destruction**
armed attacks 178
Ethiopia/Somalia 2006 245–6
frontier attacks 178
International Court of Justice 175–6
Nicaragua case 175–6
state practice 176
supply 131–2, 172, 245–6
Vietnam 177
arms embargoes
authorization for use of force by Security
  Council 329, 423
Bosnia-Herzegovina 126–7
Chapter VII of UN Charter 266–72
Ethiopia 128, 245

Kosovo 352
Liberia 128
Rwanda 127, 293
self-defence 126–8
Serbia and Montenegro 126
Somalia 245
South Africa 257–8
Yugoslavia 423
**Article 2(4) of UN Charter, prohibition on
  use of force in** 6, 30–66
customary international law 30–1
developing countries 30
economic coercion 30
humanitarian intervention 31, 32, 33–9
implied authorization of Security Council,
  doctrine of 41, 45, 50
interpretation 8, 30–2
Kosovo, use of force by NATO in 31. 39–51
meaning of use of force 30–1
national liberation movements 65
pre-colonial title 65
pro-democratic intervention, right of 55–9
responsibility to protect principle 51–5
self-determination 59–64, 65
UN, ineffectiveness of 32–3
Article 41 of UN Charter 266–72
Article 51 of UN Charter
anticipatory self-defence 160, 165, 208,
  216
armed attacks, self-defence and 141–2,
  199–200
authorization for use of force by Security
  Council 369
Bosnia-Herzegovina 126–7
collective self-defence 125, 169–71, 188–90
Ethiopia/Somalia 2006 248, 250
frontier attacks 180, 183
identification of law 7, 8
International Court of Justice 216
interpretation 8
Iranian Oil Platforms case 143–4
Kurds, protection of 141–2
nationals, protection of 157
self-defence 117, 118–21, 125–7, 157, 195,
  198
September 11, 2001 attacks on United
  States 198–200
South Africa 126
terrorist attacks, self-defence against 195,
  198
war on terror 208, 216
**Article 53 of UN Charter, regional
  organizations and**
authorization 417–18
authorization for use of force by Security
  Council 424–6
Côte d'Ivoire 425

Article 53 of UN Charter, regional
organizations and (*cont.*)
democratic government, regional right to
use force to restore 417, 418–23
ECOWAS 418
humanitarian intervention 417
interpretation 417–23, 526–7
peacekeeping operations 418
regional arrangements and enforcement
action 397, 417–23, 426–7
Security Council, *ex post facto* approval
by 417–18
AU *see* African Union (AU)
Australia
anticipatory self-defence 216, 219–20
East Timor 387
Iraq 219–20, 354–5, 358, 360–2
regional arrangements and enforcement
action 387–9
war on terror 216
authorization for use of force by Security
Council 254, 327–69
Afghanistan 343–4
Africa 334–41
African Union 376, 378
Albania 331
arms embargoes 329, 423
Article 2(4), prohibition on use of force
in 41, 45, 50
Article 51 of the UN Charter 369
Article 53 of the UN Charter 417–18,
424–6
Bosnian Serbs, safe havens for 328
Brahimi Report 366
Central African Republic 331–2
Chapter VII of UN Charter 258, 264–6,
327–32, 340–1, 366–7, 423–4
Chapter VIII of UN Charter 423–4
civil war 328
Cold War 328
Côte d'Ivoire 425, 426
delegation of operations to member
states 332–3
East Timor, INTERFET in 332
economic sanctions 329, 368
European Union 334, 340–1
ex post facto authorization 417–18
Haiti, action against 329–31, 423–4
*High-level Panel on Threats, Challenges and
Changes* (Security Council) 366
humanitarian aid, delivery of 332
implied or revived authorization to use
force 41, 45, 50, 348–66, 368–9
INTERFET 332
inter-state use of force 328–9
Iran 366–8
Iraq 348–51, 354–66, 368

Kosovo 41, 45, 50, 341–3, 351–4
Liberia 425–6
MINURCA 332
MISAB 331–2
NATO operations in former
Yugoslavia 333–4
North Korea 366–7
nuclear weapons, non-proliferation
of 366–8
Operation Desert Storm 327–9, 333, 366
Operation Iraqi Freedom 354–66, 369
permanent members 334
regional organizations 417–18, 423–8
responsibility to protect principle 52–3
Rwanda 331, 334
sanctions 329, 368, 423–4
SC resolutions 328–9, 331–3, 367–9, 424
Sierra Leone 413, 422–3, 426
Somalia, UNITAF in 333
UNITAF 333
United Kingdom 369
United States 330–1, 334, 369
UNMIH 329
Yugoslavia 333–4, 423–6
'Axis of Evil' 2, 210, 216–17, 222–7
Azerbaijan 374–5

Bosnia-Herzegovina
civil wars, intervention in 83
classification of conflict 83
European Union 385
no-fly zones 289–90, 424–5
regional arrangements and enforcement
action 385
safe havens 328, 424–5
UNMIBH 285
Brahimi Report peacekeeping reform 306–12
Africa 310–12
authorization for use of force by Security
Council 366
Capstone Document 310
Chapter VII of UN Charter 310
commitment gap 308
consent 310
consultation process 309
Democratic Republic of Congo 319
Department of Peacekeeping, changes
to 307
enforcement action 307
*High-level Panel on Threats, Challenges and
Changes* (Security Council) 311–12
impartiality 310
institutional changes to UN, proposal
for 307
mandates 309–10
Peace Operations 2010 310, 325
peacekeeping 273–4

permanent member participation 308
Rwanda, UNAMIR in 311
SC resolutions 309, 311–12
Secretariat 309
Security Council 307–12
self-defence 310
Somalia, mandates for 310
standby arrangements 307
standing army, proposal for 307
support, provision for 307–8
troops provision of 307–9
UNAMIR 311
UNPROFOR 310
Yugoslavia, UNPROFOR in 310
Brezhnev doctrine 93, 191
buffer zones, controlling 272–3
Burundi 319–20, 375–6
Bush doctrine 114, 160–5, 209–16, 252

Cambodia
civil wars, intervention in 112
opposition, forcible intervention to assist
the 106–7
peacekeeping 276–7
UNAMIC 277
UNTAC 277
Vietnam 112
Cameroon 16–17
ceasefires
Angola 275–6
enforcement 281–2
Iraq 350–1
monitoring 272–4, 275–6, 295
Mozambique 276
peacekeeping 272–6, 281–2, 295
CEMAC 421–2
Central African Republic (CAR)
authorization for use of force by Security
Council 331–2, 421–2
Bangui Agreement 386–7
CEMAC 421–2
Chad 422
civil wars, intervention in 85–6
democratic government, right to use force to
restore 421–2
European Union 340–1
FOMUC 422
France 85–6, 88–9
MINURCA 303–4, 332
MISAB 303–4, 331–2
nationals, protection of 88–9
peacekeeping operations 273, 303–4,
331–2, 422
regional arrangements and enforcement
action 386–7, 421–2
Security Council 422
centralization of use of force 254

Chad
African Union 382
Central African Republic 422
European Union 340–1, 382, 385–6
financing 398–9
France 88–9, 96–8, 341
impartiality 398–9
Libya 96–8
MINURCAT 382
nationals, protection of 88–9
Organization of African Unity 398–9
peacekeeping 273, 304, 382
regional arrangements and enforcement
action 385–6, 398–9
SC resolutions 341, 399
Sudan, insurgents from 340
troops, provision of 399
Chapter VII of UN Charter, Security Council
and 254–9
African Union 382
aggression, acts of 256, 258
Al Qaida, sanctions against 267
armed attacks, self-defence and 131
arms embargo 257–8, 267–9
Article 41 266–72
authorization of use of force 258, 264–6,
327–32, 340–1, 366–7, 423–4
Brahimi Report 310
centralization of use of force 254
Cold War 255–9, 261–5, 326
collective self-defence 170
condemnations of states by name 256
consent to peacekeeping 298
Côte d'Ivoire 335, 425
Democratic Republic of Congo 316, 318,
338
economic sanctions 256–8, 266–72
European Union 340–1
humanitarian considerations, sanctions
and 269, 270–2
Iran–Iraq war 256
Iran, sanctions against 270
Iraq 269, 271, 350–1
Korea, action against 258–9
Kosovo 341–2, 352–3
Kuwait, Iraq invasion of 264–5
legal basis for action 256, 258–9, 265
Liberia 339, 421, 425–6
Libya, sanctions against 269–70
New World Order 264–5
non-state actors, sanctions against 267
North Korea, sanctions against 270
nuclear weapons 270
Operation Desert Storm 265
Operation Iraqi Freedom 346, 356
Peace Operations 2010 325
peacekeeping 294–306, 319–20, 326

Chapter VII of UN Charter, Security
    Council and (*cont.*)
  regional arrangements and enforcement
    action 385
  Rhodesia, economic sanctions
    against 256–7
  Rwanda 293
  sanctions 256–8, 266-72
  SC resolutions 257–8, 265, 267–9
  scope of permissible action 265
  self-defence 126
  Sierra Leone 312–14, 413, 416
  Somalia 287–8, 379
  South Africa 257–8
  threats to international peace and
    security 257–8
  veto of Permanent Members of SC 255, 264
  'war on terror' 227
  Yugoslavia 282–6, 289, 291, 298, 424
Chapter VIII of UN Charter
  Abkhazia (Georgia) 410
  anticipatory self-defence 161–2
  authorization for use of force by Security
    Council 423–4
  collective self-defence 170
  Commonwealth of Independent States 388
  Côte d'Ivoire 425
  Cuban missile crisis 161–2
  Liberia 392, 400, 425
  Organization of African Unity (OAU) 376
  regional peacekeeping 161–2, 370, 372–3,
    383–8, 391–2, 426–7
  Sierra Leone 413
  Tajikistan 396, 407–8
  Yugoslavia 424
Charter for European Security 384–5
Chechnya 230–1
China 65–6
CIS *see* Commonwealth of Independent
    States (CIS)
civil law and order, maintenance of 296
civil wars 67–113
  acquiescence 80
  Afghanistan 110, 112
  aggression 85
  Angola 107–9, 111, 113
  authorization for use of force by Security
    Council 328
  Bosnia-Herzegovina, classification of
    conflict in 83
  Cambodia, Vietnam's interference in 112
  Central African Republic, French
    intervention in 85–6
  classification of conflicts 82–4
  Cold War 84–5, 110–13
  collective self-defence 69–70, 76–8, 82–3
  Colombia, United States intervention in 87

consent to peacekeeping 299–300
Cuba 108–9, 111
customary international law 68, 75–7
decolonization 82
Democratic Republic of Congo 68–73,
    78–80, 83–4
forcible intervention, prohibition on 76–7,
    81, 105–7, 113
foreign intervention, invitation in response
    to prior 92–105
Friendly Relations Resolution (1970) 68, 76,
    78–9
GA resolutions 67–8
Gabon, France's intervention in 85
Hungary, USSR intervention in 87, 88
identification of law 7
International Court of Justice 75–8, 80–1,
    83
inter-state conflict, mixed with 70
invite outside intervention, right of
    government to 80–8, 113
Kuwait, Iraq's intervention on 87–8
Liberia 74–5
Mozambique, South Africa's intervention
    in 110, 111
nationals, protection of 88–92, 159–60
Nicaragua case 75–8, 80–1, 83
Operation Iraqi Freedom 347
opposition, forcible intervention to assist
    the 105–7
Pakistan 110, 112
peacekeeping 272
regional arrangements and enforcement
    action 389–90
Rwanda 68–73, 78–80, 83–4
SC resolutions 69–72, 84, 88
Security Council 69–74, 113
self-defence 69–70, 76–8, 82–3
Sierra Leone 74–5
South Africa 107–9, 111
Sri Lanka, India's intervention in 86–7
state sovereignty 69, 79
territorial integrity 69, 79, 84
threshold for civil war 82
toleration 80
Uganda 68–73, 78–80, 83–4
United States 75–8, 80–1, 108–9, 111, 113
Vietnam 82, 112
vigilance, duty of 79–80
war on terror 112–13
classification of conflicts 82–4
Cold War
  authorization for use of force by Security
    Council 328
  Chapter VII of UN Charter 255–9, 264–5
  civil wars, intervention in 84–5, 110–13
  collective self-defence 118, 191–2

General Assembly 259–61
humanitarian law 34
peacekeeping operations 261–4, 326
regional arrangements and enforcement
    action 370–2, 391–2, 396–7
Security Council 259–61
self-defence 118
termination of Cold War conflicts 274–8,
    280
collective self-defence 167–92
aggression 178–9, 182–3
Angola, Cuban presence in 168–9
armed attacks 130, 169–86, 190
arms, provision of 178
Article 51 of UN Charter 125, 169–71,
    180, 183, 188–90
Brezhnev doctrine 191
Chapter VII of UN Charter 170
Chapter VIII of UN Charter 170
circumstances and motives 179
civil wars, intervention in 69–70, 76–8, 82–3
Cold War 118, 191–2
covert action 184–5
customary international law 171, 172–3,
    177–8, 184
declarations by victim state 184–90
Definition of Aggression 178–9, 182–3
Ethiopia, Cuban and Soviet troops
    in 168–9
foreign intervention, intervention in
    response to prior 93, 98
frontier incidents 177–83, 184
gravity of force 177, 178, 182
International Court of Justice 15–16,
    169–83, 185–90
invitations to foreign troops 168
Iranian Oil Platforms case 186
justification 168, 185
Kuwait, Iraq's invasion of 125
legality 169, 173, 186, 188, 191–2
motives 190–1
necessity and proportionality 179–80, 181
Nicaragua case 169–73, 177–84, 189–90,
    192
Operation Enduring Freedom in
    Afghanistan 169, 191
pro-democratic intervention, right of 56
reports to Security Council 172, 188–9
requests by victim state 168, 172, 184–90
Security Council 170, 172, 182, 188–9
September 11, 2001 attacks on United
    States 193–4
small states, protection of 191–2
South Africa 168–9
state practice 177, 186–8, 191–2
third state interest 169, 181, 183, 187–8
treaties 187–8, 191–2

United States 169–73, 184, 186, 188–92
Vietnam conflict 188, 191
'war on terror' 193
Colombia 87
colonialism 7, 59–60, 63–4, 82, 136–8, 139
commitment gap 308
Commonwealth of Independent States
    (CIS) 384–5, 407–11
Abkhazia (Georgia) 396, 409–10
anticipatory self-defence 214
Chapter VIII of UN Charter 388
Tajikistan 395–6, 407–9
war on terror 214
condemnations
Chapter VII of UN Charter 256
effectiveness of prohibition on force 26
GA resolutions 26
General Assembly 20–1, 23–4, 26
Israel 19
name, condemnations of states by 256
North Korea 157–8
SC resolutions 19–24, 26
self-defence 157–8
Conference on Security and Cooperation in
    Europe (CSCE) 384–5, 387–8 *see also*
    OSCE (Organization for Security and
    Cooperation in Europe)
Congo 88 *see* Democratic Republic of the
    Congo (DRC
consent to peacekeeping 294–5, 298–302
Africa 299–301
AMIS 380–1
Brahimi Report 310
Chapter VII of UN Charter 298
civil war 299–300
Darfur, Sudan 299, 301, 380–1
Democratic Republic of Congo 300–1
Egypt, UNEF in 299
Eritrea 301
Liberia 401–2
MONUC 300–1
nationals, protection of 159
Operation Iraqi Freedom 346
refusal to accept forces 299, 301
Sierra Leone 300
Somalia 300, 302
Status of Forces Agreements 298
troop contributions 301–2
UNAMID 301
UNCRO 299
UNEF 299
United States involvement in UNOSOM
    II 302
UNMEE 301
UNOSOM II 302
UNPROFOR 298–300
Yugoslavia 298–301

consultation process 309
Côte d'Ivoire
  Article 53 of UN Charter 335, 425
  authorization for use of force by Security
    Council 419–21, 425, 426
  Chapter VII of UN Charter 425
  Chapter VIII of UN Charter 425
  democratic government, right to use force to
    restore 419–21
  ECOMICI 419–21
  ECOWAS 334–5, 395, 419–21, 426
  financial and logistical support 420
  France 334–6, 419–20
  MINUCI 304–5, 420
  nationals, protection of 90
  regional arrangements and enforcement
    action 419–21
  SC resolutions 336, 419–21
  Security Council 419–21
  UNOCI 320–1, 335–6
covert action 105–6, 184–5
CSCE (Conference on Security and
    Cooperation in Europe) 384–5,
    387–8 *see also* OSCE (Organization for
    Security and Cooperation in Europe)
Croatia 285–6
cross-border action
  armed attacks, self-defence and 132–40
  Cameroon 16–17
  Chad 340
  irregular forces 132–40
  Lebanon 237–44
  state practice 11
  Sudan 340
  Turkey 140–5
Cuba
  Angola 108, 111, 275
  anticipatory self-defence 161–2
  civil wars, intervention in 108–9, 111
  Cuban missile crisis 161–2
  Ethiopia 168–9
  Organization of American States
    (OAS) 397, 403–4
  peacekeeping 275
  regional arrangements and enforcement
    action 397
customary law
  anticipatory self-defence 165
  armed attacks, self-defence and 172, 177–8
  Article 2(4), prohibition on use of force
    in 30–1
  civil wars, intervention in 68, 75–7
  collective self-defence 171, 172–3, 184
  effectiveness of prohibition on force 25
  forcible intervention, right to 8, 24
  frontier attacks 177–8
  identification of law 9

Nicaragua case 171
  necessity and proportionality 150
  reporting to Security Council 172
  self-defence 118, 165, 172, 177–8
  veto 23
cyber-attacks 128
Cyprus 94
Czechoslovakia, intervention by USSR in 92–4

Darfur, Sudan
  African Union 54–5, 380–2
  AMIS 54, 380–2
  AU/UN force, proposal for 54–5, 322
  civilians, protection of 380–1
  consent 299, 301, 380–1
  Darfur Peace Agreement 55
  France 88–9
  Genocide Convention 54–5
  humanitarian aid 54
  International Criminal Court 55
  janjaweed 53–4, 381
  mandate 382
  monitoring 380
  nationals, protection of 88–9
  peacekeeping 273, 380
  refusal to accept forces 299, 301
  responsibility to protect principle 53–4
  SC resolutions 54–5, 381–2
  UNAMID 301
  UNMIS 305
Declaration on Friendly Relations *see* Friendly
    Relations Resolution
Declaration on the Non-Use of Force 114
declaratory function of international
    law 27–8
decolonization 7, 59–60, 63–4, 82
Definition of Aggression
  armed attacks, self-defence and 130–4,
    173–4, 199–200
  frontier attacks 178–9, 182–3
  self-defence 114, 130–4, 173–4, 178–9, 182–3
  September 11, 2001 attacks on United
    States 199–200, 201–2
democracy *see* democratic government,
    regional right to use force to restore;
    pro-democratic intervention, right of
democratic government, regional right to use
    force to restore 418–23
  Article 53 of the UN Charter 418–23
  authorization of use of force by Security
    Council 418
  Central African Republic 421–2
  Côte d'Ivoire 419–21
  ECOWAS 418
  Liberia 421
  regional arrangements and enforcement
    action 418–23

Sierra Leone 395
use of force, right to 418
Democratic Republic of the Congo (DRC)
anticipatory self-defence 164, 216
armed attacks, self-defence and 132–4
Brahimi Report 319
Chapter VII of UN Charter 316, 318, 338
civil wars, intervention in 68–73, 78–80,
83–4
classification of conflicts 83–4
consent to peacekeeping 300–1
delay in deployment of UN force 280
EUFOR-RDC 337–8
European Union 337–8, 385
IEMF (Interim Emergency Multinational
Force) 317, 336
International Court of Justice 78–80, 83–4
liaison officers, deployment of 316
mandates 316, 318–19, 337
MONUC 300–1, 305, 316–19, 336, 385
Rwanda 68–73, 78–80, 83–4, 317
SC resolutions 305, 316–18, 337
self-defence 132–4, 164
Uganda 68–73, 78–80, 83–4, 132–4, 164,
216, 317
Dominican Republic 91, 92, 397

East Timor
Australia 387
authorization for use of force by Security
Council 332
INTERFET 296–7, 332
peacekeeping 295, 296–8
regional arrangements and enforcement
action 387
SC resolutions 296–7
UNAMET 296
UNMISET 297
UNMIT 297
UNTAET 295, 296–8
ECOMICI 419–21
ECOMIL 339, 421
ECOMOG 393–4, 400–7
economic sanctions *see* sanctions
ECOWAS
Article 53 of the UN Charter 418
civil war 389–90
constitutional basis 392–5, 411–16
cooperation with UN forces 405–6
Côte d'Ivoire 334–5, 395. 419–21, 426
democratic government, right to use force to
restore 418
financial support 428
impartiality 411
Liberia 338–9, 392–4, 400–7, 421, 425–6
Mediation Committee 393–4
operations, list of 375

peacekeeping 389–90
*Protocol on Mutual Assistance on
Defence* 389
Protocol on Non-Aggression 389
sanctions, Security Council approval of 403–4
Sierra Leone 58–9, 395, 411–17
effectiveness of prohibition on force 25–9
condemnations 26
customary international law 25
decision-making process 26
declaratory function of international
law 27–8
justifications 28–9
sanctions, use of 27
state behaviour, influencing 25–6
state practice 26
Egypt 161, 299
El Salvador 277
enforcement action *see also* regional
arrangements and enforcement action
Brahimi Report 307
ceasefires 281–2
CSCE 388
Liberia 403–5, 425–6
peacekeeping 281–92, 295, 326
Russia 427
Sierra Leone 313–14
Somalia 289, 291, 326
standing army, proposal for 307
Yugoslavia 284–6, 289–91, 326
Entebbe incident 32–3
Eritrea/Ethiopia conflict 30–1
consent to peacekeeping 301
gravity of attacks 148
peacekeeping 280–1
SC resolutions 281
self-defence 122
UNMEE 280–1, 301, 304–5
Ethiopia
African Union 245, 248–52
Al Qaida 249, 250
AMISOM peacekeeping force 249–51
arms embargo 128, 245
arms, supplying 245–6
Article 51 of UN Charter 248, 250
Cuba 168–9
Eritrea 30–1, 122, 148, 280–1, 301,
304–5
reporting to Security Council 248
SC resolutions 247, 250–1
Security Council 244–51
self-defence 244–52
Somalia 244–52, 379
UNITAF force 244–5
United States 244, 249–50
USSR 168–9
'war on terror' 244–53

EUFOR-RDC 337–8
European Union
    African Union 377–8, 382
    anticipatory self-defence 214–15
    authorization for use of force by Security
        Council 334, 340–1
    Bosnia-Herzegovina 385
    Central African Republic 340–1
    Chad 340–1, 382, 385–6
    Chapter VII of UN Charter 340–1
    crisis management, cooperation in 386
    Democratic Republic of Congo 337–8, 385
    EUFOR-RDC 337–8
    European Security and Defence Policy 388,
        397
    Macedonia 385
    MONUC 385
    Operation Artemis 337
    peacekeeping 273
    'war on terror' 214–15

Falklands (Malvinas) conflict 65, 123, 124,
    125
FOMUC 422
foreign intervention, intervention in response
    to prior 92–105
    Afghanistan, USSR intervention in 92–4
    Brezhnev doctrine 93
    Chad 1975–1983, French and Libyan
        intervention in 96–8
    civil wars, intervention in 92–105
    collective self-defence 93, 98
    Cyprus, Turkey's intervention in 94
    Czechoslovakia, USSR intervention
        in 92–4
    forcible interventions 94–5
    France 96–8
    identification of government entitle to invite
        intervention 98–105
    invitations to intervene 92–105
    Jordan, United Kingdom intervention
        in 95
    Libya 96–8
    Oman, United Kingdom intervention in 95
    SC resolutions 94, 98
    self-defence 93, 98
    Turkey's invasion of Cyprus 94
    USSR 92–3
France
    Central African Republic 85–6, 88–9
    Chad 88–9, 96–8, 341
    Côte d'Ivoire 334–6, 419–20
    Darfur, Sudan 88–9
    foreign intervention, intervention in
        response to prior 96–8
    Gabon 85
    Iraq 348–9

Kurds and Shiites in Iraq, protection
        of 35–8, 348–51
    nationals, protection of 88–9
    Zaire 88–9
Friendly Relations Resolution
    civil wars, intervention in 68, 76, 78–9
    self-defence 114, 198
    self-determination 61
    terrorist attacks, self-defence against 198
frontier incidents, collective self-defence and
    aggression 178–9, 182–3
    armed attacks 177–83
    arms, provision of 178
    Article 51 of the UN Charter 180, 183
    circumstances and motives 179
    collective self-defence 177–83, 184
    customary international law 177–8
    *Definition of Aggression Resolution
        (1974)* 178–9, 182–3
    gravity of force 177, 178, 182
    International Court of Justice 177–83
    necessity and proportionality 179–80, 181
    Nicaragua case 177–84
    Security Council 182
    state practice 177
    third state involvement 181, 183

GA resolutions
    anticipatory self-defence 160
    civil wars, intervention in 67–8
    condemnations 26
    humanitarian intervention 34–5
    identification of law 9–11, 18–20
    Kosovo 48
    Liberia 401
    self-defence 114
    self-determination 60–3
    September 11, 2001 attacks on United
        States 193–4
    UN Charter 27–8
    Western states, influence of 28
Gabon 85
General Assembly *see also* GA resolutions
    aggression 18–19, 22
    Cold War 261–2
    condemnations 20–1, 23–4
    Global Counter-terrorism Strategy 228
    identification of law 17–24
    recommendations 260
    regional arrangements and enforcement
        action 384
genocide
    Darfur, Sudan 54–5
    Rwanda 292–4, 334
    Yugoslavia 14
Georgia *see also* Abkhazia (Georgia)
    Abkhazia 278–9, 396, 409–12

peacekeeping 278–9
Russian intervention 230–1
war on terror 230–1
Goa 59–60, 65
gravity of attacks
  Ethiopia and Eritrea conflict 148
  frontier attacks 177, 178, 182
  Iranian Oil Platforms case 143–4, 146–7
  necessity and proportionality 147
  Nicaragua case 147–8
  self-defence 147–8, 177, 178, 182
  September 11, 2001 attacks on United
    States 202
Grenada
  anticipatory self-defence 391
  justifications 390–1
  nationals, protection of 91, 92, 157–8
  Organization of East Caribbean States
    (OECS) 390–1
  self-defence 157–8
  United States invasion 33, 56, 157–8
Guinea 395

Haiti
  authorization for use of force by Security
    Council 329–31, 423–4
  MINUSTAH 297
  Organization of American States
    (OAS) 404
  pro-democratic intervention, right of 58
  sanctions 404
  SC resolutions 424
  United States 330–1
  UNMIH 329
harbouring terrorists 200–1, 234–5, 236
*High-level Panel on Threats, Challenges and
  Changes* (Security Council)
  anticipatory self-defence 165, 212–13
  authorization for use of force by Security
    Council 332
  Brahimi Report 311–12
  purpose 3–4
  regional arrangements and enforcement
    action 373, 426–7
  responsibility to protect principle 51–2
  'war on terror' 212–13
Hezbollah 64, 237–44
hot pursuit 137
human rights 229
humanitarian considerations, sanctions
  and 269, 270–2
humanitarian intervention
  Article 2(4), prohibition on use of force
    in 31, 32, 33–9
  Article 53 of the UN Charter 417
  Cold War 34
  conditions 37

Darfur, Sudan 54
ex post facto justifications 34
forcible intervention, use of 34–6
GA resolutions 34–5
Iraq 35–8, 349
justification 36–8
Kosovo 50–1
Kurds and Shiites in Iraq, protection by UK,
  USA and France of 35–8, 348–50
Nicaragua 35
no-fly zones in Iraq 37–8, 49
peacekeeping 294, 296
Rwanda 293
SC resolutions 36
self-defence 124
Somalia 287, 291
use of force to deliver aid 282–3, 289
Yugoslavia 282–3, 289
Hungary 87, 88

identification of government entitled to invite
  intervention 98–105
  effective government 99
  Israel 100–5
  Lebanon, Syria's intervention on 99–105
  legitimate government 99
  SC resolutions 103–4
  state practice 99
  Syria 99–104
  terrorism 102
  United States 100–4
identification of law 6–24
  customary international law 9
  decolonization 7
  GA resolutions 18–20
  General Assembly 18–24
  internal conflicts 7
  International Court of Justice 14–17
  Iran–Iraq War 22
  judicial review 14
  national liberation movements 7
  SC resolutions 14, 19–24
  Security Council 13–14, 18–24
  self-determination 10
  UN Charter 6–11
  vetoes 23
IEMF (Interim Emergency Multinational
  Force) 317, 336
impartiality 310, 397–400, 402–3, 405–6,
  411, 428
implied authorization by Security Council,
  doctrine of 348–66, 368–9
  Article 2(4), prohibition on use of force
    in 41, 45, 50
  Iraq 348–51
  Kosovo 41, 45, 50, 352–4
  Kurds, protection of 350–1

implied authorization by Security Council, doctrine of *(cont.)*
  Operation Iraqi Freedom 354–66, 369
  SC resolutions 369
  United Kingdom 369
  United States 369
India 65, 86–7
INTERFET 296–7, 332
inter-governmental organizations 383
internal conflicts *see* civil wars, intervention in
International Court of Justice *see also Iranian Oil Platforms* case; *Nicaragua* case
  anticipatory self-defence 165, 216
  armed attacks, self-defence and 129–36, 173–4, 177–83
  arms, supply of 175–6
  Article 51 of UN Charter 216
  civil wars, intervention in 75–8, 80–1
  collective self-defence 15–16, 169–73, 185–90
  Democratic Republic of Congo 78–80, 83–4, 216
  frontier attacks 177–83
  identification of law 14–17
  Kosovo 44–7, 48, 353–4
  necessity and proportionality 150–5
  self-defence 119, 129–36, 165, 169–83, 185–90, 216
  Uganda 216
  war on terror 216
International Criminal Court 55
international law
  declaratory function 27–8
  regional arrangements and enforcement action 396–407
invitations for outside intervention
  civil wars, intervention in 80–8, 113
  collective self-defence 168
  foreign intervention, intervention in response to prior 92–105
  identification of government entitled to invite intervention 98–105
  nationals, protection of 88, 91
Iran *see also Iranian Oil Platforms* case
  Airbus Flight 555, United States shooting down of 162
  anticipatory self-defence 162, 224–6
  authorization for use of force by Security Council 366–8
  Axis of Evil 2, 210, 216–17, 222–7
  Chapter VII of UN Charter 270
  Iran–Iraq conflict 22, 116, 123–4, 151–4, 256
  National Security Strategy 224–5
  Non-Proliferation Treaty 225–6

nuclear weapons 225–6, 366–8
  sanctions 270
  SC resolutions 226, 270
  self-defence 162, 224–6
  terrorists, funding 225
  United States 224–7
  USSR, involvement of 13
Iranian Oil Platforms case 143–7
  accumulation of events 155
  Article 51 of UN Charter 143–4
  collective self-defence 186
  gravity, degree of 143–4, 146–7
  intent 146
  Iran–Iraq conflict 143–7, 151–4
  mine or missiles, harm caused by 145–7
  necessity and proportionality 151–5
  self-defence 146
  United States 143–7
Iran/Iraq conflict
  attribution of responsibility 22
  Chapter VII of UN Charter 256
  identification of law 22
  Iranian Oil Platforms case 151–4
  self-defence 116, 123–4
  United States 123–4
Iraq *see also* Kurds and Shiites in Iraq; *Operation Iraqi Freedom*
  Al Qaida 217–18, 221
  anticipatory self-defence 162–3, 216–27
  armed attacks, self-defence and 140–5
  assassinate United States President, plot to 196–7
  Australia 219–20
  authorization for use of force by Security Council 348–51, 354–66, 368
  'Axis of Evil' 2, 210, 216–17, 222–7
  ceasefire regime, enforcement of compliance with 350–1
  Chapter VII of UN Charter 264–5, 269, 271, 350–1
  civil wars, intervention in 87–8
  coalition 345–8, 368
  collective self-defence 125
  France 348–9
  humanitarian intervention 349
  humanitarian suffering caused by sanctions 269, 271
  imminence of threat 220
  implied authorization of use of force 348–51
  inspections 220–1
  invasion of Iraq 3, 216–27, 232–3, 252
  Iran/Iraq conflict 22, 116, 123–4, 151–4, 256
  Israeli attacks on nuclear reactor 163
  Kuwait, Iraq's invasion of 65, 87–8, 116–17, 125, 264–5

National Security Strategy (United
    States) 221
NATO 218–19
Non-Proliferation Treaty 221–2
nuclear reactor, Israeli attacks on 163
nuclear weapons facilities, raids by US,
    France and UK on 350
Operation Enduring Freedom in
    Afghanistan, precedential significance
    of 216
opposition to invasion 3
pre-colonial title, Kuwait and 65
regime change 232–3
sanctions 125, 269, 271
SC resolutions 88, 217, 219–20, 269,
    348–51
Security Council 3, 163, 348–51
self-defence 116–17, 125, 216–27, 252
United Kingdom 219–20, 348–9
United States 348–9
war on terror 1, 252
weapons of mass destruction 220–1, 269,
    350–1
irregular forces
armed attacks, self-defence and 130–40,
    172–5, 177
assistance to 130–1, 172
cross-border attacks 132–40
peacekeeping 272
ISAF (International Security Assistance
    Force) 204, 206–7, 343–4, 346
Israel
anticipatory self-defence 161, 163–4
Article 51 of UN Charter 238
ceasefire 240–3
condemnations 19
cross-border attacks 237–9
Egypt, Syria and Jordan, attacks on 171
Entebbe incident 32–3
harbouring terrorists 234–5, 236
Hezbollah 64, 234–44
identification of government entitled to
    invite intervention 100–5
Iraqi nuclear reactor, attack on 163–4
Lebanon 2006 237–44
    armed attacks, self-defence and 139
    Hezbollah 64
    occupation, Israel in illegal 235
    SC resolutions 139–40
    Syria 100–5, 234–7
    terrorism 195, 237–44, 252
necessity and proportionality 197–8, 238,
    241–3
non-state actors 239–40
Palestine 64, 135–6, 202
Palestinian Wall 135–6, 202
reprisals 197–8, 236–7

SC resolutions 103–4, 139–40, 195–8,
    234–6, 240–1, 243–4
Security Council 238–42
self-defence 135–40, 161, 163–4, 195–7,
    238–9, 241
September 11, 2001 attacks on United
    States 202
Sweden 19
Syria 100–5, 234–7, 242–4
terrorist attacks, self-defence against 195–7
Tunisia 195–6
United States 19, 100–4
'war on terror' 228–9, 234–44, 252

Jordan 95, 161
judicial review 14
justification
anticipatory self-defence 161, 164
collective self-defence 168, 185
effectiveness of prohibition on force 28–9
ex post facto interventions 34
Grenada, United State's action in 390–1
humanitarian intervention 34, 36–8
Kosovo 39–43, 45, 51, 351–2
Kurds, protection of 29
nationals, protection of 157
Operation Iraqi Freedom 355, 369
pro-democratic intervention, right of 56–7
regional arrangements and enforcement
    action 390–1
self-defence 119
Vietnam 177

Kenyan United States embassy, terrorist
    attacks on 197
KFOR 342–3
Korean War 258–9
Kosovo
1999 operation 351–4
arms embargo 352
Article 2(4), prohibition on use of force
    in 31, 39–51
authorization for use of force by Security
    Council 341–3, 351–4
Chapter VII of UN Charter 341–2, 352–3
framework for humanitarian intervention,
    proposal for a 50–1
GA resolutions 48
implied authorization of Security Council,
    doctrine of 41, 45, 50, 352–4
International Court of Justice 44–7, 48,
    353–4
ius cogens 48
justification 39–43, 45, 51, 351–2
KFOR 342–3
legality 44–7, 51, 353–4
mandates 342

Kosovo (*cont.*)
NATO 39–51, 342, 352–4
Operation Allied Force 39–41
Operation Enduring Freedom against
Afghanistan 51
Operation Iraqi Freedom 51
peace and security, threats to
international 40–3, 46, 50
precedent, as 47–8
provisional measures 45–7
SC resolutions 41–4, 50, 295, 341–3, 352
Security Council 41–50, 352
self-defence 39–40
state practice 48–9
United Kingdom 50–1, 351–2
United States 47–8, 351–2
UNMIK 273, 295–6, 343
Kurds and Shiites in Iraq
air strikes by France, UK and USA, implied
authorization of 162–3, 349–51
armed attacks, self-defence and 140–2
Article 51 of UN Charter 141–2
France 35–8, 348–9
humanitarian intervention 35–8, 349–50
justification for protection of Kurds 29
no-fly zones 37–8, 49, 162–3, 349–50
reporting to Security Council 141
safe havens 141, 348–9
SC resolutions 348–50
self-defence 141–2
terrorism 142
Turkey, cross-border operations
from 140–5
United Kingdom 35–8, 348–9
United States 35–8, 348–9
Kuwait, Iraq's invasion of finn
Chapter VII of UN Charter 264–5
civil wars, intervention in 87–8
collective self-defence 125
pre-colonial title 65
sanctions 125
SC resolutions 88
self-defence 116–17, 125

Laos 105
Lebanon
Arab Deterrent Force 399
Arab League 399
armed attacks, self-defence and 139, 174,
176
Article 51 of UN Charter 238
ceasefires 240–2
cross-border attacks 237–9
harbouring terrorists 234–5, 236
Hezbollah 64, 236–44
identification of government entitled to
invite intervention 99–105
impartiality 399
Israel 64, 100–5, 139, 195, 235–44
necessity and proportionality 238, 241–3
non-state actors 239–40
regional arrangements and enforcement
action 399
reprisals 236–7
SC resolutions 103–4, 240–1, 243–6,
297–8, 306
Security Council 238–42
self-defence 195, 238–9, 241
Syria 99–105, 234–7, 242–4, 399
terrorist attacks, self-defence against 195
UNIFIL 297–8, 305–6, 322
United States 100–4, 174, 176
legality
anticipatory self-defence 163–4
Chapter VII of UN Charter 256, 258–9,
265
collective self-defence 169, 173, 186, 188,
191–2
Israel 234–44, 252
Kosovo 44–7, 51, 353–4
Liberia 400
Operation Iraqi Freedom 354–5, 358–60,
364–5
regional arrangements and enforcement
action 370–1, 390–2, 386–407
self-defence 120–1, 124, 199
Syria 234–7
'war on terror' 237–44, 252
legitimate governments 103–4
Liberia
1990–1997, ECOWAS action in 400–7
arms embargo 128
authorization of use of force 425–6
Chapter VII of UN Charter 339, 421,
425–6
Chapter VIII of UN Charter 392, 400, 425
civil wars, intervention in 74–5
consent of host state 401–2
contributions 405
cooperation between ECOWAS and UN
forces 405–6
Cotonou Agreement 401–6
democratic government, right to use force to
restore 421
ECOMIL 339, 421
ECOMOG 393–4, 400–7
ECOWAS 338–9, 392–4, 400–7, 421,
425–6
enforcement action 403–5, 425–6
ex post facto authority 418
GA resolutions 401
impartiality 400, 402–3, 405–6
legality 400
mandate 400–1, 406

Mediation Committee 393–4
Multinational Force 339, 425
Nigeria 402–3, 421
peacekeeping operations 280, 297, 393–4,
    400–5, 420–1, 425–6
sanctions 338, 403–5, 421
SC resolutions 338–9, 400, 405, 421
Security Council 392–4, 400–4, 407, 418,
    425
self-defence 128
troop contributions 403
UN Charter 400
United States 339, 392–3
UNMIL 297, 305, 320, 405–6
Libya
Chad 96–8
Chapter VII of UN Charter 269–70
foreign intervention, intervention in
    response to prior 96–8
SC resolutions 14, 269–70
self-defence 121–2, 196
terrorism 196
United States 121–2, 196

Macedonia 284–5, 385
mandates
Abkhazia (Georgia) 410
AMIS 382
AMISOM 380
Brahimi Report 309–10
Cold War 262–3
Darfur, Sudan 380
Democratic Republic of Congo 316,
    318–19, 337
Kosovo 342
Liberia 400–1, 406
ONUC 263
Operation Enduring Freedom in
    Afghanistan 346
Operation Iraqi Freedom 347–8
Peace Operations 2010 325
reform of peacekeeping operations 306–7,
    319, 321–2
Sierra Leone 313–14
Somalia 288, 380
UNEF 262–3
mass destruction, weapons of *see* weapons of
    mass destruction
mines 128–9, 145–7
MINUCI 304–5, 420
MINURCA 303–4, 332
MINURCAT 273
MINUSTAH 297
MISAB 303–4, 331–2, 386–7
missiles 128–9, 145–7
MONUA 276
MONUC 300–1, 316–19, 336, 385

Morocco 65
motives
armed attacks 179
collective self-defence 190–1
Mozambique 110, 111, 276

Namibia
Angola 275–6
peacekeeping 274–5
Portugal 62
SC resolutions 275
South Africa 138, 275
UNTAG 275
national liberation movements
armed attacks, self-defence and 130–1,
    136–7, 172
Article 2(4), prohibition on use of force
    in 65
assistance to 130–1, 172
identification of law 7
opposition, forcible intervention to assist
    the 106
Portugal 136–7
self-determination 59–63
nationals, protection of 88–92
Article 51 of UN Charter 157
Central African Republic, French
    intervention in 88–9
Chad, French intervention in 88–9
civil wars or unrest
    intervention in 88–92
    rescuing nationals from 159–60
conditions 158–9
Congo 88
consent of state 159
Côte d'Ivoire 90
Darfur, Sudan, French intervention
    in 88–9
Dominican Republic, United States'
    intervention in 91, 92
France 88–9
Grenada, United States' intervention in 91,
    92, 157–8
invitation of government 88, 91
justification 157
necessity and proportionality 154
Panama, United States' intervention
    in 91–2, 157–8
rescuing nationals from civil wars or
    unrest 159–60
Security Council, condemnations
    from 157–8
self-defence 92, 156–60, 196–7
September 11, 2001 attacks on United
    States 202
Sierra Leone, United Kingdom's
    intervention in 88–9

nationals, protection of (*cont.*)
  Suez crisis 1956 158–9
  terrorist attacks, self-defence against 196–7
  United States 88, 91–2
  Zaire, French intervention in 88–9
NATO
  anticipatory self-defence 213–14, 218–19
  arms embargo 352
  Article 2(4), prohibition on use of force
    in 31, 39–51
  authorization for use of force by Security
    Council 333–4
  Chapter VII of UN Charter 352–3
  Comprehensive Political Guidance 214
  framework for humanitarian intervention,
    proposal for a 50–1
  GA resolutions 48
  implied authorization of Security Council,
    doctrine of 41, 45, 50, 352–4
  International Court of Justice 44–7, 48,
    353–4
  Iraq 218–19
  ius cogens 48
  justification 39–43, 45, 51, 351–2
  Kosovo 39–51, 342, 352–4
  legality 44–7, 51, 353–4
  New Capabilities Initiative 214
  *New Military Concept for Defence against
    Terrorism* 214
  Operation Allied Force 39–41
  Operation Enduring Freedom against
    Afghanistan 51, 207
  Operation Iraqi Freedom 51
  peace and security, threats to
    international 40–3, 46, 50
  precedent, as 47–8
  provisional measures 45–7
  SC resolutions 41–4, 50, 352
  Security Council 41–50, 352
  self-defence 39–40
  state practice 48–9
  United Kingdom 50–1, 351–2
  United States 47–8, 351–2
  Yugoslavia 289–91, 333–4
  'war on terror' 213–14
  weapons of mass destruction 214
naval mines 128–9
necessity and proportionality in self-
    defence 148–56, 166
  accumulation of events 155–6
  anticipatory self-defence 150, 154, 165, 208
  armed attacks 139, 147
  customary international law 150
  frontier attacks 179–80, 181
  future attacks 203
  gravity of attacks 147
  International Court of Justice 150–5

Iranian Oil Platforms case 151–5
  Israel 238, 241–3
  Lebanon 238, 241–3
  nationals, protection of 154
  Nicaragua case 151, 155
  occupation of territory 154–5
  Operation Enduring Freedom in
    Afghanistan 203–7
  proportionality 197–8
  reprisals 150–1, 155, 208
  self-defence 203
  terrorist attacks, self-defence against
    197–8
  United States 197–8
  'war on terror' 203–7
New World Order 1, 264–5
Nicaragua *see also Nicaragua* case
  humanitarian intervention 35
  opposition, forcible intervention to assist
    the 105
  self-defence 15–16, 121, 165–6
  United States 15–16, 35, 105
Nicaragua case
  accumulation of events 155
  armed attacks, self-defence and 129–32,
    138, 171–2, 175–83, 200
  arms, supply of 175–6, 178
  civil wars, intervention in 75–8, 80–1, 83
  collective self-defence 169–73, 184,
    189–90, 192
  customary international law 171
  frontier incidents 177–84
  International Court of Justice 169–73
  necessity and proportionality 155
  regime change 233
  September 11, 2001 attacks on United
    States 200
  United States 75–8, 80–1, 169–73, 184,
    189–90, 192
Nigeria
  Cameroon 16–17
  Liberia 402–3, 421
  Sierra Leone 395, 412, 414
no-fly zones in Iraq 37–8, 49, 162–3, 289–90,
    349–50, 424–5
non-state actors
  armed attacks 199–202
  Chapter VII of UN Charter 267
  Lebanon 239–40
  sanctions 267
  September 11, 2001 attacks on United
    States 199–202
North Korea
  anticipatory self-defence 210, 222–5
  authorization for use of force by Security
    Council 366–7
  'Axis of Evil' 2, 210, 216–17, 222–7

Chapter VII of UN Charter 270
National Security Strategy 223–4
Non-Proliferation Treaty 222–5
nuclear weapons, acquisition of 222–5,
  366–7
sanctions 270
SC resolutions 224, 270
United States 222–4
nuclear weapons
anticipatory self-defence 225–6
authorization for use of force by Security
  Council 366–8
Chapter VII of UN Charter 270
Iran 225–6, 366–8
Iraq 163, 221–2, 350
Israel's attack on Iraqi reactor 163
Non-Proliferation Treaty 221–6
North Korea 222–5, 366–7
SC resolutions 350

OAS *see* **Organization of American States
  (OAS)**
OAU *see* **Organization of African Unity
  (OAU)**
observer operations 295
occupation of territory 154–5
Oman 95
ONUB 319–20
ONUC 263
ONUCA 277
ONUSAL 277
Operation Allied Force 39–41
Operation Desert Storm 265, 327–8, 333,
  366
Operation Enduring Freedom in Afghanistan
Al Qaida 203–6, 344
anticipatory self-defence 209, 216
armed attacks 169
Bonn Agreement 2001 204–5
'Coalition against Terror' 206
collective self-defence 169, 191
factional fighting 205
involvement of other states 206
Iraq 216
ISAF (International Security Assistance
  Force) 204, 206–7, 343–4, 346
Kosovo 51
legal basis 206–7
mandate 346
maritime operations 206–7
NATO 207
necessity and proportionality 203–7
Pakistan, Al Qaida in 205
precedential value 208–9
pro-democratic intervention, right of 59
regime change 231–2
SC resolutions 206–7, 343–4

self-defence 208–9
September 11, 2001 attacks on United
  States 209
Taliban 203–6, 344
training camps 203–4
turning point in international law,
  as 208–9
'war on terror' 2, 194, 203–9, 228–31,
  343–4
Operation Iraqi Freedom 2–3
aggression 364
anticipatory self-defence 218, 220
armed attacks, self-defence and 142
Australia 354–5, 358, 360–2
authorization for use of force by Security
  Council 354–66, 369
Chapter VII of UN Charter 346, 356
civil war, risk of 347
coalitions forces 346, 355, 357, 358–66
consent 346
implied authorization 354–66, 369
inspections 355, 357–8
interim Iraqi government 346–7
Iraq, sanctions against 269
ISAF (International Security Assistance
  Force) 346
justification 355, 369
Kosovo 51
legality 354–5, 358–60, 364–5
mandate 347–8
material breach, existence of 362–3
multinational force 345–8
political transition 345–7
pro-democratic intervention, right of 59
reconstruction 365–6
SC resolutions 345, 346–8, 355–66
self-defence 142
UNAMI 347
United Kingdom 354–63
United States 354–63
'war on terror' 252–3, 345, 355
weapons of mass destruction 355, 357–8,
  364–5
Operation Turquoise 334
**opposition, forcible intervention to
  assist the**
Cambodia 106–7
CIA 106
civil wars, intervention in 105–6
covert action 105–6
Laos, United States' intervention in 105
national liberation movements 106
Nicaragua, United States' intervention
  in 105
Reagan doctrine 106
United States 105–6
'war on terror' 228

Organization for Security and Cooperation
   in Europe *see* OSCE (Organization
   for Security and Cooperation in
   Europe)
Organization of American States (OAS)
   Cuba 397, 403–4
   Haiti 404
   impartiality 397
   sanctions 403–4
Organization of African Unity (OAU) *see also*
   African Union
   Burundi 375
   Chad 398–9
   Chapter VIII of UN Charter 376
   constitutional bases 391
   impartiality 398–8
   *Mechanism for Conflict Prevention,
      Management and Resolution* 376
Organization of East Caribbean States
   (OCES) 390–1
OSCE (Organization for Security and
   Cooperation in Europe) 374–5,
   384–5, 387–8 *see also* CSCE
   (Conference on Security and
   Cooperation in Europe)

Pakistan
   Afghanistan 110, 112
   Al Qaida 205
   civil wars, intervention in 110, 112
   Operation Enduring Freedom in
      Afghanistan 205
   'war on terror' 112
Palestine
   intifada 64
   Israel 64
   self-determination 64
   September 11, 2001 attacks on United
      States 202
   wall, construction of 135–6, 202
Panama 57–8, 91–2, 157–8
Peace Operations 2010 274, 323–5
   Africa 324
   Article 1(1) of UN Charter 323
   Brahimi Report 310, 325
   Capstone Document 324
   Chapter VII of UN Charter 325
   Department of Peacekeeping
      Operations 323–4
   mandates 325
   Peacebuilding Commission 323–4
   prevention of conflict 323
   restraint in use of force 324–5
   SC resolutions 323–4
   Security Council 323–5
   Special Committee on Peacekeeping
      Operations 325

termination of operations, conflicts
   continuing after 323
troops, provision of 324
peacekeeping 254 *see also* particular
   operations (eg UNPROFOR)
Abkhazia (Georgia) 278–9, 410–12
Afghanistan 274, 278
Africa 5–6, 274, 376–8, 382
African Union 273, 376–8, 382
Angola 275–6, 303
Article 53 of the UN Charter 418
Bangui Peace Agreements 303
Brahimi Report 273–4, 307–12
buffer zones, controlling 272–3
Cambodia 276–7
Capstone Document 274
ceasefires 272–6, 281–2, 295
Central African Republic 273, 303–4, 422
Central America 277
Chad 273, 304
Chapter VII of UN Charter 261–3,
   294–306, 326
civil law and order, maintenance of 296
civil wars 272
Cold War 261–4, 272–326
conditions for successful operations 294
consent 294–5, 298–302
contemporaneous peacekeeping and
   enforcement operations 289–92
Côte d'Ivoire 304–5
Cuba 275
CSCE 387–8
Darfur, Sudan 273, 305, 380
Democratic Republic of Congo 280, 305,
   316–19, 336–8
Department of Field Support 274
Department of Peace Operations 274
Department of Peacekeeping
   Operations 274
East Timor 295, 296–8
El Salvador 277
enforcement role 281–92, 295, 326
Ethiopia/Eritrea conflict 280–1, 304–5
European Union 273
extension of peacekeeping 281–9
General Assembly 261–2
Geneva Accords 274
Georgia 278–9
Haiti 297
humanitarian aid, delivery of 294, 296
impartiality 397–8
irregular forces 272
Kosovo 273, 295–6
Lebanon 297–8, 305–6
Liberia 280, 297, 305, 393–4, 400–5,
   420–1, 425–6
mandates 262–3

Mozambique 276
Namibia 274–5
new conflicts, start of 278–81
number of operations 272
observer missions 295
ONUC (UN Operation in the Congo) 263
periods of peacekeeping 262
police forces, establishing local 296
reform 306–25
regional arrangements and enforcement
    action 397–8
Rwanda 292–4, 303
SC resolutions 275, 278, 281, 295–8,
    302–3, 305–6
Security Council 261–4, 272–326
self-defence 302–4
Sierra Leone 280, 395, 411–12, 415
Somalia 280, 286–9, 291–2
South Africa 275
standing army, proposal for 326
surge in peacekeeping 5
Tajikistan 279, 408
UNEF (UN Emergency Force) 262–3
use of force by peacekeeping
    operations 302–6
Yugoslavia 282–6, 289–92, 303
permanent members
    authorization for use of force by Security
        Council 334
    Brahimi Report 308
    Chapter VII of UN Charter 255, 264
    veto 255, 264
Philippines 229–30
police forces, establishing local 296
Portugal
    Africa 21, 136–8, 139
    armed attacks, self-defence and 136–8, 139
    Goa 59–60
    Namibia 62
    national liberation movements 136–7
    Senegal 13, 21
pre-colonial title 65
pre-emptive self-defence *see* anticipatory or
    pre-emptive self-defence
pro-democratic intervention, right of 55–9
    Article 2(4), prohibition on use of force
        in 55–9
    collective security 56
    Haiti, UN intervention in 58
    justification 56–7
    Operation Enduring Freedom in
        Afghanistan 59
    Operation Iraqi Freedom 59
    Panama, United States' intervention
        on 57–8
    Romania, intervention by Russia in 56–7
    Security Council 56–9

Sierra Leone, ECOWAS action in 58–9
United States 56–7
prohibition on use of force *see* Article 2(4),
    prohibition on use of force in
proportionality *see* necessity and
    proportionality in self-defence
provisional measures 45–7

rapid response capabilities 284, 374
Reagan doctrine 106
rebels *see* irregular forces; national liberation
    movements
reconstruction 365–6
reform of Security Council
    peacekeeping 306–25
    Brahimi Panel 306–12
    Burundi, ONUB in 319–20
    Chapter VII of UN Charter 319–20
    Côte d'Ivoire, UNOCI in 320–1
    Darfur, Sudan, AU/UN force in 322
    Democratic Republic of Congo, MONUC
        in 316–19
    Lebanon, UNIFIL in 322
    Liberia, UNMIL in 320
    mandates 306–7, 319, 321–2
    Peace Operations 2010 323–5
    Sierra Leone, UNAMSIL in 312–15
    Sudan, UNMIS in 321–2
    troop contributions 322–3
    refusal to accept forces 299, 301
regime change
    Iraq 232–3
    Nicaragua case 233
    Operation Enduring Freedom in
        Afghanistan 231–2
    SC resolutions 233
    United Kingdom 232–4
    'war on terror' 231–4
regional arrangements and enforcement
    action 370–428 *see also* particular
    organizations (e.g. European Union)
    Abkhazia, Georgia 409–11
    agencies 383–7
    annual meetings between Secretary-
        General and heads of regional
        organizations 374
    anticipatory self-defence 391
    Article 52 of UN Charter 370, 427
    Article 53 of UN Charter 397, 417–23,
        426–7
    Australia 387–9
    authorization of use of force by Security
        Council 417–28
    Bangui Agreement, MISAB and 386–7
    Bosnia-Herzegovina 385
    Central African Republic 386–7, 421–2
    Chad 385–6, 398–9

regional arrangements and enforcement action (*cont.*)
Chapter VII of UN Charter 385
Chapter VIII of UN Charter 161–2, 370, 372–3, 383–8, 391–2, 426–7
Charter for European Security 384–5
civil war 389–90
Cold War 370–2, 391–2, 396–7
Commonwealth of Independent States (CIS) 384–5, 388, 395–6, 407–11
constitutional bases 387–96
cooperation between Security Council and regional organizations 372–82, 383–4
Côte d'Ivoire 419–21
Cuba 397
definition 383
democratic government, right to use force to restore 417, 418–23
Democratic Republic of the Congo 385
Dominican Republic 397
East Timor 387
economic sanctions 403–4
enforcement action 388, 397
European Security and Defence Policy 385
ex post facto authorization 417–18
General Assembly 384
Grenada, United States action in 390–1
High-level Panel on Threats, Challenges and Changes (Security Council) 373, 426–7
humanitarian intervention 417
impartiality 397–9, 428
inter-governmental organizations 383
international law 396–407
interpretation 417–23, 526–7
justifications 390–1
Lebanon 399
legality 370–1, 390–2, 396–407
Liberia, ECOWAS action in 392–4, 400–7, 421
Macedonia 385
MONUC 385
peacekeeping operations 386–92, 397–8, 418
rapid response capabilities 374
sanctions 403–4
SC resolutions 372–3, 385, 399, 427
Security Council 372–3, 385, 423–6, 396–8, 422–3
Sierra Leone, ECOWAS in 395, 411–17
subregional organizations 383, 387, 389, 427–8
Tajikistan 395–6, 407–9
troops, provision of 399
UN Charter 396–407, 417–23
United States, Dominican Republic and 397

World Summit Outcome Document 373
regular armies, attacks by 130, 138, 172, 177
reporting to Security Council
armed attacks, self-defence and 141, 174
collective self-defence 172, 188–9
customary international law 172
Ethiopia/Somalia 2006 248
Kurds, protection of 141
self-defence 119–24, 141, 166, 172, 174, 188–9
Vietnam, United States' intervention in 188
reprisals 150–1, 155, 197–8, 208, 236–7
requests to member states
collective self-defence 168, 172, 184–90
genuineness of requests 187
state practice 186–7
responsibility to protect principle 51–5
African Union 53
Article 2(4), prohibition on use of force in 51–5
Darfur 53–4
High-level Panel on Threats, Challenges and Changes (Security Council) 51–2
Security Council, authorization of 52–3
state, duty of the 52
Rhodesia 256–7
Romania 56–7
Russia
Abkhazia (Georgia) 396, 409–11
armed attacks, self-defence and 175
Chechnya 230–1
enforcement 427
Georgia 230–1
Romania 56–7
Tajikistan 175, 407–8
Rwanda, peacekeeping in
arms embargo 127, 293
authorization for use of force by Security Council 331, 334
Brahimi Report 311
Chapter VII of UN Charter 293
civil wars, intervention in 68–73, 78–80, 83–4
Democratic Republic of Congo 68–73, 78–80, 83–4, 317
genocide 292–4, 331
humanitarian operations, security for 293
Operation Turquoise 334
peacekeeping 292–4, 303, 311
SC resolutions 293, 303, 331
self-defence 127
UNAMIR 292–4, 303, 311
UNOMUR 292

safe havens
Iraq 141, 348–9
Yugoslavia 284, 290, 303, 424–5

sanctions *see also* arms embargoes
Al Qaida 267
authorization for use of force by Security
  Council 329, 368, 423–4
Chapter VII of UN Charter 256–8,
  266–72
effectiveness of prohibition on force 27
General Issues of Sanctions 272
Haiti 404
humanitarian considerations 269, 2710–2
Iran 270
Iraq 269, 271
Kuwait, Iraq's invasion of 125
Liberia 338, 403–5, 421
Libya 269–70
monitoring 272
non-state actors 267
North Korea 270
Organization of American States
  (OAS) 403–4
regional arrangements and enforcement
  action 403–4
Rhodesia 256–7
self-defence 125–8
Sierra Leone 412–13
vulnerable groups, harming 269, 271
SC resolutions
Abkhazia (Georgia) 278, 409–11
aggression 18–19, 22–3
Angola 138, 140, 303
anticipatory self-defence 215, 217, 219–20,
  226
armed attacks, self-defence and 136,
  138–40
attribution of responsibility 20, 22
authorization for use of force by Security
  Council 328–9, 331–3, 367–9, 424
Brahimi Report 309, 311–12
Chad 341, 399
Chapter VII of UN Charter 257–8, 265,
  267–8
civil wars, intervention in 69–72, 84, 88
condemnations 19–24, 26
Côte d'Ivoire 336, 419–21
Cyprus, Turkish intervention in 94
Darfur, Sudan 54–5, 381–2
Democratic Republic of Congo 305,
  316–18, 337
East Timor 296–7
Eritrea 281
Ethiopia 244–52, 281
foreign intervention, intervention in
  response to prior 94, 98
Haiti 424
humanitarian intervention 36
identification of law 9–11, 14, 19–20
Iran 226, 269, 270

Iraq 217, 219–20, 345, 346–51, 355–66
Israel 100–5, 139–40, 195–6, 234–7,
  240–1, 243–4
Kosovo 41–4, 50, 295, 341–3, 352
Kurds, protection of the 350–1
Kuwait, Iraq's invasion of 88
Lebanon 100–5, 139–40, 234–7, 240–1,
  243–4, 297–8, 306
Liberia 338–9, 400, 405, 421
Libya 14, 269–70
Namibia 275
North Korea 224, 270
nuclear weapons 350
Operation Enduring Freedom in
  Afghanistan 206–7, 343–4
Operation Desert Storm 328–9, 333
Operation Iraqi Freedom 345, 346–8,
  355–66
Peace Operations 2010 323–4
regime change 233
regional arrangements and enforcement
  action 372–3, 385, 399, 427
Rwanda 293, 303, 331
sanctions 269–70
self-defence 116–21, 127
self-determination 60–3
September 11, 2001 attacks on United
  States 193, 199, 202, 208
Sierra Leone 312–15, 412–15
Somalia 244–52, 286–8, 379
South Africa 138–9
Syria 234–7
Tajikistan 408
Turkey 94
'war on terror' 209, 215, 227–8
weapons of mass destruction 350–1
Yugoslavia 282–6, 289–91, 303, 424
Security Council *see also* authorization for
  use of force by Security Council;
  reporting to Security Council;
  peacekeeping after the Cold War,
  Security Council and; SC resolutions
Abkhazia (Georgia) 409–11
African Union 377–8
anticipatory self-defence 121, 163
armed attacks, self-defence and 131–2,
  136–42, 174, 176
Brahimi Report 307–12
Central African Republic 422
Chapter VII of UN Charter 126, 254–9,
  264–72
civil wars, intervention in 69–74, 113
Cold War 259–61
collective self-defence 170, 172, 188–9
Côte d'Ivoire 419–21
frontier attacks 182
General Assembly 259–61

Security Council (*cont.*)
High-level Panel on Threats, Challenges and Changes 3–4
identification of law 13–14, 18–20
Iraq 3, 163
Israel 238–42
Kosovo 41–50, 352
Lebanon 238–42
legitimacy 2–3
Liberia 392–4, 401–4, 407, 418, 425
maintenance of international peace and security 254
nationals, protection of 157–8
Nicaragua case 169–73, 184, 189–90, 192
Peace Operations 2010 323–5
peacekeeping operations 254
pro-democratic intervention, right of 55–9
recommendations from GA 260
regional arrangements and enforcement action 372–3, 385, 423–6, 396–8, 422–3
self-defence 116–29, 157–8, 166
September 11, 2001 attacks on United States 198–9
Sierra Leone 411–17, 418, 422–3
standing army 254
Tajikistan 408–9
Uniting for Peace Resolution 259–60
'war on terror' 208–9
self-defence 114–66 *see also* **anticipatory or pre-emptive self-defence; armed attacks, self-defence and; collective self-defence**
academic debate 117–19
armed attacks, existence of 115–19, 128–48
arms embargo, impact of 126–8 13, 105–7, 207
Article 51 of UN Charter 117, 118–21, 125–7, 157
Bosnia-Herzegovina, arms embargo and 126–7
Brahimi Report 310
Bush doctrine 114, 160–5
civil wars or domestic unrest
intervention 69–70, 76–8, 82–3
rescuing nationals from 159–60
Cold War 118
condemnations 157–8
customary international law 118
Definition of Aggression Declaration (1974) 114
Eritrea Ethiopia conflict 122
Ethiopia 122, 128
Falklands War 123, 124, 125
foreign intervention, intervention in response to prior 93, 98
Friendly Relations Resolution (1970) 114
GA resolutions 9–10, 114

gravity of attacks 147–8
Grenada, United States' intervention in 157–8
humanitarian law 124
individual self-defence 122–3
inherent right 117–18
International Court of Justice 119
Iranian Oil Platforms case 146
Iran–Iraq conflict 116, 123–4
Iraq, invasion of 252
Israel 238–9, 241
justification 119
Kosovo 39–40
Kuwait, Iraq's invasion of 116–17, 125
Lebanon 238–9, 241
legality 120–1, 124, 199
Liberia, arms embargo on 128
Libya, United States and 121–2
nationals, protection of 88–9, 156–60
necessity and proportionality 148–56, 166, 203, 208
Nicaragua 15–16
Nicaragua case 121, 165–6
Non-Use of Force Declaration (1987) 114
Operation Enduring Freedom in Afghanistan 208–9
Panama, United States' intervention in 157–8
peacekeeping operations 302–4
report to Security Council, state's duty to 119–24, 166
Rwanda, arms embargo against 127
sanctions 125–8
SC resolutions 9–10, 116–21, 127
Security Council 116–29, 157–8, 166
self-determination 63
September 11, 2001 attacks on United States 198–202
Serbia and Montenegro, arms embargo against 126
Sierra Leone 415, 417
Somalia 288
South Africa, arms embargo on 126
state practice 24, 118
Suez crisis 1956 158–9
temporary right, self-defence as a 124–5
UN Charter Chapter VII, Security Council's powers under 126
unit self-defence 124
United Kingdom 88–9
United States 121–4, 166
Vietnam war 124
'war on terror' 193–4, 203, 208, 209, 227–31, 252
Yugoslavia 283–4
self-determination
armed attacks, self-defence and 138
Article 2(4), prohibition on use of force in 59–64, 65

decolonization 59–60, 63–4
Friendly Relations Resolution (1970) (GA) 61
GA resolutions 60–3
identification of law 10
national liberation movements 59–63
Palestine 64
SC resolutions 60–3
secession 64
self-defence 63
terrorism 64
Senegal 13, 21
September 11, 2001 attacks on United
    States 1–2, 198–209
Afghanistan, Taliban regime in 193–4,
    200–1, 209
Al Qaida 193–4, 200–1
armed attack, concept of 199–202
armed attacks, self-defence and 135
Article 51 of UN Charter 198–200
collective self-defence 193–4
Definition of Aggression 199–200, 201–2
GA resolutions 193
gravity, level of 202
harbouring terrorists 200–1
Israel 202
nationals abroad, attacks on 202
Nicaragua case 200
non-state actors, armed attacks by 199–202
Operation Enduring Freedom in
    Afghanistan 209
Palestinian Wall case 202
reprisals 208
SC resolutions 193, 199, 202
Security Council 198–9
self-defence 198–202
United Kingdom 200
'war on terror' 1–2, 193–4, 227–8, 252
Serbia and Montenegro 126
Shiites in Iraq *see* Kurds and Shiites in Iraq
Sierra Leone, peacekeeping operations in 280
authorization of use of force 413, 422–3,
    426
Chapter VII of UN Charter 312–14, 413,
    416
Chapter VIII of UN Charter 413
civil wars, intervention in 74–5
Conakry Peace Agreement 414
consent to peacekeeping 300
democratically elected government,
    restoration of 395
ECOMOG 395, 413–17, 422–3
ECOWAS 58–9, 383, 387, 389, 395,
    411–17, 426–8
enforcement operations 313–14
ex post facto authority 418
Guinea 395
impartiality 411

Liberia 74–5
Lomé Peace Agreement 415–16
mandate 313–14
Nigeria 395, 412, 414
peacekeeping 389, 411–12, 415
pro-democratic intervention, right of 58–9
sanctions 412–13
SC resolutions 312–15, 412–15
Security Council 411–17, 418, 422–3
self-defence 415, 417
termination of operations 315
UNAMSIL 312–15, 416
UNOMSIL 312, 415–16
small states, protection of 191–2
SOFA *(Status of Forces Agreement)* 298
Somalia 280, 286–9, 291–2
African Union 288–9
AMISOM 378–80
authorization for use of force by Security
    Council 333
Brahimi Report 310
Chapter VII of UN Charter 287–8, 379
consent to peacekeeping 300, 302
enforcement 289, 291, 326
Ethiopia 244–52, 379
humanitarian aid, delivery of 287, 291
Intergovernmental Authority on Drought
    and Development (IGAD) 378
mandate 288, 310, 380
peacekeeping 286–8, 291, 378–80
post-conflict restoration 379
resources 379–80
SC resolutions 286–8, 379
self-defence 288
Transitional Federal Government
    (TFG) 378–9
troops, securing 379–80
Union of Islamic Courts (UIC) 378–9
UNITAF 287, 291, 333
UNOSOM I 287, 291
UNOSOM II 287–8, 302
'war on terror' 244–53
sources of law *see* identification of law
South Africa
aggression 18–19
Angola 107–9, 111, 138–9, 169
arms embargo 126, 257–8
armed attacks, self-defence and 137–9
Article 51 of UN Charter 126
Chapter VII of UN Charter 257–8
civil wars, intervention in 107–9, 111
collective self-defence 168–9
hot pursuit, doctrine of 137
Mozambique 110, 111
Namibia 138, 275
SC resolutions 138–9
self-defence 126

Soviet Union *see* USSR
Sri Lanka 86–7
standby forces 307, 377
standing army, proposal for 254, 307, 326
state practice
  anticipatory self-defence 163–5
  armed attacks, self-defence and 131–2,
    173, 176
  arms, supply of 176
  collective self-defence 186–8, 191–2
  cross-border incursions 11
  declarations by victim state 184–90
  effectiveness of prohibition on force 26
  frontier attacks 177
  identification of government entitled to
    invite intervention 99
  interpretation 8
  Kosovo 48–9
  requests by victim state 186–7
  self-defence 24, 118
  United States 11–12
state sovereignty 69, 79
Status of Forces Agreements (SOFA) 298
Sudan 321–2, 340 *see also* Darfur, Sudan
Suez crisis 158–9
support, provision of *see also* troops, provision
  of
  AMISOM 380
  Brahimi Report 307–8
  Côte d'Ivoire 420
  ECOWAS 428
  Liberia 405
  Somalia 379–80
Sweden 19
Syria
  harbouring terrorists 234–5, 236
  Hezbollah 235–6, 242–4
  identification of government entitled to
    invite intervention 99–104
  Israel 100–5, 161, 234–7. 242–4
  Lebanon 99–105, 234–7, 242–4, 399
  SC resolutions 103–4, 234–6
  terrorism 102, 234–7
  United States 100–4

Taiwan 65–6
Tajikistan
  Afghanistan 140, 175, 279, 408
  armed attacks, self-defence and 140, 175
  Chapter VIII of UN Charter 396, 407–8
  Commonwealth of Independent
    States 395–6, 407–9
  consent 408
  peacekeeping 408
  regional arrangements and enforcement
    action 395–6, 407–9
  Russia 175, 407–8

SC resolutions 408
Security Council 408–9
UNMOT 279, 408–9
Taliban
  Al Qaida 193, 200–1
  civil wars 112
  harbouring terrorists 200–1
  Operation Enduring Freedom in
    Afghanistan 203–6, 344
  September 11, 2001 attacks on United
    States 194, 200–1
  United Kingdom 200–1
Tanzanian United States embassy, attack
  on 197
territorial integrity 69, 79, 84
terrorism *see also* terrorist attacks, self-defence
  against; war against terror
  harbouring terrorists 234–5, 236
  Lebanon 234–5, 236
  self-determination 64
terrorist attacks, self-defence against
  Afghanistan, Al Qaida in 197
  Al Qaida 197
  armed attacks, self-defence and 142
  Article 51 of UN Charter 195, 198
  Friendly Relations Declaration 198
  Iraq's assassination plot against George HW
    Bush 196–7
  Israel 195–8
  Kenya and Tanzania, terrorist attacks
    against US embassies in 197
  Kurds 142
  Lebanon 195
  Libya, United States' action against 196
  nationals, threats to 196–7
  necessity and proportionality 197-8
  reprisals 197–8
  UN Charter 195
  United States 195–8
third state assistance
  armed attacks, self-defence and 174, 181
  frontier attacks 181, 183
threats to international peace and security
  Chapter VII of UN Charter 257–8
  Kosovo 40–3, 46, 50
  meaning 257
  'war on terror' 208–9
training camps 194, 203–4
treaties, collective self-defence and 187–8,
  191–2
troops, provision of
  Brahimi Report 307–9
  Chad 399
  consent to peacekeeping 301–2
  Liberia 403
  Peace Operations 2010 324
  reform of peacekeeping operations 322–3

regional arrangements and enforcement
    action 399
Somalia 379–80
Tunisia 195–6
Turkey
    armed attacks, self-defence and 140–5
    cross-border operations 140–5
    Cyprus 94
    Iraq 29, 140–5
    Kurds 140–5
    SC resolutions 94
    terrorist attacks, self-defence against 29

Uganda
    anticipatory self-defence 164, 216
    armed attacks, self-defence and 132–4
    civil wars, intervention in 68–73, 78–80,
        83–4
    Democratic Republic of Congo 68–73,
        78–80, 83–4, 132–4, 164, 216, 317
    Entebbe incident 32–3
    'war on terror' 216
UK *see* United Kingdom
UN Charter *see also* Article 2(4) of UN
        Charter, prohibition on use of force in
        Article 51 of UN Charter; Article 53
        of UN Charter, regional organizations
        and; Chapter VII of UN Charter;
        Chapter VIII of UN Charter
    aims 254
    Article 1(1) 323
    Article 41 of UN Charter 266–72
    Article 52 370, 427
    changes 4
    GA resolutions 27–8
    identification of law 6–11
    interpretation 8, 18
    Liberia 400
    regional arrangements and enforcement
        action 396–407, 417–23
    state practice 8
    terrorist attacks, self-defence against 195
UNAMI 347
UNAMET 296
UNAMIC 277
UNAMID 301
UNAMIR 292–4, 311
UNAMSIL 312–15, 416
UNAVEM 275
UNAVEM II 275–6
UNAVEM III 276
UNCRO 285, 286, 299
UNEF 262–3, 299
UNGOMAP 274, 278
UNIFIL 297–8, 305–6
UNITAF 244–5, 287, 291, 333
United Kingdom

Afghanistan 200–1
Al Qaida 200–1
Albania 32
anticipatory self-defence 215, 219–20
authorization for use of force by Security
    Council 369
Iraq 35–8, 219–20, 348–51
Jordan 95
Kosovo 50–1, 351–2
Kurds and Shiites in Iraq, protection
    of 35–8, 350–1
Oman 95
Operation Iraqi Freedom 354–63
regime change 232–4
September 11, 2001 attacks on United
    States 200
Sierra Leone 88–9
'war on terror' 215
United Nations 254–326 *see also* General
    Assembly; SC resolutions; Security
    Council; UN Charter
    ineffectiveness 32–3
    legitimacy 3
    references to UN 12–13
United States 4–5
United States *see also* Operation Iraqi
    Freedom; war on terrorism
    Angola 108–9, 111, 113
    anticipatory self-defence 2, 216–27
    armed attacks, self-defence and 174–7
    authorization for use of force by Security
        Council 330–1, 334, 369
    'Axis of Evil' 210, 216–17, 222–7
    bases, establishment of new 229
    civil wars, intervention in 75–8, 80–1,
        108–9, 111, 113
    collective self-defence 169–73, 184, 186,
        188–92
    Colombia 87
    Congo 88
    consent to peacekeeping 302
    Dominican Republic 91, 92, 397
    Ethiopia/Somalia 2006 244, 249–50
    Grenada 33, 36, 91–2, 157–8
    Haiti 330–1
    identification of government entitled to
        invite intervention 100–4
    Iran 123–4, 162, 224–7
    Iranian Oil Platforms case 143–7, 151–5,
        186
    Iraq 35–8, 123–4, 216–27, 348–51
    Israel 19
    Kosovo 47–8, 351–2
    Kurds and Shiites in Iraq, protection
        of 35–8, 350–1
    Lebanon 100–4, 174, 176
    Liberia 339, 392–3

United States (*cont.*)
Laos 105
Libya 121–2
military intervention on behalf of insecure
governments to support 229
National Security Strategy 56–7, 221–5
nationals, protection of 88, 91–2
necessity and proportionality 197–8
Nicaragua 15–16, 35, 105
Nicaragua case 75–8, 80–1
North Korea 222–4
Operation Iraqi Freedom 354–63
opposition, forcible intervention to assist
the 105–6
Panama 57–8, 91–2, 157–8
Philippines, counter-terrorism activity
in 229–30
pro-democratic intervention, right of 56–7
Reagan doctrine 106
reporting to Security Council 188
reprisals 197–8
Russian intervention in Georgia against
Chechen forces 230–1
self-defence 121–4, 166, 195–8
state practice 11–12
Syria 100–4
terrorist attacks, self-defence
against 195–8
United Nations, relationship with 4–5
UNOSOM II 302
Vietnam 174–5, 177, 188
'war on terror' 113, 229–31
Uniting for Peace Resolution 259–60
UNMEE 280–1, 301, 304–5
UNMIBH 285, 291
UNMIH 329
UNMIK 273, 295–6, 343
UNMIL 297, 305
UNMIS 305, 321–2
UNMISET 297
UNMIT 297
UNMOP 285
UNMOT 279, 408–9
UNOCI 335–6
UNOMIG 278–9, 409–11
UNOMIL 405–6
UNOMOZ 276
UNOMSIL 312, 415–16
UNOMUR 292
UNOSOM I 287. 291
UNOSOM II 287–8, 302
UNPREDEP 284–5
UNPROFOR 303, 424–5
Brahimi Report 310
consent to peacekeeping 298–300
Yugoslavia 282–6, 289–90, 298–300, 303
UNTAC 277

UNTAES 285–6
UNTAET 273, 295, 296–8
UNTAG 274–5
USSR *see also* Commonwealth of Independent
States (CIS); Russia
Afghanistan 92–4, 110, 112, 174
armed attacks, self-defence and 174
Brezhnev doctrine 93
Czechoslovakia 92–4
Ethiopia 168–9
foreign intervention, intervention in
response to prior 92–3
Hungary 87, 88
identification of law 13

values change 234
veto 23, 255, 264
Vietnam
armed attacks, self-defence and 174–5, 177
arms, supply of 177
Cambodia 112
civil wars, intervention in 82, 112
classification of conflict 82
collective self-defence 82, 188, 191
decolonization 82
justification 177
reporting to Security Council 188
United States 124, 174–5, 177, 188
vigilance, duty of 79–80

'war on terror' 193–235 *see also* anticipatory
or pre-emptive self-defence, war on
terror and
Afghanistan 1–2, 194, 252
Al Qaida 193–4, 228, 267
anticipatory and pre-emptive self-
defence 2, 208–27, 252
Article 51 of UN Charter 208
'Axis of Evil' 2
Bush doctrine 209–16, 252
Chapter VII of UN Charter 227
Chechnya 230–1
civil wars, intervention in 112–13
collective self-defence 193
demonization 228–9
distraction, as 2
Ethiopia/Somalia 2006 244–53
future attacks 203
General Assembly Global Counter-terrorism
Strategy 228
Georgia 230–1
human rights 229
international response to terrorist
attacks 207–8
Iran, funding of terrorists by 225
Iraq 1, 252
Israel 228–9

Israel, Syria and Lebanon
  2001–2006 234–7
Israel/Lebanon 2006 237–44, 252
Lebanon 234–44, 252
National Security Strategy 210, 213, 215
necessity and proportionality 203–7, 208
Operation Enduring Freedom in
  Afghanistan 2, 194, 203–9, 228–31
Operation Iraqi Freedom 252–3, 345, 355
opposition forces to overthrow governments,
  states should not assist 228
Pakistan 112
Philippines, United States counter-terrorism
  activity in 229–30
regime change 231–4
Russian intervention in Georgia against
  Chechen forces 230–1
sanctions 267
SC resolutions 209, 227–8
Security Council 208–9
self-defence 193–4, 203, 208, 209, 227–30,
  252
September 11, 2001 attacks on United
  States 1–2, 193–4, 227–8, 252
Somalia/Ethiopia 2006 244–53
Syria 99–104, 234–7
terminology 1–2
threats to international peace and
  security 208–9
United States 113, 229–31
values change 234
weapons *see* armed attacks; arms; weapons of
  mass destruction
weapons of mass destruction 2–3
anticipatory self-defence 210–14, 218–22
inspections 220–1, 350–1, 355, 357–8
Iraq 218–22, 350–1
NATO 214
Operation Iraqi Freedom 355, 357–8, 364–5

SC resolutions 350–1
'war on terror' 210–14
Western Sahara 65

Yemen 13
Yugoslavia 282–6, 289–92 *see also* Bosnia-
  Herzegovina; Kosovo
arms embargo 423
authorization for use of force by Security
  Council 333–4, 423–6
Brahimi Report 310
Chapter VII of UN Charter 282–6, 289,
  291, 298, 424
Chapter VIII of UN Charter 424
classification of conflict 83
consent to peacekeeping 298–301
Croatia 285–6
enforcement operations 284–6, 289–91,
  326
genocide 14
humanitarian aid, use of force to
  deliver 282–3, 289
Macedonia, preventing conflict in 284–5
NATO, use of air strikes by 289–91
no-fly zones in Bosnia 289–90, 424–5
Rapid Reaction Force (RFF) 284
safe areas, creation of 284, 290, 303, 424–5
SC resolutions 282–6, 289–91, 303, 424
self-defence 283–4
Status of Forces Agreements (SOFA) 298
UNCRO 285, 286, 299
UNMIBH 285, 291
UNMOP 285
UNPREDEP 284–5
UNPROFOR 282–6, 289–90, 298–300,
  303, 310, 424–5
UNTAES 285–6

Zaire 88–9

Printed and bound by CPI Group (UK) Ltd, Croydon, CR0 4YY